D0536265

World History to 1648

OTHER BOOKS IN THE HARPERCOLLINS COLLEGE OUTLINE SERIES

ART
History of Art 0-06-467131-3
Introduction to Art 0-06-467122-4

BUSINESS
Business Calculus 0-06-467136-4
Business Communications 0-06-467155-0
Introduction to Business 0-06-467104-6
Introduction to Management 0-06-467127-5
Introduction to Marketing 0-06-467130-5

CHEMISTRY
College Chemistry 0-06-467120-8
Organic Chemistry 0-06-467126-7

COMPUTERS
Computers and Information Processing 0-06-467176-3
Introduction to Computer Science and Programming
   0-06-467145-3
Understanding Computers 0-06-467163-1

ECONOMICS
Introduction to Economics 0-06-467113-5
Managerial Economics 0-06-467172-0

ENGLISH LANGUAGE AND LITERATURE
English Grammar 0-06-467109-7
English Literature From 1785 0-06-467150-X
English Literature To 1785 0-06-467114-3
Persuasive Writing 0-06-467175-5

FOREIGN LANGUAGE
French Grammar 0-06-467128-3
German Grammar 0-06-467159-3
Spanish Grammar 0-06-467129-1
Wheelock's Latin Grammar 0-06-467177-1
Workbook for Wheelock's Latin Grammar
   0-06-467171-2

HISTORY
Ancient History 0-06-467119-4
British History 0-06-467110-0
Modern European History 0-06-467112-7
Russian History 0-06-467117-8
20th Century United States History 0-06-467132-1
United States History From 1865 0-06-467100-3
United States History to 1877 0-06-467111-9
Western Civilization From 1500 0-06-467102-X
Western Civilization To 1500 0-06-467101-1
World History From 1500 0-06-467138-0
World History to 1648 0-06-467123-2

MATHEMATICS
Advanced Calculus 0-06-467139-9
Advanced Math for Engineers and Scientists
   0-06-467151-8
Applied Complex Variables 0-06-467152-6
Basic Mathematics 0-06-467143-7
Calculus with Analytic Geometry 0-06-467161-5
College Algebra 0-06-467140-2
Elementary Algebra 0-06-467118-6
Finite Mathematics with Calculus 0-06-467164-X
Intermediate Algebra 0-06-467137-2
Introduction to Calculus 0-06-467125-9
Introduction to Statistics 0-06-467134-8
Ordinary Differential Equations 0-06-467133-X
Precalculus Mathematics: Functions & Graphs
   0-06-467165-8
Survey of Mathematics 0-06-467135-6

MUSIC
Harmony and Voice Leading 0-06-467148-8
History of Western Music 0-06-467107-7
Introduction to Music 0-06-467108-9
Music Theory 0-06-467168-2

PHILOSOPHY
Ethics 0-06-467166-6
History of Philosophy 0-06-467142-9
Introduction to Philosophy 0-06-467124-0

POLITICAL SCIENCE
The Constitution of the United States 0-06-467105-4
Introduction to Government 0-06-467156-9

PSYCHOLOGY
Abnormal Psychology 0-06-467121-6
Child Development 0-06-467149-6
Introduction to Psychology 0-06-467103-8
Personality: Theories and Processes 0-06-467115-1
Social Psychology 0-06-467157-7

SOCIOLOGY
Introduction to Sociology 0-06-467106-2
Marriage and the Family 0-06-467147-X

Available at your local bookstore or directly from HarperCollins at 1-800-331-3761.

HARPERCOLLINS COLLEGE OUTLINE

World History to 1648

Jay Pascal Anglin, Ph.D.
University of Southern Mississippi

William J. Hamblin, Ph.D.
Brigham Young University

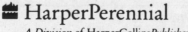

HarperPerennial
A Division of HarperCollinsPublishers

To the memory of Jay Pascal Anglin:
Global Historian

and

To Sylvie and Julie:
their father's final gift

To Loree
who did all the real work

To Alex, Karen, and Ken
who missed playing with their dad

An American BookWorks Corporation Production
Project Manager: Jonathon E. Brodman
Editor: Robert A. Weinstein

Library of Congress Catalog Card Number: 91-55404
ISBN: 0-06-467123-2

00   ABW/RRD   10   9

Contents

Preface

This book was written with the goal of providing as concise a summary as possible of the major events, people, and trends in premodern world history for use as a textbook, supplement, or reference work. We have thus focused on those developments and ideas that are widely accepted as seminal in the creation of the great civilizations and cultural traditions of the premodern world. Unfortunately, we have necessarily given less emphasis to many important events and people in order to maintain our focus on what we see as the most significant developments.

Professor Jay Pascal Anglin was instrumental in organizing and planning this project, and was kind enough to invite me to be co-author. Tragically, he was stricken with serious cancer during the early phases of writing, and died before the work could be completed. Professor Anglin was a fine friend and colleague, who is greatly missed. Professor Anglin wrote chapters 2, 3, and 4. The remaining chapters were written by William Hamblin.

I would like to thank Jonathon Brodman, Robert Weinstein, Robert Castillo, and Fred Grayson for their valuable assistance. John Clark provided useful criticism of chapter thirteen. Materials for chapter sixteen were graciously provided by J. Michael Allen and James B. Allen.

All charts and maps were designed by William Hamblin, and drawn by John Hamer and William Hamblin using a Macintosh computer and Adobe Illustrator and Aldus Freehand programs.

I would appreciate receiving any correspondence on suggested improvements for this book.

William James Hamblin

1

Basic Concepts of History

History is the study of the human past. Based on the careful analysis of surviving texts and artifacts, the historian attempts to reconstruct past events and processes which have created the world we live in.

THE STUDY OF HISTORY

Why Study History?

There are as many answers to this question as there are people who have reflected on the human condition. Several possible responses are often given by historians.

UNDERSTANDING THE WORLD

Understanding the world we live in, with its complex collection of events and developments, is impossible without understanding the past which created the present. Many past events, often from hundreds or even thousands of years ago, are still exerting important influences on the world, creating the parameters within which we live our lives.

COLLECTIVE MEMORY

Just as individuals would lose their identity if they lost their memory, so a society also loses, or more correctly transforms, its identity by its changing perception of the past. Nations, communities, groups, and individuals all understand themselves through their collective or individual memories of the past. Many modern social and political conflicts and issues arise from conflicting interpretations of the past. The historian serves as both the guardian and the interpreter of our collective memory.

INDIVIDUAL INTELLECTUAL FREEDOM

A knowledge of the past liberates the mind to view the world from different perspectives. Many of the fundamental questions concerning the problems of human existence have been asked for thousands of years. How should human groups relate to one another? Is war justifiable, and if so, under what conditions? How should society be organized? How should the benefits and responsibilities of society be distributed? Why are other communities and peoples different from us? Does God exist, and if so, how does He interact with humans? Many different answers to these and other important questions have been given by different sages and prophets throughout history. Some of their answers have been formed into intellectual or religious traditions which remain definitive for hundreds of millions of people. History forces us to recognize that, just like us, many peoples in the past have thought that their particular forms of civilization were the finest and most advanced the world has ever seen. Most of these civilizations no longer exist. History can thus serve as a mechanism to guard against temporal, geographical, or ethnic provincialism by allowing us to see the human experience from the broadest possible perspective.

HISTORY AS A HUMANISTIC STUDY

History is also an exciting branch of the humanities. It is an endlessly fascinating tale of human achievement and folly. At its finest, history is also literature, having for its plot the entire breadth of human experience. The great heroic deeds, sublime acts of selfless charity, and heinous crimes of mankind form the fundamental facets of history. Many people find a great deal of pleasure from journeying into the past. Without a knowledge of the past we cannot fully appreciate the great literature, art, architecture, and music of the world.

The Nature of Historical Study

The fundamental role of the historian is to ask questions about the past and to try to answer those questions. What happened? Who was involved? When and where did it occur? Why did it happen, and what were the results? The historian is thus often compared to a detective. A crime, such as a murder, is a historical incident: a unique event which occurred in the past. Just as a detective will examine the material evidence and question the witnesses in an attempt to reconstruct a crime, so the historian will also examine historical evidence in order to reconstruct past events.

EVIDENCE

Historians cannot directly observe the past. Nor can we create historical laboratories in which we can set up experiments in which the past can be recreated or modified. The historian's goal is to reach out and somehow comprehend and grasp a past that doesn't exist anymore; all that is left are fragmentary bits and pieces. In their attempts to reconstruct the past, historians must thus rely on the accidental survival of evidence, which they divide into two categories: artifacts and texts.

Artifactual Evidence: Archaeology. Any manmade material object which survives from the past is an artifact. Historians often divide artifacts into three categories based on the different methodologies used to analyze them, and the different types of information we can derive from them: (1) monuments and buildings which were built in the past; (2) art depicting past events, customs, gods, etc.; (3) objects, such as tools, weapons, or clothing, which were made and used in the past. The specialized study of the artifactual remains from the past is technically the domain of the archaeologist, but historians nonetheless frequently use archaeological and artifactual evidence in their attempts to reconstruct the past.

Textual Evidence: History. The most important types of artifacts from the past are those with writing on them. Indeed, written documents are absolutely crucial to the historical enterprise of reconstructing the past. In a sense a written document is a fossil idea. It is only through texts that we can enter into the minds of people long dead, to discover their hopes and hatreds, their gods and inner demons. Any document written in the past can have historical importance. Historical texts range from complete books of hundreds of pages to small inscriptions on coins. They include monumental inscriptions in rock, and obscure fragments of papyri. Private letters and journals are often as important as official government documents. The fundamental job of the historian is to read and analyze such documents in an effort to reconstruct past events and processes.

Primary Documents. Historians always attempt to get as close as possible to the actual past event they are trying to reconstruct. On occasion they go to the actual site of an event. They may attempt to handle or examine photographs of the artifacts that were involved in a particular past event. But most important, they read the surviving records of cycwitnesses in the original languages. Documents written by people who lived during or near the time of the events they are describing are called primary texts. Secondary texts are modern historians' interpretations and reconstructions of the past.

INTERPRETATION

All historical evidence requires interpretation. Evidence must be discovered, gathered together, analyzed, interpreted, and presented in the form of articles, books, lectures, or images in which the historian creates a verbal or representational reconstruction of a past event. No historian's reconstruction of the past can ever be perfect or complete. History is by no means an exact science. There are many factors which limit our ability to reconstruct the past.

The Limitations of Historical Evidence. We cannot directly observe any past events which happened beyond living memory. The surviving texts and artifacts from the past are fragmentary. By far most of the written documents from the past have been lost. On occasion, entire libraries of texts were either systematically or accidentally destroyed. The Spanish burned nearly all the books of the Mesoamerican Indians in a conscious, and basically successful attempt to obliterate Aztec civilization. Qin Shi, the first emperor of China, likewise ordered all the writings of Confucius burned in an attempt to destroy Confucianism; it survived only because Chinese scholars had memorized the texts. Alexander the Great burned the Persian imperial library at Persepolis, while Julius Caesar accidentally burned the library at Alexandria.

Of those records which survive, many are inaccurate. All documents from the past are written from the single limited perspective of an individual who cannot possible have known everything that happened, or presented a completely accurate account. Furthermore, all past writers had prejudices and biases. Many past writers had special purposes in writing; others lied about what they saw or did.

Limitations of Historical Reconstruction. After all the surviving evidence from the past has been collected and carefully analyzed for accuracy, historians still face numerous problems in interpretation. All historians bring their own philosophical assumptions and prejudices to the study of texts. Does God exist or not? Do human societies function on Marxist principles? Do humans behave according to a Freudian or some other psychological model? Furthermore, no historian, however brilliant, knows everything about the past. All historians must also be selective. To accurately describe all of the elements of a single battle—which consisted of a complex web of the actions of thousands of soldiers—would take a lifetime of writing (if the necessary evidence could be found). Thus historians are forced to select which events they wish to discuss, and which they ignore; which events or people were important, and which were inconsequential.

Reductionism. A fundamental problem facing the student of world history is the problem of selection and simplification of evidence. There are literally millions of pages of written material which survive from the past, in hundreds of languages. No single human could possibly read them all in a lifetime. But even if they could be read, how could they be adequately condensed into a single volume. Thus, a book such as this, which attempts to reconstruct the history of the entire world in a few hundred pages, suffers from unavoidable reductionism. Everything presented here has been simplified. Many important events and people are ignored. Generalizations are made which knowingly ignore many contrary examples.

The Global Perspective. Thus, what is presented here should not be seen as a completely accurate reconstruction of world history, but rather a model or map of the past. Historical reconstructions, just like maps, vary in accuracy depending on the scale. A map of the entire earth is not useful for finding a particular street in Paris, but neither will a street map of Paris aid one in discovering the location of Pakistan. The global perspective of history can be of great value, but only when we recognize its similar limitations of scale. Selected readings are provided with each chapter to direct students to more detailed historical reconstructions.

HISTORICAL CLASSIFICATION

Historians use a number of technical terms and methods of classification to help them analyze and reconstruct the past.

Technical Terms of Historical Study

CONTINUITY AND CHANGE

A central concept in history is the balance between continuity and change. Many elements of a culture—language, religion, ways of farming, social norms, technologies—may exhibit continuity for hundreds of years. Other aspects—kings, economic policy, military victory—can change quite rapidly. When forces for continuity seem more powerful than those of change, societies are said to be stable, conservative, or traditional. When the forces of change dominate, societies are often dynamic or even revolutionary. Although we in the modern West have a bias that change should be equated with progress, most ancient societies felt that stable continuity and order was preferable to uncontrolled change. Historians must always be aware of the balance between forces for change and those for continuity in any given period of history.

Events. A historical event is a discreet past occurrence which can be precisely defined in time and space. Thus a battle, the death of a king, a council of a church, or the writing of a book are all historical events. Although some events were of decisive importance in the history of the world, most past events were inconsequential. Thus the historian attempts to identify those historical events which played a decisive role in the transformations of history.

Processes. For historians a process represents patterns of change over long periods of time. Thus, while the conversion of an individual is a historical event, the spread of Christianity as a whole is a historical process. Historical processes are usually composed of numerous—occasionally millions—of discreet events, just as the spread of Christianity into western

Europe is a process composed of the individual conversion of hundreds of thousands of people. The births, lives, and deaths of the millions of peasant farmers who have toiled throughout history can each be seen as separate events, which have had, on an individual basis, very little effect on history. Collectively, however, their labors represent one of the most important historical processes, the means by which humans feed themselves.

Causality. Historians not only attempt to describe the past in their reconstructions, but also to explain why certain events or processes happened in the way they did. Attempts are made to discover the causes of each event or process. Furthermore, there are frequently chains of causality, with each cause having an anterior cause in an endless repetition back through time. Each event or process was caused by past events or processes, and in turn causes future events or processes. It must be emphasized that historical causality is extremely complex, with some events or processes having hundreds, if not thousands of causes. On a global historical level historians are frequently forced to greatly simplify extremely complex patterns of causality by focusing on what they believe are the decisive causes, while ignoring or downplaying other minor contributory causes.

CHRONOLOGICAL TERMINOLOGY

In order to precisely define the relationships between events, processes, and causes, historians need to create accurate methods of relating their historical reconstructions to time.

Calendar Systems. Calendar systems are attempts to create uniform mechanisms for measuring time. Most calendars are based on the observation of regularly repeating astronomical phenomenon, usually solar years or lunar months. Many different calendars have been devised by different societies, which are sometimes difficult to correlate. The Romans based their calendar from the legendary founding of the city of Rome in 753 B.C. Many calendars in India begin with the Shaka era in A.D. 78. The Muslims use a lunar calendar which began in A.D. 622 when Muhammad migrated to Medina.

The Modern Calendar. Our modern calendar, which has been adopted by most peoples in the world today for international use, is based on a medieval Christian calendar. It begins with the birth of Christ: the abbreviation A.D. refers to *anno domini*, the "year of [the birth of] our Lord [Jesus Christ]." The abbreviation B.C. refers to "Before Christ," and is counted backward. Although for the sake of simplicity this book uses the conventional dating system of A.D. and B.C., scholars are increasingly using the more neutral abbreviations of C.E. (in the Common or Current Era) for A.D., and B.C.E. (Before the Current Era) for B.C.

Historic and Prehistoric. Historians often use the term historic to refer to human societies which possess writing, and prehistoric to refer to

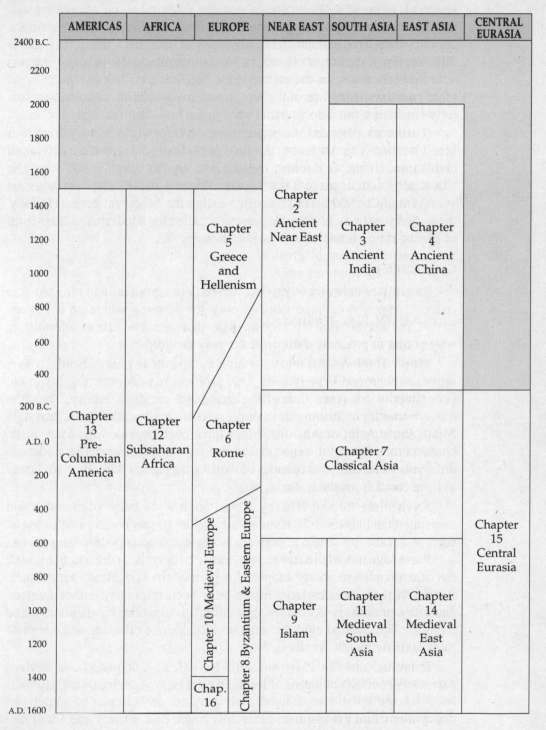

Fig. 1.1 World Chronological Chart

societies before the invention of writing. The use of these terms is not arbitrary. Historic societies which possess writing can be studied by historians who focus on texts; prehistoric societies without writing remain the domain of the archaeologist. It is important to note that history "begins" at different times in different places. In Mesopotamia and Egypt history begins with the earliest written documents in the late fourth millennium B.C. On the other hand, some regions of the world, such as Australia, remained prehistoric (without written documents) until just a few centuries ago.

Historical Periods. Historians often divide world history into four broad periods. The Ancient or Archaic period stretches from the origins of civilization in the late fourth millennium B.C. to roughly 500 B.C. The Classical period begins in 500 B.C., extending to A.D. 500. The next thousand years, from A.D. 500 to 1500, is often called the Medieval period. Finally, the period from A.D. 1500 to the present is called the Modern age. This form of periodization is useful only as broad categories.

GEOGRAPHY

Each historical event or process can be defined not only in time but also space. Geography is important not only for defining where an event occurred, but also because it played an important causative role in determining why events or processes happened the way they did.

Major Regions. An understanding of history is possible only with a proper background in geography. One problem in understanding historical geography is that place names have changed throughout history. Thus, the modern country of Turkey, for example, was anciently called Asia, then Asia Minor (little Asia) or Anatolia. Maps have been provided for each of the chapters to indicate the major places and regions discussed. If a student is unfamiliar with the basic outlines of world geography it would be advisable to have an atlas available during study.

Environments and History. There are a wide range of climates and environments in the world. Humans are unable to survive in some of these, such as oceans, the arctic regions, or waterless deserts. While humans can survive in high mountains, the steppe, semiarid deserts, or deep jungles, such environments were poorly adapted for premodern agricultural techniques. People in these regions have historically been migratory, either hunters, gatherers, or nomads. Sedentary agricultural civilizations have thus centered largely in specialized environments with temperate climates and adequate rainfall or rivers for irrigation.

Humans and the Environment. Historically, humans have devised extremely specialized means of living in each type of environment. Humans have for the most part adapted their patterns of behavior to match the necessities of the environment. It is only in the past century and a half that humans have made substantial attempts to transform as much of the planet as possible to meet their limited cultural expectations, rather than adapting their lifestyles and behavior to better match the environment. Ecological problems, however, are by no means new. Humans have caused the extinction of other species, deforestation, pollution of urban water sources, and the salinization of soils from irrigation for several thousand years.

Human Social Organization

Historians have borrowed categories from anthropologists in order to define human social organization.

KINSHIP GROUPS

The earliest and most enduring form of human social organization was the family. Since human children require a large number of years before they can take care of themselves, those humans which formed stable families tended to be most successful in reproducing and rearing. Most ancient human societies centered on extended kinship groups such as clans or tribes, which included several generations as well as cousins and uncles.

MIGRATORY PEOPLES

Migratory peoples are those who are forced to periodically move in order to obtain their food.

Hunter-Gatherers. The most ancient form of human economic organization was the hunter or gatherer clan. They obtained their food from a combination of hunting wild animals, and gathering wild nuts, fruits, and grains. Hunter-gatherer groups were forced to migrate according to seasonal patterns in order to follow the herds they hunted.

Nomads. With the domestication of animals many humans became herders rather than predators. The most important domesticated animals for nomads included cows, sheep, goats, horses, and camels. The survival of domesticated animals required that a nomadic clan migrate on a seasonal basis in order to ensure sufficient pasture and water for their herds.

SEDENTARY PEOPLES

Sedentary peoples are those who are forced to live in one place in order to obtain their food.

Agriculturalists. Agriculturalists who produce their food through farming are the foundation of sedentary human organization. The annual necessities of clearing, planting, tending, and harvesting require nearly constant human attention, forcing farmers to live in small homesteads or villages. Farming allows many more people to obtain their food from a given amount of land than either hunting, gathering, or herding.

Urban. Urban life is distinguished from agricultural life in that the urban peoples obtain their food not by directly farming themselves, but by trading with or taxing the farmers. When surplus food began to be gathered into a single center, people in that area could specialize in nonagricultural pursuits. This, in turn, led ultimately to the origins of civilization.

THE INVENTION OF CIVILIZATION

Civilization is often defined as having: (1) human societies with cities (urban centers with at least several thousand people, as opposed to villages with only a few hundred); (2) economic specialization and social stratification; and (3) a common government, language, religion, or other form of social bond and organization beyond kinship.

The Origins of Civilization

THE NEOLITHIC REVOLUTION

The Neolithic revolution is fundamentally the transformation of human groups from food collectors (hunters and gatherers) to food producers (herders and farmers). It first occurred in the Near East in the eighth millennium B.C.

Domestication of Plants. Human gatherer groups had eaten seeds of various types of grasses for thousands of years. Rather than just randomly collecting naturally growing grass seeds, some humans in the Near East came to understand the causes of plant growth and began systematically planting, protecting, and harvesting plants. New types of plants were developed through hybridization and selective breeding. As sophisticated forms of agriculture eventually developed, small human farming villages became widespread throughout the Near East, with the basic technologies of agriculture spreading to Europe, Africa, and Asia.

Domestication of Animals. Along with the development of plant domestication and agriculture many humans also began to domesticate wild animals as a food supply. Certain environments, such as semi-deserts and steppes, had sufficient pasture for herds, but were unsuitable for agriculture. In these regions animals became the primary source of food, leading to the creation of nomadic societies which specialized in herding domesticated animals, just as the new sedentary agriculturalists specialized in farming domesticated plants.

THE ORIGIN OF CITIES

The invention of agriculture and the development of small sedentary farming villages created the social conditions necessary for the development of cities and civilizations.

The Role of River Valleys. Agriculture originally arose in the regions of the Near East with adequate rainfall for farming. In certain semi-desert parts of the Near East, however—such as the Nile and Tigris-Euphrates River valleys—rainfall was inadequate for farming. In those regions farming could be successful only if the water resources of the rivers could be properly harnessed through irrigation. These same rivers provided sources of meat from fishing, reeds and mud bricks for building, and a transportation system by navigating the rivers. The necessity of irrigation for successful agriculture in river valleys provided a fundamental catalyst in the creation of civilization. The need to organize large-scale irrigation projects led to the creation of regional governments to coordinate these efforts. Thus, the earliest civilizations were either in river valleys or in swampland which required major new forms of social cooperation for irrigation.

Agricultural Surpluses. Once properly organized, irrigated agriculture in the river valleys proved far more productive than rain-fed agriculture. River valley soils were more fertile, crop yields were higher, and several crops could be harvested a year. The increase in productivity meant that individual farmers could now produce far more food than they needed for their families, creating an agricultural surplus.

Economic Specialization. Agricultural surpluses permitted the development of economic specialization. Experts in pot making, clothmaking, metalworking, hunting, warfare, or religion could now trade their specialized skills and products for the agricultural surplus. This permitted the development of a wide range of nonagricultural occupations, which became increasingly professional.

The Formation of the Temple-City. Traditional sites of religious worship naturally became the new centers of exchange and specialization. Priests collected part of the surplus as gifts and sacrifices to the gods. They gathered around them various economic specialists to protect and care for the gods. Annual gatherings of villagers to their central ancestral shrines at times of planting or harvest became the occasion of trade fairs as well as worship. Priests became specialists in knowledge, and developed forms of writing to assist them in keeping records and recording sacred lore. The shrines were thus slowly transformed from the small villages of the ancestral gods to the first true cities.

Social Stratification. Economic specialization led to the formation of social stratification. Certain crucial occupations, usually those of priest and warrior, began to consume increasing proportions of the agricultural surplus. Priests needed to continually improve the quality of the temples and rituals to ensure that the gods would continue to provide fertility for farmers. Warriors needed specialized equipment and training to protect the community. They would often return from battle with plunder, making them increasingly wealthy. The priests and warriors soon came to dominate society as a whole.

Trade. The lack of metals or other natural resources encouraged increasingly wide-ranging trading expeditions. Merchants would take the specialized crafts of civilization—metal tools, weapons, fine cloth, or other manufactured items—into semi-civilized regions to exchange for raw materials. This led to the rapid spread of the new technologies of civilization via the trade routes.

Warfare. As civilization developed, conflicts arose between temple-cities competing for land or resources. Outside barbarians might also attack the new urban centers in search of slaves and plunder. Warfare thus became a fundamental catalyst in the development of civilization. Warriors became a dominant class in society, new military technologies were invented and copied, wealth was plundered and redistributed, and larger political units began to be formed as one city-state conquered another.

Writing. A final important factor in the origins of civilization was the invention of writing. Originally devised as a mechanism to record the economic surpluses held by the temples, writing quickly became the means of storing and transmitting information through time and space. With the invention of writing the final element of civilization was in place. Ideas could now be preserved for thousands of years; writing thus became the basis for our knowledge of the past.

THE SIX PRIMARY CIVILIZATIONS

A primary civilization is one which made the transformation from neolithic agriculture to urban civilization in relative independence from outside influences. In other words, they invented, rather than borrowed, the technologies and necessary social organizations of civilization as outlined above. Historians have identified six zones of the possible development of primary civilizations which will be discussed in the following chapters: Mesopotamia, c. 3500 B.C. and Egypt, c. 3200 B.C. in the Near East (chapter 2); the Indus Valley in modern Pakistan, c. 2500 B.C. (chapter 3); the Yellow River valley in China, c. 2000 B.C. (chapter 4); Mesoamerica, c. 1500 B.C. and Peru, c. 1200 B.C. in pre-Columbian America (chapter 13).

*T*he Neolithic revolution of the domestication of plants and animals forever transformed human society. Agriculture provided a new means of producing food. When transferred to river valleys, agriculture required increasing social cooperation for irrigation while producing food surpluses. These two factors led to the formation of governments and economic specialization centering on ancestral temple-cities. By the late fourth millennium B.C., humans in Mesopotamia and Egypt had created the world's first cities and civilizations—a new form of human social organization which has continued until today.

Selected Readings

Barraclough, Geoffrey, ed. *The Times Atlas of World History* (1989)

Breisach, Ernst. *Historiography: Ancient, Medieval, and Modern* (1983)

Cotterell, Arthur, ed. *The Penguin Encyclopedia of Ancient Civilizations* (1980)

Gilderhus, Mark T. *History and Historians: A Historiographical Introduction*, 2nd ed. (1992)

Novick, Peter. *That Noble Dream: The "Objectivity Question" and the American Historical Profession* (1988)

Renfrew, Colin, ed. *Past Worlds: The Times Atlas of Archaeology* (1988)

Shafer, Robert Jones. *A Guide to Historical Method*, 3rd. ed. (1980)

Whitehouse, Ruth, and John Wilkins. *The Making of Civilization: History Discovered Through Archaeology* (1986)

2

Ancient Near East

(Unless otherwise indicated, all dates in this chapter are B.C. Those before
600 B.C. are approximate.)

3500	Pre-dynastic Sumerian culture; development of urbanization
3200–2334	Sumerian city-states in Mesopotamia
3100	Menes unifies Egypt
2686–2181	Old Kingdom in Egypt
2334–2191	Akkadian dynasty in Mesopotamia
2181–2040	First Intermediate Period in Egypt
2190–2080	Gutian dynasty in Mesopotamia
2112–2004	Third Dynasty of Ur in Mesopotamia
2040–1674	Middle Kingdom in Egypt
1900	*Epic of Gilgamesh*
1894–1595	Babylonian dynasty in Mesopotamia
1674–1552	Second Intermediate Period in Egypt
1552–1069	New Kingdom in Egypt
1415–1154	Kassite dynasty in Mesopotamia
1400	Development of the Phoenician alphabet
1380–1190	Hittite empire in Anatolia
1367–1350	Akhenaten and the Amarna period in Egypt
1260	Destruction of Troy

1200	Iron Age begins
1200–586	Hebrew kingdom
1069–332	Late Period in Egypt
911–605	The Assyrian empire
814	Founding of Carthage
750–500	Age of the Hebrew prophets
612–539	Neo-Babylonian (Chaldean) empire
586	Fall of Judah
559	Cyrus the Great founds Achaemenid dynasty
559–330	Persian empire unites the entire Near East

The world's earliest civilizations emerged in rich agricultural lands situated along the Tigris and Euphrates rivers in modern Iraq, and in the Nile River valley in Egypt. The Tigris-Euphrates valley, called Mesopotamia by the ancient Greeks, developed an eclectic urbanized culture based on Sumerian foundations. Homeland to numerous empire builders and short-lived kingdoms, Mesopotamia spread its culture throughout west Asia. Its most notable achievements were in the fields of religion, science, mathematics, writing, and literature.

The Egyptians developed an independent civilization that reached its completed stage by the Middle Kingdom. Isolated by geographical barriers, the Egyptians focused most of their creative energy on religion until they took up empire building in the sixteenth century B.C. Their architectural feats in temple and pyramid building remain their greatest cultural legacy. Following their absorption into the Persian empire, both civilizations endured to form an integral part of Hellenistic civilization.

MESOPOTAMIA

The world's first civilization emerged in the late fourth millennium B.C. in southern Iraq, developing in urban centers situated along the banks of the Tigris and the Euphrates rivers. Essential breakthroughs that allowed the inhabitants of Sumer to make a transition from the Neolithic Age had occurred in the previous millennium. In that period organized communal effort permitted the construction of elaborate irrigation and flood-control systems.

This allowed the Sumerians to transform flood-prone marshy lands and surrounding patches of desert into rich farmland. Agricultural surpluses generated population increases which in turn allowed small Neolithic villages to evolve into independent city-states. Controlled initially by priestly hierarchies, these urban centers gradually developed writing and essential political, legal, and economic structures. The transition to urban civilization was hastened by the discovery of bronze and by important technological inventions (wheeled vehicles, the potter's wheel, animal-drawn plows, and the sailboat). These in turn fostered craft specializations and class divisions.

The Greek name Mesopotamia (the land between the rivers) was commonly applied to the entire Tigris-Euphrates valley, which formed a single cultural region. Devoid of natural barriers, Mesopotamia was subject to intermittent raids by Semitic-speaking tribes from the Arabian peninsula to the southwest, and by Indo-European herders from the Zagros Mountains to the northeast. Intruders frequently settled in the region, playing a formative role in the political and cultural history of the valley. Led by warrior kings, some tribes founded empires that extended over much of west Asia. These empires facilitated cultural interchange and allowed for the extension of Mesopotamian culture throughout west Asia.

The first intruders entered the valley in the late fourth millennium B.C., when Semitic tribes settled north of Sumer and founded the kingdom of Akkad. During the next two millennia a steady influx of Semitic nomadic tribes into Mesopotamia gave them numerical, linguistic, and political dominance throughout the region. Culturally inferior to the Sumerians, the earliest tribes adopted the superior culture of their new homeland and modified it to accommodate their own unique institutions. The resultant eclectic "Mesopotamian" civilization in turn served as the foundation for its successor. As a consequence, strong cultural continuity can be seen between the various cultures within Mesopotamia and in west Asia.

The Sumerians (3200–2334 B.C.)

Although we know little about the origins of these people, it is clear that the region called Sumer was organized politically into numerous autonomous city-states or temple communities by 3000 B.C. In most communities land was commonly owned by the clan or was reserved exclusively for temple use.

POLITICAL ORGANIZATION

Initially, a secular ruler (*lugal*) and priest-bureaucrats jointly ruled each city-state. This eventually gave way to sole rule by an autocratic king who claimed to rule by divine sanction. Frequent wars between the communities over disputed water rights and land boundaries enhanced the power of warrior kings. If a powerful king attempted to impose regional political unity, his threatened neighbors tried to form military alliances to thwart him.

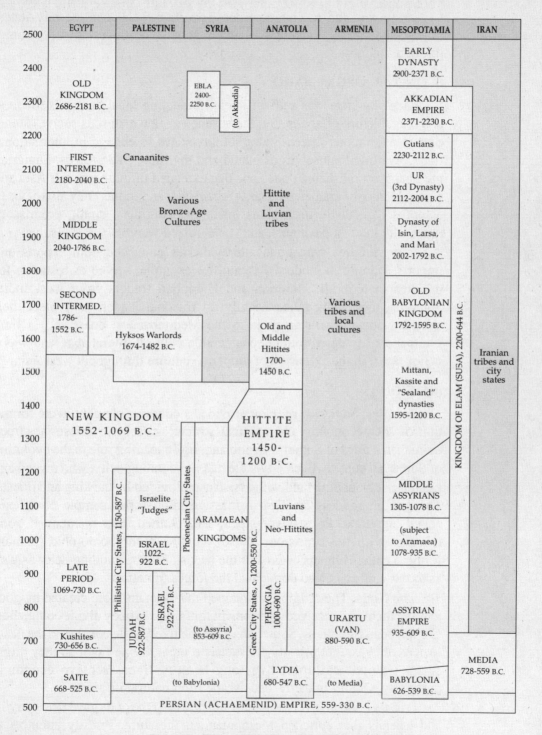

Fig. 2.1   The Middle East from 2500 to 500 B.C.

Periodic attempts to unify Sumer by kings from Ur, Umma, Erech, and Lagash proved futile. This continuous warfare weakened the city-states, setting the stage for invading Akkadians from the northwest to impose unity through conquest.

ECONOMIC ORGANIZATION

Each city-state was self-sufficient in meeting local demands for food and manufacture of goods. But the absence of raw materials such as stone, timber, and metals forced Sumerian city-states to engage in international trade. Availing themselves of inland and maritime trade routes, Sumerian merchants established a trade zone that extended throughout west Asia and eastward into the Iranian plateau, Afghanistan, and India. They also devised essential capitalistic institutions, including contracts, credit, promissory notes with interest payments, and standardized weights and measures.

Joint ventures with trade intermediaries enhanced both exports and imports. Dilmun in modern Bahrain, for example, served as a station for middleman to both Sumerian and Harappan traders from west India. Sumerian merchants relied heavily on regional leaders to protect their overland donkey caravan trade to the Mediterranean coast and in Iran. International trade permitted considerable cultural interchange and was a major factor in the extension of Sumerian culture throughout west Asia.

RELIGION

Temples. Sumerian religion provided a cohesive element in the formation of socioeconomic and political structures. Temple priests absorbed more than a third of Sumer's wealth and took a leading role in the evolution of Sumerian culture. Each city-state had its founding deity, who owned and ruled the surrounding land with assistance provided by the king and priests. The god or goddess dwelled in massive multistoried temple complexes called ziggurats. Priests worshiped, fed, clothed, and maintained good relations with the capricious and demanding anthropomorphic (human-formed) gods. Humans catered to the needs of their founding deity as well as to those of gods who dominated the forces of nature.

The Gods. The religion maintained that humans were created by gods to serve them and received punishment for failure to obey divine commands. Compared to Egyptians, Sumerians gave relatively little concern to the dead. Instead, they sought priestly assistance to incur divine favor so they might secure wanted children, live long healthy lives, achieve economic prosperity, victory in battle, and escape from natural disasters.

Priestly concern over the nature and power of the gods gave rise to myths and legends that enriched Mesopotamian literature. Priestly attempts to ascertain the will of the gods through study and observation of natural phenomena made possible a lunar calendar and the disciplines of astrology and astronomy.

CUNEIFORM WRITING

Sumerian priests responded to practical needs for establishing proof of property rights and for keeping records by inventing a complex writing system in the late fourth millennium B.C. Mastery of the hundreds of abstract signs required intensive study in formal scribal schools and severely limited its use. Now called "cuneiform" because its characters are wedge-shaped, this system was widely used throughout west Asia through the first millennium. Possibly this early system directly influenced the later writing systems devised by Egypt and the Indus. Lacking paper, Sumerian scribes wrote on soft clay tablets. Students in scribal schools produced numerous copies of important texts, many of which were housed in royal archives. From burned sites, archaeologists continue to recover whole libraries, their contents preserved as fired clay.

Mesopotamian Dynasties, 2334– 1050 B.C.

THE AKKAD DYNASTY (2334–2193 B.C.)

Sumer's peaceful coexistence with its northern neighbor, the Akkadians, ended in war in 2334 B.C. Defeated by soldiers commanded by Sargon the Great (2334–2279 B.C.), king of Akkad, the Sumerian city-states were forcibly annexed. They soon formed part of a short-lived empire that included Syria, Elam (southwest Iran), and Upper Mesopotamia. The conquerors embraced Sumerian culture and promoted it throughout the empire, but they rejected its political forms and its language. Their own Semitic language, Akkadian, displaced Sumerian and became common to the entire region. A series of ineffective rulers, internal revolts, and barbarian attacks gradually eroded Akkad's control of its empire. The empire collapsed in 2190 B.C. when tribes of Guti herders occupied the capital city of Akkad.

THE GUTIAN DYNASTY (2180–C. 2120 B.C.)

Attracted into the region by its wealth, the Guti from the Zagros Mountains in modern Iran used military force to master Akkad and Sumer and to exploit them economically. During their brief ascendancy these rude tribes maintained loose and sporadic control over Mesopotamia, but left no permanent mark on its culture. Their ineffective rule allowed the Sumerian cities of Uruk, Lagash, and Ur to revitalize themselves. After establishing itself as an independent kingdom, Uruk took the initiative in expelling the Guti. Foreign rule ended in 2119 B.C. when Utuhegal, king of Uruk, defeated the Guti in battle.

THE THIRD DYNASTY OF UR (2112–2004 B.C.)

By 2112 B.C. Urnammu, former military governor to Utuhegal, transformed Ur into an empire by occupying Uruk and taking control of most of the Akkadian territories. Declaring himself a divine ruler, Urnammu established absolutist rule through innovative administrative reforms. He and his four successors maintained law and order by forcibly deporting rebellious subjects.

By implementing political stability, a state-controlled economy, and major public-works projects, the Ur dynasty provided Mesopotamia a century of peace and prosperity. Culture flourished and the scribal schools evolved into major centers of learning. Orally transmitted myths and legends were set down in written form. Urnammu's law code, the first of its kind, marked a distinct advance in the field of law and jurisprudence by allowing monetary recompense for damages and focusing on social and economic justice.

Ur's primacy ended in 2004 B.C. when rebellious Elamites from southwest Iran destroyed the capital city and took captive King Ibbi-Sin. In part, Ur's collapse was hastened by the political and economic dislocations that accompanied the intrusion of Semitic-speaking Amorites from the Syrian desert into the empire.

THE BABYLONIAN DYNASTY (1894–1595 B.C.)

After settling in Mesopotamia the Amorites embraced its superior culture. They then built up their political base by gradually absorbing the cities of Babylon, Larsa, and Eshnunna. Once Sumuabum (1894–1881 B.C.) founded a new dynasty at Babylon in 1830 B.C., his successors extended Amorite rule over all of Mesopotamia by 1759 B.C. The main architect of the Amorite empire was Hammurabi (1792–1750), a warrior king with superb skills as a lawmaker and administrator.

By offering strong central rule and a vigorous state-controlled economy, the Babylonian kings promoted regional unity. So, too, did the use of a common Akkadian tongue, Babylonian law, and a state religion based on Marduk, the Babylonian god. As the new political and religious capital, Babylon emerged as the region's major metropolitan center.

Following the death of Hammurabi, less gifted kings failed to curb the aspirations of outlying provinces for independence. Within two decades, the southern provinces successfully severed connections with Babylon. Internal discord further weakened the ability of Babylon to defend its borders. By 1700 B.C., mountaineering Hurrians from the northeast occupied Upper Mesopotamia. This induced the Hittites from the northwest to intensify their pressures after 1650 B.C., culminating in 1595 B.C. in the sack of Babylon and temporary Hittite domination. Amorite rule ended in 1530 B.C., when

Kassite mountaineers from the Zagros mountains occupied Babylon and incorporated it into their empire.

THE KASSITE DYNASTY (1415–1154 B.C.)

Little is known of the Kassites, tribes of horse-breeding herders who shared grasslands in the Zagros mountains with the Guti. They spoke an Asian language and may have been ethnically related to the Hittites and the Hurrians. In 1500 B.C. the Kassites successfully invaded and occupied Babylon. For nearly five hundred years the Kassite kings maintained political control over the region to exploit its wealth. Kassite rule provided Babylon a long era of political stability marked by peace, prosperity, and cultural stagnation. The Kassites readily embraced Babylonian culture, but they made only minor contributions of their own. Kassite rule ended in the late twelfth century, when the militant Assyrians absorbed Babylon.

Babylonian Culture

Patronized by the Amorite rulers, scribal schools became major centers of learning which preserved many religious myths, legends, hymns, fables, and proverbs. Scholars engaged in speculative and practical studies that led to advances in mathematics and science.

EPIC OF GILGAMESH

Deriving inspiration from ancient traditions and the Mesopotamian religion, Babylonian scholars produced the world's first epic poem, the *Epic of Gilgamesh*, focused on the heroic quest for immortality by the hero, Gilgamesh, king of Uruk (2800 B.C.). Modern readers are particularly fascinated by its flood tale because it shares many similarities with that told in the Bible by the Hebrews.

MATHEMATICS AND SCIENCE

Scribal production of mathematical texts also generated practical, non-theoretical advances in arithmetic and geometry. Textbooks for classroom instruction introduced students to the place-value system of numeration; they also provided mathematical tables for multiplication, square and cube roots, exponents, and interest computations. Texts for advanced students show that Babylonians could readily handle quadratic and linear equations, compute volumes and areas of geometric forms, and use the Pythagorean theorem. Math did not serve as the language of science, but Babylonian scientists used it to devise units of time and space. Astronomy and astrology dominated the attention of scientists.

HAMMURABI'S CODE

The world's first major law code was composed on the orders of Hammurabi, king of Babylon. The 282 case laws in the code amended existing laws, integrating ancient tribal practices both in their perception of crime and in the severity of their penalties. Penalties included retribution in kind (an eye for an eye), loss of body parts, or death; some crimes allowed felons to pay monetary fines for crimes. As a historical document the code offers useful insights on Babylonian society, ethical standards, commerce and industry, the professions, property rights, and state-regulated prices and wages.

EGYPT

The Nile basin in the northwest corner of Africa was home to one of the most remarkable civilizations in antiquity. By exploiting the water and mineral nutrients from the Nile River, the ancient Egyptians transformed nearly 10,000 square miles of desert and swamp into rich arable land. Egypt's remarkably stable culture endured for 3,000 years, until eventually overwhelmed by Christianity.

The Land and Its People

GEOGRAPHY

From its sources in central Africa, the 4,000-mile-long Nile River flows unimpeded through Egypt into the Mediterranean Sea. Within Egypt the Nile flows northward through 525 miles of desert. The southernmost part of Egypt, called Upper Egypt, was an enclosed and protected river flood valley up to a dozen miles wide. Just north of modern Cairo, the river branches into several channels and forms a triangular delta of rich marshy plains called Lower Egypt. Approximately 150 miles wide, these plains contain two-thirds of the arable land of Egypt.

Until the building of the Aswan High Dam in the twentieth century, annual floods covered much of Lower and Upper Egypt between July and October. The receding nutrient-laden waters carried away accumulated salt deposits but left behind a rich alluvium that limited the need for fertilizers. Egypt's climate and an elaborate irrigation system permitted the region to produce two or three crops annually. As a consequence Egypt comprised one of the world's richest agricultural areas. The Nile unified Egypt. It served as its principal communication link and facilitated extensive trade and commerce along its banks.

Mountains and deserts surrounding these rich arable lands isolated and protected Egypt to some extent from its hostile neighbors. They allowed Egypt to produce an indigenous civilization that could fully mature before culturally inferior intruders breached the barriers. Throughout most of Egypt's history, alien conquerors eventually embraced Egyptian civilization. This combined with traditional native conservatism to minimize outside cultural influences.

Egypt's unique location at the land junction between Africa and the Near East, and the closest connection between the Mediterranean and the Red Sea, created a unique mixture of African, Near Eastern, and European cultures and ethnic groups.

PERIODIZATION

In the third century B.C., an Egyptian chronicler, Manetho, organized Egypt's history into thirty dynasties. Modern scholars have further organized Egypt's dynastic histories into four major periods or kingdoms. These periods are the Old Kingdom (2686–2181 B.C.); the Middle Kingdom (2040–1674 B.C.); the New Kingdom (1552–1069 B.C.), and the Late Period (715–332 B.C.). Each of these periods possesses a distinct political unity and is separated by periods of instability and disunity.

PREDYNASTIC EGYPT (TO 3100 B.C.)

Limited data cast few insights on the history of Upper and Lower Egypt before 3100 B.C. Once the Neolithic revolution had extended into Egypt from west Asia, the Egyptians evolved social structures, arts and crafts, and political organization. They formed into a number of independent city-states. Eventually, the need for cooperation to build large-scale irrigation works forced these local political units to merge into loose political federations. In the late fourth millennium these coalitions in Upper and Lower Egypt were transformed into kingdoms. The two halves of Egypt were unified around 3100 B.C., when Menes, king of Upper Egypt, conquered Lower Egypt.

The predynastic period produced two notable cultural contributions: the world's first solar calendar and the hieroglyphic system of writing. The foundations of many basic building blocks of Egyptian civilization can be traced to this period.

Early Dynastic (3100–2686 B.C.) and Old Kingdom (2686–2181 B.C.)

In this prosperous and creative era, six dynastic houses ruled nearly two million Egyptians from their capital at Memphis. As absolute monarchs the rulers of Egypt enhanced their authority by claiming to be the sons of Re, the sun god who ruled the universe through *Ma'at* (cosmic order). As god-kings serving as the embodiment of the theocratic state, the pharaohs mediated between the gods and the Egyptian people, maintaining harmony with *Ma'at*, thereby providing Egypt needed order and prosperity.

THEOCRATIC GOVERNMENT

The pharaohs exercised autocratic political and religious control, served as high priests, and planned and directed the economy. As sole owners of the land, the pharaohs created a command economic system which allowed them to control production and distribution through administrative means. The state also maintained a monopoly over domestic and foreign trade. To administer their realm the pharaohs relied heavily on an elaborate bureaucracy manned by royal appointees. Royal viziers (ministers) exercised supervisory control over all central administrative departments. As overseers, they curbed the power of Egypt's regional governors. They also forced the governors to comply fully with royal taxes on agriculture and to provide labor from the masses for the construction of public-works projects.

Despite the awesome attributes and powers of their office, Egyptian pharaohs continually faced the brutal realities of power politics. Failure to produce needed male heirs, incompetency, and political factionalism could lead to palace coups and even dynastic changes. Four different dynasties ruled Egypt in the Old Kingdom era. Assassinations, military coups, and factional struggles allowed interlopers to usurp the throne and to found new dynastic houses once they secured public acceptance of their divine status. During the course of its 3,000-year history Egypt accommodated former viziers, noblemen, women, and even foreigners as divine pharaohs.

THE STATE RELIGION

By monopolizing Egypt's economy, the pharaohs could divert a major portion of Egypt's wealth into the official state religion. This religion focused on the worship of various manifestations of the sun god (Re, Amon) and the pharaoh. The priests maintained that Egypt would endure so long as its people performed the proper rituals and worshiped the gods through their incarnation as the pharaohs. Religious rites were monopolized by priests and conducted in elaborate temple complexes. The state religion embraced the tenet that the dead king's soul (*ka*) departed his body and entered into the divine court of the gods in the heavens. Periodically the king's soul returned to the royal corpse. To preserve the king's body as an adequate residence for the eternal soul in the resurrection, Egyptian specialists skillfully devised means to mummify it.

THE PYRAMID AGE

The most remarkable and enduring structures in the Old Kingdom were the great stone pyramids used to house royal mummies. Imhotep's innovative use of the mud brick *mastaba*, an above-ground burial structure, gave rise in 2650 B.C. to pharaoh Zoser's step pyramid, the world's first monumental stone structure. Subsequent modifications in design permitted architects in the Fourth Dynasty to develop the true pyramid. The Old Kingdom era witnessed the construction of more than eighty pyramids, the largest of which were located at Giza. Realized through amazing engineering feats, immense costs in labor and material, but with limited technology, the pyramids served as silent reminders that deceased pharaohs continued to play a central role in Egypt's welfare.

During the annual flood season, Egyptian serfs freely performed much of the labor on the pyramids as an act of faith. Still, the extensive construction costs for these royal projects drained the state treasury. Preoccupied with their completion, pharaohs unwittingly undermined centralized control by allowing the office of provincial governor to become inheritable. Royal concessions to the governors enabled them to form a powerful nobility. Once they built private bases of power, the governors challenged each other for regional leadership and looked covetously at the office of the pharaoh.

THE FIRST INTERMEDIATE PERIOD (2181–2040 B.C.)

Between 2181 and 2040 B.C. the collapse of central rule led to political fragmentation. Some governors usurped royal political and religious authority and waged factional struggles with rivals. Political anarchy ended in 2050 B.C. when Mentuhotep, the noble ruler of Thebes, overcame his rivals and founded the Eleventh Dynasty of the Middle Kingdom.

The Middle Kingdom (2040–1674 B.C.)

After merging the local Theban god Amon with the sun god Re, the new pharaoh shifted his administrative capital to El-Lisht in the Fayum region just south of Memphis. There, he and his successors formed an alliance with men of talent from the middle class and reduced the power of the nobles. Ably assisted by their scribes, the pharaohs of the Eleventh and Twelfth Dynasties gradually restored absolutist rule. They restored social justice and democratized the state religion by promising commoners life after death on condition that they adhere to a prescribed code of moral conduct.

The pharaohs also undertook preemptive military strikes against their neighbors. Military campaigns against the Nubians in the south, against the Libyans in the west, and against the Semitic bedouins in the east temporarily secured Egypt's borders. They also revived international trade. Surplus revenues allowed them to undertake land reclamation projects in the Fayum area, which enhanced agricultural production and improved the lot of the masses.

SECOND INTERMEDIATE PERIOD (1674–1552 B.C.)

A series of weak pharaohs and the disputed ascendency of Sobekneferu (1798–1786 B.C.), daughter of Amenemhet III, led to factionalism and internal disorder. In the political vacuum that ensued, the Hyksos, Semitic warlords from Palestine, settled in the eastern delta. After embracing Egyptian culture, these "Rulers of Foreign Lands" used their superior weapons—the composite bow, the horse and war chariot, and bronze armor—to master Lower Egypt. By 1650 B.C. the Hyksos began to threaten

Upper Egypt. Faced with total subjugation, Egypt's contentious factions were united in 1570 B.C. by Thebes, which then mounted a counteroffensive against the Hyksos.

The New Kingdom (1552– 1069 B.C.)

IMPERIAL CONQUESTS

Two Theban princes, Kamose and his younger brother Ahmose, took the initiative in expelling the Hyksos from central and northern Egypt. Ahmose destroyed the Hyksos capital at Avaris and pursued the alien conquerors into Palestine. He then returned to Thebes to serve as pharaoh of a reunited Egypt.

Ahmose's reign inaugurated the imperial New Kingdom. In this period militaristic pharaohs abandoned Egypt's isolationist policy. By 1490 B.C. they forged a great empire that extended into the Sudan and west Asia. Egyptian pharaohs controlled gold-rich Nubia and the Sudan; their armies occupied Palestinian and Syrian territories. Seventeen military campaigns in west Asia by Thutmose III (1490–1436 B.C.) allowed Egypt to take a leading role in West Asian trade and politics. As a regional superpower Egypt turned to diplomacy to ease the fears of hostile neighbors and to promote international trade. Imperialism brought Egypt unparalleled prosperity, a substantial number of slaves, and unwanted cultural importations.

AKHENATEN AND THE AMARNA PERIOD

Egypt's first venture in empire building ended with the accession of Amenhotep IV (Akhenaten, 1364–1347). Having limited interest in imperial matters, this enigmatic rebel allowed Egypt's empire to be whittled away. He expended his energy in attempts to destroy Egypt's traditional religious cults and to create a formal state religion. By requiring exclusive worship of the divine sun-disc Aten he hoped to restore the ethical content in religion and to eliminate the powerful clergy. He closed traditional temple complexes throughout Egypt. His new religion, which is sometimes viewed as a form of monotheism, was unpopular with the elites and the masses alike.

Amenhotep IV changed his name to Akhenaten ("It pleases [the god] Aten"). In his new capital at Tell el-Amarna (Akhetaten), he allowed court artists and sculptors to be freed from the constraints of formal religious traditionalism, and they realistically depicted the pharaoh in a new naturalistic style. Akhenaten's religious and cultural revolution was short lived, disappearing after his death. During the brief minority rule of Akhenaten's son-in-law, Tutankhamen, court officials restored the old religion. The capital was transferred back to Thebes, where the temples of Karnak and Luxor were centers of the old religion. The officials then obliterated all traces of his reign and omitted his name from official king lists.

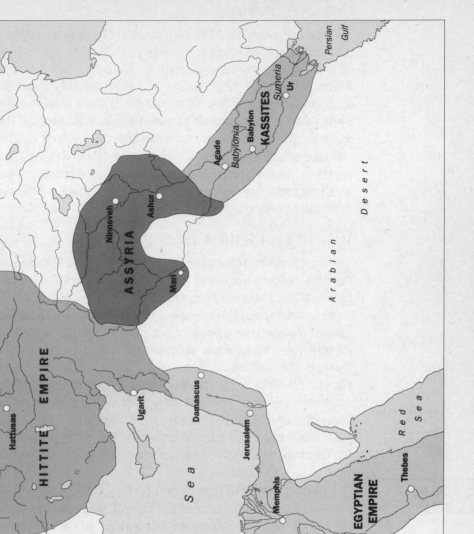

Fig. 2.2   Kingdoms of the Near East, c. 1300 B.C.

LAST DAYS OF EMPIRE

Warrior pharaohs of the Nineteenth Dynasty managed to restore Egyptian rule in their former territories in Palestine, but had limited success in displacing the powerful Anatolian Hittites, who then occupied northern Syria. Ramses II (1289–1224 B.C.) met the Hittite army at the battle of Kadesh; the battle was a draw, and the Hittites retained control of northern Syria. Successor pharaohs retained Egypt's control of Palestine until the early twelfth century, when the territory was seized by the "Sea Peoples." Comprised of Mycenaeans, Anatolians, Palestinians, and Syrians, these invaders created political and economic havoc throughout the eastern Mediterranean, destroying the international trade of the Hittite empire and nearly conquering Egypt.

THE LATE PERIOD (1069–332 B.C.)

Egypt never fully recovered from the disastrous impact of the Sea Peoples. As a consequence it entered a long period of decadence. Domestic factionalism and court intrigue often left Egypt politically fragmented. This made it increasingly difficult for the Egyptians to defend their borders against invaders; as a consequence the Egyptians were forced to submit to foreign rule. They were successively ruled by Libyans (945–715 B.C.), Nubians (760–656 B.C.), Assyrians (675–651 B.C.), Persians (525–332 B.C.), Greeks (332–30 B.C.), and Romans (30 B.C. to A.D. 330). Throughout this unhappy era Egypt retained its unique cultural identity, but became static and uncreative. During Persian and Greek rule Egyptian culture was considerably enriched by extensive cultural interchanges, which prepared Egypt for its eventual assimilation into the new Hellenistic civilization.

Egyptian Culture

In his perceptive description of Egypt, the Greek historian Herodotus (484–425 B.C.) characterized the Egyptians as the most religious people in the world. Religion dominated all aspects of their lives and served as the foundation of Egyptian civilization. Creative and innovative Egyptians focused their energies on spiritual rather than secular matters. As a consequence Egyptian cultural creativity was predominantly religious.

RELIGION

In the absence of both formal canonical sources or descriptive theological works, the fundamental beliefs of the ancient Egyptians are imperfectly known. What is clear is that they created a national religion based on the idea of individual immortality. In its advanced stage the religion conditionally offered all Egyptians the potential of life after death. From it the Egyptians derived their ethical system.

Egypt's polytheistic religion was expressed in two major forms: first, an official state religion that centered on the worship of Amon-Re and the pharaoh; second, a popular religion that incorporated worship of a large pantheon of deities including local and household gods. The state religion—the instrument by which the king and his people secured immortality—was practiced in temple sanctuaries closed to the general public. Popular religion was practiced by ordinary Egyptians near temple complexes or at local cult sites.

Egypt's pantheon of gods, many of whom represented forces in nature, assumed various forms—human, animal, natural object—that were frequently combined. Some shared common traits, since local gods were often amalgamated with regional or national gods. After 2000 B.C. the most popular god was the resurrected Osiris, who ruled over the dead. He was the instrument through which the ordinary Egyptian secured personal salvation. Most commoners believed that personal adherence to a demanding code of moral and ethical conduct was essential to salvation. This allowed their soul to pass judgment after death and to enter an agrarian paradise that shared many physical similarities with Egypt. To protect their souls in the afterlife the Egyptians relied on special omens and spells collected in *The Book of the Dead*.

THE FINE ARTS

Painters, sculptors, specialized craftsmen, and architects directed most of their creative energy into state-sponsored religious projects. Their best work was concentrated on Egypt's massive temple complexes and royal tombs which they superbly decorated with relief carvings and paintings. Their objective, reflected admirably in the stone temples of Karnak and Luxor and the enigmatic Sphinx, was to create timeless symbols of cosmic stability. With few exceptions artists and sculptors rigidly adhered to a formalized, nonnaturalistic style that changed little over the centuries.

Skilled Egyptian craftsmen exploited a variety of media to produce outstanding pieces of art. They particularly excelled in stone and metal work, the best examples of which were discovered in 1922 in the tomb of Tutankhamen.

WRITING AND LITERATURE

The Egyptians devised the nonalphabetic hieroglyphics (sacred signs) system of writing in the predynastic era. The system employed ideograms (pictures representing an idea rather than an object) and phonetic signs to represent ideas and sounds. It was extensively used in west Asia for commercial and diplomatic purposes. Scribes wrote with pen and ink on paperlike papyrus derived from the pulp of a reed. Hieroglyphics ceased to be used only in the sixth century A.D., after which the writing system remained incomprehensible until 1822 when J. F. Champollion deciphered it by using the bilingual inscriptions on the Rosetta Stone.

The ravages of time have reduced the body of Egyptian literary output. Most of the surviving texts are sacred literature: the *Pyramid Texts*, the *Coffin Texts*, *The Book of the Dead*, underworld literature, magical texts, ritual texts, omen texts, and hymns. In addition, important nonreligious works such as "wisdom" texts, chronicles and historical narratives, administrative texts, discourses covering a variety of subjects, love poetry, and short stories have survived.

MATHEMATICS AND SCIENCE

The modern assessment of Egyptian mathematicians is based mainly on two surviving papyrus rolls. These imply they lagged behind their contemporaries in Mesopotamia, since their work was limited to simple arithmetic and practical geometry. They also seem to have experienced considerable difficulty in handling fractions. Egyptian scientists by contrast were more innovative, but had little interest as a group in pure science. They derived their solar calendar in part from cumulative astrological observations on the "movement" of stars and the annual appearance of the star Sirius. Medical texts offer proof that pragmatic doctors possessed knowledge of human anatomy used various surgical techniques, and prescribed drugs. However, they shared the common ancient belief that human disease was an affliction imposed by an angry god; to cure the malady the invalid needed to appease the god.

THE HITTITE EMPIRE

Political History

The Hittites were Indo-European herders who migrated from central Eurasia into Anatolia (modern Turkey) in 2000 B.C. Using new military technologies such as horse–drawn chariots, composite bows, and heavy bronze armor, they gradually displaced native tribes throughout the region, founding a new kingdom. After building their new capital at Hattusas, the Hittites exploited their superior military system to extend their southern and eastern boundaries. This policy of expansion led in 1595 B.C. to the capture and temporary occupation of Babylon and to raids against Syria. Domestic factional struggles temporarily forced the Hittite kings to abandon their imperial policy, but it was revived by Suppiluliumas (1380–1346 B.C.) who wrested Syria from the Egyptians and made the Hittite empire the most powerful state in west Asia. Although Hittite armies could not prevent Ramses II from recovering Palestine, they did force Egypt to recognize Hittite rule of northern Syria. The Hittite empire endured until around

1200 B.C., when it collapsed in the face of combined attacks from the Assyrians, the Sea Peoples, and the Phrygians.

The Economy

Hittite strength derived principally from Anatolia's rich mineral deposits of silver, copper, and lead. By controlling regional trade routes, the Hittites marketed these prime resources throughout west Asia. They also discovered and monopolized the process of iron working. Abundant iron ore deposits and charcoal made the discovery of iron working possible and enabled them to enjoy a temporary advantage in military technology.

Hittite Culture

Hittite culture was an eclectic blend of Hittite, Hurrian, and Mesopotamian elements. The Hittites used cuneiform as well as their own hieroglyphic writing system. They embraced west Asia's religions and myths, merging them with their own deities. They patterned their laws on those devised in Babylon but tempered their severity. Only scanty remains of Hittite literature and art survive. Their most important cultural contribution was their role as transmitters and disseminators of elements from older cultures within their trading sphere.

INDEPENDENT STATES IN SYRIA-PALESTINE

Attacks by the Sea Peoples and desert nomads led to the collapse of the Egyptian and Hittite empires and the creation of a political vacuum in west Asia. As a consequence several small independent states emerged in the Syria-Palestine region between 1200 and 750 B.C. This region had been home to the Semitic Canaanites since the third millennium. The most significant new states were those founded by the Phoenicians and the Hebrews. The Phoenicians were descendants of the original Canaanites, while the Hebrews were Semitic intruders who entered Syria-Palestine from the Syrian desert between 1400 and 1200 B.C.

The Phoenician City-States (1500–330 B.C.)

The Phoenician homeland was a series of small independent city-states along the narrow coastal region of modern Lebanon. The most powerful of these—Sidon, Tyre, and Byblos—formed a loose geopolitical federation. Strategically situated, they used native maritime skills and marketing techniques to dominate commerce in the eastern Mediterranean and west Asia for several centuries.

Called "Phoenicians" (red men) by the Greeks, after their famous purple dye, they founded and colonized strategically located sites in Cyprus, Sicily, and along the North African seaboard. These served as port facilities and regional distribution centers for the sale of manufactured goods and the acquisition of raw materials. The founding of Carthage (New City) near modern Tunis by Tyre in 814 B.C. allowed the Phoenicians to extend their trade zone into the western Mediterranean and along the Atlantic coastline. Phoenician boats circumnavigated Africa (600 B.C.), transported tin from Celtic Britain (450 B.C.), and may have possibly discovered the Azores and America.

TRADE UNDER ALIEN EMPERORS

Phoenician traders preserved their dominant commercial role despite the loss of their political freedom in the eighth century. Conquered by the Assyrian empire, they pragmatically secured privileges that allowed their international trading companies to export specialized glass and metal manufactures, precious and common metal ores, Lebanese cedar, fabrics, and purple dye throughout the Mediterranean. By cooperating with Tiglath-Pileser III (746–727 B.C.), Phoenician traders secured inland markets in west Asia. Despite this advantage their share of eastern Mediterranean commerce began to decline in the seventh century because of Greek competition. Their share was further reduced in the mid-sixth century, when their city-states became part of the Persian empire. Thereafter, Carthage managed Phoenicia's former commercial empire in the western Mediterranean until it was conquered by Rome in 146 B.C.

PHOENICIAN CULTURE

Limited data, derived mainly from archaeological excavations at Carthage and from non-Phoenician sources, offer few insights on Phoenician culture. Phoenician sites in modern Lebanon are now densely populated and cannot be systematically excavated. Humidity and the ravages of time have combined to destroy the leather and papyrus texts of Phoenicia's written legacy. As a consequence the literary remains of the Phoenicians are now reduced to a few fragmentary records. Although several Phoenician gods were later incorporated into the Greek pantheon, the religious beliefs of the Phoenicians cannot be determined in detail. It is uncertain whether the Carthaginian practice of infant sacrifice was common to the Phoenician world.

The available data suggest that Phoenician culture was an eclectic blend of west Semitic, Egyptian, Mesopotamian, and Aegean elements. Despite a long symbiotic relationship between Phoenicia and Egypt, the extent to which the Phoenicians were culturally indebted to the Egyptians is uncertain. Egyptian influences are clearly visible in Phoenician art. The Phoenicians, who were renowned for their delicately carved ivories and woods and for their mass-produced glass trinkets, freely adapted Egyptian motifs, themes, and styles.

Non-Phoenician sources make clear that Phoenicia served as a major transmitter of Afroasiatic culture throughout the eastern Mediterranean, especially to Greece. In that role they introduced the Greeks to west Asian mathematics and astronomy. They also shared with them their own phonetic alphabet, their navigational arts, and their religion.

THE PHOENICIAN ALPHABET

The most important legacy of the Phoenicians was their invention of the first alphabetic system of writing. Consisting of twenty-two signs, each depicting a consonantal sound, the Phoenician alphabet proved easier to master and use than the earlier writing systems. As a consequence it gained ready acceptance in west Asia and was extensively used in international trade. The Greeks added vowels to the twenty-two consonants to form the alphabet commonly used in Europe.

The Hebrews (c. 1800– 63 B.C.)

Although the political significance of the Semitic Hebrews (the Israelites) on west Asia was slight, their religious impact was absolutely fundamental in world history. Their chief literary product, the Hebrew Bible, remains one of the basic documents of Western civiiization, and indirectly it played an important role in the origins of Islam.

According to the biblical tradition, a clan of nomadic herders left their homeland in northern Mesopotamia in the eighteenth century B.C. to settle on marginal pasture lands in Canaan. Famine eventually forced them to migrate into the Egyptian delta during the late seventeenth century B.C., where they remained for several centuries, eventually suffering semi-enslavement. In the thirteenth century the prophet Moses led a small group of Hebrew slaves into the Sinai peninsula, where they formally embraced a religious covenant which bound them to worship exclusively the god Yahweh (often rendered Jehovah, or the Lord), who transmitted laws to Moses with promise of divine protection to those Hebrews that observed them.

KINGDOMS OF ISRAEL AND JUDAH

For the next two centuries the Hebrews, their ranks augmented by other Semitic groups, successfully filtered into Canaan, coming to dominate the area. Their tribal leaders used warfare to displace the native Canaanites and to defend themselves against their powerful Philistine neighbors. About 1025 B.C. the twelve independent tribes abandoned their loose political federation to form the kingdom of Israel. Under their two powerful kings David (1000–961 B.C.) and Solomon (961–922 B.C.), Israel emergcd as a major force in west Asia. But the arbitrary restructuring of the old tribal institutions forced ten of the tribes to secede in the ninth century and regroup as the independent kingdom of Israel. Retaining control of Jerusalem, the political and spiritual capital, the two remaining tribes from the south founded the kingdom of Judah.

The northern kingdom disappeared with the revival of empire building in the region. In 721 B.C. the Assyrians occupied Israel and extensively depopulated the region. Surviving the Assyrian threat, Judah retained its independence until 586 B.C., at which time the Neo-Babylonian Chaldeans occupied Jerusalem, destroyed the Temple, and forcibly transported the most skilled Jews to Babylon. After their liberation by Cyrus the Great in 538 B.C., these captives returned to Judah to rebuild their Temple. For the next two centuries they lived under the enlightened rule of the Persians. Following their conquest by Alexander the Great, the Jews became subjects of the Greek Seleucids of Syria. They temporarily enjoyed a brief era of independence under the Maccabees (167–63 B.C.), but their homeland was eventually incorporated into the Roman empire (see chapter 6).

THE HEBREW BIBLE

Composed of a wide range of legal texts, chronicles, poetry, and oracles, the Hebrew Bible received its final written form in the fifth century B.C. (although the exact books to be included in the collection were determined only in the first century A.D.). The canonical text is traditionally divided into three parts: the Law (*Torah*, or Pentateuch), the Prophets (*Nevi'im*), and the Writings (*Ketuvim*). This text serves as the principal resource for the Hebrew religion (from which Judaism derived), and for the reconstruction of Hebrew history and law. Its authors and editors selectively chronicled key events in Hebrew history to affirm two major beliefs: the course of human history is determined by God's plan; and the fortunes of Israel are tied to the collective action of its people in adhering to their covenant with God.

The Hebrew Law or Torah contains a telescopic account of history from God's creation of the world and the earliest humans until the death of Moses. In it is contained the covenant which God made with Moses, and the laws which the Israelites must obey to fulfill that covenant. The books of the Prophets contain charismatic and literary oracles and prophecies condemning both Israel for disobedience to their covenant and non-Israelites for fighting against Israel. A series of apocalyptic prophesies about future times and a coming messiah provided the prophetic foundations for the rise of Christianity. The Writings consist of historical works, sacred and non-religious poetry, and wisdom literature.

RELIGION

In its mature form the Israelite religion advances an ethical monotheism that focuses on the exclusive worship of God. The Israelites and Jews believe that their God is the sole omnipotent, eternal, and universal god, the creator and judicious ruler of the universe. God serves as the supreme lawmaker to preserve and maintain universal order and morality. The Hebrew god has a cosmic plan for his creation, in which mankind plays a central role. The Israelites were especially honored, for God assigned them the task to serve as moral teachers to all humanity. But their role is predicated on their exclusive worship of God and entrance into a covenant or agreement with God to maintain his moral laws. Failure to fulfill their responsibilities subjects the Hebrews to God's wrath.

The focus in the Israelite religion is the observance of God's law, which served as the foundation of both the Jewish ethical value system and Jewish ritual. The laws, read and explained in the synagogue by scholarly rabbis, fostered an egalitarian moral order that promoted charity and social justice. They further promoted Jewish identity, by requiring Jews to adhere to unique observances and practices.

CULTURAL CONTRIBUTIONS

Early Israelite culture was devoid of notable contributions to art, architecture, mathematics, science, or technology. On the other hand, they excelled in the fields of religion, literature, history, and philosophy. Despite the dispersal of the Jews following the Babylonian captivity and their wars with Rome, their unique ethical monotheistic religion endured to become a great world religion. It also served as a direct source for two successor religions, Christianity and Islam. The Hebrew Bible, a world literary masterpiece and west Asia's finest attempt at historical writing, incorporates an advanced philosophy that addresses fundamental questions of the purpose of life. Later adopted as a canonical text by Christians, the Old Testament exerted a formative influence on Western ethics, political theory, and law. The unique Hebrew perception of nature as a resource for human exploitation and domination may have directly contributed to the evolution of early modern science in the West.

EMPIRES OF THE FIRST MILLENNIUM

The Assyrian Empire (911–605 B.C.)

Between 911 and 612 B.C., imperialistic Assyrian kings used their superb armies to occupy and control most of west Asia. At the peak of its power in 672 B.C., the Assyrian empire included Syria, Phoenicia, Israel, Urartu (Armenia), Babylonia, and Egypt. It ruled these territories for nearly a hundred years with a highly efficient centralized administration headed by royally appointed governors. The empire allowed Assyria to absorb most of the economic and manpower resources of west Asia. But its immense size

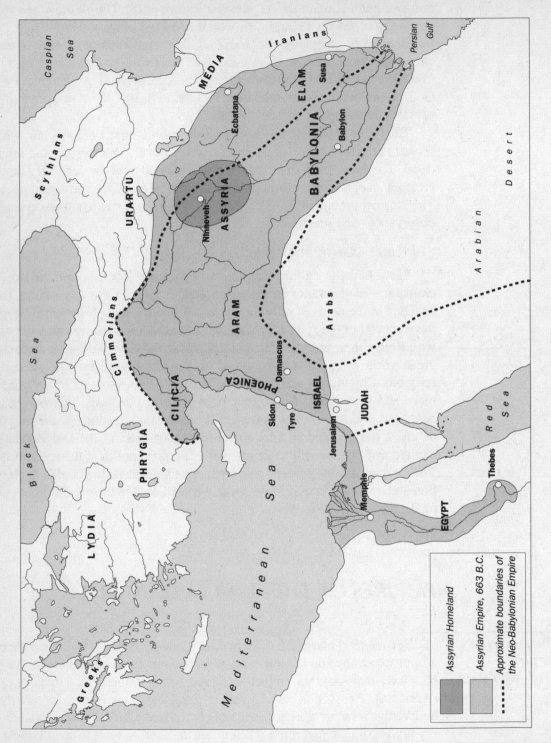

Fig. 2.3   Empires of the Near East, 800–550 B.C.

and the continuous need to quell rebellious subjects ultimately weakened the overextended Assyrians, contributing to their rapid collapse.

ASSYRIAN MILITARISM

The earliest record of the Semitic Assyrians comes from the early third millennium B.C. when they settled a strategically vulnerable plateau located between the upper Tigris and Euphrates rivers. Continuous threats from intruding nomads and hostile neighbors forced the Assyrians to turn to militarism between 1750 and 1000 B.C. Their homeland secured, autocratic warlord kings, with ideological support from the Assyrian warrior god Ashur, aggressively attacked their neighbors. Their transformation of Assyria into west Asia's greatest power was due mainly to their superb army. Organized structurally into uniform professional units under career officers, their infantry was the first in west Asia to be fully equipped with iron weapons and to have support from specialist engineering and cavalry troops.

ASSYRIAN IMPERIAL ADMINISTRATION

Efficient centralized rule in the empire derived from the domestic and imperial administrative reforms of Tiglath-Pileser III (746–727 B.C.). These curbed the power of the Assyrian nobles and placed dependable territorial governors in charge of regional administrative provinces. In addition they created a permanent imperial army and improved communications through new roads, a postal service, and common use of the Aramaic language. To preserve law and order the Assyrian rulers countered rebellions with ruthless psychological warfare: mass deportations and programs of systematic terrorization that wiped out entire cities. To counter external support to rebellious subjects they undertook wars against Egypt and Babylon. They occupied Egypt between 671 and 662 B.C. and much of Babylon in a four-year war ending in 648 B.C.

THE DISINTEGRATION OF THE EMPIRE

Due to internal stresses and external threats, the collapse of the Assyrian empire came quickly. Egypt cast off the Assyrian yoke in 662 B.C. The death of King Ashurbanipal in 627 B.C. led to factional struggles over the crown, promoting rebellions throughout the empire. Fourteen years later, the Chaldean ruler of southern Babylon undertook an invasion of Assyria. In 612 B.C. he was joined by Median forces from Iran. After sacking the capital at Nineveh in 612, the two armies won decisive victories at Balikh (609 B.C.) and Carchemish (605 B.C.) that extinguished the empire.

ASSYRIAN CULTURE

Culturally the Assyrians patronized traditional Mesopotamian styles of art and literature. Cultural eclecticism allowed them to engage artisans and artists throughout their empire to produce a unique artistic style, especially in relief sculpture. Their remarkable decorative frieze panels glorified Assyria's warrior kings in battle scenes. The Assyrians preserved and disseminated Mesopotamian literary works in massive libraries such as the royal library at Nineveh. Some theorize that the Near Eastern custom of the seclusion (veiling) of women was introduced by the Assyrians.

The Chaldeans (Neo-Babylonians) (626–539 B.C.)

About 1000 B.C. Semitic tribes settled in Chaldea, the southernmost part of ancient Babylon (a region now shared by Iraq and Kuwait). Of minor political significance, the territory eventually was integrated into the Assyrian empire, but it proved difficult to govern. In 627 B.C. Assyria's puppet king of Babylon, the Chaldean Nabopolassar, cast off the Assyrian yoke and founded the new kingdom of Babylon. With assistance from the Medes, Nabopolassar (r. 626–604 B.C.) and his warrior son, Nebuchadnezzar (r. 604–561 B.C.) mounted a counteroffensive against the Assyrians and destroyed their empire. As victors they absorbed Assyria, Syria, Palestine, and Judea, founding a new empire.

Like its predecessor, the Chaldean empire proved too large and rebellious to endure. Temporary solutions, such as a mass deportation of rebellious Jews to Babylon, could not resolve the inherent problems posed by a series of weak rulers, economic stagnation, religious conflicts, and outside threats. These problems weakened the Chaldean empire and left it vulnerable to attack by aggressive and expansionistic Persia.

NEO-BABYLONIAN CULTURE

Literature. The Chaldeans proclaimed themselves cultural successors of the Babylonians (hence "Neo-Babylonian"). As such they slavishly restored old Babylonian laws and the Marduk religion. Scholarly scribes faithfully copied and edited ancient Babylonian texts. Nebuchadnezzar renewed Babylon's old imperial splendor and transformed it into west Asia's most magnificent and dazzling city.

Astronomy. Devotion to the past severely hampered Chaldean originality, but a new celestial religion led to major advances in astronomy and timekeeping. Favored by Nabonidus, the last Chaldean king, the new religion equated the gods with the planets. It advanced the belief that future events were determined by movements of the planets in the heavens, which became the basis of astrology. This belief in turn stimulated systematic astronomical observations for the purpose of calculating predicted planetary phenomena. Chaldean astronomers made their predictions and calculations in special procedural manuals. Collectively these remarkable texts served as the foundations for future advances in astronomy. The Greeks later expressed appreciation of their work by equating the term "Chaldean" with "astronomer."

Measuring Time. The Chaldeans used their astronomical discoveries to make important contributions to the division of time. Having observed twelve heavenly constellations, they divided the day into twelve double hours. They fashioned the seven-day week by adding the sun and the moon to the five planets they had identified. The division of the hour into sixty minutes, each of which forms sixty seconds, was a natural outgrowth of the Chaldean use of sixty as the base number in mathematical calculations. Our modern system of hours, minutes, and seconds ultimately derives from Babylonian models.

Persia (2000–330 B.C.)

The ascendancy of Persia between 559 and 330 B.C. as the dominant power in west Asia ended Semitic control of the region. Egypt and west Asia were fully integrated into a new empire that stretched from Libya to Afghanistan. Persian ascendancy meant the end of the earliest cultural regions and their full integration into a larger and more complex culture.

THE INDO-IRANIAN SETTLEMENTS

About 2000 B.C., successive waves of migrant Indo-Iranians (or Indo-Aryans) came from modern southern Russia and swept into the thinly populated Iranian plateau in search of new homelands. Six Median and ten Iranian tribes settled in the plateau as cattle and horse breeders and subsidiary farmers. Others pushed eastward through the plateau to settle in Bactria and India. In their new homeland the Indo-Iranians gradually merged with the native population, imposed their Indo-European language, and founded independent tribal kingdoms. Although temporarily tributary to the Assyrians, the Iranians gained independence in the seventh century under the leadership of the clan of the Medes. As the Assyrian empire began to crumble in the late seventh century, the Medes joined the Scythians and the Babylonians in participating in the final destruction and dismemberment of the empire. The rule of the Median clan was ended by a revolt of the Persians under the leadership of Cyrus.

THE PERSIAN EMPIRE (559–330 B.C.)

Cyrus the Great (559–530 B.C.). Ascending the provincial throne of Persia in 559 B.C., Cyrus the Great united the Persian tribes in a revolt against the Medes. After defeating the Median King Astyages in 550 B.C., Cyrus proclaimed himself king of a united Persia. Cyrus pursued two objectives: securing his eastern borders and adding west Asian territories to the empire he inherited from the Medes. Superb Iranian military skills and the regional political weaknesses of his enemies enabled him to achieve both objectives.

Victory over hostile Lydia in 547 B.C. allowed Cyrus to extend Persian control over the Anatolian peninsula. After quelling rebellions in the eastern provinces of Bactria and Sogdiana, Cyrus marched his troops into Babylon

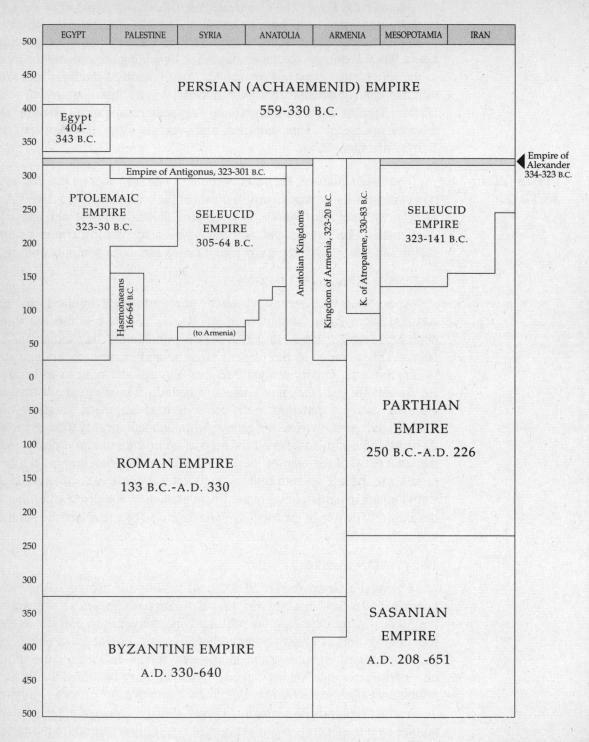

Fig. 2.4   The Middle East from 500 B.C. to A.D. 500

in 538 B.C. Cooperative assistance from Jews and Babylonian Marduk priests in the capital allowed him to absorb the Chaldean empire with little struggle. Conquest of Egypt was denied him by his death in 530 B.C. Throughout his campaigns Cyrus softened the impact of his victories with a charitable and tolerant policy toward the vanquished, recognizing local customs, laws, practices, and religions.

Cambyses (530–522 B.C.). Cyrus's son and heir, Cambyses, extended the empire's western frontiers. In five years he mastered Egypt, Libya, and part of Nubia (Sudan). During his brief reign he transformed Persia into a major sea power. In the absence of an heir his death led to factional struggles for the crown.

Darius the Great (521–486 B.C.). Darius the Great, victor in the succession struggles, added some new territory to the Persian empire. Across the Hellespont he extended Persian rule along the Thracian coast and forced Macedonia to become a Persian dependency. He expanded his eastern border by absorbing in the Indus valley. His real talents lay in the field of administration. Drawing heavily on the Assyrian model, he used his organizational skills to establish a durable imperial system of government.

As ruler of the thirty nationalities in the empire, Darius assumed the role of an absolute divinely-appointed monarch. To assist him he created a central staff and personally appointed viceroys (*satraps*) to serve as royal agents in the empire's twenty administrative divisions (*satrapies*). Exercising civil, legal, and military jurisdiction, these viceroys were normally members of the extended royal family. They collected annual tribute payments levied by the government, maintained law and order, and raised forced military levies. To assist them in curbing local revolts, royal armies of professional Median and Persian troops were posted at key sites and cities. The central staff periodically checked the activities of the viceroys and reported their findings to the emperor.

Seeking more efficient rule, Darius improved imperial communications. He built major highways to link the four capitals with the outlying provinces and established a royal postal service. He adopted Aramaic as his official imperial language, devised a common currency, and introduced uniform weights and measures. Although he left intact local economic structures, he made some attempt to create a regional economic common market. He did not impose a common legal code in the empire, preferring to give local peoples autonomy in internal legal matters.

WEAKNESSES IN THE PERSIAN IMPERIAL SYSTEM

Darius's administrative changes allowed for a centralized, but not fully integrated, imperial system. Never fully absolutist, the system operated poorly during the tenures of inept and incompetent emperors because too much power was concentrated at the center. The extensive use of royal relatives in key government offices eventually hampered administrative efficiency by inhibiting the growth of a professional bureaucracy based on talent.

Created and perpetuated by military force, the empire was much too vast, and its inhabitants and cultures too diverse, to generate a sense of patriotism and imperial loyalty. The political yoke of the Persian minority, outnumbered in their empire nearly sixty to one, was begrudgingly tolerated by the heavily taxed majority. Many nationalities resented the privileged treatment accorded the Medes, Phoenicians, and Jews. Bullion shortages, the result of royal hoarding, increasingly hampered local and regional trade and alienated businessmen throughout the empire. These grievances and oppressive government measures generated revolts throughout the empire. As we will see in chapter 5, the revolt of the Greeks in the Anatolian peninsula culminated in the Greco-Persian wars and set the stage for the eventual demise of the empire.

PERSIAN CULTURE

The practical-minded Persians excelled in the arts of war and government, but little of their cultural heritage survived the Greek conquests. Their greatest architectural monument is the splendid imperial palace at Persepolis. Their most original cultural and literary contribution was a new religion, Zoroastrianism, that survives to this day.

ZOROASTRIANISM

Founded by Zarathustra (Zoroaster), who lived in the sixth century, Zoroastrianism repudiated many of the tenets and rituals of Persia's ancient Indo-European religion. Zarathustra proclaimed himself a prophet of Ahuramazda, the universal god of light and goodness. He attributed his new religion to divine revelations sent him by Ahuramazda in two holy books, the *Gathas* and the *Avesta*. His religion advanced the belief that the physical universe was a battleground for two contending forces, Ahuramazda (good) and Ahriman (evil). By embracing a strict code of ethical conduct, Zoroastrian supporters of Ahuramazda were actively participating in God's 12,000-year struggle with the devil Ahriman. As reward for their assistance Ahuramazda granted his supporters bodily resurrection in paradise after the final victory over evil. As a promise of their redemption, Zarathustra proclaimed that a messiah (deliverer or savior) would appear in preparation for the end of the world. After their final defeat, Ahriman and his supporters would be cast into a hell of flames.

Achaemenid Persian emperors eventually adopted Zoroastrianism as their official state religion, but made only limited attempts to impose it on their subjects; it remained a minority religion. In time the religion was modified by priests to accommodate other Persian and Mesopotamian ancient rites and practices. As a consequence the religion gave rise to several denominations. It is possible that several tenets in Zoroastrianism exerted formative ideological influences in the development of late Judaism and Christianity.

*B*ronze and Iron Age Egypt and west Asia produced the world's earliest civilizations. Elaborate irrigation systems allowed farmers in these dry regions to fully exploit their agricultural potential. Accumulated surpluses quickly promoted population growth, social stratification, craft specialization, and the growth of cities and trade. In Egypt theocratic rulers diverted much of their kingdom's vast resources and energy into religion. Fully evolving in the Old Kingdom, Egyptian civilization remained static and traditionalist.

West Asian civilization was an eclectic blend of Sumerian culture and Semitic importations that proved hidebound to traditionalism. Plagued by invasions, the region witnessed numerous political conflicts, wars, and empire building that absorbed much of its creative potential. Nevertheless, this regional civilization made substantial contributions to law, literature, mathematics, science, and religion. Achieving its peak under the Neo-Babylonians and Persians, the ancient Near East gave rise to Judaism, a new world religion which would profoundly affect the course of Western and world civilizations.

Selected Readings

Baines, John, and Jaromir Malek. *Atlas of Ancient Egypt* (1980)

Bright, J. *A History of Israel*, 3d. ed. (1981)

Davies , W. D., and L. Finkelstein, eds. *The Cambridge History of Judaism*, Vol. I: *The Persian Period* (1984)

Frankfort, H. *Ancient Egyptian Religion* (1961)

Gershevitch, I., ed. *The Cambridge History of Iran*, Vol. II: *The Median and Achaemenian Periods* (1985)

Grant, M. *The History of Ancient Israel* (1984)

Gurney, O. R. *The Hittites* (1990)

Harden, D., *The Phoenicians*, 2nd. ed. (1971)

Herm, G. *The Phoenicians: The Purple Empire of the Ancient World* (1975)

Knapp, A. B. *The History and Culture of Ancient Western Asia and Egypt* (1988)

Kramer, S. N. *History Begins at Sumer*, 3d. ed. (1981)

Macqueen, J. G. *The Hittites and Their Contemporaries in Asia Minor* (1986)

Naveh, J. *Early History of the Alphabet: An Introduction to West Semitic Epigraphy and Paleography* (1982)

Nissen, H. J. *The Early History of the Ancient Near East, 9000–2000 B.C.* (1988)

Olmstead, A. T. *History of Assyria* (1975)

Redford, D. B. *Akhenaten, the Heretic King* (1984)

———. *Egypt, Canaan, and Israel in Ancient Times* (1992)

Roaf, Michael. *Cultural Atlas of Mesopotamia and the Ancient Near East* (1990)

Saggs, H. W. F. *The Might That Was Assyria* (1984)

Sandars, N. K. *The Sea Peoples* (1985)

Silver, M. *Economic Structures of the Ancient Near East* (1985)

Trigger, B. G., et al. *Ancient Egypt: A Social History* (1983)

3

Ancient India

(Note: all dates are approximate and B.C. unless otherwise indicated.)

3000	Emergence of Indus civilization
1500	Collapse of Indus civilization; Aryan invasions
1500–1000	Rig-Vedic era
1000–800	The Brahmanas and Aranyakas composed
1000–600	The era of Brahmanism
800–550	Aryans settle the Ganges river valley
800–500	The *Upanishads* composed
563–483	Siddhartha Gautama (the Buddha)
545–322	The expansion of Magadha
540–512	Persian conquests in northwest India
540–486	Vardhamana Mahavira, founder of Jainism
400	Development of the Indian writing system
327	Alexander the Great conquers territories in northwest India
322–298	Chandragupta Maurya, king of Magadha; founds Mauryan empire
303	Seleucus driven from Indian territories
298–273	Reign of Bindusara
269–232	Reign of Ashoka
250	The emergence of Hinayana Buddhism

Ancient India produced two civilizations. Emerging in the Indus River valley in 2500 B.C., the Indus civilization endured for a thousand years before it collapsed. An economic base of irrigated agriculture promoted the growth of large planned cities, whose ruins suggest the pacifist and traditionalist minded Indus people developed a sophisticated and prosperous civilization. Their Indo-Aryan successor civilization formed the foundations of modern Indian culture. Invading Aryan tribes laid the socio-economic and cultural foundations of the new civilization in the early Vedic Age (1500–1000 B.C.). By the fifth century B.C. these gave rise to elaboration of the sophisticated religious and philosophical systems of Jainism, Buddhism, and Hinduism. Indo-Aryan culture proved pliable and adaptive, allowing it to absorb numerous invaders while preserving the cultural unity of the politically fragmented subcontinent.

THE LAND

The subcontinent of India, a landmass containing over a million and a half square miles, incorporates modern India, Pakistan, Bangladesh, Nepal, and part of Afghanistan. Less than a third of this landmass is arable.

India's Regions

Approximately two-fifths the size of Europe, India consists of three distinct regions: the northernmost Himalayan mountain chain and its foothills, the plains and valleys of the Indus and Ganges rivers (Hindustan), and the southern triangular peninsula (Deccan) including the island of Sri Lanka. The Vindhyas mountains separate the northern plains from the southern peninsula.

THE HIMALAYAS

The Himalayan mountain range, the world's highest, arcs north of the 1500-mile wide Hindustani plain, severely restricting overland entry into the subcontinent. Similarly, dense jungles and mountains restrict entry from the east. The Afghan passes in the northwest Himalayas, especially the Khyber Pass, provide India's main land link with Eurasia, allowing numerous invaders to enter the subcontinent and settle there, thus contributing to its cultural, racial, and linguistic diversity.

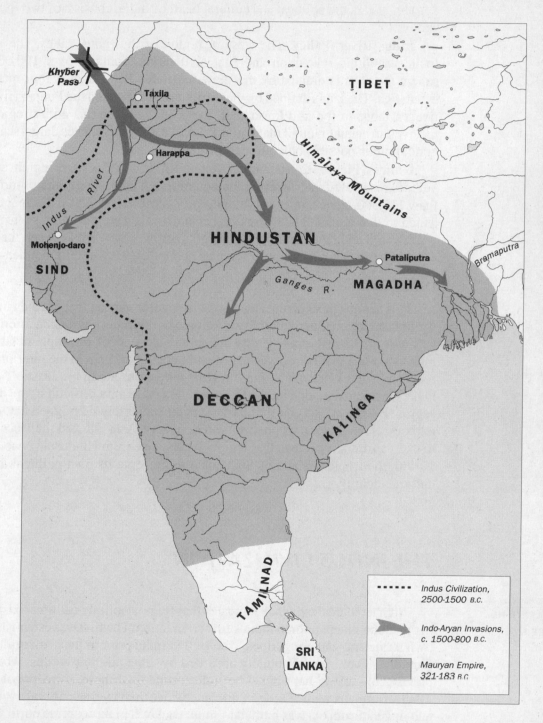

Fig. 3.1 Early India

HINDUSTAN

Hindustan, the political and cultural heart of India, consists of two river valleys.

Indus River Valley. The western region of the Indus valley, site of India's neolithic revolution and first civilization, contains over 100,000 square miles. It is drained by the snow-fed Indus River and its four main tributaries. The lands drained by these tributaries are called the Punjab (five rivers); those in the arid lower part, the Sind. Because this entire region receives an annual rainfall that varies from five to twenty inches, large-scale agriculture is possible only through irrigation.

Ganges Plains. Considerably wetter, Hindustan's eastern region envelopes the snow-fed Ganges-Brahmaputra river valleys and contains more than 115,000 square miles of India's best agricultural lands. Eminently suited to rice production, this region became India's most populous once it was cleared and developed. The strategic narrow watershed between these two great plains regions was to serve as home to several empire builders.

DECCAN

This semitropical peninsula, a large triangular plateau that extends into the Indian Ocean, is agriculturally inferior to north India, possessing inferior soil and water resources. Crops are totally dependent on unpredictable monsoon rains that fall between June and September. Rain in the interior is reduced by the Western and Eastern Ghat mountains along the coasts. This makes inland navigation on the Deccan rivers extremely difficult in the dry season. Except at Goa and Bombay, the peninsula is devoid of good natural harbors. Nevertheless, its proximity to Southeast Asia allowed the Deccan to exert a formative role in that region. Its distance from Hindustan enabled it, with the tropical island of Sri Lanka, to preserve its own political and cultural identity.

THE INDUS CIVILIZATION

Neolithic Period

Archaeological evidence indicates that four paleolithic cultures existed in the subcontinent prior to India's first civilization. The first was established by hunting and gathering tribes, who settled India prior to the sixth millennium B.C. They were eventually absorbed by three migrant groups, whose precise chronology has not yet been determined. Of these, the Mongoloid Tibeto-Burmans were of little significance since their overall cultural, racial, and linguistic impact was limited to small enclaves in the extreme north and in the Brahmaputra valley.

India's population consisted principally of Austrics and Dravidians, who freely mixed racially and linguistically after they settled in the subcontinent. By 4000 B.C. they had begun developing agriculture. The Austrics, a Mediterranean people who settled in agricultural villages scattered throughout India and Sri Lanka, engaged in hoe agriculture, farmed rice, domesticated pigs and chickens, and manufactured cotton clothing. Their modern descendants, who form a substratum in India's population, are found mainly in central and eastern India, where their language still persists. The Dravidians formed a major segment in India's population allowing them to retain their separate identity and language in the Deccan and Sri Lanka to the present.

Harappa and Mohenjo-Daro (2500– 1500 B.C.)

The Austrics and Dravidians in the Indus valley transformed small agricultural villages into cities and produced India's first civilization around 2500 B.C. A contemporary of Egypt's Middle Kingdom and Mesopotamia's Ur Dynasty, this Bronze Age civilization spread over nearly half a million square miles. Sometimes called "Harappan" from one of its key sites, the Indus civilization disappeared about 1500 B.C.

SOURCES OF INFORMATION

Archaeology. Our basic knowledge of Harappan civilization derives principally from archaeological excavations at over three hundred sites. Most assessments of the culture are based on data derived from excavations of Harappa and Mohenjo-dara, which some speculate were twin administrative capitals.

Writing. Written evidence, mainly inscriptions on cylindrical seals, remains undeciphered. The indigenous script, with its more than three hundred characters, shares no apparent similarities with Mesopotamian cuneiform. The available data preclude exact definitions of Indus social and political structures and offer few insights on their intellectual activities.

GOVERNMENT

Specialists assume the existence of a stable and conservative government, probably dominated by priests or priest-kings. The inhabitants seem to have been nonmilitaristic people, since the region failed to adopt technological advances in weaponry or to construct defensive fortifications. This suggests a conservative and traditionalist culture that intentionally resisted change and prized uniformity. These assumptions are lent credence by the fact that the region's two major cities were preplanned in identical grid-shaped block patterns. In each, common structures were built of standardized fired bricks with enclosed indoor plumbing connected to municipal sewage systems.

SOCIETY AND CULTURE

Religion. The absence of major temple complexes makes the assumption of a theocratic government tenuous. Artifacts imply an individual concern for personal piety, not a highly structured formal state religion. Harappan religion seems to have influenced later Vedic religion in areas such as ritual purity, the characteristics of the god Shiva, asceticism, and meditation.

Agriculture. A majority of the populace lived in small villages and worked in neighboring farms. Communal effort allowed them to construct flood-control and irrigation systems that allowed for substantial harvests of wheat, barley, and legumes. Surpluses, possibly extracted as taxes, were stored in large central granaries. Indus farmers were the first in Eurasia to domesticate the water buffalo and most common barnyard fowls, and to train elephants.

Economy. Local artisans and craftsmen supplied needed farm tools, instruments, and construction materials such as kiln-fired bricks. They used the potter's wheel for ceramic manufactures and produced jewelry, cloth, and weapons. Between 2350 and 1900 B.C., the Indus civilization supplemented locally produced goods with imports. Trade arrangements allowed for overland trade through Baluchistan and permitted sea trade between the Indus port of Lothal and agents in Bahrain, who acted as middlemen for the Mesopotamians.

DECLINE

The factors that contributed to the decline and eventual collapse of the civilization are uncertain. Archaeological evidence suggests the beginning of the decline as early as 2000 B.C. After the port of Lothal was abandoned in 1900 B.C., the farmlands in the region were steadily reduced during the next four centuries. Some historians attribute this to ecological disasters. They believe climatic changes and deforestation transformed much arable land in the Sind into desert. Salinization of substantial irrigated lands further reduced agricultural productivity. Recent evidence suggests a series of disastrous earthquakes may have diverted the course of the Indus River, which in turn led to massive floods and destroyed many irrigation systems. Weakened internally by these developments, the Indus proved no match to invading tribes of pastoralist Indo-Aryans, who sacked some cities and abandoned the rest as they mastered the region.

IMPACT ON INDIAN CIVILIZATION

The cultural indebtedness of the successor Indo-Aryan civilization to the Indus is difficult to determine. Common threads found in the Indus religion and Hinduism suggest the latter may have incorporated elements from the former. Notable appropriations include the Indus reverence for the pipal (fig) tree, yoga practices, ritualized bathing, representations of the god Shiva, and a mother goddess. These probably survived after the conquest in Austric-Dravidian practices and folklore, and they were absorbed into Hinduism through fusion or synthesis. Similarities in forms and designs for coinage, pottery, and weights suggest Aryan indebtedness to the Indus peoples, who were eventually integrated into the Aryan social structure.

INDO-ARYAN CIVILIZATION

The Indo-Aryans moved into northwest India in 1500 B.C. These tribes formed part of the second wave of Indo-European speaking herders, who left east-central Europe in 2000 B.C. in search of new homes. Several tribes settled in the Iranian plateau, where they gradually founded the states of Media and Persia (see chapter 2). Other Aryan ("free born" or "noble") tribes pushed eastward into Afghanistan and the Punjab in search of grasslands. As they swept into northwest India in several waves, they used their superior weaponry and horsedrawn chariots to subdue the natives, to conquer and randomly sack Indus cities, and to master the region.

The Vedic Age (1500–500 B.C.)

The history and culture of ancient India is hard to reconstruct prior to the appearance of a translatable writing system around 400 B.C. For the preliterate period, most data are derived from a body of religious literature known as the *Vedas*, authored by priests, philosophers, and poets between 1500 and 500 B.C. The texts were preserved orally by generations of priests who memorized them in special schools, until the development of writing in the fifth century B.C.

VEDIC LITERATURE

Considered inspired texts by the priests, the *Vedas* were thought to contain all sacred knowledge. The *Vedas* include four collections of hymns and rituals: the *Rigveda*, the *Artharvaveda*, the *Samaveda*, and the *Yajurveda*, composed between 1500 and 1000 B.C. Other important early Aryan religious literature includes the *Brahmanas* and the *Aranyakas* (or "Forest Books"), ritual manuals on the nature and meaning of sacrifices compiled between 1000 and 800 B.C. The *Upanishads*, a collection of 123 texts compiled between 800 and 500 B.C., relate to philosophical speculations on the nature of ultimate reality.

Although they are religious texts, the *Vedas* contain fragmentary data on worldly matters. They indicate the Aryan tribes slowly mastered all of northern India and partitioned it into numerous independent tribal kingdoms. The tribes gradually shifted from pastoralism to farming and stock breeding.

Mixing with the more populous native population, the Aryans gradually abandoned their primitive pastoral culture and created a new Indo-Aryan civilization to which they contributed their Sanskrit language, their forms of military and social organization, and their religion.

ARYAN POLITICAL SYSTEM

Conquest of North India. For nearly a thousand years (1500–500 B.C.), the various independent tribes that comprised the "Five Aryan Peoples" channeled their energies into the mastery of northwestern India and in founding small tribal republics and kingdoms. Territorial rivalry often led to tribal wars. But no single tribe possessed sufficient power to unify the entire region. From the eighth to the sixth centuries B.C. the eastern tribes crossed through the Magadha region to occupy and colonize the rich agricultural lands of the Ganges plain. They organized these regions into small kingdoms and by 550 B.C. had extended their domination to Bangladesh and the lands southward to the Narmada river.

Aryan Government. Most early tribal governments were simple and democratic. Warrior assemblies elected a tribal leader (*raja*) from within their ranks. The king, whose principal role was that of war leader, conducted important tribal business in a grand assembly of tribal dignitaries. For consultative and administrative assistance he relied on a select council. The limited scope and objectives of government required him to use a minimum of administrative machinery at both the central and local levels. As the states matured these simple arrangements gave way to monarchical rule. Some nobles successfully resisted attempts by the kings to transform their offices into hereditary kingships, instead creating republics. But persistent warfare among the states favored the evolution of monarchical governments.

Decline of the Tribal Nobility. Once they made their offices inheritable, the kings undermined the power and authority of the old nobility. They differentiated themselves from the nobles by claiming divine descent, shifting their power base from the nobility to a supportive priestly class by awarding the clergy special privileges and allowing the clerical leaders to form a royal advisory body to assist in matters of religion, law, and politics.

Bureaucracy. As their governments became more complex, the kings created new bureaucracies to administer their kingdoms at the central and village level and staffed them with royal appointees. As a consequence the ancient tribal assemblies ceased to function. To meet their financial needs, the kings devised a formal system of taxation that tapped the incomes of merchants, artisans, and peasants.

INDO-ARYAN SOCIETY

By 500 B.C. the politically fragmented Indo-Europeans had successfully established three common institutions that provided the foundations of their society. Persisting to the present day, these enduring institutions were the extended family, the autonomous village, and the caste system.

The Extended Family. The Aryans embraced a patriarchal social structure based on the extended family. Incorporating the spouses and children of adult sons, unmarried daughters, and widows, the extended family shared a common dwelling. As a close-knit corporation it was ruled by the eldest male. As head of the household, the eldest male possessed absolute power over all family members and family property; he bore the responsibility for the economic and religious well-being of his subordinates. Each member's role and responsibilities was determined by age and sex. Youths were subordinate to their elders and females to males. The collective interests and needs of the group prevailed over those of each individual.

The Autonomous Village. India witnessed the emergence of a substantial number of large cities that enjoyed political, commercial, and strategic importance. But most Indo-Aryans lived in small farming villages. These compact settlements were commonly preferred over dispersed homesteads because water supplies were limited and they offered families greater protection. Populated by several extended families, whose farms surrounded it, the village quickly became the local governmental and administrative unit.

Each village was administered by a royal appointee, the *gramani,* a local dignitary who headed one of the extended families in the village. His role was to execute military, civil, and judicial functions in the village as need arose. With assistance from an appointed council of other local dignitaries, the headsman served as a liaison between the village and the central government. As such, he was in a position to protect vital local interests, to temper the effects of harsh royal policies, and to provide stability at the local level in times of national crisis. Because it enjoyed virtual autonomy over local matters, the village became an enduring pillar in Indian society. Nearly 700,000 of them dot the landscape of modern India.

The Caste System. As a minority ethnic group in their new homeland, the Indo-Aryan tribes initially attempted to preserve their racial identity by prohibiting interracial marriages. However, miscegenation was widespread and racial distinctions soon became blurred. Political mastery allowed the Indo-Aryans to impose their own social structure in their new states. This consisted of a three-level system of classes (*varna*) divided into rulers and warriors (*kshatriyas*), priests (*brahmins*), and artisans, merchants, and agriculturalists (*vaishyas*). To accommodate the conquered native population that served as servants and slaves, the Indo-Aryans added a new caste, the *sudras.*

The Indo-Aryans justified these social distinctions by attributing them to their founding deity. Prior to 600 B.C. they evolved formal controls to curb social mobility. Each of the religiously sanctioned castes acquired its distinct religious and secular status, and the privileges and responsibilities of individual caste members were defined. They then formulated their own rules and established disciplinary procedures to preserve those rules. Many castes acquired exclusive rights to monopolize specific trades and occupations (*jati*). Since certain trades and occupations, such as those dealing with the dead, were deemed impure; those who performed such trades were denied caste status (outcastes).

This hereditary caste system discriminated against the lower castes by conferring on those in the superior castes decided economic advantages and the exclusive right of access to sacred literature. In its fully evolved form it attempted to segregate each caste by forbidding intermarriage and even eating with members of another caste. Complex rules and restrictions were devised to govern each caste member's religious and secular activities. Village caste leaders had authority to impose fines or to withdraw membership from any who violated them.

In a sense the Hindu caste system represented a society founded on a complex structure of mutual obligations and social and religious responsibilities. Unlike our modern society, where law is used primarily to define our rights, in Hindu society, *dharma* (religious law) was used to define one's responsibilities and obligations to the gods and other humans. Thus a low-caste Hindu would not feel that his rights were being violated by the limitations of his caste, but would perceive that the gods had given him a different set of responsibilities than the high-caste priest or warrior. Society could function only if each individual fulfilled their responsibilities as defined by their caste.

As a consequence, the lower castes tended to become relatively passive. This allowed India to limit the significance of class struggles and peasant revolts that commonly plagued other civilizations. The system contained sufficient flexibility to integrate new groups and new *jati* into the castes. It did so by creating "subcastes," which allowed newcomers to preserve their unique identities. This permitted the full social integration of India's numerous invaders and allowed limited social mobility when the need arose. An adverse impact of the system was that it hindered the growth of individual loyalty to the state by demanding that members give primary allegiance to their villages and castes.

Despite what we in the modern West would perceive as the inherent social and economic inequalities in the system, it offered two positive benefits. First, its control and supervision of the people served as a major factor in maintaining social stability within the subcontinent. Second, caste membership provided each group a degree of economic security, for the caste system curbed job competition by according each caste a monopoly over professions and trades. Once the system was integrated into Hinduism, one's caste status was attributed to the natural consequence of individual deeds (*karma*) in the previous existence. This made the system and its inequities tolerable to the lower castes, since they enjoyed the religious promise that in the next reincarnation the meritorious would receive an improved status.

THE RELIGIONS OF INDIA

Hinduism

VEDIC RELIGION

Religion was one of the most enduring of the Indo-Aryan contributions to world civilization. Initially sharing numerous parallels with the religions other Indo-European-speaking groups, especially the Persians, the Indo-Aryan religion adapted itself ideologically to complement the socio-political realities of the Indian subcontinent, acquiring its unique identity by 500 B.C. The main outlines of Aryan religious myths, beliefs, and practices can be found in the early Hindu scriptures, the *Vedas* and *Brahmanas*. An unusual feature in the Vedic religion was its emphasis on sacrifices with relatively little concern for ethical behavior.

Worldview. The *Rigveda* contained several creation myths but gives special prominence to the sacrificial creation of the universe by Manu, the first priest. Manu sacrificed an ox and his twin brother, the first king whose body parts were transformed into three spheres: the heavens, the earth, and the underworld. Manu's act allowed for the emergence of a hierarchical ordering of the universe with ranks of gods, humans, and other material components that evolved within the three spheres. The cosmic elements, which were continually subjected to depletion, required constant renewal by absorbing matter and energy from sacrificial victims. Hence the performance of priestly sacrifices became the most significant human endeavor, and a central feature of the Aryan religion.

Gods of the *Rigveda*. Although the *Rigveda* mentions dozens of gods and goddesses, it reduces the pantheon of gods to thirty-three major deities, eleven for each sphere. These gods took various human forms, and personified such natural forces as the sun, the moon, fire, and plants. Born after the creation of the world and initially mortal, the virile, warlike gods commonly shared the attributes of wisdom, goodness, and power. Paralleling early heroic Aryan society, the Vedic gods lived peacefully and harmoniously in an unranked democratic society. Mostly males, they wore clothes, rode chariots, ate heartily, and were willing to violate ethical principles to achieve their objectives. They entertained themselves with music, gambling, and heavy intakes of a hallucinatory drink, soma, that provided them immortality. Collectively governed by the order of nature, they forced mortals to comply with that order. They rewarded those who honored them and punished evildoers. They constantly fought against demons that generated evil in the universe.

Certain gods had unique identities and powers because they performed crucial functions for the Aryans. Among these was Varuna, the merciful and heavenly king of gods and humans, who controlled the physical order of the universe, the integrity of the sacrifice, and moral law. Over 250 hymns honor Indra, the popular warrior god who aided the Aryans in their battles against their enemies, especially against the Daysus demons. Agni, the god of fire, acted as intermediary between the gods and humans, transmitting sacrificial matter to the gods in the form of smoke ascending into heaven from a sacrificial fire. Soma, the god of plants, provided priests the ingredients for soma, the sacrificial drink that conferred immortality, promoted healing, and inspired speech for those who drank it.

The Human Condition. The *Vedas* maintain that humans, like gods, evolved from the sacrificial creative act of Manu, with possible parentage through the earth and sky or from Manu himself. Denied bodily immortality by the gods, humans are subjected to reincarnation, a cycle of recurring births and deaths. Weak and helpless, they cannot defend themselves against the evil Asuras (demons) that constantly threaten the world order. As a consequence, humans must seek protection from the gods. This was normally granted them, provided they offered the gods worship, obedience, and sacrificial gifts.

The Sacrifice. Since a sacrificial offering involved only the sacrificer and a god, it could be made at a private altar in the home. The crux of the sacrifice was the reciprocal exchange of gifts between the host and invited guest (the god). In return for providing the god sacrifices for his sustenance and renewal, the sacrificer sought blessings from the gods, such as victory in battle, the birth of a needed male heir, good crops, or restoration of health. Such simple exchanges were performed by heads of households, making group sacrifices and public cults unnecessary. Thus there was initially no need to build costly religious temples or to maintain an organized priesthood.

Eventually, however, increasing ritualistic complexity demanded by many sacrifices required the use of priests. This was especially so for those that involved the offering of soma and sacrificial animals and those used at royal coronations. These elaborate offerings required considerable expenditures on sacrificial animals, the construction of special altars, and gifts to attendant priests. Therefore, grand and elaborate sacrifices were exclusively reserved for kings, nobles, and rich merchants.

BRAHMANISM

Between 1100 and 600 B.C., priests transformed the Vedic religion into a rationalized and systematized sacrificial cult (Brahmanism) that reduced the significance of the gods. In the process, they developed ritual into a science by equating it with cosmic order. They advanced new concepts on the cosmic worldview and the nature of the sacrifice to support their claims that priests were more powerful than the gods. They also devised new theistic practices and beliefs from non-Vedic sources, integrating them into the mainstream of religious thought, and preparing the way for the emergence of Hinduism.

Priestly Status. Brahmin priests convinced their patrons that godly rewards were automatic, provided their sacrifices adhered to correct ritualistic order. To increase their wealth and power, the priests exploited their ability to control ritual order and won generous concessions from rulers and the upper castes. Their main weakness was the lack of a formal priestly hierarchy, which limited their power of collective action. To enhance their own status and vested interests the priests bestowed religious sanction on the caste system. By integrating the four stages of life as an integral part of moral law (*dharma*), they assumed a new role as religious teachers (*gurus*). To further their interests the brahmins set up specialized schools to train priests. They also wrote instructional manuals that described and defined the complex rituals.

Sacrifice. Brahmanism was heavily indebted to a creative myth centering on the self-sacrifice of Prajapati, the "lord of creatures," whose primordial self-sacrifice allowed for the creation of the cosmic order, the gods, and humans. Equating mortal sacrifices with Prajapati, brahmin theologians identified each sacrificer with that god and maintained the ritually ordered universe could be integrated into each sacrificer. Since they held ritual and cosmic order to be identical, and perceived ritualistic elements to be identifiable with the universe and self, a correctly executed sacrifice could enable the sacrificer to dominate and regulate the cosmos. Thus empowered, the sacrificer was certain to secure his requests from the gods, who, as cosmic forces, were compelled to grant them.

The *Upanishads*. In time, ritual technique degenerated into empty mechanistic formulas. Brahmin specialists increasingly preoccupied themselves with speculations on minor details of the sacrifice. Such excesses induced a small group of reform-minded intellectuals and ascetics within the priest and warrior castes to abandon studies on rituals and to focus their concerns on such matters as the nature of the universe, God, and the true self. Through this, they aspired to find the means by which the individual soul could secure permanent release (*moksha*) from the recurring cycle of births and deaths. The collective philosophical speculations of these reformers during the eighth and fourth centuries B.C. are collected in 123 *Upanishads,* marking the end of the Vedic era. It is from them that Hinduism, Indian philosophical thought, Jainism, and Buddhism subsequently derived their essential tenets.

The upanishadic thinkers expanded on the earlier priestly concept of Prajapati as the source of all being. They advanced the notion that the real substance of the universe, the impersonal eternal principle and essence of all things, is a transcendent, indescribable Brahman, or World Soul. Eternal, with no beginning and no end, Brahman existed before creation and acts as the inactive center of a godhead that incorporates Vishnu and Shiva. The basic features of life, like the physical world of time, space, and causation, are a mere illusion (*maya*); yet they serve as the cause of pain and misery.

Since each individual soul (*atman*) is a constituent part of the World Soul, it constantly seeks to free itself (*moksha*) from its mortal prison and the wheel of life. To do so it is forced to undergo a long and painful series of bodily reincarnations and transmigrations (*samsara*). The bodily form that imprisons the soul in each existence is predetermined by deeds and conduct (*karma*) perpetrated in the previous life. Upanishadic thinkers offered three paths for acquiring release and true knowledge (unity with the Absolute): right action and deeds, devotion, and the renunciation of the world through an ascetic life. They denied that true knowledge was possible through sensory and empirical means; instead, they urged ascetics to engage in psychic exercises and yoga as means of inducing trances to help achieve unity with the Absolute.

The Emergence of Reform Religions

The intellectual ferment generated by the age of the *Upanishads* culminated in the appearance of two new religions in the sixth century B.C. Founded by Vardhamana Mahavira and Guatama, sons of warrior-caste chieftains, these religions denied the authority of the Vedic scriptures, repudiating the Vedic gods, the ancient creation myths, and the merit of sacrifice. Instead they offered unique and radical guidelines for securing personal salvation.

JAINISM

Mahavira (540–468 B.C.). This non-Vedic religion, whose ascetic traditions can be traced back to the early Aryan period, was formally established in the early sixth century B.C. by Vardhamana Mahavira. Through ascetic practices, Mahavira (the Great Hero) attained his own personal enlightenment at the age of forty. Mahavira advanced an ideology of salvation that promoted strict asceticism as the means of freeing the individual soul from its material bondage. The austere practices demanded of his followers severely limited the number of practitioners. His unwritten teachings were eventually collected by his followers in the third century B.C. to form Jain scriptures.

Jain Tenets. Mahavira retained the brahmin worldview of a three-tiered cosmos but he denied the existence of a creator god or a World Soul. Instead, he advanced the concept that the cosmos consists of infinite amounts of five eternal substances—soul (*jiva*), matter, space, movement, and rest. From these elements physical creation came into being. Each corporeal being possesses a soul and is part of a hierarchical order that ranges from minerals to humans and gods. Karmic matter (actions) prevents each soul from ascending to the top of the universe, its natural resting place. Thus imprisoned until it can be liberated from the cosmic effects of karmic action, the soul is forced to undergo reincarnations and transmigrations into bodies of other corporeal beings. Its host during each existence is determined by previous karmic actions.

The Three Jewels. So that their souls might be freed to display their basic nature of perfect knowledge and bliss, Mahavira devised for his followers a spiritual path that offered hope of spiritual release. He based it on the Three Jewels (*Tri-ratna*): right knowledge, right faith, and right conduct. His program was expressly designed for monks. He required them to abandon private property and to take vows of chastity, honesty, indifference to the senses and passions, and nonviolence. He imposed on them a regimen of strict asceticism and meditative practices. He exacted compliance with minutely defined ethical and behavioral practices, including vegetarianism and strict care to avoid the unnecessary taking of life. Exceptional practitioners, including the founder, sought to eliminate the last vestiges of karmic matter by starving themselves to death.

For the spiritual needs of ordinary laymen Mahavira devised twelve vows. These promoted the moral and physical well-being of the nonmonks, and assisted them in their advancement up the spiritual ladder until they, too, could become monks. These vows promoted individual ethical conduct and morality.

Jain Sects. In A.D. 79 Jainism split into two cults, the Digambara (sky clad), who believed in absolute poverty to the extent that they refused to own or wear clothing, and the Svetambara (white clad). The more liberal Svetambara monks opened their ranks to admit women and declared them capable of securing release. The Digambara maintained an exclusive male monastic order. Despite this split, Mahavira's community and ideology remained intact. As a minority religion in India, Jainism experienced its most rapid growth during the Mauryan dynasty in the third century B.C. It continued to expand until A.D. 1200. During that time the Jains erected religious structures in western India rivaling those of Buddhists and Hindus. Since A.D. 1200, however, membership has steadily decreased. Today the nearly three million Jains in India are mainly concentrated in western India. Most pursue careers in banking and commerce to abide by the Jain ban on the unnecessary taking of life.

BUDDHISM

The Buddha. Siddhartha Gautama (563–483 B.C.), a contemporary of Mahavira, offered a more moderate path for securing release. Personal concern over the causes of human pain and suffering and the means to eliminate those causes induced Gautama, son of a nobleman in northern India, to abandon his family and to take up the ascetic life. Neither religious instruction nor ascetic excesses provided him answers to the enigma of life. Gautama turned to meditative practices which culminated in a transcendental mystical experience at age thirty-five. After securing enlightenment (*nirvana*), the charismatic Buddha ("the Enlightened One") devoted the remainder of his life to preaching the Middle Way between hedonism and asceticism as the pathway to enlightenment.

The Middle Way. Like Jainism, Gautama's Buddhism was a non-Vedic religion. It, too, sought to advance the religious goals of individual ascetics. In common with Jainism it rejected brahmin ritualism, the ancient Vedic canons, and the caste system. Similarly, it integrated into its ideology the concepts of reincarnation (*samsara*), release from reincarnation (*moshka*), and non-violence (*ahimsa*). It also used moral and ethical precepts to advance the spiritual promotion of non-ascetics, but offered them promise of release only during another lifetime.

The Four Noble Truths. The Buddha distilled the essence of his teachings into Four Noble Truths: (1) all humans endure pain and suffering; (2) we suffer because of desire, egotism, greed, and selfishness; (3) to end suffering we must end desire; (4) desire can be fully comprehended and ended by following the Eightfold Path: right view, right thought, right speech, right conduct, right livelihood, right effort, right mindfulness, and right meditation, leading to enlightenment.

Denying the existence of a soul, Buddha taught that the universe consists solely of eternal matter. An understanding of the true nature of the universe through techniques employed by the Eightfold Path enables the ascetic to realize his "non-selfness" and to secure freedom from the bonds of phenomenal existence. Additional fruits from the discovery of "non-self" are their elimination of fears, doubts, insecurities, and pains and the automatic generation of right speech, right action, and right livelihood. These in turn promote good deeds, compassion, friendship, and concord that advance universal harmony, peace, and love.

The Emergence of Buddhist Sects. Perceiving himself a reformer rather than the founder of a new religion, Buddha had little use for dogma. During his lifetime, he failed to systematize his concepts in writing, nor did he attempt to impose a common institutional structure on his community of followers. After his death the absence of a central doctrinal authority led to disputes among his followers over matters of doctrine, institutional structure, and liturgy. As a consequence, the Buddhist community splintered into several independent sects. Scholars found Buddha's ideology sufficiently flexible to accommodate cultural differences and popular religious practices. They gradually developed two major denominations, called *yana*, (vehicles). Each denomination possessed its own unique doctrines, practices, and sacred canons.

Hinayana (Theravada) Buddhism. The earliest denomination of Buddhism dates from the mid-third century B.C. Called Hinayana (Lesser Vehicle), it initially prevailed in southern India and Sri Lanka, where it enjoyed political support. It is also called Theravada (Doctrine of the Elders). This sect mandates a strict ascetic life for those following the Buddha's teachings to obtain nirvana. Hinayana doctrines advance the view that the enlightened Buddha was a human teacher, who ceased to exist after death.

Hinayana Buddhists compiled the earliest Buddhist scriptures and claimed their version of Buddhism was its purest form. They founded numerous schools, where Hinayana scholars employed the Pali language to produce a rich literature.

Mahayana Buddhism. Mahayana schools emerged in northwest India in the late third century B.C. Reacting to the extreme conservatism of the Theravadans, they devised a "Greater Vehicle" to provide the means for the enlightenment of all believers. They advanced the view of the Buddha as an eternal, compassionate, and loving savior god. In heaven he resided with a multitude of other Buddhas, who prior to their own earthly deaths had secured enlightenment and the status of *bodhissatva* (being of enlightenment). By extending the role of the bodhissatva the Mahayana opened to all Buddhist the opportunity for enlightenment. They claimed that many future Buddhas chose to postpone their nirvana so that they might help fellow Buddhists. Filled with love and compassion they retained the status of bodhissatva to become savior guides. As such they transferred their accumulated merit to those who voluntarily vowed to become bodhissatvas. Their assistance allowed ordinary Buddhists to avoid the arduous demands of the ascetic life and opened the prospects for salvation to everyone.

Spread of Buddhism. Mahayana Buddhism rapidly overshadowed its rivals and became the dominant Buddhist sect in India. Inherently flexible and adaptable, Mahayana doctrines readily submitted to continuous modifications and redefinitions by scholars in India and abroad. In the second century B.C. it spread into Central Asia. From there missionaries transported the religion to China and its cultural satellites, Korea, Japan, and Vietnam. At the same time, Hinayana missionaries played a key role in transmitting Buddhism and Indian culture to Southeast Asia. Two of Buddhism's leading intellectual centers at Nalanda and Valabhi, became international universities. Like all Buddhist centers, they virtually disappeared when Hinduism absorbed Buddhism. In the thirteenth century Muslims destroyed what remained of its schools and temples (see chapter 11).

INDIAN POLITICAL DEVELOPMENTS

*The Arduous
Road to Unity:
Seventh–Fourth
Centuries B.C.*

Between the seventh and fourth centuries B.C., intruding Persians and Macedonians absorbed several states in the northwestern corner of India. During the same period the kingdom of Magadha in the Ganges river valley expanded steadily at the expense of its neighbors. Tribal factionalism made both developments possible. The attempt of the most powerful of India's sixteen states to absorb its neighbors led to numerous wars. While foreign occupation proved short-lived and had no long term political impact, the expansion of Magadha eventually led to the formation of India's first empire.

THE PERSIAN CONQUEST

During the reigns of Cyrus the Great and Darius, Persia strengthened its ancient cultural and economic ties with India by militarily annexing tribal lands in the Indus valley. Once these frontier territories were organized as Persia's most populous and prosperous satrapy, they proved difficult to govern. Since they were never fully integrated in the empire, imperial control steadily deteriorated after the reign of Xerxes, and was virtually abandoned by the mid-fourth century. By that time the Persians had allowed local chieftains to organize small states and conferred powers on them that made them virtually independent.

The Persian conquest permanently reintegrated northwest India into the west Asian trade sphere. It also familiarized that region with the Aramaic alphabet, Persian administrative techniques, and the minting of silver coinage. Persia's name for its Indus territories, "the land of the Hindus" (India), was to serve as the future name for the entire subcontinent.

MACEDONIAN RULE IN NORTHWEST INDIA

Alexander's Conquests. After conquering the Persian empire (see chapter 5), Alexander the Great led his army across the Hindu-Kush in 327 B.C. to restore rule over Persia's territories in northwest India. Dividing the conquered Indus valley into satrapies, he stationed garrisons of Macedonian troops at strategic sites and founded numerous cities. Macedonian rule over the territories was imperfectly realized, ending in 303 B.C. when Chandragupta Maurya's army defeated Seleucus, the Macedonian ruler.

Cultural Impact. Macedonian Greeks made little impact in the Indian territories; few Indians became fully Hellenized. A few Greek words entered the Sanskrit language and Indian artists appropriated some Greek art forms and styles. The Indian indebtedness to Greek art was most obvious in Gandhara, where sculptors offered naturalistic depictions of the Buddha in Greek dress. Post-Macedonian contacts allowed for further two-way cultural exchanges between Greece and India in such fields as religion, philosophy, and science.

The Mauryan Empire

THE ASCENDANCY OF MAGADHA

Between 545 and 322 B.C., the militaristic kingdom of Magadha in the central Ganges valley gradually absorbed its neighbors. It gained domination over most of northern India as it reduced its three most powerful rivals. Magadha's ascendancy in the Ganges valley owed largely to its adoption of an efficient bureaucratic system based on the Persian model. Its rise can also be attributed to a prosperous economy that allowed its rulers to create a powerful army. Throughout this period the kings adhered to a calculated policy of territorial expansion first formulated by King Bimbisara in the mid-sixth century. By 326 B.C. this policy had enabled Magadhan kings to extend their western frontier to the Hydaspes River. Secured by its formidable army of 200,000 infantrymen and 20,000 cavalrymen, Magadha shared that border with Alexander the Great's successors.

CHANDRAGUPTA MAURYA, 322–298 B.C.

Ruled by unpopular Nanda kings since 362 B.C., Magadha experienced considerable domestic unrest during the oppressive reign of Dhana Nanda. In 322 B.C. the hated ruler was captured and killed by rebel forces commanded by Chandragupta Maurya. The young adventurer proclaimed himself king. With assistance and advice from the prime minister Kautilya, a disaffected brahmin critic of the old regime, Chandragupta quickly established himself as India's most powerful ruler. He created an efficient, highly centralized bureaucratic government and steadily enlarged his army. Thus empowered, he proceeded to enlarge his kingdom. Once he absorbed the independent states in northern India, he turned his army against Seleucus. By 303 B.C. the former Macedonian provinces of Kabul, Herat, Qandahar, and Baluchistan formed part of his empire. Before his death in 298 B.C. Chandragupta's empire stretched from central Afghanistan to the Bay of Bengal.

Kautilya. In administering his state Chandragupta relied heavily on the advice tended him by Kautilya, his chief minister. As described in the *Arthashastra*, a classical and pioneering book in political science, Kautilya's advice advanced techniques for promoting and securing universal sov-ereignty. It served as an instructional manual for rulers on statecraft and the art of government. In it Kautilya revealed the means by which a ruler could augment the wealth of his state, maintain domestic law and order, and extend his empire. That it embraced ruthless and brutal measures to achieve these objectives has led some modern critics to label Kautilya the "Indian Machiavelli."

ASHOKA: THE BUDDHIST EMPEROR, 269–232 B.C.

Chandragupta's son and successor, Bindusara (298–273 B.C.), extended the empire by occupying territories in the Deccan. Usurping the throne from Bindusara's heir, Ashoka rounded out of the empire in 256 B.C. by occupying additional Deccan territories and the coastal kingdom of Kalinga on the Bay of Bengal. Only the Tamil-speaking states in the far south remained free of Mauryan control.

Ashoka's Buddhist State. Remorse over his bloody war against Kalinga curbed further conquests. Within a year, the penitent Ashoka openly repudiated his former policy of expansion. He forswore war and became a Buddhist convert. During the last twenty-four years of his reign he committed the full powers of his state to spread Buddhism and to promote the general welfare of his subjects.

Ashoka proceeded to interject Buddhist idealism into Kautilyan statecraft; he substituted "conquest by morality" for militaristic imperialism. Without repudiating autocratic rule, he softened the harsher features of Mauryan government by using compassion, paternalism, and humanitarianism. To achieve a just and moral government and to improve his subjects' moral and spiritual welfare, Ashoka promoted the universal practice of *dharma* (morality and piety). To that effect he posted edicts, periodically undertook royal tours, and sent special overseers throughout the empire. He interjected *dharma* into the conduct of foreign diplomacy and sought its application abroad. Fully tolerant of all religious creeds, he made no attempt to make Buddhism the official state religion. But he actively propagated it throughout the empire. He transformed Buddhism into a world religion by sending missionaries to Sri Lanka, Burma, Kashmir, Nepal, Syria, Egypt, and Greece.

Economy Under Ashoka. Ashoka's benevolent and enlightened rule provided a stimulus to the economy. The resulting increase in domestic and foreign trade allowed India to become rich and prosperous. Although all mines, forests, shipyards, textile factories, and considerable farmlands were owned and operated by the state, Ashoka promoted manufacturing and trade within the private sector. Ordinary people benefitted from numerous work projects, including the construction of hospitals, public wells, roads, and roadside rest areas for travelers. Famine was virtually unknown. During his reign the elegant imperial capital, Pataliputra, emerged as a major international cultural center with its university and library. Located on a newly built road that stretched from Afghanistan to the Bay of Bengal, the capital won international acclaim for its magnificent palaces, temples, towers, and parks. It endured as India's preeminent city for the next four centuries.

THE COLLAPSE OF THE MAURYAN EMPIRE

Later Hindu and Buddhist thinkers used the enlightened rule of Ashoka as their model for an ideal king. But divergence from Kautilyan statecraft, neglect of the armed forces, and Ashoka's decision to divide the empire between two grandsons seriously undermined imperial unity. These factors contributed to the collapse of the empire during the next half century. Slack and ineffective rule by Ashoka's successors allowed outlying provinces to secede and enabled Mauryan princes to transform their provinces into sovereign territorial states. What remained of the empire continued under Mauryan rule until 184 B.C., when Pushyamitra, a military commander, assassinated the last Mauryan king and founded the short-lived Sunga dynasty. For five centuries India was to remain politically fragmented and vulnerable to a series of invaders (see chapter 11).

SOUTH INDIA

Little is known of the early history of either the Tamil-speaking Dravidians in the three ancient kingdoms of Chola, Pandya, and Kerala in southern India or the natives on the island kingdom of Sri Lanka. Like the pre-Mauryan states in the north, these rival kingdoms unsuccessfully sought to unify the region. In the second century B.C. the Chola managed to occupy Sri Lanka. Pandya used its ports at Korkai and Kayal to engage in extensive maritime trade with Southeast Asia. The most dramatic development in the region was the Indianization of its culture. This was hastened in the third century B.C. when Devanampiya, the Sri Lanka king, was converted to Theravada Buddhism by Mahendra, Ashoka's son. Following his conversion Sri Lanka became a major Buddhist center.

THE HINDU SYNTHESIS

The Development of Hinduism

Between the fifth century B.C. and the fifth century A.D., brahmin intellectuals expanded, redefined, and consolidated traditional Indian values and beliefs into a new religious and social complex called Hinduism. Hinduism provided its practitioners an integrative philosophy of life and a hierarchical social organization. As it evolved, the flexible and complex ideology assimilated select elements from Upanishadic teachings, folk traditions, and popular religions. At the same time, it reaffirmed essential doctrines from the ancient Vedic tradition, which had been repudiated by Mahavira and Gautama. Because it tended to be resistant to systematization, Hinduism failed to develop an orthodox creed, or a body of authoritative dogmas. It did not prescribe the creation of a formally structured institution, a hierarchical priesthood, or a common liturgy.

SYNCRETISM

Its innate ability to assimilate competing ideologies and practices enabled Hinduism to accept all religions and disciplines as valid approaches for seeking truth. By perceiving that all deities are manifestations of a single God (Brahma, World Soul), Hinduism came to paradoxically mix the characteristics of both monotheism and polytheism. To accommodate the intellectual and spiritual ideas and practices of its diverse sects of believers, Hinduism's caste-observing practitioners had complete freedom to believe and worship what they chose. Doctrinal flexibility provided Hinduism the capacity to absorb rival religions, to tolerate the growth and spread of sectarianism within its own ranks, and to secure and retain the loyalty of India's illiterate masses through the assimilation of popular folk cults, deities, and devotional practices.

EARLY HINDUISM

In its first stage of evolution (400 B.C. to 200 B.C.), a period sometimes called the Epic Age, Hinduism retained many traditional features of Brahmanism such as sacrifices and the worship of ancient Vedic gods. But it steadily abandoned these in the late Maurya era by shifting focus onto the worship of the Lord (usually in the forms of Vishnu or Shiva). During this stage Hindu theologians reaffirmed the canonical validity of the *Vedas* as well as the privileges and social primacy of the brahmins. The codification of the sacred laws in the *Laws of Manu* allowed them to bestow religious sanction on caste. They also provided Hindus a scheme of living to help members in all castes to perform their secular and spiritual obligations in an orderly manner. Their *Bhagavad-Gita* (The Lord's Song), served as a useful guide to selfless performance of one's duties.

By fully integrating the upanishadic tenets, Hinduism embraced the concept of the unity and the inherent goodness of all forms of life. It encouraged Hindus to comply with the concept of nonviolence (*ahimsa*). Its central message was that the soul can achieve reunification with its source, the World Soul. It can escape the physical bondage of karma and end the pain of multiple reincarnations and rebirths by complying with the sacred laws. While the ideology offered ordinary Hindus no shortcuts to that release, its plan of living provided a clear-cut and orderly path to that objective. Recognizing all aspects of life as natural parts of God's creation, Hinduism offered no dichotomy between the sacred and the profane.

By the end of the Mauryan era the Indo-Aryans had shaped many of India's fundamental cultural features. Their caste system, built on the foundations of extended families and autonomous villages, provided India's diverse population with needed societal controls in a subcontinent which rarely experienced political unity. Their primitive religion, gradually transformed into sophisticated philosophical and religious systems, gave rise to Buddhism and Hinduism. These provided the foundations for a common culture and advances in the fine arts, literature, and sciences.

Selected Readings

Allchin, B., and R. Allchin. *The Rise of Civilization in India and Pakistan* (1982)

Banerjee, N. R. *The Iron Age of India* (1965)

Basham, A. L. *The Wonder That Was India* (1959)

Chandhuri, N. C. *Hinduism: A Religion to Live By* (1979)

De Silva, K. M. *A History of Sri Lanka* (1981)

Eggermont, P. H. L., *Alexander's Campaigns in Sind and Baluchistan* (1975)

Fox, D. *The Heart of Buddhist Wisdom* (1985)

Klostermaier, K. K. *A Survey of Hinduism* (1989)

Kulke, Hermann, and Dietmar Rothermund. *A History of India* (1986)

Majumdar, R. C., ed. *The History and Culture of the Indian People, Vol. I: The Vedic Age* (1951)

Mookerji, R. K. *Chandragupta Maurya and His Times*, rev. ed. (1966)

Possehl, G. L., ed. *Harappan Civilization: A Contemporary Perspective* (1982)

Potter, K. H. *Guide to Indian Philosophy* (1988)

Sedlar, J. W. *India and the Greek World* (1980)

Thapar, R. *Ashoka and the Decline of the Mauryas* (1961)

Wolpert, S. A. ed. *A New History of India* (1989)

4

Ancient China

(Unless otherwise indicated, all dates in this chapter are B.C.)

5000	Yangshao culture
2500	Lungshan culture; appearance of writing
2000	Er-li-ton, China's first city, built
1994–1523	Xia dynasty
1523–1027	Shang dynasty
1027–221	Zhou dynasty
770–221	The Eastern Zhou
722–464	The Spring and Autumn era
551–479	Kong Qiu (Confucius)
470–391	Mozi, founder of Mohism
458–424	Partition of Qin
403–221	Era of Warring States
372–289	Mengzi (Mencius)
369–286	Zhuangzi (Chuang Tzu)
338	Death of Shang Yang
325	Qin rulers use title of king
230–221	Qin armies occupy Han, Qu, Jin, and Qi states
221–202	Qin dynasty

221   First emperor commissions Great Wall

202   Liu Bang founds Han dynasty

In sharp contrast to the river civilizations of ancient Egypt, Mesopotamia, and the Indus, Chinese civilization has endured until modern times. Having established its roots in the Shang dynasty (c. 1523–1027 B.C.), Chinese civilization acquired its most enduring elements and its unique form and style during the politically disruptive Zhou and Qin dynasties. These included linking of a humanistic philosophy and state-sanctioned religion, an imperial bureaucratic form of government based on merit, an ethical value system derived from philosophical speculation, and the foundations of an enduring social structure.

During this formative stage culture in China remained inherently Chinese, for geographical isolation denied China cultural contacts with other advanced Eurasian civilizations. As the Chinese state expanded so did its culture. Aggressive Chinese rulers peopled their occupied territories with Chinese settlers who took their culture with them. In time, the diverse population in China's empire was forged into one of the world's most advanced cultures linked by a standardized writing system.

THE LAND AND PEOPLE

Modern China occupies 3,700,000 square miles of territory and is slightly larger than the United States, and contains nearly a fifth of the world's inhabitants. Nine-tenths of its people are tightly compacted in the eastern third of the nation (China Proper) where most of China's 300,000,000 acres of arable lands lie. This rich agricultural region has allowed the Chinese to maintain the world's largest population since antiquity. Today three-fourths of China's billion inhabitants farm these lands. Its farmlands serve as home to the ethnic Han Chinese, who constitute ninety-three percent of China's population. Outside this region the land is generally unsuited to agriculture and can support only a small population. Nearly half is mountainous barren wasteland, a tenth is covered with forests, and the remainder suitable to a pastoral economy.

China Proper   During the first 3,000 years of its existence, Chinese civilization confined itself to arable basins formed by the Yellow (Huang He), the Yangtze, and the West (Xi) rivers and their respective tributaries. Originating in the Yellow River basin, which historically served as China's political and cultural heartland, Chinese civilization gradually extended southward to Vietnam and into those areas along its northern and southwestern borders wherever climate and terrain permitted Chinese-style farming. This expansion of Chinese civilization was due to conquests and to systematic colonization by emigrant Han Chinese, who slowly displaced or intermarried with native inhabitants. China acquired its natural boundaries two millennia after its origin. Called *Zhong-guo* (the Middle Kingdom) or *Zhong-hua* (Central Flower Country), its landmass contained China's eighteen historical provinces. These collectively formed "China Proper" or "China within the Great Wall."

THE NORTH CHINA PLAIN

China Proper contained two distinct geographical regions: the North China plain and South China. The flat North China plain was the site of the earliest Chinese civilization and home to the Han Chinese. Traversed by the 2,903-mile-long Yellow River, with its Wei and Fen tributaries, the flat plain owed its fertile soil to deposits of fertile loess silt left by the river before it emptied into the Bo Hai gulf. Combined with wind deposits of the yellow loess (dust) particles, this rich sediment constituted China's loessland. The climate in the plain suited the production of millet, wheat, and other dry crop cereals. Sufficient rainfall eliminated the need for massive irrigation projects. But frequent course changes by this turbulent and shallow-bedded river generated floods. These necessitated the construction of huge networks of dikes and canals. Never fully tamed and controlled, the river was often called "the River of Sorrows."

SOUTH CHINA

Separated from the North China plain by the east-west Qin Ling mountain range, South China extended southward past the Nan Ling mountains to Vietnam. Drained by the Yangtze, the Pearl (Zhu Jiang), and the West (Xi) rivers, its terrain was a diverse mixture of mountains, plains, hills, and valleys. The middle and lower delta along the deep-channeled and navigable Yangtze constituted China's richest agricultural pocket. Its full agricultural potential was not realized until several centuries after it was politically integrated by the Zhou, requiring systematic colonization by northern Han Chinese and the introduction of the Chinese system of farming. Once this was completed by A.D. 1000, abundant rainfall and a temperate climate allowed for the production of immense quantities of rice and wheat. By the next century the region housed three-fifths of China's population.

The colonization of South China's semitropical southern extremes along and below the Pearl and West rivers was first undertaken in the third century B.C. It was not fully colonized until the Tang dynasty because of diseases and the rugged terrain. Most non-Chinese inhabitants in the South eventually merged with the Han Chinese. But the multi-ethnic region retained unique cultural characteristics and dialects.

China and the Sea

While China possesses over 4,000 miles of eastern coastline with nearly 5,000 offshore islands, it remained land-oriented through the twelfth century A.D.; until then it directed little attention to its navy. This was in part due to the fact that China's political center lay inland, and that China's greatest danger came from barbarian tribes along its northern and western borders. Unchallenged by external naval threats, China was totally self-sufficient in essential mineral ores, raw materials, foodstuffs, and domestic manufactures. As a consequence, the early Chinese had little impetus to become a major maritime power, to found overseas colonies, or to engage in extensive international trade.

Excepting two exceptional periods of intensive overseas naval activity (A.D. 1127–1279 and 1405–1433), China remained to all intents and purposes a landlocked country. It used its domestic coastal and inland waterways mainly as communication links and inexpensive means for transporting inland trade. This orientation allowed the Chinese rulers to direct their main energies toward domestic and military objectives—internal stability through effective central government, territorial expansion and colonization, economic growth, and the reduction of barbarian threats along China's borders.

Outer China

The hinterland steppe provinces of Inner Mongolia (Nei Monggol), Tibet (Xizang), and Sinkiang (Xinjiang Uygur) lay outside China's political sphere until modern times, retaining their unique cultural and racial identities. The arid and barren terrain in these large provinces was unsuited to Chinese methods of farming, curbing Chinese immigration and minimizing China's cultural impact.

China's borderlands were thinly populated by tribes of nomadic herders, many of whom had migrated from Central Asia. These nomads played a formative role in Chinese history. In the absence of natural barriers, China Proper faced repeated attacks from these tribes and devoted considerable wealth, manpower, and materiel to restrain them. China resorted to military campaigns, diplomacy, bribes, and the construction of artificial barriers (the Great Wall), but these measures offered only temporary relief. Most common during periods of domestic instability, attacks from Central Asian nomads posed a serious threat to China's body politic. Inept responses by Chinese rulers to their aggressive "barbarian" neighbors could and did generate dynastic changes and, in rare cases, actual barbarian rule. The steppes served as yet another barrier that reduced China's intercourse with other great Eurasian civilizations (see chapter 15).

EARLY CHINA

Neolithic China

Archaeological evidence confirms that hundreds of Neolithic farming villages dotted China's loessland and the coasts of east and south China by 5000 B.C., forming distinct regional cultures. One of them, the Yangshao, contained villages of wattle and daub pit-dwellings, whose inhabitants used a slash and burn technique to produce millet. These villages were located along the Wei and central Yellow rivers. Noted for painted red and black pottery, Yangshao culture was gradually absorbed and displaced by a late Neolithic culture, the Lungshan, which originated in the Shangtung peninsula c. 2500 B.C. This successor culture, with its irrigated agriculture, social and craft specialization, and black burnished pottery, was widespread in the North China plain and the Yangtze valley by 2000 B.C., at which time Er-li-ton, China's earliest city, had been built. Over the next three hundred years Lungshan culture evolved city-states, a writing system, simple bronze metallurgy, and the domestication of wheat. As it made the transition toward civilization, Lungshan culture had little in common with less advanced rice-growing Neolithic cultures in the distant south.

Xia Dynasty (c. 1994–1523 B.C.)

During the late Lungshan era the Xia imposed political unity on North China's tribal city-states. Little is known of this dynasty. Recent archaeological discoveries suggest that Er-li-ton served as the Xia capital. Chinese tradition attributes the unification to Yu, who succeeded the Five Emperors that bestowed the key inventions of civilization. Early semi-legendary records indicate that Xia rule ended in 1523 B.C., when Tang the Victorious deposed King Jie for corrupt and degenerate rule. Afterward he forced the aristocratic heads of the city-states to submit to his rule and founded the Shang dynasty.

Shang Dynasty (c. 1523–1027 B.C.)

SHANG GOVERNMENT

Feudalism. Shang rule over the Xia state was tenuous. The twenty-eight kings who ruled for some seventeen generations actually controlled only those territories that lay immediately around their three different capitals. The outlying city-states in the 40,000-square-mile kingdom remained under the control of clan leaders. Shang China was a feudal state, where powerful clan rulers exercised administrative, fiscal, and judicial authority in their city-states in return for military service, tribute payments, and oaths of allegiance to the crown. Shang kings were the "first among equals" and they had to expend much of their energy in military campaigns against rebellious nobles and barbarian invaders.

Army and Kingship. They endured mainly because of the strength of their army which consisted of as many as 4,000 peasant conscript foot soldiers, and aristocratic chariot-riding archers armed with powerful composite bows. The Shang kings further exploited the claim that their dynasty possessed the exclusive spiritual power to intercede with Shang-di (the Lord on High), the supreme deity in heaven (*tien*). Shang-di, the reputed ancestor of the Shang clan, controlled the forces of nature and the human condition. Shang kings claimed that Shang-di made himself accessible only through the souls of their royal ancestors. By honoring the souls of their ancestors through ritual sacrifices, the Shang kings claimed the sole authority in acquiring the divine assistance needed to promote China's welfare.

SHANG RELIGION

Rituals. The royal cult to Shang-di was an integral part of the spiritual world of the Shang. That world was dominated by a pantheon of nature deities and human spirits, who controlled the forces of nature and made possible the procreation of humans and crops. In return for human worship, human and animal sacrifices, proper rituals, magical exercises, and other forms of appeasement, these spirits could provide suppliants with children, relief from natural calamities, good harvests, and other requested favors. The Shang resorted to divination, ritual dances, drunken orgies, and fertility rites in their quest for divine assistance, often with the assistance of shamans and priests. Because Shang religion showed little concern for ethical conduct, it played only a minor role in the later evolution of China's ethical value system.

Ancestor Worship. Ancestor worship, a domestic religious cult still widely practiced by families throughout China and the Far East, had its roots in Shang religion. Inherently ritualistic, the cult of ancestors was based on the belief that humans possess souls which depart their bodies at death for a netherworld. There they reside for six generations, after which they are absorbed by nature. During their residence in the netherworld the souls of the dead possess powers of fertility and healing. They also act as intermediaries between the gods of nature and their families. The principle of reciprocity is fundamental to the cult. To honor and worship departed souls with feasts and ritualistic practices guarantees automatic grant of favors. To dishonor them by choice or neglect incurs their hostile meddling and vengeance. The ancestor cult, which is presided over by the eldest male at a special altar in the home, allows its practitioners to embrace and practice other religions as well.

THE EMERGENCE OF WRITING

Development of the Chinese Script. The Chinese independently developed a nonalphabetical system of writing by the Lungshan era. Although none of the earliest fragile bamboo texts have survived, inscriptions on artifacts and thousands of oracle bones reveal an ideographic script in which symbols represent complete words or ideas. By Shang times the system included more than 3,000 characters employing most of the grammatical principles used in classical Chinese. Basically phonetic, each of these characters was formed by placing variously shaped lines within an imaginary square. The complex script required numerous stylistic changes before it was simplified and standardized by the first Qin ruler (see below).

The Impact of the Chinese Writing System. Mastery of the complex script required the acquisition of a minimum written vocabulary of 3,000–4,000 words. While the pronunciation of each word varied among speakers in China's seven dialect regions, its meaning was identical to all that wrote or read it. This enabled the script to serve as a common form of communication, thus making it a major cohesive force in Chinese civilization. The script fostered the growth of a literate governmental bureaucracy and made literacy a tool for social mobility.

SHANG ART

Shang metallurgists addressed the military and religious needs of the ruling class by developing a unique and exceptionally advanced technology for casting bronze weapons and a variety of highly stylized vessels. Still unsurpassed, the Shang technique allowed craftsmen to produce decorated works of remarkable beauty. Artisans employed stylized decorations, a combination of geometric designs and zoomorphic forms, to integrate religious concepts and beliefs symbolically onto their masterpieces. Similar motifs appear on other forms of Shang art, including glazed pottery, stone sculpture, and jade decorative pieces.

THE ZHOU DYNASTY (c. 1027–221 B.C.)

Western Zhou (1027–771 B.C.)   Shang rule ended in c. 1027 B.C. Wu Wang, head of the seminomadic Zhou clan of the Wei valley, sacked the capital of Anyang, killed King Zouxin, and founded a new dynasty. Like their Shang predecessors, the Zhou kings lacked sufficient power to establish national unity or to form a strong central government. As a consequence they were forced to share their power with regional leaders. The systemization of this protofeudal system of government was developed by Tan, the duke of Zhou, the younger brother of King Wu Wang and regent following his brother's death. The basic features of Tan's feudal system endured for eight hundred years. This dynastic change had only a minor cultural impact on China, since Zhou culture readily fused with that of the superior Shang.

THE MANDATE OF HEAVEN THEORY

The dynastic usurpation by the Zhou required a revision of the tradition that only Shang kings could receive the authority to rule from the supreme god Shang-di. The duke of Zhou is said to have devised the Mandate of Heaven theory to legitimize the new Zhou rule. He declared the right to rule was a gift (mandate) bestowed by Heaven (*tien*), the supreme moral force or god of the universe. This gift was conditional and could be withdrawn when a king failed to adhere to virtuous ethical conduct, or failed to promote the welfare of his subjects; the Mandate would then be conferred on a more suitable person. Although initially developed to legitimize Zhou usurpation, the theory was used throughout Chinese history to justify dynastic changes. Its standard of virtuous ethical conduct for rulers became a major intellectual component in the emergent Chinese social order.

THE ZHOU FEUDAL STATE

The duke of Zhou dismantled the Shang state and reduced Shang family holdings to the insignificant fiefdom (estate) of Song. He eliminated a large number of city-states and divided the nonroyal territories into seventy provinces, giving authority over these lands and their inhabitants to trusted noble allies who bound themselves to the crown. These noble families became the theoretical owners of their lands, acquiring full administrative, fiscal, and legal powers in return for oaths of allegiance to the crown. These oaths obligated them to fulfill fiscal and military obligations to the crown, to submit themselves to the jurisdiction of the royal courts and the royal law, and to serve the king as royal officials at the capital in Hao. These arrangements preserved royal supervisory authority over the fiefs and royal rights to terminate contractual relationships with just cause. Direct royal rule was restricted to the royal domain. To secure domestic peace, the main objective of Zhou government, the duke relied heavily on the superior royal armies.

DECLINE OF THE WESTERN ZHOU (1027–771 B.C.)

For two and a half centuries these arrangements allowed vigorous Zhou rulers to maintain essential law and order. But a combination of weak kings and persistent barbarian attacks gradually eroded royal authority and allowed the nobles to escape their contractual obligations. The remnants of royal authority collapsed with the sack of the western capital by barbarians and dissident nobles in 771 B.C. Forced to flee their home territories (which they later invested in the noble house of Qin), the Zhou leaders took refuge in their eastern capital. Since their flight to the east marked a major shift in power, historians designed the earlier era as "the Western Zhou" and the later era "the Eastern Zhou."

The Eastern Zhou (770–221 B.C.)

For nearly five centuries Zhou kings ruled China as nominal figureheads because no regional warlord could master their rivals and impose political unity in the country. This long era of nominal rule is divided into two periods: the Spring and Autumn era (722–464 B.C.) and the era of the Warring States (403–221 B.C.).

THE SPRING AND AUTUMN ERA (722–464 B.C.)

During this period, in which the territorial warlords fought each other in bids for power and the acquisition of new lands, there were only thirty-eight years of peace. These wars allowed the victors to absorb their weak neighbors and to extend China's frontiers into the Yangtze valley and southern Manchuria. While defensive alliances prevented the ascendancy of a dominant state, they could not preserve the independence of the smaller states. Using huge conscript armies with chariot and cavalry contingents, seven powerful states absorbed the rest.

Within their own states the victorious princes took measures to enhance their wealth and power. They increased agricultural productivity, promoted commerce and industry, and effected major works projects. They promoted central rule by effecting innovative bureaucratic reforms, relying on men of talent as government officials, and promulgating written codes of law. By these steps they laid the foundations for a new political, economic, and social order, while undermining the last vestiges of the Zhou feudal system of government.

ERA OF THE WARRING STATES (430–221 B.C.)

The partition of the state of Qin (458–424 B.C.) and a dynastic change in the state of Qi initiated two centuries of intermittent warfare. By the mid-third century B.C. these wars had severely weakened all the combatants except the western state of Qin, whose natural barriers and frontier location protected it from extensive devastation.

THE CULTURAL SIGNIFICANCE OF THE EASTERN ZHOU ERA

The politically unstable Eastern Zhou Era served as a major formative period in Chinese civilization. This creative era, which some call a "Golden Age," gave birth to China's traditional class structure, established the institutional framework for imperial rule, and marked the first attempt by China to extend its civilization outside the North China plain. During this time scholars produced China's classical written texts, generating considerable speculative thought that provided Chinese civilization its ethical and philosophical foundations.

The New Social Order

ZHOU GOVERNMENT

Decline of the Feudal Aristocracy. The Eastern Zhou era witnessed a substantial reduction in the number of noble houses. Those who survived lost their traditional military and political roles to nonnoble professionals. With the appearance of a new type of army nobles lost their military role to professional military commanders by the end of the fourth century B.C. They suffered an additional severe reduction in their political role in the third century when princes implemented administrative reforms to promote centralized rule. These reforms demanded skilled professional scholar-bureaucrats (*shi*) as royal officeholders and administrators.

The Foundations of the Bureaucratic State. Zhou rulers implemented bureaucratic and administrative reforms to promote unity in their states and centralized rule. They gradually established a highly centralized government based on an efficient bureaucracy. They recruited and appointed talented and specialized civil servants from the lower aristocracy to appointive noninheritable offices. Many recruits served as heads of provincial and local administrative districts. There, closely supervised by central authorities, they administered military, legal, and fiscal affairs, maintained law and order, supervised public-works programs manned by state labor recruits, and collected taxes. Their authority, circumscribing that formerly held by feudal nobles, extended to the village level. By these reforms the rulers laid the foundations for the emergence of the bureaucratic state.

SOCIAL CHANGE

Land Reform. State-sponsored agrarian and institutional reforms undermined the ancient ties between noble landowners and cultivators, promoting the evolution of a free landowning peasantry. To enhance their wealth, rulers undertook extensive agrarian reform programs and sold lands reclaimed from interior wastelands, former feudal estates, and newly acquired territories outside their borders. These measures enabled former serfs to buy and sell land. The new landowners were taxed directly by the central government, which also exacted military service and gratuitous labor obligations from them.

Agricultural Revolution and Population Expansion. With their new status the commoners began to adopt surnames and to assume self-disciplinary controls over family members. Small farms and high taxes necessarily limited family income. This curbed the size of individual households and forced younger sons to seek public employment as farm laborers, miners, soldiers, and craftsmen. Deemed socially inferior to landowning peasants, many became colonists in the new frontier territories outside the North

China plain. Colonial settlements in the Yangtze basin and Manchuria helped reduce the pressure of China's exploding population. Expanding population was a natural consequence of increased agricultural output that resulted from the introduction of animal-drawn iron plows, fertilizers, and the Manchurian soybean. China's ability to export its surplus population into neighboring regions offered the advantage of increased state revenues. It also allowed China to extend the boundaries of its civilization.

Economic Developments. Agricultural prosperity stimulated commercial, industrial, and mining activity. This in turn generated a money economy, the growth of new towns and cities, improved distribution and transportation systems, and the rise of a new merchant class. The state-controlled economic structure allowed for considerable private initiative and the accumulation of individual wealth. But the Chinese ruling class perceived rich capitalist-minded merchants and industrialists as nonproductive members in society. As a consequence they viewed the "bourgeois" inhabitants of the new towns and cities as social inferiors to the free peasant farmers. Many rich merchants sought to elevate their social status by purchasing substantial landholdings. Those with fiscal expertise sought court or local positions as ministers and advisers.

Emergence of Schools of Philosophy

The disintegration of the Zhou feudal state and the resulting political instability and immorality that accompanied it generated considerable speculative thought among Western Zhou intellectuals in the sixth century B.C. As they sought to find practical means to cure the defects in government and society, these would-be reformers founded the Hundred Schools of Thought. Of these schools the Confucianist, Daoist (Taoist), and Legalist emerged as the most culturally significant, each advancing its own unique approach for restoring social harmony and traditional values.

THE CONFUCIANIST SCHOOL

The Confucianist school urged rulers to establish a moral meritocracy to help them restore the social order and political harmony that prevailed in the early Zhou period.

Confucius, 551–479 B.C. The founder of Confucianism was Kong Qiu, known to the Chinese as Kong Fizi ("Master Kong") from which his Westernized name Confucius derives. Like his near contemporaries Gautama Buddha and Socrates, Confucius never set down his ideas in writing. His teachings are preserved in the *Analects (Lunyu)*, a collection of sayings compiled by his students after his death. Confucius based his precepts in part on ancient histories and texts, especially the Five Classics (*Book of Changes, Book of History, Book of Odes, Book of Rites*, and *Spring and Autumn Annals*) which some claim he edited. His thought was inherently humanistic and ethical. Its main notion was that humans only prosper when they comprehend and achieve harmony with the cosmic moral order.

Confucian Ethics. Advancing a social and political philosophy that promotes virtuous behavior through education, Confucius demanded that each person adhere to the moral example provided by his or her superiors, fully complying with the duties and responsibilities associated with one's status in the traditional family structure. To generate social and political harmony the state must promote the innate goodness of individuals and their economic welfare. It does this through enlightened rule by a virtuous and ethical leader who uses the assistance of educated scholar bureaucrats. As father to the state (a macrocosm of the family), the ideal ruler provides his subjects a model for correct behavior and has no need to use coercive force to achieve order.

With an ethical value system centered on the family, Confucius demanded that individuals self-cultivate traditional family virtues, filial piety, kindliness and concern for the well-being of others, loyalty, honesty, polite behavior, obedience to superiors, and courage. Individuals should correctly perform rituals and properly exercise the duties and responsibilities that are inherent in one's status. The teachings and virtuous examples of one's superiors assist individuals in achieving this code of conduct. Reciprocal fulfillment of assigned roles not only establishes harmonious relationships among family members but also motivates individual morality that leads to social cohesion.

Confucian Political Theory. Confucius embraced no particular form of government, advocating that rulers restore the benevolent paternalism favored by Shang and early Zhou rulers. Arguing that good government can only be effected by virtuous and altruistic rulers through moral persuasion, Confucius insisted that rulers must teach their subjects through personal example how to comply with the cosmic law and transform them into orderly citizens. By employing traditional family virtues, they can fulfill the basic needs of society with a minimal resort to laws. So that they might realize the maximum good for their subjects, rulers should employ the talents of well-rounded gentlemen scholars who had studied and mastered the wisdom of ancient writers. Confucius maintained that loyalty to the family supersedes that to the state. But his conservative political theory included no formal treatment of the problem of misrule and the concept of sovereignty. His theories, unsuited to the harsh realities of the competitive multistate system, attracted no immediate royal patrons; Confucius therefore never had the opportunity to hold government office. As a consequence he spent most of his life as a frustrated schoolmaster.

Mencius and the Elaboration of Confucian Thought. The Confucian school splintered into several distinct factions after the death of Confucius. In the fourth century B.C. Confucianism acquired new strength and unity through a new interpreter and theoretician, Mencius (372–289 B.C.) (Latinization of Mengzi). In the form of idealized sayings and dialogues he addressed undeveloped and disputed concepts in Confucian ideology. In his book, the *Mencius*, he expanded Confucius's treatment of human nature. He advanced that humans were innately good and declared that evil conduct was a consequence of insufficient education and harsh living conditions. Consequently, he declared rulers have a primary duty to promote the economic well-being of their subjects. Mencius placed sovereignty in the hands of the people and declared that they possessed the right to use force to depose evil rulers and to transfer the Mandate of Heaven to another. His concepts became integral parts of Confucian thought and his *Mencius* a Confucian classic.

Xunzi and the Refinement of Human Nature. Xunzi (Hsun Tzu, fl. 298–238 B.C.), the traditional "father of Han Confucianism," made further refinements and additions to Confucian ideology. As that school's first systematic philosopher, Xunzi was a scholar at Jixia Academy in Qi. He served as mentor to Han Feizi and Li Si, who took leading roles in the rival Legalist movement (see below). He frequently disagreed with concepts advanced by Confucius and Mencius, diverging most from their teachings in his radical view that humans are inherently evil, or at best possess a neutral nature that is corrupted by their environment. Only through the wisdom imparted to them by sages and by a lifestyle based on ritual (which Xunxi deemed the essence of universal order) can humans refine and perfect their character. The primary function of the state is to protect its people from wrong ideas. Incorporating important contributions to the fields of logic and psychology, Xunzi's thought exerted a major impact on Confucianism until the third century A.D., after which it steadily declined in importance.

THE DAOIST (TAOIST) SCHOOL

Origins. The Daoist school (*Daojia*), which scorned the cultural institutions of civilized society as harmful and nonproductive inventions, repudiated Confucian thought. The school was founded by the semilegendary Laozi ("Old Master," Latinized as Lao Tzu), a Zhou archivist and early contemporary of Confucius. Daoism derived its principal tenets from the *Dao De Jing (Tao Te Ching)*, a short enigmatic work of the third century B.C. (but attributed to Laozi), and from the *Zhuangzi* by Zhuangzi (Chuang Tzu, 369–286 B.C.). The latter was a philosophical text of thirty-three chapters which was edited in its current form with supplemental commentaries by Guo Xiang in the third century A.D.

Main Ideas. As classics in Chinese literature, both texts embrace a naturalistic monism (a metaphysical system in which reality is conceived as a unified whole). They declare that the *dao* (Tao, "Way") is an indescribable unified whole and the source of everything in the universe. By employing its power to concentrate (*yin*) and to expand (*yang*), this common source extends its essence to form the heaven, earth, and middle air which in turn produce all sensible beings. As part of *dao*, humans can achieve happiness by living a primitive life in harmony with nature, which offers them guidance and serves as a model. They must strive to maintain a balance of *yin* and *yang*, ignore artificial constructs of civilized life such as education and social mores, and seek knowledge of *dao*, the ultimate truth, through intuition and meditation.

Political Theory. Daoist texts frequently criticized contemporary governments and offered advice to rulers. But their authors pessimistically saw little chance that existing social and political ills would be corrected since government was the main source of most abuses. Daoists deemed government necessary provided it promoted human happiness; but they declared its role should minimally affect the lives of the people by adhering to a policy of "doing nothing" (*wu wei*) contrary to nature. For them, the ideal ruler was one who filled his subjects' bellies, kept them blissfully ignorant, and protected them from evil scholars. The best government was one that governed least.

Impact on Chinese Civilization. Zhou princes dismissed Daoist political theory as totally impractical. But the philosophy offered its small body of practitioners an escape mechanism from the harsh realities of contemporary life. As passive observers and idealizers of nature, Daoist recluses over the generations exerted considerable influence on Chinese art and poetry.

THE SCHOOL OF LEGALISM

Han Feizi (d. 233 B.C.), a prince from the royal house of Han, devised the main tenets of Legalism by adapting and expanding theories of earlier philosophers of authoritarianism. Taking from his teacher Xunzi the concept that humans are inherently evil, Feizi sought to control them by three means: strict use of uniformly applied punitive laws, group responsibility, and a system of rewards and punishments. These means had been advanced earlier by Shang Yang, the Qin prime minister, in *The Book of Lord Shang*. As a control mechanism to regiment society, Feizi recommended that rulers create a powerful absolutist state with an efficient bureaucratic organization and the administrative framework essential to its orderly operation. In his scheme of things, Feizi's system allowed for effective government in times when rulers proved weak or passive. It rested on the assumption that recalcitrant subjects can be forced to subordinate their private interests to those of the absolutist state under the continuous threat of punishment.

Feizi's pragmatic ideology found no place for conventional morality and religion. It diametrically opposed the Confucian goal of restoring early Zhou feudalism, while realistically embracing the managerial techniques and practices that several states now used to enhance their power. Nowhere was the Legalist ideology more enthusiastically received than in the state of Qin. Its rulers applied Legalist concepts both at home and to construct the foundations of their imperial government (see below).

OTHER SCHOOLS OF PHILOSOPHY

The intellectual vitality of the late Zhou era generated a substantial number of minor schools of philosophy. The most preeminent of these, the Mohists (*Mojia*) and the Yin-Yang, addressed a variety of special concerns that included the art of war, rhetoric, epistemology (the theory of the nature of knowledge), logic, cosmology, and the basic forces of nature.

Mohism. Mohism was founded by Mozi (470–c. 391 B.C.), whose goal was to organize a pacifist egalitarian society whose members practiced universal love and economic communalism. This was the first school in China to attempt the development of a theory of knowledge. Mohists made original contributions to the fields of logic and epistemology. But because they considered these fields of minor significance, they opted to use other methods and chose not to develop these intellectual tools into formal systems. Neither field became a separate division in Chinese philosophy. Like scholars at rival schools, the Mohists expended little energy on what they considered impractical and abstract philosophical concepts.

Yin-Yang. The Yin-Yang school devoted its main attention to the operation of the universe. Scholars offered systematic explanations on how it worked. They defined change in terms of nature's two mutual and complementary forces, *yin* and *yang*, and its five constituent "powers" or dynamic elements (earth, fire, water, wood, and metal). Zou Yan, the most famous of its members, employed these components for speculative analyses of historical patterns and world geography.

Military Thought. By contrast theoreticians in the school of military science focused their attention on the art of warfare. Their work culminated in the *Sunzi*, one of the world's great classics on the art of warfare. Like most of his colleagues, its unknown author drew heavily on the use of psychology and cunning.

THE QIN EMPIRE

The Rise of the Qin

The Qin rulers, who took the title of "king" from 325 B.C., used the weakness of their rivals to undertake a calculated policy of territorial expansion. In 256 B.C. Qin armies ruthlessly occupied the hapless Zhou domain and ended the Zhou dynasty. While they paused to strengthen their

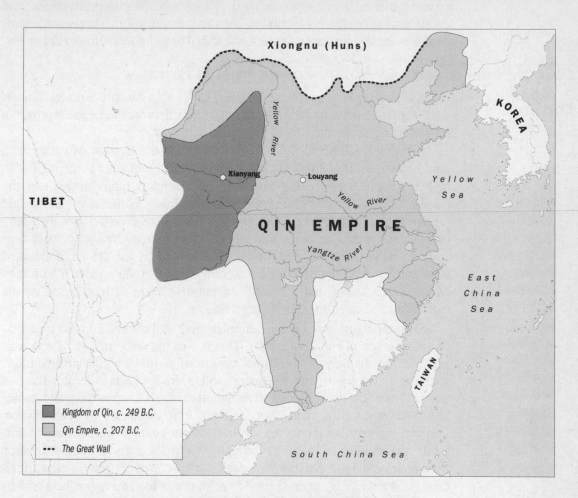

Fig. 4.1   Unification of China

armies, the Qin rulers used diplomacy to undermine defensive coalitions formed against them. In 230 B.C. Qin armies easily defeated the Han and, in quick succession, the Chao and Wei. After dispatching the southern Qu in 223 B.C., they occupied the northeastern state of Jin in 222 B.C.

Qin Shi, the First Emperor   The defeat of Qi in 221 B.C. left Qin Shi (247–210 B.C.) master of China, sole holder of the Mandate of Heaven, and ruler of a huge empire that contained 20 million inhabitants and 282,000 square miles of territory. To reduce the likelihood of revolt, he immediately disbanded all rival armies, and seized and melted down all privately owned weapons. He reduced the political and economic strength of the nobles by abolishing feudalism, selling former feudal lands to peasant farmers after he freed them from serfdom. Over 120,000 of the most powerful families were forced to take up residence near his royal palace in Xianyang. To eliminate ideological conflicts with his state-sanctioned Legalist ideology, Qin Shi proscribed all rival ideologies, burned their texts, and killed or imprisoned their supporters.

Characteristics of the Qin Dynasty

THE IMPLEMENTATION OF THE LEGALIST PROGRAM

Assisted by his capable chancellor, Li Si, Qin Shi proclaimed himself first emperor. He immediately took steps to implement the Legalist program he had successfully employed in his Qin kingdom.

Administration. To that effect, he instituted a system of centralized administration. This allowed skilled and professional staff at the capital to implement and oversee the execution of central policies throughout the empire. Bureaucratic reforms wiped out existing political divisions and replaced them with thirty-six provinces. Each new division was then subdivided into a total of approximately one thousand counties. In these new administrative units salaried officials, appointed by the crown, conducted state and local affairs under the watchful eyes of royal agents. There they administered a new and standardized punitive code of law, based on the earlier laws devised for Qin by Lord Shang.

Standardization. Legalist administrative techniques favored quantitative methods and standardization. This led to the undertaking of a census and the introduction of a uniform system of writing, a common coinage, standardized weights and measures, and even a standard length for cart axles. These new data enabled government officials to enhance tax revenues and to increase military and labor exactions from the masses. The simplification and standardization of the writing system enabled bureaucrats to surmount the problem of linguistic diversity within the empire. Standardization promoted economic prosperity. Legalist administrators promoted agricultural productivity by undertaking three massive hydraulic projects and by transporting more than 60,000 families to new colonial settlements in the Shandong peninsula at Lang-ye and in the Ordos region. To increase trade and commerce they improved overland communications by constructing 4,250 miles of imperial highways that linked most provinces to the capital.

Security and the Great Wall. By conducting military campaigns against the Xiongnu (Huns) in the north, the emperor expanded his empire into Inner Mongolia and in Gansu. In an attempt to curtail barbarian incursions along his northern and western frontiers, the first emperor commissioned General Meng Tien in 221 B.C. to join existing earthen barriers on the frontier into the Great Wall. When completed this stretched eastward nearly 1,400 miles from northeastern Heilongjiang to the seaboard of Gansu. The uninterrupted barrier required the labor of more than 300,000 convicts and conscripted laborers over the course of ten years. The emperor needed no such wall to protect his new territories in the south acquired by military expeditions. These extended southward into the Hanoi region of Vietnam and incorporated the rich agricultural lands in the modern provinces of Fujian, Guangdong, and Guangxi.

Taxes and Tyranny. To increase his state revenues the first Qin emperor imposed a poll tax and an oppressive land tax. The latter exacted one-eighth the annual yield of landowners payable in kind. More costly to the hapless populace was the constant imperial demand for free labor services. These were expended on a series of grandiose and costly works projects that included the Great Wall and the imperial highways.

The Mausoleum. These projects culminated in the construction of a new throne room and royal mausoleum, whose completion required more than 700,000 conscript laborers. Completed before his death in 210 B.C., the huge subterranean burial chamber contained a scale model of the empire and was guarded by a royal bodyguard of 7,000 terra-cotta soldiers.

The Collapse of the Qin

The death of the emperor and the usurpation of the throne by Hu-hai, a weak and ineffective younger son of the first emperor, created a power vacuum that quickly led to the demise of the Qin dynasty. Weakened within by palace conspiracies, the central government collapsed in 209 B.C. when rebellious military commanders and nobles turned against the totalitarian regime and contended for power. In the ensuing civil wars Liu Bang, a minor commander in the Qin army, captured the capital in 207 B.C. He gradually reduced his rivals, to emerge as the unchallenged leader in 202 B.C. His ascendancy owed in part to the support he received from the oppressed masses and the intellectuals victimized by the harsh regime. On February 28, 202 B.C., Liu Bang declared himself emperor and founded the Han dynasty.

Although the Qin dynasty self-destructed only fifteen years after its foundation, it had transformed the structure of Chinese society and government into the forms that were to endure until the present century. With modifications, the Legalist system of centralized bureaucratic government and imperial structure served as the framework for succeeding dynastic governments. Several facets of its laws, notably the collective responsibility of groups for the actions of individual members and the automatic assumption that an accused is guilty until proved otherwise, permanently entered the mainstream of Chinese law. By uniting the Chinese into a single empire, they reduced regional differences and promoted the growth of a common culture. They extended that culture into new regions by means of extensive colonization and through their standardized system of writing. By revealing the merits and shortcomings of Legalist ideology, the hated Qin regime offered critics a valuable example of tyrannical rule to be avoided in the future.

Selected Readings

Blunden, C., and M. Elvin. *Cultural Atlas of China* (1983)
Chan, W. T. *The Way of Lao Tzu* (1963)
Chang, K. C. *The Archaeology of Ancient China*, 4th ed. (1987)
_____. *Shang Civilization* (1981)
Cotterell, A. *The First Emperor of China* (1981)
Creel, H. G. *Confucius and the Chinese Way* (1960)
_____. *The Origins of Statecraft in China* (1970)
_____. *Shen Pu-hai* (1974)
_____. *What Is Taoism?* (1970)
Gernet, J. A. *A History of Chinese Civilization*, trans. J. R. Foster (1985)
Hanson, C. *Language and Logic in Ancient China* (1983)
Lau, D. C. *Mencius* (1970)
Li, X. Q. *Eastern Zhou and Qin Civilization* (1986)
Li, Y. N. *Shang Yang's Reforms and State Control in China* (1977)
Mote, F. W. *Intellectual Foundations of China*, 2nd ed. (1989)
Schwartz, B. I. *The World of Thought in Ancient China* (1985)
Waley, A. *Three Ways of Thought in Ancient China* (1956)
_____. *The Way and Its Power: A Study of the Tao Te Ching and Its Place in Chinese Thought* (1958)

5

Greece

(All dates are B.C.; those before 600 are approximate)

2000–1375	Minoan civilization
1550–1150	Mycenaean civilization
1500	The eruption of Thera, economic decline of Minoans
1450–1375	Mycenaean Greeks conquer Crete
1375	Mycenaean Greeks sack last Minoan palace at Knossos: end of Minoan civilization
1250–1150	Age of the Sea Peoples
1220	Mycenaean Greeks sack Troy
1200–1120	Collapse of Mycenaean civilization
1200–700	Dark Age Greece: cultural decline
1120	Sack of Mycenae
750	Homer
700–323	Classical Greece
700	Hesiod
560–527	Pisistratus rules Athens; rise of Athens
546	Persian conquest of Anatolian Greeks
512	Persian conquest of Thrace
496–406	Sophocles, greatest Greek dramatist
490	Battle of Marathon: Darius's invasion of Greece defeated

480	Battles of Thermopylae and Salamis: Persians defeated
479	Battle of Plataea: Persians withdraw from Greece
478–431	Athenian ascendancy in Greece through the Delian League
469–399	Socrates
461–429	Pericles rules Athens
431–404	The Peloponnesian War
427–347	Plato
415–413	The Sicilian Expedition: the Athenian navy and army are destroyed
404–371	Spartan ascendancy in Greece
384–322	Aristotle
378	Battle of Leuctra: Thebes defeats Sparta
359–336	Philip II: rise of Macedonia to dominance in Greece
338	Battle of Chaeronea: Philip II conquers Greece
336–323	Alexander the Great: conquest of the Persian empire
332	Foundation of Alexandria
323–30	Hellenistic Age
312–63	Seleucid empire
304–30	Ptolemaic empire
248	Parthians revolt, reconquest of Iran from the Seleucids
200	Battle of Panion: Seleucids defeat Ptolemies
200–146	Romans conquer Greece
167	Jewish revolt against Hellenistic Seleucids
63	Romans conquer Seleucids
30	Romans annex Egypt, end of the Hellenistic Age

Although originally a collection of minor barbarian Indo-European tribesmen, the Greeks eventually rose to create one of the fundamental cultural traditions of the world. The early Greek civilizations of the Minoans and Mycenaeans flourished in the Bronze Age, but disappeared in the political chaos of the twelfth century, creating a dark age lasting half a millennium.

The recovery of Greece, beginning in the seventh century B.C., led to the formation of a politically fragmented but culturally and economically vibrant civilization. Threatened with absorption by the Persian empire in the early fifth century, the Greeks managed to temporarily unite and retain their independence. However, with the Persian threat removed, the Greeks returned to their suicidal wars. Despite this military instability, the Greeks of the fifth century witnessed a golden age of cultural development. When political unity was finally imposed by Philip of Macedonia, the united Greeks turned against their old enemy Persia. Under the leadership of Alexander the Great, Persia was conquered, and Greek civilization spread throughout the eastern Mediterranean, inaugurating the Hellenistic Age.

EARLY GREECE

Based on a combination of cultural influences from the Near East and indigenous ideas, Greece was home to two splendid Bronze Age civilizations, the Minoans and the Mycenaeans.

The Minoans, 2000–1375 B.C.

Named after its semi-legendary king Minos, Minoan civilization was a maritime commercial state centered on the island of Crete. Most data used in reconstructing this civilization is derived from archaeology, which began with the famous excavations at Knossos by Arthur Evans in 1900.

THE MINOAN THALASSOCRACY

The Minoan thalassocracy (rule of the sea) was based on two features: its commercial empire and its palace-cities.

Origins. Founded by a mixture of settlers from Greece, Syria, and Anatolia, Minoan civilization was based on royal palatial centers located principally in central and eastern Crete. Although elements of Minoan culture began to appear on Crete as early as 2600 B.C., the fully developed palatial civilization began only around 2000 B.C.

Maritime Empire. Minoan kings exploited Crete's strategic geographical location, transforming their kingdom into the dominant maritime power in the eastern Mediterranean. This allowed them to engage in an extensive and profitable import and export trade with Egypt and states in west Asia.

Palace-Cities. Minoan society seems to have been a confederation of cities united under the leadership of the high king—the "Minos" at Knossos. Many of the major cities of the Minoan world were characterized by a palace complex: a combination of royal residence, economic center, barracks, and religious shrine. For the most part unfortified, these palace-cities seemed to have relied on their naval power for security. This left them open to eventual attacks from the Mycenaeans in the fifteenth century.

The Thera Eruption and Minoan Decline. About 1500 B.C. the volcanic island of Thera—home to one of the Minoan palace-cities—exploded in one of the largest volcanic eruptions in history. Many of the Minoan palace-cities were destroyed in the related earthquakes; thousands of people died. The layer of ash from the volcano may have caused long-term damage to the region's agriculture. Minoan civilization never recovered from this disaster; within decades it was overwhelmed by Mycenaean conquerors from mainland Greece.

MINOAN CULTURE

As wide-ranging merchants, Minoans were greatly influenced by the peoples with whom they traded. Minoan culture was thus an eclectic blend of Anatolian, Syrian, Egyptian, Greek, and Cretan features. Although the society was literate, their writing system has not been deciphered.

Knossos. The most important Minoan palace-city was Knossos, capital of the Minoan kings who exercised religious authority and directed the maritime economy. The best preserved Minoan archaeological site, its delightful palaces and splendid frescoes bear witness to the elegance and grace of Minoan culture.

Painting. The glory of Minoan art was their fresco painting. The remarkable brilliantly colored paintings bring numerous scenes of Minoan society to life. Themes include palace life, maritime activity, and religious worship. A wide range of sea-life, plants, and animals are also depicted.

Religion. Minoan religion centered around the worship of a mother-goddess of fertility and a male bull-god. Although details are not certain, it seems that the "Minos" was a priest-king who ruled from his palace-temple in association with the High Priestess as queen. Rather than building massive temples, the Minoans worshiped at natural shrines such as mountain tops, springs, and caves. A favorite event was the mixture of sport and religious ritual known as "bull-leaping," in which acrobats would leap over wild bulls in an arena. Modern bull-fighting may ultimately derive from such practices.

The Mycenaeans, 1550–1150 B.C.

ORIGINS

Around 1800 B.C. Greek-speaking Indo-European warrior tribes from the Balkans or Anatolia displaced and absorbed many of the neolithic inhabitants of Greece. Most of these tribes settled in southern Greece, where the mountainous terrain kept them politically divided. By 1550 B.C. several small independent states, each centering around a strongly fortified citadel (*acropolis*), had been formed under tribal warrior-kings.

THE MYCENAEAN AGE, 1550–1150

Maritime Empire. Several of the rising city-states, including Mycenae—home to the legendary Homeric hero Agamemnon—exploited their strategic locations along the Aegean Sea to engage in maritime trade. Some of them founded colonies in Cyprus, Rhodes, and Miletus. Mycenaean city-states held political and commercial domination over most of the Aegean for the next three hundred years.

The Conquest of Minoan Crete. By 1500 B.C. the Mycenaeans had entered into a trading partnership with the Minoans of Crete. Within fifty years, however, they began to conquer their former trading partner. The great palace-cities of Crete were sacked by the Mycenaeans between 1450 and 1375.

The Siege of Troy. Around 1220 the Mycenaean confederation achieved their greatest military victory. Archaeology has confirmed that the city of Troy—a major commercial rival to the Mycenaeans—was destroyed in the late thirteenth century. Legendary accounts of this siege were passed down in oral epic poetry until the eighth century, when they were collected by the poet Homer into his masterpiece, the *Iliad.*

THE FALL OF THE MYCENAEANS

The Collapse. This Mycenaean triumph at Troy was short-lived. The confederation of city-states collapsed into bitter civil wars which destabilized the region politically and ruined their economies. Non-Mycenaean Greek-speaking barbarians may also have invaded at this time, contributing to the political chaos. The great Mycenaean citadels were sacked. Mycenae itself fell around 1120, bringing an end to Bronze Age civilization in Greece.

The Sea Peoples, 1250–1150. What remained of the Mycenaean commercial empire and civilization was destroyed by a diverse horde of displaced rulers, merchants, mercenaries, pirates, and outlaws known as the "Sea Peoples," which included many Mycenaeans. Forming a loose piratical confederation, the Sea Peoples pillaged the Aegean, and disrupted trade. Their depredations sent shock waves throughout the eastern Mediterranean. The Hittite empire was pillaged by the Sea Peoples, who also invaded but failed to conquer Egypt.

MYCENAEAN CULTURE

The rediscovery of Mycenaean culture began with the archaeological discoveries of Heinrich Schliemann in the 1870s. The Mycenaeans seem to have borrowed heavily from the Minoans and the Hittites, but failed to achieve parity with their neighbors in the fields of art and technology.

Architecture. Creative use of Hittite architectural techniques allowed the Mycenaeans to produce a unique style of royal tombs, the beehive-shaped *tholoi*. Mycenaean warlords were masters of fortification, producing some of the finest surviving Bronze Age military architecture in the world.

Art. Although never achieving artistic parity with the Minoans, the Mycenaeans excelled in metal-working. The most famous examples of their gold-working come from the "treasure of Agamemnon," discovered by Schliemann at Mycenae.

Warfare. Unlike the Minoans, the Mycenaeans were an extremely warlike people, who reveled in battle and the hunt. A number of examples of arms and armor survive, including some of the earliest known examples of broadswords, and a massive suit of bronze plate armor found at Dendera. Society was dominated by the heavily armed chariot-borne aristocracy residing in their massive fortified citadels.

Writing. Deriving their own writing system (Linear B) from that used by the Minoans, the Mycenaeans kept detailed commercial and administrative records on clay tablets in palace archives. Enough of these documents survive to provide a knowledge of their palace economies. Unfortunately, no works of literature, religion, or history have been discovered.

Religion. Few details are known of Mycenaean religion. However, from incidental details in Linear B archives we know that they worshiped many of the same gods of the later Classical Greeks including Zeus, Artemis, and Poseidon.

Dark Age Greece, 1200–700 B.C.

The collapse of Mycenaean civilization initiated half a millennium of cultural decline in Greece, known as the Dark Age.

AN AGE OF CHAOS

Greek legends record the invasions of the "Heraclids" (descendants of Heracles) in the twelfth century, which some historians have attempted to equate with the coming of the Dorians, a Greek-speaking people. Although the archaeological evidence of an actual outside invasion is ambiguous, it is clear that the twelfth century in Greece was an age of political chaos as the old Mycenaean order collapsed and their citadels were sacked. Greece degenerated into a semibarbaric condition. Cities disappeared, population levels fell, and prosperity declined. Little is known of the details of the political history of this period.

COLONIZATION OF EASTERN ANATOLIA (IONIA)

The Greeks of the Dark Age retained their maritime heritage, remaining skillful seamen. The decline of Greece was paralleled by a decline in the Bronze Age Anatolian powers, especially the Hittites. A power vacuum developed on the Aegean coast of Anatolia (modern Turkey), which the Greeks moved to fill. During the Dark Ages, Greek colonists settled throughout the eastern sea coast of Anatolia, so that, by the Classical Age, the eastern Aegean seaboard had been fully integrated into Greek civilization, becoming known as Ionia. Until the coming of the Turks in the thirteenth century A.D., eastern Anatolia would remain culturally part of Greece.

THE PHOENICIAN CONNECTION

The decline of the Mycenaean maritime empire also left a commercial vacuum at sea which was filled, in large part, by the Phoenicians. During the Greek Dark Age, Phoenician sailors dominated trade throughout most of the Mediterranean. Phoenicians traded extensively with the Greeks, and may have established colonies in Greece; Greek legend maintains that the city of Thebes was founded by a Phoenician king Cadmos. What is clear, however, is that the Greeks adopted their alphabet from the earlier Phoenician models.

DARK AGE CULTURE

The Dark Age of Greece was a time of cultural stagnation. The knowledge of writing was lost until reintroduced by the Phoenicians in the eighth century. Although no surviving literature was produced, it seems clear that a bardic poetic tradition existed, which transmitted many legends including the epic tale of Troy. Few works of art or architecture survive; the most important artistic remains are geometric-style pottery.

CLASSICAL GREECE, 700–323 B.C.

The Classical Age of Greece was one of the golden ages of mankind. Although politically fragmented and chaotic, the Greek world produced a cultural and philosophical movement which laid one of the principal foundations for Western civilization.

The Archaic Age, 700–500 B.C.

In the two centuries called the Archaic Age, Greece was transformed from a cultural, political, and economic backwater into a dynamic new focus of wealth and power which rivaled the older centers of civilization in the Near East.

CITY-STATES

During the Archaic Age the city-state emerged as the center of Greek political and cultural life.

The Greek City-State. The defining feature of Classical Greece was the political, economic, and cultural centrality of the city-state (*polis*). Each city in Greece was an independent state, which included an urban center and surrounding agricultural villages. The territorial size of Greek city-states could range from 1,000 to 3,000 square miles. The population and strength of Greek city-states could vary widely, and frequently larger cities would dominate the smaller.

Greek Democracy. By the end of the Archaic Age, many Greek city-states had rejected their traditional tribal kingships, choosing instead an equally important Archaic tradition of tribal democracies. During the Archaic Age many Greek city-states experimented with various forms of democracy. Greek democracy was limited in many ways. Only adult male citizens with a certain amount of wealth and who performed military service were permitted to vote. Thus, in Athens in the late fifth century, although there were over 300,000 people living in the city, only about 30,000 were qualified to vote. There were many variations of Greek democracy, but they generally had large governing councils with rotating membership, and smaller executive councils with elected membership. Many Greek city-states wrote formal constitutions in an attempt to clearly indicate the respective powers of the various government councils and officials.

Although democratic institutions had existed in many ancient civilizations (including the archaic Sumerian city-states in the third millennium B.C.), the Greek democratic experiment served as an important source of inspiration for the rise of modern Western democratic movements in the United States and France in the late eighteenth century A.D.

Tyrants. By no means all Greek city-states were democracies. In many cases, powerful aristocrats or demagogues managed to illegally seize power, overthrowing the Archaic kingships or democracies. These usurpers, known as tyrants, became virtual dictators of their cities. Many were capable leaders who enjoyed wide popular support. Others were unscrupulous dictators who oppressed their citizens and were overthrown in revolts.

Greek Political Disunity. The combination of numerous small independent city-states, fluctuating internal political power, and constant strife among cities made the Greek political situation of the Archaic Age quite fluid and chaotic. While all Greeks felt a cultural unity based on a shared language and the worship of the same gods at pan-Hellenic (all-Greek) festivals, their political loyalty was centered on the city-state. Their inability to create a strong centralized state remained a feature of Greek history until the Roman conquests ended Greek independence.

THE RECOVERY OF GREECE

Trade. Archaic Greece was a period of tremendous economic growth. Greece became a maritime and colonial civilization for a combination of several important reasons. The irregular coastline of Greece, with its numerous fine harbors, made it a natural home for mariners. The rough terrain of the country was unsuited for growing grains, but perfect for wine and oil. This naturally lent itself to the development of an economy specializing in the export of wine and oil, and the import of grain. Finally, the limited arable land of Greece was insufficient to feed the steadily growing population. Thus, beginning in the eighth century, many Greeks began to migrate to other parts of the Mediterranean in search of new lands to farm and markets for Greek products.

Colonization. By the end of the sixth century substantial Greek colonies had been established in Sicily, southern Italy, Libya, and the Black Sea.

Smaller trading centers were established on the coasts of France and Spain, while Greek merchant communities were created in Egypt and Syria. Greeks had thus taken their place, alongside their rivals the Phoenicians, as master mariners and traders throughout the entire Mediterranean. Control of the trade and the availability of resources and markets in the colonies made the great maritime cities of Greece increasingly wealthy.

The Rise of Athens. The most important center of Greek civilization was Athens. The foundations of the Athenian democracy were made in the early sixth century by the sage Solon, whose law code and wisdom became legendary among later Greeks. Athens's rise to power occurred during the reign of the brilliant tyrant Pisistratus (560–527). The discovery and exploitations of silver mines at Laurium provided an important source of income to initiate his program. Avoiding military conflict when possible, Pisistratus extended Athens's commercial power and colonies, making it the most wealthy Greek city. Especially important were the Athenian settlements on the Hellespont (strait between Europe and Asia), which gave them control of the Black Sea trade. Beginning under the rule of Cleisthenes in 525, Athenian government was reorganized and the final forms of Athenian democracy established. Military reforms created a stronger army, which defeated an anti-Athenian alliance in 506, conquering new territory and creating the Athenian empire.

The Rise of Sparta. The major rival of Athens was Sparta, in the Peloponnese (southern Greek peninsula). Whereas Athenian power derived from its silver mines and maritime empire, Spartan power derived from its militaristic culture. During the seventh century the Spartans conquered many of the Greek city-states of the Peloponnese. The Spartans established their own citizens as an elite military caste whose full attention was devoted to warfare. The conquered Greeks of the Peloponnese became serfs who farmed the land to support the Spartan war machine. The life of the Spartan males was devoted entirely to perfection in war. The Spartans thus created the most formidable military force in Greece. So great was the strength of the Spartan military that they felt it unnecessary to fortify their capital.

THE PERSIAN CONQUEST OF THE IONIAN GREEKS

By the end of the sixth century Greece had become an extremely wealthy center of commerce. As such, it offered an irresistible temptation for conquest by the great power of the age, the Persian empire (see chapter 2). The Persians had first come into sustained contact with the Greeks following the conquest of Lydia (central Turkey) by Cyrus the Great in 546. In the following two years the Persians absorbed all of the Greek city-states in Ionia (eastern Anatolian coast of the Aegean Sea). In 512 Persian armies advanced into Europe and occupied Thrace (northeast Greece). Many of the newly conquered city-states had economic ties or political alliances with the

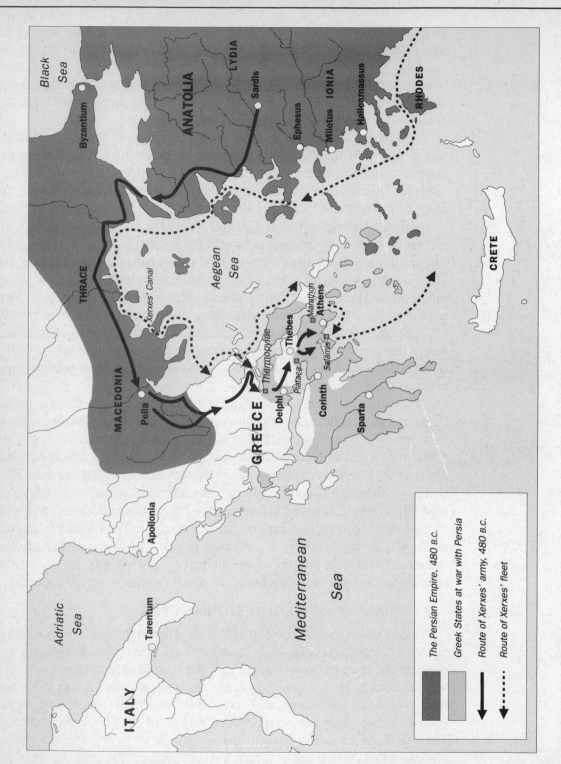

Fig. 5.1   Classical Greece and the Persian Wars, c. 500–350 B.C.

Greeks of the mainland, who were inexorably drawn into competition and, ultimately, conflict with Persia.

The Golden Age, 500–323 B.C.

The fifth and fourth centuries represent the golden age of Greek civilization. During this period the Greeks overcame the Persian threat, became masters of Mediterranean commerce, and produced some of the world's great literature, philosophy, and art. By the end of the period, Greek armies had conquered the Persian empire making the Greeks the masters of the entire Near East.

THE PERSIAN WARS, 500–479

The Ionian Greek city-states in the eastern Aegean were dissatisfied with Persian imperial rule, and took the first opportunity to revolt in 499. Between 499 and 494 the Persians crushed the rebellion, despite aid the rebels had received from Athens. The Persians correctly recognized that the mainland Greeks would continue to interfere in Ionian Greek affairs, and prepared an expedition to punish and conquer them. The first Persian army conquered Thrace and Macedonia (northern Greece), but the Persian fleet was destroyed by a storm in 492. A second force was quickly organized.

The First Persian War, 490. Underestimating the strength and resolve of the Greeks, the Persian emperor Darius prepared a relatively small expeditionary force of perhaps 25,000 men. The Athenians, under their brilliant general Miltiades, quickly mobilized a force of some 10,000 and marched to meet the Persians. The Persians had just landed their fleet at the plains of Marathon some twenty-six miles from Athens, and were unloading their men, horses, and equipment, when the Greek army advanced into view and surprised the unprepared Persians. The Persians were defeated, fled to their ships, and returned to their Anatolian bases.

The Second Persian War, 480–479. Although the Greeks had been victorious, the Persians were by no means completely defeated. A second army was mobilized by Xerxes, Darius's son. By 480 this new force, well over 100,000 strong with hundreds of ships, was prepared to march into Greece. This time the Persian army moved overland across the Hellespont and down the east coast of Greece. All independent Greek cities realized that unless they united against the Persians, they would be conquered one by one. Under the command of the Spartan king Leonidas the Greeks sent a small force to attempt to delay the Persian advance at the mountain pass at Thermopylae while the rest of the Greeks mobilized and prepared. After a valiant defense the Persians overwhelmed the Greeks and continued their advance. They marched to Athens, which had been evacuated, and sacked the city.

The Battle of Salamis. The crucial test of strength, however, was the war at sea. If the Persians could not gain control of the sea they would not be able to supply their huge army during the winter and would have to withdraw. Under the leadership of Themistocles, the Athenians had used their wealth from their silver mine at Laurium to build a massive fleet of two hundred ships. Together with the combined fleets of all other independent Greek cities, the Athenians met the Persian navy at the bay of Salamis near Athens on September 20, 480. Claiming that the Athenian fleet was ready to desert to the Persians, Themistocles laid an ambush; the Greeks drew the Persians into a narrow channel which caused the ships in the Persian fleet to be compressed together. The Greek fleet struck the disorganized Persians, destroying much of the Persian navy.

Greek Victory. The great Greek naval victory at Salamis, although of crucial importance, had not destroyed the Persian land forces, which occupied most of northern Greece. However, Greek control of the sea meant that much of the Persian army could not be adequately supplied during the coming winter; most of the Persians were therefore withdrawn. Under Spartan leadership, Greeks were victorious at Plataea in August 479, which led to the withdrawal of the remaining Persian troops from Greece.

THE ATHENIAN ASCENDANCY, 479–431

The Greek victory in the Persian wars had not only secured Greek independence, but left Athens with the strongest fleet in the eastern Mediterranean.

The Delian League. In 478 the Athenians formed 200 Greek city-states into the Delian League, a maritime alliance against possible future Persian naval attacks. The Persian threat never materialized, and the Athenians quickly turned the Delian League into a maritime empire. By controlling the treasury and foreign policy of the League, the Athenians managed to expand their trade and colonies.

Periclean Athens. The political mastermind behind the creation of the Athenian empire was Pericles, who was virtual dictator of the city from 461 to 429. Much of Athens had been destroyed by the Persians in the sack of 480; Pericles supervised the rebuilding of the city with some of the most magnificent architecture in the world. Likewise, sculpture, painting, drama, history, and philosophy all flourished during the golden age of Athens.

THE PELOPONNESIAN WARS, 431–404

Greek opposition to the overwhelming power of Athens began to coalesce around Sparta, the traditional rival of Athens. By 431 the Greek world had become divided into two opposing camps; war soon broke out.

Stalemate, 431–421. The first ten years of the war resulted in stalemate. The Athenians were supreme at sea, and raided the ports and commerce of the Spartan allies. However, the superior Spartan army was supreme on land. Thus neither power was able to defeat the other.

The Sicilian Expedition, 415–413. Unable to break the stalemate in Greece, the Athenians decided to send an expeditionary force to attempt to conquer the Greeks of Sicily. The extra wealth and resources from their Sicilian conquests could then be turned against the Spartans. After an initial victory, however, the Athenians were forced to undertake an extended siege of the Sicilian capital city of Syracuse. The Spartans sent assistance to the Syracusans, and managed to blockade and destroy the Athenian fleet. Stranded and without supplies, the Athenian army was forced to surrender. As news of the disaster spread, many cities of the Athenian empire revolted.

Spartan Victory, 408–404. The Spartans, with victory within their grasp, turned to the Persians for financial and military assistance. Delighted to see their old enemies slaughtering themselves, the Persians allied with the Spartans in 408. With the help of Persia's fleet and silver, the Spartans crushed the Athenian navy in several battles. In 404 Athens surrendered. The fortifications of the city were destroyed and its empire dismantled. The Spartans were supreme in Greece.

SPARTAN ASCENDANCY, 404–362

The Spartans managed to maintain an uneasy hegemony over Greece for the next half century. However, many Greek city-states were unwilling to simply have Athenian domination replaced by Spartan domination. Although Athens had been defeated, it had not been completely destroyed, and its numerous excellent mercantile connections allowed the city to slowly make a partial recovery.

The Rise of Thebes, 371–362. In 378 an anti-Spartan league was formed under the leadership of Thebes and Athens. Under their brilliant general Epaminondas, the Thebans defeated the Spartans at the battle of Leuctra (371). For the next decade Thebes was the dominant city-state in Greece, but its power was soon eclipsed by the rise of Macedonia under Philip II.

IMPACT

The paradox of the political history of Classical Greece is that, although the superior military system of the Spartans gave them supremacy in Greece, the Spartan emphasis on military matters in their society meant that they created little of lasting cultural significance. Thus, although they managed to dominate Greece for half a century, it was the genius of defeated Athens which changed the world, remaining a significant cultural component of Western civilization for 2,500 years.

THE HELLENISTIC AGE, 362–30

The Hellenistic Age is characterized by the spread of Greek political and economic power, language, and culture beyond the confines of Greece itself, to become the cosmopolitan culture of the entire eastern Mediterranean world. The mechanism for this development was Alexander the Great's conquest of the Persian empire.

The Macedonian Empire, 362–323 B.C.

Although Macedonia (northeastern Greece), had been increasingly incorporated into Greek culture during the fifth century, many Greeks still considered the Macedonians semi-barbarians. Under the dynamic leadership of Philip II, Macedonia managed to unite all Greeks into a single political state for the first time in history.

PHILIP II, 359–336

The Rise of Macedonia. The rise of Macedonia to military prominence was based on several factors. The discovery of new gold mines provided the funds necessary for Philip to accomplish his plans. Hiring a wide array of the finest minds in Greece—including Aristotle as tutor for his young son Alexander—Philip set about turning his capital at Pella into a splendid new center of Greek culture. At the same time, he completely reorganized his army in preparation for the conquest of Greece.

The Macedonian Military System. While most Greek states were squandering their resources in the endless struggle for dominance, Macedonia was left free to develop a new military system. Improving on the standard equipment and tactics of the Greek hoplite (armored spearman), Philip devised the *phalanx*, a formally organized corp of 16,000 men equipped with spears twice the length of the ordinary Greek spear. Marshaled in ranks sixteen men deep, this formation presented a thick wall of spears which was impenetrable to standard Greek tactics. In order to protect the flanks of his phalanx, and to deliver swift charges on enemy formations, Philip paid special attention to the creation of a strong cavalry arm, which had been neglected in traditional Greek armies. Philip also mobilized light troops specializing in missiles to harass and pursue his enemies, and to fight in terrain that was unsuited to his massive phalanx. This new use of combined arms—heavy massed infantry, light missile troops, and elite cavalry—provided Philip with the military might necessary for his conquest.

The Conquest of Greece. As the wars between Sparta and Thebes exhausted the old centers of Greek power in the south, Philip managed to turn Macedonia into the strongest power in the north through a combination of skilled diplomacy, alliances, threats, and military intervention. By the time the southern Greeks realized the danger of this new threat, Philip was on the march. Skillfully exploiting the old city-state rivalries, Philip advanced southward. When the southern Greeks finally allied together to stop the Macedonians, Philip destroyed their army at the battle of Chaeronea in 338. Thereafter, most of Greece was occupied by the Macedonians. Philip began planning the invasion of Ionia and the liberation of the Greek cities which were part of the Persian empire, but was assassinated in 336 before he could begin the next phase of his conquests. This would be left to his brilliant twenty-year-old son Alexander.

ALEXANDER THE GREAT, 336–323

One of the great generals in history, Alexander the Great led the combined Macedonian and Greek army in the conquest of the Persian empire. He thereby inaugurated the Hellenistic Age, making Hellenism one of the major cultural traditions of the premodern world. Following the assassination of Philip, Alexander took determined steps to carry out his father's plan for the liberation of the Ionian Greek city-states under the leadership of the Persian dynasty.

Decay of Persia. The Persian empire in the late fourth century was a decayed shell of the former greatness it had enjoyed under Cyrus, Darius, and Xerxes. Ruled by an incompetent emperor, divided by internal feuds, and plagued by provincial revolts, the Persian state was in a condition of severe weakness.

Alexander's Conquests. Through a combination of the powerful new Macedonian phalanx military system, brilliant generalship, the weakness of the Persians, and good fortune, Alexander conquered the entire Persian empire in an epic campaign of ten years. Driven by megalomania and a conviction that he was an instrument of the gods to inaugurate a new golden age, Alexander was victorious in all his battles. Upon reaching the Indus River Alexander was prepared to cross the river and continue his conquests to the end of the world. His army mutinied, however, refusing to campaign further. Alexander returned to Babylon, which he established as the capital of his new empire, but fell ill and died at age thirty-three.

Alexander's Legacy. Alexander had hoped that his conquests would inaugurate a new age of unity between Greeks and Persians. Instead, his early death created immediate civil war and the rupture of his empire. Although his political legacy was destroyed, culturally, Alexander's conquest formed the basis for the spread of Greek civilization throughout the Near East. For the next thousand years, until the Islamic conquests, Anatolia, Syria, Palestine, and Egypt would be culturally part of the Hellenistic Greek world.

Hellenistic Kingdoms, 323–30 B.C.

As Alexander lay on his deathbed with his generals gathered round him, he was asked, "To whom do you leave your empire?" His reply was "To the strongest." Alexander's legendary words proved prophetic.

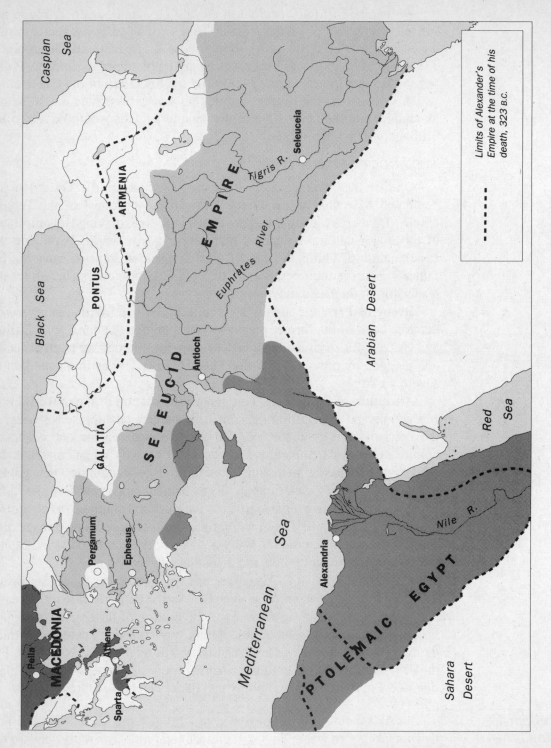

Fig. 5.2   The Hellenistic World, 362–30 B.C.

THE SUCCESSORS

Within two years of Alexander's death, civil war had rent his empire asunder. Although there were initially a dozen competitors (known as the *Diadochi*) for the empire, after fifty years of intermittent warfare, two major states emerged, each ruled by a descendant of Alexander's generals: the Seleucids and the Ptolemies.

The Seleucids of Syria, 312–63. The most powerful of the successor kingdoms was the Seleucids. The dynasty was founded by Seleucus (312–280), who initially managed to control most of the old Persian empire, including Anatolia, Syria, Mesopotamia, Iran, and the Indus valley. Recognizing this new threat, old rivals frequently made common cause against the Seleucids, and in the following decades Seleucid holdings were slowly whittled away. The Indus valley was conquered by the Indian king Chandragupta Maurya in 304; parts of Anatolia were lost in 263; the Seleucids were forced to fight a long series of costly wars against Egypt for control of Palestine; Iran revolted in 248 under the Parthians, who conquered Mesopotamia by 141; the Jews revolted in 167. The remaining Seleucid territory in Syria was conquered by the Romans in 63.

The Ptolemies of Egypt, 304–30. In the third century the Ptolemies were the major sea power in the eastern Mediterranean. Possessing the strongest fleet in the region, they gained control of most of the Mediterranean coast and many Aegean islands. Under a series of weak leaders, however, the Ptolemaic empire was lost. Confined largely to the Nile valley after their defeat at the battle of Panion in 200, Ptolemaic Egypt nonetheless witnessed a cultural flourishing. Alexandria became the cultural center and premier city of the Hellenistic world. The Ptolemaic kings also patronized traditional Egyptian architecture; some of the finest surviving Egyptian temples, such as Edfu and Dendera, were built during this period.

HELLENISM

The political divisions and military turmoil that characterized the eastern Mediterranean following the collapse of Alexander's empire masked a strong cultural unity of shared Hellenism.

The Nature of Hellenism. The word Hellenism derives from the Greek word for Greeks (*Hellen*), and can be defined as the spread of Greek political and economic power, language, culture, customs, and ideas into ethnically non-Greek areas. Hellenistic civilization was largely urban, centering on the great cities such as Alexandria in Egypt, Antioch in Syria, and Ephesus and Pergamum in Anatolia. Peasant life in the countryside of most of these areas remained largely unaffected by Hellenism. Through a combination of migration of Greeks into the Near East, the intermarriage of Greeks with local peoples, and the adoption of Greek language and customs by non-Greek aristocracies, a large Greek minority soon developed in much of the Near

East. Greeks or Hellenized Near Easterners came to dominate the military, government, economy, and scholarship.

Alexandria. The greatest center of Hellenistic culture was the glorious city of Alexandria. Founded by Alexander the Great following his conquest of Egypt in 332, Alexandria soon became the center of commerce for Egypt, and the capital of the Ptolemaic dynasty. Although almost nothing remains of its once magnificent architecture, ancient descriptions praise its glories, especially the incredible lighthouse of Pharos. Most important, Alexandria became home to the greatest library and university in the Mediterranean world, and remained the intellectual center of the Greeks, Hellenistic Jews, the Roman empire, and early Christianity.

Decline of Greece. Ironically, the victory of Hellenistic culture in the eastern Mediterranean simultaneously brought about the decline of Greek culture within Greece itself. The best and the brightest Greeks were irresistibly drawn to become mercenaries, bureaucrats, technicians, merchants, scholars, and artisans in the new centers of wealth and power in Syria and Egypt. Greece became something of a political and cultural backwater, and was conquered by the Romans in 146.

Syncretism. Although Hellenism is usually seen as the spread of Greek ideas, it also represents a period when outside ideas increasingly transformed Greek culture. Most significant in this regard was the spread of mysticism and the magic of Egypt—such as the worship of Isis, and Hermetic magic—which became greatly in vogue throughout parts of the Hellenistic world.

Reaction Against the Greeks. The non-Greek common people in the Hellenistic world served largely as farmers who provided food and taxes to supply the Greek aristocratic minority. Naturally, many of the native Near Easterners resented Greek dominance and rejected Greek culture. This could manifest itself in political or military rebellion, such as the Iranian revolt of the Parthians in 248 which reestablished the Persian empire, or the Jewish revolt in 167 against the Hellenistic tyranny of the Seleucids. On the other hand many people who rejected Hellenism and its values sought solace in new religious movements such as the Essenes of Judaism, or Christianity.

GREEK CULTURE

The Greeks produced some of the finest and most important art, literature, and philosophy in the world.

The Arts

The best examples of Greek art are in stoneworking, whether architecture or sculpture. Unlike those regions of the world that used artistic woodworking or built with clay bricks, ample supplies of fine-quality marble provided the Greeks with a resource for the creation of enduring art forms in stone.

ARCHITECTURE

Greek Temples. The supreme manifestation of the Greek architectural spirit is temple-building. Drawing on the two-thousand-year-old Egyptian and Syrian temple architecture traditions, the Greeks developed an exquisitely graceful style for temples. The central shine of the temple (*cella*) contained the cultic statue of the god or goddess. The cella was approached by a long hallway, which was surrounded by a colonnaded porch. Technological limitations prevented the use of the arch or dome, so a large number of columns were required to support the roof. Although a simple architectural form, the Greek temple's fundamental quality is harmonious symmetry. Each city-state needed at least one temple, and the ruins of dozens of examples survive.

The Acropolis of Athens. The crowning jewel of Greek architecture was the Athenian acropolis, and the outstanding building on the acropolis was the Parthenon (temple to the virgin goddess Athena). Built during the reign of Pericles, the Parthenon was universally recognized as the supreme manifestation of Greek architecture. The acropolis contained several other magnificent buildings, including temples to other gods, a massive monumental gateway (*propylaea*), and a theater. In antiquity it was also adorned by numerous statues, most of which are now lost.

ART

Sculpture. Although Greeks worked with wood, gold, ivory, precious metals, and bronze, most surviving examples of Greek sculpture are in marble, a relatively soft stone which is easy to carve and polish. The sculpture of the early Archaic period shows close resemblances to the formalized poses of Egyptian models. However, the Greeks rapidly moved toward increasing naturalism and realism. By the Classical Age, for the first time in human history, Greek artists achieved a perfectly naturalistic art form; Greek master sculptors were able to create absolutely realistic depictions of the human body. Among the most famous Greek sculptors were Phidias (490–432) whose works adorned the acropolis, and Praxiteles (c. 360).

Vase Painting. Although it is clear that the Greeks had a fresco painting tradition, most of the finest Greek painting is on vases. In many ways Greek vase painting is two-tone drawing, usually in black and white or black and red. Although some vases were decorated with geometric designs, the depiction of humans, animals, and mythical creatures was widespread. Vase painting tended to be more stylized than sculpture, because the painters were working quickly for a mass market. The themes of Greek vase painting include scenes of family life, warfare, mythological heroes, and the gods. Several different images were often painted on a single vase, representing a narration of different scenes from legend.

Literature

Greek was one of the major cultural languages of the ancient world. Works in Greek exist in a wide range of genres and topics, including poetry, myth, drama, fiction, history, religion, and philosophy.

ARCHAIC LITERATURE

The dating of the transition from the Dark Age to the Archaic Age is based on the revival of written Greek literature in the archaic oral poetic tradition. The two greatest Archaic Age literary figures were Homer (eighth century B.C.) and Hesiod (c. 700 B.C.).

Homer. One of the world's greatest poets, Homer stands at the beginning of both Greek and European literature. His two epics, the *Iliad* and the *Odyssey*, formed the foundation of the Greek cultural identity, and were widely studied in Greek schools. The *Iliad* focuses on the story of the sack of the city of Troy by Mycenaean warbands in the thirteenth century, while the *Odyssey* describes the adventures of the hero Odysseus in his ten-year journey home following the sack of Troy. Both works combine historical oral tradition with legend, mythic tales of the gods, and keen insights into human nature.

Hesiod. Hesiod's *Theogony* ("Birth of the Gods") can be loosely described as the Book of Genesis of the Greeks, providing poetic accounts of the stories of the Greek gods and the creation of the universe. His *Works and Days* is a moralizing poem on agricultural life.

POETRY

The origins of Greek poetry lie in the Archaic Indo-European epic bardic tradition as represented by Homer. By the Classical Age, however, poetry had become a mechanism for expressing individual feelings and insights.

Early Poets. The works of the earliest Greek poets have survived only in fragments. Archilochus (c. 650) describes the life-style of the Greek warrior of the period. The love poetry of Sappho of Lesbos (c. 600) offers rare insight into the world-view of Greek women.

Pindar, 518–438. Perhaps the greatest of the Classical Greek poets was Pindar, a writer of eulogies in praise of athletes, and of hymns to the gods. His poetry is noted for its complex language and vivid imagery.

DRAMA

Origins. Greek drama originated as religious rituals, dances, and songs performed in honor of the god Dionysus. Eventually these ceremonies were organized into formal dramatic competitions which occurred three times a year, at which prizes given to the best play of the season. Literally hundreds of plays were written, of which only a few dozen survive. The entire Western tradition of drama and the cinema ultimately derives from these Classical Greek models.

Themes. Although the plots of most Greek plays were based on well-known legends and myths, the Greek dramatists often focused on basic human emotions of love, hate, greed, and fear. The struggle of mankind against Fate is a recurring theme; many plots focus on a tragic flaw of the protagonists, or their descent into madness. The most important Greek dramatists were Aeschylus (525–456), Sophocles (496–406), Euripides (484–406), and Aristophanes (450–385).

Sophocles, 496–406. The greatest of the Greek dramatists was Sophocles, and his masterpiece was his *Oedipus Trilogy,* dealing with the themes of Fate, human arrogance, and justice. The third play of the trilogy, *Antigone,* provides an interesting portrayal of the role of women in Greek society, and the injustice of tyranny.

Aristophanes, 450–385. Aristophanes's plays are the supreme examples of Classical Greek comedy. Although the primary purpose of Greek comedy was to make people laugh, at times it could become deadly serious satire, making important political statements through thinly veiled mockery of the leading figures of Athens. No one was immune to the barbs of the comics. The great Athenian philosopher Socrates was parodied as a bumbling dreamer in *The Clouds*.

HISTORY

Although the writing of history is almost as old as civilization itself, Greek histories stand as the earliest examples of the Western historiographic tradition. While never denying the importance of divine intervention in history, Greek historical writing is characterized by rationalism, humanism, and naturalism. There were three Greek historians to whom we owe much of our knowledge of the Classical Age.

Herodotus, 485–425. Called the "Father of History" by Cicero, Herodotus is the earliest Greek historian whose work survives intact. Taking the Persian wars as his theme, Herodotus never fails to let his attention be distracted by anything that attracts his curiosity. His *History* thus includes lengthy digressions into ethnography, geography, natural science, and religion.

Thucydides, 460–396. Whereas Herodotus wrote from the perspective of the great Greek victories over the Persians, Thucydides chronicled the dismal story of the suicidal war between Athens and Sparta. A minor disgruntled player in the politics and warfare of the time, Thucydides wrote a detailed *History of the Peloponnesian War,* which is often seen as the earliest analytical history.

Xenophon, 430–354. Xenophon led a colorful life: a student of Socrates in his youth, he became a mercenary soldier for the Persians, and he even participated in an unsuccessful coup attempt. In his retirement, he wrote a number of important works, including *Hellenica*, a general history of Greece during his lifetime; *Anabasis*, describing his adventures as a mercenary officer for the Persians; his recollections of Socrates; and a study of horses and cavalry.

Thought

Greek philosophers and scientists provided an important intellectual foundation for Western rationalism and naturalism.

RELIGION

Greek religion derived from the worship of archaic Indo-Aryan tribal gods and goddesses. The vast array of gods and heroes were worshiped in various forms throughout the Greek world, with each city generally focusing on a patron deity of its town. There was no creed, no formal system of religious ethics, and little concern with the afterlife. Greek religion was fundamentally public and civic; worship centered on seeking temporal blessings from the gods by offering sacrifices, gifts to temples, and prayers.

The Pantheon. The Greek gods were organized into a hierarchy of the twelve Olympians (gods residing on Mt. Olympus) under the leadership of Zeus, god of heaven and storms. Each Greek god was sovereign over an element of nature or human life. Worshipers seeking blessings for a particular aspect of life would pray and sacrifice to the god or goddess who ruled over that function. Thus, Ares was the god of war, Poseidon the god of the sea, and Apollo the god of the sun. Aphrodite was goddess of sexuality and reproduction, and Athena the goddess of wisdom. Many minor gods, goddesses, spirits, and heroes were also placated in regional settings where they were thought to exercise some influence. The Greek gods, though immortal, were not seen as all-powerful. They too were subject to Fate; they had once rebelled and overthrown an earlier dynasty of gods, and would perhaps one day cease to rule the universe.

The Olympic Festivals. Although each Greek city worshiped a particular god in its own traditional ways, there were pan-Hellenic religious festivals in which all Greeks participated. The most important of these was the Olympic festival, dedicated to Olympian Zeus. According to tradition the first Olympic festival was held in 776 B.C., from which year the Greek calendar began. Along with the sacrifices, prayers, plays, and religious rituals, athletic games—celebrating military skill—were also held. Our modern Olympic games derive from these archaic ritual sports.

Oracle at Delphi. A fundamental concern of the Greek religious mind was prophecy. The Greeks believed that the gods knew and controlled the future, which they would reveal to mortals if properly placated. The most important center of prophecy was the oracle (prophet) of Delphi, where specially trained female prophetesses could be asked about the future. Great leaders from the Greek world and beyond questioned the oracle at Delphi concerning political and economic policies. Responses were often diplomatically cryptic enough to allow the recipients to make up their own minds, and to permit the oracle to claim fulfillment of the prophecy in several different ways.

The Mystery Religions. Many Greeks, seeking enlightenment and eternal life, sought spiritual wisdom beyond the traditional public and civic aspects of Greek religion. Many therefore participated in the Mystery religions, allegorical fertility rites based on the story of the death and resurrection of an agricultural deity. The most important center of the agricultural Mysteries was at Eleusis, near Athens. The nature and significance of the Mystery Religions is discussed in chapter 6.

PHILOSOPHY

The Greeks ushered in the beginnings of Western philosophy, rationalism, and science. Greek philosophy served as the basis both of medieval Christian scholastic rationalism, and for Renaissance and later philosophical thought as well.

Pre-Socratic Philosophers. In the sixth century B.C. the Greek world-view was transformed by extended encounters with non-Greeks in Anatolia, Syria, and Egypt. Many of the traditional assumptions about the gods and nature came to be questioned. A wide range of speculations arose attempting to make sense out of the observable universe. Most of these early ideas were based on speculation instead of observation, and did not have lasting effects. Nonetheless, they represent the beginnings of rationalistic inquiry into science and philosophy.

Pythagoreans. The most important pre-Socratic philosophical movement originated with Pythagoras (582–507), a Greek living in southern Italy. Pythagoras and his disciples formed a religious brotherhood which believed in reincarnation and asceticism. Their most important contribution to Greek thought, however, was their view that all things in the universe could be explained by numbers. They made significant advances in number theory, geometry, and music.

Socrates, 469–399. Socrates was the father of Western philosophy. A shoemaker by profession, he delighted in informal philosophical discussions with a close circle of friends and disciples. A master of the dialectical (question and answer) method of discussion, he was forever questioning the basic unquestioned assumptions of Athenian society. His fundamental goal was to discover what constituted the good life and good society. Professing no great knowledge in himself, he believed that the spirit of God whispered thoughts to his inner mind. Accused of blasphemy and corrupting the youth of Athens, Socrates was condemned to death by poisoning. While never creating a formal written philosophical system, his greatest impact was on his students, and his most important student was Plato.

Plato, 427–347. Much of our knowledge of Socrates derives from the writings of Plato, which consist not of organized formal discourses, but of idealized dialogues among Socrates, his students, and various prominent Athenians. In these Plato provides insights into what he saw as Socrates's basic philosophy, wrestling with many of the fundamental questions of life and society. The ideal society was to be governed by philosopher-kings, who would rule with perfect wisdom and justice. Plato founded a philosophical academy at Athens which remained in operation for nearly one thousand years. His ideas were later reformulated into a Neo-platonic philosophy which had a significant impact on medieval Christian theology. Although Plato was relatively unknown in the medieval West, the rediscovery of his works was one of the contributing factors to the Renaissance.

Aristotle, 384–322. A student of Plato, Aristotle was the most prolific and influential philosopher of antiquity. His wide-ranging intellect attempted to master all elements of philosophy and science. His writings include works on logic, metaphysics, ethics, politics, physics, natural sciences, meteorology, and geology. Translated into Latin and Arabic, his books became fundamental texts in medieval European, Byzantine, and Islamic cultures for the next two thousand years.

SCIENCE

The study of the natural world by the Classical Greeks was in some ways based more on speculation than observation. Scientific observation as a technique of study became prominent only in the Hellenistic age, when the most important Greek scientific advances occurred. In many ways Greek science represents the synthesis and formalization of three thousand years of scientific discoveries which had been occurring in the Near East since the origins of civilization. Hellenistic scientists included Egyptians, Syrians, Mesopotamians, Anatolians writing in Greek, and ethnic Greeks.

Mathematics. Pythagoreans were prominent in Hellenistic mathematical studies, being credited with the discovery of important principles in geometry such as the Pythagorean theorem. The greatest mathematician was Euclid (323–285), who codified all known geometric principles into a textbook which has remained standard until today.

Medicine. The father of Greek medicine was Hippocrates of Cos (460–377), from whom the modern profession derives the Hippocratic oath. He is noted for the use of diet and exercise in creating an entire health regimen rather than simply treating symptoms. Herophilus (c. 270) made important advances in the study of anatomy.

Engineering. The Greeks were noted for their practical application of physical principles. Greek mechanical inventions included water clocks, pumps, and a wide array of siege engines. Archimedes of Sicily (287–212) is said to have invented the pulley and catapult, discovered the basic principles of hydrostatics, and approximated the value of pi.

For almost half a millennium Greek and Hellenistic civilization was the dominant cultural force in the eastern Mediterranean. The golden age of Classical Greece produced some of the finest literature, art, architecture, and philosophy in world history. From the time of Alexander's conquest of the Persian empire, Greek colonists, ideas, language, values, and art spread throughout this region, creating a vibrant and cosmopolitan culture. Although culturally united, the Greeks were never able to unite politically, and thus became prey to the growing military power of the Romans, which ultimately absorbed the entire Hellenistic world.

Nonetheless, the strength of Hellenistic culture was such that the Roman empire itself became largely Hellenized. The eastern Mediterranean remained Hellenistic through the Roman imperial period, until the cultural transformations brought about by Christianity. Even thereafter, many Hellenistic elements were retained in medieval Byzantine civilization. Indeed, the New Testament itself is in a way a product of Hellenism, for it was written in Greek to bring Christianity to the Hellenistic world.

Selected Readings

Boardman, John, et. al. *The Oxford History of the Classical World* (1986)

Burkert, Walter. *Greek Religion* (1985)

Bury, J. B., and Russell Meiggs. *A History of Greece, to the Death of Alexander the Great*, 4th ed. (1975)

Cotterell, Arthur. *The Minoan World* (1979)

Finley, M. I. *Early Greece: The Bronze and Archaic Ages*, 2nd. ed. (1982).

Grant, Michael. *The Rise of the Greeks* (1987)

———. *From Alexander to Cleopatra: The Hellenistic World* (1982)

Green, Peter. *Alexander of Macedon, 356–323 B.C.: A Historical Biography* (1991)

———. *Alexander to Actium: The Historical Evolution of the Hellenistic Age* (1990)

Hammond, N. G. L. *A History of Greece to 322 B.C.*, 3rd ed. (1986)

Jeffery, L. H. *Archaic Greece: The City-States c. 700–500 B.C.* (1976)

Levi, Peter. *Atlas of the Greek World* (1984)

Robertson, M. *A History of Greek Art* (1975)

Sandars, N. K. *The Sea Peoples: Warriors of the Ancient Mediterranean*, 2nd ed. (1985)

Taylour, William. *The Mycenaeans*, 2nd ed. (1983)

Wood, Michael. *In Search of the Trojan War* (1985)

6

Rome

66–70	First Jewish revolt
96–180	Age of the Good Emperors
113–117	Trajan campaigns against Parthia
132–135	Second Jewish revolt; expulsion of the Jews from Judea
235–285	Period of the Soldier Emperors; empire nearly collapses
285–305	Diocletian restores order and makes reforms
305–324	Civil war; Constantine victorious
313	Conversion of Constantine
325	Council of Nicaea
330	Constantinople replaces Rome as capital
378	Battle of Adrianople; Goths destroy Roman army
393	Paganism declared illegal by Theodosius
410	Sack of Rome by Alaric and the Goths
430	Death of Augustine
476	Last Roman emperor in the west is deposed

To the spiritual heritage of ancient Israel, and the cultural and intellectual heritage of the Greeks, the Romans added the final element of Classical Western civilization, the Roman imperial political system. In the course of its twelve-hundred-year history, Roman civilization underwent a number of significant transformations. From its origins as a small city-state on the Italian peninsula, Rome became the center of one of the strongest and longest lasting empires in history. Originally relatively isolated from the centers of Hellenistic civilization in the Near East, the Romans soon absorbed many elements of Greek civilization and became the chief preservers and transmitters of Hellenistic culture. Finally, although originally the major persecutor of Judaism and Christianity, the Roman empire eventually became the political vehicle for the survival and triumph of Christianity as the major religion of Western civilization. Thus the history of the Roman empire is the history of the cultural, intellectual, and religious synthesis that was to become Western civilization.

BACKGROUND TO THE STUDY OF ROME

The Mediterranean

Although nothing is inevitable in history, the economic interdependence of the Mediterranean world in the third century B.C. meant that there were strong pressures toward closer cultural and political unity. Each region of the Mediterranean had various economic strengths and weaknesses, making them increasingly interdependent. Egypt, for example, had excellent agricultural land, which could produce plentiful surplus grain, but it lacked sufficient mineral resources. Syria and Palestine, though largely desert regions with little agricultural potential, lay astride the international sea and land trade routes to Asia; they thus became centers of trade and manufacture. Anatolia and Spain possessed metals; the Balkans lumber.

Furthermore, the spread of Hellenistic civilization throughout the Mediterranean produced increasing cultural integration. The rise of Hellenism began with the expansion of Greek merchants, colonists, and mercenaries into Sicily, southern Italy, southern France, Anatolia, and the Black Sea area, beginning in the seventh century B.C. This peaceful expansion was intensified by the conquests of Alexander the Great. The small city-state of Rome, although never a colony or conquest of the Greeks, swiftly joined the Hellenistic world by voluntarily adopting Greek literature, art, and culture. Thus by the third century B.C., various elements of Hellenistic civilization had become widespread throughout the Mediterranean.

However, this increasing economic interdependence and cultural synthesis was not matched by growing political unity. In this case, economic interdependence fostered competition rather than cooperation. Despite the conquests of Alexander, the Hellenistic world was fragmented into numerous feuding petty kingdoms, most of them short-lived.

Thus in this situation of growing economic and cultural unity but political instability and competition, the stage was set for the rise of a military power capable of creating political unity. This power was to be Rome.

Geography

The peninsula of Italy divides the oval of the Mediterranean Sea almost perfectly in half, with the city of Rome situated midway down the peninsula. At the center of the Mediterranean world, Rome was thus in the perfect position to benefit from economic exchange; and it was able to maintain military control by sending its armies by sea throughout the Mediterranean. Its central location in the Mediterranean—or *mare nostrum,* "our sea," as the Romans called it—was thus the fundamental geographical factor in the history of Rome. Since travel by water in antiquity was much faster and easier than travel by land, the Mediterranean Sea served as a vast highway for economic exchange, cultural interaction, and—most important for the creation of the Roman empire—the transport of armies and supplies. Indeed, with the exception of a few northwestern regions, all areas of the Roman empire were within a few days march of the sea.

This chapter will focus on how the Romans achieved the political unification of the Mediterranean world, the results of the creation of their empire, and the final collapse of this Mediterranean unity.

THE ORIGINS OF THE ROMAN STATE

Italy to 1000 B.C.

Early farming techniques were introduced into Italy from the Near East as early as the sixth millennium B.C. Small villages of tribal neolithic agriculturalists could be found throughout Italy during the following four millennia. Bronze was introduced in the third millennium. Thereafter, four major factors transformed Italy in the second millennium B.C.

Indo-Europeans. The migration of the Italic branch of Indo-European-speaking tribesmen into Italy occurred in the early second millennium B.C. These warriors, armed with bronze weapons, subdued the local agriculturalists, creating a large number of independent tribes. One of these was the ancestor of the Romans.

Merchant Contacts. Minoan, Mycenaean, and Near Eastern merchants frequented Italy in search of raw materials. Their contacts with the Italic peoples introduced the rudiments of Near Eastern culture to Italy.

Iron. Iron technology was introduced from Greece or the Near East about 1100 B.C., and rapidly spread throughout Italy.

Coming of the Etruscans. Sometime during the twelfth century bands of warrior-colonists known to the Egyptians as the Sea Peoples attacked Egypt. These warbands included tribes known as the Shekelesh and Teresh, who eventually migrated from the eastern Mediterranean to Italy. According to some interpretations, the descendants of these colonists thrived in Italy, becoming known as Sicilians and Etruscans. A faint legendary memory of the arrival of the Etruscans in Italy may be found in Virgil's *Aeneid*, which describes the ancestors of the Romans as refugees after the fall of Troy.

Iron Age Cultures of Italy, 1100–500 B.C.

The rise of the Etruscans in the ninth century represents the foundation of true civilization in Italy. The Etruscans and other colonists from the Near East brought with them the alphabet, stone masonry, ships and navigation, fine arts and crafts, and sophisticated political organization. Thereafter, Italy's dominant geographical position in the central Mediterranean made control of strategic Italian ports and waterways essential to commercial dominance over the western Mediterranean trade routes. Three peoples competed for hegemony on the peninsula: Italians, Greeks, and Etruscans.

PEOPLES OF EARLY IRON AGE ITALY

Italic Peoples. Italic (Italian) refers to speakers of related dialects of one branch of the Indo-European languages. The most important Italic tribe was the Romans, who spoke the Latin dialect. Italic peoples flourished in central Italy, competing with the Etruscans to the north and the Greeks to the south. They were organized into dozens of independent cities and confederations, the most important of which was the city of Rome. Many Italic tribes, including the Romans, were dominated politically by the Etruscans.

Greeks. Greek colonists and merchants settled mainly in southern Italy and eastern Sicily. Greek-style city-states were organized, the most important of which was Syracuse. They successfully competed with their cousins in Greece in wealth, culture, and warfare. They could boast of some of the great Greek philosophers (Pythagoras) and scientists (Archimedes).

Growing competition between Greeks in Italy and those in the homeland culminated in an unsuccessful Athenian attempt to conquer Syracuse in 415 B.C. However, the military power of victorious Syracuse was soon eclipsed by the rising military titans of Rome and Carthage in the third century.

Etruscans. The Etruscans were a cultural and linguistic group in north-central Italy, possibly descendants of colonists from Anatolia. Although loosely organized politically, they were the most highly developed civilization in Italy from about 900 to 400 B.C. Etruscan kings conquered Rome about 600 and ruled there for nearly a century. During this period the Etruscans contributed to the development of Rome's political and cultural ideas. Their influence, especially in religion and art, remained significant in Rome through the early empire. That the Romans adopted the Etruscan form of the alphabet, rather than the Greek or Phoenician forms, is clear indication of Etruscan cultural impact.

Decline of the Etruscans, 509–396. Although not much is known of Etruscan political history, it seems that their government was a coalition of independent city-states, much like Greece. The resulting lack of political unity weakened their overall power and military effectiveness. Meanwhile, the local Latin peoples of Italy quickly learned the arts of civilization from the Etruscans and Greeks, becoming especially adept at warfare. In 509 the Romans and other Latin tribes rebelled and threw off Etruscan lordship.

The rising military power of the Greeks in southern Italy expanded northward; in 474 a Greek fleet defeated the Etruscans at the naval battle of Cumae. This Greek intervention effectively confirmed the earlier expulsion of the Etruscans from Rome and central Italy. The Greeks, content with control of the sea routes, made no attempt to expand their political or military power on land. This political vacuum left the Romans free to become the dominant military power in central Italy. Whatever Etruscan political and military strength remained was destroyed by the invasions of the Gauls in the fourth century B.C. By 350 the Etruscan cities in the Po valley had been overrun, and Etruscan power had essentially collapsed.

THE ARCHAIC ROMAN CITY-STATE, 753–509 B.C.

The site of the city of Rome had been inhabited since at least 1000 B.C. For the first few centuries it was simply a collection of small farming villages clustered on a group of hills near the best ford over the Tiber river. The legendary date of the founding of Rome in 753 B.C. can be accepted as roughly the period in which these small villages coalesced into a unified city-state.

For the next 250 years Rome was simply one small city-state among many in central Italy, playing no unusual role. By 600 B.C. Rome had been conquered by the Etruscans, and was ruled by an Etruscan aristocracy for the next century. In 509, with Etruscan power in decline, the Romans rebelled, expelling the Etruscan aristocrats and establishing an independent republic.

The Early Roman Republic, 509–340 B.C.

By 500 B.C., the now independent city-state of Rome ruled only the small area within ten to fifteen miles of the city itself, and was part of an alliance of Latin city-states in the Tiber valley. Rome's key geographic position at the best crossing of the Tiber river, with its relative size and military strength, made it the natural leader of this Latin alliance. By 350 the other cities of the region had been absorbed by Rome, with their inhabitants becoming Roman citizens.

GOVERNMENT OF THE REPUBLIC

The Roman republic lasted in name from 509 to 31 B.C., although effective control of the government passed increasingly into the hands of military and political dictators after 133. The basic principles of Roman government were established about 450 in a document known as the Twelve Tablets of Law. Essentially, Roman republican government was a complex mixture of limited democracy and oligarchy. Although theoretically a representative republic, the Romans institutionalized two principles that in practice gave greater political authority to the wealthy.

Power of the Aristocrats. The first was that a man's political power should be proportional to his stake in the survival of the state. In other words, since a wealthy man has more to lose and less reason to sell his vote to the highest bidder, the wealthy should have greater political power. This was done by making the Roman Senate the highest authority in the state and limiting membership in it to the wealthy and noble classes. Second, the

Romans specified that only those who had served in the army received a vote in government. Since to become a soldier a man had to provide his own equipment, only those with a certain level of wealth could vote. The common people were represented in the Senate by the tribunes, who spoke for the tribe and had veto power. These characteristics of Roman government created political competition between the aristocrats and commoners.

Aristocrats vs. Commoners. Roman society was consciously divided into social classes based on wealth and noble birth. The upper class was known as the patricians, the lower as plebeians. Throughout Roman history political struggles between the patricians and plebeians were common. Plebeian power rested on three factors: the manpower needs of the state for warfare, the veto power of the tribunes who represented the plebeians in the Senate, and the ability to cause social disorder through rioting.

Celts

During the fifth century B.C. Rome continued to grow in importance as a regional power in central Italy, expanding both through military conquests and colonization. A major crisis occurred about 400 with the invasion of warlike barbarian Celtic tribes from modern France into Italy. The Celts were an Indo-European-speaking group and therefore distant cultural and linguistic cousins of the Romans. They originally settled in what is today France, Germany, Spain, and England in the early second millennium, as part of the same movement that had brought the Indo-European Italic peoples into Italy. However, the Celts had been much less influenced than the Italic peoples by the civilizations of the Near East and Greece; their society therefore remained much more like that of their warlike barbarian ancestors.

CELTIC INVASIONS

Some Celtic tribes, known to the Romans as the Gauls, crossed the Alps in the fifth century, settling in northwestern Italy and exerting military pressure on the Etruscans. Over the course of several decades, the Gauls brought about the final political collapse of the Etruscans and penetrated into central Italy. In 390 B.C. they defeated a Roman army at the battle of the Allia river and sacked Rome. The citadel of Rome withstood a subsequent siege of three months; the Gauls finally withdrew back into northern Italy, leaving the Roman city-state shaken but intact.

The Celtic invasions had thus crushed the hegemony of the Etruscans, leaving all of northern and central Italy politically destabilized. Rome was to emerge as the dominant military power following a century and a half of struggle. Although they survived politically the Celtic attack, psychologically, the Romans were convinced of the need to increase their military security to prevent future military catastrophes. This new martial mentality led to the creation and refinement of the Roman army, one of the strongest the world has ever seen.

THE ROMAN CONQUESTS, 340–31 B.C.

The Roman conquests are characterized by a series of expansions and conflicts which ultimately left them as undisputed rulers of the entire Mediterranean world. As the Romans expanded, they came to face a new set of enemies, requiring further wars. Their conquests finally ended when the Romans reached the Atlantic Ocean to the west, the deserts of the Sahara and Africa to the south, the barbaric Germanic tribes of northern Europe, and the powerful Parthian state of Persia to the east.

The Conquest of Italy, 340–272 B.C.

CENTRAL ITALY, 340–290 B.C.

By 340 B.C. the city-state of Rome was dominant in central Italy, but it was still just one small state among many. In the following seventy years the Romans conquered nearly all of Italy, becoming one of the major military powers of the Mediterranean world.

Diplomacy and Roads. The Roman conquest of Italy was not based solely on military superiority. Indeed, at this point in its history the Roman army was little different from its opponents. Rather, the Romans used skillful diplomacy to establish networks of alliances, which allowed them to overwhelm their enemies one by one. The Romans also created a system of military colonies: Roman citizens would be given grants of land in newly conquered regions of Italy and sent to farm, administer, and defend the new conquests. A sophisticated system of military roads was developed in Italy to facilitate communication, trade, and the march of armies.

Roman Citizenship. The Romans adopted a liberal policy of granting Roman citizenship to the newly conquered Italian peoples. Rather than resist and be enslaved, non-Roman Italians ultimately realized that it was in their best interest to join the Romans as nearly equal partners, thereby sharing in the benefits of military conquests. Thus by a combination of skillful diplomacy, military victories, alliances, colonization, and the extension of Roman citizenship, the Romans managed to transform Italy from a patchwork of feuding cities into a strong united state ready for further outward expansion. The ultimate success of the Roman policy of alliance and citizenship can be seen by the fact that when Hannibal invaded Italy in 218 B.C., very few of the Italian cities—most of which, only a few decades before, had been implacable enemies of Rome—joined with the African invader.

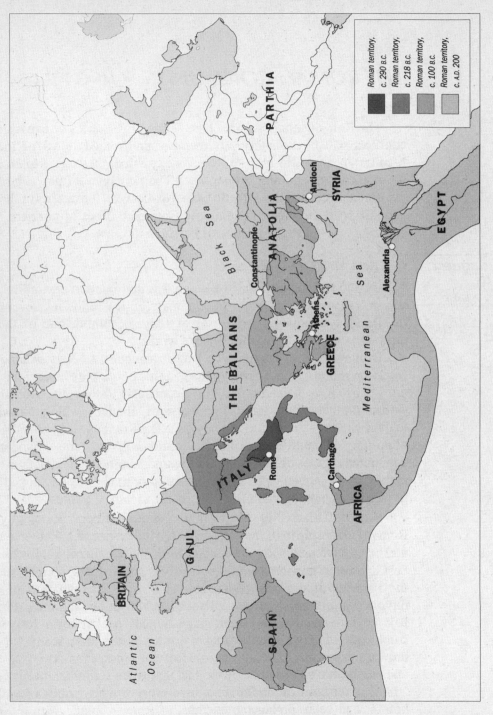

Fig. 6.1   The Roman Empire

GREEKS OF SOUTH ITALY, 282–272 B.C.

War with Pyrrhus. After the Romans had successfully conquered and assimilated their Italic cousins in Italy, they now came into conflict with the Greek city-states of southern Italy and Sicily. Unwilling to accept Roman domination, but unable to resist Roman military might, they called upon the assistance of the Greek king Pyrrhus of Epirus, heir to the military heritage of Alexander the Great. Pyrrhus arrived in southern Italy in 280 B.C. with an army of 25,000 men and 80 elephants organized in the phalanx system perfected by Alexander a half century earlier. Although defeated at first, the Romans determined to fight on rather than make an unfavorable peace settlement. This refusal to surrender and unfaltering courage in the face of defeat and hardship was a characteristic of the Romans that allowed them to prevail in situations where most other peoples invariably surrendered. The Romans defeated Pyrrhus and eventually conquered the Greek cities of Italy.

Consequences of Contacts with the Greeks. The Roman conquest of the Greeks in southern Italy had an extremely important cultural consequence. Greek ideas, language, literature, science, culture, art, architecture, religion, and philosophy began to rapidly penetrate Roman society. This process was accelerated after 146 B.C., when Greece itself became a Roman province. In the words of Horace, "captive Greece overcame her wild conquerors." In other words, although the Romans provided the political, military, legal, and administrative foundation, they became the cultural "captives" of the Greeks as their empire became increasingly Hellenized.

The Punic Wars, 264–146 B.C.

As masters of all of Italy, the Romans now began to compete with and threaten the other major power of the western Mediterranean, the Carthaginian empire.

CARTHAGE

Origins. The city of Carthage in North Africa had been founded in the ninth century B.C. by Phoenician merchants and explorers from Tyre. At first Carthage served as only a small trading post for Phoenician merchants. In the seventh century, however, when Phoenicia lost its independence, many of the aristocrats, soldiers, merchants, priests, and craftsmen fled their conquered homeland, seeking freedom and a new life in the former colony of Carthage, which became an independent city, and the new center of Phoenician military, cultural, and economic power. By the sixth century it had become the major trading city in the Mediterranean. As the financial, cultural, and political center of a dynamic mercantile empire in North Africa, the Carthaginians dominated trade in the western Mediterranean for several centuries.

The Carthaginian Empire. The former colony itself became a colonizer, establishing trading posts and cities throughout North Africa, Spain, Sicily, and Sardinia. Carthaginian merchants explored England and the west coast of Africa in their search for raw materials and markets. Initially Roman and Carthaginian interests did not conflict; indeed, they were allies against Pyrrhus in 278 B.C. However, the expansionist policies of both states meant that their interests would eventually collide.

THE PUNIC WARS

The Roman conflict with Carthage for domination of the western Mediterranean was known as the Punic (Latin for "Phoenician") wars. This conflict lasted over a century (264–146 B.C.), punctuated by three periods of major conflict. The strength of the competing sides was relatively well balanced. The Romans had a superior army and greater population and manpower base; the Carthaginians had a superior navy and greater wealth from trade.

First Punic War, 264–241 B.C. Beginning with a minor dispute in Sicily, the First Punic War soon snowballed into a major war lasting over twenty years. The central issue was domination of Sicily. Initially Carthage, with its superior navy, gained the upper hand and came close to victory. The Romans, who had previously maintained only a small navy of coastal patrol vessels, rose to the challenge; in four years they'd managed to create a powerful navy of one hundred large warships. Victorious in several battles, this new Roman fleet was destroyed in a great storm. After a brief stalemate the Romans won a decisive naval victory at the Aegates islands in 241. In the resulting peace settlement, the Carthaginians agreed to evacuate Sicily, which was added to the expanding Roman empire.

Second Punic War, 218–201 B.C. Though defeated, the Carthaginians were not conquered. Over the next two decades they more than made up for the loss of Sicily by the conquest of much of Spain, which again brought them into conflict with the Romans, who claimed northeastern Spain for themselves. This time, however, the Carthaginians were led by one of the great generals of history, Hannibal. With a splendid grasp of strategy and tactics, Hannibal avoided the war of attrition in Sicily that had characterized the First Punic War. He decided instead to strike directly at Rome by a surprise attack over the Alps into Italy. Between 218 and 216, Hannibal destroyed four Roman armies, nearly bringing the Romans to defeat. However, his lack of siege equipment and insufficient supplies prevented him from achieving his final aim of capturing Rome itself.

For the next thirteen years (215–203 B.C.), Hannibal remained in Italy, controlling much of the south but unable to bring the war to a decisive conclusion. In the meantime the Romans, using Hannibal's own tactics, had prepared an expedition to invade Carthage, under the leadership of a twenty-four-year-old general, Scipio. The Carthaginian senate panicked at the approach of a Roman army, and quickly recalled Hannibal, who was defeated by Scipio at the battle of Zama in 202 B.C.—the only defeat of his career. Carthage surrendered, and Hannibal fled to Anatolia where he later committed suicide rather than face capture by the Romans.

Third Punic War, 149–146 B.C. Thereafter Carthage was reduced by treaty and Roman annexation to only a small fragment of its former empire, which posed no real threat to Rome. When Carthage began showing signs of economic revival in the mid-second century, the Romans agreed with Cato that "*Delenda est Carthago*, Carthage must be destroyed." After a bitter struggle, they sacked and completely obliterated the city, which remained an unoccupied wasteland for another century.

Results of the Punic Wars. The Punic wars had four major effects on world history. First, the Romans became undisputed masters of the western Mediterranean, making them the most powerful military force in the region. Second, the new conquests provided the necessary resources for further expansion. During the decades of constant campaigning, the Roman army became an efficient, well-organized, and effective military force, capable of defeating the Hellenistic armies of the eastern Mediterranean. Third, the wars against Carthage also resulted in the creation of a Roman navy, which ultimately became the most powerful in the Mediterranean. This gave the Romans the capacity to intervene overseas against the Hellenistic kingdoms to the east. This combination of manpower and resources, a strong army, and a powerful navy provided the basis for the final phase of the Roman conquests. Up to this point, the Romans had gone to war essentially out of necessity, in order to defend themselves against real or perceived threats from enemies. By the end of the Carthaginian wars, however, there was no power in the Mediterranean world capable of threatening Rome. But the victories over Carthage had given the Romans a taste for imperialism. Victory in battle brought wealth from plunder, slaves for cheap labor, new lands to farm, control of trade routes, provinces for taxation, and glory and power for the generals. Finally, in many ways the Roman victory in the Punic wars laid the cultural foundation for European civilization. Latin, rather than Phoenician, was to become the language of culture, law, and religion in Europe for the next 1,800 years.

The Conquest of the East, 192–31 B.C.

HELLENISTIC SUCCESSOR KINGDOMS

Following the death of Alexander the Great, his empire collapsed into a dozen fragments, known as the Hellenistic successor kingdoms, each ruled by one of his former generals. In the following century and a half, warfare became endemic in the eastern Mediterranean as these kingdoms competed for domination. Each of the kingdoms held the others in check by a pattern of shifting alliances: if any one kingdom began to threaten the others, the threatened states would quickly ally against the would-be Alexander. While thus engaged in interminable squabbles, a new military power was rising in the west. The Hellenistic kingdoms became aware of the Roman threat only after it had become too powerful for any one state to defeat. Generations of jealous bickering had sapped their strength, preventing the Hellenistic kings from allying themselves against this new outside threat. One by one, the kingdoms were conquered by the Romans. The surviving Hellenistic kings applauded the downfall of their former enemies, seemingly oblivious to the fact that their kingdoms were next on the Roman imperial agenda.

ROMAN IMPERIALISM IN THE EAST

At first the Romans intervened in the affairs of the Hellenistic states only as the ally of one side or the other. They soon recognized the political and military weaknesses of the Hellenistic kingdoms, however, and became conquerors. In the century and a half between 197 and 63 B.C., the Romans made themselves masters of the entire eastern Mediterranean.

Greece, 200–146 B.C. Roman conflicts with the Greeks began in 280 with the invasion of Italy by Pyrrhus of Epirus. After the defeat of Pyrrhus and the conquest of the Greeks in southern Italy in 272 B.C., Rome's military attention was directed against Carthage. By 202 B.C. however, with Carthage reduced to impotence, the Romans were ready to deal with the Greeks. At the battle of Cynoscephalae in 197, the now fully developed Roman legions defeated the Macedonian phalanx of Philip of Macedon; at the battle of Magnesia in Anatolia in 190 the Seleucid king Antiochus III was also decisively defeated. Between 191 and 171 the Romans conquered Greece, creating a system of client states, whereby local rulers were left in nominal charge of affairs with the unwritten understanding that any anti-Roman policies would be harshly dealt with. By 146 B.C. a series of anti-Roman rebellions resulted in the pillage, destruction, enslavement, and annexation of Greece and the imposition of direct Roman imperial rule.

Anatolia and Syria. Following the defeat of the Seleucids at Magnesia in 190 B.C., the Hellenistic kingdoms of Anatolia disintegrated into almost a dozen small principalities, the most powerful of which were Pontus and Armenia in the east. In the next century Rome managed to annex or form protectorates of nearly all these small principalities. The independent states finally formed a coalition against Rome in 89 under the leadership of Mithridates VI (121–63 B.C.) of Pontus. This coalition was ultimately defeated and their territories finally annexed by Rome under Pompey in 62; at the same time Syria and Palestine were brought under Roman domination.

Egypt. The major remaining Hellenistic kingdom was Egypt, which had been ruled for nearly three centuries by the Ptolemaic dynasty, descendants of one of Alexander's generals. Although Egypt had been a powerful military state in the third century B.C., it had declined to relative impotence by the mid-second century. The conquest of Egypt in 168 by the Seleucid king Antiochus IV was prevented only by the intervention of Roman envoys who informed Antiochus that Seleucid annexation of Egypt would be grounds for war with Rome. Antiochus withdrew his army. Thereafter Egypt remained in a state of semi-independence under the protection of Rome. A brief resurrection of imperial ambition under Cleopatra and Antony was crushed by Augustus at the battle of Actium in 31 B.C., after which Egypt became a Roman province.

Thus by 31 B.C., almost exactly three hundred years after the triumphs of Alexander, the entire Hellenistic world had been conquered by Rome.

Social Disintegration and Civil Wars, 135–31 B.C.

SOCIAL CONSEQUENCES OF THE ROMAN CONQUESTS

Two centuries of nearly constant warfare and imperial expansion had created profound changes in the nature of Roman society.

Wealth. Plunder and taxation of new provinces produced a new, immensely wealthy aristocratic class. The wealth from conquests was used to fuel new conquests, for massive building projects, and for the creation of huge agricultural estates for the aristocrats.

Decline of the Free Farmers. The Roman peasant class of free farmers began to disappear. During two centuries of almost continuous warfare, a great deal of the Roman population was constantly under arms: perhaps as many as half the adult male farmers were in the army at any one time. This drain of free manpower from the farms greatly decreased agricultural productivity; many farms ceased to be productive and competitive. At the same time, the vast influx of riches from imperial conquests produced a wealthy class ready to buy up farmland. The resulting large estates were farmed not by free farmers but by slaves acquired through warfare. Displaced free farmers fled to the large cities seeking work. The net result was the decline of the free peasant farmers, the rise of slave agriculture, and the creation of a rootless day-laborer class in the large expanding cities.

Professional Army. As warfare became a permanent state of affairs, many peasant farmers became professional soldiers. The development of a professional army created a new and potentially dangerous political situation, as the soldiers became increasingly loyal to the generals who brought them plunder and victory in battle, rather than the Roman state.

CRISIS IN THE ROMAN REPUBLIC

These and related social changes created a crisis in the Roman society culminating in peasant uprisings, slave revolts, civil wars, and the ultimate turn to dictators to restore the crumbling social order.

The Gracchi Brothers. The first political manifestation of the social problems facing Rome came about because of the attempted reforms of the

Gracchi brothers, who served as tribunes between 137 and 121 B.C. Their reforms included a call for the distribution of state land to displaced peasants, a variety of programs to improve the conditions of the commoners and army, laws against corruption, and the extension of the franchise to certain groups of non-Romans. Their plans aroused great fear among the aristocrats, who correctly recognized that they would lose a great deal of power and control over Roman society if the reforms were enacted. Though the Gracchi were killed in political riots, their attempted reforms demonstrated both the seriousness of the social problems facing Rome and the rising power of the mob, which could be increasingly manipulated by the promises of demagogues.

Marius and Military Reforms. The crisis of Roman society was further compounded by a series of military defeats in northern Italy, northwest Africa, and Anatolia. The major threat came from a confederation of barbarian tribes known as the Cimbri and Teutons. Foreshadowing the more massive and dangerous Germanic migrations some four centuries later, these tribes invaded northern Italy and defeated several Roman armies in a series of battles between 113 and 105 B.C. At the same time, the king of Numidia, Jugurtha, threatened Roman possessions in North Africa.

Roman power was restored under the leadership of Marius, a general who in 107 was given what essentially amounted to dictatorial powers. He defeated Jugurtha in 105, then the Cimbri and Teutons by 101 B.C. In the process, he reformed the Roman army, completing a transformation which had begun two centuries earlier. A citizen-army called to temporary service according to military necessity, had become a professional, well-disciplined standing army, for which military service was now a full-time career. The motivation for this new professional army became increasingly money rather than a sense of public duty.

On the one hand, this new professional army was of great benefit to the Romans. It was now without question the strongest force in the Mediterranean world, capable of defeating any enemy, civilized or barbarian. On the other hand, the creation of a professional army serving for pay laid the foundation for the final step to dictatorship. The military services of the ordinary Roman farmer and citizen were no longer necessary. They became progressively marginalized as they lost political power, eventually turning into the mob of Rome, expressing their displeasure by rioting, and supporting any tyrant who would provide "*panem et circenses*, bread and circuses." The power of the Senate and Roman aristocracy also declined, with decisive power resting in the hands of generals whose military prowess and plunder won them the loyalty of the army. The pathway to Roman dictatorship was now open, awaiting only a tyrant with the skill to seize absolute power.

War of the Allies (Social War). The increasing social, economic, and political tensions in Roman society in the first century B.C. were also manifest in various rebellions within the Roman empire. Between 91 and 89 B.C., the Italian allies—who provided full tax and military service, but who were not Roman citizens—revolted, demanding full citizenship. Nearly half the territory of southern Italy joined the rebellion, which gravely threatened the security of Rome. The Romans were able to end the rebellion only by meeting most of the allies' demands, who thereby became full Roman citizens.

Slave Revolts. During this same period, the Romans faced a series of dangerous slave revolts (135–132, 104–99, 73–71 B.C.), as tens of thousands of armed slaves formed themselves into makeshift armies and rampaged throughout southern Italy and Sicily. The most famous and serious of these rebellions was led by a gladiator, Spartacus, who defeated several Roman armies. This rebellion was crushed with the utmost ruthlessness by Crassus in 71; over 6000 crucified slaves lined the Appian Way.

Sulla, 88–79 B.C. A final threat to the Roman republic came from the king of Anatolia, Mithridates VI (121–63 B.C.). The greed, misrule, and oppression of Roman governors and merchants in the provinces created increasing anti-Roman sentiment, especially in Greece. Capitalizing on this widespread feeling, Mithridates liberated most of Anatolia and part of Greece from the Romans in 88 B.C. Sulla, a Roman general who had served under Marius in earlier wars, was placed in command of the campaign. The aged Marius rightly felt that this move was an attempt to weaken his authority; he initiated a coup in 87, and seized control of Rome, massacred all opponents and established a dictatorship, declaring Sulla a traitor.

Sulla managed to defeat Mithridates in 86, and returned to Rome with his army. He ousted the supporters of Marius and became a dictator himself in 82. Another reign of terror followed, in which hundreds of Roman aristocrats were executed without trial. After attempting to reform the rapidly disintegrating government, Sulla retired in 79. He was succeeded by such henchmen as Pompey and Crassus, who had made their fortunes by confiscating the estates of Roman aristocrats murdered by Marius and Sulla.

Dictatorial power in Rome was now available for the taking. In the following decades Rome descended into a series of civil wars as warlords competed for absolute authority.

THE FALL OF THE ROMAN REPUBLIC, 79–31 B.C.

The complex history of the civil wars leading to the fall of the Roman republic and the establishment of the Roman empire can be divided into three periods, each dominated by a different warlord.

Pompey, 79–49 B.C. Initially power in Rome fell into the hands of one of Sulla's followers, Pompey, who campaigned successfully against rebels in Spain (81–72), and against Cilician pirates (67). Next he defeated Mithridates VI, adding all of Anatolia, Syria, and Palestine to the empire by 63. Military success, wealth from plunder, and, most important, the loyalty of the army allowed Pompey to become the most powerful man in Rome. Nonetheless, his power was not absolute, and he found it useful to form a political alliance with two other powerful generals, Crassus and Caesar, creating the dictatorship of the First Triumvirate (61–49 B.C.).

Caesar, 59–44 B.C. Each of the three *triumvirs*—Pompey, Crassus, and Caesar—immediately set about attempting to secure absolute power for himself by establishing a military reputation and creating a personal army. As senior ruler, Pompey remained the master of Rome. Crassus, perhaps the richest man in Rome, was made governor of Syria and the eastern Mediterranean. There he mobilized an army to conquer the Parthians of Iran (see chapter 7), but was disastrously defeated and killed by the Parthian mounted archers at Carrhae (Harran) in 53. This left Pompey and Caesar as the only viable military leaders of Rome.

Caesar, meanwhile, had conquered Gaul (modern France) from 58 to 52 B.C. Through skillful propaganda in his book *The Gallic Wars*, he presented himself as the greatest living Roman, and created a powerful army loyal only to himself. Caesar was ordered by the pro-Pompey Senate to disband this force. When he refused, civil war broke out, lasting from 49 to 47 B.C., which raged in Italy, Spain, North Africa, Greece, and Egypt. In the end, Pompey was defeated and assassinated, and Caesar emerged victorious.

Although never assuming the title of emperor, Caesar was absolute dictator from 47 to 44 B.C., during which time he established a series of important government, economic, and social reforms. His political enemies joined those who desired the return of republican government and assassinated Caesar in the Senate building in 44 B.C.

Augustus, 44–31 B.C. The death of Caesar did not result in a restoration of the republic. Rather, Antony, Caesar's most important general, and Caesar's nephew Octavian, rallied Caesar's armies. They decisively defeated the republicans at the battle of Philippi in 42, then murdered all remaining republicans. Naturally enough, Antony and Octavian quarreled, and another civil war broke out. The forces of Antony, joined with those of Cleopatra of Egypt, were crushed at the naval battle of Actium in 31 B.C.; the defeated rulers fled to Egypt, where they committed suicide. Egypt was annexed, and Octavian returned to Rome in triumph, where the battered remnants of the Senate proclaimed him Augustus, and supreme ruler of the empire. The republic had been replaced by imperial dictatorship.

Reasons for the Success of the Roman Conquests

The success of the Roman conquests was based on a number of factors:

(1) The Romans developed a military ethos and martial mentality that glorified war and conquest.

(2) The Roman army was one of the finest military systems in the pre-modern world.

(3) The agricultural population base of Italy was much larger than that of any opponents. This provided the Romans with manpower reserves, which allowed them to raise new armies after seemingly crushing defeats.

(4) Their diplomatic skill allowed them to create a system of alliances that permitted the destruction of enemies one by one whom they could never have conquered all at once. The Roman policy of expanding citizenship and colonization, especially in Italy, caused many of the conquered peoples to join the Roman imperial efforts.

(5) Roman victories created a snowball effect. Each campaign resulted in a more efficient army, with more land and resources available for future campaigns. The military system eventually became so large and powerful that none of Rome's neighbors except the Parthians could hope to withstand its attacks.

THE ROMAN EMPIRE, 31 B.C.–A.D. 284

Julio-Claudian Period, 48 B.C.– A.D. 96

AUGUSTUS (31 B.C.–A.D. 14)

Dictatorship. After decades of costly civil wars and numerous purges, the Romans, both aristocrats and commoners, were ready for peace. Augustus's victory at the battle of Actium (31 B.C.) left him as the sole remaining warlord in the Mediterranean. He returned to Rome in triumph and assumed absolute rule. Remembering the fate of his uncle and adopted father, Julius Caesar, Augustus wisely adopted the policy of maintaining the fiction of old republican institutions such as the Senate, while retaining all real authority in his own hands. Thus Augustus always consulted with the Senate on major decisions; on the other hand, he was sure to make his wishes clear to the Senate, and they were more than happy to honor the First Roman by agreeing to institute all of his policies.

Administration. As the true founder of the Roman empire, Augustus established a working imperial system which would last for nearly three centuries, until finally modified significantly by Diocletian. His major policies and achievements included the creation of a professional standing army designed for the defense of the frontiers; regularization of taxes and administration; and the utilization of the old senatorial ruling class as military commanders, provincial governors, and administrators, thus gaining their cooperation by providing them profits and power through the new imperial system.

Creation of the Empire. Augustus made a conscious decision to end imperial expansion. Instead he established the boundaries of the empire along strong defensible frontiers such as rivers (Rhine and Danube), mountains (in Anatolia), and deserts (Syria and North Africa). Although Britain was added to the empire by Claudius in 43, the imperial boundaries established by Augustus remained for the most part unchanged for the next 400 years. Augustus's long reign of forty-five years provided the Roman empire the peace and security it needed to recover. The unification of the Mediterranean basin had created a zone of economic cooperation, security, and exchange. Once established and functioning, the advantages of the new Roman imperial system became clear to nearly everyone: with the exception of the Jews and some Iberians, all of the peoples of the Roman empire came to accept its burdens as the price of its benefits.

THE LATER JULIO-CLAUDIANS

The successors of Augustus, though not his direct descendants, were mostly members of his extended family. Unfortunately, none of them had his genius or moderation; on the contrary, several—most notably Caligula—were quite probably insane. Nonetheless, despite the corruption, promiscuity, intrigue, sycophancy, executions, and assassinations that plagued the imperial court, Augustus's imperial system was strong and stable enough to continue functioning. Ultimately, however, the excesses of the emperors became intolerable, and a rash of military coups ensued; in A.D. 68 four emperors were established and deposed.

In 96 a strange scene unfolded: the imperial throne, which had formerly been the cause of numerous civil wars, coups, and assassinations, was left unoccupied. Even stranger, the Senate, which a century earlier had been the center of pro-republican opposition to dictators, now decided to elect a new emperor rather than regain its autonomy by restoring the republic. Thus the aged Nerva (96–98) was elected, initiating over a century of stable rule and peaceful succession to the throne.

Good Emperors, 96–180	The period of the Good Emperors was one of relative peace, stability, prosperity, and general good government. Although there were some outside attacks by Germans and Persians, and some imperial expansion was attempted under Trajan, for the most part the emperors of this period were willing to enjoy the peaceful fruits of empire. This century of peace was accompanied by prosperity and the flourishing of literature, the arts, philosophy, and science.
Decline and the Soldier Emperors, 180–284	This century of excellent emperors was ended by the disastrous reign of the tyrant Commodus (180–192). His misrule compelled a general named Septimus Severus (193–211) to usurp the throne, the first time in over a century that the imperial succession was determined by military coup. Severus attempted to create a hereditary dynasty, but ultimately other

generals followed his example. A series of coups, assassinations, usurpations, and civil wars ensued. Between 180 and 284, there were twenty-six different emperors, with an average reign of only two years each; none of them died of natural causes.

At the same time, the military power of the Germans and Sasanid Persians was increasing. The Goths crossed the Danube river and plundered the Balkans in 251, while other Germans plundered Gaul and Spain in 256. The emperor Valerian was captured in a disastrous defeat at the hands of Shapur of Persia in 260. At this point the empire nearly collapsed, but it was rescued by the rise of Diocletian to the throne (see below).

During the period of the Soldier Emperors, a combination of decreasing military and administrative efficiency, bloating bureaucracy, economic stagnation and depression, corruption, and civil and military strife began to weaken the empire, just as its Persian and Germanic enemies were growing in strength. Despite a temporary recovery under Diocletian and Constantine, the foundation for the eventual collapse of the empire had been laid.

THE ELEMENTS OF ROMAN CIVILIZATION

The Roman Political System

GOVERNMENT

The Greek historian Polybius considered the Roman republican government an ideal combination of the three forms of government recognized by the ancient Greeks: monarchy or rule by one; aristocracy, rule by a few (the "best"); and democracy, rule by the people. Each form of government was thought to have its strengths and weaknesses. In part the founders of the United States government saw republican Rome as its model, dividing power between the "monarchical" executive branch and the "aristocratic" legislature (named the Senate after the Roman consultative body), while democratic participation was ensured by the vote of the common people.

The government of the Roman republic was based on the separation of powers among the different classes of society: the aristocracy—patricians— held the upper hand in the Senate; and the plebeians (commoners) could serve in the assembly and were represented in the Senate by the tribunes. Two elected consuls served for a limited period of time (usually one year) as executive officials; in times of war and crisis they served as warlords and could be given essentially dictatorial powers for the duration of the crisis.

The Fall of the Republic. This republican form of government failed to survive the political and social crises of the first century B.C. The common people lost their share of power when the Roman army became a professional force and the free farmers ceased to play a vital role as a source of manpower for the state. The Senate lost its influence through a combination of indifference, corruption, and ultimately assassination. The civil wars of the first century B.C. resulted in numerous purges of the Senate and aristocracy; as "enemies of the state" they were summarily executed. The end result was the creation of a docile Senate, eager to please whichever military warlord came to power. This allowed Augustus to create an imperial dictatorship under the thin guise of republican institutions, retaining the Senate to rubber-stamp his imperial decrees.

Thus although the Senate survived throughout Roman imperial history and even into Byzantine times, it ceased to serve as a functioning consultative and legislative body, becoming increasingly an aristocratic club from which manpower could be drawn to serve as officials in the military and bureaucracy. Real power rested only in the hands of the emperor, and the emperor's power rested on the loyalty of the army.

Succession to the Throne. With so much power in the hands of the emperor, and with the security and prosperity of the state so dependent on the skill and wisdom of this single man, the selection of a new emperor (or the removal of an incompetent one) became the major political issue for imperial Rome. There were four basic options: election by the Senate, hereditary succession, adoption, and military coup. Although each of these methods were used at various times, in the long run the military could determine who would be emperor.

Social and Economic System

SOCIAL CLASSES

The fundamental social reality of the Roman empire was its division into classes, each with vastly different power, influence, and wealth. Class differentiations were based on numerous factors. Although Roman women had some rights, fundamentally the male head of an extended family had absolute patriarchal authority over his wife and children; he could even execute them without trial for certain offenses. Many class distinctions were based on noble birth, with certain noble Roman families playing important roles in politics and the army for centuries. Wealth was probably the most important factor in the creation of social classes. The conquest of the empire created a class of enormously wealthy families; some had wealth equal to the annual income of the state itself—a trillionaire by modern-day standards. Such men could buy anything—even, on occasion, the imperial throne.

Social Tensions. Roman society, like any other, contained a number of social tensions and contradictions, creating a range of social conflicts, from slave wars to mob riots. Though generally tolerant, the Romans were nonetheless quite prejudiced against non-Romans, including the Greeks. Thus social distinctions also arose on ethnic lines. Slavery obviously created a major class distinction. It should be noted that although the vast majority of Roman slaves were used for agriculture, mines, and industry, the slaves of the wealthy and powerful could often become extremely wealthy themselves. This was especially true for the slaves of the emperors, who were often notoriously corrupt, asking extravagant "gifts" from those seeking the ear of the emperors.

ECONOMY

Agriculture. As in all premodern societies, agriculture formed the basis of the economy in the Roman world. Perhaps as much as 80 to 90 percent of the population of Rome was directly or indirectly engaged in agriculture. Initially Roman agriculture centered on small farms run by free farmers who also served in the military. As the Roman conquests expanded, however, the wealthy aristocrats increasingly purchased or confiscated the land of the small farmers, creating massive plantations known as *latifundia*. These plantations were farmed by slaves, and designed to produce cash crops. Ultimately, in the late Roman empire, most of the land ended in the possession of the state or the aristocratic farmers. The common farmers merged with the slave class to be eventually transformed into the serfs of the Middle Ages—people with imited rights who could not be sold like a slave, but who were legally bound to farm the land of a landlord.

Trade. By the first century A.D., the city of Rome had become the largest in the Mediterranean world, with a population as high as half a million people. To feed this massive population, the Romans were required to import grain from Sicily, North Africa, and most important, Egypt. The long-term effects of this grain dependency were twofold. On the one hand, it meant an increasing integration of the economy of the Mediterranean, by which all areas became dependent on one another for specialized products. Each region tended to specialize in specific products and exchange them for the specialities of other regions. On the other hand, this economic interdependency meant that the entire Roman Mediterranean economic system as a whole was somewhat fragile. An economic depression in one region could have repercussions throughout the Roman empire. Ultimately, following the economic and political crises brought about by the Germanic invasions of the fourth and fifth centuries, the entire economic system of the Mediterranean collapsed into smaller regional units. Each eventually achieved relative economic self-sufficiency, laying the basis for the economic system of early medieval Europe.

International Trade. During the Roman period international trade also expanded significantly. Trading connections were made into parts of Africa (especially the east coast), Arabia, India, and China. It was thus during this period that all of the great civilized regions of the Old World—Rome, the Middle East, India, and China—were for the first time connected together by trade. The importance of this development will be discussed further in chapter 7.

TECHNOLOGY AND SCIENCE

Science. Some significant advances in the sciences were made during the imperial period. Aside from engineering, most Roman science was directly borrowed from the Greeks, and indeed, most "Roman" scientists were in fact ethnically Greek. Pliny (A.D. 13–79) composed a massive encyclopedia of the natural sciences, which remained a standard work on the subject for the next 1500 years. Galen (A.D. 129–199) was the most renowned doctor of his age, whose writings likewise influenced dozens of successive generations. Unfortunately, so important was Galen's reputation as the master of medicine, that his errors and mistakes also went unchallenged for centuries. Strabo (64 B.C.–A.D. 21) composed a massive work on geography, showing the extent of the Roman's knowledge of the world, and preserving important descriptions of ancient places which now are only piles of rubble. Astronomy flourished under the Roman empire under the influence of the most famous astronomer of antiquity, Ptolemy (fl. A.D. 121–151). His geocentric description of the earth as the center of the universe, with all heavenly bodies revolving around it, remained the standard interpretation of the cosmos until Copernicus introduced the concept of heliocentrism in the sixteenth century.

Engineering. The Romans were masters of engineering, both civil and military. Roman roads and fortifications can still be seen throughout Europe, the Middle East, and North Africa. Their monumental civic architecture is among the most magnificent in the world, especially when we remember that it was all built without the benefits of modern technology.

Roman Culture

The fundamental elements of Roman culture derived largely from Greek and Hellenistic models, and as such, Roman civilization can in many ways be seen as Hellenistic—an extension of earlier Greek civilization. Indeed, the Classical civilization of the entire Mediterranean world from the time of Alexander to Constantine is often described as Greco-Roman. The main center of all branches of learning, both the humanities and sciences, during the imperial period was not Rome, but Alexandria in Egypt. Home of the largest university and library in antiquity, Alexandria was the literary and philosophical capital of the empire. In a sense, Rome provided the political, military, and legal elements of the empire, while Greece provided the cultural, philosophical, literary, and artistic elements. This can be seen in each of the four areas of Roman culture discussed below.

HISTORY

By the second century B.C. most aristocratic Romans received a dual education in both Latin and Greek; Greek literary models thus served as the basis for later Roman productions in the writing of history, prose, poetry, and drama. "Roman" literature included many authors writing in Greek as well as Latin, since most well-educated Romans were expected to read Greek, and many Greeks participated in the Roman cultural achievement. Thus a good deal of important Greek literature was created during the Roman empire. A large number of works of Roman literature have been preserved, making Rome one of the best documented societies of antiquity.

Livy (59 B.C.–A.D. 17). The earliest major Roman historian was Livy who wrote a massive work on the entire history of Rome entitled *From the Founding of the City [of Rome]*. Although he occasionally mixed legend with fact, Livy's work remains fundamental for our knowledge of republican Rome, and makes excellent reading.

Caesar (102–44 B.C.). The famous general and tyrant Julius Caesar was the author of several important military commentaries. The most important was *The Gallic Wars*, describing his conquest of Gaul (modern France). Caesar's purpose in writing was entirely propagandistic; he wished to demonstrate to the Roman literate public that he was the greatest living Roman, destined for imperial rule. He was nonetheless an excellent writer, and brilliant general.

Tacitus and Suetonius. Tacitus's (c. A.D. 55–115) *Histories* and *Annals* and Suetonius's (A.D. 75–110) *Twelve Caesars* provide a remarkable feel for the history of the first century A.D., including the decadence and indeed insanity of many of the early Roman emperors.

Late Roman Historians. Later important Roman historians, although not as polished or analytical as their predecessors, include Cassius Dio and Ammianus Marcellinus. All in all, surviving Roman histories provide a splendid account of their civilization.

LITERATURE

Classical Roman literature includes some of the world's masterpieces.

Cicero (106–43 B.C.). Cicero was one of the greatest minds of Roman civilization. During his lifetime he was recognized as the greatest prose writer and orator in Rome. His skill at rhetoric and oratory made him the most important lawyer and politician of his age. As such he made powerful enemies, and was gruesomely murdered during one of the bloody purges following the death of Julius Caesar. His surviving works include collections of legal and political speeches, philosophical essays, and letters. He was considered the finest Latin prose stylist, especially by writers of Renaissance Italy. He was imitated by would-be authors for the next 1700 years, until Latin began to decline as the universal language of the educated classes in Europe.

Virgil (70–19 B.C.). Virgil's *Aeneid* served as the literary exemplar for Europe for 1600 years, inspiring the poetic epics of Dante, Ariosto, and Milton. Virgil, in turn, was imitating Homer, telling the tale of Aeneas, a refugee from the sack of Troy. According to Virgil, Aeneas, with the help of the gods, and after a series of adventures, was brought to the future site of Rome, and became the ancestor of the Roman people. He thus provided the Romans with legendary links to ancient Greek mythology.

Satire. Satire flourished among the Romans both as a form of social and moral commentary, and for sheer entertainment. Horace, Persius, and Juvenal are especially noted for their scathing attacks on the corruption and immorality of the Roman aristocracy. Their critique of human weakness and hypocrisy is remarkably timeless in its application.

PHILOSOPHY

Although Roman philosophy generally represented modifications and extensions of the philosophical schools of the Greeks, there nonetheless were several major philosophers writing in Latin. Cicero wrote several philosophical essays, as did Seneca, the tutor of Nero. The most important philosophers of the Roman age were the Epicurean Lucretius (94–55 B.C.), and the Egyptian Plotinus (205–270). Lucretius wrote a long philosophical speculation called *On the Nature of Things*, which, although pagan, had a significant impact on later medieval Christian thought. Remarkably, Lucretius wrote his philosophical works entirely in verse. Plotinus mixed the thought of Plato with mystical speculation, creating the final form of a philosophical movement known as Neoplatonism. Plotinus and Neoplatonism greatly influenced later Christian ideas on the nature of God and the Trinity.

By the late third century Greco-Roman philosophy had become unable deal with the significant issues facing the Roman world; the best minds of the fourth and fifth centuries were drawn to Christianity (see below).

THE ARTS

Art. The classical forms of Roman art are fundamentally derived from Hellenistic models. There is a wide variety of Roman art forms, the most important of which include sculpture, mosaic, and painting.

Architecture. Roman architecture also derived largely from Classical Greek models. In many ways, however, Roman architecture better represents the technological rather than the artistic skill of the Romans. Many feel that Roman architecture gives one the feeling of imperial grandeur rather than the sophisticated aesthetic grace found in Classical Greek architecture.

The Romans also introduced several new forms of public architecture such as the coliseum (center for sporting events), the circus (for chariot and horse racing), public baths (a mixture of gymnasium, swimming pool, sauna, and bath), and aqueducts to supply clean water to large cities. These Roman architectural forms spread to the Hellenistic cities of the eastern Mediterranean. The Romans were also great temple builders. Roman forums—the centers of economic, cultural, and political life in a Roman city—were also centers of magnificent public architecture. Memorial columns and victory arches could be found in many Roman cities.

An important new imperial Roman style of building was the basilica, which served as a type of town hall for business and government functions. The secular Roman basilican style of architecture was adopted by Constantine and transformed into a place of Christian worship when the empire was Christianized in the fourth century.

RELIGION IN THE ROMAN EMPIRE

Greco-Roman Religion

INDO-EUROPEAN RELIGION

Both Greek and Roman religions derived from forms of earlier Bronze Age Indo-European religions, and as such bore some fundamental similarities in world view. Both religions were polytheistic, with numerous gods ruling over all of the various aspects of nature and life. Mythological tales of gods and heroes served both religions as the foundation for moral and political behavior. For Romans, Rome conquered the world not only because of superior political, economic, and military power, but because the gods had predestined Rome to rule the world.

INFLUENCE OF GREEK RELIGION

When the Romans began to absorb many elements of Hellenistic culture beginning in the third century B.C., they quickly merged their gods with the myths and powers of related Greek gods. Thus, the supreme god Jupiter became equated with the Greek Zeus, god of the sky and storm; the Roman war god Mars was equated with the Greek Ares; Roman Venus was seen as simply a different manifestation and name for the Greek goddess Aphrodite. By the end of this process, Greek and Roman religions had merged into a single fundamentally unified system, although retaining many local variations in practices and beliefs.

ROMAN RELIGION

Greek and Roman religions were fundamentally civic religions; the worship of the gods of the city in which you were born was the civic duty of each citizen. As the Roman empire expanded, the worship of Roman gods was required of newly conquered peoples. Thus, in a sense, the Roman state religion can be linked with modern concepts such as patriotism and loyalty to one's country. Today, most people feel that religion is a matter of private choice. To a Roman the worship of the Roman gods was considered a matter of civic duty, loyalty, and patriotism.

Sacrifice. The fundamental religious act in the Roman world was sacrifice, usually of animals and plants (and on rare occasions, human beings). A complex system of sacrifices on holy days and sacred festivals dominated the Roman calendar and religious life. Romans were characterized as superstitious by the Greeks, since their political and personal lives revolved around their religious calendar and divination. Much of what passed for religion among the Romans we today would view as magic.

Deification. Drawing on the religious traditions of the deification of Alexander and other Hellenistic kings, as well as the Egyptian concept of the pharaoh as an incarnation of god, Roman emperors were often worshiped as an incarnation or manifestation of the gods. Ultimately, offering sacrifices to the divine spirit of the emperor became an important public ritual of loyalty.

Salvation. For the most part, Roman religion was concerned with this life, not the hereafter. Romans worshiped their gods for the benefits of security, prosperity, and fertility that the gods could bring to the living. There was no salvation in the hereafter; indeed, there was nothing to be saved from. Although there were various views of the afterlife held by Romans, none of them included a Judeo-Christian style concept of a heavenly existence in the presence of God. Thus, perhaps the greatest revolution in the Roman religious world-view was the introduction of the idea—via the Mystery religions and Christianity—that an ordinary person could obtain eternal life with God (see below).

Philosophy. As time progressed, many aristocratic Romans ceased to believe the traditional myths of Rome, turning instead to Greek philosophy as the basis for their understanding of the world and the purpose of life. For followers of Greco-Roman philosophy, the myths of the gods were simply tales to inculcate fear and morality in the masses. In a sense, Roman philosophy amounted to the "deification" and justification of traditional Roman virtues—courage, honor, and frugality—in the guise of Greek rationalism. The major philosophical development of the Roman era was the creation of Neoplatonism (the new interpretation of Plato)—a mixture of the ideas of Plato with mystical interpretations of the nature of god, the natural world, and the human soul. Many Neoplatonic ideas greatly influenced medieval Christian theology and mysticism.

Syncretism. A final important characteristic of Roman religion was its syncretism—mixing together different religious ideas and practices. The Romans believed that their gods were obviously the most powerful in the world; after all, they had led the Romans to world conquest. Nonetheless, the gods of all other peoples also existed, and had power, especially in their homelands. This belief had two major effects. It caused the Romans to equate their gods with similar gods of conquered peoples. Most important, it allowed the Romans to worship these other gods as manifestations of their own gods. Indeed, as long as a Roman continued his required worship of the gods of Rome, he was free to worship any foreign god he pleased. Thus, during the imperial period, the worship of the gods and goddesses of many different religions from various conquered regions became widespread throughout the Roman empire.

Oriental Mystery Religions

As the Romans conquered the eastern Mediterranean and the cultures of all peoples of the Mediterranean increasingly merged into a more homogeneous form, the Romans began to participate in Oriental religious rituals and beliefs. The most important of these are called the Mystery religions by historians.

Rituals. The name "Mystery religion" derives from a Greek word meaning "secret," because the fundamental rituals and beliefs of the religion were revealed only to initiates in secret ceremonies, consisting of elaborate rituals including purification, teaching, a sacred drama reenacting the life of the god or goddess, dancing, and in some cases a symbolic marriage or sexual orgy. So important was this secrecy that many of the doctrines and practices were never openly described. Today we are left with only a vague understanding of many details.

Gods. Mystery religions originated in the eastern Mediterranean: Greece, Anatolia (Turkey), Syria, and Egypt. The most well known examples of mystery religions include the Mysteries of Dionysus, Eleusus (Greece), Cybele (Anatolia), Isis (Egypt), and Mithra (Persia and Anatolia).

Fertility Rites. Their rituals and beliefs grew out of allegorical interpretations of fertility cults, whose purpose was to ensure agricultural fertility. Ultimately, however, the growth, harvesting, and planting of crops became allegorical symbols for the birth, death, burial, and resurrection of the human soul, which was equated with the god or goddess of grain.

Salvation. The rituals of the Mystery religions allowed the initiate to become associated with a god or goddess of death and resurrection. Partaking in the death and resurrection of the god of the Mysteries brought the promise of personal salvation, resurrection, and immortality.

Social Bonds. Those who were initiated into a Mystery religion were accepted into a special community of believers, who shared feasts, ideas, and close social bonds. Mystery religions were highly organized into social and civic groups, often with clearly defined priesthoods, temples, and holy days. Thus the life of the initiate often became centered on the beliefs and fellowship of the religion.

Unlike traditional Roman religion, the Mystery religions promised the believers eternal life. Since both the Roman and Mystery religions permitted believers to worship other gods, one could continue to worship Roman gods after initiation into a Mystery religion. Indeed, one could be a member of several Mystery religions simultaneously. Thus, as time progressed, these religions became extremely widespread throughout the Roman empire. For example, the worship of Mithra essentially became the official religion of the Roman army. The mysteries of Eleusus and Isis became very popular among upper-class Romans. However, the most important Oriental religion offering eternal life to believers was Christianity.

Judaism

The most unusual religion of the Roman empire was Judaism. Indeed, so strange was Judaism from the Roman point of view they were forced to create a series of special laws and exemptions to accommodate Jewish beliefs and customs.

ORIGINS

Although Judaism grew out of the Israelite religion as described in the Bible (see chapter 2), it went through several important transformations. First, the Assyrian and Babylonian conquests had begun a diaspora (scattering) of the Jews away from their original homeland. By the time of the Roman conquest, more Jews lived outside of Judea than inside, becoming merchants, craftsmen, and mercenaries in foreign lands. Alexandria in Egypt had more Jews than any other city in the world.

HELLENISM

The conquest of Judea by Alexander the Great in 333 B.C. brought the Jews under the influences of Hellenism. The Jews were just as susceptible to the brilliance of Hellenistic culture as any other people, and many were ultimately adopted into Judaism. By the time of Jesus, Greek had become the major intellectual language of the Jews, and Hellenistic Alexandria the center of Jewish learning. The Bible had been translated into Greek; the two greatest Jewish writers of the age, Philo the Alexandrian philosopher and Josephus the historian, both wrote in Greek.

HASMONEANS AND HERODIANS

Jewish political aspirations for an independent state were revived under the Hasmonean dynasty (167–63 B.C.), when Judea successfully rebelled against the intolerant tyranny of the Hellenistic Seleucids of Syria. By 63 B.C., however, Judea, along with all other small kingdoms of the eastern Mediterranean, was absorbed by the Romans. Herod the Great (40–4 B.C.), a convert to Judaism, usurped the throne, becoming a loyal vassal of the Romans. His reign was noted for the brilliance of his building projects.

DENOMINATIONS

By the time of Jesus, Judaism was an extremely diverse religious movement, with numerous political and religious sects. The most important included Pharisees, who emphasized strict obedience to Jewish law and oral tradition and opposed Hellenism; Sadducees, supporters of the Herodians and the Temple priesthood in Jerusalem; Essenes, extremists who rejected the authority of the Jewish establishment at Jerusalem, and had their own set of scriptures and interpretations known as the Dead Sea Scrolls; and Zealots (Sicarii), advocates of armed rebellion against Rome. Early Christians can also be seen as a messianic Jewish sect.

JEWISH UNIQUENESS

There were several elements of Jewish religion which were unique in the Roman world. First, the Jews were monotheists. However, not only did the Jews themselves worship only one god—the Romans could probably have tolerated a peculiar attachment to a single ethnic god—the Jews insisted that their god was the only one that existed at all. The gods of the Greeks, Romans, and all other peoples were either demons, or were figments of the worshipers' imaginations. Naturally, to the Romans this was a laughable absurdity. After all, it was the Romans who had conquered the Jews: Why would this all-powerful Jewish god have allowed the Romans to conquer his chosen people? Needless to say, it was a question many Jews found difficult to answer. The most successful Jewish response was that of the Christians: God's kingdom was not of this world; God sought victory over the souls of mankind, not over their armies.

JEWISH REBELLIONS

It is a remarkable example of Roman religious tolerance (or perhaps indifference) that they ultimately created a special set of laws which allowed the Jews the right to worship their one God, and even excused them from the necessity of sacrificing to the gods of Rome and the Roman emperors—a requirement imposed on all other peoples of the empire.

Although the Romans may have been willing to tolerate what they saw as the silly religious eccentricities of the Jews, they were absolutely unwilling to tolerate the slightest semblance of political disloyalty. Many Jews were willing to submit to Rome in return for a guarantee of religious and ethnic survival. The extremist messianic and militant Jews, such as the Zealots and Essenes, were unable to reconcile political submission to Rome with their religion. This inherent Jewish antagonism to Rome was greatly intensified by the mismanagement, greed, incompetence, and corruption of Roman governors. Ultimately a social, political, and religious crisis developed in Judea, culminating in the Jewish rebellions of A.D. 66–70, and A.D. 132–135. The first rebellion ended with the Roman sack of Jerusalem in A.D. 70, and the destruction of the Jewish temple. The second rebellion ended with the expulsion of the Jews from Judea and the leveling of the city of Jerusalem. Nonetheless, scattered Jewish communities survived throughout the Roman world as a tolerated eccentric minority.

RABBINIC JUDAISM

Out of the ashes of this political disaster, two important religious movements developed. The Jewish Christians saw the destruction of Jerusalem and the Temple as a fulfillment of Christ's prophecy and a vindication of the spiritual over the temporal kingdom of God. They therefore redoubled their missionary efforts throughout the Roman world. As will be described below, they eventually triumphed spiritually over the Romans.

Other Jews, led by the Pharisees, suppressed the dream of political independence, and set about to preserve the Jews as a people and religion. This they achieved by creating a religion centered on learning instead of sacrifice, scholars (rabbis) instead of priests, and a unique religious law (the Talmud) which would allow them to abide by the ethical and spiritual principles of the Jewish religion in whatever country or city they lived.

The synthesis of these new ideas, known as Rabbinic Judaism, allowed the Jews to survive centuries of political impotence and frequent persecution as a small minority in Europe and the Middle East. Indeed, of all the multitude of gods which were once worshiped in the Roman empire, only the Jewish god is still worshiped today. On the other hand, Jewish political and messianic aspirations, although dormant for centuries, were never entirely abandoned. The revival of nationalistic Judaism (Zionism) in modern times has created one of the great world political crises of the second half of the twentieth century—the Arab-Israeli conflict.

Christianity

For the study of world history, the development of Christianity was certainly one of the most important and long-lasting consequence of both Judaism and the Roman empire. In the course of two thousand years Christianity has grown from a few hundred persecuted followers of an eccentric Jewish sect into the most important religion in the world.

THE ORIGINS OF CHRISTIANITY

The Messianic Idea. Christianity derived many of its ideas and practices from Judaism, especially from the Jewish concept of the messiah. *Messiah* means the "anointed one," or king, referring specifically to the Near Eastern custom of anointing kings with olive oil at their coronations. In most Jewish circles during the early Roman empire, the messiah was conceived of as a mighty eschatological warrior-king destined to bring political deliverance and supremacy to the Jews. During the first century of Roman dominance in Judea there were numerous unsuccessful militant false messiahs.

Jesus (c. 4 B.C.–A.D. 30). The most important claimant of the title messiah was Jesus of Nazareth, who is still worshiped by hundreds of millions throughout the world. Jesus' career as an itinerant rabbi in Judea spanned only a few years, but his influence on his followers and on world history has been remarkable. Rejecting the traditional Jewish understanding of a militant messiah, Jesus proclaimed that he was the Son of God. His messianic mission was to bring spiritual salvation and eternal life to individuals, not political or military salvation to the Jews. His messianic claims were rejected by most Jews of his day, and he was ultimately executed for blasphemy and sedition. His followers (apostles and disciples), however, were convinced that Jesus was resurrected from the dead, confirming his status as the Messiah and Son of God. Based on his impact on world history, Jesus—in company with Muhammad, the Buddha, and Confucius—is widely regarded as one of the most important people ever to have lived.

The Apostles and Paul. The conviction that Jesus had been resurrected from the dead, combined with the profundity of his moral teachings, inspired his twelve closest companions, the Apostles, to spread his message. Initially preaching the story and teachings of Jesus was limited to Jews. With the visionary experience of Peter, and the conversion of the Hellenized Jew Paul (Saul) of Tarsus, however, Christianity began to be preached to a wider gentile (non-Jewish) audience in the Roman empire. Paul's discussion of the doctrines of Christianity in his letters and his missionary efforts among the Greeks and Romans make him the most important Apostle, who laid the foundation for the transformation of Christianity from a minority sect among the Jews to a world religion in the Roman empire.

CHARACTERISTICS OF CHRISTIANITY

Christianity had a number of important characteristics which contributed to its success as a religious movement.

Monotheism. Christianity inherited the monotheism of Judaism (though eventually transformed into a Hellenized philosophical trinitarianism). As such, it was perceived by many in the Roman empire as philosophically modern and enlightened compared to the mythological polytheism of the traditional Greek and Roman religions.

Miracles. Christians professed the reality of both miracles and of God's direct intervention in the present, replacing the vague claims of the intervention of the Roman gods at unspecified times in mythological antiquity.

Exclusivism. The exclusivism of Christianity—once you became a Christian you could no longer worship any of the numerous other Hellenistic gods—was originally a negative factor, limiting its acceptability to the Romans, who perceived it as arrogant and irrational. Ultimately, however, each convert to Christianity represented a weakening of the Roman religion.

As Christianity grew it eventually gained momentum, and slowly strangled paganism.

Moral Ideas. The principles of Christianity, as taught by Jesus, include some of the most profound moral ideas in religious history. Although today they may seem commonplace, the ideas were revolutionary in the world of moral decay in the Roman empire; many were therefore drawn to the teachings of Christ.

Brotherhood. Christianity provided a feeling of brotherhood, stability, purpose, and organization in the increasingly chaotic times of the late Roman empire.

Proselytizing. Unlike most other religions in the Roman empire, Christianity was missionary oriented, seeking to convert all who would listen. The very fact that Christians attempted to convert non-Christians, even if only with moderate success, meant that over the decades the number of Christians would increase while the number of pagans decreased.

Promise of Salvation. Finally, Christianity provided a promise of salvation and eternal life, something with which Roman religion was relatively unconcerned. In this regard, the greatest competition to Christianity came not from the official state religion, but from the Oriental Mystery religions described above.

THE SPREAD OF CHRISTIANITY TO 450

Early Spread of Christianity. Christianity initially spread by word of mouth among the lower and middle classes of the Roman empire. Many enthusiastic preachers, often with a limited knowledge of Christ's teachings, carried the message of the birth of God's son and the possibility of eternal life throughout the Roman empire. Within a few decades of the death of Jesus, small Christian communities had appeared in most of the provinces of the Roman empire.

Roman Reaction. Initially the Roman authorities paid very little attention to Christianity, considering it a strange and eccentric sect of Judaism. Aside from sporadic persecutions, the Romans for the most part left the early Christians alone. Ultimately, however, as Christians increased in number, the Romans began to perceive Christianity as a threat, both to society and the state, and organized persecutions broke out. In the long run these persecutions were ineffective, and Christianity continued to spread and flourish. When Christians took control of the state, the persecuted in turn became persecutors.

Denominations and Heresy. As time progressed, these small Christian communities grew through conversion, creating numerous regional denominations of Christianity, often divided on linguistic and doctrinal grounds. As the leaders of Christianity attempted to maintain some semblance of order within these Christian communities, there arose a series of disputes over doctrinal, practice, and administration. The ultimate consequence was the creation of a remarkable number of denominations within early Christianity, including Judeo-Christianity, Hellenistic Christianity, Gnosticism, Arianism, and Monophysitism. Although important in their own day, with disputes between denominations often leading to persecution and bloodshed, most of these early denominations of Christianity have disappeared. The major surviving branches will be discussed below.

Constantine (324–337). The decisive event in the rise of Christianity was the conversion of the Roman emperor Constantine. His conversion had a major impact on the development of Christianity. First, state patronage of Christianity allowed the religion to spread more rapidly among the Romans. Many Romans, accustomed to worshiping the state gods, were transformed into nominal Christians when the emperor became a Christian. Others joined because they saw Christianity as a mechanism for promotion and power. Ultimately, under Theodosius (379–395), non-Christian religions were outlawed, and slowly disappeared.

The second effect of Constantine's conversion was the establishment of religious orthodoxy as a state issue. It was not sufficient to be a Christian; rather, one had to be a member of the "politically correct" (i.e., imperially patronized) branch of Christianity. Thus one effect of Constantine's conversion was the elimination of religious diversity within the Christian movement. Another effect was that the old decaying Roman empire was revitalized and reunified by the new imperial ideology, Christianity, which would remain the ideology of the Byzantine empire for over one thousand years.

Church Councils. Despite occasional outbursts of interdenominational strife between different Christian groups, more rational attempts were also made to reconcile differences and define Christian doctrines through holding councils of Christian bishops and leaders. The most important of these councils were the council of Nicaea, which convened in 325 under the direction of Constantine, and the council of Chalcedon in 451. The outcome of these councils was paradoxical. On the one hand, they laid the foundation for all future doctrine, practice, and theology for the Greek Orthodox and Roman Catholic branches of Christianity. Thus, in a sense, they can be seen as having been successful in their attempts to promulgate Christian unity. On the other hand, dissenters from the newly proclaimed orthodoxy were branded as heretics, expelled from the Church, and persecuted. Ultimately these and related councils, which sought to unify Christianity, also served to formalize and institutionalize the already existing divisions, causing a permanent split between European Christianity, and the branches of Christianity in the Middle East, Asia, and Africa.

Church Fathers. As Christianity spread a growing group of late Roman intellectuals, known as the Church Fathers, became prominent leaders of the

Church. The Church Fathers attempted to achieve a number of goals: (1) clearly define Christian doctrine; (2) intellectually defend Christianity against attacks by pagan scholars; (3) make Christianity intellectually understandable and acceptable to pagan Romans; and (4) create a synthesis of Christian ideas with Hellenistic philosophy and culture.

Thus throughout the second and third centuries, the Church Fathers created a series of writings in Greek and Latin which laid the foundation for subsequent theology in both the Greek Orthodox and the Roman Catholic traditions. Eusebius (d. 340), a councilor to Constantine, wrote a history of early Christianity, celebrating its victory through the conversion of Constantine. Jerome's (d. 420) Latin translation of the Bible (the Vulgate) became the most important cultural and religious book of the next thousand years in western Europe.

Augustine. Most important, perhaps, was Augustine (d. 430). His conversion from Manichaeism (a form of Zoroastrianism) is recounted in his *Confessions*, while *The City of God* attempts to explain why God preserved a pagan Roman empire for nearly a thousand years only to let the Christian Roman empire be destroyed by the barbarians. His writings laid the foundation for the theology of medieval Roman Catholicism, and greatly influenced the ideas of the German Protestant reformer Martin Luther in the sixteenth century.

Patriarchs. The formal organization of Christian denominations became focused on the Christian leaders (patriarchs) of five major cities: Jerusalem, Rome, Alexandria, Antioch, and, after 325, Constantinople. Four of these patriarchs became the leaders of independent Christian churches and ethnic groups. The three eastern churches (Jerusalem, Alexandria, and Antioch) were initially by far the most important in early Christianity: the patriarch of Jerusalem received his prestige from his association with the Holy Land; the patriarch of Alexandria, the intellectual center of early Christianity, governed Egyptian Christians. In the seventh century, however, these capitals were conquered by the Arab Muslims, and declined in significance among Christians thereafter. Nonetheless, two of the major branches of Eastern Christianity are today still centered on these ancient patriarchates: Alexandria remains the seat of the patriarch of the Coptic Christian Church, with Antioch the traditional center of the Syrian Jacobite Church.

It was the patriarchs of Rome and Constantinople, however, who were to play the major role in later Christian history. The patriarch of Rome derived his prestige from his authority over the capital of the Roman empire, as did the patriarch of Constantinople when the capital of the empire was transferred there in 325. These two European churches became the most important in the history of Christianity, with the patriarch of Rome becoming the pope, the leader of the Latin Roman Catholic Church, and the patriarch of Constantinople the leader of the Greek Orthodox Church.

Schism. The division of the Roman empire into a western Latin half and an eastern Greek half (see below) was paralleled by the division of European Christianity into a western Latin Roman Catholic half centered at Rome, and eastern Greek Orthodox half centered at Constantinople. Although these two branches of Christianity remained united for several centuries, they increasingly drifted apart in doctrine, practice, and administration, until they eventually split into two distinct denominations.

Missionary Efforts. Christian missionary efforts in the early period can be divided into two phases: missions within the Roman empire, and missions to peoples outside the Roman empire. As Christian and Classical culture became increasingly merged in the fourth century, missionary efforts became in part an attempt to extend Christian-Roman culture beyond the boundaries of the Roman empire. Thus they eventually obtained by conversion what had been unattainable by military conquest—the integration of the Germanic barbarians into Roman civilization. Along with their new religion, Christian missionaries often brought literacy, new forms of social organization, and improved international contacts to converted peoples. The major early Christian missionary efforts included missions to the Germanic and Celtic tribes, Arabs, Persians, Nubians, and Ethiopians. The most successful and historically significant missions were those to the Germans and Celts. It is ironic that the barbarian German tribes which invaded and destroyed the Christian empire were for the most part themselves Christians, although of the Arian denomination. Ultimately, Christianity spread both by conversion and conquest, until it became the universal religion of Europe.

THE DECLINE AND FALL OF ROME, 284–476

Temporary Recovery

DIOCLETIAN, 284–305

The age of the Soldier Emperors ended with the reign of Diocletian, who set about reforming and temporarily stabilizing the empire. Diocletian's major success centered on his reorganization of the administration of the empire into a more manageable system of provinces. His division of the empire into eastern and western halves made excellent sense from an administrative point of view. However, this policy also contributed to a number of problems, as will be noted below.

Although Diocletian and many other Romans recognized the grave problems facing the empire, they were unable to see deeply enough into the fundamental causes of those problems. Thus they attempted to solve the problems by regulating the symptoms rather than the causes. Diocletian instituted a wide range of legislation attempting to establish state control over many aspects of life: production, prices, military draft, and even ideas. Although these absolutist attempts achieved a limited and temporary success, they ultimately failed to solve the problems of Rome, and in the long run contributed to its decline, by creating expanding disaffection.

CIVIL WAR, 305–324

Diocletian had hoped that his new administrative system would create an orderly succession to the throne by creating formal hierarchy among two co-emperors (augusti) and two assistant emperors (caesars). In reality it simply created four men ready to compete for absolute authority. Thus when Diocletian retired, a period of twenty years of civil war ensued between his designated successors and their assistants. Ultimately, Constantine, who had been given responsibility for the western half of the empire, emerged victorious.

CONSTANTINE THE GREAT, 324–337

Constantine was the son of a Roman general and a Christian mother, who served a military career, eventually reaching the highest ranks in the empire under Diocletian. After his victory in the civil war, he instituted reforms which changed both the nature of the Roman empire and subsequent European history in a number of ways.

Christianization of Rome. Constantine was convinced that his victory at the battle of the Milvian bridge (312) was due to the intervention of the God of the Christians. In 313 Constantine became a Christian and issued a proclamation allowing freedom of worship. Christians flocked to his banner supplying men, wealth, administrators, and, most important, a new imperial ideology.

Imperial Christianity: The Unification of Church and State. Constantine's conversion paved the way for a rapid expansion of Christianity within the Roman empire. It also led to the union of church and state, creating a fundamental tension which has existed in Western society until the present day. For centuries Christianity had been at odds with the secular Roman government. Now, under a Christian emperor, Christians had a stake in the survival of the empire. Eusebius, Constantine's chief Christian councilor, developed the idea that it had been a foreordained part of God's plan of salvation to save the Roman empire and Christianity by the merger of the two. Although the union of Christianity with the Roman empire brought numerous benefits to Christians, it also created the problems of corruption, simony (selling of ecclesiastical offices), and government intervention in church affairs.

Constantinople. For a number of reasons, Constantine decided to move the capital of the empire from Rome to Constantinople ("Constantine's City," modern Istanbul). There he created a completely Christian capital, highly defensible, and in an ideal position for commanding trade routes and the movement of troops and supplies between the Near East and Europe. Constantinople was to remain the capital of the Eastern Roman or Byzantine empire for over 1000 years. As such it was the center of Christian and European culture, and one of the major cities in the world for centuries.

CONSTANTINIAN DYNASTY

Constantine's descendants ruled the empire only from 337 to 363, barely managing to hold together the deteriorating situation. They faced a decaying economy and social situation at home and barbarians and Persians threatening from without. Modern historians have long been intrigued by Constantine's last successor, Julian the Apostate (361–363), who converted from Christianity to paganism, and unsuccessfully attempted to reestablish the old traditional religion of the Romans. Julian launched an ill-conceived campaign against Persia, and was killed in battle. His troops thereupon elected a Christian general as the new emperor.

The Fall of Rome

REASONS FOR THE FALL OF ROME

The cause of the fall of the Roman empire is a complex problem which has intrigued historians for centuries and still elicits debate. The following are some of the widely accepted factors which contributed to the fall of Rome.

Administrative Problems. Diocletian's division of the empire into two administrative halves eventually led to the formation of two separate states. Although there were instances of cooperation, the co-emperors of the two halves naturally began to see their colleagues not as allies but as potential rivals. This rivalry occasionally developed into civil wars, weakening the Roman army.

The two administrative halves of the empire had vastly different economic and military resources. The Eastern Roman empire was more wealthy and populous, providing a stronger base for security and prosperity, especially when they were no longer required to use much of their wealth and manpower for the defense of the crumbling Western Roman empire. The West, on the other hand, was in a far more dangerous strategic situation; it faced the brunt of the attacks of the Germanic barbarians. Thus, at a time of growing military requirements for the West, it lost access to much of the military resources of the East. In the long run, the emperors of the East, already conceiving of the empire as divided into two halves, found it easier to simply surrender the West to the Germanic tribes, rather than risk the loss of the East in an attempt to save the West. Thus paradoxically, the division of the Roman empire into two halves served to prolong the empire in the short run, but contributed to the ultimate fall of the West.

Bureaucracy. Additional administrative problems included the bloating of the bureaucracy, which increasingly absorbed the resources of the state without providing increased efficiency or benefits. Corruption became widespread throughout the Roman administration and society, further decreasing resources available for defense and economic growth.

Economic Problems. An important factor in the economic decay of the empire was decreasing population and productivity. This was partly a consequence of the half century of civil strife and mismanagement during the period of the Soldier Emperors, but was also due to environmental and agricultural deterioration, including overgrazing, depletion of the soil, and deforestation. Thus, at the same time that population and land under cultivation was decreasing, the productivity of the land also declined. During this same period of decreasing productivity, the requirements of the state, both the bureaucracy and army, were increasing, leading to overtaxation. Thus, a vicious cycle was created: a recession led to the need for more funds for the government, which increased taxes. The increase in taxes further lowered productivity, creating a deeper recession and need for higher taxes. In an attempt to circumvent the need for cash to pay soldiers and bureaucrats, the government resorted to giving tax exemptions to the estates of the rich and the Church in return for service to the state. This further lowered the tax base, increasing the burden on the poor. Ultimately, the poor farmers became clients of the rich in order to escape the burden of taxes.

Military Decline. By the late empire the Roman army had been transformed. Mobile forces of heavily armored cavalry, based on Persian and Germanic models, became the central striking force; the infantry legions were increasingly limited to garrison duty on the frontiers. As a result, the discipline and training standards of the infantry declined.

Barbarian Invasions. The Romans were finding it cheaper to hire Germanic and other barbarian soldiers to serve in their armies, creating the ironic situation where Germanic mercenaries inside the Roman boundaries were defending the empire against their barbarian cousins outside. Frontier troops became little more than border militias. Needless to say, this frontier defense system ultimately collapsed, and the Germanic warriors flooded and pillaged the empire. Thus the decline of training, discipline, and morale of the army ushered in the fall of the empire. In the end two Germanic armies, one paid by the emperor, the other seeking plunder, fought over the corpse of the Roman empire.

THE COLLAPSE

The Huns. Following the death of Julian the Apostate, the empire rapidly deteriorated. Part of the problem, remarkably enough, originated in

East Asia. A series of inner Eurasian wars, invasions, and tribal migrations associated with the collapse of the Han dynasty in the third century initiated a chain reaction across the steppes of Asia which culminated in the migration of the Huns into Europe (see chapter 15).

Germanic Invasion. By about 350 the Huns had arrived in eastern Europe, attacking and defeating a Germanic tribe known as the Goths. Trapped between the Hunnic horde and the decayed legions of the Roman empire, the Goths decided to do battle with their weaker enemy, the Romans. They crossed the Danube into Roman territory, and in 378 completely crushed the Roman army at the battle of Adrianople, killing the emperor. The Roman army was never to recover.

In the following centuries, numerous Germanic tribes invaded the Roman empire, seeking plunder, land, and safety from the Huns. Germanic warlords were hired by the Romans to lead the deteriorating Roman army, which was increasingly manned by German mercenaries. The German warlords established themselves as the power behind the throne, making and unmaking emperors at will.

The Eastern half of the empire, with greater resources, and a smaller border to defend, managed to survive by buying off the Germans, bribing them to leave the East and attack the West instead. The Western empire was not as fortunate. In 410 Alaric the Goth attacked and sacked Rome. Puppet emperors continued to rule a fragmentary Roman state in Italy, but for all practical purposes, the Western empire had collapsed. The last emperor, Romulus Augustus, a virtual captive of his German troops, was murdered in 476.

Despite the imperial Roman pagan propaganda that the Roman empire was destined to be eternal, no state or civilization lasts forever. Considering the numerous problems facing the Roman empire in its final two centuries, perhaps the question should not be why did it fall, but rather why it lasted as long as it did.

The fall of the Roman empire was in many ways a dreadful catastrophe. Thousands died and prosperity declined during decades of constant warfare. Many great cultural and intellectual treasures were lost. Nonetheless, the fundamental elements of the Roman heritage survived for centuries and still influence the world today. The Byzantine empire was the direct political heir of Rome, lasting over 1,000 years. Roman imperial ideology and law formed part of the basis of ideas of kingship and empire in the European Middle Ages. Christianity remained the major religion of the West since its adoption as the imperial religion under Constantine. Roman exemplars in art, architecture, literature, history, and philosophy became the Classical pattern upon which the European Renaissance was built.

Selected Readings

Boak, A. E. R. *A History of Rome to A.D. 565*, revised by W. G. Sinnigen (1977)

Boardman, John, et al. *The Oxford History of the Classical World* (1986)

Cary, M., and H. H. Scullard. *A History of Rome*, 3rd ed. (1979)

_____. *The Oxford Classical Dictionary*, 2nd ed. (1970)

Christ, K. *The Romans: An Introduction to Their History and Culture* (1984)

Cornell, Tim, and John Matthews. *Atlas of the Roman World* (1982)

Ferrill, Arthur. *The Fall of Rome* (1986)

Frend, W. H. C. *The Rise of Christianity* (1984)

Gibbon, E. *The Decline and Fall of the Roman Empire*

Scullard, H. H. *From the Gracchi to Nero*, 5th ed. (1982)

(Translations of all the major Roman historians can be found in the Loeb Classical Library series and in Penguin paperback editions. Various editions of Gibbon's classic work are also in print.)

7

Classical Asia

97	Chinese expedition under Ban Chao reaches the Black Sea
184–205	Revolt of the Yellow Turbans in China
208–265	Age of the Three Kingdoms in China
216–277	Mani, founder of Manichaeism in Iran
224–651	Sasanid empire in Iran
239–272	Shapur I, Sasanid emperor of Iran
259	Defeat of Romans by Shapur, capture of Valerian
311–316	Xiongnu sack Chinese capitals at Louyang and Changan
320–535	Gupta empire in India
335–375	Samudragupta conquers much of India
375–415	Chandragupta II, golden age of Gupta culture in India
399–413	Travels of Chinese Buddhist monk Faxian to India
c. 400	Kalidasa, India's greatest dramatist, at the Gupta court
440–554	Hephthalite (White) Huns
460	Defeat of Huns' first attack on India
500–27	Huns overrun northern India, end of Classical Age
531–579	Khosrow I Anusharvan, emperor of Iran
581–604	Sui Yang Jian reunites China and founds Sui dynasty
591–628	Khosrow II Parviz, emperor of Iran
614–616	Sasanids (Iran) conquer Syria, Jerusalem, and Egypt
627	Dastagird, Sasanid palace-city, sacked by Byzantines
636–651	Arab conquest of Iran

The Roman empire laid the cultural, religious, and political foundation on which subsequent Western civilization developed. During the same period in Asia, three great classical civilizations arose—Iran, China, and India—which laid the foundation for nearly all subsequent Asian ocieties. These three great classical Asian civilizations each went through similar phases of empire building, cultural synthesis, cultural expansion, and eventual decay and collapse. Although the dynasties and political institutions of Classical Asia did not endure, their cultural and religious impact in Asia was as fundamental as the impact of Greek, Roman, and Jewish civilization in the West.

CLASSICAL IRAN

Background

Iran rests in a strategic central location in the Old World. The Near East lies at the crossroads of China, India, Africa, and Europe, and was significantly influenced by cultural, economic, and military developments in all four regions. More than any other region in the world, the Near East is a zone of synthesis and interaction. On the other hand, its central location means thau the Near East is also subject to military and political pressures from all sides. As such it is a region of complex political and military history.

During the Classical Age (c. 500 B.C.–A.D. 500), the Near East was divided into three major political and cultural spheres: the Hellenistic in the West, the Iranian in the East, and a Semitic culture which was divided between the other two political zones. Land, wealth, and political power were roughly balanced between the Hellenistic and Iranian political zones. The Hellenistic or Western cultural zone was chronologically divided into three dynastic periods: the Hellenistic kingdoms (330–31 B.C., see chapter 5), the Roman period (200 B.C.–A.D. 330, see chapter 6), and the Byzantine period, (330–1453, see chapter 7). The East was divided into two dynastic periods: the Parthian (248 B.C. to A.D. 226), and the Sasanid (226–651). Both the Hellenistic and the Iranian regions were ultimately reunited and absorbed into Islamic civilization following the Arab conquests (see chapter 9).

Parthian (Arsacid) Empire, 248 B.C.– A.D. 224

HELLENISTIC KINGDOMS

The genesis of the Parthian empire is linked to the collapse of Achaemenid Persian political power following the conquests of Alexander. His early death cut short his attempts to create a single unified empire by merging Greek and Iranian cultures; his generals shattered the empire into a dozen fragments as they struggled with one another to become sole heir to Alexander's domain. Greek mercenaries and merchants were established in small colonies throughout much of the former Persian empire by Alexander and some of his successors. Outside the Mediterranean basin and Mesopotamia, however, only a few of these colonies flourished. The most powerful Hellenistic kingdom—dominating Syria, Mesopotamia, and much of Iran—was the Seleucid empire, named after Seleucus, a general of Alexander. For the most part the Iranians were dissatisfied with Seleucid domination; in the period of civil wars following Alexander's death, they attempted to regain their former political independence. The most successful resurgent Iranian group was the Parthian dynasty.

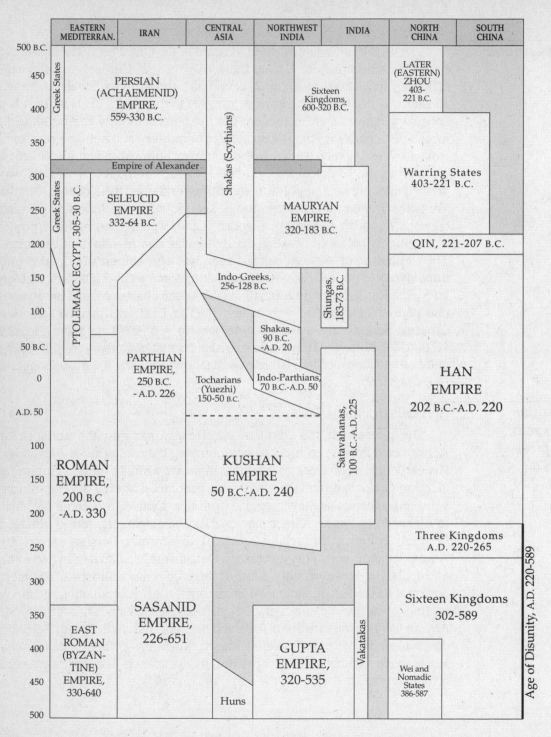

EASTERN MEDITERRAN.	IRAN	CENTRAL ASIA	NORTHWEST INDIA	INDIA	NORTH CHINA	SOUTH CHINA

Fig. 7.1   Classical Asia from 500 B.C. to A.D. 500

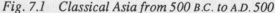

ORIGINS OF THE PARTHIANS

The Parthians were a nomadic tribe in northeastern Iran which had been under nominal allegiance to the former Achaemenid emperors, having often served as mercenaries in the imperial army. They had never been fully subdued by Alexander, and from 250 to 248 B.C., under their king Arsaces, they drove out the Seleucids and formed the nucleus of a state in northeastern Iran. During the next seventy years they relentlessly battled the Hellenistic Seleucids for control of Iran, slowly expelling the Greeks from Iranian territory. Ultimately, under their brilliant kings Mithradates I (171–138 B.C.) and Mithradates II (124–87 B.C.), the Parthians conquered all of Iran and Mesopotamia; at this point they ruled over half the former Iranian Achaemenid empire.

RELATIONS WITH ROME

Pompey's conquests of Anatolia and Syria in 66–63 B.C. brought the Romans into direct military contact with the Parthians. After several decades of warfare, Parthia and Rome divided the former domain of the Hellenistic kingdoms between themselves: Parthia dominated Iran, Mesopotamia, and Armenia, while Rome controlled Anatolia, Syria, and Egypt. Both sides attempted invasions of the other's territories on several occasions, but a military stalemate ensued. Parthia, with its army of mobile horse archers and heavy cavalry, could generally defeat the Roman legions in the field. The Romans, on the other hand, were superior in fortifications and siege-craft. By about the time of Christ, a relatively permanent boundary had been established between Rome and Parthia. This balance of power lasted for nearly two centuries, with the major exception of the Roman emperor Trajan's ultimately unsuccessful attempt to annex Armenia and Meso-potamia in 114–117.

DECLINE AND FALL

Parthian power declined during the second century A.D. for three major reasons. The Romans discovered and exploited the Red Sea trade route to India. This effectively decreased Parthian control of Asian trade, thereby decreasing their wealth and power. Turmoil in Central Eurasia also made the Silk Road trade to China more difficult and expensive. The Scythian (Shaka) and Tocharian nomads exerted increasing pressure on the eastern boundaries of Parthia, culminating in the establishment of the Kushan empire which absorbed much of Parthia's former territory in the east (see section on India below), and constantly threatened their eastern boundary. Interminable internal strife among different feudal factions over the succession to the throne intensified, leading to a period of political chaos and military weakness. Ultimately a vassal of the Parthians, known as Ardashir

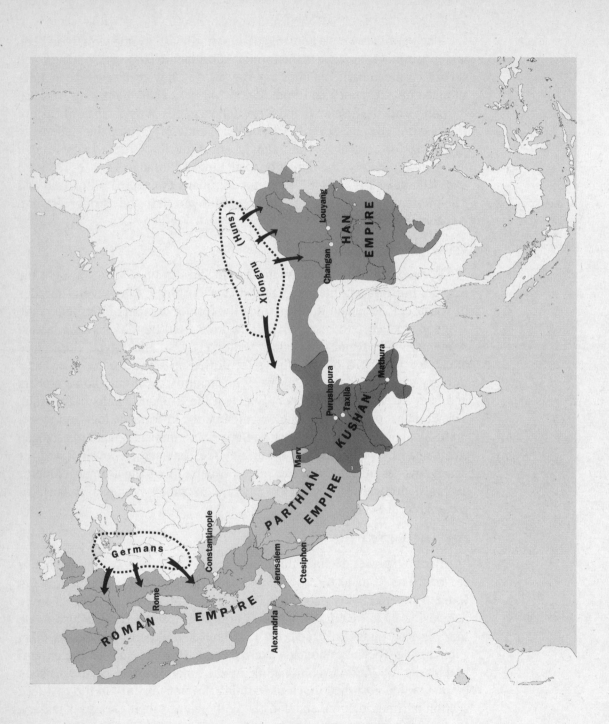

Fig. 7.2   *Eurasia in the Second Century* A.D.

of the Sasanid clan, rebelled and overthrew the last Parthian emperor, establishing a new dynasty which would rule Iran for the next four centuries.

Sasanid Empire, 224–651

Most of the reign of Ardashir (224–240) was spent in subjugating the former domain of the Parthian empire. By his death the new dynasty had been established on a sound basis; his son Shapur I (240–270) used his newfound power in war with the Romans. In 259 Shapur won a great victory over the Romans, capturing the emperor Valerian as recorded on the famous rock reliefs at Naqsh-i Rustam in Iran. The ex-emperor Valerian spent the rest of his life as a slave laborer on a dam in Iran, which is still known today as "Caesar's Dam."

FOREIGN RELATIONS

Romans. Relations with the Romans and Byzantines continued to be stormy throughout most of Sasanid history for several reasons. The Sasanids were much more expansionist than the Parthians. This was in part because, while the Parthians faced the Romans at the height of their power, the Sasanids faced the decaying and collapsing Roman empire. The Sasanids developed a centralized bureaucracy which could provide greater resources for the state, creating a stronger army. They also developed a concept of divine legitimization of kingship through Zoroastrian ideology, which included a militant element. Although there were numerous wars, and boundaries fluctuated occasionally, for the most part the balance of power remained intact.

Nomads. Much like the Romans, the Iranians faced a major political and military problem on their nomadic barbarian frontier. Unlike the Germanic tribes, however, the inner Eurasian barbarians were cattle-, horse-, and sheep-raising nomads, many speaking Iranian dialects. Like that of the Roman empire, official Iranian policy was to establish a frontier—usually the Oxus river—and prevent nomadic penetration into settled Iranian lands.

There were two major nomadic enemies of the Iranians: the Indo-European Scythians (Shakas) and related Tocharians (Yuezhi and Kushans) dominated the western steppes from c. 800 B.C.–A.D. 250; the Hunnic tribe known as the Hephthalite (or White) Huns ruled from c. 440–560 A.D., when they were displaced and absorbed by Turks. The Scythians and Tocharians were Iranian nomads, closely tied culturally and linguistically with the settled Iranians. The Huns, on the other hand, were a Turkic people, with no cultural ties to the Iranians, therefore representing a greater threat to Iranian civilization. In the fourth and fifth centuries different Hunnic tribes simultaneously threatened the Roman, Han Chinese, Gupta Indian, and Sasanid empires (see chapter 15). After numerous battles, only the Sasanids proved powerful enough to escape the collapse and fragmentation of their empires as a direct or indirect result of the invasions of the Huns.

SPLENDOR AND DECLINE

Khosrow (Chosroes) Anusharvan I (531–579). Khosrow I was a king of legendary stature in Iranian history and literature, playing a role similar to that of Caesar or Alexander in the Western tradition. He is remembered as the ideal example of Iranian kingship, just, wise, and courageous. His major accomplishments include the reorganization and centralization of state finances, taxes, provinces, irrigation, and the army. Many of these administrative reforms were adopted by the Muslims, forming the basis for Iranian government throughout the Middle Ages.

Khosrow was also a great warrior. His campaigns against the Byzantines proved indecisive and ended with an "eternal peace," which naturally was broken shortly thereafter. On other fronts, he was more successful. He defeated and subjugated the Hephthalite Huns in 554, ending their power, but paving the way for the advance of the Turks. He also conquered southwestern Arabia (modern Yemen) in a brilliant sea campaign.

Khosrow (Chosroes) II (591–628). The second Khosrow paradoxically brought Sasanid Persia to the height of its power, while at the same time paving the way for its eventual downfall to the Arabs. Khosrow's father, Hormizd, had been overthrown, blinded, and executed in a rebellion, forcing Khosrow to flee to the Byzantine court in 590. There the emperor Maurice (582–602) equipped Khosrow with an army, which reinstated him on the throne of Iran. A few years later, when Maurice himself was overthrown and killed in a Byzantine coup, Khosrow swore to revenge the death of his former benefactor. (Khosrow's sincerity in this can certainly be questioned; it may simply have been a pretext for invading the Byzantine empire which was in chaos following the coup.)

War with Byzantium. Raising a massive army, Khosrow conquered eastern Anatolia (612), Syria (614), and Egypt (616). He also scored a great psychological blow by the conquest of Jerusalem (615). In 617 his army was within a few miles of Constantinople, but was unable to besiege the city effectively at that time. The Byzantine emperor Heraclius, however, out-flanked Khosrow by attacking into the heart of Mesopotamia through Armenia. In 626 the fate of the Classical world hung in the balance as a combined army of Avars and Sasanids besieged Constantinople while Heraclius's army advanced on the Sasanid capital of Ctesiphon. Byzantine control of the sea prevented the Sasanids from taking Constantinople, but in 627 the Persian army was defeated near their captial of Ctesiphon, forcing the withdrawal of the Persians from their conquests. Khosrow was murdered by rebellious nobles the next year.

The Fall of the Sasanids, 635–651. Following the sack of Ctesiphon and the loss of captured Byzantine territory, the Sasanids entered a period of civil war and anarchy as various factions struggled for domination. By 634 Yezdigird III (634–651) had emerged as king. He immediately faced a

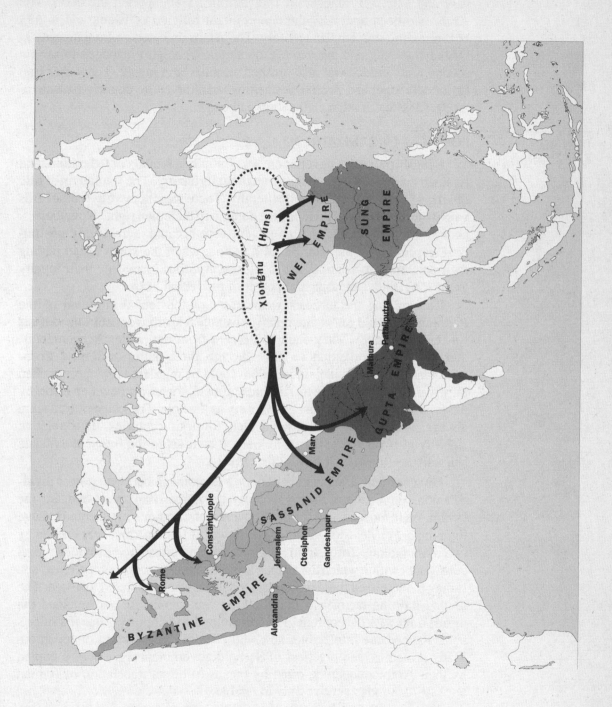

Fig. 7.3   Eurasia in the Fifth Century A.D.

new and extremely dangerous threat from an unexpected direction. The Arabs had been united by the new militant religion of Islam, and in 633 began raiding into Persian territory. The Arabs defeated an Iranian army at Qadisiya in 637, and overran Mesopotamia. Yezdigird managed to raise a second army, which was also crushed at Nihawand in 642. Thereafter Iran lay undefended, and Arab tribesmen overran the entire country (see chapter 9). Classical Iranian civilization had ended.

Iranian Civilization

POLITICAL ORGANIZATION

Kingship. Iranian government was initially a feudal confederation, and retained many feudal elements throughout its history. The Iranian royal title of king of kings was meant quite literally. There were numerous feudal lords who were also kings of their private domain in their own right. Nonetheless, as time progressed, the Iranian government became increasingly centralized, especially in the later Sasanid period, when the kings began paying their soldiers directly from the royal treasury, thus increasing their loyalty to the king, and decreasing the power of the feudal lords.

Recognizing the inherent weaknesses of the feudal kingdom of the Parthians, Sasanid rulers attempted to establish a stronger centralized basis for their monarchy. They claimed descent from the earlier Achaemenids, and divine authorization to rule through their patronization of Zoroastrianism. Although individual rulers could be murdered or deposed when they were thought to have lost divine approval, there was never an effort by the priests or nobility to oust the dynasty as a whole. The kings of Iran were always chosen from the Sasanid clan for four centuries. This relative stability in royal succession is in marked contrast to the frequent dynastic shifts in the Roman and Byzantine empires.

Government. Iranian government was monarchical, with power divided among three groups: the royal family, the Zoroastrian priesthood, and the nobles. As in most ancient forms of government, commoners seemed to have little impact on decision making. The power of Iranian kings was limited by two main factors. Zoroastrian religious law and priesthood provided moral constraints within which the Iranian kings and nobles were compelled to act. If they transgressed these principles, rebellion was considered justified. The second limiting factor was that the king was chosen for and retained the throne only with the consent of the priesthood and nobility. Thus if a ruler's behavior became intolerable, he could be removed by coup or rebellion. Many principles and practices of Sasanid government were in turn copied by their Arab conquerors, often by means of direct translation of Iranian books which today survive only in Arabic.

Military. The Iranians created a highly efficient military system which was a match for the more famous Roman legions, and Central Eurasian nomadic warriors. Although some infantry was used, the Iranian army centered on cavalry of two types. Nomad mercenaries supplied light bow-armed cavalry, whose tactical mobility allowed them to literally ride circles around Roman infantry, while raining arrows upon them. The main striking force consisted of heavily armored cavalry armed with bows, lances, and swords. When the light cavalry had disrupted an enemy with archery, the heavy cavalry would charge, attempting to destroy the foe.

The skill of the Iranian horse archers was legendary. They were able to shoot arrows from horseback at a gallop in any direction, including backward—the famous "Parthian shot." At the battle of Carrhae in 53 B.C., the Romans under Crassus suffered one of their worst defeats in history at the hands of the Parthian mounted archers.

Perhaps the greatest testimony to the strength of the Iranian military system was the fact that by the late third century the Romans had gradually abandoned their legionary system, adopting Iranian armor, weapons, terminology, techniques, and organization. By the fifth century the standard warrior in both the Eastern Roman and the Sasanid empires was the heavily armored horse archer. There were, nonetheless, two main weaknesses in the Iranian army. First, organization remained feudal, with troops serving under local lords. This created problems in recruitment, maintaining an army in the field for long periods, and the possibility of rebellion. Second, the Iranians tended to be weak in siegecraft, making it difficult for them to conquer fortifications or walled cities.

SOCIAL AND ECONOMIC ORGANIZATION

Society. The social structure of classical Iran revolved around two factors. First was the division of society into settled agriculturalists and nomadic pastoralists. In many ways the Iranians were successful in synthesizing agricultural and pastoral lifestyles. The Parthian kings were themselves descendants of nomads who integrated themselves into settled society. But under weak rulers or in times of trouble, nomads could become a disruptive element in society through raids, plunder, and the disruption of agriculture and trade. In the end the Sasanids were overthrown by nomadic Arab warriors.

Iranian society was structured into three main classes. The nobility served both as warriors and as government officials. Zoroastrian priests and scribes controlled religion, education, and the bureaucracy. The commoners included farmers, artisans, and merchants. Although never as highly structured as the Hindu caste system, Iranian social organization derived from similar archaic Indo-European antecedents.

Economy. The economy of the Sasanids was based on several elements. As in all ancient societies, agriculture formed the basis of the economy. The rich Mesopotamian farmlands and some fertile regions of Iran provided most government revenues in taxes. Since the Iranian state encompassed a great deal of desert and marginal agricultural land, a sophisticated system of irrigation and canals was developed, requiring a strong central government and stability to maintain. Iran was famous for its underground canal system which carried water from mountain springs to arid farmland. This complex irrigation system was very fragile. Once disrupted it could take years to restore; decreased agricultural production, depression, and even famine could result. Marginal lands which could not be farmed were used by nomads for pasture. The Iranian economic system thus maximized the use of marginal resources, and provided an internal exchange system in which agricultural and manufactured products were traded for nomadic products such as meat, wool, leather, and horses.

International Trade. International trade played a major role in Iranian history. Iran served as the terminal for overland trade on the Silk Road from China. As such, Iranian merchants would purchase products brought from East Asia, and sell them at an enormous profit to the merchants of the Roman empire. A fully developed overland Central Asian trade system was in place by the first century A.D. The Iranian monopoly on east Asian trade was somewhat broken when the Romans established direct sea trade with India. Nonetheless, the Iranians also controlled much of this sea traffic.

Iranian Culture

Although the transition between the Parthians and the Sasanids was significant politically, culturally the two dynasties are characterized by a great deal of continuity. Despite some differences and developments, the cultures of the two dynasties nonetheless represent variations of a single Iranian civilization.

LITERATURE

Most classical Iranian secular literature has been lost. That which does survive exists largely in either Arabic translations or in later medieval Iranian reworkings of classical themes and stories. Three pieces of classically influenced literature deserve special attention. The most important is the collection of classical Iranian tales and legends found in Firdawsi's poetic epic *The Book of the Kings (Shahnameh)*, the masterpiece of medieval Persian literature. The medieval Persian romance *Vis and Ramin* derives much of its story from a Parthian original. Likewise, some of the tales from the famous Arabian *One Thousand and One Nights* derive from Sasanid originals. On the other hand, a large collection of Zoroastrian religious texts have survived among the Parsis and other Zoroastrian communities.

HISTORY

Historical records are very sparse for the Parthian period; historians are forced to rely for the most part on references to Parthian affairs in Greek and Latin sources. The Sasanids, on the other hand, are known to have kept court histories. The original Persian version of these records has not been preserved, but an abridged version exists in Arab, especially in the writings of al-Tabari and al-Tha'labi. Many semihistorical legends of Persian kings are also preserved in Firdawsi's *Book of the Kings*.

ART

The art of classical Iran is only imperfectly preserved. There are several splendid surviving monumental sculptured reliefs depicting royal triumphs. The most famous, at Naqsh-i Rustam, shows the captured Roman emperor Valerian kneeling before the Sasanid king Shapur I. The most beautiful sculptured reliefs, however, are those at Taq-i Bustan. Sasanid precious metal working, being a durable medium, is particularly well represented. Themes of classical Iranian art focus on royal life: the court, feasting, the hunt, and warfare. Enough classical Iranian art has survived to demonstrate that they had a splendid artistic tradition, which greatly influenced later Islamic art styles.

ARCHITECTURE

The surviving monumental architecture of the classical Iranians gives a glimpse into the magnificence of the royal court. Especially noteworthy is the royal palace of Taq-i Kisra, probably built by Shapur I in the third century at Ctesiphon (near Baghdad), the main capital of both the Parthians and Sasanids. Only one wing survives, which includes a monumental throne room with a massive arch 75 feet wide (wider than any in Europe), a remarkable engineering feat for the technology of the time. Zoroastrians usually worshiped in the open air, and often exposed their dead. Therefore, unlike the Romans and Christians, there is relatively little Iranian surviving religious architecture.

Classical Iranian Religion

ZOROASTRIANISM

The origins and early development of Zorastrianism under the Achaemenids have been discussed in chapter 2. Here the focus will be on developments in Zoroastrianism in the classical period. Zoroastrianism had been patronized by both the Achaemenid and the Parthian emperors, but was never established as the only official state religion. The Parthians were quite eclectic and tolerant of religions; during their dynasty there is evidence of the flourishing of Zoroastrianism, Judaism, Christianity, Buddhism, and several polytheistic religions in Iran.

Sasanid State Religion. Under the Sasanids, however, this situation changed dramatically. It is quite likely that the Sasanids were descendants of a Zoroastrian priestly family, and their entire culture and monarchy was deeply affected with Zoroastrian ideas and practices. Non-Zoroastrian religions were generally tolerated, but were occasionally persecuted. When

Christianity became the official religion of the Roman empire, the conflict between Iran and Rome took on increasing cosmological and religious meaning as a struggle between the God of the Christians and the God of the Zoroastrians. The Zoroastrians therefore welcomed and protected dissident pagans, Christian, and Jewish refugees from the Byzantine empire. Nestorian Christianity, considered heretical by the Byzantines, was patronized by the Sasanid kings.

During the classical Iranian period Zoroastrianism took on its final form which it has retained until today. The scriptures and commentaries were codified, as were religious laws, practices, and beliefs.

MANICHAEISM

Like all religions, Zoroastrianism spawned many different sects and interpretations, the most important of which was Manichaeism. Manichaeism was founded by Mani (216–277), who claimed to be a prophet sent to unite Zoroastrianism, Christianity, and Buddhism into a single perfected religion. Initially patronized by the Sasanid king Shapur I, he was ultimately imprisoned and executed. His teachings, however, spread to both the Roman empire and Central Eurasia. Mani's most famous disciple was Augustine, who was a Manichaean before becoming a Christian, and whose theology was influenced by Manichaean ideas. Although they were persecuted in both Iran and Rome, Manichaeans found refuge among the nomads and oases of Central Eurasia where they survived until the sixteenth century.

DECLINE OF ZOROASTRIANISM

Since Sasanid kings had closely aligned their imperial ideology with Zoroastrianism, the defeat and capture of Iran by the Muslim Arabs created a major religious crisis from which Zoroastrianism never recovered. Although small Zoroastrian communities have survived even to the present, over the centuries most Iranians converted to Islam. Many Zoroastrian doctrines and practices survived in an Islamic form, especially among some of the medieval Islamic heretical movements. Zoroastrians number nearly 300,000 today, mainly in the Bombay area in India, where their ancestors migrated in the Middle Ages to escape Islamic persecution. There, like the Jews in Europe, they thrived, faithfully preserving their religious ideas, laws, and scripture. Some Zoroastrians have also migrated in recent times to the United States and Europe. Despite the fall of the Sasanids and the decline of Zoroastrianism, all other elements of Iranian culture played a fundamental role in the formation of Islamic civilization.

Importance of Classical Iranian Civilization in World History

The Iranians had several significant effects on world history.

CULTURE

Iranians preserved and expanded the ancient cultural and political heritage of the Achaemenids. Through the Parthians, Iranian language, art, literature, and religion survived the conquests of Alexander, laying the foundation for nearly a thousand years of Iranian civilization. The Classical Near East thus was influenced by three major cultural traditions: the Iranian as represented by the Parthians and Sasanids; the Hellenistic, as represented by the Greek kingdoms and the Roman and Byzantine empires; and the Judeo-Christian, represented in the Byzantine empire and other minority Jewish and Christian communities.

MOUNTED ARCHERY

Although the basic military tactics associated with mounted archery were developed in Central Eurasia, the classical Iranians transformed these techniques into a professionalized form. Military systems based on the Iranian model of the heavily armored mounted archer became widespread throughout the Near East, northern India, and eastern Europe.

INTERNATIONAL EXCHANGE

The Iranians played a crucial role in establishing economic and cultural links between Europe, India, and China. Long-distance overland trade from China to the Roman empire was maintained under the direction of Iranian merchants, thereby facilitating the flow of goods and ideas between the major classical civilizations of the Old World.

SYNTHESIS WITH ISLAM

After the coming of the Arabs in the early seventh century, a fourth cultural tradition was added, the Islamic (see chapter 9), which ultimately absorbed and synthesized all these traditions into a new single unified Near Eastern civilization. Iranian ideas, practices, and culture became a major element in Islamic civilization.

CLASSICAL CHINA

Although the tyranny of Qin Shi prevented his dynasty from ruling China for more than a few years, nonetheless, many of the reforms he instituted—especially the centralization of Chinese government, society, and economy—had an enduring impact on the Chinese, and were followed by many succeeding dynasties.

Han Dynasty, 206 B.C.– A.D. 220

ORIGINS

From 207 to 202 B.C. China was plunged into a civil war between two major factions. The aristocrats were led by Xiang Yu and were supported by the Legalist ideologues. The oppressed Confucianists, commoners, and disaffected aristocrats gathered around the banner of Liu Bang, a peasant who had risen to the middle ranks of the army, but who had become a rebel brigand during the last days of Qin Shi. Xiang was arrogant and brutal, and although a brilliant general, his supporters were ultimately alienated by his capricious cruelty. Liu Bang, although an unlettered commoner, was nonetheless a just and charismatic leader. He gained the support of many aristocrats, especially after his magnanimity in victory ensured their survival and participation in his new regime. Ultimately Xiang's support dwindled to the extent that he committed suicide, and Liu Bang was proclaimed emperor in 202 B.C. under the throne name of Han Gao-zu.

EARLY HAN, 206 B.C.–A.D. 23

Gao-zu, 206–194 B.C. As founder of the Han dynasty emperor Gao-zu is remembered for establishing the pattern of the ideal emperor in direct contrast to the image of Qin Shi, the archetypal tyrant. Gao-zu lowered taxes, eliminated dictatorial control of the economy, and made decisions only after consultation with his advisors. He established an important precedent of selecting his advisors and bureaucrats on the basis of skill and learning rather than noble birth. This principle laid the foundation for the rise of the Chinese Confucian meritocracy which was to dominate Chinese bureaucracy and education for over two thousand years. In the next half century of peace China recovered economically and culturally, developing into a stable and prosperous empire.

Wu, 140–86 B.C. Wu's long reign is remembered as one of the greatest in Chinese history. He further centralized the government, decreasing the power of the feudal lords. This laid the foundation for strong state finances and a powerful army. In the economy, he instituted state monopolies on several important products such as iron and salt, and ordered taxes on wealthy merchants; both policies increased government resources and decreased the tax burden on the poor.

Wu is rightly famous for his military conquests. During his reign northern Vietnam, parts of southwestern China, Manchuria, most of Korea, and parts of Central Eurasia were all added to the empire. The greatest military threat to China came from the Xiongnu (Hun) nomadic barbarians from Central Eurasia. From 133 to 115 B.C. Wu campaigned relentlessly against the Xiongnu Huns, ultimately conquering much of their territory and reducing them to submission. These campaigns were successful in opening up the Silk Road trading route from China to Iran. An official Chinese embassy arrived on the borders of Iran in 102 B.C. to trade for horses.

Wang Mang, A.D. 9–23. Wu's successors managed to maintain the empire for half a century, but eventually corruption and mismanagement increased, and the prestige and power of the imperial family declined drastically. In hopes of correcting the problems facing the government, the prime minister, Wang Mang usurped the throne in A.D. 9 Wang's rule was an ambiguous mix of hopelessly idealistic Confucianist antiquarianism—for example, trying to replace coins with the archaic Chinese currency of cowrie shells—and inept Legalist despotism. His numerous economic and social reforms were successful only in alienating both the aristocracy and the commoners. The dikes of the Yellow River collapsed in A.D. 11 causing tremendous flooding. The river changed its course, hundreds were left homeless, with their farms ruined; a depression ensued. The Xiongnu took advantage of the chaos in China to establish complete independence, again becoming a military threat. All of these developments indicated to the Chinese that Wang Mang had lost the Mandate of Heaven; a populist band of Daoist (Taoist) brigands called the Red Eyebrows rebelled. Wang Mang was overthrown in A.D. 23, and a collateral branch of the Han family was restored to the throne.

LATER HAN, A.D. 23–220

In the next century China was ruled by a series of vigorous and competent emperors who managed to restore economic prosperity and military power. The territory lost under the rulers of the previous century was regained. In order to secure overland trade on the Silk Road, a Chinese army under Ban Chao even reached the Caspian Sea in A.D. 97, sending a scouting party on to the Black Sea.

Decline. In the second century, however, new problems emerged. The empire was ruled by a series of young, indolent, and incompetent emperors. The court became dominated by factions of corrupt eunuchs (castrated servants and guards) and bureaucrats. Government officials who protested the excesses of the court were rewarded with imprisonment and torture. Wealthy merchants and land-owners seized most of the land, reducing the peasants to near serfdom. The peasants were finally overwhelmed in the decade of the 170s by famine and plague. In 184 they revolted under the banner of a Daoist-inspired religious revolutionary movement called the Yellow Turbans. This rebellion lasted until 205, hastening the collapse of the moribund Han dynasty.

The End of the Han, 184–220. The rebellion of the Yellow Turbans caused panic in the imperial court, which summoned their generals to suppress it. One of the generals rebelled in 190, captured the imperial capital of Louyang, and murdered the emperor. Civil war ensued in which the general Cao Cao was ultimately victorious, becoming the real power behind the Han imperial throne. Cao Cao was successful in suppressing the Yellow

Turbans in 205, but the empire was falling apart. Cao Cao's son deposed the final Han emperor in 220, declaring himself emperor of the new Wei dynasty. Other regions refused to accept his rule and China split into three feuding kingdoms.

Comparison with Rome. Paralleling the experience of the Roman empire in the third century, the Han dynasty faced a serious crisis in the second century A.D. As in Rome, corruption and mismanagement of the empire seriously undermined its efficiency and support by the aristocracy, bureaucrats, and commoners. In its weakened condition, the Xiongnu barbarian nomads from Central Eurasia seized the opportunity to intervene in Chinese affairs, and ultimately invaded and conquered northern China, just as Germans overwhelmed the western Roman empire. Confidence in the empire and in Chinese imperial ideology was undermined in this age of crisis, paralleling a similar crisis in confidence in Rome. Many Chinese began to seek solace in the new worldview of Buddhism, paralleling the rise of Christianity in Rome.

Age of Disunity, 220–589

THE THREE KINGDOMS, 208–265

Civil War. The capture of Louyang in 190 and the collapse of the Han dynasty initiated a three-way power struggle in China; civil war ensued. Cao Cao, nominally representing the Han emperor but in reality seeking his own power, raised an army in an attempt to reunite China, but was defeated at the battle of the Red Cliff in 208. Thereafter, China was split into three regional states known as the Three Kingdoms. Although most of China was briefly reunited in 265, China remained fundamentally divided into feuding regional states for almost 400 years.

Legends. The period of the Three Kingdoms has passed into Chinese legend and history as a mythic age of adventure, rather similar to the tales of King Arthur in Europe. The legends of the Three Kingdoms were collected together in their final authoritative form in the early fourteenth century as *The Romance of the Three Kingdoms*. Such was the importance of these legends in Chinese culture that one of the heroes of the period, the warlord Guan Yu, was ultimately deified, becoming the war god of China.

XIONGNU (HUNS)

Conquests. In the early fourth century the barbarian nomadic Xiongnu, recognizing the growing weakness of the Chinese, began to penetrate into northern China. In 311 they sacked the Chinese capital at Louyang, and in 316 the capital at Changan. With northern China in their hands, the Xiongnu spent the next decades consolidating their conquests and mobilizing their forces preparing for an invasion of southern China. But their army was defeated at the battle of Fei River in 383, effectively ending the Hun threat to the south.

Fragmented Kingdoms. Thus, for the next two and a half centuries China was divided into two cultural zones: Northern China was dominated by various Central Eurasian nomadic warlords, while the south was ruled by a succession of short-lived and fragmented Chinese dynasties. In the north an increasing cultural synthesis developed between nomad and Chinese, while in the south the older Chinese culture and civilization were preserved. China was ruled by small states and short-lived dynasties which were constantly struggling with one another for political domination. Decentralized feudalism reemerged, with real power resting in the hands of feudal warlords.

REUNIFICATION BY THE SUI

By the late sixth century the northern Toba Wei Turkish dynasty had become sinicized (copied Chinese customs and language). A Chinese warlord, Sui Yang Jian (581–604), in the service of the Toba Wei kings, managed to usurp the throne from an infant ruler in 581 and established the Sui dynasty (581–618). Although lasting less than forty years, the Sui emperors played a crucial role in Chinese history. After centuries of decentralization and fragmentation, the Sui emperors managed to conquer all other Chinese states; by 589 China was reunited.

COMPARISON WITH ROME

The major difference between the collapse of the Classical civilizations among the Roman and Chinese is that the attempt at reunification of the Roman empire by the Byzantine emperor Justinian was ultimately a failure (see chapter 8), while China's Justinian, Sui Yang Jian, successfully restored the unity of the Chinese empire. Thus in China, a restored empire under the Sui and Tang dynasties preserved Chinese culture and brought a reunified Chinese society to new heights of splendor (see chapter 14); the Roman and Byzantine empires were eventually overwhelmed and destroyed. Indeed, of the four great Classical empires—Roman, Iranian, Indian, and Chinese—only the Chinese managed to restore imperial unity after the collapse of their empire.

Government and Military

GOVERNMENT

The government of China was theoretically in the hands of the all-powerful emperor. In practice, however, the actual governing and policy making was in the hands of the ministers. The government was divided into three branches: the military, the ministers, and the censors. Most of the day-to-day affairs were controlled by the prime minister and his nine chief ministers, and governors of the various provincial subdivisions. The role of the censors was to serve as the eyes and ears of the emperor, inspecting provincial bureaucrats to ensure that they were obeying imperial policy and governing justly. In practice, of course, the censors became a type of secret police.

INFORMAL POWER STRUCTURE

In addition to this formal hierarchical bureaucracy, the imperial court also contained an informal structure of power which was often more important than the formal. The emperor was surrounded by a group of eunuch servants and scribes, whose function was to serve the emperor's every need. In practice, however, the eunuchs frequently attempted to isolate a young or weak emperor from all meaningful outside contacts, limiting his interaction with the noneunuch bureaucrats to formal ritual audiences. The eunuchs decided what information was received by the emperor, who could meet with him, and what form the imperial policy pronouncements would take. By thus controlling the flow of information and decrees to and from the emperor, this inner court of eunuchs could often effectively control the emperor and govern the empire. This led to the creation of factions both among the eunuchs and between the eunuchs and outside bureaucrats.

WEAKNESSES

Corruption. Chinese government in the classical period evolved from a set of conflicting tensions in Chinese society. On the one hand, the ideal Chinese state was to be ruled by a divinely appointed emperor, the Son of Heaven. On the other, the great warlords and merchant and agricultural families continually sought to increase their own independence, wealth, and power. The Chinese sought to establish a bureaucracy where influence and power rested with the wisest and most able. Frequently, however, the bureaucracy was wracked with corruption and nepotism, where wealth and patronage, rather than competence, led to success.

Empress Dowager. If emperors were powerful they could personally direct government policies. On the other hand, a young, weak-willed, or hedonistic emperor would often be incapable or uninterested in government, turning over policy-making decisions to his servants and staff. Factions would then develop within the bureaucracy, each struggling to gain control over a weak emperor, thereby controlling the state, and its wealth and power. In the end, these contradictions led to a succession of weak Han emperors, who were dominated by the empress dowager (mother of the emperor) and court eunuchs. Han government policy making was thus paralyzed by factionalism, corruptions, and indecision, leaving the path open for usurpation by warlords and the collapse of the dynasty.

Decentralization. In the Age of Disunity, each small state attempted to recreate the government structure of the old Han imperial court in miniature, thus preserving the basic institutional framework of the empire. In practice, however, decentralization prevailed, and real power lay in the hands of wealthy regional families and warlords, contributing to the frequent shift of rulers and dynasties as different strongmen struggled for the throne.

MILITARY

Development. The Chinese military was divided into two separate categories: the nobility and the commoners. The nobility frequently served in the army as officers or cavalry, but increasingly the noble class came to prefer bureaucratic service as the means to power and wealth. In theory all Chinese males were supposed to serve in the military during part of their lives, and in the early Han dynasty this system was partially put into practice. As time progressed, however, the needs of a professional standing army which could serve as permanent garrisons, or on long campaigns away from home began to limit the usefulness of the citizen militias. Thus the army became professionalized, increasingly serving for pay, plunder, and power. As centralized power collapsed, provincial generals became local warlords, under only nominal control of the imperial court. Ultimately, in the third century A.D. when the Han dynasty disintegrated, the more powerful warlords established their own independent kingdoms.

Barbarian Frontier. The Xiongnu threat also created a new military reality on the northern barbarian border. The Central Asian mounted horse archers placed the Chinese infantry at a disadvantage. Precisely as in the analogous Roman situation, the preferred Chinese solution was to hire Central Asians as mercenaries to defend the borders against other nomads. In the end this facilitated the nomadic conquest of north China, and increased the importance of both cavalry and mounted archers in Chinese armies, further decreasing the importance of militia infantry.

Terracotta Army. An idea of the equipment and organization of an early Han army can be derived from the famous life-size terracotta warriors recently found in the tomb of Qin Shi. Many Chinese infantry were armed with the crossbow—a Chinese invention of the fourth century B.C.—which gave them a powerful missile weapon. Chinese military technology of this period also included the use of noxious smoke and gas.

Social and Economic Life

SOCIETY

Chinese society was divided into three tiers: the imperial family, the noble families, and the commoners.

Imperial Family. The extended imperial family could be enormous, including uncles, cousins, and numerous children. More important, members of the noble aristocracy could gain admittance into the imperial family through marriage, especially the marriage of a daughter to the emperors, who as polygamists could have numerous wives and concubines. The role of the dowager empress (mother of a reigning emperor) was very important in the Chinese imperial family and court politics. If an emperor died as a relatively young man, leaving an infant heir, the dowager empress could take de facto control of the government as regent of the infant emperor. In this situation the family of the dowager—the uncles and cousins of the infant emperor—would quickly become the chief ministers and generals of the court, attempting to isolate and control the young emperor. This happened under the empress Lu, wife of the first Han emperor Gao-zu, in the period following the emperor Wu, and in the last century of the Han dynasty. In such circumstances court intrigue and factionalism tended to abound, to the detriment of good government

Nobility. The noble families of China attained their power and influence through various combinations of noble birth, wealth, land, education, influential positions in government, and ties by marriage to other noble families or the imperial family. As in all premodern societies, wealth was fundamentally derived from ownership of land, but could be supplemented by trade, monopolies on natural resources, and government office. Many noble families amassed huge fortunes and large estates, becoming essentially independent princes in their provincial palaces, surrounded by a small "court" of clients, slaves, and a private army. In the period of decentralization and feudalism following the collapse of the Han, such noble families often became regional warlords, even creating their own small kingdoms.

Commoners. The Chinese commoners, as always, had little access to power and wealth. Some could rise to positions of importance, usually by amassing wealth from land or trade, or more frequently by rising through the ranks of the army, which tended by necessity to allow greater social mobility than the court and government. Indeed, there are two cases where Chinese commoners eventually ascended the imperial throne as the founders of new dynasties: Liu Bang, the first emperor of the Han, and Zhu Yuanzhang, first emperor of the Ming. Such cases were exceptional; for the most part the Chinese peasants—as was the case with peasants everywhere before modern agricultural technology—remained condemned to a life of hard manual labor in their villages, only to see most of their produce taken as taxes and rents by the government and landlords. When conditions became intolerable, their only recourse was to turn to the escapism of Buddhist monasteries, or rebellion and brigandage, which plagued classical China on a regular basis.

Examination System. Chinese society was theoretically a meritocracy, where power and position was given according to skill and merit rather than wealth and birth. During the early Han empire, advancement in government bureaucracy became based on a standardized exam system. One could attain an appointment in the government only after passing the examination, which in theory was open to anyone. In practice, however, the exam system functioned to exclude the poor from participation. The Chinese written language was difficult, requiring extensive study to master. Only the wealthy could afford to give their children the luxury of such extensive periods of leisure to ensure literacy. Thus, the examination system, while posing as a meritocracy, became in practice a mechanism for excluding the vast majority of Chinese from a meaningful chance at upward social mobility. China became an aristocracy based on education, and since wealth was a prerequisite to education, it remained, as most other societies in history, an aristocracy of wealth.

Women. The role of women in classical and medieval China is interesting. Peasant women shared the burdens of unremitting toil and poverty with their husbands and children. Upper-class women, however, did have some potential for a life of luxury, cultural achievement, or power. The important role of the dowager empress has been noted above. Since marriage to the right family—and hopefully into the imperial family—was an important avenue to wealth and power, Chinese women were frequently given excellent educations to make them fit companions for emperors and nobles. As such they participated in many cultural practices of the Chinese nobles, especially the writing of poetry, literature, and the arts. The most educated, refined, and successful woman intellectual in Classical Chinese history was Ban Zhao (45–114), who completed the famous history of her brother Ban Gu upon his death. She is especially noted for writing an account of the proper training, behavior, and role in life of the ideal Chinese noblewoman, which remained standard reading for centuries. This work provides a fascinating insight into the mentality of late Han China.

ECONOMY

The Han Chinese faced a paradox in establishing their economic policy. Many emperors favored what we would call a market economy, allowing the merchants and landlords to buy and sell without government interference. Unfortunately, this frequently led to the amassing of vast estates and fortunes, the creation of monopolies and corruption, and the general impoverishment of the peasants at the hands of the wealthy. The wealthy were able to evade taxes, thereby increasing the tax burden on the poor and decreasing government revenues. Many important natural resources, such as salt and iron, eventually became government monopolies.

Chinese Culture

LITERATURE

Chinese literature during the Han dynasty centered around poetry and the short story.

Poetry. Poetry played a fundamental role in Chinese society. An educated person demonstrated his knowledge and wit through poetry. Eloquence and erudition, highly prized skills in government circles, were also manifest in poetry writing. More poetry was probably written per capita among aristocrats in ancient and medieval China than in any other society in the world. Although Chinese poetry can be found on almost every conceivable subject, descriptions of the beauties of nature are favored. Two poets stand out as masters during the Classical Age in China. Sima Xiangru (179–117 B.C.) is most noted for his flattering descriptions of Han court life. Tao Qian (365–427) is the greatest of early landscape poets whose themes emphasize descriptions of natural beauty.

Short Story. Short stories written during the Classical period include fables, court gossip, wit and frivolity, and fantasy. The greatest short-story writer of the age was Tao Qian (365–427), the nature poet mentioned above, whose "Peach Tree Spring"—the tale of a fisherman who finds a marvelous paradise in a cave, but cannot find it again after he has left—is perhaps the most famous of all Chinese short stories.

HISTORY

Sima Qian. The writing of history flourished during the Han dynasty, based on the example of the greatest of all Chinese historians, Sima Qian (145–87 B.C.). One of the great historical minds of all time, Sima served as the Han court historian under the emperor Wu. His history, the *Shi Ji* (*Book of Records*) laid the foundation and pattern of all later Chinese dynastic histories. His work covers the history of China from the earliest legendary Xia times until his own day. His work is know for his deft characterizations of important figures, and his attempts to draw moral lessons from historical events. Following his example in style and organization, all later Chinese dynasties kept meticulous histories, carefully preserving the records of previous dynasties. This unequaled tradition of historical continuity means that more historical information is preserved about China than any other premodern civilization in the world.

Ban Gu. The other great historian of Classical China was Ban Gu (A.D. 32–92), who, closely followed the pattern established by Sima Qian in his history of the later Han dynasty. His history was finished by his sister Ban Zhao (A.D. 45–114), the most famous female intellectual of the age.

ART

Tomb Art. Little of what was once a great body of splendid Classical Chinese art has survived, much of it coming from tombs. The best surviving examples of early Chinese art include sculpture, ceramics, and painting. Only a few free-standing sculptures have been preserved from Classical times, most frequently "guardian" figures used at the entrances of palaces and tombs. The small ceramic figures preserved in several tombs provide an interesting view of day-to-day life. Another important source of information comes from funerary tiles and stones, with shallow-relief sculptures on a wide variety of subjects; the most important come from the Wu family tombs in Shantung province.

Buddhist Art. The best-preserved examples of Chinese sculpture and painting come from the great caves and grottos of the magnificent Buddhist sites of Yungang and Longmen, which include monumental rock-cut images of the Buddha, and some fine fresco paintings on the walls of the caves.

ARCHITECTURE

Since the Chinese built predominantly in mud brick and wood, no building survives from Han times. A general understanding of Classical Chinese architecture can be derived from representations of buildings on low-relief sculptures. The stone pagoda at Mount Song is an exception, indicating the spread of pagoda architecture in China, ultimately based on the Indian Buddhist architectural form of the *stupa*. Furthermore, early Japanese buildings are said to have faithfully copied the pattern of Chinese originals, the most important example coming from Horyuji, Japan.

THE INVENTION OF PAPER

China was the place of origin for many of the world's most significant new technologies in premodern times. The most important Chinese invention of the Classical period was paper, invented in the first century A.D. Paper made the dissemination of knowledge cheaper and easier. Previously the Chinese had written on silk and bamboo, which were expensive and cumbersome. This meant that books, and therefore literacy and knowledge, were limited to the elite few who could afford them. The invention of paper made book production cheaper and easier, therefore allowing more people to have books, and literacy and knowledge to spread. Ultimately paper made its way to the Middle East in the eighth century, and from there to Europe, where it eventually replaced writing on papyrus and animal skins. The irony of the invention of paper is that it cannot be preserved as well as animal skin, papyrus, silk, or bamboo. Thus, although more books could be written, fewer would survive the ravages of time.

Chinese Thought

The main currents of Chinese thought in the Classical period were divided among the three great schools, the Confucian, Daoist (Taoist), and Buddhist. Each of these interacted and influenced each other in various ways during Classical times. By the beginning of the Sui and Tang dynasties, however, Buddhism had made great headway, nearly to the point of replacing Confucianism as the official state ideology. The ultimate revival and triumph of neo-Confucianism will be discussed in chapter 14.

CONFUCIANISM

The Han period witnessed the rise to supremacy of Confucianism as the official state ideology of China, a status it retained until the twentieth century.

Dong Zhongshu (179–104 B.C.). The greatest Confucianist of the Han period was Dong Zhongshu, who led the movement to canonize Confucianist thought, created the first Confucianist university, and initiated the prototype for the later examination system. Thus the foundations for the Confucianist domination of both the state ideology and bureaucracy were established, which would endure for over two thousand years.

Chinese intellectuals of the Classical period were engaged in four major activities which laid the foundation for all future Chinese thought.

Text Preservation. Chinese scholars attempted to reconstruct the texts which had been destroyed by the great book burning of Qin Shi. Some were written from memory, others from copies intellectuals had managed to hide. Some texts were found hidden in obscure places, or in fragments.

Confucian Classics. Various versions of these texts were compared and edited, arriving eventually at the standard Chinese Confucian Classics, which became the basis for Chinese education and examinations for government service.

Commentaries. Massive commentaries on these texts were written for two purposes. First, the language, script, or meaning were often obscure, and needed explanation. Second, many of the ideas in the ancient texts were at variance with Han understanding of Confucianism. Therefore, the texts were reinterpreted and modernized.

Synthesism. Scholars of the Classical period attempted to synthesize the ideas of Confucius with Daoism and later Buddhism.

Innovation. It should be noted that, although the greatest efforts were directed at restoring and synthesizing the ancient heritage—especially the writings of Confucius—not all Confucianist thought during this period was simply antiquarianism. The most important work of Chinese scholarship of this period was the *Classic of Filial Piety*, a brief but remarkably influential text describing the fundamental importance of the Confucian concept of filial piety to society as a whole. This work became the traditional introduction for new students to Confucian thought.

Crisis. The progress of Confucianism, however, was not without difficulties and setbacks. The crisis in society and government in the late Han and Age of Disunity created an intellectual crisis as well. Many Chinese intellectuals became pessimistic, withdrawing from public life for private meditation. In this period of intellectual crisis, Buddhism seemed to offer a method of both retreat and escape from the problems of life, with the promise of a better life to come. As such Buddhism made tremendous progress among Chinese in the Age of Disunity.

DAOISM

Daoism took its classical form during the Han empire and Age of Disunity, with the final commentaries and interpretations of the two most important Daoist texts, the *Yi Jing* (Book of Changes), and the *Dao de Jing* (Book of the Way). Daoism had two major manifestations.

Philosophical Daoism. Philosophical Daoism was practiced by the intellectuals as an attempt to understand the nature of the universe and to bring themselves into harmony with it. Philosophical Daoist thought included many different strands: Some took to meditation, others to hedonism, still others to anarchism. An example of the hedonistic branch of Daoism is the Seven Sages of the Bamboo Grove, a group of men who met together to drink wine, play music, and recite poetry. They believed that the proper method of following the Dao (Way) was to hedonistically indulge their every desire; this was the "natural" path for mankind.

Religious Daoism. Religious Daoism was widespread among commoners and aristocrats alike. In this movement Daoists absorbed the ideas and practices of a wide range of Chinese religions: Magic, shamanism, local nature gods, Confucianism, and Buddhism were all combined together in an eclectic synthesis.

Religious Daoism had three major manifestations: (1) Magic and divination (fortune telling) were widespread, in the belief that those who understood the nature of the universe thereby gained power over it. Nearly all Chinese courts had Daoist diviners who would foretell the future through astrology and the Daoist divination manual, the Yi Jing. (2) The search for the elixir of immortality, a drug or plant which would provide the body with eternal life, was central to Daoist thought. Daoists believed both that there was an island in the west where immortal humans lived, and that certain Daoist sages had themselves achieved immortality. (3) Alchemy derived from the search for the magic drug of immortality, but soon developed additional goals like synthesizing gold. Daoist alchemical thought would eventually lead in later times to some substantial scientific discoveries, most importantly gunpowder.

Daoist Organizations. As Daoism developed, Daoist practitioners eventually organized themselves into a formal hierarchy—a church of sorts—with leaders drawn from the Zhang family residing at the Daoist monastery at Kiangsi. Eclectic Daoism, with its capacity to absorb and synthesize beliefs and practices from all levels of Chinese society, became the popular and universal religion of China. Many Chinese scholars, while appearing as orthodox Confucianists in public life, would nonetheless follow many Daoist ideas and practices as a private religion.

BUDDHISM

The most important intellectual and religious development during the Han dynasty and Age of Disunity was the introduction and spread of Buddhism in China. As has been noted before (chapter 4), Buddhism originated in India in the sixth century B.C.; by the third century it had penetrated into Central Eurasia. The earliest mention of Buddhism in China comes in the first century, when an emperor is said to have had a Buddhist-inspired dream. The introduction of Buddhism into China undoubtedly came from Central Eurasian merchants.

Branches of Buddhism. Buddhism had split into two major branches: Hinayana, which dominated in southern India and Southeast Asia, and Mahayana Buddhism, which was important in northern India and Central Eurasia. Because of the contacts with Central Eurasia, it was the Mahayana form of Buddhism which was introduced into China. Since Mahayana Buddhism is more eclectic and willing to accept the existence of a variety of local gods and boddhisatvas, Mahayana Buddhism was better able to absorb many elements of Chinese life and thought into a Buddhist framework.

Spread of Buddhism. Although occasionally persecuted, for the most part Buddhism spread widely and rapidly in China during the Age of Disunity. This was in part because the Central Eurasian warlords who dominated the north were themselves influenced by Buddhism and saw the religion as a mechanism to counteract the cultural and intellectual power of the Chinese Confucianist and Daoist scholars. Furthermore, the social and intellectual crises of the Age of Disunity created an atmosphere where the promise of escape from the problems of this life and a better life in the hereafter were appealing to many people.

Buddhist Scholars. The earliest Buddhist teachers in China were probably Iranian Central Eurasians with strong ties to India. Ultimately, as the Chinese themselves came to understand Buddhism and Indian languages, they took the lead in the Buddhist hierarchy and scholarship in China. Chinese scholars made lengthy pilgrimages to Buddhist holy sites in Southeast Asia and India. The most important in the Age of Disunity was Faxian, who traveled widely from 399 to 413, returning with hundreds of Buddhist texts which he translated into Chinese. His adventures provided the Chinese with both a better knowledge of the world outside China, and the foundation for a more profound understanding of Buddhism through the availability of numerous texts in translation.

CLASSICAL INDIA, 180 B.C.–A.D. 550

The Classical millennium in India is bracketed by two major empires—the Mauryas and the Guptas—which laid the foundation for all subsequent Hindu tradition. The role of the Mauryas has been discussed in chapter 3.

This section begins with the situation in India following the fall of the Maurya empire around 183 B.C.

After the Mauryas

SHUNGAS AND FRAGMENTATION

Shunga Dynasty. The last Mauryan emperor was assassinated by one of his generals, Pushyamitra Shunga, who usurped the throne, founding the short-lived Shunga dynasty (183–73 B.C.). Although claiming to be heirs to the imperial Mauryan throne, Shunga power was swiftly limited to the Ganges valley as the Mauryan provinces became independent and as Central Eurasian nomads flooded across the northwest frontier into the Indus valley.

Decline of Buddhism. The most important policy of the Shungas was to abandon Ashoka's Buddhist ideology, reverting to the official patronage of Hinduism. Although Buddhism continued to play an important role in India for the next millennium, its failure to fully replace Hinduism and maintain royal patronage meant that ultimately Buddhism would be absorbed by syncretistic Hinduism.

Fragmentation. In the following centuries, India was fragmented into numerous regional kingdoms. The most dynamic states were located in the region of modern Pakistan and Afghanistan, where a marvelously cosmopolitan synthesis of Greek, Iranian, Middle Eastern, Central Eurasian, Buddhist, and Hindu cultures developed. The age of this northwestern cultural synthesis is divided into three main periods: Indo-Greek (256–128 B.C.), Shaka (c. 150 B.C.–A.D. 20), and Kushan (c. 50–A.D. 240).

INDO-GREEKS, 256–128 B.C.

Following the death of Alexander in 323 B.C., his general Seleucus attempted to exert authority over the eastern Iranian provinces, but was quickly checked by the armies of Chandragupta Maurya, and driven from the Indus valley (304). Thereafter the eastern Iranian provinces broke from the Seleucids, becoming independent states. Bactria (modern Afghanistan) became the center of a state with a mixed Greek, Iranian, and Indian culture known to modern historians as the Indo-Greek. Taking advantage of the collapse of the Guptas, the Indo-Greeks conquered much of the Indus and western Ganges river valleys beginning in 183 B.C. They managed to retain northwestern India only for a few decades; their state ultimately divided into several small kingdoms which were dismembered and conquered by the Parthians and Shakas.

Culture. Although initially strongly Hellenistic, the Indo-Greeks became increasingly merged with the surrounding Iranian and Indian cultures. This process is exemplified by the last important Indo-Greek king, Menander (c. 155–145 B.C.), who was converted to Buddhism. The Indo-Greek period is noted for a wonderful synthesis of Hellenistic, Iranian, and Indian art and culture. This is most apparent in the statues of the period, where Hindu and Greek gods merge together, and statues of the Buddha appear very much like the Greek Apollo. With the decline of their kingdom, the last survivors of Alexander's famous march to India were ultimately absorbed into the indigenous cultures, losing their independent ethnic and cultural identity by the time of Christ.

SHAKAS (SCYTHIANS) AND CENTRAL EURASIANS, C. 150 B.C.–A.D. 20

The Shakas. The Shakas (known as Scythians to the Greeks) were an Indo-European Central Eurasian nomadic group living to the north of modern Iran and Afghanistan. Their culture was typical of the Central Eurasian nomads: they were breeders of horses and sheep, excellent horsemen and hunters, fierce warriors, and experts at mounted archery. They had dominated the western Central Eurasian steppes for centuries, until around 150 B.C.

Nomadic Invasions. The rise of the Xiongnu north of China in the early second century B.C. created a chain of events among the nomads of Central Eurasia which eventually affected India. In about 170 B.C. the Xiongnu attacked and defeated the Tocharians (Yuezhi), driving them westward. The Tocharians in turn attacked and defeated the Shakas about 150 B.C., who invaded the territory of the Indo-Greeks and Parthians between 141 and 128 B.C. The Parthians ultimately defeated the Shakas, while the Indo-Greek kingdom was destroyed by the new invaders. By about 90 B.C. under their king Maues, the Shaka nomads had coalesced into a kingdom in former territory of the Indo-Greeks in the Indus valley, which they dominated until c. A.D. 20. Thereafter they were briefly absorbed by the Parthians.

KUSHANS, C. A.D. 50–240

Origins. Parthian rule in the Indus valley was not to last long, however, for turmoil in Central Eurasia was precipitating the new wave of nomadic migrations of the Tocharian (Yuezhi). Having been driven westward by the expanding power of the Xiongnu, the Tocharians ultimately settled around 80 B.C. in modern Afghanistan. Around the time of Christ the five original tribes had been welded together into a single powerful kingdom under the leadership of the Kushan clan, who gave their name to the dynasty they founded in northwestern India. Thereafter, succeeding kings followed the aggressive policy of empire building.

Kanishka, c. 78–103. The power and splendor of the Kushans reached its height under their most important king, Kanishka. The extent of his empire was such that during his reign, his armies fought against Indians, Persians, and Chinese; his empire certainly ranked in power and wealth as the equal of Rome, Persia, or China. Some of his achievements as a patron of Buddhism and the arts will be noted below.

Decline. During the century following Kanishka, the Kushan empire seems to have been prosperous and powerful. However, by the early third century their empire declined. Unable to resist the rising military might of the new militant Sasanid empire in Iran, the western half of the Kushan kingdom was overwhelmed and conquered by the Iranians following 226.

Gupta Empire, 320–535

The Gupta Empire was the shortest-lived of the great Classical empires of the Old World, but its cultural impact on India was the equivalent of the impact of the other great empires in their respective regions. The patterns of thought, culture, society, and politics which originated in the Gupta age remained definitive for Hindu India during the next thousand years, until the invasions and ultimate conquest of India by the Muslims (see chapter 11).

RISE OF THE GUPTAS

The Gupta dynasty was initially one of numerous petty kingdoms in the Ganges valley in the fourth century. Through a combination of diplomatic marriages and brilliant military conquests, the Guptas ultimately managed to conquer all of northern India.

Samudragupta, 335–375. One of the greatest conquerors of Indian history, Samudragupta laid the political and military foundations for Gupta power. In campaigns ranging throughout the subcontinent, Samudragupta subdued nearly all the kings of India. His career culminated with the great Horse Sacrifice, a traditional Hindu ritual by which a king was crowned universal emperor. Although some regions of India remained outside Gupta political control, Gupta supremacy was unchallenged.

Splendor. Throughout the fifth century, as the Roman empire was collapsing, Gupta kings ruled over a large, powerful, and prosperous empire which incorporated most of India. The Gupta period is especially noted for the creation of the classical patterns of Indian literature, art, and architecture (see below).

Fall. The fall of the Gupta dynasty resulted from a combination of struggle for succession to the throne, rebellion of vassals, weak rulers, and the invasion of the Hephthalite Huns. Although initially defeated in their invasion around 460, the Huns returned again around 510 following a Gupta civil war. In their weakened condition the Guptas were defeated. As with the Chinese, Iranians, and Romans, the invasion of the Huns in northern India had drastic negative effects. It contributed to political disunity, creating a fragmented political situation with many small kingdoms competing for power. The Huns also destroyed many cities, decreasing population, urbanization, and trade. Many Buddhist monasteries were destroyed, contributing to the slow decline of Buddhism as a major independent system of thought in India.

GUPTA GOVERNMENT

Gupta Feudalism. The Gupta system of conquest and government created the pattern for subsequent medieval Hindu feudalism. Through military conquests the Guptas demonstrated their power over all rivals; but once conquered the Gupta rulers sought to demonstrate their magnanimity by allowing conquered rulers to remain on their thrones as vassals. Indeed, the power of an Indian ruler was demonstrated not so much by the amount of territory he ruled, but by the number of kings who were his vassals. This system had several advantages: it created minimal economic and cultural disruption through conquests, it simplified the problems of government by allowing local rulers to remain in place, and it allowed local cultures to flourish, contributing to the tremendous cultural diversity of India. Another fundamental policy of Gupta statecraft was the forging of alliances through diplomatic marriages. This was especially important in their relations with the Vakataka dynasty of central India, which remained closely tied with the Gupta royal family throughout the period.

Weaknesses. But Gupta feudalism was effective only as long as the Gupta rulers were strong. Under weak emperors, vassal kings were tempted to rebel. Thus the seeds of regionalism and political fragmentation were sown in the Gupta form of government, which persisted throughout the medieval period in India.

ECONOMY

The Gupta period was noted for its prosperity and security. Seaborne trade flourished, especially with the opening of the sea routes through Southeast Asia (see chapter 11). Guilds or castes of bankers, traders, and craftsmen became major factors in India's prosperity. The Chinese Buddhist pilgrim Faxian described the prosperity of India under the Guptas in glowing terms.

Indian Culture in the Classical Age

KUSHAN CULTURAL SYNTHESIS

The Indo-Greek, Shaka, and Kushan periods represent several centuries of cultural integration in northwestern India.

Economic Synthesis. The Kushan sovereigns were probably the most cosmopolitan of their age, with strong international trading contacts with India, Iran, the Romans, and China. Indeed a central policy of the Kushans seems to have been monopolizing world trade. Their wealth is exemplified by the numerous hoards of splendid gold coins that have been found throughout their domain.

Kingship. The cosmopolitan perspective of the Kushan kings can be seen in their attempts to legitimize their authority through the assumption of grandiose titles and divine attributes from all the surrounding cultures. Royal titles on their inscriptions include the Hindu "Great King" (*maharaja*), the Iranian "King of Kings," the Roman "Caesar," the Chinese "Son of God (Heaven)," and the Greek *basileos* (king), and *soter* (savior, a title also used by Christ). The Kushan kings introduced the ideology of the deification of the king as a manifestation or incarnation of the Hindu god Shiva. This ideology would become a fundamental part of Hindu kingship throughout the Middle Ages, and was ultimately introduced into Southeast Asia as well (see chapter 11).

Art. The Kushans patronized the Gandhara and Mathura styles of art which, after further refinements during the Gupta period, would become definitive for subsequent Hindu civilization. Their patronage of Buddhism produced one of the wonders of Asian architecture. Though now destroyed, the great stupa (Buddhist memorial shrine) built by Kanishka at Peshawar was 286 feet in diameter and reportedly nearly 700 feet high.

Religion. All religions seemed to have been welcomed and tolerated in the syncretistic atmosphere of Classical northwestern India. Nearly every religion of the Classical Age was represented in northwestern India. Greco-Roman gods were worshiped alongside the Hindu pantheon; priests of Zarathustra debated Buddhist monks. Kanishka was a patron of Buddhism, convening the Buddhist council of Kashmir; it was in this period that Buddhism spread throughout Central Eurasia, ultimately making its way to China. Christianity even received its hearing in this tolerant age. According to tradition, the apostle Thomas (the Doubter) converted the Indo-Parthian king Gondopharnes (c. A.D. 20–46) to Christianity, establishing a small Christian community on the east coast of India which survived until the coming of the Portuguese.

GUPTA CULTURE

Kalidasa. Poetry, drama, and fiction all flourished, as represented by the greatest of all Indian writers, Kalidasa (fl. c. A.D. 400). Known as one of the Nine Jewels of the Gupta court, Kalidasa, like Shakespeare, excelled at both poetry and drama. His most famous work, *Shakuntala*, is considered the masterpiece of Sanskrit drama.

The Epics. The Gupta period also saw the creation of the final editions of the two massive Indian epics, the *Mahabharata* and the *Ramayana*. Based on epic traditions dating back over a thousand years, the *Mahabharata* tells a tale, much like the *Iliad*, of an epic battle between two armies from legendary times. The *Ramayana* is the story of an incarnation of the god Vishnu as the warrior Rama, and his struggle against a demonic king of Sri Lanka who has kidnaped his wife. These two tales serve the role of both Homer and the Bible in subsequent Hindu culture, providing religious mythology, a classical literary pattern, and entertainment for countless generations.

Puranas. The final major literary development of Gupta India was the creation of the *Puranas*, encyclopedic collections of Hindu culture. The numerous elements of the *Puranas* represent an odd mixture of Hindu myth, ritual, legend, history, science, and law.

Art and Architecture. The Gupta period also laid the foundation for the subsequent millennium of Indian art and architecture. Surviving examples of sculpture show a cultural synthesis and creativity which resulted in the definitive Indian style. Most notable is the beginnings of the rock-cut temples and sculpture at sites such as Ajanta.

CLASSICAL INDIAN THOUGHT IN THE GUPTA PERIOD

The Gupta age, like the period of the Kushans before them, was one of religious tolerance. Buddhism, Jainism, and Hinduism flourished side by side, each patronized in turn by the Gupta emperors and wealthy citizens. However, in the long run the Guptas began a fundamental shift from the patronage of Buddhism to Hinduism. Though the process was slow, Hindu temples increasingly flourished, while Buddhism began its slow decline. In the long-run the kings of India saw Hinduism as a superior base on which to establish their ideologies of kingship.

The Spread of Indian Thought in the Classical Age. The Classical Age in Asia could be called the Age of India; during this period Indian ideas spread from their homeland in the Ganges valley throughout Asia. Buddhism made its way into Tibet, China, Mongolia, Korea, and Japan. Hinduism and Buddhism spread throughout India, and into Southeast Asia, which in many ways became a cultural satellite of India for nearly a thousand years. All throughout Asia Indian gods were worshipped, Indian texts translated, and Indian art forms imitated. Indian cultural forms remained dominant throughout Asia until the coming of Islam in the eighth century, when India itself succumbed to outside cultural influences (see chapter 11).

The Rise of Southern India

NORTHERN INFLUENCES

Southern India emerged from prehistory during the Classical Age. The most important development in the region was the spread and adaptation of northern Indian civilization throughout the south, as manifest at several levels.

Literature. Sanskrit, the classical language of the north, was adopted as the official court language by many south Indian kings, though a great deal of literature was produced in the native south Indian scholarly language Pali. Intellectual academies (*sangams*) were patronized by south Indian kings, where Sanskrit and Pali studies flourished.

Religion. Hinduism and Buddhism spread throughout south India, merging with local religions, and eventually receiving official royal patronage. Buddhism flourished during the Classical period, especially in

Sri Lanka, which became a major center of Buddhist studies. Buddhist scripture was translated into Pali, with numerous commentaries added. Indeed, Buddhist scriptures in Pali remain one of the most important sources for our understanding of early Buddhist thought.

Politics. Politically south India remained fragmented. Although the Guptas occasionally exerted military power in the region, for the most part the southern Indians remained politically independent, while becoming increasingly culturally dependent. Small local princes established regional states which would ultimately develop into full-fledged kingdoms. The most important of these were the Cholas, and Pallavas.

TRADE

The prosperity of the southern Indian kingdoms was based on a two-fold trade. First, the maritime trade with Rome consisted of the export of Indian products such as gems, spices, incense, and cloth. Roman geographers made numerous references to the wealth and splendor of India during this period. Second, the southern Indians participated extensively in the growing trade with Southeast Asia and China (see chapter 11).

The Classical period in Asia is characterized by the creation of three powerful cultural entities: Iran, China, and India. Each region was initially united by military conquest. Thereafter the emperors of each region selectively patronized specific types of religion, scholarship, and art, which became definitive for the next thousand years. The imperial ideologies and mythologies, as well as court, administrative, and government practices, also created a pattern which was consciously imitated by subsequent dynasties.

Each region also began to generate cultural satellites, as their languages, religions, art forms, and practices were adopted by other peoples. Iran's major cultural heir was the Muslim empire (see chapter 9). Chinese influences spread to Central Eurasia, Korea, Japan, and Vietnam (see chapter 14). India generated the most important cultural influences during this period. Northern Indian language, culture, religion, and political institutions spread into south India and Southeast Asia. Most important, however, was the spread of Buddhism to Central Eurasia and China, thereby becoming the international religion of East Asia.

Selected Readings

Agrawal, Ashvini. *The Rise and Fall of the Imperial Guptas* (1989)

Basham, A. L. *The Wonder That Was India*, 3rd ed. (1959)

Boyce, M. *Zoroastrians, Their Religious Beliefs and Practices* (1979)

Debevoise, Neilson C. *A Political History of Parthia* (1938)

Farmer, Edward L., et al. *Comparative History of Civilizations in Asia*, Vol. 1 (1986)

Frye, Richard N. *The Heritage of Persia* (1963)

Gernet, J. *A History of Chinese Civilization* (1982)

Harvey, Peter. *An Introduction to Buddhism* (1990)

Hucker, Charles O. *China's Imperial Past* (1975)

Kulke, Hermann, and Dietmar Rothermund. *A History of India* (1986)

Majumdar, R. C., ed. *History and Culture of the Indian People, Vol. 2, The Age of Imperial Unity* (1951)

Sullivan, Michael. *The Arts of China*, 3rd ed. (1984)

Watson, Burton. *Records of the Grand Historian of China*, 2 Vols. (1961)

Yarshater, Ehsan, ed. *The Cambridge History of Iran, vol. 3. The Seleucid, Parthian, and Sasanian Periods* (1968–1986)

8

Byzantium and Medieval Eastern Europe

1204–1261	Latin empire of Constantinople
1236–1242	Mongol conquest of eastern Europe
1261–1453	Palaeologi retake Constantinople, restore Byzantine empire
1380	Battle of Kulikovo; Moscovite Russian expansion begins
1386	Unification of Poland and Lithuania
1453	Fall of Constantinople to the Turks

The collapse of the Roman empire in the fifth century left Europe divided into two cultural zones. Western Europe included a mixture of Germanic and Latin peoples, with Latin Roman culture, and Roman Catholic Christianity. Eastern Europe developed from a mixture of Slavic and Greek peoples, Greek culture, and Eastern Orthodox Christianity. The result was that, despite many shared characteristics, western and eastern Europe developed into two related but distinct cultural zones. This chapter analyzes the Byzantine empire and medieval Slavic eastern European states. The history of medieval western Europe is described in chapter 10.

Four major developments occurred in eastern Europe during the Middle Ages. First, the Byzantine empire was the major cultural, economic, and religious force in the region. Second, the Slavic peoples migrated throughout eastern Europe, were Christianized, and formed medieval Slavic kingdoms. Third, Turkic and Mongolian nomads from Central Eurasia penetrated and dominated parts of eastern Europe. Fourth, Byzantium declined and fell to the Muslim Ottoman Turks. Thereafter, late medieval Slavic kingdoms, especially Moscow, arose as the dominant political and cultural powers in eastern Europe.

THE BYZANTINE EMPIRE, 330–1453

The Byzantine empire can be simply defined as the Christian state which had its capital at Constantinople. As such, it existed for eleven centuries, from the founding of Constantinople as the New Rome by Constantine in 330, until the conquest of the city by the Ottoman Turks in 1453. Throughout this millennium, the Byzantine empire endured numerous transformations, and the steady diminution of its boundaries until, when Mehmet the Conqueror besieged the city in 1453, the empire consisted solely of the decaying shell of the former glorious capital city of Constantinople.

The Byzantine empire can be described by three major characteristics. First, the Byzantines were the heirs of imperial Roman law, government, and administration; indeed, throughout their history they consistently called themselves Romans. Second, in distinction to the Latin cultural basis of the earlier Classical Roman empire, the Byzantine Roman empire was fundamentally Greek in both language and culture. Finally, and perhaps most importantly, the Byzantine Roman empire was a Christian state, in distinction to the earlier paganism of the Classical Roman empire. Thus the Byzantine empire was the political heir to Rome, cultural heir to Greece, and the spiritual heir to Christianity.

Political History

EASTERN ROMAN EMPIRE, 330–643

Constantine (324–337). The transformation of the Roman into the Byzantine empire began with the crowning of Constantine as emperor, his conversion to Christianity, and his foundation of Constantinople as the new capital of the empire (see chapter 6). There was, of course, a great deal of continuity with the earlier Roman empire—which survived in western Europe for another century and a half. Nonetheless, the two significant changes of the Christianization of the empire and the transfer of the capital from Rome to Constantinople are sufficient to justify dating the beginning of the Byzantine empire to 330.

A Christian Empire. Constantine's role in Roman history has been discussed in chapter 6. From the perspective of Byzantine history, Constantine is not seen as one of the last strong rulers of a collapsing Roman empire. Rather, as described by Constantine's councilor and biographer Eusebius, he was the "equal of the Apostles [of Christ]," who transformed the decadent pagan tyranny of Rome into a Christian kingdom, the purpose of which was to defend and propagate Christianity and prepare the earth for the Second Coming of Christ. Thus, a new imperial ideology developed which borrowed the earlier pagan Roman idea that the Roman empire had been chosen by God to eternally rule the earth. However, the emperor was demoted from being a god himself in the pagan Roman empire, to being the chief minister and representative of God on earth.

Administrative Reforms. Constantine's achievement was not solely limited to the Christianization of the empire and the creation of a new imperial ideology. Rather he laid the foundations for the Byzantine empire through reform of the army and the creation of a Christianized civilian bureaucracy. Constantine's currency and economic reforms allowed the survival of the Byzantine state through the economic chaos and depression of the next centuries. Indeed, the gold coinage created by Constantine remained the standard medium of international exchange in the Mediterranean for centuries.

Survival of Byzantium. Under the successors of Constantine, the Byzantine empire was largely spared the disaster of the Germanic invasions and conquests of western Europe. In the West, urban life, population,

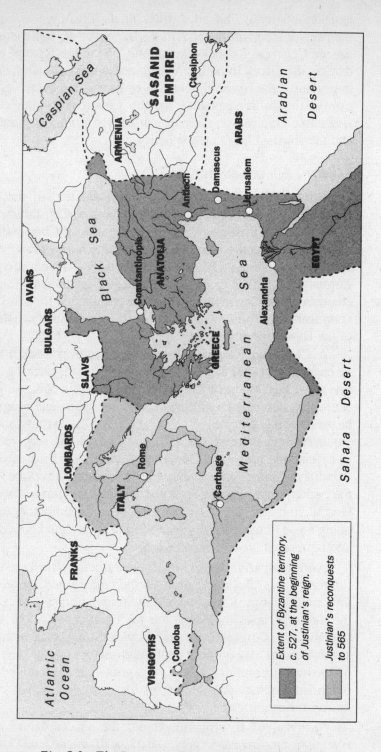

Fig. 8.1   The Byzantine Empire in the Sixth Century

culture, and the economy declined dramatically in the wake of the Germanic invasions (see chapter 10); the Roman empire ceased to exist and political power was fragmented among several Germanic kingdoms. Although the Byzantine empire also suffered a decline, it nonetheless survived with its cities, population, economy, culture, and state relatively intact. In large part the administrative and fiscal stability of the empire in the coming century was due to the administrative, tax, and currency reforms of Anastasius I (491–518), who left the empire with a vast reserve of gold in the treasury, which served as the economic foundation for the brilliant age of Justinian.

Justinian (527–565). The sixth century was dominated by the emperor Justinian, and his equally famous wife Theodora. Although initially facing unrest and discontent as manifest by the popular Nika revolt in Constantinople (532) in which 30,000 people were killed, Justinian ultimately secured his throne, initiating a policy of imperial aggrandizement and expansion.

The power and wealth of the sixth-century Byzantine state is demonstrated by the fact that Justinian was able to contemplate, even if overoptimistically, an attempted restoration of the Roman empire by the reconquest of the West. Under the command of Belesarius, one of the great generals of history, Byzantine armies managed to retake North Africa (533), Italy (535–554), and southern Spain (552). However, bubonic plague decimated the Byzantine army and population, while Slavic enemies in the Balkans and the Persians in the east attacked. The Byzantines ultimately lost most of Italy; the dream of Byzantine imperial reunification of both halves of the old Roman empire was ended forever.

Although Justinian's attempts at military expansion were ultimately unsuccessful, two achievements had a lasting impact. His codification of Roman law, under the direction of the jurist Tribonian, represents the final culmination of nearly a thousand years of Greek and Roman legal thought and practice, and was extremely influential for many centuries in both Byzantium and the West. Justinian's program of monumental building is best represented by the great church Hagia Sophia (see below).

Civil Wars and Collapse. However, all of Justinian's achievements were purchased at a price. His military campaigns and monumental building programs left the state bankrupt. Furthermore, bubonic plague struck the Mediterranean in 541; thousands died, and plagues regularly reappeared for decades. The subsequent decline in population, state revenues, and morale created serious social and economic problems.

In addition, in ensuing decades of imperial mismanagement combined with constant military threat from the Slavs in the Balkans, Persians in the east, and Lombards in Italy created a major economic and military crisis. The ultimate result was rebellion, civil war, and anarchy (602–610). The Sasanid Persians, taking advantage of this situation, invaded the empire from the east in alliance with the Avars and Slavs who struck into the Balkans from the north. By 626 the Byzantine empire faced almost certain destruction, having been reduced to the city of Constantinople, North Africa, and a few regions in Greece and Italy (see chapter 7).

Heraclius (610–641): Triumph and Catastrophe. The empire was saved by the emperor Heraclius. The churches of Constantinople donated their wealth to raise a new army, which ultimately defeated the Persians and restored the empire to its former boundaries by 628. Heraclius also reformed both the provincial administration and the army, laying the foundation for a military system which would provide an army strong enough to survive a forthcoming century of strenuous Arab Muslim assaults. However, despite his initial victories, he lived to see the land he had regained from the Sasanid Persians again lost to the Arab onslaught in 636.

THE AGE OF CRISIS, 636–802

The following century and a half of Byzantine history represents a period of continual crisis. Bubonic plague, social discontent, theological disputes, and civil wars were combined with persistent attacks by the Arabs, Slavs, and Bulgars. Disaster and destruction were only narrowly averted several times. People in despair began to talk of the end of the world and the coming of the Antichrist.

The Arab Threat. Following the death of the Arabian prophet Muhammad (570–632), the Arab tribes, now united by a new religion, began invading the neighboring Sasanid and Byzantine empires (see chapter 9). After having permanently lost the wealthy provinces of Syria (638), Egypt (642), and North Africa (698) to the Arab conquerors, the Byzantine empire barely survived direct attacks on Constantinople. The Arabs mobilized huge fleets and armies to besiege Constantinople itself in 673–678 and 717–718. The city was saved by a combination of the strength of its massive fortifications, the invention of a new secret superweapon, Greek fire (a type of flame-thrower which burned the Arab fleet), and the indomitable will of Leo III (717–741), who usurped the throne from the tyrant Justinian II, and successfully led the resistance.

Although the Arabs were ultimately unsuccessful in completely destroying the Byzantine empire and conquering Constantinople, they were nonetheless the clear victors in these wars. Over half the territory of the empire was lost to the Arabs; Anatolia was repeatedly raided and left devastated and depopulated. The economy and military power of the empire was permanently damaged.

The Slavic and Bulgar Threats. Slavic incursions into the Balkans and Greece began as early as 540. Justinian had managed to limit the destruction of these invasions by building an extensive network of fortification and payment of bribes to forestall threatened attacks. By the end of Justinian's reign, however, the treasury was exhausted, plague had decimated the army, and the Slavs began a second wave of invasions in the Balkans beginning in 582. Within a few decades they had overrun all of the Balkans, and most of Greece. The deteriorating situation in the Balkans was compounded by the invasions of the Central Eurasian nomadic Bulgars (Onogur Huns), culminating in their establishment of the kingdom of Bulgaria (681) which ruled most former Byzantine territory in the Balkans for decades.

Survival. The empire managed to survive largely due to the efforts of great military emperors such as Leo III (717–741) and Constantine V (741–775); by the late eighth century, the assaults of the Slavs, Bulgars, and Arabs had all been halted. But the state which emerged from these crises was quite different from that of earlier centuries. Over half of the former domain of the empire, and therefore its wealth and military power, had been lost. All administration was now under the authority of military commanders; military service began to be paid for in land rather than money. Although these reforms provided a strong army at minimal cost, in the long run they laid the foundations for increasing decentralization and ultimate feudalism.

Irene, 780–802. The great victories of Leo and Constantine were almost undone by the tyranny and mismanagement of the empress Irene. One of three women to rule Byzantium, Irene initially acted as regent for her ten-year-old son Constantine VI (780–797), during which time she effectively ruled the state. When her son reached maturity and began to exercise his own will, she had him blinded, ascending to the throne as independent ruler from 797 to 802. Charlemagne's efforts to woo and marry the empress, thereby uniting the Carolingian and Byzantine empires, were rebuffed. When her neglect of the army and military affairs ultimately led to disastrous defeats by the Bulgars and Arabs, she was deposed by her court ministers and military officers.

THE IMPERIAL AGE, 867–1071

Beginning in the early ninth century, the condition of the Byzantine empire began to improve. This revival derived from several factors. The Arab caliphate had begun to fragment into several competing kingdoms; although still dangerous, they never again threatened the very survival of the empire. The Slavic invaders in the Balkans and Greece were ultimately converted to Christianity, and slowly brought within the realm of Byzantine authority. The plagues which had depopulated the empire ceased; combined with new agricultural techniques and the expansion of farmland, this created a substantial rise in population, taxes, wealth, and military power. The Iconoclast controversy (whether Christians should venerate images) ended in 843 with the Greek Orthodox Church definitively deciding to allow the use of icons in Christian worship, thereby providing much-needed ideological unity.

Macedonian Warrior-Emperors, 867–1025. The rising power of the Byzantine state was paralleled by the rise to power of the dynamic Macedonian dynasty (867–1025), initiating a new age of imperial splendor for the Byzantine empire. The dynasty was founded by Basil I (867–886), a peasant adventurer who had found favor as a groom of the emperor Michael III, murdered him, and usurped the throne. But despite such an inauspicious beginning, his reign and the Macedonian dynasty he founded were both successful.

Military Expansion. During the ninth century, civil wars and fragmentation had greatly weakened the power of the Arab caliphate (see chapter 9), allowing the Byzantines to turn to the offensive in the east. In the course of the next century a series of able soldier-emperors and their generals made substantial territorial gains against the Arabs, including most of Syria and parts of northern Mesopotamia. In the spirit of later Crusades, plans were even laid for the reconquest of Jerusalem itself. Ultimately, however, a renewed threat from the Bulgars in the Balkans required that most military attention be devoted to that region. Basil II (976–1014) was called *Bulgaroktonos* (the Bulgar Slayer) because he destroyed the Bulgar empire in a series of brilliant military campaigns between 996 and 1014. Through a combination of diplomacy, threat, and evangelization, he managed to reincorporate nearly all of the Balkans into the Byzantine empire. The Bulgarians adopted Christianity in 870, and the Russians in 988 (see below).

By 1025 this newly revitalized empire was secure on all fronts, and was the most powerful state in Europe or the Near East. It is all the more remarkable, therefore, that the empire would once again be on the verge of destruction within a few short decades.

THE CRISIS AND COLLAPSE, 1025–1261

Decline of the Military. Although seemingly supreme during the early eleventh century, the security of the Byzantine empire was not firmly established. Threatened by numerous enemies on all sides, the survival of the Byzantine empire was clearly dependent on the maintenance of the powerful army which had been developed during the tenth century. This pillar of the state was undermined in the mid-eleventh century during a struggle between the landed military aristocracy and the civil bureaucracy of Constantinople. Both parties attempted to control imperial policy to the benefit of their factions: the bureaucrats by utilizing funds for civic and cultural developments; the military by using funds to raise troops, and by enlarging their own estates. For several decades the bureaucratic party dominated Constantinople, and thereby the government. During this period, the efficiency and size of the army declined drastically, with the bureaucrats

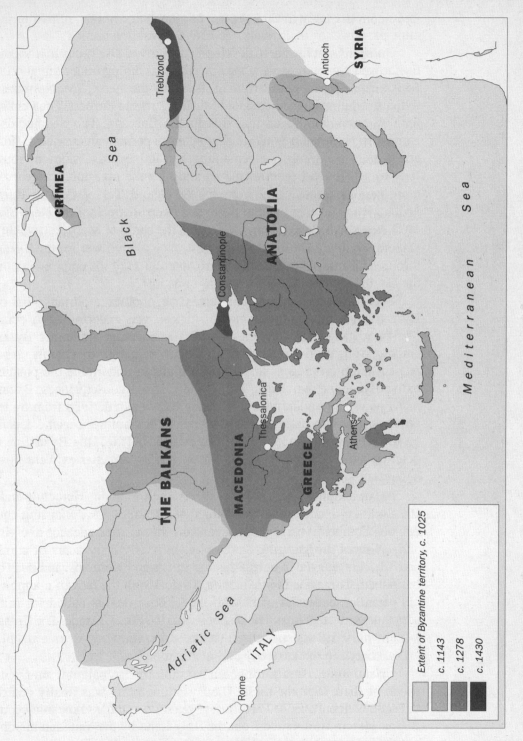

Fig. 8.2   Decline of the Byzantine Empire, 1025–1453

turning increasingly toward the use of mercenary troops, in part to undermine the power of their rivals, the native Byzantine army.

Outside Attacks. These developments proved disastrous for the empire. By the mid-eleventh century the empire was coming under threat on three flanks: the Pecheneg and Cuman Turks to the north, the Normans and Italians in the west, and Selchuqid Muslim Turks to the east. The Pechenegs limited themselves to costly raids in the Balkans. The Selchuqids and Normans, on the other hand, attempted more permanent conquest. Norman adventurers conquered the remaining Byzantine possessions in southern Italy by 1071, and began raising an army for the invasion of Greece. The more serious threat came from the Selchuqid Turks, Central Eurasian nomads who had converted to Islam and overrun much of the Near East. In 1071 they crushed the Byzantine army at the battle of Manzikert, taking the emperor prisoner. During the ensuing decade of civil war for the Byzantine throne the Turks overran nearly all of Anatolia. Half the empire—including the heartland of its military strength—was lost.

Decline of the Navy. At this same time, another important pillar of the Byzantine society, its strong merchant class, was undermined by competition from Italian maritime city-states. To encourage trade, the Byzantine emperors began giving special privileges to Italian merchants. As time passed, these privileges allowed the Italians to undermine the position of native Byzantine merchants. This had disastrous consequences: Byzantine naval power was undermined, allowing the wealth derived from trade and tariffs to pass into Italian hands. Second, the Byzantines became dependent on the Italians for trade goods from overseas. Third, the Byzantine navy deteriorated to the point where Italian naval mercenaries were hired to defend the ports and seas of the empire.

Alexius Comnenus (1081–1118). As before under Heraclius and Leo III, a military leader arose who rallied and restored the collapsing empire. Alexius Comnenus managed to ascend the throne after a decade of civil war, and set about reorganizing the empire. In nearly forty years of continual warfare, he managed to defeat the Pechenegs and Normans, and push back, but not crush, the Turks in Anatolia. To deal with the lack of manpower in his partially successful wars with the Turks, Alexius called for military assistance from the West. The response was the First Crusade. The Crusaders initially provided assistance against the Turks, allowing Alexius and his son and grandson to retake nearly half of Anatolia.

Crisis. But the strains of continual military campaigning on a reduced economic base took their toll. The Byzantine army was finally decisively defeated by the Turks in 1176. A few years later, the unthinkable occurred. A Crusader army, diverted from the Holy Land by the Venetian merchants, attacked Constantinople in 1204, ostensibly to assist a deposed emperor. In fact, the city was conquered, sacked, and the empire collapsed.

The Latin Empire, 1204–1261. The Latin conquest of Constantinople was a disaster for both the Greeks and, ultimately, for the western Europeans. The former unified territory of the empire was fragmented into several competing states, some ruled by Byzantine princes, others by Latin feudal lords. Warfare among these small competing states became constant—the only beneficiaries were the Muslim Turks in Anatolia, who used the feuding of the Christians to extend their domain to the shores of the Aegean Sea. It again appeared that the empire was on the verge of extinction.

PALAEOLOGI AND TURKS: THE LATER BYZANTINE EMPIRE, 1261–1453

Once again, however, a military savior arose to rally the last vestiges of Byzantine power. Michael Palaeologus (1259–1282), the emperor in exile at Nicaea, managed to reconquer Constantinople from the Latins in 1261, establishing the last Byzantine imperial dynasty.

Weakened Condition. The term empire, however, is a misnomer, given the new condition of the Byzantine state. Limited in territory, with a weakened economy, and debilitated by the Black Death, the state was constantly threatened on all sides by powerful enemies, its territories overrun by Italian merchants, Western mercenaries, Slavic princes, pirates, and, most important, Turkish warlords. The story of the last two centuries of Byzantine history is one of steady diminution of territory and power, until, at the end in 1453, only the city of Constantinople itself remained in the hands of the Byzantines as their empire.

The Rise of the Ottoman Turks. As Westerners and Greeks feuded over the corpse of the dying empire, the great benefactors were the Muslim Turks in Anatolia, who steadily encroached on Byzantine territory, until their armies ultimately crossed into Greece for the first time in 1354. Under the leadership of a dynasty of warlords known as the Ottomans, the Turks rapidly overran much of Greece and the Balkans in the late fourteenth and early fifteenth centuries (see chapter 9). Western European attempts to relieve the beleaguered Byzantines were disastrously crushed at the battles of Nicopolis (1396) and Varna (1444), leaving the Turks as masters of the Balkans. Their impending conquest of Constantinople was forestalled only by their defeat in 1402 at the hands of another Muslim Turkish warlord from Central Eurasia, Tamerlane. The Ottomans quickly revived, however, and were able to conquer Constantinople in 1453 with a massive army and the new technology of cannons.

Last Cultural Flourishing. In this time of crisis, some Byzantines attempted to withdraw from the troubles of the world into a life of monastic contemplation as symbolized by the Hesychast mystical movement at Mount Athos. Others, however, attempted to revive the cultural splendor of the empire even as they lost political and economic power. The court at Constantinople was home to an array of brilliant scholars in all fields; Classical

Greek studies and history writing especially flourished, describing in detail the sad tale of the empire's fall. This final intellectual revival was especially important in western European history; some of these scholars ultimately fled the Byzantine empire in the wake of the Turkish conquests, bringing with them their knowledge and Greek manuscripts. Many, such as Bishop Bessarion of Nicaea, ultimately received positions in Italy, where they shared their books and knowledge of the Classical Greek heritage with their Italian students, thereby contributing to the formation of the Italian Renaissance and the transformation of western European culture.

Byzantine Civilization

Byzantine civilization was one of the most brilliant and enduring of the Middle Ages, perhaps the best representation of the ideal of a medieval Christian state. The Byzantine state rested upon a triple foundation: the emperor and his bureaucracy, the Greek Orthodox Church, and the military. Although the state itself eventually disappeared, its cultural influences continued in Italy during the Renaissance, and among the late medieval Slavic states in eastern Europe.

GOVERNMENT

The Emperor. The government of the empire was centered around the absolute authority of the emperor. As representative of God on earth, the emperor was imbued with a sacred aura symbolized by splendid court rituals and ceremonies. As representatives of God, emperors had to be without physical imperfection, a quality which explains the frequent resort to blinding and mutilation to remove possible contenders to the throne. Although theoretically elective, in practice the imperial throne was usually passed from father to son. As a form of divine kingship, the Byzantine emperors were necessarily closely allied to the Greek Orthodox Church, upon which they were dependant for their ideological foundation and their legitimization. Despite the facade of this imperial ideal, the reality of the Byzantine court was frequently one of plots, coups, and murder—giving rise to our modern use of the adjective byzantine to refer to complex intrigue.

The Bureaucracy. Another characteristic of the Byzantine state was its highly effective and centralized bureaucracy, probably the most efficient in the European Middle Ages. Bureaucrats were trained at the University of Constantinople, serving in a wide range of posts—jurists, secretaries, diplomats, governors, accountants—both in Constantinople and the provinces. The common background and training of the Byzantine bureaucratic corps was the sinew which held the empire together. One of the major functions of the bureaucracy was to provide for the financial needs of the empire through taxation and the imposition of tariffs. Although not without problems, the Byzantine tax and legal systems during the early and middle periods were generally fair and efficient.

THE BYZANTINE MILITARY SYSTEM

Faced with numerous enemies on many fronts, the survival and success of the Byzantine empire was dependent on an efficient military system. At its height, the army of the empire was composed of disciplined, well-trained and equipped farmer-soldiers, who fought from a sense of patriotism and in defense of their homelands. Adapting the military techniques of their Persian and Central Eurasian enemies, the main striking force of the Byzantine army was the heavily armored horse archer known as the *kataphraktos*.

Military Technology. The Byzantines were also noted for their technological skill in warfare. The fortifications of Constantinople stand as one of the world's great monuments of military architecture. On many occasions the walls prevented the conquest of the city. In a thousand years they were only breached on two occasions: by the Crusaders in 1204, and the Turks in 1453. The Byzantines are also noted for the invention of Greek fire, and their skill at siegecraft. Many Byzantine military ideas and practices have been preserved in a highly sophisticated series of military training manuals.

Decline. Beginning in the late eleventh century, this military system began to decline. In part this was the fault of the military aristocracy itself, which slowly usurped the lands of the farmer-soldiers in an effort to enlarge their own estates. As the farmer-soldiers declined in number, their ranks were replaced with mercenaries, thereby increasing the cost of maintaining an army. At the same time, the bureaucratic corps attempted to undermine the authority of the military aristocracy by decreasing the size and power of the army through limiting funds. The strength of the navy was undercut by trade privileges granted to the Italians, who soon provided naval defense for pay. Ultimately the standing professional army declined, to be replaced by mercenaries who, like the infamous Catalan Company, were not adverse to switching sides on the eve of battle, selling their services to the highest bidder, or betraying the empire.

SOCIETY AND ECONOMY

Greek Orthodoxy. The core of the Byzantine society was the Greek Orthodox Church. In a sense, membership in the Orthodox religion can be conceived of as citizenship in the Byzantine empire. Although Greek was the language of culture, religion, and government in the empire, many different ethnic groups were included—Armenians, Egyptian, Syrians, Slavs—as long as they were part of the Orthodox fold. Even barbarians, such as Bulgars or Turks, could be incorporated into the Byzantine social system through conversion to Christianity. Thus, Byzantine missionary efforts can in part be seen as an attempt to expand and defend the empire through the conversion of its enemies.

Social Structure. Byzantine society was divided into three classes, the aristocracy, the merchants and artisans, and the peasants. The aristocracy itself was divided into three classes, the court bureaucracy, the military, and the clergy, with wealthy merchants occasionally gaining influence as well. Social mobility was not uncommon in the empire, with peasants rising to the throne, or becoming important military officers or monks. Although never considered the equal of men, women occasionally played an important role in Byzantine life. Some, like Irene, rose to the throne; others, like Anna Comnena, became scholars, writers, or artists; many had important positions in female monastic life.

Economy. Like all premodern economies, the Byzantine was based fundamentally on agriculture. During the early centuries, the Byzantine empire was well served by a strong patriotic peasant class, who were protected by special agricultural legislation. With the loss of Egypt and North Africa, which had supplied Constantinople with grain, the city had to find new sources for food, resulting in a tremendous agricultural expansion. The tax system was generally fair and balanced, although there were periods of abuse. The Byzantine government established a policy of state monopoly over mineral resources and certain types of industry and manufacturing. In the short run this provided the state with a valuable source of income, but ultimately Byzantine industry ceased to be competitive, and was over-whelmed by Muslim and Italian competition.

Trade. Trade played an important role in the early Byzantine empire. A key element of Byzantine success in trade was the central geographical location of Constantinople at the transit point for overland trade between Asia and Europe, and sea trade between the Black and Mediterranean seas. The gold coinage of the empire served for centuries as the international medium of exchange in Mediterranean trade until it was devalued in an economic crisis and eventually replaced by the Venetian ducat in the thirteenth century. The Byzantines recognized the importance of international trade, making trading agreements with the Khazars (of southern Russia) and Axum in the Horn of Africa, in attempts to break the Sasanid Persian monopoly on silk from the Orient. Ultimately, in an early example of industrial espionage, Justinian sent secret agents to China, who managed to smuggle silkworms back to the empire in 561. Thereafter, the Byzantine state silk industry provided a major source of wealth to the empire.

Economic Decline. By the twelfth century the Byzantine economic position was in decline. Land was slowly passing from the free peasants into the hands of the aristocracy and large Church estates. Trade and manufac-turing were passing into the hands of the Italians. The deteriorating political situation combined with this economic decline to create a spiral of declining wealth and power, leading ultimately to the fall of the empire.

Constantinople. For all Byzantines, Constantinople was the center of political, social, military, economic, religious, and cultural life. Indeed, it was often referred to in Byzantine writings simply as The City. For over a thousand years Constantinople stood in the Byzantine mind as the ideal city. It was adorned with hundreds of churches filled with exquisite works of art; its university was the center of intellectual life; its monasteries were filled with prayers, contemplation, and theological discourse; its court boasted the most wealthy, beautiful, and powerful people in the empire.

EASTERN ORTHODOX CHRISTIANITY

The official state religion of the Byzantine empire became know to historians as Greek Orthodoxy. To the Byzantines, however, it was simply the one true form of Christianity. In structure, doctrine, and practice, the Byzantine Church was broadly similar to medieval Roman Catholicism (though with significant differences); its ecclesiastical leader was the patriarch of Constantinople, who regarded the Roman Catholic pope as simply the patriarch of Rome. Throughout the Byzantine period Greek Orthodoxy remained the definitive characteristic of a Byzantine citizen; all Byzantines were Orthodox, and all Orthodox were somehow subjects of the emperor no matter where they lived.

Schism with the West. Initially united with Roman Catholicism, the Greek Orthodox Church eventually diverged over issues of doctrine, liturgy, and especially ecclesiastical administration and jurisdiction—the Byzantines rejected the Roman Catholic pope's claims of ecclesiastical primacy as laughably arrogant. These issues finally came to a head in the ninth century. After numerous disputes and mutual excommunications, the Greek and Latin churches split, first in 867 (the Photian schism), with a final schism in 1054. Attempts at reunification of the two churches in the fifteenth century under the threat of Muslim Turkish invasions proved fruitless; the attitude of the Byzantines was reflected in the saying "Better the turban of the Turk than the tiara of the Pope."

Theological Controversies. Numerous difficulties arose as Christian scholars attempted to develop a sophisticated coherent theology, trying to combine often ambiguous statements from the Bible with centuries of pagan Hellenistic philosophical speculations about the nature of God. A wide range of theological interpretations naturally arose. The fundamental issues centered on questions about the Trinity: the nature of Christ's humanity, divinity, and his relationship with God the Father and the Holy Ghost.

To many modern readers, the bewildering array of theological controversies in the Byzantine empire—to which so many medieval thinkers devoted so much effort—seems remarkably dull. For the Byzantine citizens, however, such issues were not theological nitpicking. The fundamental ideology of the Byzantine empire was that it represented the ideal Christian state, established by God on earth. As such, it was crucial that the empire serve God faithfully, and worship Him in the orthodox manner. Deviation from Orthodoxy would undermine not only the fundamental nature of society, but would risk God's wrath. Thus questions of theology were as fundamental to the Byzantines as issues of civil or women's rights are to twentieth-century Americans. In both cases, the issues determined the very nature of society and its fundamental values.

Christological Controversies. The two major (though not the only) theological controversies in the empire include Arianism (viewing Christ as subordinate to the Father and not eternal) and monophysitism (belief that Christ has only a Divine nature, rather than a mixed divine and human nature). Ultimately Arianism disappeared, but monophysitism became the dominant theology in Syria and Egypt, where the Syriac and Coptic Christian monophysite churches still exist.

The Greek Fathers. The numerous theological debates during the Byzantine empire created a flourishing of Christian theological writings in the defense and definition of Greek Orthodoxy. The most important Byzantine theologians include Basil (329–379); John Chrysostom (347–407), the "golden mouth," the greatest orator of his day; Gregory of Nazianzus (330–389); and Gregory of Nyssa (335–394).

The Iconoclast Controversy. The political and military crisis of the eighth century was mirrored by a spiritual crisis. Seeing the collapse of their empire around them, many Byzantines began reexamining their spiritual life in an attempt to explain why God had seemingly abandoned his empire. One explanation was that the empire had violated the biblical commandment against the worship of images through the use of icons (religious images). In the Byzantine context, icons were paintings of Christ or saints which were revered during religious ritual, and frequently carried into battle as symbols of divine protection. Beginning under Leo III in 730, and enduring for over a century, the religious controversy over the efficacy and morality of icons raged in Byzantine society. Ultimately, the faction supporting the use of icons prevailed. Icons have remained an important element of all Orthodox religious services and worship until the present day, thereby serving as one of the finest forms of Eastern European religious art.

Monasticism. Monasticism—the withdrawal from the secular world for a life of devotion, prayer, scholarship, meditation, celibacy, and poverty— was a fundamental feature of Byzantine society. Drawing on various ascetic traditions from both the Jewish and pagan Near East (and possibly from Buddhism and Hinduism as well), Christian monasticism made its first appearance in Egypt in the third century. Beginning as isolated hermits seeking withdrawal from the sins and corruption of the cities, monks eventually organized themselves into small communities.

Monasteries became major spiritual, cultural, welfare, and intellectual centers in the Byzantine empire. The monks' life centered on worship, study, and service; their days were spent in prayer, study, theological discussion, the celebration of liturgies, meditation, teaching, preaching, and providing health care, food, and shelter for the poor.

Monks throughout the empire also played other vital roles in Byzantine society. Many served as teachers for noble or wealthy families, or in the great university of Constantinople. Others served as government bureaucrats, officials, or even councilors to emperors. The most significant impact of the monks was their ability to direct the emotions and opinions of the common people. Viewed as holy saints who could miraculously heal the sick or cast out demons, monks could sway the opinion of the masses, thereby causing occasional shifts in government policy.

Caesaropapism: The Unity of Church and State. Another important characteristic of medieval Greek Orthodoxy is Caesaropapism, the alliance, and indeed the complete identification of the State (Caesar) with the Church (pope, or papism). In the Byzantine empire Church and State were closely linked and mutually interdependent. The State existed to defend and propagate the Faith; the Church's role was to guide, bless, and support the policies of the emperors. Church officials received special privileges including exemption from taxes and military service, and the use of special ecclesiastical courts. Many ecclesiastical officials received appointments from the emperor, while all emperors needed to be anointed and crowned by the patriarch of Constantinople. Monks and priests served as bureaucrats and officials in the state government, and would routinely bless Byzantine armies as they marched to war.

There were many potential abuses of this close unity between Church and State, including nepotism, simony (the purchasing of Church offices), corruption, and the installation of incompetent and immoral men in high ecclesiastical offices to serve as lackeys of the state. Nonetheless, this successful symbiosis of Church and State remained a fundamental characteristic of Byzantine civilization.

Conversion of the Slavs. The most important impact of Byzantine Christianity on world history was the conversion of the Slavs. Over the course of several centuries, Byzantine monastic missionaries carried the religion, culture, and writing system of the empire throughout eastern Europe. The Cyrillic alphabet, used by most Slavic peoples today, was invented by St. Cyril (827–869), a missionary to the Slavs who developed it from the Greek alphabet in order to translate the Bible and liturgy into Slavic languages. Further analysis of the impact of the Byzantine conversion of the Slavs can be found below.

ART AND ARCHITECTURE

Art. The fundamental inspiration for Byzantine art was religion. They particularly excelled in two religious art forms: mosaics and icons. The mosaics at the Byzantine church of Ravenna in Italy are some of the most magnificent in the world. Likewise, icons represent a fundamental feature of Eastern Orthodox worship, laying part of the foundation for medieval Italian schools of painting.

Architecture and Hagia Sophia. The splendor of Byzantine architecture was its churches. Hundreds of medieval churches, many with splendid mosaics and frescoes, still exist throughout Greece and other former Byzantine territories. The greatest monument of Byzantine culture is the splendid church of Hagia Sophia (Holy Wisdom). Built by order of Justinian, and completed in 537 after only six years of construction, Hagia Sophia remained the largest and most beautiful Christian church in the world for nearly a thousand years. The vast low-arching dome stands as one of the great monuments of engineering, art, imperial arrogance, and the human quest for the Divine. Upon completion of the church, Justinian is reported to have proclaimed, "Solomon, I have surpassed thee," claiming to have built a building more splendid than Solomon's temple as described in the Bible. The 1,500-year-old church, now a museum in Istanbul, remains one of the architectural wonders of the world.

Music. The writing of hymns and religious music also flourished in Byzantine churches, ultimately having an impact on western European musical development. In a way, medieval Byzantine liturgy can be seen as a type of archaic opera, providing a spectacular pageant in a brilliant acoustical and artistic setting such as the church of Hagia Sophia. This "operatic" style of liturgy included a combination of drama (the retelling of the tales of Christ and the saints through the liturgical readings), music in the hymns, and art in the icons, mosaics, and religious dress.

LITERATURE

Preservation of Greek Classics. One of the greatest Byzantine contributions to world literature was the preservation of the manuscripts of the Classical Greek literary heritage. Indeed, without the efforts of hundreds of dedicated Byzantine scholars and monks, nearly all of the literature of Classical Greece—Homer, the dramatists, Plato, Herodotus, and others— would have been lost.

Religious Writing. Most Byzantine literary and intellectual effort centered on theological writings, which remain of interest largely to Greek Orthodox Christians and scholars. An interesting form of Byzantine religious literature was the odd mixture of biography and legend known as the saint's life (hagiography). As predictable as a modern television serial, the saint's life provided a combination of entertainment and moral teaching, as well as a revealing look at the social world of the time. Other important devotional and theological works, as well as hymns, remain important and widely used in the Greek Orthodox tradition until today.

History. The greatest Byzantine literary contribution was in history. The entire Byzantine period is remarkably well documented, but several historians stand out as especially important. Byzantine and Christian historiography began with Eusebius's, *History of the Church*, which attempted to show that the foundation of the Byzantine state by Constantine the Great was the ultimate logical development of Christianity. Justinian's era was chronicled by perhaps the most brilliant Byzantine historian, Procopius, whose *History of the Wars* and *Secret History* provide a remarkable view of this complex age.

Anna Comnena, 1083–1153. The most famous woman scholar of the Byzantine empire was Anna Comnena, the daughter of the emperor Alexius. A brilliant and highly educated woman, she was confined to a nunnery following her husband's abortive attempt (which she instigated) to usurp the throne of her brother. Deprived of the throne, she turned to history, composing a brilliant biography of her father, *The Alexiad*, an important literary and historical work.

Scholarship and the University of Constantinople. Although there had always been a court school at Constantinople, with its reorganization in the mid-ninth century it developed into a true university. Interest in Classical Greek studies created an intellectual renaissance; Plato and Aristotle were a fundamental part of the philosophical curriculum, along with the Christian Fathers.

Michael Psellus, 1018–1078. One of the most remarkable intellectuals of the period was Michael Psellus. During his long and active life he served as a monk, university professor (1045–1054), bureaucrat, and prime minister (at various times from 1055 to 1078). A brilliant scholar, he wrote important works on poetry, theology, philosophy (including commentaries on Plato), grammar, law, medicine, mathematics, natural sciences, and the occult. He is most famous for his history, the *Chronographia* (often called in English *Fourteen Byzantine Emperors*) which contains fascinating character studies of the Byzantine rulers of the tenth and eleventh centuries. His career indicates the amazing intellectual vitality of Byzantine culture.

Influence on the Renaissance. Ultimately, as the Byzantine state was collapsing in the fifteenth century, Greek scholars fled to Italy, where they took up positions in Italian schools, bringing with them Greek manuscripts, ideas, and art styles which had been unknown in the West for centuries;. These ideas found rapid acceptance in the West, contributing significantly to the development of the Italian Renaissance.

MEDIEVAL EASTERN EUROPE

Background

GEOGRAPHY

Geography played a major role in the historical development of eastern Europe. Two main factors were important. First, most of the river systems of eastern Europe flow basically north and south, either into the Black Sea or Baltic Sea. Since Byzantine Constantinople dominated access to the Black Sea, this meant that communications and trade—and therefore cultural influences—in the Balkans and Russia tended to be linked to the Byzantine empire. Those regions bordering Germany and the Baltic Sea, however, had better communications with Germany, and ultimately largely became Roman Catholic and more Westernized.

Second, the steppes of southern Russia (the Dnieper and Volga plains) provided perfect pasture land for Central Eurasian nomads from the east. The constant westward push of these warlike tribesmen put continual military pressure on the eastern and southern Slavic peoples. This military tension meant that population and prosperity increased less rapidly than in western Europe

THE SLAVS

Origins. The Slavs are an Indo-European ethnic and linguistic group which includes several major languages such as Polish, Russian, Ukrainian, Bulgarian, Czech, Slovak, and Serbian. The Slavs participated in the last great Indo-European tribal migration. Beginning from their homeland in the Pripet marshes (in west-central Russia) in the fifth and sixth centuries, they expanded out in a broad hemisphere to the east, west, and south, eventually settling in and giving their tribal names and languages to most of the modern states of eastern Europe. Eastern Europeans were also the last people of Europe to become civilized (that is, to begin to settle in cities), and the last to be Christianized. Some tribes of eastern Europe, such as the Balts in modern Estonia and Latvia, remained pagan until the middle of the thirteenth century, when they were finally converted only under extreme military pressure from their conquerors, the German Christian Teutonic Knights.

Thus the origin of eastern European civilizations represents the final phase in the old order—the migration of pagan Indo-European tribal warbands—and a cultural victory for the new order of medieval Christianity. After finally being absorbed into medieval Christian civilization, the Slavs developed their own states and civilizations, to be described below, and which laid the foundation for most of the modern states of eastern Europe.

Cultural Groups. Culturally the peoples of eastern Europe can divided into three major groups. The western Slavs (Poles, Czechs, Slovaks, and non-Slavic Hungarians) are Roman Catholic and distinguished by their close cultural and religious ties to western Europe. The eastern Slavs (Russians, Ukrainians) are mainly Eastern Orthodox in religion, and are culturally influenced by Byzantium and the Turko-Mongolians. The southern or Balkan Slavs (Serbs, Bulgarians and non-Slavic Romanians) are also largely Eastern Orthodox. They are distinguished from other Slavs by having been incorporated into the Byzantine empire at various times, and later being conquered and ruled by the Ottoman Turks for three centuries.

NON-SLAVIC PEOPLES

Although the Slavs represent by far the major cultural and ethnic group in eastern Europe, there were several other important peoples which influenced the course of medieval eastern European history. There are three regions in eastern Europe which are linguistically not Slavic, but are culturally closely tied to Slavic peoples. Romanians speak a Latin-based language derived from the ancient Roman colonization of the region in the second century. Hungarians speak a Central Eurasian language derived from the Magyar invaders of the tenth century. The Baltic peoples (Lithuanians, Estonians) are a distinct branch of Indo-Europeans. Thus, despite Slavic dominance of the area, there is a great deal of linguistic and cultural complexity reflecting the numerous migrations and conquests throughout eastern European history.

Historical Development of Medieval Eastern Europe

AGE OF MIGRATION, c. 350–750

The Germanic invasion of the Roman empire in the fourth and fifth centuries was part of a much larger world-wide phenomenon. In eastern Europe this had four major phases. First, several Central Eurasian tribes—Hun, Avars, and Bulgars—migrated into the region. Second, this stimulated the migration of Germanic peoples in the fourth century, beginning with the Gothic flight into the Roman empire in response to attacks from the Huns from the east. Third, these Central Eurasian and Germanic migrations served as a catalyst for the later Slavic migrations. In the fifth and sixth centuries the Slavs migrated throughout eastern Europe, penetrating the Danube border of the Byzantine empire and settling in the Balkans and Greece. During these chaotic centuries of migration and invasions, the Slavs became the major ethnic group throughout nearly all of eastern Europe. However, major pockets of Turko-Mongolian nomads remained in four zones: the Hungarian plains in modern Hungary and northwestern Romania, the lower Danube plains, the Dnieper plains, and the Volga plains. For the most part, both Slavs and Turko-Mongolians remained pagan, illiterate, and without cities. Government remained on a tribal level, although massive tribal confederations did on occasion develop under the domination of powerful Turko-Mongolian warlords. Fourth, to this complex ethnic mosaic, a new Germanic people arrived in the eighth century, Vikings from Scandinavia.

THE VIKINGS AND KIEVAN RUSSIA, 750–1054

The Viking Migration. The Vikings are most noted for their plundering raids against western Europe, and their conquest and settlement of parts of Ireland, England, and Normandy in the ninth and tenth centuries. At this same time other Vikings, known as Varangians, made their way eastward, sailing their longships from the Baltic Sea up the eastern European rivers, raiding the Slavic peoples, and eventually conquering and settling among the Slavs. Between 800 and 1050 they dominated the river valleys of much of what is now central-western Russia. Indeed, the name *Russia* derives from the name for one Varangian group, the Rus.

Kiev, 858–1054. The greatest achievement of the Scandinavians in Russia was the foundation of the principalities of Kiev and Novgorod, the first powerful states in the region. From these two centers the Varangians grew wealthy by the control of the trade from Scandinavia to the Mediterranean on the Dnieper river. Following the conversion of Prince Vladimir I of Kiev to Christianity in 988, the Kievan empire became increasingly Slavic, with strong influences from Byzantium. The Kievan empire was strong enough to challenge Constantinople itself in three unsuccessful naval assaults in 860, 944, and 1043. After 1054 Kiev began to fragment under pressure from Central Eurasians and Poles. During the next two centuries the region was divided into small principalities.

Significance. The coming of the Varangians had three major effects on Slavic peoples. First, they conquered and dominated certain regions, establishing the earliest cities and states in eastern Europe. Second, in order to deal with the Varangian attacks, the Slavs were forced to organize themselves into military alliances beyond the simple clan level, leading to the creation of independent Slavic principalities along the pattern of the Varangian states. Third, Varangian invasions began to link the Slavs to the outside world through trade routes into the Baltic and Black seas. Ultimately, by the eleventh century, the Viking warriors in eastern Europe were absorbed by the local Slavic populations, just as their cousins were in England and Normandy.

TURKO-MONGOLIANS

Major Invasions. The major competitor of the Slavs in the regions of modern Hungary, Romania, Bulgaria, and the areas north of the Black Sea were inner Eurasian Turko-Mongolian tribesmen. From the fourth through the fifteenth centuries many different Turko-Mongolian tribes migrated through this region; the most important were (with approximate dates): Huns (375–452), Avars (557–805), Khazars (568–965), Volga Bulgars (460–1236), Danube Bulgars (605–870), Magyars (830–988), Pechenegs (915–1091), and Cumans (1050–1237). One after another these tribes migrated into southern Russia and the Balkans, each dominating various zones for several centuries before being replaced by another invading tribe from Central Eurasia. (Details of the origin and nature of Turko-Mongolian societies and states will be given in chapter 15.)

Impact. Their major impact on Slavic civilization was in many ways negative; Turko-Mongolian invasions often meant wars, devastation, and decades of serving as vassals to the conquerors. On the other hand, Central Eurasian forms of government, social organization, and military practices all influenced medieval Slavic peoples. The Central Eurasians brought with them trade links to east Asia via the Silk Road; much of Russia's subsequent ties with Asia were initially forged by Turko-Mongolians. The autocratic, brutal, and expansionist mentality of Moscovite Princes in the fourteenth and fifteenth centuries is based in part on their need to organize a strong militarized society to combat the Turko-Mongolian threat.

Thus, throughout most of the Middle Ages, most of southern Russia and the northern Balkans were dominated not by Slavic, but by Turko-Mongolian states. Only from the fourteenth through the seventeenth centuries were many of these regions pacified, conquered, and ultimately Christianized.

EARLY SLAVIC PRINCIPALITIES, 900–1300

Following the collapse of the Kievan empire, political power was diffused in eastern Europe among several different states. Each of these medieval kingdoms formed the cultural and ethnic nucleus for the eventual development of modern states in eastern Europe.

Early Poland, 960–1386. A Polish kingdom emerged in the middle of the tenth century, followed by two centuries of struggles with Germans, Russians, and Mongols.

Hungary, 997–1241. Following their Christianization about 990, the Magyars began to adapt their customs and culture to medieval European norms, while maintaining their expansionist military tradition. Between 997 and 1241 Hungary became the dominant state in the northern Balkans. The kingdom fell into disarray following its disastrous defeat by the Mongols at the battle of Sajo river in 1241.

Bohemia (Czechoslovakia), 973–1278. Bohemia was an important Slavic state with close ties to Germany, and ultimately was absorbed by the Holy Roman Empire.

Lithuania, 1250–1386. Under pressure from the Teutonic Knights, whose aim was both to conquer Lithuania and convert the pagan people to Christianity, the Baltic Lithuanians organized a state in the mid-thirteenth century. In a period of rapid and widespread expansion, they conquered all of the Slavic principalities along the Dnieper river. Although threatened by the Mongols, by 1386 they had become the most powerful state in eastern Europe.

Serbia (Yugoslavia), 1151–1396; and Bulgaria, 1186–1396. With the collapse of the Byzantine empire following the sack of Constantinople in 1204, Slavic rulers in the Balkan provinces established independent states; the two most important were Serbia and Bulgaria. Both experienced periods of power as Byzantium declined, only to be eventually crushed and absorbed in the late fourteenth century by the expanding Ottoman Turks.

MONGOLS AND TARTARS, 1223–1478

Conquests. A watershed in eastern European history was the Mongol conquests in the mid-thirteenth century, and the establishment of the Tartar Yoke (Turko-Mongolian domination). The Mongol invasion of eastern Europe lasted from 1236 to 1242, during which time all of southern Russia came under Mongol domination (see chapter 15). Shortly thereafter, the Mongol empire fragmented into four major successor states; Chingis (Genghis) Khan's grandson Batu (1235–1255) gained control of eastern Europe, founding the Golden Horde (Kipchak Khanate) which lasted until 1502.

Significance. Several major developments occurred as a result of the empire of the Golden Horde. Russia and other parts of eastern Europe which were dominated by the Mongols became culturally and economically stagnant for several centuries. Eastern European princes who submitted to the Mongols were allowed to retain their domains as vassals of the khan; such principalities became increasingly autocratic and militarized. Moscow and Novgorod, the major cities on the northern fringes of the Golden Horde, were only partially within the sphere of Mongol domination. As such they replaced Kiev as the cultural, political, religious and economic centers of non-Mongol Russia. Moscow eventually became the center of anti-Mongol military resistance, laying the foundation for its eventual rise as the principal state in Russia. Russian ties with Central Eurasia became significant during the Mongol period, culminating in the sixteenth and seventeenth centuries in Russian colonialism to the east.

LATE MEDIEVAL SLAVIC KINGDOMS, 1300–1500

By about 1300 the political situation in eastern Europe was highly complex and fragmented. The Balkans was politically fragmented among Serbs, Bulgars, Greeks, Latins, and Hungarians. Hungary and Poland were both politically weak; Lithuania was the strongest Slavic power, but was still overshadowed by the Mongol Golden Horde. Within two centuries this situation had been drastically changed.

The Rise of Russia. In the east, the Golden Horde began to disintegrate, and although it remained powerful, the Principality of Moscow—which had led the opposition to the Mongols—was able to go on the offensive. In 1380 the Moscovites defeated the Golden Horde at the battle of Kulikovo, beginning expansion eastward at Mongol expense. By 1480 the Golden

Horde fragmented into several states, allowing Moscow to begin its major period of eastward expansion. The introduction of firearms began to give the Moscovites an additional significant military advantage over the Mongols. By 1600 all of southern Russia was in Slavic hands; the Central Eurasian threat to the Slavs had been ended forever and Moscovite Russia had emerged as the major power in eastern Europe.

A major element of Russian expansion was their adoption of Byzantine imperial ideology following the fall of Constantinople in 1453. Ivan III (1462–1505) married Zoe, a Byzantine princess, taking the Byzantine/Roman title Czar (Caesar) following the fall of Constantinople. Moscow became the Third Rome (after Rome and Constantinople), gaining religious sanctification as the new center of Eastern Orthodoxy.

Poland-Lithuania. At the same time Russia was beginning its expansion against the Mongols, the kingdoms of Poland and Lithuania merged through dynastic alliance in 1386. With an empire extending from the Baltic to the Black seas, Poland-Lithuania was the major Slavic state until the rise of Moscow in the late fifteenth century. It played a leading, but unsuccessful role in attempting to halt Ottoman expansion in the Balkans. Internal weakness and divisiveness in their political system robbed the Polish kings of much needed administrative power, leading to a decline in their position in the sixteenth century in the face of German and Russian expansion.

The Ottoman Empire. The third major power to arise in eastern Europe in the fourteenth century was the Ottoman empire, which in geographic and strategic terms replaced Byzantium. As the Byzantine empire collapsed in the fourteenth century, Ottoman expansion in the Balkans progressed rapidly. By 1354 they had established their first base in Europe. By 1389 the Slavic kingdoms of Bulgaria and Serbia had been crushed. They defeated major Western Christian armies at Nicopolis (1396), and Varna (1444), and conquered Hungary following the battle of Mohacs in 1526.

The New Order. Thus by the end of the sixteenth century, three major powers dominated eastern Europe: Russia in the east, which had absorbed the other small eastern Slavic principalities and driven out the Mongols; the Muslim Ottoman Turks in the south, who had destroyed and replaced the Byzantine empire, and absorbed the Christian kingdoms of Bulgaria, Serbia, and Hungary; and Poland-Lithuanian in the northwest. The Russian and Ottoman empires survived into the twentieth century (although the Ottomans lost the Balkans in the nineteenth). Poland-Lithuania was to be dismembered and divided among Russia and various German principalities in the seventeenth and eighteenth centuries.

Eastern European Civilization

GOVERNMENT AND SOCIETY

Nobility. Although there were many local variations, medieval eastern European governments were generally monarchical, and frequently autocratic. Societies tended to be sharply divided into the noble (*boyar*) and serf classes. The noble class, whose main function was warfare, tended to have a militaristic, frontier mentality. Turbulent and militant, the nobles imbued many Slavic societies with a warlike flavor. This, combined with frequent threats from enemies such as the Mongols and Ottomans, caused many Slavic societies to become militaristic.

Lower Classes. The middle class of artisans and merchants tended to be small and wield relatively little political power. Following the Byzantine example of Caesaropapism, eastern European Christian clergy tended to be closely tied to the interests of the noble class. There were thus few legitimate mechanisms for political opposition and reform; significant social changes tended to come either from autocratic decree, palace coups organized by the nobles, or by peasant uprisings.

Underdevelopment. By most social and economic criteria eastern Europe lagged behind the west. It was substantially more rural than the west, centered on villages based on strong ties of kinship and communal values. Population density and prosperity was lower in the east than west; cultural achievements were less spectacular. Finally, there was a fundamental social discontinuity on several levels between the Turko-Mongolians and Slavs: the Central Eurasians were pagan or Islamic and nomadic, while the Slavs were Christian and sedentary. These and related differences created an endless array of social tensions which were not finally resolved until the Moscovite Russian conquest of the Central Eurasians beginning in the sixteenth century.

Literature. Following the creation of the Cyrillic alphabet after about 900, written Slavic literature began, primarily in various dialects of Old Church Slavonic. As with Byzantine and other medieval cultures, the vast majority of medieval Slavic literature remained religious throughout this period. The most notable work of history is the *Russian Primary Chronicle*, which gives details on the early history of Russia. An important type of secular literature is the *bylina*, or heroic folk song, which is best represented by *The Song of Igors Campaign*, describing the heroic deeds of the prince Igor of Novgorod's ill-fated campaign in 1185.

RELIGION IN EASTERN EUROPE

In a sense the early Middle Ages represents a time of struggle for the soul of eastern Europe between many different religious groups. Originally Slavic and Baltic polytheism—ancestral religions related to similar forms of Indo-European polytheism—were the dominant religions of the area. Certain peoples of eastern Europe continued worshiping their pagan ancestral gods well into the thirteenth century. Ultimately, however, these forms of paganism were replaced and absorbed by the three major forms of Near Eastern monotheism: Judaism, Christianity, and Islam.

Judaism. Judaism became an important religion in eastern Europe through a remarkable development; the ruling class of the Turko-Mongolian Khazars (582–1060) of the Volga valley converted to Judaism in the mid–eighth century, creating a Jewish state in southern Russia for several centuries. Jewish descendants of the Khazars may have formed local Jewish communities in eastern Europe following the collapse of the Khazar dynasty. Within a few centuries, however, persecution of Jews in western Europe led to their gradual migration eastward into Slavic lands, where major Jewish settlements began to develop from the twelfth century. Thus, by the end of the Middle Ages there were substantial Jewish communities in Poland, Lithuania, and western Russia, each of which developed important centers of Jewish religion, thought, and culture. Other than the Khazars, however, Jews never held significant political power in eastern Europe.

The Byzantines and Eastern Orthodoxy. The Byzantines contributed four major elements to eastern European civilization. First, Byzantine missionaries—the two most important being Cyril (827–869) and Methodius (825–884)—converted the eastern and southern Slavs to Eastern Orthodox Christianity. The Bulgarians were converted beginning in 865, the Serbs in 879, and Kievan Russia (Varangians and Slavs) in 988. Second, these same missionaries developed the Cyrillic alphabet (named after Cyril), and translated the Bible and other Christian writings into Slavic languages, thereby bringing literacy to the Slavs. Third, Byzantine forms of government administration and imperial ideology laid the political foundation for the development of medieval Slavic kingdoms. Finally, Byzantine types of art, architecture, and literature formed models for medieval Slavic art and literature. Thus, in a very important sense, eastern Europe is the cultural heir of Byzantine civilization; Eastern Orthodoxy became the fundamental cultural characteristic of the southern and eastern Slavs.

A major feature of the conversion to Eastern Orthodoxy was the establishment of autonomous church hierarchies among the Slavs. Although recognizing the moral leadership of the patriarch of Constantinople, each major Slavic community established its own independent Orthodox hierarchy. Thus, today, we find that the Eastern Orthodox Church is administratively divided into several branches—e.g., the Greek, Russian, Bulgarian churches—all of which remain in communion. On the other hand, all western Slavs accepted the primacy of the pope at Rome, remaining within the hierarchy of the Roman Catholic Church.

Western Europe and Roman Catholicism. Western Europeans—mainly Germans and Italians—had an important impact on the Western Slavs. The Western European role among the western Slavs was fundamentally the same as that of the Byzantines among the southern and eastern Slavic peoples: providing Catholic Christianity, the Roman alphabet, and models of government, literature, and the arts. Eastern Europeans who converted to Roman Catholicism include (with approximate dates of earliest conversions): Croats (879), Czeches (890), Magyars (990), Poles (966), and the non-Slavic Balts (1240). On the other hand, the Slavs often served as a source of plunder for Westerners—indeed, our word slave derives from the name Slav, since raids against the pagan Slavs were a major source of slaves in medieval times. Wars between German and Slavic princes were frequent throughout the entire Middle Ages, with German warlords and settlers slowly advancing eastward into Slavic territories.

Islam and the Turko-Mongolians. The final major religion to have an impact on eastern Europe was Islam (see chapter 9). In the initial Islamic conquests, Arab warriors stopped their expansion at the Caucasus mountains, and did not penetrate directly into eastern Europe. The eventual expansion of Islam into that region came indirectly, through the conversion of the Turks and Mongols. By 922 some of the Volga Bulgars had converted to Islam, and from that time on Islam made steady progress among the inner Eurasian nomads.

There were two major avenues for the spread of Islam into eastern Europe. First, the Ottoman Turks were Muslims, and they spread Islam among the southern Slavs during their conquest of the Balkans in the fourteenth through the sixteenth centuries. Islam declined in the Balkans following the expulsion of the Turks in the nineteenth century, but substantial Islamic communities still exist in Albania, Bosnia, and Bulgaria. Second, the Golden Horde, the successor state to the Mongol Empire in southern Russia, converted to Islam around 1340. Thereafter, southern Russia remained largely Islamic for several centuries. The areas northeast of the Black Sea were Christianized only following the Russian conquest of that region in the sixteenth century.

THE IMPACT OF MEDIEVAL SLAVIC CIVILIZATION

Relations with the West. In eastern Europe in the late Middle Ages, a major cultural division arose between the western and eastern and southern Slavs. The western Slavic peoples—Poles, Czechs, Hungarians—who bordered on Germany and who had been converted to Roman Catholicism, tended to share in the cultural and economic developments of the West, including the decline of feudalism, the Renaissance, the Reformation, and the scientific revolution. Indeed Copernicus (1473–1543), a leading figure in sixteenth-century astronomy, was Polish.

These close ties with the West were possible for three reasons. Western Slavs bordered on western Europe, which was therefore physically more accessible. As Roman Catholics, the western Slavs used Latin as the major language of education and culture, and therefore had access to all the new ideas of the Renaissance and early modern Europe. Finally, the eastern Slavs shielded the western Slavs from the invasions of the central Eurasians, allowing them to develop more prosperous and less militaristic societies.

Isolation of the Eastern Slavs. Eastern and southern Slavs, on the other hand, were physically more isolated from the West, creating relative difficulties in communication. Their use of the Cyrillic alphabet, and the absence of Latin as a language of culture, meant that they were much less affected by early modern Western intellectual trends. Finally, their constant wars with the Turks and Mongols created a tendency toward militaristic and autocratic states, with much of their attention focused on warfare and national survival. Indeed, the southern Slavs of the Balkans were part of the Ottoman empire for over three hundred years, and thus were fundamentally isolated from intellectual, cultural, and social trends in the West.

The Byzantine empire played a vital role in the development of western European civilization, with consequences which still affect us today. Byzantine scholars preserved Classical Greek literature and culture. Without Byzantium nearly all of the works of Greek literature, drama, history, philosophy, and science would have been irretrievably lost. The military strength of the Byzantines stood for centuries as a bulwark against the Islamic invasion of Europe. If Constantinople had fallen to the Arabs in 717, it is quite certain that most of eastern and central Europe—and quite possibly all of Europe—would have been eventually conquered by the Muslims. Western civilization as we know it would never have existed.

The survival of Byzantine cities, industry and trade during the early Middle Ages provided an important economic stimulus to the later growth of western European economies. Byzantine theological and religious writings have served as an important source of doctrine and inspiration for the Eastern Orthodox branch of Christianity. The Byzantines created splendid works of medieval Christian art, architecture, and history. Byzantine missionaries brought literacy, Byzantine cultural forms, and Christianity to the pagan Slavic peoples of eastern Europe. Byzantine imperial ideology was selectively adopted by the princes of Moscow which laid the foundations for the imperial claims of the Russian czars (caesars). Byzantine manuscripts, scholars, art forms, and ideas played a significant role in the development of the ideas of the Italian Renaissance.

In many ways, the Byzantine empire stands on the crossroads of time and space, and as such its chief role was a transmitter of ideas between different cultures, peoples, and times. Geographically, it stands on the boundary between Europe and Asia, serving initially as a bulwark against the penetration of Persian, Arab, and Central Eurasian peoples and ideas into Europe. Ultimately it was transformed into the highway for the Ottoman Turkish conquests of the Balkans. Chronologically it spans the entire medieval period: Its history begins with the simultaneous fall of Rome in the

West and the triumph of Christianity. The fall of Constantinople a thousand years later in 1453 was on the verge of modernity: a world of cannons, printing, and the Renaissance, which was within decades of the beginnings of the Reformation and the discovery of the New World.

The eastern Slavs developed societies which tended to be autocratic and militaristic. Cities for the most part remained small, with weak merchant and middle classes. Vast aristocratic landed estates were worked by serfs rather than a free peasant class. It was not until the eighteenth and nineteenth centuries that the eastern Slavs began creating closer ties with the West.

Selected Readings

Crummey, Robert O. *The Formation of Muscovy, 1304–1613* (1987)
Dvornik, Francis. *The Slavs in European History and Civilization* (1962)
Fine, John V. A. Jr., *The Early Medieval Balkans* (1986)
_____. *The Late Medieval Balkans* (1987)
Halperin, Charles J. *Russia and the Golden Horde* (1987)
Mango, Cyril. *Byzantium, the Empire of New Rome* (1980)
Nicol, Donald M. *The Last Centuries of Byzantium* (1972)
Norwich, John Julius. *Byzantium: The Apogee* (1992)
_____. *Byzantium: The Early Centuries* (1989)
Ostrogorsky, Georg. *A History of the Byzantine State*, 2nd. ed. (1969)
Riasanovsky, Nicholas. *A History of Russia*, 4th ed. (1984)
Vernadsky, George. *Kievan Russia* (1948)

9

Islam

945	Shi'ite Buyid dynasty occupies Baghdad, dominates Abbasids
1031	Fragmentation of Muslim Spain, beginning of Christian Reconquista
1040	Battle of Dandanqan: Selchuqid Turks invade Iran
1055	Selchuqid Turks occupy Baghdad
1071	Battle of Manzikert: Selchuqid Turks crush Byzantines
1099	First Crusade: Crusaders take Jerusalem
1130–1269	Al-Muwahhidun (Almohades) dominate North Africa and Spain
1187	Battle of Hattin: Saladin takes Jerusalem from Crusaders
1218	Beginning of the Mongol conquests in the Near East
1250–1517	Mamluk sultanate in Egypt and Near East
1258	Sack of Baghdad by the Mongols
1291	Fall of Acre to the Mamluks: end of the Crusades
1325–1353	Travels of Ibn Battuta
1354	Ottoman invasion of the Balkans begins
1370–1405	Conquests of Tamerlane
1389	Battle of Kosovo: Ottomans conquer southern Balkans
1453	The fall of Constantinople to the Turks
1498	Vasco da Gama reaches India
1501–1524	Shah Ismail founds the Safavid dynasty in Iran
1517	Ottomans conquer Egypt from Mamluks
1520–1566	Sulayman the Magnificent, Ottoman sultan
1526	Battle of Mohacs, Ottomans conquer Hungary
1526	Battle of Panipat, Babur founds Mughal dynasty in India
1556–1605	Akbar, Mughal emperor of India
1571	Battle of Lepanto, Ottoman navy defeated
1588–1629	Shah Abbas I, emperor of Safavid Iran

*T*he Arabian peninsula is the home of Islam, one of the world's great
religions. Founded by the prophet Muhammad in 610, Islam spread, via
the Arab conquests and conversions, throughout the Near East and North
Africa. The Islamic empire of the Umayyad and Abbasid periods created a
cultural synthesis of Byzantine, Iranian, and Arab elements which combined
to form classical Islamic civilization. Despite a period of fragmentation and
outside invasions, Islamic civilization remained vital. Scientific advances

were coupled with a golden age of literary and artistic achievement. With political power restored in the fifteenth century, Islamic civilization spread into subsaharan Africa, Central Eurasia, India, and Southeast Asia.

PRE-ISLAMIC ARABIA

Although the impact of Arabia and the Arabs on world history stems from Islam and the Arab conquests in the seventh century A.D., Arabs had long played a significant regional role in the Near East.

Land and People

CLIMATE

Desert. Arabia is a huge peninsula, equal in size to nearly all the rest of the Near East. Most of Arabia is desert; in some parts pastoral nomadism is possible, but vast regions—such as the Empty Quarter and Nafud—are completely uninhabited stone and sand deserts.

Agricultural Zones. Agriculture is possible only in four parts of Arabia: the Hejaz in the central western coast; Yemen in the southwestern corner; Oman in the southeastern corner; and in a few scattered oases. Even in those regions the agricultural potential is limited; irrigation is often necessary and many of the inhabitants of the agricultural zones live seminomadic or nomadic lifestyles. The Hejaz and Yemen have historically formed the most important centers of Arabian agricultural civilization.

THE ARABS

Arabs are a Semitic people, speaking a language related to Hebrew, ancient Akkadian, and Babylonian. Historically Arabia has been a land of emigration, not immigration, and therefore has only few minority ethnic groups. There were numerous tribes and dialects of Arabic in pre-Islamic Arabia: classical Arabic derives from the dialect spoken by Muhammad as preserved in the Qur'an (Koran).

DOMESTICATION OF THE CAMEL

A crucial event in the history of both Arabia and the world was the domestication of the camel. Just as the horse played a major role in trade and warfare in the steppes of Central Eurasia, the domestication of the camel was an important part of civilization in the Near East and north Africa.

The Arabian Camel. Although camels must drink as much water as any other animal, their importance for desert travel derives from the fact that they can go without drinking much longer than any other pack animal. The camel was domesticated in Arabia perhaps in the early second millennium B.C., but came into widespread use only in the eleventh century B.C., when camel-riding nomads (such as the biblical Midianites) began to raid the agricultural communities on the desert fringes in Israel, Syria, and Mesopotamia.

The Impact of the Camel. The camel gave the Arabian nomads three crucial advantages. First, it extended the possible range of human habitation, allowing camel herding in marginal zones with inadequate water resources for either agriculture or traditional sheep or goat raising. Second, the ability to cross long stretches of desert allowed the nomads to become merchants, developing new desert trade routes. Finally, the camel provided a military advantage for logistics and transportation in arid zones.

The Camel in North Africa. The introduction of the camel into North Africa about the middle of the first millennium B.C. played a major role in subsaharan African history by creating trans-Saharan trade routes which connected west African kingdoms with North Africa (see chapter 12).

Pre-Islamic Arabian peoples

Although the major role of the Arabs in world history begins with the coming of Islam in the seventh century A.D., there were important pre-Islamic Arab kingdoms as well.

SABEANS

Early Kingdom. The most important pre-Islamic Arabs were the Sabeans in modern Yemen. The introduction of agriculture and civilization into this region dates back to the late second millennium B.C. Sabeans mastered irrigation techniques and controlled the overland and sea trade from southern Arabia to Mesopotamia and Egypt. The famous Queen of Sheba, who visited Solomon, was a ruler of the Sabean kingdom in the tenth century B.C. Culturally, they developed their own script for writing Arabic, as well as a unique style of art and architecture; their culture played an important role in the development of civilization in Ethiopia.

Sabeans in the Sixth Century A.D. Many Sabeans converted to Christianity or Judaism after the fourth century A.D.; religious disputes culminated in a civil war between Christian and Jewish factions in the early sixth century. Exhausted by these wars, their society was further devastated by the collapse of the Marib dam around 580, which destroyed much of the irrigation system, bringing economic decline. Sabean Yemen was occupied by Ethiopians between 525 and 575, and by the Sasanid Persians from 575 to 628. Thereafter the region was integrated into Islamic civilization.

NABATAEANS

Another important pre-Islamic Arab people were the Nabataeans of modern Jordan. Having settled in southern Jordan in the fifth century B.C., the Nabataeans prospered as caravaneers controlling trade between Yemen and the Mediterranean Sea. The capital of the Nabataean kingdom was the magnificent city of Petra. Nestled in an oasis in a mountain gorge, Petra boasts some of the most magnificent rock-cut temples and tombs of antiquity, indicative of the vast wealth they derived from their trading enterprises. They were conquered and absorbed into the Roman empire in A.D. 106, after which their civilization slowly declined.

PALMYRA

Another important Arab trading city was Palmyra. Located halfway between Mesopotamia and Syria, Palmyra's strategic location allowed it to prosper in the third century A.D. through its control of camel-borne desert trade. Palmyra's most famous ruler was Queen Zenobia (264–273), who challenged the Roman empire for control of the east, briefly ruling most of Syria, Egypt, Mesopotamia, and Anatolia. Like Petra, the ruins of Palmyra contain magnificent examples of Hellenized Arab architecture.

ARABIA ON THE EVE OF ISLAM

At the birth of Muhammad Arabia was a peninsula with severe social, political, and religious divisions. Indeed, there had never been an Arabian culture or state which encompassed the entire peninsula. In the north, the Ghassanid and Lakhmid Arabs were client states of the Byzantines and Sasanids. The desert regions of Arabia were controlled by desert nomads, while the oases and fertile zones on the western and southern coasts were politically divided into several small kingdoms or city-states. Religiously, most Arabs were pagans, worshiping traditional tribal gods. However, there were small but important Christian, Jewish, Zoroastrian, and nondenominational monotheistic communities. Religious wars between Jewish and Christian factions had plagued the Sabeans of Yemen for decades. Outside military forces from Persia, the Byzantine empire, and from Abyssinia had been interfering in Arabian politics as well.

MUHAMMAD AND ISLAM

Muhammad, the Prophet of Islam, 570–632

EARLY CAREER, 570–622

Early Life. Born in 570, Muhammad was a member of a minor trading clan in the city of Mecca (Makka) in the Hejaz. Orphaned as a young man, Muhammad was raised by his uncle, playing an undistinguished role in the mercantile affairs of Mecca until his marriage, at age twenty-five, to a wealthy widow named Khadija. Under Muhammad's guidance, Khadija's trading enterprises flourished, until at about age forty he was able to enter into semiretirement and devote an increasing part of his time to religious meditation.

Prophetic Calling. In 610 Muhammad was meditating in the mountains near Mecca. There he believed that the angel Gabriel appeared to him, revealing to him part of the Qur'an (Koran), and summoning him to become God's prophet. Muhammad was so shaken by this experience that, fearing for his sanity, he fled to his home; his wife Khadija convinced him to act upon his revelations. As he preached God's message to his fellow citizens of Mecca, the revelations which were to become the Qur'an began to come with increasing frequency.

RISE TO POWER, 622–632

The *Hijra* (Hegira), 622. Although Muhammad convinced a small group of friends and relatives, few Meccans believed the new self-proclaimed prophet. As Muhammad began to denounce their sins and disbelief, many turned to active persecution and threatened Muhammad's life. In 622 he and his followers were forced to flee Mecca in the wake of an assassination attempt. He found refuge in the city of Medina, where most of the local inhabitants accepted him as a prophet and the leader of their community. Muhammad's flight (*hijra* or hegira) from Mecca to Medina is considered a seminal event by Muslims, representing the transition from a small persecuted band of believers to a fully established Muslim religious and political community. Year one of the Islamic calendar therefore dates from 622.

Muhammad at Medina. As political and religious leader of Medina, Muhammad initiated a policy of proselytizing other Arab tribes and cities, and opposing his old enemies at Medina. War soon broke out between pagan Mecca and Muslim Medina. Although things initially went badly for the Muslims, Muhammad personally led his small army to several remarkable victories over the vastly superior forces of Mecca at the battles of Badr (623) and the siege of Medina (627). These victories were widely seen throughout Arabia as miraculous signs of God's blessings on the Muslim community; thousands flocked to Muhammad's banner and became Muslims.

The Conquest of Arabia. By 630 Muhammad had raised an army of about 10,000 men and marched on Mecca. Unable to resist, the Meccans surrendered and accepted Islam. For the most part, Muhammad treated his old enemies with great generosity, even though they had once tried to assassinate him. He insisted on cleansing the Ka'aba—an ancient temple at Mecca which was said to have been built by Abraham—of pagan worship. He thereafter rededicated it as the central shine of Islam, instituting an annual pilgrimage of Muslims to worship there. Thereafter, by a combination of military action and religious conversion, nearly the entire Arabian peninsula had converted to Islam or allied with Muhammad by his death in 632.

THE IMPACT OF MUHAMMAD

In the company of Jesus, the Buddha, and Confucius, Muhammad is the founder of one of the world's great religions and civilizations. However, no other great religious leader had Muhammad's combined success in both spiritual and political affairs. In a short twenty-year period Muhammad created a united nation of the disparate and feuding Arabian tribes. He produced a book of scripture which is accepted by hundreds of millions as the word of God, who also accept his life as their model for an ideal human being. Combined with his personal teachings, the Qur'an formed the basis of a legal system which would be normative among Muslims for the next 1,300 years. Finally, Muhammad's religious, social, and political ideals succeeded in creating the first global civilization: within five hundred years of his death, the Muslim call to prayer could be heard in every continent in the Old World.

Basic Principles of Islam

THE QUR'AN (KORAN) AND THE SUNNA

The Qur'an. Muslims accept the Qur'an not only as the revelation of God to the prophet Muhammad, but as the perfect and eternal manifestation of God's word. As such, it is the definitive scripture of Islam, and the foundation for all Islamic beliefs and practices. Although not strictly poetry, the Qur'an is written in an elegant elevated style of Arabic, and it is universally considered to be a literary masterpiece.

The Sunna. While the Qur'an is considered the word of God Himself, Muslims also find an important source for doctrine and practice in the words of Muhammad, known as the Sunna. While not considered scriptural revelations, the teachings and practices of Muhammad have historically played an important role in the development of Muslim law and ethics.

THE FIVE PILLARS OF ISLAM

The basic beliefs and practices of Islam have been traditionally summarized in the "Five Pillars."

Faith. The basic article of faith of Islam is "There is no god but God (Allah) and Muhammad is the Messenger of God." This statement implies strict monotheism, acceptance of the Qur'an as the revelation of the word of God, as well as belief in angels, a final judgment, and the hereafter. Although differing in many details, the basic Muslim ideas on these latter matters roughly parallel traditional Jewish and Christian thought.

Prayer. Muslims are required to perform five ritual prayers daily; at set times each day faithful Muslims will face the central shrine of the Ka'aba at Mecca and perform a short ritual prayer. In addition, Muslims are required to come to a mosque (place of prayer) each Friday at noon for prayer and sermons.

Alms. Care of the poor is enjoined on Muslims, and generally takes the form of a standardized almsgiving of 2.5 percent of yearly income. This money can be directly distributed to the poor, or donated through religious institutions.

Fasting. The fast of Ramadan (the ninth month of the Islamic lunar calendar) is celebrated throughout the Islamic world as a fundamental religious duty. The fast consists of daily abstinence from food and drink (and other physical pleasures such as sexual intercourse), each day from sunrise to sunset for a lunar month. Meals are taken before sunrise, and after sunset. The fast is designed both to celebrate the revelation of the Qur'an (which occurred during the last ten days of Ramadan), and to serve for spiritual purification and discipline.

Pilgrimage. While Arab pilgrimage to the Ka'aba at Mecca antedates Islam, Muhammad turned a regional religious festival into an annual act of global religious unity. If physically and financially able, each Muslim should participate in the annual pilgrimage to Mecca once in his lifetime. Muslims find great spiritual power in the simultaneous worship of over two million people from all over the world.

Jihad. Although not one of the Five Pillars, the concept of *jihad* is important in Islam. Widely misunderstood in the West to mean "holy war," jihad literally means "struggle": the command to work for the good of Islam. This religious struggle includes study and meditation, preaching and missionary work, and a wide variety of good deeds. Fighting for the faith—the typical understanding of jihad—is thus only one element of jihad. At times—such as the Arab conquests and the counter-Crusade—the Holy War aspect of jihad has played an important part in Islamic history.

SHARI'A

Foundations. Social and political order in traditional Islamic societies based on a code of religious, civil, and criminal law known as the *shari'a*. Unlike the modern West, where legal codes are usually limited to secular criminal and civil issues, the traditional Islamic legal system proscribes proper behavior for nearly all aspects of life; there is no separation between religious, civil, or criminal law. The basic legal precepts of the *shari'a* derive from the Qur'an and the Sunna, but are interpreted and expanded to deal with new situations by use of principles of precedence, methods of legal reasoning, and the consensus of legal scholars.

The Four Schools. Islamic legal interpretations have by no means been monolithic. Although there have been many schools of legal thought, four have become widespread: the Hanbali, Hanafi, Shafi'i, and Maliki. Although each of these groups share the same basic legal sources (Qur'an and

Sunna), methods of legal reasoning and resultant legal interpretations can differ widely.

The Shari'a and Islamic Fundamentalism. In the late nineteenth and early twentieth centuries many Islamic countries adopted Western-style legal codes under the influence of European colonial powers. One of the principal demands of modern Islamic fundamentalists is to return to the medieval legal roots of Islamic society by reinstating the traditional *shari' a* legal system, making Islamic political and legal thought normative for Islamic societies.

ORGANIZATION AND DENOMINATIONS

Succession Crisis. Following the death of Muhammad in 632, the Muslim community faced a major political and religious crisis. Muhammad had left no clear instruction for succession. While all agreed that no one could succeed to the prophetic authority of Muhammad, a spiritual and political leader needed to be selected for the Islamic community.

Two opposing movements developed. The first, known as the Sunnis, followed the principles of traditional Arab tribal democracy, attempting to elect the most pious Muslim as the successor to Muhammad through a vote of the Islamic leaders. The second group, the Shi'ites, followed an equally strong tradition of Arab patriarchal government, believing that succession to leadership should fall to Muhammad's eldest male relative.

The majority Sunni faction elected Abu Bakr (632–634), Muhammad's closest associate, as his successor, while the Shi'ites chose Ali, Muhammad's adopted brother, cousin, and son-in-law. At this point the Shi'ites agreed to accept the majority position, and followed Abu Bakr. But these two communities eventually split, creating Islam's two major denominations.

Sunnis. The Sunnis have historically been the largest and most significant Islamic denomination: today they include roughly 90 percent of Muslims. A guiding principle of Sunni Islamic thought has been the concept of consensus: Islamic doctrine and practice should be based on the consensus of the majority of the believers.

Shi'ites. Shi'ites make up roughly ten percent of the world's Muslims. They are mainly centered in Iran (which is 90 percent Shi'ite), with scattered minorities in Lebanon, Iraq, and Arabia. The Shi'ite movement has been characterized by religious extremism, factionalism, and frequent political activism. Doctrinally they believe in a line of divinely inspired successors to Muhammad (the Imams), in esoteric interpretations of Islamic thought, and in an apocalyptic eschatology.

Sufis. A final important religious movement in Islam is sufism (Islamic mysticism). Sufis believe that it is possible to attain spiritual unity with God through mystical doctrines, meditation, and rituals. Sufism is not a denomination in Islam, but a religious system of thought and behavior which appears in a multitude of forms in all Islamic denominations. Sufis are widely regarded by Muslims as being extremely pious, often having special spiritual and miraculous powers.

ISLAM AND OTHER RELIGIONS

Islam is a conscious part of the Near Eastern monotheistic religious tradition which includes Judaism and Christianity. Muslims worship the same god as Christians and Jews; Allah is simply the Arabic name for God. Muslims accept the authenticity of most biblical prophets, although they believe the Bible itself has been inadequately transmitted and interpreted. While Jesus is accepted as the Messiah and a great prophet, he is not seen as the divine Son of God. Accepting the divine origins of Judaism and Christianity, Muslims see Muhammad as the last and greatest of the prophets, and believe that the Qur'an supersedes the Bible as scripture. Muslims are admonished to be tolerant of non-Muslims; forced conversion is technically prohibited, but, as with all religions, fanaticism and intolerance are not unknown. Historically this religious tolerance has been only partially extended to "idolatrous" religions such as Hinduism and Buddhism. Islam is a proselytizing religion, with a fundamental goal of converting the world.

THE ARAB EMPIRE, 632–861

In one of the most remarkable conquests in world military history, within a few years of Muhammad's death Arab armies had conquered the entire Near East and were fighting on the borders of China, India, and Europe.

The Arab Conquests

THE RASHIDUN CALIPHS

The first four successors to the prophet Muhammad—known as the *rashidun*, or "rightly guided" caliphs—are widely regarded by Muslims as ideal examples of leadership. Austere and pious bedouin rulers, the rightly guided caliphs guided the early Arab conquests of the Middle East.

CONQUEST OF THE MIDDLE EAST

Syria and Palestine were conquered from the Byzantine empire following the Arab victory at the battle of Yarmuk in 636. Jerusalem, the sacred city of Jesus for Christians, surrendered to the caliph Umar (634–644) in 637. The city would be in Muslim hands for the next half a millennium, a fact which contributed to the origins of the Crusading movement and western European militarism. Egypt was conquered from 639 to 642.

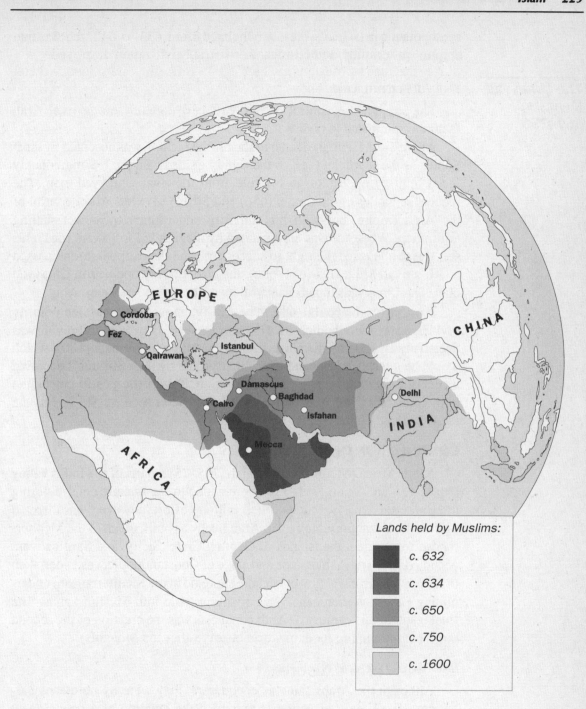

Fig. 9.1 The Islamic World

Mesopotamia and Iran were overwhelmed from 633 to 642, the Sasanid empire was crushed, and classical Zoroastrian civilization destroyed.

The Umayyad Dynasty, 661–750

THE FIRST CIVIL WAR

The struggle for control of this vast new domain among rival Arab factions culminated in civil war.

Ali, 656–661. Ali, the leader of the Shi'ite faction, was accepted by most Sunnis as the fourth and last of the rightly guided caliphs. He immediately faced military opposition to his rule from the rival Umayyad clan. The indecisive battles of the Camel (656) and Siffin (657) left Ali in control of the Arab empire, but with his authority undermined by power-sharing arbitration. When Ali was assassinated by disgruntled followers (661), his son Hasan abdicated the right to succession, and the caliphal throne passed to Ali's rival, Mu'awiya (661–680), the leader of the opposition Umayyad clan. The Umayyads thus became rulers of the entire Arab empire.

Husayn at Karbala, 680. The Shi'ite movement was temporarily revitalized by the rebellion of Ali's son Husayn. However, the revolt was decisively crushed by the Umayyads at the battle of Karbala (680), which would be interpreted as a sacrificial martyrdom by later Shi'ites, becoming a central historical event in Shi'ite religion. This battle is still celebrated with ceremonies and passion plays in Iran, and is seen by Shi'ites as the ideal example of martyrdom for the Faith.

CONTINUATION OF THE CONQUESTS

North Africa (647–698), Turkestan (705–751), parts of the Indus valley (710–713), and Spain (711–732) were added to the Islamic empire during the Umayyad dynasty. Much of their military effort, however, was directed against the Byzantine empire. An Arab fleet was built, much of the Mediterranean was raided, the islands of Cyprus, Crete, Sicily, and Sardina were occupied, and a naval blockade and siege of Constantinople was undertaken (672–679). Arab naval power became supreme in the Mediterranean, undermining European merchants, and diverting trade into Muslim hands. The final result of this century of Arab conquests was the creation of the second largest empire in pre-modern world history (after the Mongols).

EARLY CULTURAL SYNTHESIS

Although the Arabs came as conquerors, they were by no means barbarians. The Umayyad period is noted for the creation of a new elegant cultural synthesis. Having a great appreciate for the cultural heritage of the Byzantines and Persians, the Umayyads rapidly incorporated many elements of those two civilizations. Byzantine and Iranian systems of government, taxation, coinage, and administration were all adopted.

Damascus. Damascus was made the capital of the Umayyad caliphs, becoming a new center of culture and learning. Local artists and architects were patronized, creating a new Byzantine-Islamic style which produced two masterpieces of world architecture: the Great Mosque in Damascus, and the Dome of the Rock in Jerusalem.

THE END OF THE CONQUESTS

The high-water mark of the Islamic conquests came by the mid-eighth century, focusing on three major battles. Constantinople was unsuccessfully besieged from 717 to 718, with the loss of a massive fleet and army. Thereafter, the Muslims were not able to threaten the Byzantine capital for another seven centuries. In the west, the Arab army which repeatedly raided southern France was defeated by Charles Martel and the Franks at the battle of Tours (732), ending the threat of permanent Arab occupation north of the Pyrenees mountains. In Turkestan in Central Eurasia an Arab force with Turkish allies defeated a Chinese army at the battle of Talas (751). Thereafter, Chinese power in the region collapsed, leaving Islam to become the dominant religion and culture of the Turks in the ensuing centuries.

REVOLTS AND CIVIL WAR

Although the Umayyad rulers were noted for their fine aesthetic sense, they were widely perceived by most Muslims as cruel and oppressive tyrants. Despite defeats at Constantinople and Tours, the fundamental reason for the cessation of the Islamic conquests was not European military victory. Rather, the Umayyad empire rapidly decayed due to a series of coups, revolts, and civil wars. Revolts against oppressive Umayyad taxation and administrative policies occurred in Egypt (725), Iran (734–746), and North Africa (740), as rival Umayyad claimants struggled for the throne. In 744 a revolt in Iran under the leadership of the Abbasid family led to civil war and the downfall of the Umayyads (750).

The Abbasid Dynasty, 750–1258

The first century of the Abbasid dynasty represents the high point of classical Islamic culture and political power. Ruling from their capital at Baghdad, the Abbasids ceased major efforts at expanding the empire by military conquest, focusing their attention instead on cultural and economic activities.

THE CREATION OF ISLAMIC CULTURE

The Abbasid period witnessed the final stages in the creation of classical Islamic culture and civilization. Classical Islamic culture derived from the combination of four major elements

Islamic Religion. The foundation of Islamic civilization is the religion of Islam. Its influences permeate all aspects of Islamic society: social, legal, economic, political, artistic, and philosophical.

Arabic Language and Literature. Since the Qur'an was written in Arabic, knowledge of that language became a prerequisite of membership in the Islamic religious and intellectual elite. Arabic thereby became the universal language of scholarship in the Islamic world, playing a role similar to that of Latin in the West. All Islamic scholars, whether ethnically Persian, Turkish, Indian, or African, were required to know Arabic. Arabic secular literary forms also became widespread throughout the Islamic world. Although Arabic continued to be the dominant language in religion and law following the decline of the Abbasid empire, Persian (from the tenth century) and Turkish (from the fifteenth century) also became important literary languages in the Islamic world.

Iranian Arts and Culture. A fundamental cultural influence, especially in art and architecture, came from the Iranian world. Although Byzantine artistic influences predominated in the early Umayyad period, Iranian styles of art and architecture eventually became normative, spreading throughout the Near East, North Africa, Central Asia, and India.

Hellenistic Philosophy and Science. A final element in the Islamic cultural synthesis was the adoption of Greek philosophy and science. The caliph al-Ma'mun (813–833) sponsored an intellectual academy at Baghdad which attempted to translate all of the major Greek scientific and philosophical works into Arabic. The most important figure in this translation effort was the Nestorian Christian Hunayn ibn Ishaq (809–873). The influx of new ideas created an intellectual renaissance in the Islamic world, leaving a permanent imprint on classical Islamic philosophy and science. Throughout the rest of Islamic history Plato and Aristotle were often studied in Islamic universities along with the Qur'an.

From Arab to Muslim. A final important development in the formulation of classical Islamic civilization was the transfer of power from the hands of Arab tribal elites to the larger Muslim community as a whole. During the Umayyad period non-Arab converts to Islam were often treated as second-class citizens, with the most important positions in government and society being held by ethnic Arabs. Under the Abbasid dynasty, Islamic civilization became truly global: Arabs, Iranians, Turks, and Africans now all participated equally in Islamic politics, society, and culture.

THE GOLDEN AGE

Baghdad. The Abbasids transferred their capital from Damascus to Baghdad, which was founded in 762. Thereafter, until its destruction by the Mongols in 1258, Baghdad remained one of the leading intellectual, religious, and cultural centers of the world. The new city grew rapidly until reaching a population of several hundred thousand, attracting the greatest scholars from throughout the Islamic world.

Harun al-Rashid, 786–809. The most famous Abbasid caliph was Harun al-Rashid, whose fictional adventures are immortalized in a collection of Arabic folk tales, the *Thousand and One Nights*. The historic Harun al-Rashid ruled over the Abbasid empire at the height of its power; his court was a renowned center of intellectual and cultural brilliance. The great literature and philosophy which was written during the Abbasid Golden Age has played a cultural role in the Islamic world similar to that of the Greek and Roman literary classics in the West.

FRAGMENTATION AND DECLINE, 850–1200

Political Disintegration, 850–1000

THE DECLINE OF THE ABBASID EMPIRE

Although the Abbasid period witnessed a cultural golden age, politically the Abbasids were faced with numerous serious problems which undermined the strength of the dynasty.

Rebellions. Some Muslims—such as the Umayyads in Spain, various Shi'ite groups, and the Rustamids (777–909) and Idrisids (789–926) in North Africa—never accepted Abbasid authority. Rebellions periodically erupted throughout the Islamic world, including a massive slave revolt in Iraq (869–883).

Struggle for Power. Rival members of the Abbasid clan struggled for succession to the caliphal throne, resulting in a civil war (809–813). As central political control weakened, provincial governors increasingly asserted their independence (Aghlabids in Tunisia, 800–909; Tahirids in eastern Iran, 821–873; Tulunids in Egypt, 868–905). Finally, after 861 the Abbasid caliphs fell increasingly under the domination of their Turkish palace guards, who struggled among themselves for control of the palace and the puppet caliphs. Although the Abbasid dynasty remained in nominal power for several centuries to come, and some elements of their religious authority were preserved, they had become simply one rival state among many.

RESULTS

Political Fragmentation. By the tenth century the Abbasids had become mere figureheads, while the Arab empire had fragmented into numerous successor states. Political and religious unity of the Islamic world was never regained. Political feuding between rival Muslim states has remained a major political problem in the Near East until today.

Regional Cultures. On the other hand, the development of regional political states also contributed to the creation of regional cultural developments. Thus, throughout the Islamic world new centers of cultural, economic, and political life grew up in the capitals of the regional kingdoms. Cordoba in Spain (756), Fez in Morocco (808), Qairawan in Tunisia (800), and Cairo in Egypt (969) all became homes to both independent kingdoms and regional cultures. Thus, although political unity was lost, Islamic culture continued to flourish, developing regional styles and variations.

Invasions and Crisis, 950–1300

As the Arab empire fragmented its political and military power declined, leaving the Muslim world vulnerable to outside intervention. The combination of internal struggles and outside invaders brought the Islamic world to the point of collapse.

INTERNAL STRUGGLES

Rival Dynasties. The disintegration of the Abbasid empire left the Islamic world divided among numerous feuding dynasties. Numerous petty dynasties rose and fell as they were conquered by outside rivals or overthrown by internal opposition. Much of the economic and military strength of these kingdoms was absorbed in such conflicts. The result was an age of political and military chaos.

The Rise of Shi'ite Political Power. Some of the more important political struggles in the Islamic world took the form of ideological conflict between the decaying Sunni caliphate of the Abbasids, and rival Shi'ite groups which attempted to overthrow the old order completely and recreate the Islamic empire on the basis of Shi'ite leadership and ideology. Three major Shi'ite movements developed. The Buyid dynasty from Iran (945–1055) managed to capture Baghdad from the Abbasids in 945. However, they did not feel confident enough to abolish the Sunni Abbasid caliphate, preferring instead to keep Abbasid caliphs as their puppets. The Qaramatians (tenth century), a radical egalitarian peasant Shi'ite movement, arose in Arabia and raided various Sunni cities, even sacking the holy city of Mecca (930), which was under the protection of the Sunni Abbasid caliphs.

Fatimids, 909–1171. The most important Shi'ite dynasty, however, was the Fatimids, who claimed descent from Muhammad's daughter Fatima. A group of Fatimid subversives in Tunisia staged a coup and established the dynasty in 909. Within a few decades all of North Africa had been conquered; in 969 they founded the city of Cairo in Egypt as their capital. Their forces pushed on into Syria and Arabia, and briefly ruled the Abbasid capital of Baghdad itself from 1059–1060. For a few decades it seemed as if the Fatimids might succeed in reuniting most of the Islamic world under a Shi'ite caliphate. However, provincial rebellions and palace coups undermined Fatimid military strength, and by the end of the eleventh century their authority was reduced to Egypt. Thus the rival Shi'ite political and religious movement failed to become dominant in the Islamic world, remaining in the minority until today.

OUTSIDE INVADERS

This period of internal strife and weakness opened the path for outside powers to invade the Islamic world.

Byzantines. The history of the Byzantine empire after 636 is one of almost continual warfare against Islamic states, until the final conquest of Constantinople by the Turks in 1453. During most of this period the Byzantines were on the defensive. However the period of Islamic weakness and disunity provided the Byzantines an opportunity to counterattack. Between 956 and 996 Byzantine emperors led campaigns against the Arabs, reconquering much of eastern Anatolia, Armenia, and Syria. The reconquest of the holy city of Jerusalem was contemplated in 976, but the rise of the powerful Fatimid dynasty in Egypt prevented it. The Byzantines remained a major threat to the Islamic world until the coming of the Turks into Mesopotamia, who crushed the Byzantine army at the battle of Manzikert in 1071, initiating the decline of the Byzantine empire and the Turkish conquest of Anatolia.

Turks. The origin of the Turkish people and their role in world history as a whole is discussed in detail in chapter 15. The Turkish tribes on the northeast borders of Iran had been nominally converted to Islam in the late tenth century. A tribal coalition under the leadership of the Selchuqid clan was formed in the early eleventh century. Defeating the Ghaznavid Iranian army at the battle of Dandanqan in 1040, the Selchuqid Turks conquered Iran, entering Baghdad in triumph in 1055 as the restorers of Sunni orthodoxy against the Shi'ite Buyids and Fatimids. Their armies crushed the Byzantines at Manzikert in 1071, and occupied Syria and Palestine by 1078.

Although their empire disintegrated into several rival dynastic factions shortly thereafter, the Selchuqid Turks had succeeded in stopping the Byzantine and Fatimid advance, thereby reestablishing Sunni ideology as the dominant political force in the Near East. The Turkish invasion of the Near East was a mixed blessing, causing a great deal of social, political, and economic disruption. However, the Turks in many ways revitalized the Islamic world militarily. From the twelfth century on Turkish sultans and warbands formed the core of Islamic military power, leading the Islamic conquests of Anatolia, the Balkans, and India.

Crusaders. Since the original Islamic conquests in the seventh century, many Christian and Muslim religious leaders saw warfare between Muslim and Christian kings as a type of holy war. The military weakness of western Europe left it in no position to oppose the Muslim conquest of the Holy Land, Spain, and Sicily. However, the decline of the Islamic world was contemporary with the revival of European economic and military power in the eleventh century. Beginning in that century, Spanish Christians initiated the Reconquista, a five-century war against Spanish and North African Muslims. Norman adventurers conquered Sicily from the Muslims between 1061 and 1091. The major European assault against the Islamic world, however, was the Crusades. Between 1095 and 1291 seven major armies from Europe repeatedly invaded Syria, Palestine, and Egypt in attempts to capture and hold the holy city of Jerusalem. Although ultimately unsuccessful, the Crusades brought two centuries of turmoil to the Near East, which culminated in the rise of jihad ideology and militaristic Islamic dynasties which ousted the Europeans from the Near East, taking the holy war into the Balkans in the form of the Ottoman Turkish conquests.

Mongols. The most dangerous and devastating outside invaders were the Mongols (see chapter 15). In the century between 1218 and 1336, Mongol armies conquered Islamic Turkestan, Iran, Mesopotamia, Anatolia, and Syria, while threatening Islamic kingdoms in Egypt and India. Baghdad, which had been the spiritual and cultural capital of the Islamic world for half a millennium, was brutally sacked in 1258, and the last Abbasid caliph was executed. It was centuries before Iran and Mesopotamia fully recovered from the slaughter and economic destruction of the Mongols. In the end the Islamic world survived this onslaught, however, both through the military resistance of the Mamluks of Egypt and the sultanate of Delhi in India, and by the eventual conversion of the Mongols to Islam, and their integration as defenders, rather than destroyers, of Islamic civilization.

RECOVERY AND RENEWED EXPANSION, 1200–1500

The threats from Europeans and Mongols led to a military revival in the Islamic world, and the foundation of a number of militaristic dynasties which initiated a second period of Islamic conquests.

Military Dynasties

AL-MUWAHHIDUN (ALMOHADS), 1130–1269

Internal developments in North Africa, combined with the threat of resurgent Christian power in Spain, led to the foundation of the militant al-Muwahhidun dynasty. Their repeated military intervention in Spain succeeded in temporarily stopping the Christian advance. They also participated in spreading Islam into subsaharan Africa, both through conversion and conquest.

AYYUBIDS, 1169–1250

The Crusader invasions led to the formation of an anti-Crusader dynasty, the Ayyubids. Led by Saladin (1169–1193), Ayyubid armies managed to crush the Crusaders at the battle of Hattin and reconquer Jerusalem (1187).

Factional infighting by Saladin's successors prevented the Ayyubids from completely driving the Crusaders from the Holy Land.

MAMLUKS, 1250–1517

A Crusader invasion of Egypt (1249–1250) and the rise of the Mongol threat in the east gave a military clique in Egypt the opportunity to initiate a coup which overthrew the Ayyubids, and established the Mamluk dynasty. The Mamluks were Turkish military slaves who had been purchased as young men, raised in a rigorous military training program, and enrolled in elite military units. These Mamluk warriors were renowned for their military skill in horsemanship and archery, and proved the equal of both the European knight and the mounted Mongol archer. Under their brutal but brilliant sultan Baybars (1260–1277), the Mamluks managed to stem the Mongol advance into Syria and expel the Crusaders from all but a few coastal cities. The last Crusaders were massacred by the Mamluks at the city of Acre (1291). Thereafter the Mamluks ruled Egypt, Syria, and western Arabia for two centuries.

The Second Age of Conquest

The revitalization of the Islamic military system in response to the military and political crises of the tenth and eleventh centuries led to a renewal of the Islamic conquests and conversions throughout much of the Old World.

AFRICA

Islamic military forces reached the Niger valley in west Africa in the eleventh century, conquering the kingdom of Ghana in 1076. Thereafter, Islam became the dominant ideology in the kingdoms of Mali and Songhai. Other Islamic forces conquered Nubia and much of Ethiopia in the fifteenth and early sixteenth centuries (see chapter 12).

BYZANTIUM

After the battle of Manzikert in 1071 Anatolia and the Byzantine empire remained the site of a seesaw battle between Muslim Turks and Christian Greeks for two centuries. By the fourteenth century most of Anatolia was firmly in Turkish hands, and the Ottoman empire began its conquests of the Balkans. Constantinople fell in 1453, and by the early sixteenth century Muslim armies were invading Austria (see chapter 8).

CENTRAL EURASIA

Islam was first established in Turkestan in Central Eurasia in the early eighth century. Thereafter, Islam slowly spread among the Turks, culminating in the conversion of the Selchuqids in the late tenth century. The subsequent conversion of the Mongol Golden Horde, the Chaggatai Horde, and the Ilkhanids in the early fourteenth century made Islam the dominant religion in the western Central Eurasian steppe. The conquests of Tamerlane (1363–1405) confirmed Islam's dominant role in Central Eurasia (see chapter 15).

INDIA

Islamic plundering raids into north India during the eleventh century turned into permanent conquest following the great victory of Muhammad of Ghur at the battle of Thanesar in 1192. By the end of the thirteenth century most of northern India had been conquered by the Muslim sultans of Delhi. Thereafter Muslim power and religion spread by both conquest and conversion into south India and Southeast Asia (see chapter 11).

CLASSICAL ISLAMIC CIVILIZATION

Islamic Social Order

SOCIETY AND ECONOMY

Agriculture. The Near East was home to the earliest agricultural societies in the world, and agriculture remained the primary occupation and source of revenue for most Muslims. The vast majority of people in the Islamic world lived in small farming communities, often on land that was owned by absentee landlords.

Agriculture in the Near East faced two major difficulties due to the arid climate. First, the lack of water meant that there was only limited agricultural land available, nearly all of which had been under cultivation for thousands of years before the coming of Islam. Thus, there was no opportunity to increase the population or tax base by bringing new lands under cultivation. Whereas in Europe, the progressive expansion of agriculture into previously unfarmed lands allowed a tripling or quadrupling of the population during the Middle Ages, in the Near East population levels remained relatively stable. Second, much of the most productive agriculture required intensive irrigation with high levels of labor and government control. In times of chaos, governmental incompetence, or neglect by nomadic regimes, the irrigation system could decay, undermining productivity, and destroying the work of generations of agriculturalists.

The limited agricultural resources meant that the strength of most dynasties rested on their ability to control and exploit the agricultural productivity of the better watered regions such as Egypt or Mesopotamia.

Urban Life. Whereas the economic foundation of Islamic Near Eastern society was agriculture, the cultural and intellectual heart of the civilization was in the cities. Urban life flourished throughout the Islamic world. Many of the great centers of medieval Islamic culture remain important cities today, including Mecca, Damascus, Baghdad, Cairo, Istanbul, Isphahan, Cordoba, Samarkand, and Delhi. Islamic cities were centers of government, manufacturing, trade, religion, fortification, art, and literature. The battle for political power always centered around the struggle for control of the great cities.

Trade and Manufacturing. Trade and manufacturing played a major role in Islamic civilization. From the eighth to the fourteenth centuries Muslim traders controlled most of the major international trade routes of the world, including the west African trans-Saharan trade, the east African sea trade, and the Silk Road. Muslim merchants also played a significant role in the Mediterranean and Indian Ocean trade. A tremendous amount of wealth flowed into the Islamic economy from these trade routes; when Muslim control over these routes was lost to the Europeans beginning in the sixteenth century, it created a major economic depression in the Islamic world.

Manufactured goods from the Islamic world also played an important role in the world economy. For centuries Muslim products such as weapons, metalwork, carpets, textiles, glass, perfumes, and jewels dominated international trade.

Classes and Social Structure. Islamic society was remarkably egalitarian by medieval standards. There were no formal class barriers to prevent social mobility. Commoners frequently rose to high positions in society based on their military or religious achievements. Indeed, slaves were known to have risen to the highest ranks of government, and even overthrown their masters and assumed the throne. Nonetheless, as in any society, groups with power—religious, economic, political, or military—devised various ways to retain that power, and to pass that power on to their descendants.

The bonds which held Islamic society together were not based chiefly on ethnicity, but on kinship groups (tribes or clans), urban and occupational ties, or on religious allegiance. Thus a city or region might have a diverse population which was internally divided into various groups based on clan relationships, guild ties, religious affiliation with different Islamic denominations or Christian or Jewish minorities, and ethnicity. Successful political and social movements needed to be able to mobilize the loyalty of widely diverse social, ethnic, and religious groups. The dynastic instability of much of the medieval Near East is in part based on the weakness of these bonds of allegiance.

Nomadism. Unlike medieval Europe, much of the social, economic, and political history of the medieval Islamic world is tightly tied to the nomadic peoples of the region. Nomadic peoples in the Islamic world centered in three regions: the Berbers of North Africa, the Arabs of Arabia and the Syrian desert, and the Turks and Mongols of Central Eurasia.

On the one hand, relations with the nomads were often mutually beneficial. Indeed, the rise of Islam and the great Arab conquests occurred in the bedouin context of Arabia. Nomads produced meat, wool, and other products from marginal land which could not be farmed. Nomads provided an important source of horses, camels, and mercenaries for service in Islamic armies. As masters of desert travel, nomads were indispensable in maintaining the trade routes across the Sahara, in the interior of Arabia, and on the Silk Road.

However, nomads could also create serious problems for many Islamic kingdoms. Nomad raiders would frequently attack farms and cities, killing people, ruining crops, and plundering property. On occasion, nomadic tribal confederations—such as the original Arab conquests (622–751), the Selchuqid Turks (1040–1170), the Mongols (1218–1310), or the al-Murabit (Almoravid) Berbers in North Africa (1056–1147)—could invade and conquer sedentary dynasties, creating new nomadic kingdoms.

UNITY AMID DIVERSITY

The Arab conquests brought together a wide range of peoples from remarkably different social and cultural backgrounds—including Arabs, Egyptians, Berbers, Africans, Turks, Iranians, Europeans, Mongols, Afghans, Indians, Malays, and Indonesians—and succeeded in forming them into a single global civilization. One of the greatest strengths of Islamic civilization is its remarkable ability to absorb conquered peoples as equals, and adapt itself to a wide range of social structures without losing its intrinsic cultural unity and identity. The basic mechanism of this social unification was the Islamic religion.

Government

THE CALIPHATE

Origins. Leadership of the early Islamic community centered on the caliph, or "successor" of the prophet Muhammad. Although generally interpreted as not possessing any prophetic powers, the caliphs did combine secular and religious authority, and ruled as emperors of the early Arab empire. Because of the immorality and tyranny of some of the caliphs, many Muslims believed that the caliphs lost their legitimacy.

Decline. In the mid-ninth century, the political power of the caliphate was usurped by various bodyguards and warlords as the Abbasid empire disintegrated. Thereafter, caliphs continued to rule only as figureheads in the Abbasid caliphate at Baghdad, but were able to exercise limited moral authority throughout the Islamic world. In 1258 Baghdad was destroyed by the Mongols: thereafter, although a line of "shadow" caliphs and the Ottoman sultans claimed to be successors to caliphal power, for practical purposes, the caliphate had ceased to exist.

THE ULEMA

With the collapse of the moral and political authority of the caliphate, leadership in the Islamic community fragmented. Political power was usurped by warlords and sultans (see below). Religious authority, however, became centered in the Islamic intellectual elite known as the *ulema*. Although technically there is no formal hierarchy or clergy in Islam, the scholars and *qadis* (judges) became the functional leaders of Muslims. Playing a role similar to that of rabbis in Jewish communities, Muslim scholars and judges have exercised practical and doctrinal leadership among Muslims throughout most of Islamic history.

SULTANS

With the decline of the real authority of the caliphate, political power became diffused into the hands of regional *sultans* (authorities). In theory a sultan was a representative of the caliph, requiring official investiture with robes and banners. Sultans always made sure to invoke blessings on the caliph in weekly prayers. However, in reality, whatever warlord managed to usurp political power in a region could expect to receive an investiture from the powerless caliphs.

Real political power in the Islamic world thus came to rest in the hands of the strongest military dictators, creating frequent wars, coups, and assassinations. Sultans maintained their armies (upon which their power rested) by a combination of salaries paid by the central treasury, and by the feudal distribution of land to officers and soldiers. Most governments in the Islamic world were absolutist monarchies, although considerable autonomy was given to cities and villages in internal affairs. Nevertheless, in order to establish their legitimacy among their Muslim subjects, sultans were required to submit to the jurisdiction of pious scholars and judges in all matters of religion and law, thus providing a limitation on their absolutist authority.

Science and Technology

During the Middle Ages, Muslims were among the leading scientists in the world: indeed the Islamic medieval scientific and technological achievement is rivaled only by the medieval Chinese.

MATHEMATICS

Muslim scholars had translated the major Greek works on mathematics into Arabic by the ninth century. Thereafter, they made many impressive advances. One of the greatest Muslim mathematicians was al-Khwarizmi (d. 846), who did the first systematic study of algebra in history. Important discoveries were also made in geometry, trigonometry, and number theory. The impact of Muslim mathematics in the West can be seen by the fact that our Arabic number system was copied from the Muslims; likewise, mathematical terms such as *algorithm* and *algebra* are Arabic words.

ASTRONOMY

As in mathematics, the foundation for Islamic astronomy came from the translation of Greek astronomical works into Arabic. Although retaining a basically geocentric view of the universe, Muslim astronomers made significant advances in both accuracy and theory over their Greek predecessors. Some Muslim astronomers had begun to grapple with the same problems which ultimately led Copernicus to devise his heliocentric view of the universe. The astrolabe was an Islamic invention, which greatly facilitated both astronomical observation, and navigation. Its adoption by the West permitted the beginning of the exploration of the west African coast and the Atlantic. Many of our astronomical terms such as *azimuth*, *zenith*, and *nadir*, are likewise of Arabic derivation.

MEDICINE

Again based originally on Greek sources, Islamic civilization made many important advances in medical science. The two greatest Islamic physicians were al-Razi (865–925), Ibn Sina (980–1037), both of whose works were translated into Latin and remained fundamental medical textbooks in the West until the seventeenth century.

GEOGRAPHY

The Muslims were unrivaled masters of geographical knowledge during the Middle Ages. They had basically accurate descriptions and geographical guidebooks for nearly the entire Old World. Muslim geographers and merchants traveled from the borders of Scandinavia to the Zambezi River in Africa, and from Morocco to China. By far the most famous Muslim geographer was Ibn Battuta (1304–1369), the greatest traveler of premodern times. During his lifetime he visited all of the civilized regions of Africa, the Near East, India, and Southeast Asia. He also traveled widely in eastern Europe, Central Eurasia, and visited China.

OTHER SCIENCES

Muslims excelled in many other areas of technology and science. Irrigation techniques of the Near East were unsurpassed in the world. Military science and technology flourished, with special advances in archery, siegecraft, fortification, and gunpowder weapons. Many of the basic principles of modern chemistry were first discovered and described by Muslim scholars. Muslims were also noted for their textiles, development of paper industries, and metallurgy.

Classical Islamic Culture

LITERATURE

Languages. Islamic literature incorporates works in three major languages. Arabic, the original tongue of the Qur'anic revelation, has remained the most significant cultural and religious language of Islam. Beginning in the tenth century, secular literature began to be written in Persian, which soon developed into the second cultural language of the Islamic world. In the fifteenth century, with the rise of the Ottoman empire, Turkish also became a great literary language.

Poetry. Throughout the Islamic world poetry was considered the supreme literary form. Using complex meters and rhyme systems, with very intricate patterns of grammar and vocabulary, classical Arabic and Persian poetry has remained the standard of eloquence for Muslims. Hundreds of volumes of splendid medieval Arabic and Persian poetry have survived. Themes include the drunken wine-songs of Abu Nuwas (d. 810), the heroic verse of al-Mutanabbi (915–965), the love poetry of al-Hafiz (d. 1389), philosophical quatrains of Omar Khayyam (d. 1132), the sublime mystical meditations of Jalal al-Din Rumi (1207–1273). The greatest work of Persian literature is widely thought to be the *Shahnameh* (Book of Kings) of Ferdowsi (940–1020), recounting in 60,000 verses the legendary exploits of pre-Islamic Iranian kings.

Short Stories. Short stories were widely told and written. The most well known work of Islamic literature in the West is the *Arabian Nights*, or *A Thousand and One Nights*. This amusing collection of folk and fairy tales is generally considered of secondary literary importance by most Arabs. Cycles of legendary heroic tales were composed around famous historical figures such as the caliph Harun al-Rashid, the pre-Islamic bedouin warrior Antar, and the Egyptian sultan Baybars.

Essays. The essay was the most prestigious form of prose in the Islamic world, and its greatest practitioner was al-Jahiz (d. 869). A descendant of black African slaves, al-Jahiz rose to be the master of Arabic prose of the golden age of Baghdad. His works include essays—both serious and comic—on rhetoric, animals, politics, aesthetics, racism, misers, and warfare.

HISTORY

One of the greatest achievements of Islamic literature is in history writing. The works of literally hundreds of major historians have survived, making Islamic history extremely well documented. For the first time in history attention was paid to the sources of information, which were critically evaluated to identify discrepancies in received accounts. One of the great historians of all time was al-Tabari (839–923) whose massive world history covers the age of the Islamic empire. One of the first philosophers of history in the world was Ibn Khaldun (1332–1406), whose *Introduction to History* is still widely regarded as a valuable theoretical introduction to general principles of historical thought.

PHILOSOPHY

The fundamental issue in Islamic philosophy was the relationship between reason and revelation, a question which has vexed philosophers in all traditions. The most significant Muslim theologian and philosopher was al-Ghazzali (1058–1111), whose attempts to answer these questions in favor of revelation became normative for the Muslim world. Many Islamic philosophers carefully studied translations of Plato and Aristotle; the leading Muslim Neoplatonist was al-Farabi (870–950), who wrote a commentary on Plato's *Republic*. The writings of Muslim philosophers, such as Ibn Sina (Avicenna, 980–1037) and Ibn Rushd (Averroes, 1126–1198), were translated into Latin and played a major role in the western European renaissance of the twelfth century and in scholasticism.

ART AND ARCHITECTURE

Art. Most of the surviving art from premodern times is religious. In the Islamic world, the prejudice against representing humans or animals in a religious setting limited the development of some art forms. Sculpture, for example, is quite underdeveloped in the Islamic world. Religious ornamentation tended to concentrate on intricate abstract geometric patterns (arabesques), and the use of exotic styles of calligraphy. Using largely secular themes, manuscript illumination developed beginning in the twelfth century, creating a splendid school of Islamic painting, especially in the later Middle Ages. Highly ornamental styles of metalwork, glasswork, and ceramics are also well known.

Architecture. The most important forms of Islamic architecture are mosques and tombs. The Dome of the Rock in Jerusalem (692) and the Great Mosque of Damascus (715) are the best examples of the early Islamic-Byzantine style of the Umayyad period. The great mosque of Cordoba (tenth century) is illustrative of the cultural splendor of the age of the Islamic empire. The architectural achievements of the later Middle Ages will be discussed below.

THE AGE OF THE GUNPOWDER EMPIRES, 1450–1650

The Military Revolution

GUNPOWDER WEAPONS

In the late fifteenth century a military revolution swept over the Islamic world, following much the same patterns as in the West. The development of effective gunpowder weapons—first artillery and later muskets—created new political and social power structures, which contributed to the disappearance of the older chaotic medieval order. Artillery greatly reduced the military effectiveness of castles and fortified cities, which in turn diminished the independence of decentralized feudal lords. This facilitated the rise of powerful centralized empires which maintained their power by their relative superiority in artillery over regional warlords. Second, muskets further diminished the military power of the medieval mounted military aristocracy. Before the invention of muskets, the military aristocrat, with his superior training and equipment, generally had the capacity to defeat a poorly armed and trained peasant. With a musket, however, a partially trained peasant could kill the most highly trained and costly armed mounted aristocratic warrior. Ultimately, the finest armor proved incapable of stopping a musket ball. Thus, in competition between various armies, those with the best and most numerous cannons and muskets generally proved able to defeat their enemies.

RESULTS OF THE MILITARY REVOLUTION

In the Islamic world this new military situation led to five major developments. First, Islamic governments were able to become increasingly centralized and autocratic. Second, small Islamic states and principalities proved unable to compete in new gunpowder technologies, and were overwhelmed by their stronger and larger neighbors. Third, Islamic states with superior gunpowder technology were able to conquer non-Islamic neighbors in the Balkans, India, and parts of Africa. Fourth, the Central Eurasian nomads, whose military power depended on their skills at mounted archery, were eventually defeated by musket-armed infantry. Finally, although the Ottoman Turks were initially among the world leaders in the development and applications of gunpowder technology, the Muslim world slowly lost ground to the western Europeans, leading to the complete collapse of Islamic military power in the early eighteenth century. This inaugurated nearly two centuries of European domination over nearly all Muslim peoples.

These developments led to the formulation of three "gunpowder empires" in the Islamic world. The Safavids in Iran and the Ottomans in the Near East and Balkans are discussed below. Islamic mughals of India will be discussed in chapter 11.

Safavid Iran, 1501–1753

ORIGINS

Following the collapse of the Timurid empire in Iran in the late fifteenth century, Iran was rent into numerous small unstable principalities, constantly at war with each other. The political and social chaos of the age lent itself to apocalyptic religious fervor. In the mountains of Azarbaijan in northwestern Iran, a small band of fanatical Shi'ite sufis known as the Red Turbans (Qizilbash) were galvanized by their leader Ismail (1501–1524). Proclaiming himself a quasi-messianic figure, Ismail led his troops to a sweeping conquest of Iran and Mesopotamia in the first decade of the sixteenth century. In spite of his defeat by the Ottoman army at the battle of Chaldiran in 1514—after which Mesopotamia was conquered by the Ottomans—the Safavids had become firmly established in Iran, which their dynasty would rule for the next two centuries.

THE SHI'ITE CONVERSION

Origins. Prior to the Safavid conquest, Iran had been largely a Sunni Muslim society, with only small non-Sunni minorities. Nonetheless, Iran had always served as a center of Sufism, esoteric Islamic thought, and heresy. Ismail had risen to power based on his claims to be an incarnation of the twelfth Shi'ite imam, a claim which aroused great excitement throughout Iran. Twelver Shi'ism was declared the official state religion, and a massive proselytizing program was undertaken, both by conversion and coercion. In the end, nearly all Iranians converted to the Twelver branch of Shi'ism.

Significance. The conversion of Iran to Shi'ite Islam in the sixteenth century was to have important effects on world history. First, within Iran itself, Shi'ite culture, thought, mysticism, and philosophy became a fundamental element of Iranian society. Unlike the Sunni branch of Islam, Iranian Shi'ism developed a quasi-clergy, in which the ulema (scholars) were organized into a regular hierarchy; a great deal of social, legal, educational, economic, and political power was usurped by the scholar class in Iran.

Shi'ite Fundamentalism. The conversion of Iran to Shi'ism laid the foundation for the radical political revolution led by the Shi'ite Islamic fundamentalists, who overthrew Shah Mohammed Pahlavi in 1979, and transformed the balance of power in the Middle East in the late twentieth century. Today, the Iranian Shi'ite fundamentalist movement is still a major force in the Islamic world.

THE GOLDEN AGE OF SHAH ABBAS I, 1588–1629

Shah Abbas. Iran reached its political and cultural height during the reign of Shah Abbas I. A man of tremendous energy and brilliance, Abbas led Iran into perhaps its most glorious golden cultural age. Having established a strong military and efficient administration, Abbas set about making his capital at Isphahan one of the great centers of commerce and culture in the world. At its height the population of the city numbered over one million, making it one of the largest, wealthiest, and most splendid cities of the seventeenth century.

Persian Culture. Iranian art especially flourished in the age of Abbas. Iranian painting, architecture, tile working, carpets, tapestries, brocades, metalworking, and ceramics all became internationally renowned. The architectural masterpieces of the age are the Lutf Allah and Royal mosques. The cultural power of this golden age was felt throughout most of the Islamic world. Iranian models in poetry, literature, art, and architecture were adopted throughout the rival Ottoman and Mughal empires. For several centuries Persian became the international language of culture, finance, and diplomacy in the Islamic world. The education of most Muslim gentlemen would include a healthy dose of Persian poetry, much like their contemporaries in Europe were gaining a Classical education based on Greek and Roman models.

The Ottoman Empire, 1299–1924

THE RISE OF THE OTTOMANS

Origins. Various bands of Turkish nomads had settled in the Anatolian highlands following the great Turkish victory over the Byzantines at Manzikert in 1071. In the early fourteenth century these Turks were divided into numerous petty tribes, which vied with each other in attacking and plundering the collapsing Byzantine state. The most important and successful of the tribal warlords was Osman (1281–1326), whose successors would rule Turkey for over six hundred years as the Ottoman dynasty.

Conquest of Constantinople. The Ottomans made steady military progress during the fourteenth and fifteenth centuries, conquering most of Anatolia from rival Muslim Turkish princes, and conquering nearly all of the Christian Balkans as well. Constantinople, the capital of the Byzantine empire, with its massive walls, proved unconquerable until the Turks developed artillery; in 1453 Constantinople fell. Renamed Istanbul, the new capital of the Ottoman empire was destined to become the greatest center of Islamic culture for the next several centuries.

Creation of the Empire. As masters of the new military technologies, Ottoman military expansionism did not cease with the fall of Constantinople in 1453. During the next century and a half they conquered most of modern Serbia, Croatia, Hungary, Romania, Moldavia and southern Russia from the Europeans. Syria and Egypt were conquered from the Mamluks by 1517. Mesopotamia and much of Arabia were added by 1538. Most of North Africa was conquered by 1574. Throughout the sixteenth and early seventeenth centuries, the Ottomans were not only the most important Islamic empire, but the largest and most powerful European state as well.

THE GOLDEN AGE

Sulayman the Magnificent, 1520–1566. The greatest ruler of the Ottoman empire was Sulayman the Magnificent. His policies and personality left a permanent stamp on all facets of Ottoman life. His early career was marked by his modernization of the Ottoman army, and his great military conquests in the Balkans, eastern Mediterranean, and North Africa, creating a vast, prosperous, and secure empire. The political boundaries

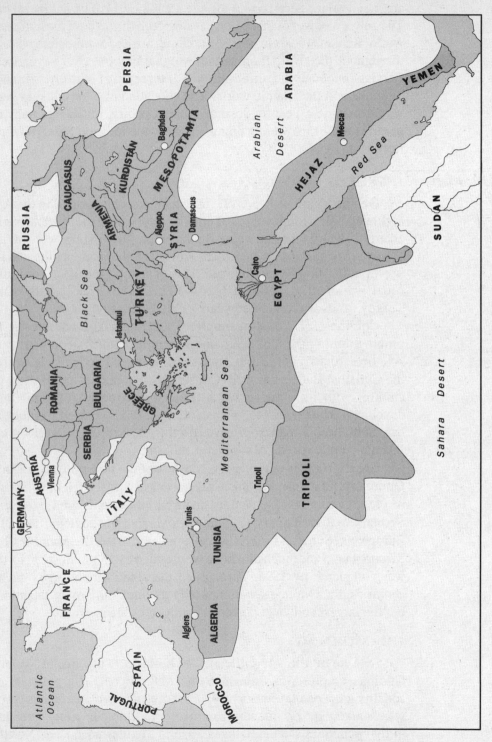

Fig. 9.2   The Ottoman Empire at Its Greatest Extent, c. 1650

established by Sulayman remained essentially unchanged for the next century and a half.

Administration and Law. His second great contribution was the establishment of a sound Ottoman administrative system. Known in Turkish as Sulayman the "Lawgiver," he supervised the creation of an administrative and legal structure for the empire under the direction of the legal genius Khoja Chelebi (1490–1574). Sulayman's and Chelebi's legal and administrative system would last until the great Westernizing reforms of the nineteenth century.

Janissaries. The early Ottoman empire was renowned in Europe for its powerful military, efficient bureaucracy, and autocratic imperial authority. Recruitment for the army and bureaucracy was based in part on the *devshirme*, a "tax" on young Christian boys who were taken in a state of quasi-slavery to the great palace-university at Istanbul for a grueling training course in military and administrative skills. The elite soldiers who emerged from this training program, known as the *janissaries* (new soldiers), were among the finest in the world. The success and longevity of the Ottoman empire is in large part due to its superb administration and army.

Culture. Sulayman presided over a golden age in Islamic culture. The crown of Ottoman culture was its architecture, based on a delightful and harmonious blend of Byzantine, Arab, and Persian styles. The master builder of Sulayman was Sinan (1491–1588), one of the greatest architects in world history. A product of the *devshirme* system, Sinan first served for nearly twenty years as a military engineer in the janissaries. His skills in engineering won him the position of royal architect in 1538; he designed over 300 buildings in the course of his fifty-year career. His masterpiece is the Selimiye mosque at Erdine, in which his engineering skills managed to surpass the size of the great Byzantine dome of Hagia Sofia. The entire architectural "feel" of Istanbul is essentially the extension of the artistic vision of Sinan.

The Arts. Other arts and literature also flourished in the Ottoman empire. Following Persian models, painting and manuscript illustration became an important art form. Metal and tile working were also highly developed. The Ottomans created a complex semi-artificial literary language from a mixture of Turkish, Persian, and Arabic; indeed the educated Ottoman could speak all three languages fluently. Poetry was an integral part of Ottoman aristocratic society; historical writing also flourished.

During the Middle Ages Muslim peoples produced one of the great civilizations of the world, which still has a tremendous impact on modern life. In the year before Columbus set out on his voyage to the New World, most objective observers would have predicted that Islamic civilization, rather than western Europe, was the wave of the future. Muslims controlled most of the major trade routes in the world and were expanding militarily in Europe, Africa, Central Eurasia, and India. From the fifteenth through the sixteenth centuries, the Islamic world witnessed a remarkable period of expansion based on a combination of religious proselytizing, control of trade routes, and military power.

Yet it was the European Christians, rather than the Muslims, who were to transform the world from its medieval to its modern social, economic, intellectual, and political structures. The seventeenth century witnessed the first signs that the Islamic world was beginning to collapse in the face of expanding European economic, technological, and military power.

Selected Readings

Dunn, Ross E. *The Adventures of Ibn Battuta, a Muslim Traveler of the 14th Century* (1986)

Endress, Gerhard. *An Introduction to Islam* (1988)

Ettinghausen, Richard. *The Art and Architecture of Islam, 650–1250* (1987)

Fakhry, Majid. *A History of Islamic Philosophy*, 2nd ed. (1983)

Faruqi, Isma'il R., and Lois Lamya. *The Cultural Atlas of Islam* (1986)

al-Hassan, Ahmad Y., and Donald R. Hill. *Islamic Technology: An Illustrated History* (1986)

Hodgson, M. G. *The Venture of Islam*, 3 vols. (1974)

Holt, P. M. *The Age of the Crusades: The Near East from the Eleventh Century to 1517* (1986)

Hourani, Albert. *A History of the Arab Peoples* (1991)

Ikram, Sheikh Mohamad. *Muslim Civilization in India* (1964)

Itzkowitz, Norman. *Ottoman Empire and Islamic Tradition* (1972)

Kennedy, Hugh. *The Prophet and the Age of the Caliphates: The Islamic Near East from the Sixth to the Eleventh Century* (1986)

Kritzeck, James. *Anthology of Islamic Literature* (1964)

Lapidus, Ira M. *A History of Islamic Societies* (1988)

Lewis, Bernard. *Islam: From the Prophet Muhammad to the Capture of Constantinople* (1987)

Morgan, David. *Medieval Persia, 1040–1797* (1988)

Otto-Dorn, Katharina. *The Art and Architecture of the Islamic World* (1991)

Rahman, Fazlur, *Islam*, 2nd ed. (1979)

Savory, R. M. *Iran Under the Safavids* (1980)

Schacht, Joseph, and C. E. Bosworth. *The Legacy of Islam*, 2nd ed. (1979)

Shaw, Stanford J. *History of the Ottoman Empire and Modern Turkey*, 2 vols. (1976)

Watt, W. M. *Muhammad: Prophet and Statesman* (1961)

Williams, John Alden. *Themes of Islamic Civilization* (1971)

10

Medieval Western Europe

378–476	Germanic invasions, the fall of Rome
481–511	Clovis, king of the Franks, founds Merovingian dynasty
496	Clovis converts to Christianity
597	Beginning of the conversion of the Anglo-Saxons
711–718	Arab conquest of Spain
732	Battle of Tours; Charles Martel defeats the Arabs
768–814	Reign of Charlemagne
800	Charlemagne crowned emperor by Pope Leo III at Rome
843	Treaty of Verdun divides Charlemagne's empire
871–899	Alfred the Great
896–955	Magyar raids in Europe
787–1066	Age of the Viking raids
1016–1035	Reign of Canute, king of Denmark and England
1066	Battle of Hastings, William conquers England
1077	Investiture controversy, Henry IV submits to Gregory VII
1099	The First Crusade conquers Jerusalem
1204	The Fourth Crusade sacks Constantinople
1211–1250	Frederick II, Holy Roman Emperor
1215	The signing of the Magna Charta
1225–1274	Thomas Aquinas, greatest medieval philosopher and theologian

1226–1270   Louis IX, king of France

1229   Teutonic Knights begin conquest of the Baltic region

1265–1321   Dante Alighieri, author of the *Divine Comedy*

1291   Fall of Acre, end of the Crusades to the Holy Land

1305–1378   "Babylonian Captivity," popes at Avignon

1338–1453   Hundred Years' War between France and England

1340–1400   Chaucer, author of *The Canterbury Tales*

1347–1349   The "Black Death," bubonic plague in Europe

1453   Fall of Constantinople to the Ottoman Turks

1455–1485   War of the Roses, civil war in England

1492   Columbus reaches the Americas

The Middle Ages in western Europe is defined as the roughly thousand-year period from the fall of the western Roman empire during great Germanic migrations of the fifth century, until the beginnings of the Italian Renaissance in the fifteenth century. It began with the disintegration of the Roman empire, the decline of urban social order, and the decentralization of political power. It ended with Europe entering a period of tremendous social and intellectual transformation, on the verge of global exploration and expansion. Despite complexity and regional differences, medieval Europe can be broadly characterized as having a monarchical and feudal political structure, an aristocratic feudal military system, a manorial agrarian economy, scholastic intellectual patterns, and Roman Catholic Christian religion.

It was a time of great paradox. Europeans witnessed both the rise of Roman Catholicism and the papacy to its greatest intellectual and political power, as well as warfare, plunder, torture, and inquisition in the name of God. The crucial transformations of western European society during the Middle Ages laid the foundation for the rise of the intellectual, social, economic, and political conditions of the modern world.

EARLY MEDIEVAL EUROPE, 378–c. 1000

Germanic Migrations and Kingdoms, 378–750

GERMANIC SOCIETY

The Germanic (or Teutonic) peoples of the fourth century A.D. originally lived in what are now Germany, Hungary, and Romania. Speaking related Germanic dialects of the Indo-European language group, the Germanic tribes shared the following social characteristics: their economy was essentially nonurban, based on cattle herding and agriculture; their political structure was tribal; their religion was Germanic paganism; their social system was dominated by a militaristic aristocracy.

GERMANIC INVASIONS AND THE FALL OF ROME

Beginning in the late fourth century A.D., under mounting pressure from the Huns from central Eurasia, a large number of German tribes broke through the Roman imperial frontier on the Rhine and Danube rivers, destroying the Roman army. In succeeding decades, they overran Roman provinces in modern Italy, France, Spain, and North Africa, sacking Rome in 410. Although the pretense of imperial Roman authority was maintained for a few decades in the West, for all practical purposes, the western half of the Roman empire was subjugated to Germanic warlords.

THE GERMANIC SUCCESSOR STATES

In the East the Roman state survived as the Byzantine empire (see chapter 8). In the West, however, the Roman state was replaced by six kingdoms created from the amalgamation of Germanic tribes with conquered Roman peoples: the Franks and Burgundians in France, the Visigoths in Spain, the Vandals in North Africa, the Ostrogoths in Italy, and the Anglo-Saxons in Britain. In these regions a new civilization arose, synthesizing Germanic tribal culture and values with Roman civilization and Roman Catholic Christianity. Modern Germany and Scandinavia, however, initially remained relatively unaffected by Roman civilization; some Germanic peoples and the Vikings of Scandinavia continued their traditional warlike pagan culture until the eleventh century (see below).

The Formation of the Six Western European Cultural Zones

Three of the five Romanized and Christianized Germanic kingdoms were destroyed in the sixth and seventh centuries. The Vandals of North Africa and the Ostrogoths of Italy succumbed to the imperial ambitions of Justinian the Great; their kingdoms were conquered and partially absorbed by the Byzantine empire. In Spain, the Visigothic kingdom was overwhelmed in 711 by Arab and Moorish invaders, leading to the establishment of the splendid Muslim Andalusian civilization in Spain. In the meantime, western Europe was transformed into a politically fragmented civilization sharing mixed Germanic, Roman, and Christian characteristics. Politically and culturally western Europe was divided into six major zones.

FRANCE

As the most successful and important Germanic tribe, the Franks settled in France beginning in 482 under their great warlord Clovis (481–511). By the mid-sixth century, the descendants of Clovis, known as the Merovingians, had conquered all of France, extending their domain back across the

Rhine into Germany. For the next three centuries they remained the pre-eminent Germano-Roman state. Their culture well represents the amalgamation of Germanic, Roman, and Christian civilizations, as related in the remarkable history of Gregory of Tours. This Frankish kingdom would eventually serve as the basis for the attempted restoration of unity in Europe by Charlemagne (see below).

IBERIA (SPAIN AND PORTUGAL)

Under Visigothic kings, Spain witnessed a period of relative prosperity, with a fine cultural center developing at Seville under its brilliant archbishop Isidore (560–636). However, in 711 a combined army of Muslim Arabs and Moors (Moroccan Berbers) invaded Spain, crushing the Visigothic army and conquering nearly the entire peninsula. Christian warlords survived only in the mountainous north. Spain entered a period of three centuries of Islamic rule.

GERMANY

The homeland of the original Germanic tribes which overwhelmed Rome, Germany slowly merged culturally with the other Germanic kingdoms of the West. Parts of Germany were incorporated into the Merovingian Frankish kingdom in the sixth century. Additional regions of the old Germanic homelands were conquered and Christianized by Charlemagne, so that by the ninth century the entire region had been culturally and politically merged with the lands of the former Roman empire. Thereafter, imperial Roman ideology, as filtered through the Carolingian empire, served as the basis for attempts to create a Christian German empire.

ITALY

After the Ostrogothic Germanic kingdom was crushed by the Byzantines in the sixth century, Italy suffered a second wave of Germanic invasions under the Lombards, beginning in 568. Thereafter Italy remained politically fragmented among Lombard warlords, Italian princes, the Papal States, and the Byzantines. The northern and central parts were incorporated into Charlemagne's empire in 773. As a whole, Italy remained less affected by Germanic civilization than the rest of western Europe, retaining stronger Roman and Christian influences, and a more urban and mercantile social order.

ENGLAND

When Britain was abandoned by the Roman legions around 400, political authority devolved to local Romano-British military and ecclesiastical leaders. Although an island, Britain was not spared the destruction of the Germanic invasions. In a foreshadowing of the Viking invasions two centuries later, the pagan Germanic tribes of the Angles and Saxons invaded and conquered much of Britain in the late fifth and sixth centuries. (The legends of King Arthur apparently derive from tales of a local British warlord's attempts to battle these invaders.) British civilization as a whole declined during this period of warfare, but in the long run the Anglo-Saxon tribes were converted to Christianity, merging with the local British to form seven small kingdoms by the end of the seventh century. A new Viking-Danish element was added to this mixture of British and Anglo-Saxons in the ninth century, culminating in the formation of a united kingdom of England in the eleventh century, which in turn was to be conquered by the Normans in 1066.

SCANDINAVIA

Scandinavia retained its unique warlike pagan Germanic identity for centuries after the rest of Europe had been Christianized. By the late eighth century the Scandinavians had begun the final phase of the Germanic migrations known as the age of the Vikings (see below).

Carolingian Empire, 751–870

By the late eighth century the authority of the Merovingian Frankish kings had deteriorated to the point where a palace coup in 751 placed one of their officials, Pepin, on the throne. In 772 he was succeeded by his son Charlemagne (772–814) who initiated a policy of imperialism aimed at uniting all Christian lands and forming a new Roman empire. Through a series of bold military conquests and cultural reforms, Charlemagne came close to achieving his goal.

CHARLEMAGNE'S MILITARY POLICY

Charlemagne's fundamental political policy was military expansionism. During the four decades of his rule, he campaigned relentlessly. In Spain, against the power of the Muslim Umayyad caliphate, he secured a strip of territory south of the Pyrenees mountains (795). In Germany he conquered and forcibly converted the Saxons (772–804), and other Germanic and Slavic tribes. In central Europe he defeated the Central Asian Avars who had settled in modern Hungary, and who had long plagued Europeans with their raids (796). He also conquered the kingdom of the Lombards, thereby absorbing northern Italy as well (774). On his death in 814 western Europe was more united and stronger militarily than it had been in over four centuries.

CHARLEMAGNE, THE CHURCH, AND THE IMPERIAL IDEAL

By 800 Charlemagne was supreme in Europe, and was recognized as a world leader of equal status with the Byzantine emperor and Muslim caliphs of Baghdad. After he helped Pope Leo III (795–816) retain his disputed papal throne, the pope reciprocated by crowning Charlemagne Roman emperor on Christmas Day, 800. There were three important implications

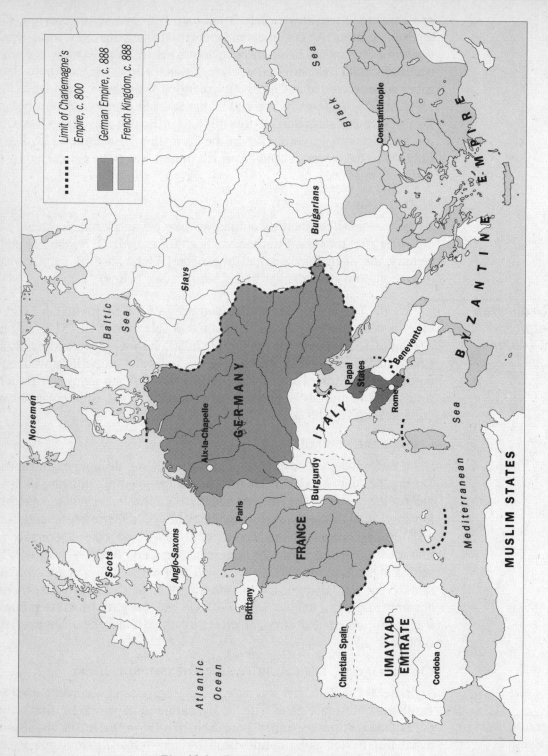

Fig. 10.1   Europe in the Ninth Century

of this event. First, it increased a growing rift between the West and the Byzantine emperors (who claimed the sole right to the imperial Roman title), thereby contributing to the animosities which culminated in the Photian schism in 867. Of greater long-term significance, however, was the creation of an imperial title and ideology in the West, from which would derive the Holy Roman Empire in Germany. Finally, after Charlemagne, western emperors had to be crowned in Rome by the popes, who could thus lay claim to ecclesiastical authority over kings and emperors. This contributed to the growing controversy between Church and State in the West.

THE CAROLINGIAN RENAISSANCE

The most long lasting and significant impact of Charlemagne was intellectual and cultural. He established a court school at Aachen in 781 which was essentially designed to create an educated body of bureaucrats and clerics to administer his kingdom. Under the leadership of the Anglo-Saxon monk Alcuin (735–804), however, the school became the center of a brief cultural renaissance which would have lasting impact on medieval civilization. Among the achievements of the school at Aachen were the modernization of the education system, the regulation of Latin monasticism under the Benedictine rule, and the standardization of provincial government. More important, however, was the development of the Caroline minuscule script which facilitated reading and writing and, thereby, the preservation and editing of earlier Roman and Latin Christian manuscripts. Indeed, most pre-Carolingian books survive only in Carolingian manuscript form.

DISINTEGRATION OF THE CAROLINGIAN STATE

Charlemagne's empire did not long outlast him. Continuing the Germanic tradition that inheritance should be divided equally among all sons, Charlemagne's empire was eventually split among his three grandsons, who immediately commenced a struggle for supremacy. The chaos caused by these wars of dynastic succession, and the related decentralization of political and military authority into the hands of regional warlords, was compounded by a new wave of outside invaders. The empire was first officially divided by the treaty of Verdun in 843. Another three decades of conflict among the descendants of Charlemagne culminated in the final division into three units (roughly equivalent to modern France, Germany, and Italy) by the treaty of Mersen in 870. The final collapse of the empire followed shortly thereafter.

Second Age of Invaders, c. 700–1000

During this period of both imperial strength and decline, outside invaders began threatening western Europe again. These invasions began even before Charlemagne's accession to the throne, and continued during his reign. The military strength of the Carolingian empire at its height proved capable of subduing the Avars, and holding off the early Vikings and Muslims. As the empire dissolved, however, the central army ceased to be effective, allowing the invaders to capitalize on the disintegrating situation.

VIKINGS

Origins. From the north arose the Vikings, the last of the Germanic pagan warrior tribes, as well as the last phase of the Indo-European migrations which had begun almost three thousand years earlier. Expert seamen, the Vikings combined features of explorers, merchants, warriors, and pirates. From their havens in Scandinavia, they set out on nearly annual expeditions to trade and pillage.

Raids. Initially focusing their unwanted attentions largely on the British Isles, they soon spread further abroad to the coasts of France, Spain, and even occasionally into Italy. Others moved eastward to the Baltic Sea, and thence down the broad rivers of Russia where they conquered local Slavic peoples, founding the city-states which developed into the principalities of Russia (see chapter 8). Some even reached the Caspian Sea, raiding Iran, while others took service in the court of the Byzantine emperors, campaigning throughout the eastern Mediterranean. A final group moved westward, discovering and colonizing Iceland and Greenland; some Vikings even established temporary contact and colonies in northeastern North America over four hundred years before Columbus.

Impact. The impact of the Vikings was twofold. First, their raids caused political and economic disruption, especially in England and northwestern France, contributing to the collapse of the Carolingian state. Second, Viking colonists who settled in northwestern France created an independent duchy of the "Northmen," or Normandy as it became known. The Normans, descendants of the Vikings who had become assimilated to feudal French society, became the leaders of the military expansion of Europe in the twelfth and thirteenth centuries, conquering England, southern Italy, playing a major role in the Crusades, and nearly conquering the Byzantine empire.

Ultimately, the Vikings were Christianized in the late tenth and eleventh centuries; their raids ceased, and their society merged with the Christian civilization of western Europe, adding, in the process, a fascinating literature of Viking sagas, myths, and poetry.

MAGYARS

The Magyars were Central Eurasian nomads who migrated eastward out of the southern Russian steppe into Europe in the eighth century. The Magyars arrived in modern Hungary about 896, replacing the Central Eurasian Avars, who had been conquered by Charlemagne. From there they commenced a period of nearly six decades of plundering raids throughout

Germany, northern and central Italy, and eastern France. Their offensive power was finally crushed at the battle of Lechfield (Augsburg) in 955; thereafter they retained their lands in Hungary, and were rapidly sedentarized, Christianized, and culturally assimilated into western Christendom as the kingdom of Hungary. By the year 1000 the new kingdom of Hungary was largely integrated into western European ecclesiastical, cultural, and political circles.

MUSLIMS

Conquests. The Muslim invasion of Europe was part of the greater worldwide expansion of Muslims into the Near East, Africa, and Asia during the Arab conquests in the seventh and eighth centuries (see chapter 9). The invasions of Europe occurred along three fronts. From Morocco Muslims invaded Spain in 711, penetrating into southern France in 732. The Muslims were successful in conquering and integrating the Iberian peninsula into their massive empire; for three hundred years Spain was a major center of Islamic culture, with Muslims politically dominating all but the northern mountains. Sea raids from Tunisia conquered Sicily (823) and pillaged the coasts of Italy. Nearly all of the islands of the Mediterranean were also conquered, with the development of a major political and cultural center in Sicily. Italy was raided frequently, and some coastal towns taken; Rome itself was sacked in 846. The major thrust, however, came from Syria and Mesopotamia into Anatolia, with the ultimate goal of conquering Constantinople and the Byzantine empire.

Battle of Tours. The Merovingian Frankish victory by Charles Martel over Muslim forces at the battle of Tours in 732 is often credited as a decisive factor in stemming the Muslim advance. In reality, the decline of Muslim attacks on Europe was much more due to the breakup of the Umayyad and Abbasid caliphates and the subsequent decades of warfare among rival Muslim successor states, which diverted and absorbed Muslim military strength. By the beginning of the tenth century, Muslim raids into Europe had essentially ceased; within another century the revitalized and militant Christians would take the offensive against Islam.

HIGH MIDDLE AGES, 1000–1450

Charlemagne's grand attempt at the unification of Christendom was ultimately unsuccessful; he never managed to incorporate Spain, England, or Scandinavia at all, while his unification of France, Italy, and Germany was only temporary. Within a few decades of his death, Europe had again politically fragmented into the six fundamental cultural zones which had predated his empire.

The most important characteristics of late medieval western European civilization include: Roman Catholic religion; Latin as the international language of scholarship; Christian influences in thought, literature, and the arts; agrarian economy; and feudal political structures. Despite these shared characteristics, however, many unique developments in the six cultural sub-zones led eventually to the rise of the modern nation-states of Europe.

France

CAPETIAN DYNASTY, 987–1328

Under the Capetian dynasty medieval France achieved a period of prosperity and power. The twelfth and thirteenth centuries witnessed the consolidation of royal power in France, the beginnings of constitutional and parliamentarian institutions, and the growth of a national consciousness. In the thirteenth century Louis IX (1226–1270) led two Crusades, and was considered the most powerful ruler in Europe. The power of the French monarchy culminated in the early fourteenth century under the brilliant if unscrupulous rule of Philip the Fair (1285–1314).

HUNDRED YEARS' WAR, 1337–1453

A succession crisis brought the Valois family to the throne. Earlier English kings had married French princesses, which provided a rationale for English royal claims to the French throne. This succession dispute culminated in the disastrous Hundred Years' War in which English armies, unpaid mercenaries, and peasant rebel bands devastated much of France, while the Black Death and famine swept through Europe.

Joan of Arc. By 1420 it seemed that France would soon succumb to the English. At this point, however, the remarkable Joan of Arc, a young French peasant woman who claimed to have visions from God, led the French to a series of victories over the English. Although ultimately captured and burned as a witch by the English, Joan's faith and example revitalized the morale of the French, who subsequently defeated the English and reestablished a strong monarchy. By the end of the fifteenth century France was again one of the strongest states in Europe.

Iberia

RECONQUISTA

The High Middle Ages witnessed massive changes in Iberian civilization. The fundamental development was the amazing resurgence of Christian principalities on the peninsula in the face of the disastrous disintegration of the Umayyad caliphate into numerous warring Muslim principalities. Muslim political disunity ensured the success of the Reconquista, accelerating the expansion of the new major Christian principalities in the north— Leon, Castile, and Aragon. Despite setbacks caused by the military intervention of North African Muslims, the Christian princes made steady headway. By 1300 they had reconquered most of Iberia from the Muslims, creating in the process a fourth Christian kingdom, Portugal.

UNIFICATION AND INQUISITION

In the fifteenth century the Spanish continued their military expansionism; Aragon conquered southern Italy and the islands of the western Mediterranean. In 1479 the crowns of Aragon and Castile were politically united by marriage. Attempts at cultural unification soon followed. Jews and Muslims were forced to convert to Christianity or be expelled; the infamous Spanish Inquisition attempted to ensure that such forced conversions were authentic, and that Spain harbored no heretics.

EXPLORATION OF THE NEW WORLD

Despite this intellectual and spiritual tyranny, the newly united Spanish kingdom remained vital and powerful. The last Muslim state in Iberia, Granada, was captured in 1492. In that same year, Columbus began the exploration of the Americas, beginning the final phase of Iberian expansionism, the conquest of the New World.

Germany

THE HOLY ROMAN EMPIRE

The fundamental political characteristic of medieval Germany was the perpetual tension between the imperial ambitions and claims of the Holy Roman emperors, and the desire for independence on the part of the German and Italian feudal nobility. Power constantly fluctuated between the emperors and the feudal nobles. Ultimately, however, imperial ambitions in Italy and the desire by the emperors to dominate the papacy led to a rift with Rome. A series of popes undermined the authority of the Holy Roman emperors, contributing to the ultimate fragmentation of Germany into small feudal principalities.

SAXON DYNASTY, 919–1024

Germany in the tenth century was dominated by the Saxon emperors, who had been elected to replace the defunct Carolingian dynasty in 919. The first half of the century was spent in subduing the semi-autonomous dukes of Germany, and in wars with the Magyars who were finally decisively defeated at Lechfield in 955. Thereafter, Otto the Great (936–973) carried out expansionist military operations, conquering northern Italy, and subduing the Slavs to the east, culminating in his being crowned Holy Roman emperor in 963 by the pope in Rome. The Carolingian imperial title, which had lapsed elsewhere, thereafter became the exclusive domain of the Germans.

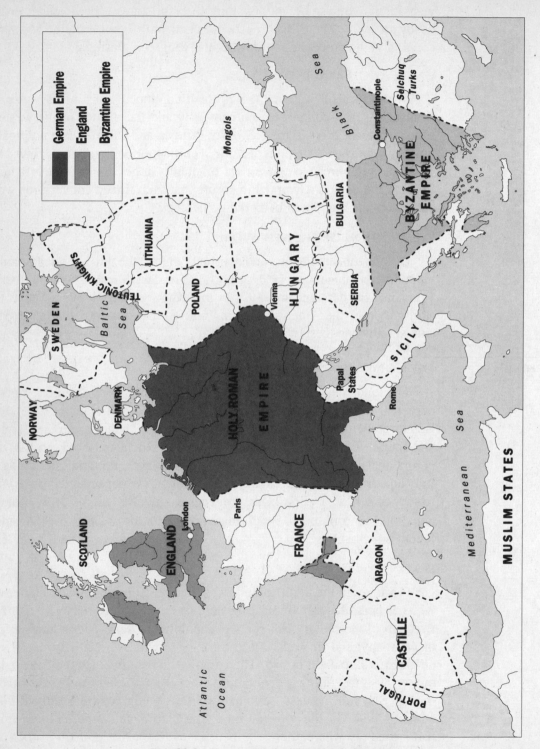

Fig. 10.2   Europe in the Thirteenth Century

SALIAN DYNASTY, 1024–1125

In the eleventh century, the Salian emperors maintained and expanded the territorial domain of their empire. However, the popes resented imperial control over Rome, which threatened to turn the papacy into a dependent imperial ecclesiastical office. They therefore strongly opposed German control over the Church and northern Italy. This conflict culminated in the investiture controversy of 1077 (see below), which was only temporarily ended when Emperor Henry IV submitted to Pope Gregory VII.

HOHENSTAUFEN DYNASTY, 1137–1268

The ongoing conflict between pope and emperor, and Church and State, came to a head during the rule of the Hohenstaufen dynasty. The struggle between popes and emperors continued unabated. Emperor Frederick II nearly achieved his aim of creating a single united empire of Germany and Italy.

DECLINE OF GERMANY

After the death of Frederick II in 1250, however, German power in Italy collapsed. Thereafter, the Holy Roman emperors limited their ambitions to Germany itself, where an electoral system for selecting emperors weakened imperial authority. In the fourteenth century Germany increasingly became a confederation of independent principalities loosely bound by an elected emperor, whose authority had been undermined. The international power of Germany therefore declined.

Italy

POLITICAL DISUNITY

Although perhaps the most prosperous and culturally vibrant region of Europe throughout the Middle Ages, Italy suffered from continual political disunity often verging on anarchy. The fundamental political institution remained small regional states and city-states. The fundamental political issue was the role of the German Holy Roman Empire in Italy. Those supporting German claims were known as the Ghibellines, those supporting papal independence, and thereby Italian independence, became known as the Guelfs. German ambitions in Italy collapsed in the early fourteenth century; northern Italy was left a patchwork of independent states whose economic and cultural vitality led to the Renaissance (see chapter 16).

SOUTHERN ITALY

In 1000 southern Italy was divided into three cultural spheres of influence. Muslims from Tunisia had conquered Sicily, creating an independent Muslim state there. The Byzantines still controlled parts of the south which had been conquered in the days of Justinian the Great. Other regions were in the hands of local Italian warlords. Into this politically fragmented scene a band of Norman mercenaries arrived, seeking employment in the petty wars of the region. Recognizing the opportunities for conquest, one of these Normans, Robert Guiscard, betrayed his employers and began creating a small independent principality for himself. By 1091 the Normans had conquered most of Sicily and southern Italy, creating a powerful state. Culturally, the Norman kings patronized all three of the conquered southern Italian peoples—Muslims, Greeks, and Italians—creating the most tolerant, cosmopolitan, and creative court in western Europe.

FREDERICK II, 1212–1250

Sicily flourished as the center of this new civilization, serving as the base for one of the most controversial and intriguing of medieval rulers, Frederick II. A brilliant man, conversant in half a dozen languages, Frederick reigned over a court in Palermo where Muslim, Jewish, Greek Orthodox, and Catholic scholars held free discourse on all subjects. Hailed as a messianic figure by his supporters, and as the anti-Christ by his papal opponents, Frederick was the most powerful ruler of his day.

Imperial Ambitions. Politically he attempted to unify all of Germany, Italy, and the Crusader states into a single empire, envisioning the popes playing a supportive role similar to the Orthodox patriarch's role in Byzantium. In these plans he was a failure, for the popes consistently and correctly saw Frederick as a threat to their independence. He was twice excommunicated, even though he regained Jerusalem for the Crusaders in 1229. His death in 1250 marked the beginning of the collapse of the imperial ambitions of the Holy Roman Empire.

Sicily. A brief attempt by the French to dominate Sicily ended in the disaster of the Sicilian Vespers (1282), in which the French were either massacred or expelled by their Sicilian subjects. Thereafter southern Italy fell increasingly into the hands of the expansionist Iberian kingdom of Aragon, which solidified its control by the mid-fifteenth century.

GROWTH OF MERCANTILE STATES

A remarkable characteristic of the Middle Ages in Italy was the strength of Italian cities, industry, and trade. Despite problems and periods of decay, Italy's urban and economic life remained vibrant, and substantially superior to the rest of Europe. This was manifest in the growth of the great maritime city-states of Genoa, Pisa, and especially Venice. Holding only small amounts of territory in Italy, the wealth and power of these states derived from industry and control of the trade from the Orient to Europe. The wealth from trade allowed Venice and Genoa to create massive and beautiful cities, with navies, colonies, and conquests ranging throughout the eastern Mediterranean. Venetian merchants such as Marco Polo traveled throughout the entire Old World in search of trade and profit. The wealth and power of these Italian maritime city-states rivaled that of the larger kingdoms and empires of Europe; in 1204 the Venetians even managed to orchestrate the conquest of Constantinople. The cultural manifestations of medieval Italian wealth culminated in the creation of one of the golden ages in world thought and art—the Italian Renaissance (see chapter 16).

England

NORMANS AND PLANTAGENETS

English Expansion. Five major political developments occurred in England during the late Middle Ages. First, William the Conqueror, duke of Normandy (in France), conquered England in 1066, destroying the old Anglo-Saxon monarchy, and creating in its place an Anglo-Norman society with close cultural and political ties to France. For the next five centuries England would play a fundamental role in continental politics. Second, the dynamic Plantagenet royal dynasty (1154–1399) created an increasingly centralized and powerful monarchy. Third, these Plantagenet kings managed to conquer Ireland (1171), Wales (1172), and Scotland (1173), creating a single kingdom of the entire British Isles. Fourth, as both kings of England and dukes of Normandy, Plantagenet kings pursued a policy of continental expansion in France, culminating in their abortive attempts to unite the crowns of France and England during the Hundred Years War (see above).

Parliament and the Magna Charta. Two important new political institutions developed in England during this period. The Magna Charta was a prototype of the U.S. Bill of Rights, a document guaranteeing basic privileges to the nobility. English parliament developed as an early form of representational government. These institutions laid the foundation for modern British parliamentary democracy which had a subsequent fundamental impact on democratic ideology and institutions throughout the world.

WAR OF THE ROSES

English royal ambitions in France came to a disastrous end. With French unity restored by Joan of Arc, and using new military techniques and cannons, the French drove the English from the continent. Meanwhile, England itself was plunged into the War of the Roses (1455–1485), a civil war over succession to the English throne. In the end, strong central government was restored under the Tudor dynasty (1485–1603), which again made England a major power in Europe, and laid the foundation for eventual English global expansion.

Scandinavia

RISE OF MEDIEVAL CHRISTIAN KINGDOMS

The close of the Viking age at about 1000 brought three new elements to Scandinavia: Christianity, cultural and economic ties with Germany and western Europe, and the rise of centralized monarchies. The old Viking homeland was divided into three medieval kingdoms—Denmark, Norway, and Sweden—which eventually developed into modern nation-states.

IMPERIAL AMBITIONS

During the eleventh through the thirteenth centuries various Scandinavian kings attempted to establish their authority over all of Scandinavia. Canute the Great (1016–1035) managed to unite Denmark, Norway, and England into a northern empire which did not survive his death. Imperial ambitions were again raised by Harold Hardrada (1047–1066), whose unsuccessful invasion of England in 1066 weakened the English army, thereby indirectly assisting William the Conqueror's later victory. The Danes revived imperial ambitions, temporarily uniting all of Scandinavia through the union of Kalmar in 1397, but were able to retain a tenuous hold on Sweden only until 1471.

Military Expansion of Europe in the Late Middle Ages

Militarism has been a characteristic of western European civilization from the time of its Greek and Roman origins. During the early Middle Ages much of Europe's military strength was used to defend Europe against outside invaders, or in a seemingly endless array of wars among regional warlords. By the eleventh century, however, Europeans managed to redirect much of the military effort against "outsiders," initiating a period of military expansionism which in various modified forms has lasted until the twentieth century.

REASONS FOR EXPANSION

There are several reasons why western European states began military expansion in the eleventh century. First, most political policy making in Europe was dominated by the martial values of the feudal military aristocracy, who saw war as their legitimate occupation. Second, Europe's major military enemies—the Vikings, Muslims, Central Eurasians, Slavs, and Byzantines—all had entered periods of decline or had disappeared completely by the eleventh century, giving Europeans the opportunity for military expansionism. Third, the growing population and economic wealth of Europe provided the manpower and resources for successful military campaigns. Finally, the Catholic Church provided the ideological basis for military expansion through the concept of the crusades. Medieval imperialism took several forms: wars against the Muslims of Spain and Italy, the crusades, wars against Slavs and Balts in eastern Europe, and campaigns against the Byzantine empire.

THE RECONQUISTA

In Spain, ongoing centuries of warfare between Muslims and Christians led to the eventual slow reconquest of the entire peninsula from the Muslim Arabs and Moors. The Reconquista led to the creation not only of the kingdoms of Spain and Portugal, but to the development of a militant Christian mentality among the Spanish nobility, which would later manifest itself in their conquest and colonization of Latin America in the sixteenth century.

CRUSADES

The most fascinating form of Christian warfare against the Muslims was the Crusades. Conceived as a mixture of pilgrimage and holy war, the goal of the Crusades was the capture of Jerusalem and other holy places in Palestine from the Muslims. Through two centuries and seven major expeditions, the Crusaders fought a relentless war against Islam, only to be eventually defeated and driven from the Near East by 1291. The long-term political impact of the Crusades was to contribute to the revitalization of militant expansionist Islam in the guise of the Ottoman Turks. The Ottomans would ultimately conquer the Balkans in the fourteenth century, and Constantinople in 1453. They thereafter continued to pose a major military threat to western Europe throughout the seventeenth century.

EASTERN EUROPE

Expansion into eastern Europe took the form of a campaign focused on converting the Slavic and Baltic pagan peoples. Germanic imperial ambitions, aided by the militant Christianity of the Teutonic Knights, brought Roman Catholicism and western European cultural and economic influences to the modern regions of Poland, Lithuania, and Estonia.

IMPACT

Medieval western European imperialism nearly doubled western European territory through the conquest or conversion, most of Iberia, Sicily, Croatia, Hungary, Bohemia, Poland, Scandinavia, and the Baltic states (and temporarily, parts of Greece and the Near East). The militant expansionist mentality which originated in this period carried on into the sixteenth century in the conquests and explorations of the Spanish and Portuguese conquistadors in the New World, Africa, and Asia. The Age of Exploration is thus in part the continuation of medieval expansionist policies and ideologies into new regions of the world, and with the aid of new military and naval technologies.

MEDIEVAL CIVILIZATION

The Political Order

FEUDALISM

Origins. By the end of the ninth century Charlemagne's empire was gone; there was no longer a central authority capable of defending the inhabitants of western Europe from its internal and external enemies. In its place was a patchwork of small principalities and kingdoms ruled by warlords who had taken upon themselves the task of defending their provinces from the invaders as the military strength of the central government had collapsed. Forged on the anvil of constant political turmoil and threatened invasion, these warlords organized a decentralized military system which provided maximum manpower for defense at the local level, with minimal control from higher central authorities. This new social, economic, and political order became known as feudalism.

Characteristics. The medieval European feudal system consisted of four major elements. First, the basic structure of feudal society was bound together by an interlocking network of oaths of loyalty and mutual obligation. Feudalism was based on vassalage, by which a warrior would swear to obey and defend his lord; in return, the lord agreed to provide for his warrior vassals' sustenance. Second, wealth in society was largely based on agriculture; wealth derived from control of land. The vassals of the great lords were therefore usually given land rather than direct cash payments in return for their military service and vassalage. Third, political and military power was decentralized to local levels, often giving regional dukes and counts practical independence. One of the major themes of medieval history is the ongoing struggle between royal attempts at centralization, and the nobility's attempts to retain regional independence. Fourth, military power became dominated by aristocratic heavily armored cavalry known as knights. Since the horse, arms, and training of the knight was expensive, military power was monopolized by wealthy aristocrats.

Extent and Impact. Although feudalism was the dominant political institution of the Middle Ages, it is important to recognize that medieval society was composed of a patchwork of overlapping social and political institutions. These included monasteries, church hierarchy, cities, free rural villages, kings, emperors, mercenaries, merchants, and guilds. Various regions of Europe were influenced by the feudal political order at different levels, which varied through time. Thus, for example, France eventually became, for the most part, a highly feudalized agrarian society dominated by a landed military aristocracy. Italy, on the other hand, tended to be more urban, dominated by a wealthy mercantile aristocracy supported by mercenary armies paid in gold and silver. But despite such regional variations, feudalism remained the definitive military, political, social, and economic institution in medieval western Europe.

MONARCHY

Medieval Kingship. An integral part of the medieval European political order was the concept of monarchy. The ideology of monarchy derived from three sources. Concepts of kingship from the Roman empire and pagan

Germanic society were merged during the Germanic invasions. This new synthesis of ideas was then bound together by the Christian idea that kingship was divinely ordained, drawing its power from Heaven through authorization from God's representative on earth, the pope. As a divinely ordained institution, there was little or no questioning of the validity of monarchy during the Middle Ages; there was, however, a great deal of debate about the nature and extent of royal power.

Limitations of Monarchy. Medieval monarchical power was not absolute. It was limited and shared in a number of ways. In theory kings were ultimately subject to the laws of God as interpreted by the pope. Medieval kings could suffer excommunication when they were perceived to have transgressed these laws; disputes between kings and the Church were widespread. At a more practical level, the power of kings was limited by the feudal system, with its decentralized military. Although kings had their own personal lands, revenues, and troops, they were fundamentally dependent for military power on their feudal vassals. They therefore had to govern with the consultation and consent of the feudal nobility. The merchant classes also could influence government policy, since the king was frequently dependent on the merchants for supplies, transportation, and loans.

Attempts at Absolutism. Authority therefore fluctuated among different segments of medieval society; some kings might be extremely powerful, while others were simply one lord among many in a feudal confederation. Some kings attempted to increase their authority by forming consultative coalitions with the nobles and merchants in the form of parliaments. Others attempted to secure obedience by building an independent powerful base of royal lands and mercenaries. The invention of cannons in the late fourteenth was a major factor in increasing royal power, since kings were able to effectively besiege the castles of their feudal vassals which had previously been able to withstand royal assaults with relative impunity. Thus, by the end of the Middle Ages, European monarchy was moving in two contradictory directions. On the one hand, members from different classes of society were increasingly concerned with participation in government in proto-democratic parliaments. On the other hand, kings were attempting to absolutize their power. Tension between representational and absolutist forms of government would continue in Europe into the twentieth century, contributing to various civil wars and the French Revolution.

Society and the Economy

AGRICULTURE

Agrarian Life. As with all premodern societies, the economy of medieval Europe was fundamentally agricultural. The vast majority of people, as many as 90 to 95 percent, worked directly on the land in agricultural pursuits, eating the produce of their own labor. Agriculture was organized into relatively self-sufficient units known as manors, which served as the basis of feudal government and taxation. In the early Middle Ages, agriculture remained relatively primitive and unproductive. As time progressed, however, various agricultural innovations, developing over long periods of time, combined to produce a remarkable agricultural revolution which had numerous important long-term social and political effects.

Agricultural Revolution. The agricultural revolution of medieval Europe was based on several important technological and social developments. The invention of a heavy plow which turned soils deeper during plowing permitted both the replenishing of vital minerals and plant nutrients, and farming in more difficult lands. The development of new yokes and the horse collar allowed the use of the horse in pulling plows; animals could thereby pull heavier plows without choking. New types of crops, introduced from Asia and eastern Europe, provided a superior diet and a healthier population. Methods of crop and field rotation allowed the planting of multiple crops per year, with some lands lying fallow and becoming fertilized by grazing animals. Finally, as population and agricultural technology expanded, new lands which had previously been unproductive—forest, marsh, or rugged terrain—were turned into farm land. The combined result of these developments was that more land was placed under cultivation, and cultivated land became more productive. Population, wealth, and military power therefore increased. There was, however, a serious environmental problem which derived from the medieval agricultural revolution which still plagues us today—deforestation. Estimates are that as much as half of Europe was deforested during the Middle Ages.

Effects of the Agricultural Revolution. There were two major effects of the agricultural revolution. The first was a population increase; more land under cultivation and greater productivity meant that more people could be fed. This brought greater revenues for feudal lords and kings, and increased political and military power for European rulers. Second, and more important, increased agricultural productivity meant that a larger number of people could be fed by the same number of agricultural workers. This contributed both to the rise of cities, and to the development of industry and trade.

URBAN LIFE

Cities. Following the collapse of the Roman empire in the fifth century, urban life and international trade in western Europe declined drastically. The numerous wars accompanying the fall of Rome made international trade dangerous and expensive; it therefore declined. Without international trade, small regional kingdoms and states were forced to become increasingly self-sufficient, further decreasing the demand for trade. Kingdoms thereby suffered economic depression, making them weaker militarily and more susceptible to attack. Cities, whose economic function was to serve as centers for industrial production and exchange, also suffered when they were no longer able to exchange their surplus industrial produce. Cities retained their administrative and cultural functions, but decreased drastically in size.

Revival of International Trade and Industry. The recovery of medieval cities and international trade began in the ninth century, centering initially in Italy, where economic ties with the Byzantine empire had prevented urban life from declining as drastically as in other parts of western Europe. As the western economy began to recover, become more productive, and have surplus products, Oriental trade with Byzantium, the Islamic world, and eastern Europe became increasingly profitable. Italy became the conduit through which most of this trade was channeled. Other regions of Europe began to specialize in certain products for which their environments were especially suited: England for sheep and wool, France for wine, Scandinavia for wood. Specialized regional crafts and skills also developed, such as weaving in Flanders (Belgium).

The Black Death. Economic growth and recovery in medieval Europe was not continuous, nor without social costs. Problems of uncontrolled urban growth and population expansion created pollution and unsanitary conditions in many medieval cities. In 1347 the bubonic plague, known as the Black Death, appeared in Europe, brought by traders from the Near East. The polluted, unsanitary, and rat-infested cities of Europe were havens for the spread of the disease which was spread by fleas on rats. Within a few years all of Europe was infected; one third of the population died. The subsequent psychological and social dislocation created widespread panic, suffering and social disturbances in Europe, culminating in peasant rebellions. Ultimately, however, the inherent strength of the European economy led to eventual social and economic recovery.

Results. By the late fourteenth century, western Europe had begun its economic recovery, with population levels and wealth equaling or surpassing those of the former Roman empire. The reintroduction of gold coinage in this period was a sure sign that wealth was increasing and that international trade was flourishing. Politically, however, Europe remained a disunited patchwork of rival states. The economic recovery and transformation of medieval Europe laid the foundation upon which the later European industrial, social, and technological revolutions would occur.

SOCIETY

Hierarchy. Medieval society was fundamentally hierarchical and aristocratic. Hierarchy—the ordering of society into graded levels—was manifest in all medieval institutions: ecclesiastical, political, and economic. Church hierarchy was organized around ranks of popes, archbishops, bishops, priests, abbots, and monks. Political hierarchy was developed through the feudal system, with its ranks of kings, dukes, counts, and knights, and its detailed network of feudal oaths and obligations. Economically the idea of hierarchy manifested itself in the guild system, which controlled the manufacture, quality, and prices of goods produced, as well as the training and qualifications of artisans and craftsmen.

Aristocracy. Medieval aristocracy was technically hereditary; birth into the noble knightly class provided certain privileges and obligations. However, two alternative aristocracies also existed: that of the Church, and the merchants. Clerical celibacy (priests were not allowed to marry) precluded the transfer of ecclesiastical office from one generation to the next. The ecclesiastical aristocracy was therefore based fundamentally on the merit of individuals as manifested by learning, administrative skills, or piety. This offered an important avenue for social advancement. The mercantile aristocracy was based on wealth. Since wealth could be inherited and derived from land as well as trade, the mercantile aristocracy in many ways was also hereditary and frequently tied to the noble military aristocracy. On the other hand, any family which gained enough wealth through craftsmanship or trade could eventually blend into the ranks of the aristocracy of wealth.

Classes. Medieval society was traditionally divided into three classes: those who fight (knights), those who pray (priests), and those who work (farmers). In reality there was a fourth class, the craftsmen, artisans, and merchants. Although technically part of the working class, the wealth of this segment of society gave it enormous power in cities and certain regions of Europe. Movement between the classes was often difficult, but not impossible. Wealth, skill, and luck could often bring commoners into the ranks of the clerical, feudal, and mercantile nobility.

Religion in Early Medieval Europe

Religion was a fundamental element of medieval Europe, coloring all aspects of society, including politics, war, economic activity, and cultural and intellectual life.

RELIGIOUS DIVERSITY IN MEDIEVAL EUROPE

Throughout most of the Middle Ages religion in western Europe was very closely tied to Roman Catholicism. However, there were numerous minority or rival religious groups within the framework of the dominant Catholic majority.

Non-Christians. Various non-Christian religions existed in Europe. Germanic and Slavic paganism persisted in Scandinavia and the Baltic regions into the thirteenth century. The Hungarians were converted only in the tenth century. Muslims were dominant in Spain and Sicily into the eleventh century; the final Muslim city-state in Iberia, Granada, was conquered only in 1492. Despite frequent persecution, the Jews were also an important and vibrant religious minority in Europe throughout the Middle Ages.

Non-Catholics. Non-Catholic denominations of Christianity existed at various times in western Europe. In the early period, many of the early Germanic invaders of Rome were Arian Christians, who believed that Christ had a fundamentally different nature from God. In Ireland and Britain, Celtic Christianity was dominant through the eighth century. Although generally on friendly terms with the Catholics, the Celtic Christians retained many unique doctrines and practices. Greek Orthodox Christianity also remained important in parts of Italy throughout the Middle Ages.

Dissent. Forces of religious and intellectual dissent, religious renewal, and reform, as well as new religious movements (so-called heresies), all developed within Roman Catholic Europe. Dissent and reform often appeared within the framework of Catholicism, such as the attempts by the Cluniac and Franciscan monastic orders to reform the Church. Other dissenters might formally break with Catholicism, such as the Cathars of southern France (twelfth through thirteenth centuries), and the Hussites in Czechoslovakia (fifteenth century). The forces of dissent and dissatisfaction with Roman Catholicism culminated in the Protestant Reformation of the sixteenth century (see chapter 16).

ROMAN CATHOLICISM

Origins of Roman Catholicism. The Roman empire which disintegrated in the West in the fifth century is often thought of as being Christianized, but it should perhaps more accurately be seen as an empire going through the final stages of Christianization. The fact that the political Empire in the West collapsed just as Christianity was becoming dominant had a tremendous impact on the ideas and institutions of medieval Catholicism. The greatest early Catholic theologian, Augustine (354–430), lived during the sack of Rome in 410 by Alaric the Visigoth. He died in 430 during the siege of the city of Hippo in North Africa by the Vandals. One of his theological masterpieces, *The City of God*, was written to explain why God would allow a Christian Roman empire to fall shortly after it replaced a pagan Roman empire which had lasted for nearly a thousand years.

In the Byzantine empire, the ideology of Eastern Orthodox Christianity was in part based on the writings of Eusebius, who viewed the conversion of Constantine and the foundation of the Byzantine empire at the city of Constantinople as the historical triumph of the Christian empire in this world. But the ideology of the western Catholic Church was founded in an age of crisis and collapse. No empire existed in the west to sustain or dominate the papacy until the ninth century, four hundred years after the fall of Rome.

Christianization of Western Europe. In the first centuries after the fall of Rome, western Christianity reached its lowest ebb. Spain was lost to the Muslims, and England to the pagans. Only France, northern Italy, and parts of western Germany remained firmly Catholic throughout these centuries. The ultimate triumph of Catholicism in the West, despite these setbacks, was due to several factors. First, monasticism provided a mechanism for the preservation of Christian culture, ideas, and literature during periods of political collapse or chaos. Second, for liturgical and ecclesiastical purposes, the Church maintained a literate, educated, and administratively trained clergy. These clerics provided the best available source of valuable bureaucratic expertise to the nascent Germanic kingdoms. Kings therefore allied themselves with the Church in order to avail themselves of the administrative services of the Catholic clergy. Third, the conversion of Clovis (481–511), pagan king of the Franks and founder of the Merovingian Frankish dynasty, to Catholic Christianity in 496 was a crucial event. Had Clovis remained a pagan or become an Arian Christian, Catholicism may not have become the dominant religion of the West. The political alliance between the Franks and the papacy continued throughout the Carolingian dynasty, guaranteeing the survival and triumph of Catholicism. Finally, the faith and missionary efforts of the early medieval Catholics allowed them to convert (often with accompanying military force) the Irish (fifth century), Anglo-Saxons (from 597), Germanic peoples (ninth century), Hungarians (ninth century), northwestern Slavs (tenth century), Scandinavians (eleventh century), and Baltic peoples (twelfth century).

Catholicism Triumphant. Thus, by the eleventh century Roman Catholicism had become the definitive religion of western Europe, replacing, absorbing, or dominating all competing religious systems. During the next five centuries forces of dissent were generally manifest within the framework of Catholicism. Ironically, however, at the height of its spiritual, intellectual, cultural, political, and economic power, the Church was overtaken by a series of crises which ultimately culminated in the Protestant Reformation (see chapter 16).

MONASTICISM

Origins. Monasticism was an attempt by individuals to completely abandon worldly life and devote themselves entirely to the quest for perfection through the worship and service of God. Christian monasticism originated in Egypt in the late third century under the influence of desert hermits such as St. Antony (251–356). From there it rapidly spread throughout the Christian world. By the early sixth century monastic life in western Europe received its classical form through the Rule of St. Benedict (480–543) of Italy, which became the basis of all later monastic orders in the West.

Monastic Institutions. Monasticism required that monks abandon all secular ties by taking three oaths: poverty, chastity, and obedience. The life of the medieval monk was dedicated to prayer and work: prayer referring to the worship of God in various forms, while work included both manual labor as well as scholarship, teaching, and charitable service. Following basic medieval social concepts of hierarchy and aristocracy, monasticism soon became highly organized. Many branches (orders) of monasticism developed, each with its unique organization, hierarchy, regulations, practices, philosophy, and goals. The following are the more important medieval monastic orders (with approximate dates of origin): the Benedictines (540), Cluniacs (909), Cistercians (1098), mendicant orders (whose members were forbidden to own property) such as the Franciscans (1209) and Dominicans (1220), and the Jesuits (1534) of the Counter Reformation.

Impact. The impact of monasticism in medieval Europe cannot be over-emphasized. It spread rapidly, with monasteries becoming major centers of not only worship, scholarship, and culture, but also of economic life and welfare services such as almsgiving to the poor, and hospital care. Many of the greatest artists, scholars, leaders, and saints of the medieval period were monks.

THE IDEA OF CHRISTENDOM

As noted above, by the early eighth century, each of the major regions of western Europe had developed on distinct lines, creating six major zones which have remained the primary cultural and political regions of Europe until today. The distinctions between these regions were in part linguistic, social, geographical, cultural, and political. The major factor binding these six regions together was their common acceptance of Roman Catholicism. Thus arose the fundamental medieval concept of Christendom: spiritual unity within political diversity. Despite vast political and cultural differences in western Europe, all peoples and kingdoms felt they were bound together by a higher power which transcended those differences—their allegiance to Christianity. This concept remained a fundamental political and cultural idea in Europe until the Protestant Reformation in the sixteenth century.

THE QUESTION OF CHURCH AND STATE

Independence of the Papacy. In the Byzantine East, the empire survived the Germanic invasions. There, Greek Orthodox Christianity became intimately linked to the Byzantine empire in a system known as Caesaropapism. The Church became almost a department of the State, with the emperors selecting patriarchs and determining issues of doctrine (see chapter 8). In the West, on the other hand, there was no equivalent political power capable of either dominating or protecting Rome and the papacy, which rapidly passed through the hands of various political powers: Goths, Byzantines, Ostrogoths, Lombards, Franks, and Germans. In the end, the popes emerged as independent political rulers of the Papal States in central Italy.

Conflicting Authority. According to papal theory, all kings of Europe were subordinate to ecclesiastical authority; in reality they were frequent political rivals. Furthermore, as more and more land was donated to the Church as pious offerings, the Church became the major landowner in Europe. In medieval times land equaled wealth and military power; kings therefore wished to control, tax, or otherwise benefit from land within their domain which was owned by the Church. They therefore attempted to select loyal bishops and abbots who controlled Church lands. Such bishops would in effect be feudal vassals of the king, owing the king military and economic support like any other feudal vassal. Thus bishops and abbots could well become feudal nobles; like secular lords, they were often concerned more with their own wealth and power than with the spiritual needs of the Church. Indeed, the papacy itself could be infected with greed and corruption as it passed under the control of emperors and kings. These developments contributed to the growing tension between Church and State.

Investiture Controversy. These tensions culminated in the eleventh century in the investiture controversy. Efforts at clerical reform by the new Cluniac monastic order created a series of conflicts and confrontations. Pope Gregory VII (1073–1085) led the effort for both internal reform and external papal supremacy, advocating the idea that the pope's leadership of Christians extended to kings as well. Henry IV (1050–1106), the Holy Roman Emperor, opposed Gregory's efforts to assert papal control over the investiture (selection) of high clergymen within the German empire. The dispute culminated with Henry being excommunicated by Gregory, which freed all his feudal vassals from their oaths of loyalty, creating political chaos in Germany. To regain authority over his rebellious vassals Henry submitted and did penance to Gregory at Canossa in Italy in 1077. But the dispute was not really resolved; after Gregory's death in 1085, the struggle continued, with German invasions of Italy and the election of rival popes. Ultimately, the struggle between the papacy and the Holy Roman Empire was never fully resolved, greatly weakening not only the political stability of the German state, but also the authority of the popes. In general, however, a power-sharing compromise was reached, allowing the pope absolute supremacy in all spiritual matters, but sharing political authority with the kings.

Crisis and Reform in Medieval Catholicism. By the late fourteenth century medieval Catholicism entered a period of severe spiritual and political crisis. Problems such as clerical corruption and immorality, simony (selling Church offices), heresy, political control over popes (the Babylonian Captivity), and the simultaneous election of several rival popes contributed to the crisis which shook the Church to its foundation. Ultimately medieval

Christendom was split in two during the Protestant Reformation. (These developments will be discussed in detail in chapter 16.)

Significance. In spite of internal problems and rival political and religious movements, Roman Catholicism has remained the dominant religion of Europe to the present. Indeed, although the institutions of Roman Catholicism are often seen as conservative and traditional, it is the only medieval institution which has survived into the twentieth century, making it by far the most significant, flexible, versatile, and enduring institution and system of thought in European history.

MEDIEVAL CULTURE

Medieval cultural history can be divided into two roughly equal periods. The early medieval period from roughly 400 to 1000 is characterized by relative cultural decline. The later medieval period from around 1000 to 1500 is the age of high medieval cultural achievements.

Early Medieval Period

The seeming cultural stagnation of early medieval Europe is in large part a relative phenomenon, due to comparison with the splendid periods of creativity of the preceding Roman empire, and the succeeding late Middle Ages. There were many important cultural developments in the early period.

PRESERVATION OF THE PAST

For the most part, the political insecurity and economic stagnation of the early medieval period did not encourage cultural creativity. One of the major cultural concerns of this period was the preservation of the heritage of past centuries, which was in serious danger of being lost. Indeed, much was lost. Nonetheless, nearly all copies of Roman or early Latin Christian writings which exist today survive because of the efforts of early medieval monks and scholars to preserve the heritage of the past as their world was seemingly collapsing about them.

CREATIVE SCHOLARSHIP

Philosophy and History. Individual genius can be manifest in ages of economic depression and political chaos as well as in periods of stability and prosperity. Three great figures are representative of creative scholarship of the early Middle Ages: Boethius, Gregory of Tours, and Bede. Boethius (480–524) was a minister and educator in the court of the Ostrogothic kingdom in Italy. Falsely accused of treason, he was imprisoned and ultimately executed. While in prison, he wrote his famous *On the Consolation of Philosophy*, which describes how the soul can attain a knowledge of God through philosophy. Gregory of Tours (540–594) was a French clergyman in the service of the Merovingian kings, who wrote the *History of the Franks*. Bede (673–735) was an early medieval English monk who devoted his life to teaching and scholarship. He is most famous for his *Ecclesiastical History of the English People*, which is our major source for the history of England during the early Middle Ages.

Alfred's Court. Various royal courts of the early Middle Ages, notably Charlemagne's, became centers of learning. One outstanding example was the court of Alfred, king of Wessex (871–899) in England. Alfred achieved success not only in putting an end to the violent Danish military raids of the ninth century, but also creating a remarkable renaissance of culture at his court. In addition to promoting Christianity, patronizing learning, and codifying laws, Alfred is noted both for his translation of Latin works into Old English, and his own scholarly writings.

Celtic Christian Culture. One of the remarkable characteristics of this age was the flowering of Celtic or Irish Christianity. Originally a separate denomination of Christianity which eventually merged with Roman Catholicism, the Celtic Christians were known for their highly developed monastic life, their missionary efforts, their preservation of the myths and legends of pagan Ireland, and for their ornamental artwork.

High Middle Ages, 1000–1450

The High Middle Ages was a period of tremendous cultural vitality and creativity. The intellectual, artistic, and literary culture of Europe was completely transformed, in the process creating numerous pieces of magnificent art and literature.

RENAISSANCE OF THE TWELFTH CENTURY

The economic and political revitalization of Europe in the twelfth century—characterized by prosperity, the growth of agriculture, cities, and trade, and military expansionism—was paralleled by equal developments in culture, often called the renaissance of the twelfth Century (in distinction to the more well-known Italian Renaissance of the fifteenth century). Stimulated by fresh readings of the Latin Church Fathers, rediscovery of texts on Roman law and Aristotle, and the translation of Arabic works on philosophy and science from Muslim Spain, the twelfth century was a period of tremendous intellectual development. Unlike the later Italian Renaissance, which was dominated by non-clerical humanists, the renaissance of the twelfth century was almost entirely the province of Catholic monks and clergymen such as Anselm (1033–1109), Abelard (1079–1142), Bernard (1090–1153), and Thomas Aquinas (1225–1274).

Universities. The intellectual revolution of the twelfth century was intimately linked to new educational, intellectual, and cultural centers known as universities. Originating as teachers' guilds (trade unions) at the cathedral school in Paris in the late twelfth century, universities existed largely to regulate salaries, administration, admissions, standards, and curriculum for the training of clergy. As time progressed, however, the fundamental goal of the medieval university became the systematization of all human knowledge on rational principles to improve its teaching and application in the affairs of the world and Church. The medieval university laid the foundations for the eventual rise of the modern university system of higher education.

SCHOLASTICISM

Scholastic Philosophy. The culmination of the medieval intellectual revolution in the thirteenth century was the philosophical system known as scholasticism (the origins of which can be traced back as far as Augustine). The fundamental premise of the medieval scholastics was that the revelation of the scriptures and teachings of the Church (*auctoritas*) are conceptually superior to, but ultimately compatible with, human reason and logic (*ratio*), as found in writers such as Aristotle. Indeed reason can be used to validate the truths of revelation. The relation between reason and revelation is determined through logical argumentation (*quaestio*). Such attempts at rationalizing European cultural and religious norms has become characteristic of European civilization until the present.

Thomas Aquinas, 1225–1274. The greatest proponent and systematizer of scholastic thought was Thomas Aquinas. Despite initial controversy, his works eventually became the basis of much later Roman Catholic theology. Aquinas is still standard reading for a Catholic education, and he has exerted an immeasurable impact on all subsequent Catholic thought.

LITERATURE

Medieval Europeans produced some remarkable works of literature. The barbaric and warlike spirit of the age of Germanic conquests and early Middle Ages is well preserved in the Old English epic *Beowulf*, and in Scandinavian sagas and Irish legends. The medieval epics of the High Middle Ages—such as the French *Song of Roland*, the Spanish *Poem of the Cid*, and the German *Niebelungenlied*—well reflect the aristocratic spirit of the militant feudal nobility of Europe. The lifestyle of the common people of the Middle Ages is brilliantly recreated by Geoffrey Chaucer's *Canterbury Tales*, and Boccacio's *Decameron*.

Chivalrous Romances. Perhaps the most enduring form of medieval literature was the chivalrous romance—tales of knightly adventures, love, and magic. Popular throughout Europe, the most famous cycle of stories centers around the legendary King Arthur and his court, as popularized by Chretien of Troyes, and later Mallory. Arthurian tales have since been retold for centuries, including modern retellings in novels and movies. The medieval chivalrous romance is also the direct literary antecedent of the popular fantasy literary genre of today.

Dante, 1265–1321. The outstanding literary work of the Middle Ages is Dante Alighieri's *Divine Comedy*. In this vast poetic work, Dante describes an allegorical vision of the Afterworld through his descent to Hell, slow progress through Purgatory, and on to a vision in Paradise of God Himself. The *Divine Comedy* perfectly captures the spirit of the medieval mind and soul: deep spirituality, mystical speculation, hierarchical conception of the universe, rationalization, humor, tragedy, and the ceaseless quest for the Divine.

History. History was widely written and read throughout the Middle Ages. The early medieval historians Bede and Gregory of Tours have already been mentioned. Many monks and clerics diligently wrote yearly lists of events in their vicinity in the form of medieval annals. Other writers, however, attempted to analyze, comment upon, and make sense of the historical developments of their age. Important medieval historians include William of Tyre (1130–1185), author of a fascinating history of the Crusades; Matthew Paris (1199–1259), author of a world history; and Ordericus Vitalis (1075–1142), a chronicler of the Normans. Biography was a major historical form in medieval Europe; numerous lives of kings and saints have been preserved, such as the *Life of St. Louis (IX)* by Joinville (1224–1319). The aristocratic and militant spirit of the late Middle Ages is best captured in the *Chronicle* of Froissart (1335–1405), a detailed history of the Hundred Years War.

ART AND ARCHITECTURE

Art. During the Middle Ages murals, mosaics, sculpture, and icons were considered the books of the illiterate, who formed the vast majority of the population. The major patron of medieval art was the Church; the major themes are therefore retellings of the stories of the Bible and Christian history. Numerous art forms flourished; particularly noteworthy are gothic sculpture, manuscript illuminations, and tapestries. Painting was especially important in pre-Renaissance Italy under such masters as Giotto of Florence. Their techniques and styles blend seamlessly with later Renaissance traditions.

Architecture. The two most enduring architectural symbols of the Middle Ages are castles and cathedrals. The numerous huge stone fortresses which dot the landscape of Europe are quintessential representations of feudalism, with its decentralized regional states dominated by knightly aristocracies whose main function was warfare. Cathedrals represent another side of medieval life, the omnipresent quest for God. Cathedral architecture (also known as the Gothic style) developed in twelfth-century France, but it soon spread throughout Europe. Characterized by pointed arches, flying buttresses, huge columns, ribbed domes, gothic sculpture, and vast stained-glass windows, cathedral architecture is a masterful combination of technology, art, and spirituality. It is impossible to enter a cathedral without standing in awe at the splendid concept and design of the buildings, and the literal centuries of human labor and devotion which went into building them.

Politically medieval Europe never recovered from the destruction of the Roman empire. Western Europe remained politically divided, with regional feudal centers of power. Warfare between European states was widespread, causing great human suffering and economic loss. Nonetheless, despite this loss of political unity, cultural unity was retained through the ideal of Christendom. Furthermore, medieval Europe eventually revived economically and culturally. Urbanization, trade, manufacturing, population levels, and prosperity all eventually surpassed Roman levels by the late Middle Ages.

Although the achievements of medieval western Europeans are important in their own right, the new civilization which was coming into being in the late Middle Ages was to have global significance. The civilization of late medieval Europe laid the foundation for the rise of the Renaissance, the Reformation, the Age of Exploration, the scientific revolution, and the Industrial Revolution which, in the coming centuries, would transform western Europe into the first truly "modern" civilization on earth, leading eventually to European political and economic domination of much of the world.

Selected Readings

Barraclough, G. *The Medieval Papacy* (1968)

Bloch, M. *Feudal Society* (1961)

Calkins, Robert G. *Monuments of Medieval Art* (1979)

Contamine, Philippe. *War in the Middle Ages* (1980)

Cook, William R., and Ronald B. Herzman. *The Medieval World View* (1983)

Hollister, C. Warren. *Medieval Europe: A Short History*, 5th ed. (1982)

Knowles, M. D. *The Evolution of Medieval Thought* (1962)

Matthew, Donald. *Atlas of Medieval Europe* (1983)

Riley-Smith, Jonathan. *The Crusades* (1987)

Southern, R. W. *The Making of the Middle Ages* (1953)

Wallace-Hadrill, J. M. *The Barbarian West, 400–1000* (1967)

11

Medieval India and Southeast Asia

535	Fall of the Gupta empire; beginning of medieval India
c. 600	Polynesians colonize Hawaii
606–647	Reign of Harsha in India
c. 650	Beginnings of Bhakti mystical movement in south India
c. 700–1250	Srivijaya maritime empire in Southeast Asia
711	Arabs conquer the Indus valley
740–1310	Chola dynasty in southeast India
753–973	Rashtrakuta dynasty in central India
788–820	Shankara, greatest Hindu philosopher
c. 800	Building of the rock-cut temples at Ellora
c. 800	Polynesians colonize New Zealand
802–1369	Angkor (Cambodia), greatest kingdom of Southeast Asia
849–1287	Kingdom of Pagan (Burma) in Southeast Asia
c. 900	Building of Borobudur Buddhist temple in Java
939	Nam Viet (Vietnam) establishes independence from China
939–968	Krishna II, greatest king of the Rashtrakuta dynasty
c. 1000	Beginning of the decline of Buddhism in India
1000–1027	Seventeen raids of Mahmud of Ghazni into India

1022	Rajendra I of the Cholas conquers the lower Ganges valley
1026	Chola maritime invasion of Southeast Asia
c. 1130	Construction begins on temple of Angkor Wat (Cambodia)
1173–1206	Muhammad of Ghur conquers northern India
1192	Battle of Thanesar, Muhammad of Ghur defeats Hindu kings
1206–1526	Islamic sultanate of Delhi, Muslim expansion in India
c. 1250	Building of the Sun Temple of Konarak
1253	Invasion of the Thai peoples, founding of Thailand (Ayuthia)
1283–1293	Mongol invasion of Southeast Asia and Java
1296–1306	Mongol invasion of north India repulsed by sultans of Delhi
1330–c. 1500	Majapahit (Java) maritime empire in Southeast Asia
1346–1564	Vijayanagar: last Hindu resistance to the Muslim conquest
1398	Tamerlane invades India, sacks Delhi
1403–1433	Ming Chinese naval expeditions visit Southeast Asia and India
1403–1511	Muslims found Malacca, establish control over the strait
1469–1539	Nanak, founder of Sikhism
1485–1533	Chitanya formalize the bhakti worship of Krishna
1498	Vasco da Gama of Portugal arrives in Calicut
1504–1530	Babur of Ferghana (Afghanistan) conquers northern India
1511	Portuguese conquer Malacca, begin to usurp trade
1526–1707	Muslim Mughal dynasty dominates India
1634	Building of the Taj Mahal, finest Islamic monument in India

*T*his chapter focuses on medieval India and Southeast Asia—collectively called South Asia—during the period from roughly A.D. 500 to 1650. The period begins with the invasion of the Huns (c. 455) and the collapse of the Gupta empire (c. 500) (see chapter 3), which brought about political fragmentation in India. It ends with the reign of the last of the great Mughal emperors (Aurangzeb, 1658–1707), the resurgence of political Hinduism under Maratha warlords, and the rise of European power in India.

There were several important developments in medieval South Asia. Hindu political power remained fragmented, and unable to resist Islamic penetration of India. Nonetheless, medieval India was an age of tremendous Hindu cultural creativity in both literature and the arts. Beginning in the thirteenth century, Muslim armies invaded and conquered northern India, *coming to political and cultural dominance. Muslims politically dominated most of India during the next four hundred years, creating a brilliant synthesis of Islamic and Hindu cultures. Indian culture, both Hindu and Buddhist, spread to Southeast Asia, where numerous Indianized kingdoms flourished during the medieval period. Buddhism has remained one of the major cultural influences in Southeast Asia until the present. By the fourteenth century Islam was beginning to make major advances, especially in Indonesia. By the early sixteenth century, the Europeans arrived, providing the final major cultural component of Southeast Asia.*

MEDIEVAL HINDU INDIA

The medieval period in India is characterized by several features. Politically India was divided into numerous regional kingdoms with complex political and military histories, with numerous dynastic changes and military struggles. No region or dynasty was ever able to control all of India for any length of time. Each of the dynasties of medieval Hindu India shared common social, religious, political, and military assumptions, which allowed this unstable political situation to continue indefinitely.

The archaic Brahmanic (Vedic) religion of India was transformed into Hinduism and the popular Bhakti movements. Still, each of these regions developed its own cultural achievements within the greater tradition of Hindu India. The medieval period is noted for important works of art, literature, and architecture.

International trade with the Near East, Central Eurasia, Southeast Asia, and China became an increasingly important economic factor in the power and prosperity of the regional kingdoms. The economy of India became interdependent with the rest of Eurasia.

Medieval Indian Kingdoms

THE MEDIEVAL HINDU FEUDAL SYSTEM

The medieval Indian political system can be described as feudal; it was broadly similar to that of medieval Europe. Political and military authority was decentralized into a large number of small regions, each with local autonomy under warlords. By dominating his neighbors, any of these warlords could eventually rise to supremacy in his region, becoming a great king (*maharaja*). The great king was thus one who had the capacity to control a large number of feudal vassals. These vassals were required to provide tax revenues and military service to their overlord. A strong king with loyal vassals could quickly rise to a position of military power and dominate large regions of India. But under weak successors, the system could just as easily disintegrate back to decentralized local autonomy.

Thus in India we see frequent repetition of a dynastic pattern. A regional warlord rises to power, extending his kingdom by conquest. Eventually the kingdom disintegrates through rule of incompetent successors, social and economic imbalance, internal rebellion of vassals, or external invasion. Thereafter, another warlord would rise to dominance in the region, and the cycle would be repeated. However, this political instability tended not to have long-lasting negative effects on the culture and economy of India, which remained relatively stable throughout the period, despite continual dynastic change.

A great king's control over his feudal vassals was based on a combination of factors. The royal religious ideology allowed kings to legitimize their rule by patronizing the brahmans (priests) and by building temples and monasteries. Great kings could bestow advantages to their vassals through gifts, military protection, privileges, titles, and marriage. Great kings, with superior military resources, could use force to subdue rebellious vassals.

HARSHA

The invasion of the Huns and the collapse of the Gupta empire brought a period of political chaos in northern India during the sixth century. By 600 the Pushyabhuti dynasty had replaced the Guptas as the dominant force in the Ganges valley. Harsha (606–647) became ruler of the Pushyabhuti state, initiating the last major effort of a Hindu king to conquer the entire Indian peninsula. Although successful in his attempts to conquer northern India, Harsha was never able to subdue the south. Following his death, northern India again split into numerous warring regions. The age of Harsha is noted for the great flowering of Sanskrit literature and religious studies, as exemplified by the biography of Harsha, the *Harshacharita*.

REGIONAL FEUDAL KINGDOMS

Development of Regional Kingdoms. Following the death of Harsha, India entered a period of nearly six hundred years of political disunity. During these centuries there were five main political regions in India (Fig. 11.1): (1) The Ganges River valley, centered on the city of Kanauj; (2) the Ganges delta, roughly equivalent to the modern country of Bangladesh; (3) The Indus valley, which was conquered by Arab-Muslim invaders in 711 and thereafter became the center for Muslim power in northwest India; (4) the northwestern Deccan; and (5) the southeast coast of India. Each of these regions was ruled by a succession of dynasties with complex histories. But despite frequent dynastic changes and numerous wars, these five regions remained as the major cultural and political units of India throughout the Middle Ages.

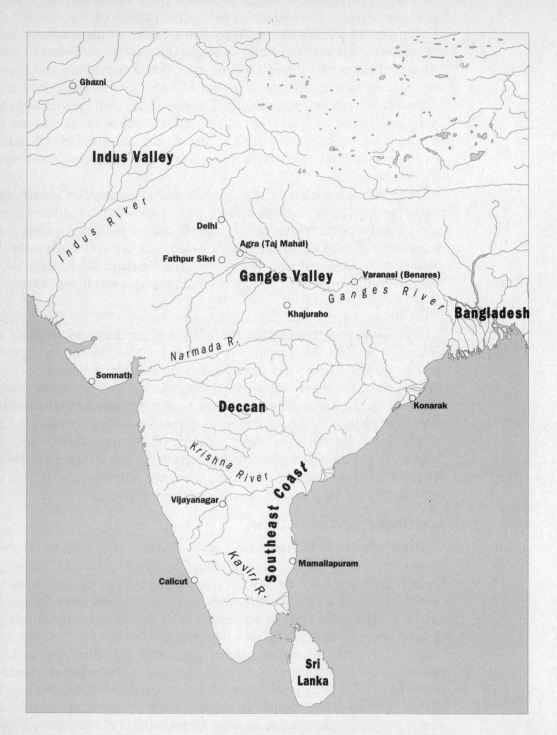

Fig. 11.1   Medieval India

Dynastic Wars. The eighth through the tenth centuries in northern India were characterized by a continuous power struggle between the three major dynasties of the north: the Rashtrakutas in the western Deccan, the Palas in the east centering in modern Bangladesh, and the Gurjara-Partiharas in the northwest. Each of these kingdoms struggled for control of the rich central Ganges plains, creating a cycle of wars lasting several centuries. Each kingdom in turn managed to briefly conquer the Ganges plain, only to be displaced by one of the other three competitors. The politics of this age were described by the political maxim the "law of the fishes" (*matsya-nyaya*)— just as big fish eat little fish so large states are meant to conquer and devour smaller states.

The Rashtrakuta Dynasty, 753–973. The Rashtrakuta dynasty dominated western central India from 753 to 973. Their most successful king was Krishna II (939–968). A great military leader, Krishna II managed to force most of the kings of India to become his vassals. Although he subdued most of his enemies, he was unable to establish firm or lasting control in India. Upon his death his empire collapsed as each regional kingdom reasserted its independence. Ultimately the Rashtrakuta dynasty itself disappeared due to rebellion and civil war in 973. The most famous cultural achievement of the Rashtrakutas was the splendid rock-cut temples at Ellora.

The Rajputs and the Gurjara-Pratihara Dynasty, 725–1050. In the fifth century the Huns invaded and plundered much of northwestern India. In the wake of these invasions many Central Eurasian tribes settled in this area. Their descendants became known as the Rajputs, meaning "sons of kings." Although originally Central Eurasians, the Rajputs soon became Hindus. In 747 they held a great religious ceremony where they were fully adopted as kshatriyas (the Hindu warrior caste), thereby becoming an integral part of Hindu society.

Rajput princes became the founders of several important dynasties in northwestern Indian, such as the Gurjara-Pratihara (c. 725–1050). Just as the Germanic tribes of northern Europe merged with and later supplanted the Roman empire, so the Rajputs eventually merged with the local peoples of northern India, where they became the dominant political force. They were noted for their martial life-style, their tribal social system, and their feudal political organization. Rajput dynasties in the northwest served as one of the major military forces resisting the Islamic conquest of India.

The Pala Dynasty, 750–1199. Although the Pala dynasty of Bangladesh also participated in the military struggle for control of northern India, they were noted especially for their patronage of Buddhism. Buddhist scholarship in India saw its last flowering at the Pala university of Nalanda, which became the leading center of Buddhist thought and scholarship in the world. Pilgrims from all parts of Asia flocked to Nalanda to study Sanskrit and obtain copies of important Buddhist scriptures. Nalanda was in reality a complex city in the form of a massive monastery in which thousands of Buddhist monks and scholars lived, worked, and taught.

The Chola Dynasty, 740–1310. A small feudal family named the Cholas rose to power in south India following the collapse of the Rashtrakutas and Pallavas. The Chola kingdom centered on the southeastern Indian coast and was noted for their control of international trade and their powerful navy. The Chola king Rajendra I (1016–1044) initiated a policy of conquest by land and sea. In 1022 he conquered the entire eastern coast of India up to the Ganges river. In 1026 he continued his conquest by sending a fleet and army to Southeast Asia, raiding Sumatra and Malaya. These military conquests gave the Cholas control of much of the trade between the Near East, India, Southeast Asia, and China for the next century. Numerous embassies were exchanged between China, the kings of Southeast Asia, and the Cholas. These military conquests, and the wealth derived from their control of trade, made the Cholas one of the major powers in Asia, and a cultural center of India in the eleventh century.

The Economy of Medieval India

Merchant Guilds. Control of international and local trade in medieval India was exercised by great merchant families and guilds which enjoyed much power in Indian social life, politics, and culture. These guilds served as allies of the royal families of India, providing wealth through taxation, important products from foreign lands, lending money to kings, and financing cultural activities such as temples and monasteries. Many guilds were powerful enough to create their own armies which could defend the interests of the guilds or be hired as mercenaries by kings.

International Trade. The great merchant guilds of South Asia had trading contacts throughout the Old World. Indians, Arabs, Persians, Turks, Jews, Africans, Malays, Sumatrans, Javanese, Chinese, and even a few Europeans such as Marco Polo intermingled and exchanged products and ideas in thriving market towns of coastal India. A ruler who gained the support of these Indian merchant castes, and controlled major trade routes, thereby gained a significant economic advantage in his struggles with rival dynasties.

Agriculture. Despite the importance of international trade and merchant guilds in medieval India, most of the people—perhaps 90 percent— were peasant farmers, living in small villages. Like all premodern societies, medieval India was basically agricultural. Despite whatever additional wealth and prosperity could be obtained through trade, each state required a strong agricultural base, usually centered in one of the river valleys or deltas. Furthermore, the vast wealth acquired through trade for the most part did little to improve the status or life-style of the common farmers.

Religion and Culture

Archaic Hinduism (often called Brahmanism, referring to its domination by the Brahmans, or caste of priests) underwent significant development during the medieval period, laying the foundation for modern Hindu practices and beliefs. Hindu ideas and art forms dominated the culture of all regions of India until the coming of Islam.

RELIGION

There were several major changes in Indian thought during the medieval period, which differentiate medieval Hinduism from its Vedic antecedents.

Decline of Buddhism. A combination of several factors led to the decline of Buddhism in India. Following the fall of the Palas of Bangladesh, no other major dynasty in India patronized Buddhism. Without the wealth and prestige derived from royal patronage, the influence of Buddhism declined. Only in the fringes of India such as Sri Lanka and Nepal did royal patronage of Buddhism survive. Also, the Muslim invaders of India frequently plundered the wealth of Buddhist temples and monasteries. Without royal patronage to rebuild these institutions, organized Buddhism suffered a serious blow.

Another major factor in the decline of Buddhism in India was its absorption into Hinduism. Medieval India witnessed an ongoing philosophical and religious debate between Hindus, Buddhists, and Jains. In the long run Hinduism seems to have won this debate by absorbing many of the ideas of Buddhists and Jains. Ultimately the Buddha himself was adopted into the Hindu religion as an *avatar* (incarnation) of the Hindu god Vishnu. Thus by the end of the medieval period, Buddhism had declined to a minor religion in India, with many of its ideas having been absorbed into Hinduism.

Shankara, 788–820. A major religious development in Hinduism was the rise of the philosophical system of Vedanta under the influence of the greatest medieval Indian philosopher, Shankara. Shankara played a role in medieval Hinduism similar to that of Thomas Aquinas in medieval Europe. He traveled throughout India writing, teaching disciples, debating Buddhists, and establishing centers for Hindu scholarship. He preached a monistic philosophy, maintaining that all the multitude of Hindu gods were manifestations of a Divine Soul. Indeed, each individual soul was also ultimately a part of the single Divine Soul. His teachings laid the foundation for the eventual rise of neo-Hindu philosophy of the nineteenth and twentieth century. Shankara's philosophical system facilitated the combination of archaic orthodox Brahmanism, ritual, scholarship, the practices of popular Hinduism, and many Buddhist ideas.

Bhakti. Archaic Hinduism centered around dominance of society by the Brahman (priest) caste, emphasizing the study of the Vedas, proper performance of ritual, and correct moral behavior (*dharma*) (see chapter 3). Many of the lower castes of India were unable to fully participate in this complex system of scholarship and ritual, and were thus in a sense excluded from the possibilities of salvation. Beginning in southern India in the sixth century, many commoners began practices which eventually developed into the Hindu religious system known as Bhakti.

The fundamental principle of Bhakti is the emphasis on love of and devotion to God. Bhakti devotees (worshipers) believe that salvation comes through absolute devotion to one of the principal gods of Hinduism, usually either Vishnu or Shiva. Ultimately the Bhakti movement rejected the necessity of both the Brahmanic system of salvation through proper behavior and ritual, and the philosophical system of salvation through knowledge and scholarship. Instead the Bhakti mystics believed that salvation could be attained through meditation, ecstatic trances, absolute faith, and devotion to God.

Naturally, Bhakti found many adherents among lower-caste Hindus and commoners, who where thereby freed from the dominance of the Brahman caste. Many of the saints of the Bhakti movement were ordinary farmers, fishers, or hunters; women were often included in their number. The important scriptures of the Bhakti movement are poetic works and hymns of devotion and praise for the incarnation of the gods Shiva or Vishnu.

Krishna. The most important incarnation of the god Vishnu was Krishna, a hero in the great Indian epic the *Mahabharata*, whose primary religious teachings are found in the *Bhagavad-Gita*. Krishna's rise to importance in medieval Hinduism was linked to the production of several major devotional texts, especially the *Bhagavata Purana* and the *Gitagovinda*, which are still widely read in India. These two books established a complete mythology of Krishna/Vishnu. The worship of Krishna was frequently associated with erotic symbolism and ritual derived from an interpretation of the love affair of Radha and Krishna as an allegory of the love between God and Mankind. Ultimately the worship of Krishna was centralized in Mathura, a city near the legendary birthplace of Krishna. The greatest of the saints of Krishna was Chitanya (1485–1533), who is himself considered by many devotees as an incarnation of Vishnu/Krishna. An ecstatic and eccentric version of the worship of Krishna was introduced to the United States in the mid-1960s as the Hare (lord) Krishna movement.

Culture

Just as in medieval Europe, medieval Indian cultural achievement cannot be separated from religion. Nearly all of the surviving works of art and literature are religious in form and content. The two greatest cultural achievement of medieval India occurred in temple building and associated art forms, and religious literature.

TEMPLE CITIES AND PILGRIMAGE

Royal Patronage. Attempts to legitimize kingship through religious ideology were very important in medieval India. Religious legitimization included performing the proper Hindu rituals and supporting the Brahman caste with grants of land, money, villages, trading advantages, and high positions at court. However, the construction of temples ultimately became the major mechanisms of religious legitimization in medieval India. Paralleling the political, religious, and cultural roles of cathedrals in medieval Europe, Hindu temples became centers of religion, culture, art, and learning. Royal patrons of temples expended enormous wealth in attempting to create temples that would serve not only as signs of their devotion to the gods, but as manifestations of royal wealth, power, and high culture.

Pilgrimage. Following the decline of a dynasty, royal temples often remained major independent centers of political power, economic activity, culture, and religion. The last great Hindu state of medieval India, Vijayanagar (see below), is the best preserved example of a royal temple city. Pilgrimage to many of these splendid temples became an act of great piety and merit. Special festival seasons drew tens of thousands of Hindu worshipers to the temples, which thus came to serve as centers of economic exchange, scholarship, and the exchange of ideas.

Muslim Raids. A vast program of temple building occurred in the eleventh through the thirteenth centuries, with the construction of hundreds of temples throughout India, which remain today as the major works of art of this period. Grants of land and money to these temples made them tremendous repositories of wealth. They thereby became magnets for raids by Muslims beginning in the eleventh century, leading to widespread pillaging and destruction of these cultural monuments.

The Great Temples of Medieval India. Several temples in India are especially noteworthy. The rock-cut temples at Ellora, built by the Rashtrakutas in the eighth century, are an excellent example of Indian engineering and artistic skill. Khajuraho in Orissa, built by the Chandelas, 950–1050, is especially famous for its sculpture, which celebrates the manifestation of the divine presence through human sexuality. The Temple of the Sun at Konarak in Orissa was built by Narasimhadeva I (1238–1264) to represent the massive chariot of the sun god. One of the great temple centers on the southeast coast of India was Mamallapuram (Mahabalipuram), built by various kings of the Pallava dynasty. The "Descent of the Ganges," a splendid rock-cut sculpture over 150 feet high and 220 feet wide, depicts various mythic scenes. The temple complex at Vijayanagar, abandoned following the collapse of the dynasty in 1564, is the best-preserved medieval Hindu temple city.

ART

Many of the great Indian artistic achievements, especially in sculpture, occurred during this period. Sculpture became formalized into a complex system of Hindu iconography, as exemplified by the detailed symbolism of the famous "dancing Shiva" (*Nataraga*).

LITERATURE

Royal patronage of culture in India brought to a peak not only architecture, sculpture, and painting, but poetry and literature as well. There were several important developments in Indian literature during this period. Serving a role similar to Latin in medieval Europe, Sanskrit remained the great unifying cultural and religious language of India, even into the twentieth century. However, by the end of the medieval period, important works of literature began appearing in several regional languages, especially Marathi, Bengali, and Tamil. The rise of these languages was usually associated with both the development of regional kingdoms, whose rulers patronized literature in their regional language, and with the development of popular Bhakti movements, whose saints and teachers—often uneducated commoners—taught in the local languages. Eventually some of the important classical Sanskrit epics and religious writings were translated into regional languages.

Puranas. Another important literary development was the ongoing production of the great Puranas, massive encyclopedias of religious, mythical, historical, and cultural lore. Eighteen major Puranas were written in Sanskrit; some were ultimately translated into the regional languages as well.

ISLAM IN MEDIEVAL INDIA, 1000–1650

The Islamic Conquest of India

THE EARLY ISLAMIC CONQUESTS

The Islamic conquests were one of the most remarkable military achievements in history (see chapter 9). By 711 an Arab Muslim army had conquered the western portion of the Indus valley. In the following decades the Arabs attempted an invasion of India across the Indus River, but a confederation of Indian kings managed to drive them back. Thereafter, the threat of direct Arab intervention into India subsided for several centuries, during which the great rulers of India squandered their wealth and military resources in continual warfare among themselves. Thus the Hindus retained control of northern India for the next four centuries, with the defense of the region against Islamic raids resting largely in the hands of the Gurjara-Pratihara and Hindu Shahi dynasties.

MAHMUD OF GHAZNI (998–1030)

Conquests. By 1000 the Muslims of Iran, with the help of newly converted Turkish mercenaries and warlords, resumed Islamic expansion with

India as a prime target for conquest. Mahmud, the son of a Turkish slave-soldier of Ghazni, became the warlord of most of Afghanistan and Iran. From 1000 to 1027 he launched seventeen campaigns into northern India, striking with an army composed largely of horse archers, armed and trained in Turkish, Central Eurasian fashion. Mahmud's army, with greater strategic and tactical mobility than his Hindu enemies, managed to defeat the Hindu rulers in northwestern India, and to pillage much of the Indus and Ganges regions. Many magnificent Buddhist and Hindu temples were plundered, and the wealth derived from these raids was used to raise more troops for additional expeditions. Thus a cycle of military intervention, plunder, and renewed recruitment was initiated which culminated in the devastation of northern India and the rise of an extremely wealthy and powerful Islamic military state in Afghanistan and eastern Iran.

Culture of Ghazni. From the sack of the temple of Somnath in 1025, Mahmud was said to have plundered 20 million gold coins, the equivalent of nearly six and half tons. With this and other plundered wealth, Mahmud made his capital of Ghazni one of the great cities in the world, a center of culture and military power. Here the great Persian poet Firdausi (940–1020) composed his historical epic the *Shahnameh*, considered by many to be the finest work of Persian literature. Likewise, one of the greatest scientists and historians of medieval Islam, al-Biruni (973–1050), worked under Mahmud's patronage.

Effects. There were several major effects of Mahmud of Ghazni's military expeditions. While bringing great prosperity and wealth to Islamic Afghanistan, his devastation of northern India created an economic crisis in India. His plundering raids, centering on Hindu and Buddhist holy sites, caused a collapse in the cultural, religious, and scholarly life of northern India, creating a spiritual crisis for India as well. As noted above, Buddhism in India never recovered from this crisis. Many of the great cultural monuments of the early Middle Ages were ruined in Mahmud's plundering raids and his fanatical attempts to destroy the forbidden idols of Hinduism. Most important, Mahmud's military victories caused a decline in the political and military strength of northern India, and the rise of Islamic Afghanistan to military predominance.

Decline. Mahmud's kingdom ultimately fell into disarray following his death, and Islamic intervention in northern India slowed for nearly a century. Mahmud's splendid capital at Ghazni was itself plundered in 1173, and today is a ruin. During the twelfth century the Hindu kingdoms of India were thus able to restore their power and wealth to a certain degree, but again squandered much of their resources in warfare among themselves. Although Mahmud's invasions brought no lasting Islamic conquests in India, his raids sapped the strength of the Hindu kingdoms, while bringing power and wealth to the Muslims of eastern Iran, thereby laying the foundation for the final conquests under Muhammad of Ghur.

MUHAMMAD OF GHUR, 1173–1206

By 1173 the Ghaznavid dynasty in Afghanistan had collapsed and was supplanted by the Turkish Muslim warlord Muhammad of Ghur. In 1175, following the earlier pattern of Mahmud, he initiated his first raid across the Indus River. But unlike Mahmud, Muhammad strove for permanent conquest rather than simply raiding India, plundering the available wealth, and retreating back to Afghanistan. In 1192 Muhammad's Muslim army defeated the Rajput king Prithviraja at the battle of Thanesar (Taraori), near Delhi. This victory left all of the Ganges valley defenseless; in the following decade Muhammad's armies swept down the Ganges River valley, ultimately conquering Bangladesh and establishing permanent Islamic rule over all of northern India. Muhammad established the capital for his new state at Delhi, which became the cultural, political, and economic center for Muslims in India for the next several centuries. The resulting sultinate of Delhi lasted from Muhammad's death in 1206 until the rise of the Mughals in 1526.

REASONS FOR ISLAMIC MILITARY SUCCESS

There were several reasons why the Muslims were successful in conquering northern India: (1) Islamic armies adapted the Central Eurasian military tactics of mounted archery into a formalized system which gave them superior firepower and mobility over Hindu armies. (2) The Islamic ideology of *jihad* provided a religious justification for the conquest of the polytheistic Hindus of India. (3) The great wealth of India attracted many warriors from throughout the Islamic world intent on plunder. (4) Islamic society was relatively egalitarian. Islam preached the equality of all worshipers and could thus be attractive to some elements of Hindu society. Some low-caste Hindus, who in many ways were economically oppressed by the higher castes, found conversion to Islam appealing. (5) Rather than uniting to face the outside Muslim threat, the medieval kingdoms of northern India continued to battle one another, thereby undermining their own security and military strength as the outside threat continued to grow and eventually overwhelmed them.

The Sultanate of Delhi, 1206–1526

CHARACTERISTICS

The period of the sultanate of Delhi was one of frequent political upheaval. There were, however, several characteristics of continuity. Islamic administrative and feudal practices replaced the older Hindu system, becoming a permanent feature of Indian society until the coming of the British in the nineteenth century. Hundreds of thousands of Muslims migrated into India, some fleeing from the Mongol conquests and massacres, others seeing India as a "frontier" land of opportunities in government, scholarship, trade, and warfare. Many Indians converted to Islam, creating a truly international society, with a mixture of Turks, Persians, Afghans, Arabs, and many Indian ethnic groups. Ultimately, one quarter of the population of the subcontinent became Muslims. India was thus brought into cultural and financial contact with the wider Islamic world. At the same time the older commercial and cultural ties with Indianized Southeast Asia and Buddhist East Asia declined in significance. Although the initial territory of the sultanate included mainly northern India, Muslim armies continually pressed southward, creating several centuries of ongoing warfare between the Islamic sultanates of the north, and the Hindu kingdoms of the south.

CONSOLIDATION

Administration. The first rulers of Islamic India were the Mamluks (military slaves) of Muhammad of Ghur who usurped power upon their master's death. The Mamluk sultans consolidated the conquests of Muhammad of Ghur into a permanent state, introducing Islamic administrative practices. Large numbers of Muslim scholars from throughout the Middle East flocked to India to obtain government, educational, and military positions in the new kingdom. In the long run, despite the frequent coups and dynastic struggles, the Islamic administration of the sultanate remained relatively stable, with bureaucrats being willing to serve whatever new warlord rose to power.

The Mamluk dynasty was essentially a meritocracy, with the most capable (and frequently the most ruthless) ruler rising to the throne, regardless of any dynastic principle. Indeed, the sultana Razia (1236–1240) was a woman, raised to the throne by a palace coup to replace her incompetent brother.

The Mongol Wars. One of the major contributions of the Mamluk dynasty was its resistance against a series of Mongol invasions of India which occurred sporadically throughout the late thirteenth century (see chapter 15). The Muslim armies of India, having adapted Central Eurasian military practices similar to the Mongols, were one of the few armies in the world which were capable of defeating them. They thereby spared India the devastation which followed in the wake of the Mongol conquests in the Middle East, eastern Europe, and east Asia.

Wars with the Hindu Kingdoms. Under the sultan Ala al-Din Khalji (1296–1316) all Hindu resistance to the Muslims in northern India was finally suppressed. In 1303 he besieged and conquered the final Rajput Hindu stronghold of Chitor, only to find that the Rajput queen Padmavati and thousands of other Rajput women had burned themselves to death rather than be captured by the Muslims. With north India finally subdued, Muhammad ibn Tughluq (1325–1351) began a series of campaigns aimed at extending Muslim rule over all of India. By 1335 he had conquered all but the southern tip of India.

THE COLLAPSE OF THE SULTANATE

However, it would be another two centuries before the Muslims would finally establish long-term rule over all of India. Three factors contributed to the decline and collapse of the power of the sultanate of Delhi. Hindu military resistance to Muslim attacks in the south was galvanized by the rise of the kingdom of Vijayanagar (see below). Following the death of Muhammad ibn Tughluq, a dynastic crisis split the sultanate into a group of feuding successor states. Tamerlane (1307–1405), a descendant of Chingis Khan, who ruled Iran, invaded northern India, defeated the army of the sultanate, and sacked the capital of Delhi in 1398. Thereafter the prestige of the sultanate collapsed, and Muslim India was racked by a series of revolts, coups, and wars between rival sultans.

The Mughal Dynasty, 1526–1707

The fifteenth century in India was a period of extreme political fragmentation and conflict, with numerous small states, both Hindu and Muslim, struggling for the prize of the domination of India.

BABUR (1504–1530) AND THE RISE OF THE MUGHALS

Babur, the founder, and one of the most remarkable rulers of the Mughal dynasty, was a descendant of two other famous conquerors—Tamerlane and Chingis Khan. A man of enormous energy and talent, Babur is noted both for his scholarship (he wrote a massive autobiography), military genius, and excellent artistic sense. He inherited only the small principality of Ferghana, but quickly rose to military dominance in Afghanistan. He modernized his army, mixing traditional Central Eurasian horse-archer tactics with new gunpowder weapons and tactics derived from Ottoman Turkish mercenaries. With this powerful new military system, Babur invaded northern India in 1523. His campaign culminated in 1526 at the battle of Panipat, where Babur's powerful army crushed the more traditional Muslim army of the moribund sultanate of Delhi. By his death in 1530 Babur was master of most of northern India, and had founded the Mughal dynasty which would dominate India for the next two centuries.

AKBAR (1542–1605)

Conquest. Local Indian Muslim rulers took up arms against the Mughal invaders, and nearly expelled them. But in the reign of Akbar, Mughal power was reasserted. In his sixty-three-year reign Akbar subdued all of northern India and Afghanistan, and created a powerful centralized administration and modern army. A system of land reform provided peasants with fair taxes, laying the basis for agricultural prosperity. New wealth was provided by a rising class of artisans and traders, and by international trade with the newly arriving Europeans.

Religious Views. Although raised a Muslim, Akbar took a great interest in all the religions of India, sponsoring a series of debates between the various denominations of his realm, even inviting European Jesuits to participate. In an attempt to unite his Hindu and Muslim subjects into a new united society, he created his own religion, the Divine Faith, with himself as the high priest. His efforts, understandably, were accepted by neither Muslims nor Hindus.

SPLENDOR AND DECAY

In the century following Akbar, Indian Islamic culture reached its highest form. Nearly all of India was united into a single prosperous state and Islamic arts flourished. However, the tyranny, oppressive taxes, and failed conquests of Aurangzeb (1658–1707) ultimately led to the collapse of Mughal power, sparking massive rebellions of the Rajputs, Sikhs, and Marathas under Shivaji (1627–1680). By the eighteenth century India was again in political chaos, and was ripe for the eventual conquest by the British. Mughal emperors continued to rule at Delhi as powerless puppets until the last ruler was finally deposed by the British in 1858.

Islamic Culture in India

The cultural achievements of Islamic India derive from two main sources of inspiration: Islamic Persian culture, and indigenous Hindu cultural forms, adapted to the tastes and requirements of Islamic rulers.

LITERATURE

Islamic literature in India was based on the models supplied by the courts of Islamic Persia. Numerous scholars and administrators from Persia were hired by the sultans of Delhi, bringing with them their Persian cultural heritage. Poetry and history writing in Persian especially flourished. Among the notable works of history in Islamic India are the *Baburnama*, an autobiography by the conqueror Babur, and the *Akbarnama*, a biography of Akbar. Some Sanskrit literature, most notably the *Mahabharata*, was translated into Persian for the entertainment of Muslim sultans.

PAINTING

The arts of Islamic India flourished in two major areas: painting and architecture. The Mughal emperors patronized a splendid school of painting combining influences from Persia, China, and India. Numerous large albums of miniatures and illuminated manuscripts depict delightful details of Mughal court life and military campaigns.

ARCHITECTURE

Indian Islamic architecture includes mosques, palaces, and tombs. Even the fortifications of medieval India were often built with a style and beauty which renders them works of art. Among the best examples of the vibrant Islamic architecture of the early sultanate is the Qutb mosque at Delhi with its splendid minaret (c. 1200), and the Mughal palace complex at Fathpur Sikri.

Taj Mahal. However, the most splendid example of Indian Islamic architecture is the magnificent Taj Mahal. Built by the Mughal Shah Jahan (1627–1658) in 1634 as a tomb for his beloved wife Mumtaz Mahal, the Taj Mahal is considered by many to be the most beautiful building in the world.

The Hindu Reaction to Muslim Domination

The Hindus of India reacted to Muslim domination in various ways. Ultimately, however, Hindu religion and culture survived both five centuries of Muslim domination, and an additional two centuries of European domination to reemerge in the late nineteenth century to lay the foundation for the modern state of India.

CONVERSION

Many Hindus and Buddhists reacted to the Islamic conquests by conversion. Conversion to Islam by Indians came about for many reasons. Some members of the lower castes saw Islam as a path to social advancement by freeing them from the domination of the Hindu higher castes. Others believed that the Islamic victories in battle were a sign of the superiority of Allah over the gods of India. Still others converted because they became convinced that Islam was the true religion. Ultimately, by a combination of conversion of Indians and migration of Muslims from the Near East, a quarter of the population of the Indian subcontinent became Muslim.

ACCOMMODATION

Other Hindus managed to accommodate their lives to the new invaders. Hindus could be found serving as administrators, soldiers, and artisans for the Muslim sultans. Although some of the initial Muslim conquests were motivated by religious fanaticism, and there were cases of religious intolerance and persecution (under Aurangzeb, for example), for the most part Muslims and Hindus learned to live in relative peace with each other.

BHAKTI

Although the Bhakti movement of Hinduism had its origins in southern India in the sixth century, the beliefs and practices of the Bhakti devotees facilitated the survival of Hinduism in the period of Islamic domination. By focusing on personal devotion to God, the Bhakti devotee could continue his worship even when the great temples, priesthoods, and ritual systems of Hinduism had been disrupted by Islamic rulers.

SIKHS

Hinduism has always been a flexible religion, and some Hindus absorbed many Muslim religious ideas and practices during the period of Islamic domination. The most important syncretistic movement was founded by the Bhakti saint Kabir (1440–1518), who felt that Hinduism and Islam were both different forms of the worship of the same god. His teachings were expanded by his disciple Nanak (1469–1539). However, rather than serving as a mechanism to unite Hinduism and Islam, the teachings of Nanak led to the foundation of an entirely new religious community, the Sikhs. Ultimately, Sikhs became the major ethnic group in northwest India, and they remain an important minority in India today.

VIJAYANAGAR AND MILITARY RESISTANCE

A final reaction to the Islamic conquest was continued military resistance. No Muslim ruler was ever able to conquer all of India; throughout the Islamic period Hindu kingdoms continued to exist and resist. The most important of these was the kingdom of Vijayanagar (1336–1565) in southern India. Founded in the wake of the invasions of Muhammad ibn Tughluq, the kingdom of Vijayanagar led the Hindu resistance against Islam for two centuries. Their capital, Vijayanagar, was a splendid and wealthy center of Hindu culture. Its ruins remain today as the best example of a medieval Hindu temple-city. Although the kingdom was destroyed by Muslims equipped with firearms in 1565, other independent Hindu states continued military resistance against the Muslims until all of India was eventually subdued by the British in the nineteenth century.

RESULTS

The centuries of conflict between Hindus and Muslims created numerous problems for the eventual creation of modern states in the Indian subcontinent. When independence came after World War II, it became necessary to divide the region into a Hindu state (India) and two Muslim states (Pakistan and Bangladesh). Interreligious conflicts remain a social and political problem today.

SOUTHEAST ASIA

During the medieval period Southeast Asia emerged from relative cultural backwardness into a major civilization. Adapting the cultural and religious influences of Hinduism and Buddhism from India to its own native traditions, the Southeast Asians created numerous kingdoms, splendid temples, and beautiful works of art. They were especially important as middlemen in trade and cultural interaction between India and China.

Geography

The history of Southeast Asia was greatly influenced by its geographical setting.

MAINLAND AND ISLANDS

Southeast Asia can be divided into two roughly equal regions: the mainland, consisting of the modern countries of Burma, Thailand, Malaysia, Cambodia, Laos, and Vietnam; and the island complex, including the countries of Indonesia, Brunei, and the Philippines.

RIVER SYSTEMS

The geography of the mainland is dominated by four relatively isolated river valleys and delta systems (from west to east): the Irrawaddy, Chao Phraya, Mekong, and Red. Each of these river systems was home to one of the major cultural groups in Southeast Asia: Burmese on the Irrawaddy; Thais on the Chao Phraya; Khmers on the upper Mekong near the Great Lake; Champas on the lower Mekong delta; and Vietnamese on the Red River delta at the Gulf of Tongking. Ranges of mountains and hills separating these river valleys discouraged communications between the river systems.

RAINFALL AND WATER MANAGEMENT

The tropical vegetation of Southeast Asia provided the region's inhabitants with important natural resources such as spices and tropical woods. Ample rainfall meant that a wide variety of plants could grow in the area. However, excessive tropical rainfall brought flooding, erosion, and the spread of plants and animals which made human settlement and agriculture difficult. Unlike the Near East, where irrigation was necessary to provide water for desert regions, in Southeast Asia irrigation was necessary to drain swamps and provide the proper balance of water for rice horticulture.

MONSOONS AND TRADE

The monsoons—seasons of strong directional winds and rains—greatly facilitated trade in Southeast Asia. The prevailing winds are to the northeast during summer, and to the southwest during winter. Thus merchants were able to organize their maritime trade based on these seasonal rhythms of changing wind patterns. Merchants awaiting the shift in prevailing winds needed safe ports for their ships and products. These ports soon developed into the major centers of Southeast Asian wealth, culture, and political power.

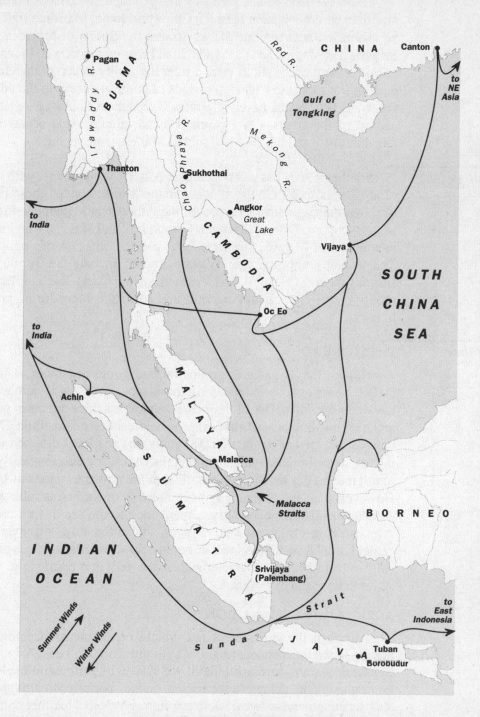

Fig. 11.2 Medieval Southeast Asia

STRAITS AND TRADE

Southeast Asia can be seen as a mass of land and islands complicating maritime communication between China and India. Maritime traffic had to be channeled between one of two straits: the Straits of Malacca between Sumatra and Malaya, and the Sunda Strait between Sumatra and Java. Control of one or both of the straits gave a ruler the ability to tax all merchant ships passing from India to China. In periods of political decay, on the other hand, the straits became the haven of pirates. Throughout Southeast Asian history, control of the straits was a major political, military, and economic issue; kingdoms rose and fell based on control of these trade routes.

Ethnology

Southeast Asia has a very complex pattern of ethnology, with hundreds of languages spoken in the region. Linguists have divided these languages into two major groups. One group, the Austroasiatic peoples, include the Mons (southern Burma), Khmers (Cambodia), and Malays, who include the inhabitants of Malaya, Sumatra, Java, and the other islands of Indonesia. The second group, the Sino-Tibetan peoples, include the Burmans (north Burma), Thais (Thailand), and Vietnamese (Vietnam). Each of these ethnic groups created important kingdoms and cultural centers during premodern history.

Prehistory

THE STONE AGE

Human hunter-gatherer groups migrated into Southeast Asia at least 50,000 years ago, as indicated by the discovery of fossil human remains known as Java man. One of the most remarkable achievements of paleolithic and neolithic Southeast Asians was the colonization of Australia. During the various ice ages of the last 50,000 years, the sea level dropped up to 100 meters, exposing low-lying continental shelves, and allowing early humans to migrate on dry land into much of what are now the islands of Indonesia. However, this land bridge did not completely connect Australia with Asia. About 40,000 years ago, early humans took to the sea in frail canoes and rafts, making dangerous sea voyages, and ultimately "discovering" and "colonizing" Australia. As will be noted below, such daring feats of seamanship were to become characteristic of the skill and courage of Southeast Asian sailors and explorers.

AGRICULTURAL REVOLUTION

Although the evidence is not conclusive, some archaeologists have argued for an independent origin of agriculture in Southeast Asia. Certainly Southeast Asians developed their own system of agriculture exploiting the numerous plants unique to the region. Some specialized cultivated plants, such as the banana and yam, were eventually exported to other parts of Asia, the Near East, and Africa.

DONG SON AND THE BRONZE AGE

Bronze was introduced into the region during the second millennium B.C.; iron made its first appearance by 500 B.C. The most famous prehistoric site in Southeast Asia is at Dong Son, in northern Vietnam. A large collection of finely crafted ritual bronze drums was discovered there, along with evidence of the beginnings of civilization and social stratification. Dong Son drums have been found throughout Southeast Asia, indicating that there was widespread trading contact in the first millennium B.C.

RICE AGRICULTURE

The Southeast Asian bronze age also saw the development of sophisticated agricultural techniques, especially wet-rice farming, laying the agricultural foundation for all future kingdoms. Improved rice productivity allowed greater exploitation of the human and agricultural potential of the region, ultimately leading, under the stimulus of international trade from India, to the formation of true cities and states.

The Origins of Southeast Asian Civilization

Civilization in Southeast Asia is derived from a combination of the indigenous developments mentioned above, and outside stimulation. Even before the major impact of Indian ideas in Southeast Asia, many of the prerequisites of civilization could be found: agriculture, pottery, metal working, trade, and the beginnings of urbanization and social stratification. Nonetheless, contact with India and China proved to be the catalyst which transformed the tribal peoples of Southeast Asia into civilized states. Indeed, the impact of Indian culture on Southeast Asia was so great that, during the medieval period, the region can in many ways be seen as an extension of Indian civilization.

THE INDIANIZATION OF SOUTHEAST ASIA

Contacts with India. The fundamental reason for contacts between India and Southeast Asia was trade. Trade between the regions rapidly expanded in the first centuries after Christ. Thereafter, cultural contacts with India became constant. Eventually occasional traders gave way to large numbers of Indians who permanently settled in Southeast Asia, intermarrying with the local peoples. These Indian traders brought with them Hindu and Buddhist priests, scholars, and missionaries. The skills of these settlers in writing, government, law, architecture, agriculture, politics, and warfare made them invaluable servants of the local rulers, who competed to hire Indian scholars, craftsmen, and soldiers. Through conversion and intermarriage, local Indianized families were soon found throughout Southeast Asia in prominent positions in government, religion, finance, and culture. Local Southeast Asians also traveled frequently to India as pilgrims, merchants, and scholars in search of education at Indian universities. Ultimately some Indian military adventurers intervened in local politics. Occasionally some

Indian kings, such as the Cholas, sent fleets and armies into Southeast Asia, although such military intervention did not produce long-lasting conquests.

Trade. The fundamental goal of Indian contact with Southeast Asia was trade. The region had a number of products which the Indians sought: tropical timber, oils, resins, minerals, gold, gems, and exotic plants for dyes and medicines. Although the Indians seem to have initiated the international trading contacts, local peoples soon took their share of the profits. Local networks of trade developed, connecting the major centers of international trade (such as Palembang in Sumatra) with the sources for various specialized products from the islands and interior. Southeast Asian ships also sailed the international trade routes, and could be found in the major ports of India, the Near East, and China. Indian cultural influence naturally centered on regions associated with international trade: the deltas of the major river systems (except the Red river delta, which was under Chinese cultural influence, see below) and the islands of Sumatra and Java.

Hydraulic Technology. A combination of local techniques and inventions and the introduction of Indian hydraulic technology led to the creation of some of the most sophisticated irrigation and hydraulic systems in premodern times. The prosperity of many parts of Southeast Asia was founded on complex and enormous irrigation systems, including a wide range of canals, dikes, basins, and artificial lakes. The Khmer agriculture system centered on the Great Lake (Tonle Sap) and middle Mekong river of Cambodia. It eventually became so extensive and efficient that, at its height, it supported a population of about one million people in the area surrounding Angkor. Utilizing this vast reservoir of manpower, the kings of Angkor initiated a building program unequaled in Southeast Asia, creating one of the most famous cultural sites of the world, the temple complex at Angkor.

Culture and Religion. Indian scholars and craftsmen did not just bring technical skills to Southeast Asia. Rather, they brought an entire world-view which saw success in agriculture based not just on proper irrigation techniques, but on a proper relationship with the gods. Many different Indian denominations were transported to Southeast Asia. Up through the fourteenth century, Shaivite Hinduism and Mahayana Buddhism were the most important religions, often peacefully coexisting in a kingdom with both sects receiving patronage from the kings. Indian priests and scholars brought with them their ideas and practices on kingship, law, religion, art, architecture, literature, language, and writing. These ideas were then adapted to local Southeast Asian traditions, creating their own style of Indianized religion.

Devaraja Ideology. Politically, the most important idea brought from India was the idea of divine kingship known as *devaraja* (god king). Devaraja ideology centered around the concept that the king was either an incarnation or a descendant of a god. As such he had divine sanction to rule his kingdom, and was to be treated with divine respect. This devaraja ideology obviously provided a strong basis for royal rule, and was widespread throughout Southeast Asia from the fifth through the fourteenth centuries. A central feature of the devaraja cult was the construction of temple-cities in honor of the kings as incarnations of the gods. Many of the great temple complexes of Southeast Asia, notably Angkor Wat, were constructed for this purpose (see below).

CHINESE INFLUENCE

Extensive Chinese influence was largely limited to the area of Annam, (northern Vietnam), which was directly ruled by China from 111 B.C. to A.D. 939. Thereafter Chinese influence remained strong in the region. In the rest of Southeast Asia, Chinese influence was much more limited, centering basically on the establishment of "tributary" relationships, which essentially meant creating diplomatic ties and trading agreements. The major political intervention of China into Southeast Asia came during the Mongol-Chinese invasions of 1283–1287, and the famous voyages of the Ming Chinese fleets between 1403 and 1433.

The Devaraja Kingdoms of Southeast Asia

The medieval political history of Southeast Asia is extremely complex. There were numerous small kingdoms and city-states, for which the surviving historical sources are frequently sparse. In this section we can examine only a few of the major states. All of these early states were founded on the religious and political ideology of devaraja, incorporating Indian culture and various strands of Hinduism and Buddhism as the state religions.

FUNAN, C. 100–550

The earliest major state in Southeast Asia was Funan (in modern Cambodia). Although few details are known of its history, it initiated the pattern which would become characteristic of Southeast Asian states for the next millennium. Its prosperity derived ultimately from the control of trade routes between India and China, centered on their port city of Oc Eo, and their military and economic dominance of the portage routes across the upper Malay peninsula. The rulers of Funan adopted Indian devaraja ideology, and their cultural achievements in the arts were based on Indian models. According to reports of Chinese visitors, Funan was prosperous and well governed.

ANGKOR (KHMER, KAMBUJADESA), 802–1369

The kingdom of Angkor perhaps represents the highest cultural achievement of medieval Southeast Asia. Founded by Jayavarman II (802–850), Angkor reached its height in the eleventh century when its emperors ruled over most of modern Cambodia, Thailand, and Malaya. In the period of imperial splendor, Suryavarman II (1113–1150) began construction of the temple at Angkor Wat, celebrating the king as an incarnation of the Hindu god Vishnu. The monuments there remain the most splendid architectural and artistic achievements of Southeast Asia; the reliefs provide invaluable historical data on life in medieval Cambodia. After several centuries of imperial splendor, the kingdom of Angkor declined during the crisis of the fourteenth century (see below). Thereafter the Cambodian kingdom survived in weakened condition, under constant threat from the Thais.

PAGAN, 849–1287

Although founded in 849, the city of Pagan remained one of numerous small states in Burma until the reign of Anawrahta (1044–1077). He defeated Khmer attempts at conquering Burma (1057–1059), and proceeded to subdue all the other principalities of the region. For the next two centuries Pagan was the political and cultural center of Burma. The state crumbled following the invasion of the Mongols in 1287.

SRIVIJAYA, c. 700–c. 1250

In the early eighth century the port city of Srivijaya (in modern Sumatra) rose to prominence as a center of trade. Through a series of diplomatic maneuvers, dynastic marriages, and military conquest, Srivijaya eventually gained control of both the straits of Malacca and Sunda, thereby establishing a monopoly over trade from China to India. This monopoly gave the kings of Srivijaya vast wealth, which in turn provided the military resources necessary to retain their monopoly. Srivijaya's control was threatened in 1025 when a vast fleet and army from the Chola kingdom of India conquered the straits of Malacca and plundered Sumatra. Although the Cholas were unable to retain long-term direct control over their conquests, the basis of Srivijaya's power had been undermined. Thereafter, they began a period of slow decline, in which kingdoms on the island of Java challenged Srivijaya's maritime supremacy.

The Crisis of the Fourteenth Century

In the decades surrounding 1300, the Indian-based devaraja temple-state system, which had dominated Southeast Asia for over eight hundred years, collapsed. Three factors contributed to its demise.

ECONOMIC OVEREXTENSION

The devaraja ideology required the construction of massive monumental temples as acts of piety and worship for the god-kings. Paralleling the economic effects of pyramid building in Old Kingdom Egypt, these massive construction projects produced severe internal economic and social stresses because of the insatiable demand for resources to build the temples.

MONGOL CONQUESTS

In 1279 the Mongols finally completed their nearly seven-decade conquest of Sung China (see chapter 15). They immediately mobilized the massive military and economic resources of China in an attempt to extend their conquests overseas. Mongol armies conquered northern Vietnam in 1257, and destroyed the kingdom of Pagan in Burma in 1287. Their military intervention culminated in a massive naval invasion of Java (1292–1293). Although the Mongol-Chinese invasions of Southeast Asia were ultimately repulsed, many of the devaraja kingdoms collapsed in the aftermath.

Decline of Trade. Another major effect of the Mongol conquest was to divert sea-borne trade, which had passed through Southeast Asia, to the overland Central Eurasian Silk Road, which was controlled by the Mongols. As Silk Road trade increased, trade passing through Southeast Asian ports declined, bringing economic depression.

THAI INVASIONS

In 1253 the Thai-Shan peoples, living in what is now upper Burma and Thailand, became Mongol vassals. Many Thais fled the Mongol conquest of their homeland, and moved southward into the older civilized regions. These Thai migrations and invasions eventually led to Thai warlords ruling in Burma, and the establishment of the Thai kingdom of Ayuthia (see below). Angkor, once the greatest cultural center of Southeast Asia, was sacked by the Thais in 1369, and eventually abandoned. Thus, although new stable kingdoms eventually arose, the initial result of the Thai migrations was political and economic disorder.

Late Medieval Southeast Asia

After several decades of political chaos, a new political order began to appear in Southeast Asia. On the mainland, a series of Theravada Buddhist kingdoms, often headed by new ethnic groups and elites, replaced the older devaraja kingdoms. In the islands, Islam began to make headway, and by the end of the sixteenth century, most of the major states of the islands were Islamic. The old devaraja temple-state ideology survived only in parts of Java and Bali.

AYUTHIA, 1350–1767

Thai warlords eventually consolidated political power in the Chao Phraya river valley (in modern Thailand). Under the command of Rama Khamheng (the Brave, 1275–1317), the Thais established a kingdom based on the city of Sukhothai, and soon dominated most of what is now Thailand. In 1350 the capital was shifted to Ayuthia under a new dynasty. A series of wars with the Khmer kingdom of Angkor ended with the sack of Angkor in 1369. The great Thai king Trailok (1448–1488) created a well-ordered administration and legal system for the kingdom. Under several dynasties of kings, this Thais state lasted until the twentieth century. For the most part the Thai contributed military and political ideas to their new kingdom, while adopting some of the cultural and religious institutions of previous states. Theravada Buddhism became the state religion.

MAJAPAHIT, 1330–c. 1500

The islands of Indonesia were left in a state of political fragmentation following the Mongol invasions of 1292–1293. From 1330 to 1364 the prime minister Gaja Mada became the effective ruler of Java and initiated an expansionist policy which made the kingdom of Majapahit the major political and economic power in Indonesia for the next century. Majapahit declined in the late fifteenth century under the impact of the rising power of Islamic and European island principalities.

NAM VIET, FROM 939

The area of modern Vietnam was divided into two major cultural regions during the Middle Ages. In the south, the kingdom of Champa was a traditional devaraja state. In the north, from 111 B.C. to A.D. 939, the Chinese ruled the region as their southernmost province. This area was largely sinicized (adopted Chinese customs and culture), maintaining a combination of Confucian and Buddhist cultural characteristics ever since. The main theme of Nam Viet history in the latter Middle Ages is a five-century struggle with Champa for political control, and repeated threats of the reimposition of Chinese military dominance. The Vietnamese were briefly conquered by the Mongol-Chinese invasion of 1257, and by the Ming Chinese (1409–1428), but they ultimately retained independence. By 1471 Nam Viet military expansion at the expense of the kingdom of Champa had created the basis for the modern state of Vietnam.

ISLAM IN SOUTHEAST ASIA

The Coming of Islam. Islam made its first penetration into Southeast Asia in the late thirteenth century. The Islamic conquest of northern India established bases of operation for Muslim merchants in Bangladesh and Gujerat. From there, Muslim traders brought Islamic ideas and practices into the islands of Indonesia. By 1403 a Muslim warlord controlled the strait of Malacca from his base at the newly founded city of Malacca. From there Islamic commercial and political power, religion, and culture spread throughout Indonesia and into the southern Philippines. Although the spread of Islam was temporarily slowed by the coming of the Europeans, it eventually became the dominant religion in all of the islands of Southeast Asia except the Philippines, which were Christianized by Spanish colonizers.

Malacca, 1403–1511; and Achin, 1496–1834. Islamic power in Southeast Asia initially centered on Malacca in Malaya, and Achin in Sumatra, giving the Muslims control of the strait of Malacca. Under the patronage of Chinese admirals commanding the seven great Chinese naval expeditions from 1403 to 1433, Malacca became the new major center for international trade. The wealth derived from this trading monopoly was used to extend Islamic commercial and political power throughout the Southeast Asian islands. By the end of the sixteenth century much of Sumatra and Java had come under the control of Islamic princes. Thereafter, however, the newly arrived Europeans became the major economic and political competitors of the Muslims.

THE PORTUGUESE

Arrival. The final important historical development in the history of premodern Southeast Asia was the coming of the Portuguese and other Europeans. Portuguese intervention in the region began shortly after Vasco da Gama's discovery of the sea route around Africa to India in 1498. From 1505 to 1515 the Portuguese initiated a policy of conquering strongly fortified strategic ports in an attempt to gain control over the sea trade of China, India, and Southeast Asia. In 1511 they conquered Malacca and established domination over the straits, thereby bringing much of the East Asian trade under their control as well. In 1557 they had captured a base in Macao in China, and in 1571 the Spanish had built a port at Manila in the Philippines. The Portuguese remained a major economic and military power in the region for the next 130 years.

Domination. During this period the greed, brutality, mismanagment, and lack of concern for local inhabitants on the part of Portuguese traders and pirates in Southeast Asia essentially guaranteed strong opposition to their presence. Although some Christian missionaries attempted to alleviate the problems, in the long run Christianity made little headway in Southeast Asia, due largely to the poor examples of the European colonists. Instead, Islam expanded, and in many ways became the ideology behind resistance to the Europeans.

Decline. Throughout most of the sixteenth century the Portuguese were at war with neighboring Malay Muslim states. They survived largely due to superior gunpowder weapons and their ability to reinforce their ports through their unassailable dominance at sea. Portuguese attempts to expand their conquests onto the mainland and other islands invariably met with disaster. Nonetheless, despite their many problems, the Portuguese managed to control a significant portion of the East Asian trade throughout the sixteenth century. Ultimately the Portuguese were overthrown by the Dutch, who captured Malacca in 1641. The Dutch thereafter controlled Southeast Asian trade, and began the colonization and conquest of Indonesia.

Religion

The religions of Southeast Asia played a fundamental role in the nature of their civilizations. There were several major religious traditions which had an impact in the area.

LOCAL RELIGIOUS TRADITIONS

Before the coming of Indian religions, Southeast Asia had a wide range of local religious traditions. These were characterized by animism, ancestor worship, and a strong ritual magic element. Many of these archaic ideas and practices have survived to the present day in various Buddhist and Islamic forms. Thus the Hinduism, Buddhism, and Islam of the region gained a uniquely Southeast Asian flavor.

HINDU AND MAHAYANA BUDDHIST TRADITIONS

According to legend, Buddhism was introduced into Southeast Asia in the third century B.C. when the Mauryan emperor Ashoka (272–232 B.C.) sent missionaries into the region. Although this specific event may be legendary, it is certain that Hindu and Buddhist influences in Southeast Asia were becoming important in the first centuries after Christ. These religious traditions declined beginning in the fourteenth century, and were eventually replaced by Theravada Buddhism and Islam. It seems that Hinduism and Mahayana Buddhism were patronized largely by the elites of Southeast Asia, the common people continuing with their traditional religions under a veneer of Indian ideas and practices.

THERAVADA (HINAYANA) BUDDHISM

It was with the introduction of Theravada Buddhism that Buddhism finally penetrated to the daily lives, beliefs, and practices of the commoners of Southeast Asia. Although Theravada was introduced into Southeast Asia along with Hinduism, its major impact did not occur until the eleventh century, when new Theravada ideas from Sri Lanka took hold in Burma. Following the fall of the Pagan dynasty and the collapse of the devaraja political ideology, new Burmese and Thai warlords adopted Theravada as their state religion. Under Burmese and Thai patronage, Theravada eventually spread throughout mainland Southeast Asia at the same time Islam was coming to dominate the islands.

ISLAM

Muslim merchants and sufis (Muslim mystics) introduced Islam into Southeast Asia beginning in the thirteenth century. It spread in conjunction with the spread of Islamic political and economic power, and today dominates southern Malaya and Indonesia. In those regions Islam provided the ideological foundation for resistance to European colonialism in the eighteenth through twentieth centuries.

CHRISTIANITY

Christianity was introduced into Southeast Asia by the Portuguese in 1511 with their capture of Malacca. Ultimately, however, Christian missionary efforts made little headway. Only in the Philippines, which became a Spanish colony beginning in 1571, did Christian missionaries have any substantial success.

Culture

The art of Southeast Asia during the eleventh through the fourteenth centuries is the equal of any in the world. The finest manifestations of Southeast Asian culture are the great temple complexes.

Borobudur. Borobudur (Java, 9th–10th centuries) is one of the finest Buddhist shrines in the world. Built in the form of a *stupa* (Buddhist shrine) atop a cosmic mountain, it includes splendid bas-reliefs of various legends and stories from Buddhist scriptures.

Angkor Wat. The empire of Angkor (Cambodia, 9th–13th centuries) included over 900 temples. The most important are found in the urban/ritual complex of Angkor, covering nearly 250 square kilometers.

Pagan. Pagan (Burma, 11th–13th centuries), the urban-ritual center of Burma, rests on a plain of some 41 square kilometers, and includes 2,000 Buddhist temples, perhaps the densest accumulation of religious buildings in the world.

Palembang. Palembang (Sumatra, 7th–10th centuries), the capital of the Srivijayan state in Sumatra, was a center of Buddhist and Sanskrit culture, boasting a large university and library. It attracted numerous pilgrims and students from East Asia.

Polynesian Migrations

ORIGINS

Southeast Asian peoples are noted also for their remarkable colonization of the Pacific islands and Madagascar. Beginning in the second millennium B.C., Southeast Asian seamen, in small canoes and rafts, embarked on an incredible migration which would eventually carry their descendents to Africa and the Americas. One group of explorers turned westward, and by about A.D. 500 had migrated to Madagascar, bringing new crops such as bananas to the east African coasts.

COLONIZATION OF THE PACIFIC

Others turned eastward, and began "island hopping" across the Pacific Ocean. By about A.D. 300 they had reached the Society islands. From there, other groups spread to Hawaii by 600, and New Zealand by 800. Easter Island was colonized by Polynesians about A.D. 500, where they eventually created an incredible array of monumental stone sculpture. Other Polynesians undoubtedly reached the Americas as well, to be absorbed by the local American Indians. Polynesian oral traditions have preserved accounts of some of these migrations, such as the tale of Roy Mata and his expedition in the thirteenth century to the Islands of vanuatu near New Caledonia. Archaeologists have discovered Roy Mata's tomb precisely at the location claimed by the oral traditions. Given their technological level—they were all neolithic peoples with no sophisticated navigational tools—the Polynesian colonization of the Pacific certainly ranks as one of the major exploration achievements of mankind.

*M*edieval South Asia experienced great cultural and political transformations. Although India was politically fragmented into numerous warring dynasties, culturally there was a great flourishing, especially in the building of splendid temple-cities. Buddhism declined, while Bhakti mysticism became increasingly widespread among the common people. The Muslim invasions in the eleventh century represent a major watershed in Indian history. Politically India was conquered by the Muslims in a series of wars lasting five centuries. Muslim control of India culminated with the rise of the Mughal dynasty in 1526, which reunited all of India into a single state for the first time since the Mauryas. Culturally, the coming of Islam included the conversion of a quarter of the population to Islam, and the creation of a brilliant literature, art, and architecture based on a synthesis of Hindu and Islamic elements.

Southeast Asian states and civilizations began to emerge in the first century based on wealth from trade from China to India, and on Hindu ideas of religion, kingship, and irrigation. The great Indianized civilizations lasted until the fourteenth century, when they were transformed to Theravada Buddhist cultures, which have endured to the present. The coming of the Muslims in the fifteenth century, and the Europeans in the sixteenth century, represent the final cultural elements which make up the modern states and societies of Southeast Asia.

The medieval period in South Asia ends with coming of the Europeans. The Europeans initially explored and traded, but soon conquered ports and dominated the trade routes of South Asia, and finally sent armies inland to establish kingdoms and colonies. Thus a period that began with Hindu states and cultural dominance throughout the entire region ended with the political and cultural supremacy of Islamic and European peoples.

Selected Readings

Aung-Thwin, M. *Pagan: The Origins of Modern Burma* (1985)

Basham, A. L. *The Wonder That Was India* (1959)

Briggs, L. *The Ancient Khmer Empire* (1951)

Chaudhuri, K. N. *Trade and Civilisation in the Indian Ocean: An Economic History from the Rise of Islam to 1750* (1985)

Coedes, G. *The Indianized States of Southeast Asia* (1968)

Eck, Diana L. *Banaras: City of Light* (1982)

Gesick, L., ed. *Centers, Symbols, and Hierarchies: Essays on the Classical States of Southeast Asia* (1983)

Groslier, B. P., and J. Arthaud. *Angkor: Art and Civilization* (1966)

Hall, D. G. R. *A History of Southeast Asia*, 4th ed. (1981)

Harle, J. C. *The Art and Architecture of the Indian Subcontinent* (1986)

Ikram, S. M. *Muslim Civilization in India* (1964)

Kulke, Hermann, and Dietmar Rothermund. *A History of India* (1986)

Majumdar, R. C. *The Delhi Sultanate: The History and Culture of the Indian People* (1967)

Rawson, Philip. *The Art of Southeast Asia* (1967)

Singhal, D. P. *A History of the Indian People (1983)*

Stein, B. *Peasant, State, and Society in Medieval South India* (1980)

Thapar, R. *A History of India*, vol. 1 (1969)

Warner, Michael Freeman. *Angkor: The Hidden Glories* (1990)

Wolters, O. L. *Early Indonesian Commerce: The Origins of Srivijaya* (1967)

12

Subsaharan Africa

451	East Africans adopt Monophysite Christianity
c. 500	Beginning of Malaysian emigration to Madagascar
517	Caleb of Axum invades and conquers Yemen
543–569	Conversion of Nubians to Christianity
570	Battle of the Elephant at Mecca: Axumite invasion repeled
572	Sasanid Persian fleet drives Axumites from Arabia
640–709	Arab Muslim conquest of North Africa
700	Beginnings of Muslim trade in east Africa
702	Axumites sack Jidda, war with Muslims
957	Foundation of Kilwa, Arab Swahili trading town
1076	Almoravids conquer Kumbi, Ghana declines
c. 1200–1600	Kingdom of Mwenemutapa
1235–1255	Sundiata, founder of kingdom of Mali
1312–1337	Mansa Musa, king of Mali
1314–1344	Amda Seyon, king of Ethiopia
1352–1353	Ibn Battuta visits Africa
1405–1433	Chinese maritime expeditions explore east Africa
1464–1492	Sunni Ali founds empire of Songhai
1483	Portuguese arrive at Kongo (Congo)
1497	Vasco da Gama explores east coast of Africa
1504	Fall of Soba, last Christian state of Nubia
1506–1543	Alfonso I, king of Kongo
1542	Ethiopians and Portuguese defeat Muslim invasion
1571–1603	Idris III founds empire of Kanem Bornu
1578	Defeat of Portuguese invasion of Morocco at Kasr al-Kabir
1591	Battle of Tondibi: Moroccans conquer Songhai

*T*he history of premodern subsaharan (south of the Sahara desert) Africa was conditioned by its relative geographical isolation, caused by the Sahara desert. The most advanced civilizations in Africa developed at the end of the great trans-Saharan trade routes: in the northeast, in Nubia and Ethiopia, and in the west, in the Niger River valley; in the south, Bantu warrior tribes consolidated kingdoms such as Mwenemutapa, while Islamic merchant trading city-states, with contacts as far away as China, flourished on the

Swahili coast. The power and cultural achievements of these kingdoms reached their peak from the thirteenth through the sixteenth centuries. Their wealth derived in large part from their participation in international trade. When the Portuguese, with their superior ships and artillery, began to usurp control of African international trade routes in the sixteenth century, the great medieval African kingdoms began to decline.

BACKGROUND

Geography and Environment

An understanding of African history before A.D. 1600 must be based on an appreciation for the role of geography. Although the geography and environments of Africa did not "determine" the course of African history, they laid the framework within which African peoples created their various civilizations by influencing agriculture, natural resources, communications, and culture.

SIZE OF AFRICA

Africa is a vast continent, much larger than the United States or Europe, containing a wide range of ecological environments. To speak of "African civilization" is thus inaccurate, since many of the peoples living in the different regions of Africa had no direct communication with each other in premodern times. Indeed, the people of Zimbabwe and Kilwa on the southeast coast of Africa had much more contact with the peoples of Arabia, India, and China than they did with the inhabitants of the Niger river valley in west Africa. As will be discussed below, although there are no common linguistic or religious bonds that united all Africans in premodern times, there are broad cultural characteristics that most premodern subsaharan Africans shared.

DIVERSITY IN ECOLOGICAL ZONES

In order to understand African history, it is vital to have a basic understanding of the main features of African geography.

North Africa. The coastal regions of North Africa are distinguished by a Mediterranean climate, with adequate rainfall and reasonable agriculture potential. Isolated from subsaharan Africa by the Sahara, this region was culturally part of the Mediterranean and Middle Eastern civilizations.

Sahara Desert. The Sahara desert, the largest in the world, separates North Africa from subsaharan Africa. Although for the most part uninhabited, in premodern times there were various Berber bedouin tribes who migrated among the oases and semi-arid regions. There is another swath of desert, the Kalahari, in the southwestern part of Africa.

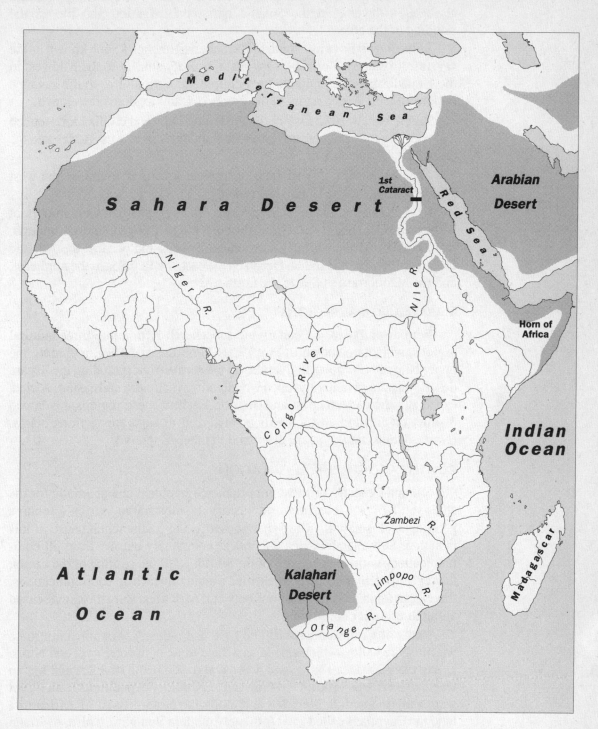

Fig. 12.1   The Geography of Africa

Nile Valley. Only in the east, in the Nile valley, could an agricultural civilization develop in the Sahara, based on irrigation and the annual flooding of the Nile.

Subsaharan Savana. South of the Sahara stretches a zone known as the savanna, or steppe, a broad grassy plain, broadly similar to the Midwest in the United States and suitable for herding and agriculture. In the savanna regions of west Africa many of the great African kingdoms developed.

Throughout African history the great kingdoms and civilizations tended to develop in the savanna and open woodland regions of west Africa and the east coast.

Tropical Forest. A vast zone of tropical forests is found on the west African coast, and the Congo river valley.

River Systems. There are five major river systems that were important in the premodern history of Africa: the Nile, Niger, Congo (Zaire), Limpopo, and Zambizi. Africa is nearly surrounded by seas and oceans: the Atlantic Ocean on the west, the Indian Ocean on the east, the Red Sea to the northeast, and the Mediterranean Sea to the north.

MAJOR CULTURAL REGIONS

For our purposes, we can divide subsaharan Africa into three cultural regions, which are shown in Fig. 12.1: (1) northeast Africa, including the upper Nile and Ethiopian highlands; (2) western Africa, including the Sahara desert, western savanna and open woodland; (3) southern and eastern Africa, especially the eastern coast and interior. Each of these regions developed distinct civilizations, which will be analyzed in separate sections below. (North Africa and Egypt are discussed in other chapters.)

RELATIVE GEOGRAPHICAL ISOLATION

Sahara Desert. The most important geographical characteristic for the study of Africa's role in world history is subsaharan Africa's relative geographical isolation. The Sahara desert is the fundamental cause of this isolation. Subsaharan Africa was never completely cut off from all communications with other regions of the world. Until the coming of the camel, however, the Sahara desert represented a major obstacle to communications, travel, and trade. Communications between Africa and Eurasia were focused along three major corridors.

Paths of Communication. The first, and oldest, communication route was the Nile valley, which served as a trade route between Egypt and Nubia as early as 3000 B.C. The second was naval traffic in the Red Sea and Indian Ocean. As early as 1500 B.C. trading and exploratory expeditions from Egypt were sailing down the Red Sea and along the eastern coast of Africa to a land the Egyptians called Punt (probably modern Somalia). Third, overland trans-Saharan communications were established by horse chariots perhaps as early as 1100 B.C. The introduction of the camel into the Sahara in the first century B.C. represents the major and permanent opening of relations between North Africa and the subsaharan savannah. Even so, caravans from North Africa required over forty days of travel through some of the harshest conditions on earth to reach the Niger River valley.

Atlantic Sea Route. The western coasts of Africa were occasionally visited by outsiders, but due to the prevailing northern winds, contact by sea from the Atlantic was difficult before the development of new sail technology by the Portuguese in the late fifteenth century A.D. that allowed them to travel against the wind down the west African coast. From that time on the Atlantic seaboard represented a fourth corridor of contact between Africa, Europe, and the Americas. In the modern period this communication corridor increasingly became the most important.

ETHNOLOGY

Although Africa is often thought of as the continent of blacks, in reality it has a very complex and diverse mixture of ethnic groups. In the north and northeast we find Semitic peoples, now largely Arabic speaking, but originally including numerous Phoenicians and Jews. Indeed, Amharic, the major modern language of Ethiopia, is a Semitic language. The Sahara region is inhabited by Berbers and Egyptians. Black Africans, the majority ethnic group (perhaps 70 percent of all Africans), inhabit most of Africa south of the Sahara. However, there are small enclaves of Khoisan peoples (also known as Bushmen and Hottentots) in the Kalahari region. Malaysians (Malagasy) migrated from Southeast Asia to Madagascar and southeast Africa as early as the fifth century A.D. Finally, beginning in the sixteenth century, Europeans began to migrate to the continent, followed, in the nineteenth and twentieth centuries, by Chinese and Indian Asians, who today make up a small percentage of African peoples.

Prehistory

Africa is generally recognized as the cradle of the earliest hominids, who slowly, over the course of hundreds of thousands of years, migrated out of Africa and into Europe, Asia, and the Americas. Some of the earliest and finest neolithic rock art is to be found in Africa, indicating the continent's importance in human cultural origins. During this period parts of the Sahara were grassy plains, which provided excellent hunting grounds for early human groups. Following the most recent Ice Age, however, a decrease in rainfall caused a progressive drying of the Sahara, which continues to this day. The Sahara thus became a barrier to communications and Africa was only slowly brought back into continuous contact with the rest of the world.

Past Misunder-standings About Africa

The study of subsaharan Africa during the past two centuries has been plagued by numerous misunderstandings of the nature of Africa, its peoples, and history. Part of this problem was due to simple lack of information. However, the unique circumstances of Africa's interaction with Westerners has added other dimensions to the problems of misunderstanding. Since many of the false stereotypes of Africa are still with us today in various forms, it is worth mentioning the origins of these distortions.

RACISM AND SLAVERY

Relations between Westerners and Africans in the nineteenth and twentieth centuries have been plagued by slavery and racism. Westerners' interpretations of Africa and its history were frequently distorted by racist views of black African inferiority. This was in part a rationale for slavery; the misapplication of Darwinian theories of evolution added to the problem. It is really only in the past few decades that these biases have been corrected and a nonracist view of African history has been presented in the West.

IMPERIALISM AND COLONIALISM

Although the problems of the Atlantic slave trade were in the process of being resolved throughout the nineteenth century, racist concepts of Africa did not end, but were compounded by new forms of exploitation: colonialism and imperialism. As Europeans competed for political dominance in Europe and vied for control of African resources and markets, they eventually came to believe that they had to take direct military control over Africa. Once again, Europeans' views of Africa were distorted: In order to justify conquest and colonization, claims were made of African inferiority, and it became the "White Man's burden" to bring civilization to the "Dark Continent."

RADICAL AFROCENTRISM

Although most scholars believe that the major intellectual problems of racist and colonial ideologies have been corrected, a new intellectual movement, sometimes called radical Afrocentrism, has emerged in some circles. Believing that the true role of Africans has been systematically suppressed by inherently racist whites, these scholars have called for a radical reinterpretation of the role of Africa in world history. In essence the radical Afrocentrists believe that pharaonic Egypt was a "black" civilization that was the source of most of the civilizing impulses that spread to Greece and Europe. Thus black Africans were the true creators of civilization, and this information has been systematically suppressed by whites. These more radical claims have not won acceptance in the broader scholarly community.

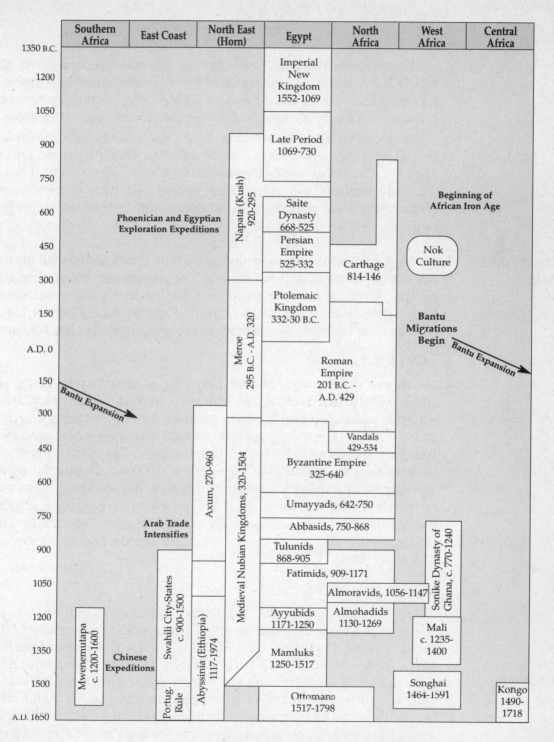

Southern Africa	East Coast	North East (Horn)	Egypt	North Africa	West Africa	Central Africa

1350 B.C.

Imperial New Kingdom 1552-1069

1200

1050

Late Period 1069-730

900

Napata (Kush) 920-295

750

Phoenician and Egyptian Exploration Expeditions

Saite Dynasty 668-525

600

Beginning of African Iron Age

Persian Empire 525-332

450

Nok Culture

300

Carthage 814-146

Meroe 295 B.C. - A.D. 320

Ptolemaic Kingdom 332-30 B.C.

150

Bantu Migrations Begin

A.D. 0

Bantu Expansion

Roman Empire 201 B.C. - A.D. 429

150

Bantu Expansion

300

Axum, 270-960

Medieval Nubian Kingdoms, 320-1504

450

Vandals 429-534

Byzantine Empire 325-640

600

Umayyads, 642-750

750

Arab Trade Intensifies

Abbasids, 750-868

Tulunids 868-905

900

Swahili City-States c. 900-1500

Sonike Dynasty of Ghana, c. 770-1240

Fatimids, 909-1171

1050

Almoravids, 1056-1147

Abyssinia (Ethiopia) 1117-1974

1200

Mwenemutapa c. 1200-1600

Ayyubids 1171-1250

Almohadids 1130-1269

Mali c. 1235-1400

Chinese Expeditions

1350

Mamluks 1250-1517

1500

Portug. Rule

Songhai 1464-1591

Kongo 1490-1718

Ottomans 1517-1798

A.D. 1650

Fig. 12.2   African Civilizations, 1350 B.C.–A.D. 1650

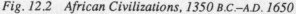

NORTHEAST AFRICA

Northeastern Africa can be divided into two major cultural zones. The middle Nile encompasses the region of the Nile valley in modern Sudan. It was inhabited by a number of ancient peoples who can broadly be called Nubians. The Ethiopian highlands include the modern states of Ethiopia.

Unlike other areas of Africa, both of these regions were in constant contact with the civilizations of the Middle East from the second millennium B.C. The earliest civilizations in subsaharan Africa are to be found in these two regions. Civilization in the middle Nile dates to the fifteenth century B.C., while civilization in Ethiopia dates to about the fourth century B.C.

The Middle Nile

Upstream (southern) navigation on the Nile is unhindered until the first cataract (rapids). Navigational hazards here prevent easy travel, creating a natural boundary between Egypt and the modern country of Sudan. Geographically, the region south of the first cataract was called the middle Nile, and was inhabited by numerous ethnic groups loosely called Nubians.

EARLY NUBIA

As one of the cradles of civilization, Egypt served as the model and stimulus for the oldest subsaharan African civilization. As early as 3000 B.C. Egyptian traders and warriors had penetrated the middle Nile in search of gold and slaves. These early sporadic contacts soon gave way to permanent fortresses and garrisons in Nubia, culminating in Egyptian conquest and occupation of the middle Nile from 1500 to 1000 B.C. During this period Nubian peoples acquired knowledge of irrigation, metalworking, monumental building, writing, government, and religion from the Egyptians, adapting these skills to their own needs, culture, and environment. From this time on, the history of Nubia can be divided into three periods: Napata, Meroe, and Christian Nubia.

NAPATA, 760–295 B.C.

By the eighth century B.C. the dynasty of Napata (Kush) had become roughly equal to the Egyptians in military power. The greatest king of this period, Piankhy (751–716), conquered Egypt and was proclaimed pharaoh of the Twenty-fifth (Kushite) dynasty. Nubian pharaohs and warlords ruled Egypt for nearly a century until the Assyrian conquest in 671 B.C. Thereafter the kings of Napata continued as independent rulers of the middle Nile despite invasions by Egyptians and Persians. Following the sack of Napata by the Egyptians, the capital was moved to the more secure site of Meroe, initiating the second phase of Nubian civilization.

MEROE, 295 B.C.–A.D. 320

In Meroe the Nubians, though still heavily influenced by!Egyptian practices, adopted elements of Hellenism following the Greek conquest of Egypt by Alexander. The basis of their prosperity in this period was the control of the gold and ivory trade. Their mastery of irrigation technology allowed agriculture in otherwise barren regions of the middle Nile. Meroe is noted for its splendid temples, royal burials in pyramids in imitation of earlier Egyptian pharaohs, and for their massive iron industry.

Role of Women. An interesting feature of Meroitic civilization was the important role of women in the ruling dynasty. Five women ruled as independent queens of Meroe, with many others playing important roles as dowager queens and regents for their sons. One of the most famous is Amanitere (12 B.C.–A.D. 12), immortalized at the Lion Temple at Naqa. There the plump, matronly looking queen stands in the classic pose of the ancient Egyptian warrior-pharaohs, grasping a dozen male enemies by the hair and raising a sword in her other hand, prepared to dispatch the cowering prisoners.

Decline. The collapse of the kingdom of Meroe was brought about by declining prosperity because of shifting trade patterns and the invasion of the Axumites, under the newly Christianized king Ezana. He sacked Meroe sometime around A.D. 350 (see below), which opened the area to nomadic invaders from the Sahara. Thereafter Nubia entered two centuries of decline and political disunity.

CHRISTIAN NUBIA, 543–1504

Feudal Kingdoms. In the sixth century Christian missionaries from Egypt and the court of Justinian in Constantinople converted the nobility of the region, initiating the Christian Nubian or medieval period (543–1504). Nubia during this period was divided into several feudal kingdoms, the most important being Dongola (Makuria) and Alwa. Here, isolated from all other Christians, one could find a Christian society with monasteries, cathedrals, and castles ruled by African bishops and knights. Christian Nubia is especially noted for the outstanding painting tradition of the cathedral at Faras.

Islamic Conquest. These feudal Christian kingdoms of Nubia were unable to withstand the assaults by Islamic armies from Egypt. By the late thirteenth century the Nubians had become vassals of the Mamluk sultans of Egypt. Soba, the capital of the last Nubian Christian state, was sacked in 1504 by an Islamic tribe known as the Funj. From the sixteenth century on, the region became increasingly Islamic, with Arabic becoming the dominant language.

Ethiopian Highlands

South of Nubia, and outside the Nile valley in the high plateaus of Ethiopia, the second oldest African civilization emerged. In the sixth cen-

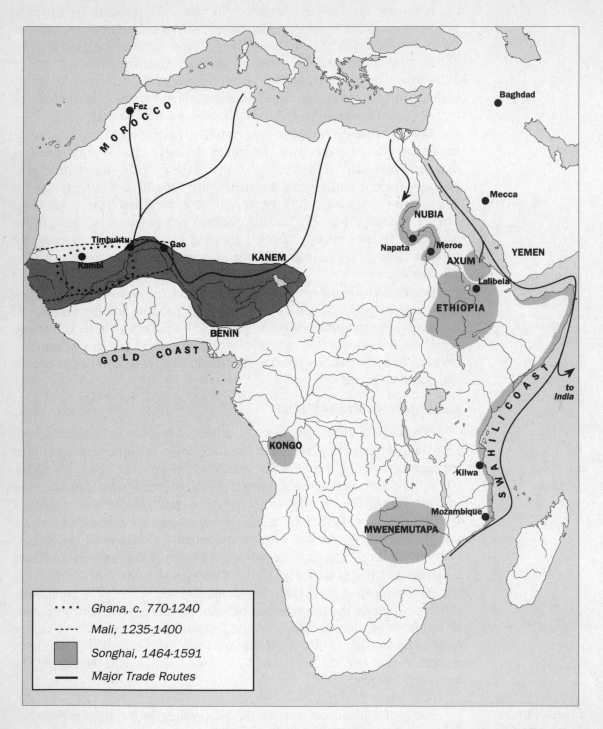

Fig. 12.3   Medieval Africa

tury B.C. Sabean Arabian traders from the region of modern Yemen migrated to the west shore of the Red Sea to establish trading colonies. These Arab colonists brought with them their religion, writing system, building techniques, ironworking skills, irrigation methods, and system of government. Within a few centuries, the Sabean Arab colonists had intermarried and were absorbed by the local African peoples. From this mixture of African and Arabian cultures, the state of Axum (c. 100 B.C. to A.D. 960) emerged.

AXUM

Origins. The kings of Axum were merchant princes who derived their wealth and power from the control of trade in the Red Sea. Axumite traders dealt with products from east Africa, India, China, Arabia, the African interior, Egypt, and the eastern Mediterranean. In an attempt to control the access to the Red Sea, King Aphilas (c. 270–300) conquered the southwest corner of Arabia (modern Yemen).

Ezana, 325–356. The most famous king of Axum was Ezana, who converted to Christianity about 350. A mighty warrior, Ezana conquered the weakened state of Meroe, establishing Axum as the sole military power of the region and creating an environment for the spread of Christianity.

Height of Power. The Axumites continued to play a major economic and political role in the region until the coming of Islam. They exchanged embassies and made alliances with Justinian the Great of Constantinople. In 570 (the traditional date of the birth of the prophet Muhammad) they even attempted the conquest of the Arabian city of Mecca. The failure of this assault permitted the subsequent rise of Mecca as the major military and economic state in Arabia. This had a profound consequence for world history, contributing to the ultimate success of Muhammad's preaching and the Islamic conquests.

Decline. It is ironic that, in an attempt to undermine the power of the Meccans by supporting their rivals, the kings of Axum welcomed early Islamic refugees from Mecca, thereby assisting the rise of Islam. Following the Islamic conquests in the seventh century, and the consequent shifting of trade routes, Axum began a period of economic and political decline.

Gudit and the Falasha. Axum was ultimately overthrown by a fascinating semilegendary woman warrior, Gudit (Judith), queen of the Falasha clan. The Falasha, African converts to Judaism, survived in Ethiopia until they recently migrated to Israel. Gudit's armies sacked the city of Axum around 960.

ABYSSINIAN PERIOD, 1117–1974

Following their defeats by Gudit and Islamic warlords who had established bases on the coast of Africa, the Christians of Axum and the Ethiopian highlands withdrew inland, establishing a new capital around the city of Lalibela, inaugurating the Abyssinian or Ethiopian period. The Christian Ethiopian state became increasingly feudalized and militarized during this period in an effort to resist the encroachment of Islamic African sultanates of Ifat and Adal on the Horn of Africa (modern Somalia and Ethiopia). Great warrior-kings such as Amda Seyon (1314–1344), and Zara Yaqob (1434–1468) established Ethiopia as the major military power of east Africa. The culture of Ethiopia during this period represents one of the most splendid achievements of premodern Africa (see below). The military strength of the Ethiopians, combined with military assistance from Portugal in the mid-sixteenth century, permitted the survival of this isolated Christian state until the twentieth century, when Haile Selassie, the last Christian emperor of Ethiopia, was overthrown in a military coup.

KINGDOMS OF WEST AFRICA

Characteristics of West African Society

Like most subsaharan societies, the foundations of the great kingdoms of west Africa were based on agricultural techniques adapted to their environment, the herding of cattle in marginal lands, and the use of iron tools and weapons. In west Africa, however, several additional factors led to the development of some of the largest and wealthiest African kingdoms of premodern times.

THE USE OF THE HORSE IN WARFARE

The horse was introduced into west Africa perhaps as early as 1100 B.C. Initially the horse was used only with chariots by Berber tribesmen, but eventually cavalry began to appear. By A.D. 1000 western Africans had developed a military system whose power rested, like that in contemporary medieval Europe, on heavily armored mounted knights.

TRAVEL BY CAMEL

The introduction of the camel into the Sahara in the first century B.C. was one of the major events in African history. The camel's ability to cross the desert with relative ease facilitated trans-Saharan trade with North Africa. Without the camel, west Africa would have remained basically isolated from the rest of the civilized world. With the camel, west Africa was able to become fully integrated with Islamic civilization.

DIVINE KINGSHIP

Traditional ideas of divine kingship (that the king was an incarnation of, or descended from, the gods) were used to establish an ideology for the centralization of political and economic power under great kings or emperors.

GOLD TRADE

A flourishing gold trade developed between subsaharan and North Africa. The success of the gold trade rested on the spread of organized camel caravans, the discovery of new gold fields in west Africa, and the development of kingdoms capable of exploiting, controlling, and transporting these gold resources.

ISLAM

The introduction of Islam into west Africa, beginning in the ninth century A.D., brought significant change to west African societies on several levels. Although local religions survived among the common people (often disguised under a veneer of Islamic practices), the elite classes of west Africa became increasingly Muslim. Muslim merchants and scholars who settled in west Africa introduced the Islamic alphabet, culture, art and architecture, government, and law, leaving a major imprint on life in the area until the present day.

Major Kingdoms of West Africa

The three major kingdoms of medieval west Africa were Ghana, Mali, and Songhai. Historical knowledge of western African states derives from the reports of Arab historians and geographers and indigenous oral traditions, first committed to writing in the sixteenth century by African historians of Timbuktu and Kanem.

GHANA, c. 350–1240

Origins. Ghana is the oldest historical kingdom of west Africa. Its origins may go back as early as A.D. 300, but its period of greatness extended from the tenth through the thirteenth centuries. The rise of Ghana was closely linked to the wealth derived from the development and expansion of the gold trade. In this period Ghana was the largest, wealthiest, and most powerful state in west Africa. Throughout most of its history, the kings of Ghana followed traditional African religions, basing their power on local concepts of divine kingship.

Coming of Islam. Islam was introduced into subsaharan Africa by Muslim merchants from North Africa in the ninth century. Originally Muslim merchants had their own towns and mosques, interacting with the Ghanans largely for trade. But eventually the Ghanan kings learned to capitalize on Muslim skills of writing and administration, and the traders and Ghanans began to merge into a single society. In 1076 Kumbi, the capital of Ghana, was sacked by Muslim Berbers from the Sahara known as the Almoravids. Thereafter Ghana lost its position of preeminence in west Africa.

MALI, 1230–1390

Sundiata, 1230–1255. Within a century of the collapse of Ghana, a new imperial power had united most of west Africa. The empire of Mali was founded by Sundiata I (Sun Jata, 1230–1255), sometimes known as the "Alexander of Africa." Through a series of brilliant military campaigns, he transformed the small city-state of Mali into the dominant power in the region, ultimately conquering the weakened state of Ghana itself. The legendary memory of these campaigns led Sundiata to become the epic hero of west Africa. His exploits have been remembered by west African epic poets for over seven hundred years, and tales continue to be told today of his military adventures and legendary combat with monsters and magicians.

Mansa Musa, 1312–1337. Sundiata's most famous descendant was Mansa Musa I, who ruled Mali at the height of its power. As Muslims, the kings of Mali were obligated to perform the pilgrimage to Mecca. Mansa Musa's display of wealth and power so dazzled the Muslims of Egypt and Arabia that he and his kingdom became well known throughout the Muslim world. The glory of Mali was such that it was visited by the most famous traveler of premodern times, Ibn Battuta, who during his lifetime journeyed to every civilized region of the Old World, traveling about twice as far as Marco Polo.

SONGHAI, 1464–1591

Sunni Ali, 1464–1492. The final and greatest kingdom of west Africa was Songhai. Taking advantage of Mali's increasing internal weakness, the brilliant ruler of the small tributary kingdom of Songhai, Sunni Ali, launched a series of military campaigns that culminated in the overthrow of Mali and the establishment of Songhai as the dominant power in west Africa.

Muhammad Askia, 1493–1528. Under Muhammad Askia the Great, Songhai reached the height of its power, with a strong military, and control of regional and international trade. Great centers of Islamic learning and culture were established at the imperial capital, Gao, and the international trading center of Timbuktu.

Fall of Songhai. Following the reign of Askia, the empire of Songhai entered a period of internal religious conflict between animists and Muslims, each group supporting rival contestants for the throne. By the late sixteenth century the sultan of Morocco, tempted by the weakness of Songhai and the superiority of his musket-armed troops, sent a daring expeditionary force of five thousand men across the Sahara desert in 1590. Although only half his army survived the grueling journey, the Moroccans crushed the Songhai at the battle of Tondibi in 1591. The Moroccans were unable to retain control of the region, and political disintegration followed. No African state was ever again able to unify all of west Africa into a single empire.

The Forest Kingdoms

Not all west Africans became Muslim, nor were all west African peoples merged into the great states described above.

HAUSA AND MOSSI

Many African communities, such as the Hausa and Mossi, formed their own confederations and kingdoms, developing urbanized governments. These confederations could be broadly compared to Dark Age Greece. Peoples originally organized on a tribal basis began to coalesce into small city-states. While retaining their related cultural and religious unity, each city-state competed with the others for political and economic dominance. Only when threatened by outside powers would the Hausa or Mossi city-states unite to face the threat. When the larger empires of Mali or Songhai were weak, the Hausa and Mossi could raid and plunder beyond their borders. When the great states were powerful, the Hausa and Mossi often became tributaries.

BENIN

One of the most famous and important of these smaller west African city-states was Benin, in the Niger delta region. The city of Benin is most famous for its brass statues and its huge fortification system of earthen embankments and "living" fortifications of hedges, trees, and thorn bushes. Benin and its neighbor Ifo produced some of the finest art in all premodern Africa.

The Decline of West African Civilization

The civilizations of west Africa were destined to fall victim to shifting patterns of world trade and new military technologies.

SHIFTING GOLD TRADE

The coming of the Portuguese to the west coast in the late fifteenth century affected the gold trade: Gold could now be transported by European ships instead of camel caravans crossing the Sahara. This broke the monopoly of the west African kingdoms on the gold trade, undermining their economic foundations. Furthermore, the vast influx of gold and silver from the Spanish conquest of the Aztecs and Incas and their mines in the New World created a decline in the world value of gold. These two factors combined to create an economic crisis in west Africa.

POLITICAL DISUNITY

This crisis was partially resolved by the creation of the Songhai empire, which united all regions of west Africa into a single state and trading community, with the ability to control trade and the value of African products. But when musket-armed Moroccans crushed the Songhai in 1591, west Africa disintegrated into dozens of small competing states, all of which were ultimately at the mercy of European and North African merchants.

SLAVE TRADE

The insatiable demand for cheap labor to work the plantations in the New World caused a vast increase in the Atlantic slave trade. Thus the great imperial system of the thirteenth through the sixteenth centuries was replaced in the seventeenth century by small competing west African kingdoms. This political disunity led to greatly increased internal warfare, the main purpose of which was to capture enemies to be sold as slaves to the Europeans.

THE BANTU PEOPLES

There are numerous ethnic groups in central and southern subsaharan Africa. Most of these peoples are collectively known as Bantu, a linguistic term referring to the cluster of related languages spoken in these regions. Bantu-speaking peoples are not indigenous to these areas of Africa but seem to have migrated from the Niger River region in west Africa beginning perhaps as early as 400 B.C.

Origins and Characteristics of the Bantu

Three main technological and cultural developments led to a revolution in the lives of the inhabitants of subsaharan Africa: cattle herding and agriculture, and the introduction of iron, and new forms of social organization.

AGRICULTURE

Agriculture seems to have been introduced into subsaharan Africa from the Nile valley and Tunisia perhaps as early as the fourth millennium B.C. Although the idea of agriculture seems to have derived from Near Eastern sources, the methods and types of crops harvested were quickly adopted to meet the wide range of environments, needs, and technologies of subsaharan Africa.

IRON

As in Asia and Europe, the introduction of iron greatly changed the nature of African society. Iron tools transformed African society in two ways. First, iron axes allowed the spread of agriculture into forested areas. A man with an iron ax could more swiftly clear land for farming, thereby greatly increasing agricultural productivity. In some regions iron also allowed for the development of better plows. Second, iron weapons provided a fundamental military advantage. States and tribes with iron weapons could dominate, enslave, conquer, and ultimately destroy any enemy lacking this technology. Thus with the introduction of iron Africa witnessed; (1) an increase in population, agricultural productivity, and prosperity; (2) the development of powerful military states; and (3) the migrations of iron-armed communities from the Niger valley region and northeast Africa throughout central and southern Africa. Thus arose the migration of Bantu-speaking iron-working agriculturalists from west Africa south and eastward from c. 400 B.C. to A.D. 500.

SOCIAL ORGANIZATION

A final factor contributing to the success of the Bantu tribes in their migrations was their social organization. The males of many Bantu tribes were organized into warrior societies, centered around male solidarity, the maintenance of martial values and skills, and religious and magical practices. Young men were trained in military skills, often accompanied by brutal initiation ceremonies testing their courage and endurance. They were also taught secret religious knowledge of the way of the warrior, ritually initiating them into the spiritual powers that lay behind success in battle and hunting. This martial mentality contributed to their desire for migration and conquest, as well as to their ability to defeat enemies and successfully expand their power and land.

Bantu Migrations

SCOPE OF THE MIGRATIONS

As Bantu populations increased, many tribes began to migrate in search of new lands for herding and agriculture. Beginning about the time of Christ, Bantu tribes moved eastward and southward, reaching the east coast of Africa by about A.D. 200. From there they continued their migrations southward, reaching the Kalahari desert and the Orange river by about 500. The intermixing of various Bantu tribes within this region made the final linguistic and archaeological picture somewhat complex. the final result was that by 500 Bantu peoples had come to dominate most of the southern half of Africa. With them they brought their mixed cattle-herding and farming economy, iron tools and weapons, and new forms of social and military organization.

NON-BANTU PEOPLES OF SOUTHERN AFRICA

Throughout their migrations the Bantu encountered various neolithic hunter-gatherer peoples inhabiting southern and eastern Africa, collectively called Khoisans (Bushmen, Hottentots). These groups, having neither the technology nor the economic resources and population levels to resist, were either absorbed by the Bantu, destroyed, or driven into marginal lands, such as the deep forests of the Congo or the deserts of the Kalihari, which were ill adapted to Bantu agricultural and herding techniques. There the Khoisans survived, continuing their neolithic lifestyle centered on hunting and gathering into the twentieth century.

State Formation

Beginning in the sixth century the Bantu communities of central and southern Africa witnessed a series of internal migrations, intermixing, and wars, culminating in the formation of a group of Bantu states and tribal confederations from the thirteenth through the seventeenth centuries. The most important of these was the kingdom of Mwenemutapa (also called Zimbabwe or Muene Motopo).

MWENEMUTAPA

The medieval state of Mwenemutapa centered in the region of the modern African state of Zimbabwe between the Zambezi and Limpopo rivers, flourishing between the thirteenth and early seventeenth centuries. It was the most important of a number of kingdoms of the Shona people, a sub-group of the Bantu.

Basis of Power. The power of Mwenemutapa was derived from three sources. First, the royal and martial traditions of the Bantu-speaking Shona tribes laid the political and military foundation of Mwenemutapa. Second, the discovery and efficient exploitation of the gold fields of the region, combined with agricultural production, provided wealth and prosperity. Finally, control of trade routes to the Islamic Swahili cities of the east coast of Africa provided additional wealth and prestige. This gave the kings of Mwenemutapa control of luxury products and ideas imported from the Islamic world and Asia. Although Mwenemutapa and the other Shona kingdoms of southeast Africa were in relatively continuous contact with the Islamic Swahili city-states, they seem to have been relatively little affected by Islam.

Great Zimbabwe. The most famous feature of the Shona culture was the walled palace complex at Great Zimbabwe, the capital and religious center of the Mwenemutapa kingdom. An outstanding example of indigenous African architecture, the stone towers, walls, palaces, shrines, and homes of Great Zimbabwe present the picture of a sophisticated local culture.

Decline. The decline of the Shona kingdoms in the mid-seventeenth century can be attributed to shifts in trading patterns due to Portuguese intervention, a worldwide decline in the value of gold following the discovery of the New World, environmental degradation due to overutilization of agricultural resources, internal warfare, and wars with the Portuguese, the most important of which occurred in the 1580s. These wars ended with the Portuguese establishing control over the old Swahili coastal cities, while the Shona tribes were left with control of the interior. Nonetheless, the age of Mwenemutapa domination had ended.

Swahili City-States

Trading contacts between the east coast of Africa and the Middle East began as early as 1500 B.C. As the centuries passed, traders and explorers worked their way south down the east coast of Africa, establishing small trading posts to serve as depots for goods from the interior. These trading posts developed into cities, which in turn became independent city-states.

ARAB INFLUENCES

The period of the most intense international commercial activity on the east coast began in the ninth century. Muslim Arab merchants began to dominate the trade routes, thereby linking the east African coastal cities into the international Muslim trading system. The thirty-seven merchant towns were collectively known as the Swahili (coastal) cities, a term also applied to a mixed Arabic-Bantu dialect of the region.

Kilwa. By the thirteenth century Kilwa had become the major commercial city. Under the Mahdali dynasty, Kilwa gained international importance, becoming the center of Islamic culture in east Africa. The traveler Ibn Battuta described it as "one of the finest and most substantially built towns" he had seen. The ruins of its palaces and mosques remain as the major architectural monuments of this period.

International Trade. The merchants of the Swahili city-states served as middlemen in an international trading system, shipping the gold, ivory, skins, iron, copper, rare woods, and slaves of east Africa to the Middle East and Asia. In return, they imported pottery, glass, cloth, weapons, and luxury items from as far away as China. The Swahili coastal cities thus linked the inland kingdoms such as Mwenemutapa with the wider world.

PORTUGUESE IMPACT

This period of international importance ceased with the arrival of the Portuguese in the early sixteenth century, who established control over the trade routes and most of the Swahili cities. The Swahili cities were left impoverished until the late seventeenth century, when Omani Arab fleets defeated the Portuguese and reestablished Muslim independence. The Portuguese were left in control only of the region around Mozambique. By this time, however, most international trade routes had come under European control. The Swahili cities never again witnessed the prosperity and importance they had enjoyed in the fourteenth and fifteenth centuries.

RELIGION IN AFRICA

Religion played a dominant role in culture, society, law, and intellectual life in all premodern societies; it was frequently the unifying and definitive cultural characteristic of premodern peoples. Subsaharan Africa was no different in this regard. There were four major religion in premodern Africa: African polytheism, African Christianity, Islam, and European Christianity.

African Polytheism

What is frequently called African polytheism or animism (the worship of spirits) is in fact a complex array of religions, often varying widely in doctrine and practice. Each of the hundreds of African communities and linguistic groups had its own unique religion. Nonetheless, there are a set of related characteristics found in most African polytheisms.

SUPREME GOD

Traditional African religion was polytheistic, with a vast number of gods, goddesses, and lesser spirits. There was also a widespread believe in a supreme god, the true creator and ruler of the universe. The various spirits of the lesser gods were often seen as manifestations of a single supreme power. When Christianity and Islam began to have an impact on the continent, many Africans readily accepted monotheism as another manifestation of their own supreme god. This allowed them to become Muslims or Christians while retaining many of their previous beliefs and rituals.

DIVINE KINGSHIP

Another widespread belief was the divine or semidivine nature of kingship. Throughout Africa kings were seen as possessing sacred power. This power derived from noble birth, control of the rituals necessary for communication with the gods, and from the king's own power and charisma as shown by prosperity and victory in battle. The divine status of the kings was seen in numerous widespread African practices, such as secluding the king from contact with commoners, elaborate court ritual, sacrifices, and taboos.

SHAMANS

African religions often centered on the powers of mediums and prophets. Certain individuals, usually including the king, were thought to have special access to the spirit world. Although frequently called "witch doctors," they are now generally described as shamans. African shamans could use their access to the spirit world for healing, divination (foretelling the future), and cursing. Animal sacrifice to obtain power over or from the spirits and gods was widespread in African religion.

African Christianity

Africans of the upper Nile and Horn region adopted Christianity at a very early stage, adapting it to their local traditions and worldview.

ORIGINS

From the very beginning, African Christianity established its own traditions, quite independent of European developments. Small communities of

Christians began appearing in Egypt in the first century A.D. Christianity was adopted as the official religion of Axum (in Ethiopia) by King Ezana about 350. It has remained the religion of Ethiopia ever since, so that Ethiopians form one of the oldest Christian communities in the world. Nubia was evangelized from Egypt in the sixth century. Thus by 600 the entire Nile valley, the Ethiopian highlands, and Yemen in Arabia had been Christianized, forming an interrelated Christian community. For the most part African Christians refused to yield to mounting political pressure from the "orthodox" European Christians to abandon their traditional doctrines and practices.

ISOLATION

With the Islamic conquests in the seventh century and the shifts in political power and religious orthodoxy in the Middle East, African Christianity began a long period of slow decline. African Christians retained and developed their traditions in isolation from the Christians in Europe for almost a thousand years. Today African Christianity is still the majority religion in Ethiopia, and the faith of a large minority (perhaps as high as 10 percent) in Egypt.

CHRISTIAN CULTURE

Christianity played a major part in the cultural and intellectual life of the communities of Egypt, Nubia, and Ethiopia. African monks and scholars maintained a long tradition of Christian scholarship and writing in the three major ecclesiastical languages of the region: Coptic (Egypt), Nubian, and Ge'ez (medieval Ethiopian). African Christians developed their own traditions of art, iconography (in which Jesus and other biblical figures frequently appear black), and church architecture.

Islam

The coming of Islam was one of the most significant cultural events in African history, ranking along with European colonization and conquests. The Muslim conquests brought Arab soldiers, merchants, and scholars into the communities of North Africa. Within a few centuries Islam had become the dominant religion of North Africa.

THE SPREAD OF ISLAM

The spread of Islam into subsaharan Africa followed the three major trade routes: the caravan trails across the Sahara; up the Nile River and the Red Sea; and along the oceanic trade routes on the east coast. Islam made its greatest impact in west Africa. There the great African empires of Mali and Songhai were ruled by Islamicized leaders from the twelfth century onward. In the Swahili city-states of east Africa, Islam became the religion of the Arab-African elite, predominating in the coastal cities but apparently not spreading extensively inland. In the upper Nile and Horn, Islamic penetration was much slower due to the establishment of strong Christian communities in the area. Islam did not penetrate into Nubia and Ethiopia until the fourteenth century, when it came in the wake of conquering Islamic armies from Egypt and Arabia.

IMPACT OF ISLAM

Although in all of these regions, the king, his court, nobles, merchants, and scholars were for the most part Muslim, many of the common people remained polytheists, following their ancestral religions. Even so, the impact of Islam in Africa was widespread and profound. The written language of scholarship was Arabic. When Africans outside of the Christian zone first began to write their native languages, they used the Arabic script, in much the same way that the Christianized Germanic tribes adopted the Roman alphabet for writing their languages. Islamic law, economics, and social concepts were adopted into African society with the conversion of the African elite to Islam. Timbuktu became one of the leading centers of Islamic learning, boasting a university where, for example, Africans could be found discussing the philosophy of Aristotle. Islamic architecture, as exemplified by mosques, palaces, and fortifications, also had an impact. In all of these cases, however, the Africans adapted Islamic civilization to their own preexisting cultures.

European Christianity

European Christianity was introduced largely under the influence of the Portuguese. Its greatest impact was in the Congo River basin and Ethiopia.

KONGO

European Christianity was most successful among the Kongo in modern Zaire. King Nzinga a Nkuwa was converted to Christianity by Portuguese missionaries, taking the name Alfonso I (r. 1506–1543). By the time of his death, Christianity had become strongly entrenched in the royal and noble families of the Kongo. In the long run, however, the exploitative policies of the Portuguese undermined their attempts at evangelization. Portuguese missionary efforts in east Africa were also notably unsuccessful.

ETHIOPIA

In 1529 Ahmad Gran, the Muslim sultan of Adal on the Horn, invaded Christian Ethiopia. Equipped with muskets, his army conquered most of the country in the next decade, leaving the Ethiopian king a refugee hiding in the mountains. In 1541 the Portuguese sent an expeditionary force of 400 musket-armed men to assist Ethiopia. With the help of their Portuguese allies, the Ethiopians defeated and killed Ahmad Gran in 1543. Ethiopian Christianity was thus preserved, and continued to the present.

STAGNATION OF CHRISTIANITY

By the mid-seventeenth century European Christianity had had relatively little impact on the religions of Africa. Rather, Islam continued to make progress throughout much of the continent through the early nineteenth century. It was only in the nineteenth century, when the Europeans gained complete political control of Africa, that European Christian missionaries began to have significant success among Africans.

THE SIGNIFICANCE OF AFRICA IN WORLD HISTORY

Africa's relationship with the rest of the world was dependent on its relative geographic isolation, which meant that its global interaction and role in cultural exchange and development was somewhat limited. Nonetheless, Africans contributed to the development of world civilization in a number of important ways.

Contacts with Other Civilizations

As previously noted, there were three main channels of contact: trans-Saharan, the Nile and Red seas, and the east coast. In the fifteenth century a fourth corridor was added by Portuguese explorations: the Atlantic seaboard. The relative importance of these routes varied through time in relation to changing patterns of political dominance and trade.

CONTACTS WITH THE MIDDLE EAST AND NORTH AFRICA

Eastern Corridor. Egyptian merchants and slavers first penetrated beyond the first cataract before 3000 B.C. From then on, Egyptian influence and occasionally political power spread south up the Nile and down the Red Sea coast. By the late second millennium B.C., ships from Egypt were beginning to make their way south of the Horn of Africa. The Greek historian Herodotus claims that a combined Egyptian and Phoenician expedition circumnavigated Africa in the sixth century B.C.

Trans-Saharan Corridor. The earliest record of trans-Saharan contacts with North Africa date to about 1000 B.C., when horse-drawn chariots apparently crossed the Sahara. In the first century A.D. camel caravans began to cross the Sahara. By the coming of Islam in the seventh century, caravans crossed the Sahara nearly every year. As discussed above, these regions were greatly influenced by the cultures of the Middle East, especially through the absorption of Christianity and Islam. Through trade with Muslim merchants, the peoples of Africa were brought into extensive commercial contact with all parts of Eurasia. Muslim armies also occasionally intervened in African affairs, such as the Almoravid conquest of Ghana in the eleventh century and the Moroccan destruction of the kingdom of Songhai in the late sixteenth.

CONTACTS WITH ASIA

Although Asians did not influence Africa nearly to the degree that the people of the Middle East did, there were important Asian contacts with Africa as well.

Early Contacts. The earliest seems to have been the migration by sea of Southeast Asians to Madagascar about A.D. 500. The Southeast Asians settled there, mixing with Bantu peoples. Later merchants from India and Southeast Asia brought a wide variety of important crops to Africa, such as bananas and Asian breeds of yams and rice, which proved effective new food sources in the African tropics.

Chinese Expeditions. The most important Asian contacts with Africa were the two Chinese expeditions of 1417–1419 and 1421–1422 which explored and traded with the Swahili cities of Africa. The Ming emperors eventually decided it was unwise to continue expeditions to Africa, leaving the east coast open for Portuguese domination eighty years later.

THE COMING OF THE EUROPEANS

Early Contacts. After the fall of the Roman empire and the rise of Islam Europeans were cut off from direct cultural and economic contacts with subsaharan Africa for almost 1,000 years. Although some European merchants sailed the Red Sea and thus may have had contact with Africans in the Horn region, the first direct sustained contact of Europeans came in the late fifteenth century.

Portuguese Explorations. The development of new sailing ships allowed the Portuguese to navigate south into the head winds. By the 1460s they had explored the southern Gold Coast of west Africa. In 1488 they rounded the southern tip of Africa, and in 1497–98 explored the east coast of Africa and reached India.

Beginnings of European Colonization. The Portuguese established trading forts on the Gold Coast, in the Congo, and at Mozambique on the east coast. These trading forts were established as ports for ships on their way to India, to control the gold trade from the interior, as missions for the evangelization of Africans, and as slaving posts. Despite several military expeditions into the interior, the Portuguese were generally unsuccessful in penetrating deep inland: The total number of Portuguese in Africa never exceeded a few thousand men. They did, however, manage to transform the previous trading patterns and increase the slave trade. By 1650 Dutch, English, and French merchants were beginning to intervene in Africa.

Full-scale European conquest and colonization of Africa did not begin until the nineteenth century.

Slavery in Premodern African History

THE NATURE OF PREMODERN SLAVERY

Slavery. Slavery was an ancient, accepted, and nearly universal human institution in premodern times. In antiquity people were enslaved for a number of reasons: failure to pay debts, punishment for crimes, or as prisoners of war. It was a widespread practice that people captured in war were released only if ransomed by friends and families. If no ransom was paid, the prisoners were sold into slavery. Slaves were used to supplement labor resources. Occasionally this took the form of agricultural slavery, as in the plantation system in the United States. But in the premodern world there were usually ample numbers of semi-free peasants to provide the needed agricultural labor.

Royal Slaves and Warrior-Slaves. Slaves were therefore frequently used for specialized labor: working mines, special craftsmen, and personal servants. Many slaves managed to rise to positions of importance and power. This was especially true of slaves of kings, who often ended up serving as high ministers in royal government. In the Islamic world, slaves were frequently trained as soldiers, creating a warrior-slave caste known as *mamluks*. These slaves increasingly usurped power and took control of governments in some regions of the Middle East.

Slavery in Africa. Most premodern societies accepted slavery as an institution, but generally enslaved only foreigners. Africans were thus only one among many ethnic groups that were enslaved by their enemies. Indeed, there are accounts of Europeans being enslaved by Africans. The premodern slave trade, although brutal and inhuman, was not particularly devastating to African civilization, largely because the number of people enslaved was relatively limited. The growth of the European plantation system in the Americas, however, brought an insatiable need for cheap labor. This in turn created the massive African slave trade of the eighteenth and early nineteenth centuries. This demand for slaves led to continual warfare, as different black communities attacked each other in search of slaves to sell to the Europeans. The net result in Africa was political and social disruption, and economic decline.

THE FIRST AFRICAN DIASPORA

Africans in the Ancient Near East. Until the twentieth century the fundamental cause of African migration was the slave trade. In the first diaspora (scattering of a people)—which began in the Bronze Age and continued through the coming of Islam in the Near East—Egyptians and North Africans used subsaharan Africa as a source for slaves and mercenaries. For the most part the slaves were dispersed throughout the Middle

East, with a few ending up in southern Europe and Asia. African mercenaries served in all major military systems of the Middle East and southern Europe up to the Middle Ages. African soldiers participated in the campaigns of Ramses into Syria, Xerxes's invasion of Greece, and in Roman imperial armies.

Africans in the Islamic World. The coming of Islam brought a shift in the patterns of the slave trade. African slaves were retained for the most part within the Islamic world. Under the Islamic slave system many Africans rose increasingly to positions of prominence in Islamic society. Many ministers and rulers in Islamic North Africa and the Middle East were African or part-African; large regiments of African slave-soldiers served in many Islamic armies. Indeed, an east African warlord serving in India, Muzaffar Shah, instituted a palace coup, ruling Bangladesh from 1491 to 1494.

African and the Premodern Global Economy

Although a wide range of products were exported from Africa, the global impact of Africa on the premodern world economy was the export of gold and slaves. Africa contained the largest source of world gold until the opening of precious metal resources from the Americas. International trade and coinage systems of the Middle East, Europe, and, to a lesser extent, Asia were all dependent on African gold. Islamic dominance of trade during the Middle Ages was in part due to their control over gold exports from Africa. The African slave trade was of less importance in global terms before the coming of the Europeans, but nonetheless, African slaves supplied a major source of labor during Islamic times, especially in the specialized field of slave-soldiers.

African Cultural Achievement

Africa's relative isolation meant that African culture did not have a great impact on other regions of the world in premodern times. However, the indigenous cultural tradition created numerous important works of literature, art, and architecture.

LITERATURE

Most African societies were non-literate during the premodern period. Unfortunately, most of this premodern oral literature has not survived. There were, however, four major literary traditions in premodern subsaharan Africa.

Nubian. The oldest subsaharan literature comes from the kingdom of Napata and was written in Egyptian hieroglyphics. The subsequent cultures of Nubia were all literate, although the Meroitic script cannot be translated. Nubian Christian literature is, unfortunately, fragmentary, since Christian writings ceased to be copied and cared for after the Islamic conquest of the middle Nile in the fifteenth century.

Ethiopia. Ethiopia provides a wealth of African literature during the Middle Ages. While most Ethiopian writings center on religious issues, there are a number of legends and historical chronicles. Ethiopians also preserved a number of interesting religious books: the Book of Enoch, which was quoted in the Epistle of Jude in the New Testament, has survived as part of the canonical Ethiopian Bible.

Arabic. Arabic was the most important literary and scholarly language in Africa during the Middle Ages, playing the same role in Africa that Latin played in medieval Europe. Arabic was the language of scholarship in North Africa and Egypt, and dozens of important accounts of life in Africa survive by Arab historians and geographers. Arabic became the language of court administration, religion, law, and scholarship in several centers of African culture. Timbuktu became a famous center for history writing in the sixteenth century, as did the prosperous merchant city of Kilwa.

Al-Jahiz, 776–869. The most famous African literary figure in premodern times was al-Jahiz, a Muslim black living in Baghdad. The descendant of Africans, al-Jahiz received an outstanding education and became the leading literary and philosophical figure at the court of Baghdad. He is frequently considered one of the best prose writers of classical Arabic.

Oral Tradition. Although not committed to writing until the nineteenth and twentieth centuries, the African oral traditions contain tales and histories extending back into premodern times. These tales were transmitted by professional poets (called *griots* in west Africa) in much the same way that the tales of Homer and parts of the Bible were passed down to succeeding generations. These tales were finally written down, often centuries after having first been composed. The most famous of these African oral tales is the *Epic of Sundiata*. African oral traditions have been used by many modern scholars to reconstruct the history and customs of premodern times.

ART AND ARCHITECTURE

Art. Africa is noted for its extensive tradition of rock painting, spanning thousands of years. Christian Ethiopia and Nubia developed manuscript illumination and church painting. Ife, in the Niger delta, is famous for its magnificent naturalistic bronze sculptures, especially ritual busts of royalty. Benin, also in the Niger delta, has a remarkable style of royal bronze busts. African tribal art includes examples of wood, ivory and metalwork. In the twentieth century a positive reexamination of traditional African art and music inspired the development of several modern Western art forms and certain styles of music.

Architecture. Since most African architecture was built in wood, relatively little survives from premodern times. However, there are several important surviving examples of premodern African architecture. The pyramids and temples of Meroe were built in imitation of Egyptian styles, but with indigenous modifications. At Lalibela, the capital of Christian Ethiopia, a large number of delightful churches were excavated from solid rock. The whole city of Lalibela was reportedly built following the pattern for New Jerusalem outlined in the Book of Revelations. The great mosque at Timbuktu is a good example of the adaptation of Islamic architecture to the African architectural tradition. Kilwa contains the ruins of a splendid mosque and palace. The stone ruins of Great Zimbabwe represent the culmination of southern Bantu architecture.

RELIGION

During the premodern period, Africa was largely influenced by Islam and Christianity, creating unique fusions of those two religions with local African traditions. However, with the diaspora of Africans to the New World during the European slave trade, African religious ideas were transported outside of Africa. In the Americas these ideas were adopted and transformed, largely in connection with Catholicism, leading to the development of two new religious movements: Afro-Brazilian religions, as characterized by Umbanda, and Afro-Caribbean religions, such as voodoo, both of which are widespread among blacks of these regions. Both consist of a core of African religious ideas and practices overlaid with a veneer of Catholicism. Although popularly associated with black magic, a more accurate view of these religions is ritual mediumship. By a set of rituals the priest or priestess is able to contact the spirit world to obtain knowledge or blessings for the worshipers, and, on occasion, allow a spirit to possess the body of a worshiper.

Unlike the rest of Africa, northeast Africa was characterized by ancient and continuous contacts between Egypt and Nubia, and Arabia and Ethiopia. The kingdoms of the northeast were dependent on control of trade routes from the interior of Africa to the Red Sea for their prosperity. The civilizations of these regions were literate, highly advanced, and produced splendid cultural achievements. Christianity was adopted as the state religion in Ethiopia in the fourth century and in Nubia in the sixth. Their relative isolation from other Christian communities following the rise of Islam in the seventh century created a period of nearly one thousand years of struggle between these African Christians and Muslims. This struggle culminated with the ultimate collapse of Nubia and the withdrawal inland of Ethiopia in the face of repeated Islamic attacks from the thirteenth to the sixteenth centuries.

The introduction of the camel, the opening up of the gold trade, the rise of the mounted knight, and the coming of Islam to west Africa all combined to create a sequence of the most advanced, wealthy, and powerful states in premodern African history. The great empires of west Africa from A.D. 1000–

1600—Ghana, Mali, and Songhai—rivaled their early contemporaries in Europe in wealth and power, and were treated by the sultans of North Africa and Egypt as equals. With the collapse of Songhai and the rise of the slave wars, the region that had once boasted some of the wealthiest empires of the world degenerated into relative political chaos, continual war, and depression, leaving the way open for eventual European colonization in the nineteenth century.

The coming of cattle herding, agriculture and iron to Africa gave the Bantu peoples the economic and military base that allowed them to migrate throughout most of southern Africa, displacing or merging with local neolithic peoples. This period of tribal migrations gave way to the growth of states and tribal confederations beginning in the thirteenth century, culminating in the formation of powerful Bantu kingdoms such as Zimbabwe and Kongo. The arrival of the Portuguese and other Europeans beginning in the late fifteenth century would eventually modify, but not completely destroy, the Bantu system of tribal confederations and states. Indeed, the most famous Bantu warrior state, the Zulu, established their kingdom in the face of European opposition in the nineteenth century.

Selected Readings

Adams, William Y. *Nubia: Corridor to Africa* (1977)

Ajayi, J. E. Ade, and Michael Crowder, eds. *Historical Atlas of Africa* (1985)

Beach, D. N. *The Shona & Zimbabwe, 900–1850: An Outline of Shona History* (1980)

Buxton, David. *The Abyssinians* (1970)

Chittick, H. Neville, and Robert I. Rotberg. *East Africa and the Orient: Cultural Syntheses in Pre-Colonial Times* (1975)

Curtin, P., et al. *African History* (1978)

Davidson, B. *A History of West Africa, 1000–1800* (1966)

Fage, J. D. *A History of Africa* (1978)

Garlake, P. S. *Great Zimbabwe* (1973)

_____. *The Kingdoms of Africa* (1978)

Levitzion, N. *Ancient Ghana and Mali* (1973)

Niane, D. T., ed. *Africa from the XIIth to the XVIth Century* (1984)

Oliver, Roland, and J. D. Fage, eds. *The Cambridge History of Africa*, 8 vols. (1975)

Oliver, R., and J. D. Fage. *A Short History of Africa* (1962)

Tamrat, Taddesse. *Church and State in Ethiopia: 1270–1527* (1972)

Trimingham, J. S. *A History of Islam in West Africa* (1962)

_____. *Islam in East Africa* (1964)

UNESCO. *General History of Africa* (1981)

Willett, F. *African Art: An Introduction* (1971)

13

Pre-Columbian America

(Most dates are approximate.)

3000 B.C.	Beginnings of Old Copper Culture in North America
1700–700	Ritual Center at Poverty Point, Louisiana
1500	Earliest use of gold in the Andean mountains
1500–400	Olmec civilization in Mesoamerica
1200–900	San Lorenzo, earliest temple-city in the Americas
c. 1000	Maize introduced into North America from Mesoamerica
850–200	Chavin, earliest temple-city in the Andean region
200 B.C.–A.D. 400	Hopewell culture in Mississippi valley
200–650 A.D.	The empire of Teotihuacán
200–700	Monte Alban dominates the Oaxaca valley in Mesoamerica
200–850	The Classic Maya period
c. 300	Teotihuacán conquers highland Guatemala
c. 400	Teotihuacán conquers Petén region
500–900	Empires of Tiahuanaco and Huari
615–683	Pacal, king of Palenque
628–734	Ah-Cacaw, king of Tikal
750–850	Collapse of the Classic Maya
c. 800	Introduction of metallurgy into Mesoamerica

900–1150	Chaco Canyon civilization
900–1250	Toltec empire in highland Mexico
900–1450	Hohokam civilization
900–1476	Chimu kingdom dominates the Andes
970–1000	Topilzin, Toltec high priest of Quetzalcoatl
987	Topilzin migrates to Yucatán, captures city of Chichén Itzá
987–1187	Toltecs at Chichén Itzá
982	Vikings first reach the Americas
1156	Fall of Toltec capital of Tula
1187–1446	Mayapan dynasty of northern Yucatán
1193	Aztec barbarians found city of Tenochtitlán
c. 1200	Height of Cahokia, largest city in North America
1325–1519	Aztec empire
1426–1440	Itzcoatl, king of Aztecs, begins Aztec military conquests
c. 1400	Navajo and Apache migrations into Southwest
1463–1471	Pachacutec founds the Incan empire
1487	80,000 people sacrificed at dedication of temple of Tenochtitlán
1492	Columbus discovers the Americas
1503–1520	Montezuma II, last emperor of the Aztecs
1519–1524	Cortés conquers the Aztec empire
1521	The Aztec capital of Tenochtitlán plundered by Cortés
1531–1533	Pizarro conquers the Incan empire

*P*re-Columbian civilizations seem to have originated and developed in nearly complete isolation from the Old World. Civilization in the New World ranged from the small regional ritual centers of Chaco Canyon and Snaketown to vast metropolises like Teotihuacán, with population levels nearly reaching those of the great cities of the Old World. Political organization ranged from the independent city-states of the Maya to empires like the Aztecs. In many ways pre-Columbian American civilizations were the social and cultural equals of those in the Old World. The art and architecture of Mesoamerica includes some of the finest in the world. Only in metallurgy and some forms of technology did they lag seriously behind. The first permanent encounter of pre-Columbian Americans with the

*peoples of the Europe proved a disaster which culminated in the destruction
of their civilizations by brutal adventurers like Cortés and Pizarro.*

BACKGROUND TO PRE-COLUMBIAN AMERICA

Pre-Columbian American civilizations represent something of a
paradox for world historians, since they don't fit the traditional Old World
models of civilization. The cultures of Mesoamerica (modern Mexico and
Guatemala), for example, attained levels of cultural development com-
parable with those of the Old World, yet remained at a neolithic technological level until the ninth century A.D. The cultures of South America nestled
in some of the world's highest mountains, likewise developed to levels as
sophisticated as the Old World, but without a written language. Thus the
study of pre-Columbian societies is valuable not only for its own sake, but
as a test case for theories about patterns of world history.

Geography

The American hemisphere includes examples of every type of climatic
and geographic environment on Earth. Arctic tundra dominates the far north.
In southwest North America we find extensive deserts; the Amazon is a
region of vast tropical rain forests. Interestingly, pre-Columbian civilizations often developed in some of the more difficult types of terrain: the harsh
deserts in the southwest U.S., tropical forests in the Petén, and mountain
highlands in the Andes. Oddly, civilizations of the Indians in the fertile and
temperate Mississippi River valleys—which in many ways are more fertile
than the Nile, Indus, or Yellow rivers—were among the less sophisticated
in the New World.

There are several major geographical features which had an important
effect on pre-Columbian civilizations. The entire hemisphere is divided by
a series of mountain ranges running north to south: the Rocky mountains in
North America, the Sierra Madre in Mesoamerica, and the Andes in South
America. The two major river systems are the Amazon in South America
and the Mississippi in North America. Civilization developed only in the
latter. Pre-Columbian civilizations can be divided into three cultural zones,
roughly corresponding to North America, Mesoamerica, and South America.

**Limits of
Knowledge**

Pre-Columbian civilizations remained largely prehistoric; we lack written records for most of their history. No surviving writing systems ever
developed in North and South America. Mesoamerica, on the other hand,
did have a hieroglyphic writing system. Unfortunately, most pre-fourteenth

century Mesoamerican records were destroyed by a combination of natural decay, Spanish vandalism, and religious suppression. A study of pre-Columbian civilizations before the fifteenth century is therefore largely dependent on archaeological data. Thus, although a good deal can be said about pre-Columbian economic, social, and technological history, much less is understood about their ideas and feelings; we know the names of no one living before about A.D. 400. Nor are most of the original pre-Columbian place names known. Most of the place names mentioned below are not the original names of the sites and cultures, but European or archaeological names given only in the last few centuries. Furthermore, many of the conclusions of archaeologists are hypothetical, controversial, and subject to rapid change as new discoveries are made.

The Earliest Americans

The western hemisphere was the last region of the world to be inhabited. During the various ice ages of the past 100,000 years, the ocean level decreased up to 90 meters, creating a broad land bridge between Asia and Alaska in the region now known as the Bering Sea. Although the issue is disputed, there is no conclusive evidence of extensive human occupation in the New World before 13,000 B.C. Beginning about that time, northeast Asian arctic hunting and fishing bands migrated from Asia to Alaska, and began to move southward into North America. The successors of the early Stone Age immigrants are know to archaeologists as the Clovis peoples of North America, and were essentially big-game hunters. These same human communities slowly migrated throughout the continent, adapting their lifestyles to the new environments they encountered. By at least 9000 B.C. human hunting bands had reached Terra del Fuego at southern tip of South America.

PRE-COLUMBIAN CONTACTS WITH THE OLD WORLD

Columbus's discovery of the New World in 1492 is often misunderstood. In fact, he was by no means the first person from the Old World to visit the western hemisphere. The Bering straits in Alaska remained a pathway for primitive fishermen to sail between Asia and the New World throughout pre-Columbian times. The Vikings established small colonies in eastern Canada in the twelfth and thirteenth centuries, but the long-term impact of this contact was very limited and the colonies ultimately disappeared. There is also controversial evidence of possible Phoenician, Roman, Irish, Chinese, Japanese, and South Asian contacts with the New World. Although uncertain, the possibility that Old World ships were blown off course in storms and marooned in the New World should not be discounted. But whatever the exact nature of these possible early pre-Columbian contacts with the Old World, Columbus's discovery was unique. Columbus established the first permanent and extensive contact between the Old and New worlds. In doing so, he radically transformed the nature of all the civilizations on earth.

NORTH AMERICA

Early Hunters

Throughout the pre-Columbian era, most regions of North America were inhabited only by hunters and gatherers. Following the end of the last Ice Age, climatic change and overhunting by humans contributed to the extinction of many of the large mammals (such as mammoths), which had served as the main source of food for many of these hunting bands. This caused human groups in some regions to develop specialized hunting and gathering techniques for particular environments. Although there were variations and changes in technologies and lifestyles throughout pre-Columbian times, most parts of North America remained at a hunting and gathering level of social organization.

In two regions of North America, however, civilizations did develop: among the Indians of the Southwest, and the Woodland cultures of the Mississippi and Ohio river systems. Although neither of these groups ever reached the levels of sophistication found in Mesoamerica or South America, their achievements are nonetheless noteworthy.

Southwest Civilizations

ORIGINS

The name "Southwest Indians" is used by archaeologists to designate the pre-Columbian Indian societies of the southwest United States and northwest Mexico. Their precise relationship to the historic ethnic groups of this area is not certain. Some tribes, like the Zuñi, Puma, and Hopi, are probably descendants of earlier peoples. Others, like the Navajo and Apache, migrated into the southwest from the north only in the fifteenth century.

Hunting and gathering groups inhabited this region for thousands of years until the introduction of maize (corn) agriculture and irrigation techniques from Mesoamerica about 1000 B.C. During the next thousand years, strains of maize were bred which were adapted to the harsh semi-arid environment of the southwest. Between A.D. 200 and 900 people called Basketmakers by archaeologists organized small agricultural villages. By 900 these scattered agricultural villages of the southwest began to coalesce into distinct cultural zones, each centering around an important ritual center (a place of religious pilgrimage, festivals, and rituals). The following are the three most important Southwest Indian cultures.

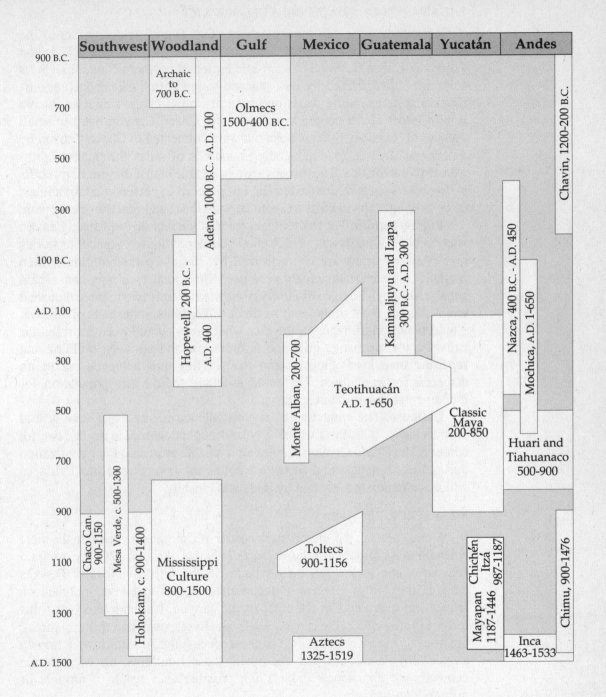

Fig. 13.1   Pre-Columbian Civilizations, 900 B.C.–A.D. 1500

THE ANASAZI OF CHACO CANYON, 900–1150

Anasazi is a Navajo term meaning "Old Ones," which refers to the ancient Indians of northern New Mexico and Arizona and southern Utah and Colorado. Chaco Canyon is a semi-arid region of northern New Mexico. Its culture is characterized by well-planned towns (often called pueblos), irrigation systems, and a focus on important ritual centers such as Pueblo Bonito. Most of the people associated with Chaco Canyon lived in small villages of less than 1,000 people, but were connected to Chaco Canyon by a network of ritual roads extending hundreds of miles throughout northwestern New Mexico. These roads are remarkable in that they make no shifts in direction to accommodate terrain, but proceed in perfectly straight lines, often carving stairs in cliffs to avoid curving the road to take an easier path.

Pueblo Bonito. The main ritual center of the Anasazi of Chaco Canyon was Pueblo Bonito. It was a hemispheric cluster of houses, some four stories high. Anasazi ruins are characterized by *kivas*—round buildings, often partially subterranean, which were used for social meetings and sacred rituals. Although Pueblo Bonito was inhabited by only two to three thousand people during most of the year, at times of festivals, thousands of Anasazi would make pilgrimages to the city where they would perform religious rituals, trade, exchange gifts and information, and work on building and repairing their kivas, houses, and roads. They thus achieved maximum dispersal for agriculture, but could mobilize their entire population for monumental construction projects.

Collapse. The environment of New Mexico is harsh and semi-arid at best. Evidence indicates that a fifty-year drought occurred in the late twelfth century. The Chaco Canyon peoples were unable to sustain their civilization during this drought, and their culture collapsed, reverting to small villages which were only loosely tied by trade and kinship.

MESA VERDE, 500–1300

Mesa Verde, in the southeastern corner of Colorado, is home to the most splendid pre-Columbian ruins in North America. Around 1200 the Anasazi Indians of the region left their villages in the fertile valleys of Fewkes canyon, moving to clusters of fortresslike houses and kivas perched on ledges and overhangs in the cliffs of the canyon. It seems likely that this move to fortresses in the canyon walls was in response to a military threat, but its exact nature is unknown. The most spectacular Anasazi town is known as the Cliff Palace. As with the other Anasazi cultures, the Mesa Verde centers were abandoned about 1300, possibly as a result of drought or military conflict.

THE HOHOKAM AND SNAKETOWN, 900–1450

The Hohokam culture developed in a well-watered floodplain of the Gila river basin in southern Arizona, centering on the ritual center of Snaketown. As with other Anasazi cities, Snaketown (near modern Phoenix, Arizona) was a small settlement of about 1000 inhabitants, but served as the ritual center for the Hohokam people of much of southern Arizona. It is characterized by a well-developed irrigation system, and ritual monumental architecture.

Mesoamerican Influences. The most intriguing monumental buildings at Snaketown are the ball courts which have been found at several Hohokam sites, designed for playing the ritual ball game of Mesoamerica (described below). Snaketown probably served as a trading post for merchants or products from central Mexico, and in many ways it can be seen as the northernmost manifestation of Mesoamerican culture. Long distance trade to Mesoamerica was frequent, though not continuous, focusing on luxury items such as exotic bird feathers and copper bells. From Snaketown, Mesoamerican products and ideas were dispersed throughout the Southwest Indian cultural zone.

Collapse. The reason for the collapse of the Hohokam culture is unknown. It may have included drought, the disruption of trade from Mesoamerica due to war, or the military incursions of the early Apache and Navajo, who entered the region in the late fifteenth century. Whatever the exact cause, Snaketown was abandoned around 1450.

Woodland Civilizations

The term "Woodland Civilizations" defines a sequence of cultures throughout the Mississippi river basin. It is divided into four major periods.

ARCHAIC (TO 700 B.C.)

During the Archaic period the Woodland peoples were hunters and gatherers with sparse populations. Sophisticated agriculture was not present. One of the major achievements of the Archaic period was the development of Chalcolithic technology, using unsmelted beaten copper for tools, weapons, and luxury items. This Old Copper Culture began about 3000 B.C. in the Keweenaw peninsula of the Great Lakes area, where naturally occurring copper can be found. The major impact of the development of copper-working was to contribute to the creation of increasingly wide exchange networks, which eventually would encompass the entire midwest and eastern United States, and southern Canada. The most intriguing archaeological site of this period is Poverty Point, Louisiana (1700–700 B.C.), where groups of Archaic peoples created a ritual center consisting of a central shrine surrounded by six concentric semicircular dirt ridges. It was probably built for astronomical observation and the celebration of annual festivals.

ADENA OR EARLY WOODLAND PERIOD (1000 B.C.– A.D. 100)

The Adena culture centered in the Ohio river valley. This period is characterized by the beginnings of archaic agriculture, pottery, the development of long-distance exchange routes, and the creation of a wide range of earthworks, including burial mounds, ritual mounds, and perhaps fortifications. Some splendid artistic funerary goods have been discovered from the Adena period.

HOPEWELL OR MIDDLE WOODLAND PERIOD (200 B.C.–A.D. 400)

Around the time of Christ a combination of increasing population, improved agricultural techniques and expanding exchange networks led to the development of an advanced culture called Hopewell. In a sense, the Hopewell period is a more sophisticated and geographically extensive version of the Adena culture, with increasingly complex religious practices and social organization. Although there are regional variations, the Hopewell is noted for similar cultural patterns throughout the Mississippi river basin.

Trade. Informal trade networks developed, including the exchange of obsidian from Wyoming, copper from the Great Lakes, silver from Ontario, and ocean products from the Gulf. The use of natural unsmelted copper continued, with the creation of numerous copper tools and works of art. The Hopewell period is also noted for its splendid funerary art, discovered in the hundreds of burial and ritual mounds found throughout the region. Ritual earthworks, such as the Great Serpent Mound in Ohio, indicate the growing importance of religion and ritual in Hopewell societies, and their capacity to organize relatively large groups of people for cooperative efforts. By about 400 the Hopewell exchange system had collapsed, shattering the previous cultural continuity. During the next 400 years the Woodland Indians continued at roughly the same technological level, but were divided into numerous small regional cultures, with much more limited interaction.

MISSISSIPPIAN OR LATE WOODLAND PERIOD (800–1500)

Origins. The climax of pre-Columbian civilization in the eastern United States was initiated by the introduction of maize and bean agriculture from Mexico. This was made possible by the development of new hardier strains of maize which could flourish in the colder North American climates. Combined with the cultivation of indigenous plants, maize agriculture revolutionized Woodland Indian life in many ways.

Growth of Cities. Over several centuries following 800, these improved crops brought an approximately five-fold increase in population. Mississippian communities centered on river valleys and floodplains, where maize agriculture was most successful, and where irrigation was not necessary. Whereas previous Woodland cultures had remained at the village and primitive chiefdom level of social organization, Mississippian peoples developed true urban centers and more sophisticated forms of government. Society was stratified, and military conflict spread rapidly as chiefdoms competed for prestige and the control over the best agricultural land. Many of the major Mississippian sites were fortified with mounds, moats, and wooden stockades, indicating frequent military conflict.

Cahokia. The most important Mississippian site is Cahokia, in southwestern Illinois, the largest city in pre-Columbian North America. Cahokia and its surrounding floodplain contained up to 30,000 people in the thirteenth century—as many as contemporary London. The focus of the city was on a large ritual square called the Grand Plaza. This plaza was dominated by Monk's Mound, a huge earthen temple mound. It is the largest earthwork in pre-Columbian North America, with a base greater than that of the Great Pyramid of Egypt. Over 100 smaller mounds have been discovered at Cahokia which were used for temples, tombs, or elite dwellings. The area surrounding Monk's Mound and the Grand Plaza was fortified by a wooden palisade with towers and gates; much of the population lived outside the fortifications, to which they could retreat in times of crisis.

There is clear evidence from burials that Cahokia was ruled by a powerful stratified elite class. One king was buried with 800 arrows and several beheaded male sacrifices; fifty young women were strangled and buried with the king to accompany him into the afterlife. Although disputed, some archaeologists see Cahokia as the center of a primitive state, ruling the smaller cities and villages surrounding it, and extending its power through trade, colonization, and conquest. Religion was a major force in the life of the Mississippian peoples, as indicated by the vast effort applied to building temples and burial mounds, and the high value and quality of grave goods.

Decline. By the time of the coming of the Europeans, the Mississippian culture was in decline, and Cahokia had been abandoned. The previous extensive exchange networks had disappeared, and political units fragmented into small chiefdoms. The Natchez Indians of the lower Mississippi are the best documented historical example of late Mississippian Indians. They were still building temples and burial mounds like their ancestors, when, in the seventeenth century, they were visited by the French. A combination of European disease and colonial expansion finished the destruction of the already declining Mississippian peoples. Thereafter, the history of North America becomes the story of the European colonists' conquest of the continent.

MESOAMERICA

Background to Mesoamerican Civilizations

Mesoamerica is an archaeological term used to describe the region of modern Mexico and Guatemala. It contained the most complex, sophisticated, and highly developed civilizations of pre-Columbian America.

GEOGRAPHY AND ETHNOLOGY

There are five major cultural regions of Mesoamerica (see map): (1) the Guatemalan highlands; (2) the Yucatán peninsula; (3) the Gulf coast and Veracruz region; (4) the Oaxaca valley; and (5) the Mexican highlands.

Mesoamerica contains a wide range of environments, leading to the development of numerous types of human adaptation and cultures. A range of mountainous highlands runs up the entire region, somewhat hindering communications between the Pacific and Atlantic sea coasts. Environments include the dense tropical forests of the Petén, swamps and marshes, coniferous forest of some highland regions, tropical savannah, grassland, arid zones, and deserts.

Although the ethnolinguistic patterns of Mesoamerica are very complex, we will deal with only four major ethnic groups: the Maya of the Guatemala highlands and the Yucatán and Petén peninsula, the Zapotec-Mixtec of Oaxaca, and the Toltecs and Nahuatl-Aztec of the central Mexican highlands.

CHARACTERISTICS OF MESOAMERICAN CIVILIZATIONS

Historians and archaeologists divide Mesoamerican history into five periods: Archaic (7000–1500 B.C.), Formative (1500 B.C.–A.D. 150), Classic (150–900), Early Postclassic (900–1250), and Late Postclassic (1250–1519). Many of these periods are further subdivided into early, middle, and late phases. Mesoamerican civilizations have the following broadly shared characteristics:

Agriculture. A complex, intensive, and highly organized agricultural system developed by the Classic period, including intensive use of swampland (raised field system) and lakes (*chinampas* or "floating gardens," i.e., raised fields in the lake). Agriculture was based on combinations of three principal crop—corn, beans, and squash—and a wide range of specialty crops. Few domesticated animals were used for food.

City-States. Although larger political units could be found, Mesoamerican civilization centered around city-states and temple centers. Urban life was highly developed; Teotihuacán had as many as 250,000 people, making it not only the largest city of pre-Columbian America, but one of the largest cities in the premodern world. Most people lived in smaller agricul-

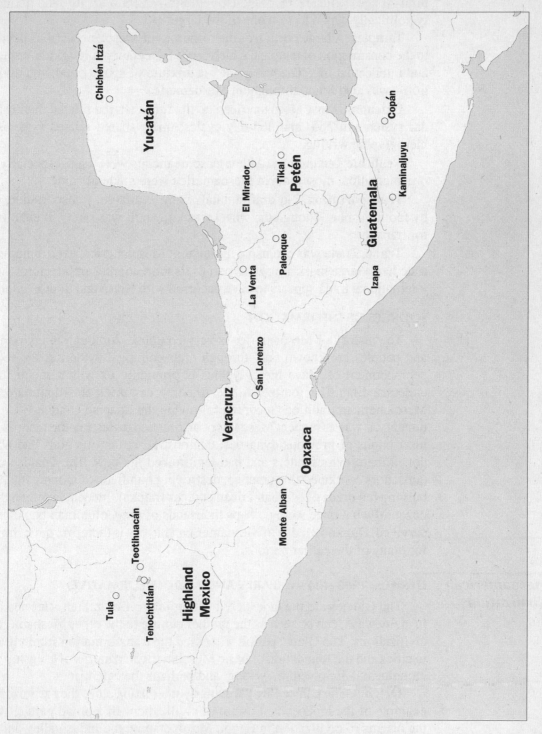

Fig. 13.2   Mesoamerica

tural villages which were religiously, culturally, economically, and frequently politically dependent on one of the larger cities.

Temples. A large portion of the resources of Mesoamerica was devoted to the construction of temples, which served as centers of religious, cultural, and intellectual life. The ball game—a mixture of sport, ritual, and divination—was also found throughout Mesoamerica.

Calendar. Most Mesoamerican civilizations shared related dual calendar systems of 260- and 365-day cycles; many shared related systems of hieroglyphic writing.

Neolithic Technology. Although some metals were used, especially for ornamentation, most tools in Mesoamerica were made of stone.

Transportation. No draft animals were available; transportation was by foot or canoe. Though the wheel was known, it was rarely, if ever, used for transport.

Trade. Trade was extensive throughout Mesoamerica; each major city-state had a large market plaza as part of its monumental architecture. Some international trade appears to have occurred with North and South America.

SOURCES OF INFORMATION

The history of Mesoamerica is very complex. Although many periods and peoples are known only through archaeological evidence, the recent decipherment of Maya hieroglyphics is providing us with a much fuller understanding. The fourteenth and fifteenth centuries are illuminated by Mesoamerican traditions recorded following the Spanish conquest. Unfortunately, it was a frequent Mesoamerican practice to destroy the records and inscriptions of previous dynasties, demonstrating that the gods had abandoned the previous rulers and had legitimized the new. The Spanish conquistadors continued this practice, destroying hundreds of monuments, and burning hundreds of Mesoamerican codices (books). Indeed, less than three dozen of what once were perhaps thousands of pre-Columbian books have survived. Our knowledge of Mesoamerican history is therefore quite limited for many of the earlier periods.

Mesoamerican Civilizations

OLMECS, 1500–400 B.C. (EARLY AND MIDDLE FORMATIVE)

The Olmecs are the oldest civilization in pre-Columbian America and, in many ways, can be seen as the mother culture to the other Mesoamerican civilizations. The Olmec period witnessed the transformation from villages to cities and the foundation of basic Mesoamerican patterns of kingship, art, monumental architecture, writing, and perhaps the calendar.

Origins. The Olmecs are particularly interesting since they represent an example of the independent origin of civilization. In a broad parallel with the origins of civilization in Egypt, Mesopotamia, the Indus valley and the Yellow river valley, Olmec civilization was based on the development of agricultural techniques adapted to river basins and swamplands. The Olmecs transition from small farming villages to civilization came as a reaction to the stresses created by new social and economic developments: intensification of agricultural production to feed an expanding population; the need to organize labor for large and complex irrigation projects in the swampy deltas; the creation of a religious ideology justifying the collection of surplus produce by the elites; and the collective use of surplus labor for monumental religious architecture.

Olmec Civilization. Olmec civilization centered around the two ritual centers of San Lorenzo and La Venta in the Gulf region of Veracruz, Mexico. Political power seems to have shifted between these major city-states. San Lorenzo dominated the region from 1200 to 900 B.C., creating the first Mesoamerican monumental architecture. It was destroyed in war about 900 B.C., after which political power centered at La Venta from 900 to 400 B.C. There the Olmec reached their cultural height, with a massive program of temple and tomb construction and splendid sculpture. La Venta became the most important Olmec site, the center of culture, religious pilgrimage, and perhaps political and military control. The famous colossal stone heads, probably portraits of Olmec rulers, exemplify the magnificence of their civilization.

Influence. The Olmecs influenced many other early cultures in Mesoamerica; their art and artifacts can be found throughout the region. Archaeologists debate whether this influence reflects a political and military expansion beyond the Olmec homeland, or merely a network of trade and cultural contacts. Whatever the case, it is clear that Olmec ideas and religious ideology had a great influence on most regional cultures of Mesoamerica. The Olmecs contributed to the development of the oldest known writing system in the Americas, and probably created the calendar system used by most subsequent Mesoamerican peoples.

Decline. Ultimately, the city of La Venta was sacked around 400 B.C., either by outside invaders or civil war. Thereafter, although earlier Olmec ideas and culture continued to influence other regions, Olmec political power collapsed.

REGIONAL CENTERS, 400 B.C.–A.D. 200 (LATE FORMATIVE PERIOD)

Following the collapse of the Olmecs, Mesoamerican civilization continued to develop independently in the five regions. This was a period of city-states and political regionalization. Each of these cultural regions developed its own traditions in relative independence; none of them obtained the cultural or political dominance held previously by the Olmecs.

Guatemalan Maya Sites. Kaminaljuyu and Izapa were the most important centers of highland Maya civilization. It appears that many of the basic elements of Maya culture developed in this region in the Late Formative period, later spreading to the lowland Maya. These cities are especially noted for their splendid carved monuments. Kaminaljuyu was ultimately conquered by Teotihuacán about 300, and declined following the collapse of the Teotihuacán empire after 650.

Petén and Yucatán (Lowland Maya). The late Formative period saw the rise of city-states among the lowland Maya, laying the foundations for classic Maya civilization. Petén was dominated by the site of El Mirador, which boasts the largest pyramid in the entire western hemisphere, as well as numerous temple mounds and ritual roads, indicating that it must have dominated the labor resources of a large region. Becan is noted for its massive fortification system. The fundamental cultural patterns which would flourish during the classic Maya period were established at this time. It is probable that some Maya cities were politically tributary to Teotihuacán in the fifth and early sixth century (see below).

Oaxaca Valley. The Oaxaca valley, inhabited by the Zapotec and Mixtec peoples, flourished from 200 to 700. By at least 200, the cities and villages of the valley were united into a single state under the domination of Monte Alban. For the next five hundred years, Monte Alban remained one of the great cultural centers of Mesoamerica. It is especially noted for its hundreds of sculptures of captured, tortured, and dead enemy leaders (called *danzantes*, or dancers), graphically demonstrating Monte Alban's military expansion. The city includes excellent examples of temple architecture, ball courts, and an early astronomical observatory (probably for calendar purposes). The Zapotec civilization at Monte Alban collapsed around 700.

Ultimately, these early regional centers were eclipsed by the rise of two of the most important civilizations in classic Mesoamerica: the empire of Teotihuacán in the valley of Mexico, and the Maya in the Yucatán peninsula.

TEOTIHUACÁN, 100–650 (CLASSIC)

Imperial Conquests. The highland valley of Mexico was united under the authority of the city of Teotihuacán (near modern Mexico City) at about the time of Christ. With a strong military and aggressive merchant class, Teotihuacán initiated a period of imperial expansion and conquest. By about 200 they had established hegemony over most of highland Mexico. Only the state of Monte Alban in the Oaxaca valley and some parts of the northern Gulf region escaped their control. By 300 Teotihuacán merchants and soldiers were dominating highland Guatemala. By 400 they were overlords of Petén.

Empire. Due to lack of written records, the exact nature of Teotihuacán hegemony is not clear. It seems certain, however, that their empire was founded as much on military conquest as on control of trade. The Teotihuacán empire dominated most of Mesoamerica for about two hundred years, but began to decline by the late sixth century. Ultimately, the city of

Teotihuacán itself was destroyed by warfare around 650. Thereafter only small bands of people lived in its ruins.

The City of Teotihuacán. At its height Teotihuacán was the largest city in pre-Columbian American history, and one of the largest in the premodern world. The city covers eight square miles, organized on a well-planned grid system. Most of the population lived in standardized housing complexes in the suburbs. The center of the city was dominated by the massive Pyramid of the Sun, built about 100, around which were seventy-five other temples. The Imperial Palace, known today as the Citadel, included defensive walls, royal apartments, a large platform for ceremonies, and a temple to the god Quetzalcoatl. The city is especially noted for the brilliant mural paintings depicting religious and military themes found in many of its buildings. A huge plaza served as the central marketplace; a section of the city was inhabited by foreign merchants, indicating the importance of international trade in the Teotihuacán empire.

Impact. Though the Teotihuacán empire collapsed in about 650, the political and cultural patterns established by the empire seem to have provided the basis for the subsequent pre-Columbian highland Mexican states of the Toltecs (900–1250) and Aztecs (1325–1519) (see below). All three states were fundamentally militaristic and predatory; their splendor was built on a combination of plunder, the tribute of conquered peoples, and the control of trade.

MAYA, 200–850 (CLASSIC)

Maya Civilization. The period of the classic Maya in Yucatan can be broadly compared to classical Greece. The political foundations of both societies were built upon city-states. Political history revolved around military, economic, and cultural competition among these city-states. At various times different cities dominated the region, only to be eventually replaced by their rivals. No one city-state ever managed to completely control the entire peninsula. Cultural competition among city-states, in the form of monumental architecture and royal patronage of the arts, led to a period of splendid artistic creativity. The religion and culture of both Greece and the classic Maya became the pattern for subsequent civilizations in their respective regions.

Early City-States. By 200 several Maya cities in Petén and the Yucatán, such as El Mirador, Tikal, Edzna, and Becan, had become major powers, and had come into conflict with their neighbors. Warfare intensified, as indicated by the widespread building of fortifications. By about 300 El Mirador was apparently conquered by Tikal, and declined as a major city-state. Thereafter regional coalitions grew around Tikal and Calakmul. The empire of Teotihuacán seems to have intervened in Petén from its newly acquired base at Kaminaljuyu about 350. By 400 many of the cities of Petén, including Tikal, Uaxactun, and Becan, had become tributaries of Teotihuacán.

Golden Age. By the early sixth century, however, Teotihuacán's authority in Petan was declining. Thereafter, from about 600 to 850, we see the flowering of the classic Maya civilization, producing some of the most splendid art and architecture in the world. Tikal retained its position as one of the most important city-states throughout this period. It flourished in the seventh century under the dynasty of Ah-Cacaw (682–734) when many of its great monumental plazas and temples were built. Palenque was ruled by the dynasty of Pacal (615–683), who is buried there in a magnificent tomb in the Temple of the Inscriptions. Calkmul and Copan were also important city-states. The populations of the larger Maya cities at their height ranged from fifty to one hundred thousand.

At its peak in 700 Maya society was characterized by an extremely intensive agricultural system, and maximal exploitation of natural resources at the Maya technological level. A militaristic state and religious ideology, combined with intense competition for resources, led to frequent warfare among city-states.

Maya Astronomy and Calendar. Maya scientific thought is especially exemplified in the development of their calendar, astronomical observations (largely for calendar purposes), and fairly sophisticated mathematics, including the concept of zero and place notation. The Maya idea of history, like many other archaic systems of thought, centered around a cyclical concept of time and prophecy. Maya lords were seen as living fulfillments of an ancient cyclical pattern of divine kingship. Maya historical stelae (monumental inscriptions) frequently center on the divine ancestry of the kings, their great conquests, and ritual sacrifices.

Maya Art. The greatest cultural achievement of the Maya is in art and architecture. Although the Maya style of art is strange and somewhat difficult to comprehend for modern Westerners, when its basic artistic assumptions and practices are understood, the true genius of Maya art becomes apparent. Maya art and architecture usually focused on religious or royal themes. Surviving artforms include sculpture, bas-reliefs, mural painting, ceramic decoration, and jade jewelry. Although all Maya sites include monumental architecture, the temples and tombs of Tikal and Palenque are especially noteworthy. The Temple of the Inscriptions at Palenque and Temple I at Tikal are among the finest examples of Maya pyramidal temple-tomb architecture. The Maya were a literate society, which undoubtedly produced works of poetry, literature, history, and religious thought. However, only relatively short historical and religious inscriptions carved in stone have survived.

Collapse of the Maya. Beginning about 750, the classic Maya social, political, and religious system collapsed. The elites were overthrown, the great palaces and temples were abandoned, monumental art and architecture ceased, and the entire region was depopulated. Although the exact reasons for this collapse are not known, the following basic pattern can be discerned.

The population of Petén had reached the maximum sustainable under Maya technology. This delicate balance seems to have been upset by a combination of famine and warfare. Analysis of tree rings indicates a major drought around 850; several years of crop failure could have initiated widespread famine, followed by warfare to obtain scarce food resources. There was a wide social gulf between rulers and commoners; the elites took increasing amounts of economic and labor resources for their monumental building projects. Existing social tensions between rulers and ruled increased, bringing coups, revolts, and ultimately perhaps revolution. Warfare among Maya city-states, revolution, and outside invasion became widespread; these new levels of violence and social conflict further decreased agricultural productivity, intensifying the social and economic crisis.

In the end, the Maya proved unable to find solutions to this cycle of crises, and their civilization collapsed. The overall population level declined from 12 million in 750 to 1.8 million by 900. Much of Petén reverted to tropical jungle, and was not repopulated until the twentieth century. The city-states of the northern Yucatán, especially Uxmal, seem to have survived longer, but ultimately also fell to Toltec conquest. Nonetheless, vestiges of Maya civilization survived this decline until the coming of the Spanish (see below).

TOLTECS, 900–1250 (EARLY POSTCLASSIC)

Barbarian Origins. The fall of the empire of Teotihuacán in the seventh century can be roughly compared to the fall of the Western Roman empire in the fifth. Both empires collapsed into small regional states and cultures. Both regions faced a period of economic and cultural decline, with falling populations. Wandering barbarians and war bands frequently ravaged both regions, eventually establishing new city-states and kingdoms, laying the foundation for the recovery of the economy and culture in later times.

Conquests. The Toltecs were the most important of these barbarian warbands, playing a role in Mesoamerica roughly similar to the Merovingian Franks in western Europe. They migrated into central Mexico following the fall of the Teotihuacán empire, settling at Tula, and eventually formed a new militarized and predatory state.

Topiltzin, c. 970–1000. Later legend records the interesting story of the religious reformer Topiltzin, high priest of Quetzalcoatl, who has been compared to Akhenaton of Egypt. Topiltzin attempted to transform Toltec religion, subsituting the sacrifice of flowers and fruits for rituals of human sacrifice to the war god Tezcatlipoca. Topiltzin was defeated in a political and religious struggle with the priests of Tezcatlipoca, and he and his followers were exiled to the Yucatán about 987. Thereafter, Toltec and later Aztec religion centered on continuous ritual warfare to provide for the insatiable need for human sacrifice.

International Trade. Toltec militarism led to the foundation of a powerful predatory state in the Mexican highlands which dominated northern Mesoamerica for nearly two centuries. The Toltecs had an extensive trading network, including possible military colonies, extending throughout Mesoamerica and beyond. It is possible that during the Toltec era, or perhaps a little earlier, sea trade began to become important, especially the routes through the Gulf of Mexico and around the Yucatán. Land and possibly sea trade routes down the Pacific coast to South America also became important. Metallurgy was introduced from South America into Mexico by about 800. Toltec traders established militarized trading colonies in northern Mexico, developing an expanding trade with the Anasazi Indians of the southwest U.S. By 1050 Casas Grandes had become the main trading center between the southwest U.S. and central Mexico. As noted above, Mesoamerican cultural and religious influences can be found in Southwest Indian architecture, religion, and technology.

Chichén Itzá and the Yucatán Toltecs. The most important colony of the Toltecs was established at Chichén Itzá in the northern Yucatán. The arrival of the Toltecs at Chichén Itzá was associated with the previously mentioned Topiltzin, who was exiled from Tula around 987. It is clear that about this time, a band of Toltec warriors, traders, and priests invaded the northern Yucatán and seized control of Chichén Itzá, making it the center of a second Toltec militaristic state; the god Quetzalcoatl was the primary deity of the city. At Chichén Itzá, however, the Toltec military aristocracy merged with local northern Maya elites to create a new synthesis of Maya and Toltec culture. The Toltec-Maya state of Chichén Itzá dominated the northern Yucatan for the next two centuries. In the process, the city became the cultural center of Mesoamerica, outshining the Toltec capital of Tula in central Mexico. Its mixture of Toltec and Maya artistic styles led to the creation of some of the finest Postclassic art and architecture of Mesoamerica.

Collapse. The Toltec states collapsed into war and rebellion in the late twelfth century. A combination of drought, nomadic barbarian attacks from the north, and rebellion and revolution within the Toltec state created this crisis. The last Toltec king, Heumac, abandoned Tula in 1156, leaving the capital to be sacked and destroyed. The Toltec state in central Mexico completely collapsed shortly thereafter. A similar fate awaited the Toltecs at Chichén Itzá. Led by the Maya lord Hunac Ceel, the Maya rebelled and sacked Chichén Itzá in 1187. Hunac Ceel then established the capital of his new Maya dynasty at Mayapán, which dominated the northern Yucatán from 1187 to 1446.

AZTECS, 1325–1521 (LATE POSTCLASSIC)

Origins. The fall of the Toltec empire brought two centuries of political decentralization to highland Mexico. The sack of Tula was attributed to the invasion of nomadic barbarian tribes from northern Mexico known collectively as the Chichimecs, (meaning literally "dog lineage"), who were traditionally divided into seven tribes. As seminomads their lifestyle consisted of wandering, hunting, and raiding, mixed with occasional farming in semipermanent villages.

The Chichimec barbarian interaction with the civilized centers of central Mexico roughly parallels the relationship of Germanic barbarian tribes with the Roman empire. Some Chichimec warriors served as mercenaries for their civilized neighbors. Others served as traders, guides, and porters for merchant caravans to the north. When the civilized states were weak, Chichimec confederations would raid the settled villages and cities. Ultimately, as Toltec power collapsed in the late twelfth century, these raids turned into full-scale invasion and migration.

Conquest and Empire. The most important of the seven Chichimec tribes were the Aztecs (also known as Mexica). They are by far the best known Mesoamerican civilization due to the abundance of native Aztec historical sources and Spanish chronicles which have survived. In 1193 the Aztecs settled around the shores of Lake Texcoco (the site of modern Mexico City), forming a small city-state. They were later forced to an island in the lake, where they established their final capital of Tenochtitlán. For the next two centuries the Aztecs were simply one minor city-state among many, often vassals to, or serving as mercenaries for, their more powerful neighbors. By the late fourteenth century they had established a network of alliances through intermarriage with the families of several other city-states in their valley. During the reigns of Itzcoatl (1426–1440) and Moctezuma I (1440–1468) the Aztecs initiated a policy of military conquest. In the course of the next century and a half they established themselves as masters of central Mexico.

Military Tyranny. Their empire was a militaristic tyranny founded on five basic principles: (1) frequent, if not annual, military raids on unsubdued enemies for plunder; (2) demands for large payment of tribute from subdued neighbors; (3) control of regional trade routes through groups of Aztec warrior-merchants; (4) the institution of the "flowery war," the major purpose of which was to capture enemy warriors for human sacrifice to their war god Tezcatlipoca; and (5) an overall policy of terror in governing conquered peoples. If enemies resisted or rebelled, reprisal would be certain, swift, and bloody. Thus their empire was based on, and survived by, the plundered wealth and sacrificial blood of their neighbors.

Montezuma II, 1503–1520. At the accession of Montezuma (Moctezuma) II the Aztec empire was at the height of its power. The Aztecs ruled nearly all of highland Mexico, obtained vast wealth by annual tribute and trade, and had the most powerful army of the region. Their capital at Tenochtitlán was one of the most magnificent cities in the world, with a population numbering nearly 200,000. Within two decades, however, their entire civilization had disappeared, destroyed by a band of 500 Spanish adventurers in alliance with oppressed Aztec vassals.

Mesoamerican Religion and Culture

Mesoamerican religion was polytheistic and focused on the temple as the ritual center of the universe. All aspects of Mesoamerican life—the agricultural cycle, trade, kingship and government, warfare, art and architecture, even sports—centered on the temple, its festivals, ideology and ritual. Temples and religion were the ideological cement that held Mesoamerican societies together.

SOCIETY

Agriculture. As the center for astronomical study and measuring time, the Mesoamerican temple played a major role in determining when and how to plant crops. Much of the agricultural produce of the peasant farmers was donated to the gods in the form of taxes. A complex mythology of fertility and rain gods and goddesses provided an explanation for the workings of the natural world.

Economics. Trade was influenced by temple centers in several ways. The great trading fairs usually also coincided with important religious festivals. Furthermore, many of the products transported and traded were used mainly for the religious art and ritual of the temple centers.

Government. Kingship and government was also centralized in temple-cities. The focus of people and products at a temple made it the natural site for the creation of a royal capital. If a king could control a major temple, he could control many of the people who worshiped there. Most of the bureaucrats, technicians, and artists who ran the government were priests, educated at temple schools. But most important, the temple mythology provided a legitimization for the rule of a royal family through the ideology of divine kingship. Kings ruled not because of merit or power, but because they were descended from the gods and had been chosen and blessed by them.

Warfare. Although Mesoamericans went to war for secular motives—the desire for plunder and glory—warfare was nonetheless fundamentally sacred. A battle between two city-states was a battle between the patron gods of those cities; victory was obtained not by the more powerful army or brilliant general but by the will of the gods. Decisions of when to fight were based on the need for sacrificial victims, the mythological calendar, and prophetic omens. War was a sacred ritual, where the fallen in battle were human sacrifices on a monumental scale. War was also a great divination mechanism, whereby the will of the gods became manifest as nations rose and fell.

RELIGION

Gods and Goddesses. There are a bewildering array of gods and goddesses in Mesoamerican mythology, who are generally recognizable only by their artistic representations. Many of their names are not known today; they are prosaically called "god 1" and "god 2." The major deities existed in several different forms among the various peoples of Mesoamerica. Quetzalcoatl ("feathered serpent") was one of the more beneficent gods of Mesoamerica, who gave humans the gift of civilization and law; Tlaloc was the god of rain and water; Tezcatlipoca ("smoking mirror"), the god of warfare and human sacrifice, was the mythological opponent of Quetzalcoatl; Xilonen was the goddess of maize.

Human Sacrifice. A morbidly fascinating element of Mesoamerican religion was the widespread practice of human sacrifice. It is certain that the Mesoamericans sacrificed more humans than any other civilization in history. The blood of human sacrifice was seen as the food of the gods, and it was necessary to appease them. Victims were taken to the tops of temple pyramids, where their hearts were cut out and offered to the sun; their blood was poured over the sacrificial priests as a type of baptism; the flayed skin of dead bodies was occasionally worn by priests as ritual clothing; skulls of sacrificed humans were hung on racks by the thousands; the flesh of the victims was distributed and eaten. For many, to be sacrificed was seen as the greatest honor, ensuring a happy afterlife with the gods; others, no doubt, saw matters differently. Nearly 80,000 people were said to have been sacrificed by the Aztecs at the dedication of the Great Temple of Tenochtitlán in 1487. Even if this figure is exaggerated, hundreds of people were clearly sacrificed each year. The cultural vandalism of the Spanish, who destroyed most of the books and much of the art and architecture of Mesoamerica, is a tremendous blow to historians. However, given their medieval Christian perspective, it is perhaps understandable that they could interpret these elements of Mesoamerican religion as demonic.

Time. Temples were believed to be a portal for communication with the world of the gods. Through temple rituals, Mesoamericans believed they could contact the gods and goddesses and obtain information and blessings from them. As gateways through time, temples were the mechanism for contacting the world of the royal ancestors (themselves often gods) and for receiving prophecies for the future.

The Ball Game. Even Mesoamerican sports were religious, and associated with the great temples. The ball game was the universal sport of pre-Columbian Mesoamerica. At one level it was simply a sporting event, a mix of soccer and basketball, in which two opposing teams attempted to bounce a rubber ball through hoops or to an opponent's goals, without using their hands. But on a ritual level, the ball court was a cosmic diagram of the universe; the game itself was a great ritual mythological drama; the players represented the gods in mythological conflict; the course and outcome of the game were interpreted as prophetic of future events; the losers were often sacrificed to the gods.

THE ARTS

Art and Architecture. Nearly all art and architecture in Mesoamerica derived from temple centers. The great themes of art were mythological stories of the gods, divine kingship, sacred warfare, and sacrifice. The most splendid works of Mesoamerican architecture are temples.

Literature. The Olmec may have had a writing system, which unfortunately cannot be fully interpreted today. Most other Mesoamerican hieroglyphic systems seem to have been derived from the Olmec. The oldest significant body of literature is Maya hieroglyphic inscriptions from the sixth through the ninth centuries, which give us insights into the royal ideology and religion of the classic Maya.

Actual books survive only from the fifteenth and sixteenth century, although they record a great deal of older traditional material. Among the most important books describing pre-Columbian Mesoamerica are the *Popul Vuh* (Book of Council), a Maya mythological story of the creation of the universe and the origin of mankind; the *Books of Chilam Balam* (Jaguar Prophet), a mixture of legend, history, mythology, and prophecy from the Maya of northern Yucatan; and the *Florentine Codex* of Bernard de Sahagun, which was written by a Spaniard, and was based on Aztec informants. It contains a wide range of Mesoamerican history and mythology, together with nearly 2,000 native illustrations.

SOUTH AMERICA

Background   GEOGRAPHY

South America is a vast continent with a wide range of environments. The two dominating features of South American geography are the Amazon River basin and the Andes mountain range. The Amazon drainage basin—one of the largest river systems in the world—covers most of the northern half of South America. It is characterized by dense tropical rain forests. Grassland and subtropical forests predominate in the southeastern zone, with a large area of semidesert covering much of Argentina. The northwest (Colombia and Venezuela) includes a complex mixture of mountain highlands, tropical forests, grassland, the Orinoco River basin, and desert. The Andes mountains run like a spine along the western coast of the continent. Surprisingly, it is here that the great pre-Columbian civilizations of South America developed.

ETHNIC GROUPS

The complexity of the environments and geography in pre-Columbian South America also contributed to an extremely complex ethnic and linguistic mosaic. Although Spanish and Portuguese have become the dominant languages since the European colonization, many Indian ethnic groups remain. Indeed, until recently some Indian tribes in the Amazon rain forests continued living in their traditional ways well into the twentieth century, relatively untouched by modernization.

CULTURAL ZONES

For the most part, civilization in South America focused on Peru (the northern and central Andes mountains) and some parts of modern Ecuador and Colombia. The other regions of South America never advanced beyond small primitive agricultural villages and tribal chiefdoms.

METAL

Unlike other parts of the Americas, metal was extensively used by Andean peoples for both tools and ornamentation. By 1500 B.C. Andeans had begun experimenting with gold; by 800 B.C. they had succeeded in creating splendid gold metalwork. Ultimately copper, bronze, and other alloys were used by Andean peoples. From its origins in Peru and Ecuador, metal working ultimately spread northward into Mesoamerica.

ANDEAN GEOGRAPHY AND THE ORIGIN OF CIVILIZATION

The unique geography of the Andean region contributed to the origin of civilization in South America. There are several environmental strips running parallel to the coast, totaling about 120 miles wide. Ascending from west to east there are a coastal desert, a semi-arid zone of scrub and thorn forests, Andean highlands of sparse grassland, and Andean mountain summits (the peaks of which reach over 20,000 feet). Descending from the mountain peaks from west to east there are more Andean highlands, Andean tropical forests, and, finally, the Amazonian tropical rain forests.

This mixture of parallel environmental strips created a rich range of accessible resources for early Andean peoples to use. As in other parts of the world, civilization in the Andes originated in the small river valleys that descended from the mountains to the coastal plains. Unlike the Nile, Tigris and Euphrates, Indus, and Yellow river systems, the Andean river valleys were short streams dissecting steep mountain valleys, offering relatively limited opportunity for agriculture. Early humans were attracted to these valleys for a wide range of food and resources. Furthermore, the river valleys provided a relatively easy means of ascent into the mountain highlands.

Early Andean Civilizations

INITIAL PERIOD (2000–1200 B.C.)

Most of the small coastal river valleys in Peru became home to early irrigation-based farming villages by 2000 B.C. As in the rest of the Americas, maize was the most important crop, supplemented in South America by the manioc root and potato. Another important innovation was mountain terracing for agriculture. Domesticated animals included guinea pigs, ducks, and dogs; llamas and alpacas were used for pack animals, food, and wool.

EARLY HORIZON (1200–200 B.C.): CHAVIN

By 1200 B.C. these small river valley farming villages had begun to coalesce around major ceremonial temples, which became the centers of religious ritual, pilgrimage, trade, and ultimately government. Cultural interaction, trade, and possibly military competition drew the entire Andean region together into a loosely united cultural system, called Chavin. Although the exact nature of this cultural interaction is uncertain, it is clear that many sites shared a related religion and art forms. The most important site in this period was the temple center at Chavin de Huantar (flourished from 850 to 200 B.C.), which included a large temple complex with a sophisticated ritual water system. Echoes of the art styles and deities of Chavin can be seen in all subsequent Andean civilizations.

EARLY OR FIRST INTERMEDIATE (400 B.C.–A.D. 600): NAZCA AND MOCHICA

By about 400 B.C., the unity of cultural forms which had been characteristic of the Chavin period began to fragment into different regional variations. In the next centuries, several early states formed, the most important being the Nazca and the Mochica.

The Nazca, 400 B.C.–A.D. 450. The Nazca centered on the south coast of modern Peru. Their capital seems to have been the ceremonial center of Cahuachi. There is evidence of military struggle and expansion by the Nazca, culminating in the formation of a primitive state. The importance of taking the heads of slain or sacrificed enemies as trophies (a characteristic trait of many American Indians) is common in Nazca art. The Nazca are most famous for their monumental desert designs, consisting of lines and human and animal figures etched in the desert floor. Fully visible only from the sky, these lines were formed by removing a layer of loose dark gravel from the ground, exposing the light soil underneath. Some are perfectly straight lines extending for over seven miles. Others are designed to represent figures, including monkeys, birds, spiders, and humans, but are recognizable only from the sky. The precise purpose of these lines and figures is unknown, but they seem to have had religious significance (being visible to the sky god), and perhaps were used for astronomical and calendar observation.

Mochica (Moche) (1–600). The Mochica state began about the time of Christ at their ceremonial center of Moche in the Moche river valley. The site contains the enormous Pyramid of the Sun, but since construction was largely of adobe bricks, most of the city of Moche is today only disintegrated mounds. They are noted especially for some of the finest pre-Columbian metalwork and pottery. The Mochica were a militaristic people; at its greatest extent at around 500, their state extended about 450 miles along the Pacific coast of Peru. Their splendid pottery shows interesting scenes of the ritual chewing of coca-leaves (from which modern cocaine derives) and frequent depictions of warfare and human sacrifice. By about 600 the site of Moche was abandoned, perhaps due to shifting sand dunes disrupting agriculture. Eventually the Mochica region was absorbed by the empire of Huari.

MIDDLE HORIZON (500–900): TIAHUANACO AND HUARI

Two states came to dominate the Andean region beginning about 500: Tiahuanaco in the highland Andes on the southern shore of Lake Titicaca; and Huari, in the highlands of central Peru. Both states seem to have had related cultural and religious ideas; some archaeologists believe they may even have been the two major cities of a single empire.

Tiahuanaco. Tiahuanaco was the more culturally advanced of the two cities, with finer art and architecture. One of the highest urban settlements in the world, Tiahuanaco is located above the timber line near the southern shore of lake Titicaca in Bolivia. The site is noted for its monumental stone temples, monolithic sculptures, and complex irrigation system. Tiahuanaco's influence was more cultural and religious than military.

Huari. Huari, on the other hand, was a militaristic state. Its initial period of conquest extended from about 600 to 700. Huari expansion ranged throughout most of the coastal region of Peru, and into the Andean highlands, as shown by Huari-style fortifications, garrisons, and administrative buildings throughout the conquered area. Their expansion slowed thereafter, and ultimately their empire collapsed and their capital was abandoned in 800.

LATE INTERMEDIATE PERIOD (900–1476): CHIMU (CHIMOR)

The fall of Tiahuanaco and Huari initiated another period of regional fragmentation in the Andean zone. Several city-states competed for power and developed their own regional cultural traditions within the larger framework of the heritage of Chavin, Mochica, and Huari.

Origins. The most important and powerful of these was the kingdom of Chimu, based on their capital at Chan Chan. Founded by their legendary first king Tacaynamo around 900, Chan Chan remained a regional city-state until the twelfth century and the beginnings of military expansion under Nancenpinco. By 1370 they had conquered most of the coastal region of northern Peru.

Chan Chan. The Chimu capital of Chan Chan was the largest pre-Columbian city in South America, covering over six square miles. It is notable for its ten palaces, which, according to legendary history, are associated with the ten Chimu kings. Archaeologists have speculated that each of the palaces was occupied by a different king; when a king died, he was buried in his palace, which was sealed and converted into a mausoleum.

War with the Incas. Around 1460 the last Chimu king, Manchancaman, came to the throne, initiating the final period of Chimu expansion and military competition with the Inca. Ultimately, the Chimu were defeated and conquered by the Inca ruler Tupac Yupanqui around 1470, and absorbed into the expanding Incan empire.

The Incan Empire

HISTORY

The largest, most splendid, and last of the civilizations of the Andes was the Incan empire. The Inca were originally one of numerous small city-states which developed in highland Peru following the collapse of the Huari and Tiahuanaco about 800. For several centuries the Inca were simply a small chiefdom at their city-state of Cuzco. It was not until 1438 that imperial expansion began. Under their greatest ruler, Pachacutec (1463–1471), the Inca conquered most of highland and coastal Peru. Expansion continued under his son Tupac Yupanqui (1471–1493), who doubled the size of the empire by military conquests of parts of modern Ecuador, Bolivia, and Chile. These Incan rulers were divine kings, descendants of the sun god Viracoca.

GOVERNMENT

Road System. In order to administer their empire and facilitate the collection and distribution of taxes, the Inca developed a massive communication system of nearly 25,000 miles of roads extending the length and breadth of their empire. The only comparison in premodern times is with the Roman network of military roads. The Incan road system included large tracts of extremely mountainous terrain traversed by narrow roads, and remarkable suspension bridges spanning vast chasms. The roads were designed mainly for military and administrative purposes, but they might have been used by merchant traffic and llama caravans.

Administration. Garrison towns were created on the Incan highway system to serve as residences for royal officials and troops, and as storage and transportation centers. Taxation rates were enormous; one third of the produce went to the king, one third to the gods and their priests, with only one third left to the workers. In addition, the Incan kings could call upon their subjects for forced labor in numerous Incan building projects. A remarkable feature of Incan administration is the absence of a written language—no system of writing is known in pre-Columbian South America. For administrative purposes the Inca bureaucrats used a remarkable system called quipu, consisting of a string with various colors and styles of knots recording the king's possessions.

ARCHITECTURE

The Inca are especially noted for their magnificent architecture.

Cuzco and Sacsahuaman. The royal city of Cuzco includes the nearby fabulous palace-fortress of Sacsahuaman, with its terraced ramparts and inset towers. The fortress, though under construction for nearly a century, was not completed when the Spanish attacked. Nonetheless, it was the site of several battles between the Inca and the conquistadors. The masonry techniques of the Inca are fascinating; the fortification of Sacsahuaman consists of huge blocks of irregular-cut stones fit together like a gigantic jigsaw puzzle. The irregular stones were assembled without mortar, yet they fit together so precisely that a knife blade cannot be inserted between the blocks.

Machu Picchu. The expansion of agricultural land in the Andean highlands required the construction of narrow agricultural terraces on the steep slopes of mountains, as exemplified by the magnificent city of Machu Picchu. Built on the spur of an almost inaccessible ridge some 2,000 feet above the surrounding valley, Machu Picchu includes a plaza, palace, and an important temple to the sun god. Surrounding the city are a sequence of agricultural terraces, descending down the steep ridge like giant steps.

SPANISH CONQUEST

Upon the death of the Incan ruler Huayna Capac in 1525, a civil war broke out between two of his sons, Huascar and Atahualpa. In this unstable situation, Atahualpa invited Francisco Pizarro and his few hundred Spanish conquistadors to assist him as mercenaries in 1531. Instead, Pizarro decided to conquer the Inca empire. By a combination of guile, treachery, murder, bravado, military superiority, and sheer good fortune, Pizarro managed to crush the Inca in only two years. Although Indian resistance continued in various regions for decades, the Spanish soon ruled all of the Andes.

THE COLLAPSE OF PRE-COLUMBIAN CIVILIZATIONS

Weaknesses in Pre-Columbian Societies

The early collapse of the Olmec is paralleled throughout pre-Columbian history by other similar collapses of civilizations: Teotihuacán, the classic Maya, the Toltecs, the cultures of the Southwest, the Woodland Indians, and several South American cultures all collapsed after periods of cultural brilliance. This may indicate that pre-Columbian political units were organized on a fragile and sophisticated social, economic, and ideological basis that could not withstand severe disruption.

But whatever the inherent weaknesses in pre-Columbian societies, the coming of the Europeans brought disastrous consequences to the American Indians which are unparalleled in world history. Moving beyond the internal dynamic of the rise and fall of civilizations within the ancient pre-Columbian traditions, the Europeans brought about the nearly complete eradication of Indian cultures. The following are the most important factors in the destruction of the pre-Columbian civilizations.

Reasons for the European Conquest

DISEASE

Certainly the greatest calamity which befell the Indians was the introduction of new European diseases to which the Indians had no biological resistance. It has been estimated by some historians that in the century following the arrival of the first Europeans, smallpox, measles, and tuberculosis killed as many as 80 percent of the inhabitants of the Americas. This was the most devastating plague in the history of the world, more than twice as deadly as the Black Death in medieval Europe.

TECHNOLOGY

The Europeans had superior technology, including steel weapons, firearms, horses, and cannons. The pre-Columbians could not compete with these military technologies, nor with the industrial technologies which produced these weapons. The Spanish conquistadors Cortés and Pizarro were brutal men, but brilliant and bold conquerors. Their numbers were few, but they were well disciplined and highly motivated in their search for gold and glory.

CAPTURE OF DIVINE KINGS

The invasion of the Spaniards, both in Mesoamerica and Peru, was a complete surprise, both culturally and strategically. The Indian worldview simply could not accommodate such an event. For a while, the Aztecs saw Cortés as the reincarnation of their god Quetzelcoatl, a fact which Cortés used to great advantage. The culture shock which afflicted the Aztecs and

Incas gave the Spaniards the opportunity to consolidate their positions. Both Cortés and Pizarro had the good fortune to conquer the emperors of the Aztecs (Montezuma) and the Incas (Atahualpa). As both societies saw their rulers as divine kings, the capture of the king paralyzed resistance.

REBELLION

Both the Aztec and Incan empires were tyrannies, ruling over oppressed peoples who initially welcomed and supported the Spaniards as liberators. When the Spanish arrived in Mexico in 1519, the Tlaxcala, one of the tribes subject to the Aztecs, immediately joined the Spanish army with thousands of soldiers. Their hopes for liberty were short-lived, since Aztec tyranny was simply replaced by Spanish tyranny. Nevertheless, it was the combination of the rebellion by oppressed peoples, in conjunction with the Spanish invasion, which destroyed the Aztec empire.

RELIGION

From the pre-Columbian religious perspective, defeat by the Spanish was tantamount to defeat by the god of the Spaniards. Through his military victory, the god of the friars had demonstrated that he was more powerful than the god of the Aztecs. The logical extension of this idea was that pre-Columbian Indians came to accept the new, more powerful god of their conquerors. In the process, they ended up largely abandoning their own ancient cultural heritage, and creating the new civilization of Hispanic Latin America—a combination of the Indian heritage with the new religion, ideas, plants, animals, practices, and technologies of Europe.

In general, the pre-Columbian civilizations of North America shared the following characteristics. Most of the people lived in small farming villages. Larger towns developed from ritual urban centers which were used as sites of pilgrimage and trading fairs during annual festivals. Social stratification, large-scale political organization, long-distance trade, cities, and massive monumental architecture all existed among the peoples of the Mississippi valley, but they lacked a writing system, and thus have no recorded history. Religious pilgrimage festivals were the ideological bond which held these cultures together. North American Indians achieved a basic knowledge of astronomy, designing special astronomical observatories in which the solstices and other calendar events could be determined by examining the movement of shadows on earthen ramps, stones or pictoglyphs.

The Indians in Mesoamerica achieved the highest levels of culture of the entire New World. The oldest cities in the New World were found among the Olmecs, who laid the foundation for all subsequent Mesoamerican civilizations. The fundamental unit of social, economic, political, and cultural organization in Mesoamerica remained the city-state, although there were periods of imperial ambition. While separate politically, the various city-states of Mesoamerica shared a wide array of common cultural characteristics. The first Mesoamerican empire was formed by the great city of Teotihuacán, which dominated most of the region for several centuries. The greatest cultural age was that of the Classic Maya, which lasted until about 850. The militaristic empires of the Toltecs and Aztecs were the major powers of the post-Classic age. Mesoamerican civilizations were noted for their relative instability; throughout their history there are several examples of massive collapses of civilization in the face of severe economic, social, or military problems. The final permanent collapse of Mesoamerican civilization occurred with the coming of the Spanish.

Archaeologists and historians divide the history of the Andean civilizations of South America into five periods. The Initial period is characterized by the establishment of agricultural villages, small ceremonial centers, and the early use of pottery, metal, and textiles. The Early Horizon period is exemplified by the site of Chavin de Huantar; the basic cultural, religious, technological, artistic, and political characteristics of Andean civilization were established at this time. The Early or First Intermediate period witnessed the fragmentation of cultural styles into several regional variations, the most important of which were the Mochica and Nazca. The Middle Horizon period was dominated by the expansion of the states of Tiahuanaco and Huari to near imperial status. The Late Intermediate period was again characterized by the breakup of the Andean zone into small regional states, the most important being Chimu. Finally, in the Incan period, the entire Andean region was conquered by the Incan kings, creating the highest manifestation of civilization in South America. The Inca were conquered by the invasion of Pizarro in 1531, initiating the Colonial Spanish period.

Selected Readings

Adams, Richard E. W. *Prehistoric Mesoamerica*, 2nd ed. (1991)

Brotherston, Gordon. *Image of the New World: The American Continent Portrayed in Native Texts* (1979)

Cameron, Ian. *Kingdom of the Sun God: A History of the Andes and Their People* (1990)

Carrasco, David. *Religions of Mesoamerica* (1990)

Coe, Michael, Dean Snow, and Elizabeth Benson. *Atlas of Ancient America* (1986)

Conrad, Geoffrey W., and Arthur A. Demarest. *Religion and Empire: The Dynamics of Aztec and Inca Expansionism* (1984)

Davies, Nigel. *The Aztecs* (1972)

_____. *The Toltecs Until the Fall of Tula* (1977)

_____. *The Toltec Heritage* (1980)

Fagan, Brian M. *Ancient North America: The Archaeology of a Continent* (1991)

Hassig, Ross. *Aztec Warfare: Imperial Expansion and Political Control* (1988)

Hemming, John. *The Conquest of the Incas* (1970)

Hemming, John, and Edward Ranney. *Monuments of the Incas* (1982)

MacCormack, Sabine G. *Children of the Sun and Reason of State: Myths, Ceremonies, and Conflicts in Inca Peru* (1990)

Miller, Mary Ellen. *The Art of Mesoamerica from the Olmec to Aztec* (1986)

Morley, Sylvanus G., George W. Brainerd, and Robert J. Sharer. *The Ancient Maya*, 4th ed. (1983)

Schele, Linda, and Mary Ellen Miller. *The Blood of Kings: Dynasty and Ritual in Maya Art* (1986)

Schele, Linda, and David Freidel. *A Forest of Kings: The Untold Story of the Ancient Maya* (1990)

Soustelle, Jacques. *The Olmecs: The Oldest Civilization in Mexico* (1979)

Tedlock, Dennis. *Popul Vuh: The Mayan Book of the Dawn of Life* (1985)

14

Medieval East Asia

1192–1333   Kamakura period in Japan

1211–1279   Mongol conquest of China

1250–1337   Wang Shifu, greatest Chinese dramatist

1260–1294   Kublai Khan, emperor of China

1281   Failure of the Mongol invasion of Japan

1355   First rebellion of the Red Turbans in China

1368–1644   Ming dynasty in China

1392–1910   Yi (Choson) dynasty in Korea

1405–1433   Ming exploration expeditions to South Asia and Africa

1406   Construction of the Forbidden Palace begun

1419–1450   Sejong the Great rules Korea

1467–1477   Onin War, Japan enters century of fragmentation

1543   Arrival of the Portuguese in Japan

1592   Koreans defeat Japanese naval invasion

1598–1616   Tokugawa Ieyasu reunites Japan

1638   Japan is closed to foreigners

Medieval East Asia has several important distinguishing characteristics. Unlike western Europe, where the early medieval period was an age of political decentralization and economic decline relative to the Roman empire, the civilizations of medieval East Asia developed economically, politically, and culturally beyond their own classical predecessors. China continued to culturally dominate East Asia throughout the medieval period. Chinese government, philosophy, writing system, religion, and cultural forms were adopted in varying degrees by all the other East Asian civilizations. China likewise remained the most important political force in the region, overshadowing all other states. Central Eurasian Turks and Mongols, while adopting many Chinese ideas and practices, remained the major political and military competitor to China.

Buddhism flourished and spread throughout East Asia; in each new area of conversion Buddhists accommodated their doctrines and practices to local custom, thus supplementing, rather than replacing, local religions. Buddhism thereby became the universal religion of East Asia. While strongly influenced by Chinese culture, independent civilizations developed in Japan, Korea, and Tibet, laying the foundations for modern nation states. International contacts through trade, Ming explorations, and the coming of the Europeans became a major factor shaping the history of East Asia from the fifteenth century on. The fundamental East Asian reaction to these new international contacts was rejection of Western cultural influences and isolationism.

MEDIEVAL CHINA, 589–1644

Political History

SUI, 589–618

As noted previously (chapter 7) China was reunified after four centuries of fragmentation by Sui Yang Jian (581–604). His reign and that of his successor are characterized by the establishment of a pragmatic and uniform system of government throughout China, laying the administrative foundations for the succeeding Tang dynasty. The capital city at Changan was designed by the architect Yu-wen Kai; it remains the largest planned city ever created. The country was further unified by the creation of the Grand Canal system, the longest man-made waterway in the world. Connecting the Yellow and Yangtze rivers, it economically linked the north and south, ensuring food supplies to the new capital at Changan. Confucian values were infused into the administration through an extension of the Confucian examination system. The failure of Sui military expeditions against the Turks in Central Eurasia and Korea undermined imperial authority, resulting in a series of rebellions; the Sui ruling family was ousted and replaced by the Tang. Despite its short duration, the Sui dynasty played an important role in Chinese history. It reunified China, created a well-organized government and unified economic infrastructure, and laid the cultural foundation for the golden age of the Tang.

TANG, 618–907

Origin and Expansion. Although the reunification of China after the Age of Disunity was achieved by the Sui dynasty, the benefits of reunification were to be reaped by the Tang. A power struggle developed in China following the death of the last Sui emperor. Gao-zi (618–626), a powerful general, emerged triumphant, subduing all rivals in a series of military campaigns throughout China from 618 to 624. Adopting and building upon the administrative system of the Sui, Gao-zi, and his son Tai-zong (626–649) created a rational, efficient, and equitable system of government, law, and taxation. Until 755 Tang rulers consistently pursued an aggressive and expansionist foreign policy, with significant military campaigns into Central Eurasia to gain control of the Silk Road, and into Tibet, Korea, and Vietnam; this militarism made China the most powerful state in East Asia.

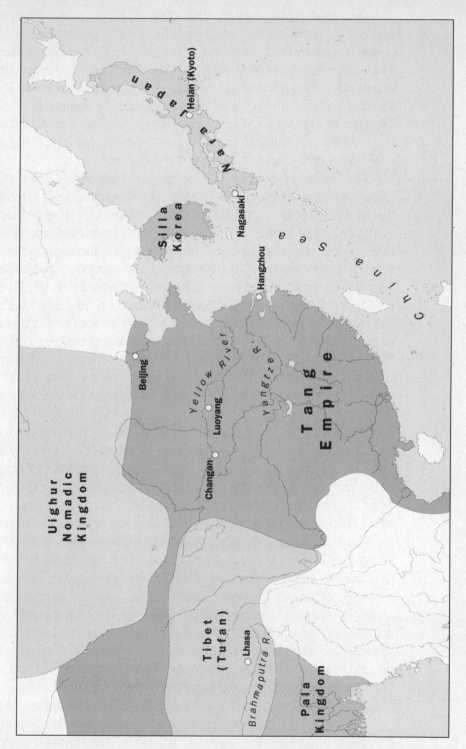

Fig. 14.1   East Asia, c. 750

The Tang Achievement. The Tang emperors and bureaucrats were masters at organization, administration, and standardization; the Tang period represents the culmination of centuries of Chinese administrative and educational developments and the final formulation of the definitive Confucian gentleman-bureaucrat (see below). By the Tang period all aristocratic Chinese received similar educations and held the same world view. The Tang period is recognized as the greatest age in premodern Chinese history, not only for its political expansion and power, but also for its cultural achievements in literature, art, and architecture.

The Glory of Changan. Throughout the Tang period, the capital city at Changan was undoubtedly the largest, wealthiest, and most splendid city in the world. Indeed, it was probably the greatest city of premodern times, surpassing even Rome. It was also the most cosmopolitan; thousands of foreign merchants and students from all of Asia could be found in Changan, seeking wealth and wisdom. The Tang dynasty was thus a period of expansion of Chinese ideas and cultural styles into Central Eurasia, Tibet, Korea, Japan, and Southeast Asia. Chinese influence on all forms of East Asian culture cannot be overemphasized. The Tang aristocracy is also noted for having been intrigued with non-Chinese ideas and culture. Turkish, Arab, Korean, Jewish, Japanese, Indian, Southeast Asian, and Persian merchants, scholars, and holy men could be seen in many major Chinese cities, bringing with them the products, music, dances, art styles, and ideas of their homelands.

Women at the Tang Court. One of the most remarkable and ruthless women in Chinese history was Empress Wu (690–705), the only woman to rule China as an independent sovereign. Wife of the emperor Gao-zong, she utilized her power at court to place her relatives in key government positions, while systematically banishing all opposition. Since her relatives held power based solely on her control of court policy, she became the effective ruler for China for several decades, ruling in her own name after 690. Finally grown feeble in her eighties, she was deposed by an aristocratic reaction to her excesses and nepotism; her relatives were executed or exiled.

Another famous Chinese woman was Yang Guifei, concubine of Xuan-zong (713–756). The emperor was reportedly so enamored of her that she managed to control court policy for the last years of his reign. The subsequent discontent among the aristocrats culminated in the disastrous rebellion of General An Lushan (755–763), which nearly toppled the dynasty and left China in anarchy for decades. Xuan-zong was forced to flee his capital at Changan; he abdicated the throne and his officers strangled Yang Guifei.

The examples of these two remarkable women indicate the fundamental perceived inferiority of women in medieval China. Women could achieve political power only through court intrigue and by associating with and ultimately dominating an emperor. Nonetheless, the general status of women was higher at the Tang court than in many other premodern societies.

Weaknesses of the Tang. In a sense the Tang dynasty became a victim of its own success. One major problem was simply that the empire expanded beyond the capacity for effective communications and control. Provincial generals and administrators were thus able to gain increasing autonomy, and ultimately could rebel. As wealth increased the court and bureaucracy became riddled with corruption and intrigue; court eunuchs (castrated servants) controlled access to the emperor, thereby effectively becoming power brokers and policy makers. Under such conditions, the size and cost of the bureaucracy expanded and efficiency decreased. The insatiable demands of the ever-expanding court, army, and bureaucracy led to increased taxation and impoverishment of the peasant class. Wealthy aristocrats were thus able to purchase the lands of the indebted peasants; many farmers turned to robbery rather than serfdom under rich landlords.

Rebellion of An Lushan, 755–763. The revolt of An Lushan clearly demonstrated these problems. A Turkish mercenary commanding troops on the northwestern frontier, An Lushan recognized the weakness of the imperial court and rose in rebellion, attempting to establish himself on the throne. Although ultimately unsuccessful, the rebellion left the Tang dynasty in crisis. Other provincial governors likewise rebelled, and it was not until 818 that imperial authority was finally reestablished throughout China.

Fall of the Tang. Thereafter, although the dynasty remained in power for almost another century, it was greatly weakened by internal dissension; the power of the provincial governors increased, while the central government was plagued by mismanagement and corruption. Both peasants and aristocrats rebelled, and Huang Chao was able to sack and destroy the magnificent capital of Changan. The dynasty collapsed shortly thereafter, and China entered a period of fifty years of political anarchy (907–960).

SONG DYNASTY, 960–1279

Northern Song, 960–1127. Order was ultimately restored, however, by the founder of the Song dynasty, General Zhao Kuang-yin, who unified northern China and began campaigns into the south. Reunification was completed under his successor, and reintegration of China was begun through administrative reforms and standardization. The Song dynasty was constantly threatened by outside Central Eurasian nomads from the north, and never achieved the military power or geographical extent of the Tang. Nonetheless, they made important achievements in administrative reforms, thought, and culture.

Southern Song, 1127–1279. The overriding problem facing the Chinese during the twelfth through the fourteenth centuries was the military threat from Central Eurasian nomads. Beginning in the late eleventh century, the

Khitan (Liao, 907–1124) and Juchen (Jin, 1115–1234) nomadic confederations repeatedly attacked northern China; the Song capital at Bianjing was sacked in 1126, after which all of northern China was overrun by the Juchen nomads in 1127. The Song forces retreated southward, making the Yangtze River their new defensive line which they managed to hold for another century and a half.

During the Southern Song period all of southern China was united under a single stable Chinese dynasty, while the north was dominated by foreigners. Thus it was not an age of Chinese internal disunity, but of foreign domination of the northern part of China. The Southern Song is characterized by tremendous economic growth, including an expansion of iron working, agricultural innovation, and a system of aggressive merchant guilds. Urban life flourished, with several cities having populations of over a million. The port city of Hangzhou was a center of bustling economic activity. Paper money was introduced successfully, until the government began printing more than they could redeem; inflation naturally followed.

Despite the cultural and economic successes of the Song, they were unable to resist the military threat of the northern barbarian nomads. Nomadic assaults into the south were temporarily held in check by the forests, marsh lands, and rivers of the south, all of which presented natural obstacles to nomadic armies; and the superiority of the Song navy, which gave the Chinese control of the rivers and canals. However, with the coming of the Mongols in the early thirteenth century, the balance of power shifted against the Chinese.

YUAN (MONGOL) DYNASTY, 1279–1368

Mongol Conquest of China, 1211–1279. Background on the origin of the Mongols, the nature of their social system, and the history of their conquests under Chingis Khan can be found in chapter 15. Here the focus is on the period of Mongol domination in China. The Mongol conquest of China began in 1211 as a conflict between the Mongols and the sinicized Jurchen (Jin) who ruled northern China. Initially, then, the Mongol invasions can be seen as a power struggle between nomadic factions stemming from Chingis Khan's attempt to unify all of Central Eurasia under his authority. By 1234 the Jurchen in northern China had been subdued. In the following forty years, the Mongols continually pressed the Song in the south, finally conquering all of China by 1279.

Khublai Khan, 1260–1294. The greatest ruler of the Yuan dynasty was Khublai Khan, grandson of Chingis. Khublai's reign is noted for his attempts to conquer all of East Asia, creating the most expansionist period in Chinese history. Khublai inherited the powerful Mongol army from his grandfather; into it he incorporated Chinese military forces, technology, and, most important, the Chinese navy. Korea was conquered by 1258. Massive but unsuccessful and disastrous naval expeditions were sent to Japan in 1274 and 1281. Vietnam and Burma were subdued in the 1280s, with a naval expedition to Java in 1292. Despite these successes, Khublai's Mongol control of most of these regions did not long outlast death in 1294.

Decline. The breakup of the Mongol empire in the late thirteenth century left Yuan China as one of four Mongol successor states. Mongol-Chinese expansionism essentially ceased following the death of Khublai. The Mongols were never fully accepted by their Chinese subjects, creating instead what essentially amounted to a caste system, with Mongols occupying the highest levels, foreign allies of Mongols the next, and southern Chinese the lowest. Confucian scholars frequently refused to serve the Mongols. Although partially sinicized, the Mongols never completely abandoned their Central Eurasian traditions, patronizing Buddhism over Confucianism.

Fall of the Yuan. In the 1340s the Yellow River flooded and shifted its course, creating widespread suffering and economic chaos as farms were destroyed and the Grand Canal ruined. The Mongol emperor Toghto managed to restore the canal, but the social and economic stresses intensified widespread discontent with Mongol rule, culminating in a Buddhist rebel movement known as the Red Turbans. Temporarily subdued in 1355, the movement resurfaced in the following decade, culminating in the expulsion of the Mongols by 1368.

MING, 1368–1644

Hung-wu, 1368–1398. The founder of the Ming dynasty, a former peasant, beggar, and Buddhist monk, was Hung-wu (1368–1398). As a military leader of the Red Turban movement, Hung-wu had subdued all rivals, and driven the Mongols from China by 1368. In a series of campaigns he succeeded in reuniting all of China by 1382. Backed by a vast array of Confucian scholars, Hung-wu restored Confucianism and the examination system as fundamental parts of his new administration. The old Mongol military aristocracy was deposed and replaced by a native Confucian Chinese bureaucratic aristocracy. However, Hung-wu was autocratic and tyrannical. Following the Mongol example, he centralized all authority in the hands of the emperor; autocracy remained a characteristic of Ming rulers throughout the dynasty.

Wars with the Mongols. Even though they had been expelled from China itself, the Mongols continued to represent a serious threat, and regular campaigns were carried out in Mongolia to subdue the nomads. Although originally constructed in the third century B.C., and repaired many times since, the Great Wall of China took its final form and was extended by 600 miles during the Ming dynasty in order to prevent Mongol raids. Major Mongol invasions between 1550 and 1570 were successfully defeated.

Ming Exploratory Expeditions, 1405–1433. The chaos of the final decades of the Yuan dynasty allowed numerous pirate bands to operate on the coasts of China. The Ming emperors developed a substantial naval power to exterminate the pirates, then turned their naval strength to outward explorations and conquests. Between 1405 and 1433 seven massive naval expeditions explored Southeast Asia, India, the Persian Gulf, the Red Sea, and the east coast of Africa. Compared with the few hundred men and three small ships of Columbus's expedition in 1492, the first Ming expedition included nearly 28,000 men, 63 large vessels, and 255 small vessels. Exploring, trading, and even conquering as they went, the Ming expeditions clearly had the technology to reach Europe. But they lacked the desire. Deciding that the expeditions were too costly and there was nothing to be gained or learned from foreigners, the emperor Xuan-zong discontinued Chinese explorations in 1433, leaving the Europeans free to eventually discover the Americas and Asia, and reap the economic benefits from control of international trade for the next four centuries.

Decline of the Ming. The fifteenth and early sixteenth centuries represent the high period of Ming power, wealth, and cultural achievement. From the late sixteenth century, however, the Ming emperors tended to withdraw into a world of private pleasures, essentially ignoring matters of state. Administration deteriorated into feuding court factions unable to resolve their differences. Deteriorating conditions in the government were reflected, naturally, in poor administration and oppression in the provinces. Outlaw rebel bands arose and eventually seized Beijing; the last Ming emperor committed suicide. The path was open for the invasion of a new Central Eurasian power, the Manchus.

Chinese Government and Society

Although there were many developments, the Chinese system of government fundamentally continued on the pattern which had been established during the Han. The emperor was the center of authority, served by a corps of palace eunuchs and supported by a vast bureaucracy. Under strong emperors, government could be efficient and reforms could occur; under weak emperors administration often degenerated into harem and eunuch intrigues, corruption, and factionalism. The common people were, for the most part, left without a substantial voice in national government; their only recourse when abuse became intolerable was rebellion, which occurred with some regularity throughout medieval Chinese history. Two important features of Chinese government reached their final forms in medieval times.

THE EXAMINATION SYSTEM

Origins. The Chinese university examination system—one of the most complex in premodern times—reached its full development under the Song dynasty. No one could obtain a government office unless he had passed the examination. Candidates were usually in their mid-thirties, having obtained the rough equivalent of a modern Ph.D. The Thirteen Chinese Classics had to be memorized perfectly; candidates were graded on knowledge, writing style, and calligraphy in a series of essays. Thus, only those with an excellent education could hope to pass. Chinese literature abounds with tales of the sorry state of students who were preparing for, or had failed, the examinations. This system remained in effect in China until 1905.

The Confucian Bureaucratic Aristocracy. The Song period witnessed the culmination of the development of the Chinese bureaucratic aristocracy, whose power in society was based on a combination of wealth, education, and government office. Wealth was necessary to obtain an education; sufficient education to pass the examination was necessary to obtain government office; government office in turn could be used to obtain wealth. Although ownership of land remained a fundamental source of wealth, the new bureaucratic aristocracy of China obtained its power and wealth through control of the government. This Chinese system was always theoretically an open meritocracy; anyone could take the government examinations, and could thereby obtain a government office. In practice, however, the complexities of the Chinese educational and examination systems ensured that education (and thereby government offices) remained, for the most part, an aristocratic privilege.

Medieval Chinese Culture

All forms of Chinese culture—religion, philosophy, literature, art, music, and architecture—flourished in the medieval period, becoming the models for cultural expression for all the civilizations of East Asia.

BUDDHISM

Buddhism remained a major religious force throughout the medieval Chinese period, becoming the most important and successful Chinese cultural export. There were three significant developments in Chinese Buddhism in the medieval period.

Period of Dominance. Chinese Buddhism reached its greatest influence during the Tang dynasty, when Chinese art, architecture, and literature were dominated by Buddhist themes. Tang emperors patronized Buddhism, resulting in the proliferation of temples and monasteries. Likewise, Central Eurasian Turks and Mongols patronized Buddhism as an international religion and an ideological counterpoise to the dominance of the Chinese Confucian bureaucracy.

Division into Denominations. East Asian Buddhism derived from the Mahayana tradition of northwestern India, but swiftly developed many unique East Asian denominations. Several major denominations appeared in the sixth through eighth centuries. Tiantai emphasized mystical meditation; the Pure Land sect sought salvation through absolute faith and devotion to the Boddhisattva Amida (*A-mi-to-fu*). Chan Buddhism, with its emphasis on discipline and sudden enlightenment, spread to Japan in the form of Zen, where it became extremely influential.

Expansion Throughout East Asia. Although indigenous to India, Buddhism quickly developed independent centers of thought in China in the medieval period, from which it spread to Korea and Japan. Korean, Japanese, and Chinese Buddhists frequently visited each other's monasteries, sharing ideas and practices. Most sectarian developments in medieval China were quickly reflected by similar movements in Korea and Japan. Buddhism in Tibet, however, derived directly from India, and developed on a unique course (see below).

NEO-CONFUCIANISM

Beginning in the ninth century under the influence of Han Yu (768–824), the medieval Confucian revival, known as Neo-Confucianism, became the dominant ideology during the Song dynasty. Neo-Confucianists had several important goals and effects.

Confucian Classics. A fundamental feature of the Neo-Confucianist revival was the creation of the Confucian Classics (or Canon) by Zhu Xi (1130–1200). The Confucian Canon consisted of the basic writings of Confucius, other early Chinese writings, and several important later Confucianist texts. These documents served both as fundamental sources for Confucianist ideas, and as the basic texts for a classical Chinese education. Memorization of the Confucian Classics became a requirement for all educated Chinese, and for passing the government examination.

Accommodation with Buddhism and Daoism. For centuries Confucianism had competed with Buddhism and Daoism for the hearts and minds of the Chinese people. By the Song period, however, Confucian thought had become strongly influenced by Buddhist and Daoist ideas, successfully synthesizing Confucian ethical, political, and philosophical thought with Buddhist and Daoist metaphysics and speculations. The result was the development of a new religious and mystical dimension to Neo-Confucianism.

Statecraft. Nonetheless, the fundamental concern of the Confucianist scholar remained the organization of the ideal state. Confucian influence on the day-to-day running of Chinese government was absolutely fundamental. The development of Chinese governmental policy was determined by the ministers and bureaucrats; the bureaucrats were selected through the examination system; the examination system was based on a Confucian education in the Confucian Classics. Thus, by controlling education, the Confucianists came to dominate the Chinese government and state as a whole.

Scholarship. Medieval Confucianists made important contributions to scholarship in three major additional areas: philosophical thought; the editing and preservation of ancient Chinese texts; and historical writing. The finest historian of the medieval period was probably Sima Guang (1019–1086), who was noted for his analytical powers, his attention to detail, his fine writing style, and his ability to abstract moral principles from historical events.

LITERATURE

Chinese literature flourished during the medieval period, producing not only important works within the Chinese tradition itself, but works which can easily be classified as world classics.

Poetry. Poetry flourished throughout medieval China; indeed, the three skills of the Confucian gentleman-scholar were calligraphy, painting, and poetry. The poetic output of the medieval Chinese was enormous. Nearly 50,000 poems by 2,000 authors have survived from the Tang period alone, many times the surviving poetic heritage of Greece or Rome. The two most famous medieval poets are Li Bo (701–762) and Du Fu (712–770), who are noted for their vivid imagery, use of nature themes, and the political overtones of some of their work.

Prose. The short story became an important literary form in the Tang period. Originally tales emphasized fantasy and the supernatural, but by the ninth century more realistic stories began to appear. The most famous is perhaps the story of "Ying-ying," a tale of love between a student and the woman whom he seduces and ultimately deserts. The standard medieval Chinese fictional work would be classified today as fantasy and adventure, focusing on history, romance, adventure, and the supernatural. The Ming period is especially noted for *The Romance of the Three Kingdoms*, a historical fantasy of the collapse of the Han dynasty in the third century A.D., and *Journey to the West (Monkey)*, a satirical and allegorical fantasy about a Buddhist monk's pilgrimage to India accompanied by a supernatural monkey which the Buddha sends to guide and protect him.

Drama and Opera. China witnessed the full development of drama during the Yuan period. Chinese Yuan drama was essentially operatic, including important poetic and musical elements. The greatest Yuan play was *The Romance of the Western Chamber*, by the finest Yuan dramatist, Wang Shifu (1250–1337). This opera was based on the famous tale of Ying-ying, mentioned above.

ART AND ARCHITECTURE

The artistic creativity of medieval China was represented in numerous genres and styles, which were widely imitated by artists in Korea and Japan. During the early Middle Ages much Chinese art was influenced by Buddhist themes, especially in religious statuary and the development of pagoda architecture.

Art. Among the outstanding achievements of Chinese art, painting and ceramics stand out as unique. Chinese painting often drew themes from landscapes and nature—trees, animals, a lone human walking in a vast background. Although colored paints and inks were used, the Chinese excelled in evocative black ink drawing, which were often accompanied by related poetry. Chinese ceramics are frequently considered the finest in the premodern world; the texture of the clay, methods of firing, elegant shapes, and exquisite painting were all of unrivaled quality, making Chinese ceramics a product sought by merchants throughout the Old World.

Architecture. Medieval Chinese architecture, like other premodern traditions, is best represented by temples, pagodas, and palaces. One of the great architectural masterpieces of the world is the Forbidden Palace at Beijing (Peking), which was begun in 1406 during the Ming dynasty and remained the principal residence of most Chinese emperors for the next 500 years.

CHINESE TECHNOLOGY

The Chinese were undoubtedly the most technologically innovative civilization of premodern times; their achievements were surpassed by the Europeans only in the sixteenth century. There were five technological advances made in China which have fundamentally altered the way we live in the modern world.

Paper. Paper was invented in China about A.D. 105, creating a significant intellectual and economic revolution throughout the world. The Chinese had traditionally used silk or bamboo strips for writing, both of which—like the papyrus and leather parchment used in the West—were expensive. The invention of paper created a new and relatively inexpensive medium for writing, which meant that more books could be written, copied, and preserved, with more people thus having access to books and ideas. The manufacture of paper reached the Middle East around 750 and Europe by 1150, where it produced similar social changes.

Printing. The intellectual changes initiated by the invention of paper were multiplied many times by the invention of printing, which first appeared in China in the eighth century A.D. The idea slowly spread eastward, reaching Europe in the fifteenth century, culminating in Gutenburg's development of the moveable-type printing press. The existence of printing in China 700 years earlier than in Europe meant that the Chinese were able to print and preserve copies of many more books than any other region in the world; some have estimated that half of all surviving books in the world from before A.D. 1500 are in Chinese. Nonetheless, their complex writing system, with thousands of characters, minimized the ultimate social implications of the discovery of printing. Literacy expanded, but gaining an education or buying a book was still prohibitively expensive for most of the population. In the West, however, with its alphabetic writing system, the introduction of printing created an intellectual, educational, and social revolution (see chapter 16).

Iron and Steel. The use of iron developed in the Near East in the early second millennium B.C. The Chinese, however, invented several new iron technologies which created better and cheaper metals, including new ways of smelting and casting iron, strengthening steel, and the use of coal rather than wood for furnaces. The Song period was renowned for its numerous iron factories, and its fine steel. Some of these improved Chinese methods of iron working reached Europe in the late fourteenth century, where they added to the ongoing economic revival, contributing to the foundation for the European Industrial Revolution.

Gunpowder. Gunpowder was invented in China around A.D. 850. Initially it was used mainly to create smoke and noise for entertainment or to expel demons. Gunpowder reached Europe in the fourteenth century, where it was quickly adapted to create powerful cannons for besieging fortresses. It was thus the western Europeans who maximized the potential of this new military technology, which allowed them to conquer the Americas and dominate much of Africa and Asia in the sixteenth and seventeenth centuries.

Mariner's Compass. Magnetism had been understood by the Chinese for centuries, but was initially used mainly for divination. By the twelfth century the Chinese had developed the mariner's compass which could be used for finding direction at sea, thereby allowing much more accurate sailing, and sailing farther from land. The principles of the compass may have been invented independently in Europe, or may have been borrowed from the Chinese through intermediaries; in either case the compass was a fundamental element of the Age of Exploration which ultimately brought the entire globe within the range of sailing ships.

Lack of Scientific Method. Despite their technological creativity and advances, the Chinese never fully developed the scientific method which would eventually institutionalize scientific thought and change in the West. Thus, Chinese technological developments were essentially practical rather than theoretical; they emphasized brilliant creative solutions to specific problems. But unlike the West, China never reorganized its entire society and way of viewing the universe to maximize the capacity for technological change, which we call the Scientific Revolution. Thus, the West ultimately achieved a technological superiority and military dominance over East Asia, which lasted until the twentieth century.

JAPAN

The history of Japan was influenced by two major geographical factors. First, like England, Japan is an island, close enough to the mainland to be influenced by cultural developments in China and Korea, but far enough away to be able to avoid direct political domination or interference by China. Thus, although occasionally threatened by other East Asian powers, Japan was never conquered by outsiders until the twentieth century. Second, Japan is a collection of mountainous islands, with limited agricultural land. This promoted the growth of regionalism, competition between regions, and ultimately militarism.

Political History

PREHISTORY TO A.D. 250

Human beings migrated to Japan in neolithic times, establishing small hunting and farming communities throughout many of the islands. Archaeological and linguistic evidence points to strong influences from Korea, including the introduction of metals, pottery, and other technologies. By the early centuries A.D. Japanese culture was beginning to take on some of the characteristics which would last for the next two millennia. Emphasis on the status of the royal family and its genealogical connection with the sun goddess can be deduced from the creation of massive royal funerary complexes, the most famous being that of the emperor Nintoku (c. 395–427). The warrior class was already playing an important role in Japanese society. The basic features of the native Japanese religion, Shinto, were also in place (see below). Chinese records from this period speak of the possible existence of matriarchy (rule by women), mentioning a queen Pimiko as the ruler of Japan. Nonetheless, early Japan should not be seen as a unified monarchy, but as a tribal confederation of numerous military clans.

YAMATO PERIOD, 250–710

The clan rulers of the Yamato plain gained special significance in the forth and fifth centuries through a combination of force of arms, diplomatic marriages, alliances, and by their special status as descendants of the sun goddess. By the sixth century, they had established their lineage as the imperial family of Japan. Although in the ensuing centuries their descendants often occupied a position of little more than pawns and puppets of powerful warlords, they nonetheless remained the only imperial family of Japan until the present; the current emperor is the direct descendant of these early rulers, the longest-ruling family in history.

Chinese Cultural Influences. The Yamato period is especially noted for the impact of numerous cultural influences from China and Korea, which played a fundamental role in shaping subsequent Japanese culture. The two most important were the introduction of Buddhism and the Chinese writing system. Chinese influence on Japan was intensified during the administration of the prime minister Suiko (592–628), who actively sponsored several cultural missions to China seeking new ideas, bringing back a wide array of social practices and court etiquette. He built numerous Buddhist temples, including the famous shrine of Horyuji. Chinese influences in art, architecture, poetry, and literature were extensive; indeed, many art historians find the best examples of early Chinese architecture have been preserved in Japanese copies of Chinese styles. Suiko is also credited with centralization of government power and reform of the legal system as reflected in his seventeen points of government written in 607. The influence of Chinese ideas, practices, and culture on the formation of Japanese civilization cannot be overemphasized.

Shinto. The native Japanese religion of Shinto developed during the early historical period in Japan. Deriving from animism and the belief that there were numerous *kami* (divine beings) in the land of Japan, Shinto is the formalization and rationalization of native Japanese religious beliefs. Focusing on seasonal agricultural festivals, rituals of purity, and the worship of the sun goddess, Shinto remained an important part of Japanese religious belief and practice even after the introduction and spread of Buddhism.

NARA PERIOD, 710–784

These developments culminated in the Nara Period with the creation of a new capital, court, and bureaucracy at the city of Nara. During these important decades, the religious, cultural and political changes which had transformed the late Yamato were fully integrated into a classical pattern of Japanese civilization which would last in its fundamentals until the nineteenth century.

Chinese Influences. Cultural influences from China continued; the capital and court system at Nara was designed in conscious imitation of the Tang Chinese capital and court at Changan. Despite the importance of Chinese culture in the formation of Japanese civilization, the Japanese adapted Chinese influences to meet their own cultural traditions. Most notably, they never abandoned the importance of hereditary aristocracy in favor of a Chinese-style Confucianist meritocracy; indeed, Confucianism as a whole was never enthusiastically or fully accepted by the Japanese. Furthermore, the position of the Japanese emperor, as descendant of the sun goddess, was inviolate. The Chinese concept of the Mandate of Heaven was thus unacceptable to the Japanese. Since there could only be one imperial family for Japan, power struggles centered on who would control the emperor and the court.

Buddhism. Buddhism and Shinto continued to co-exist in Japan; by the eighth century Buddhism was widespread and had great influence on the court elite. Numerous temples and monasteries were constructed, the most famous being Todaji temple at Nara, which housed a fifty-three-foot-high cast metal statue of the Buddha weighing over a million pounds.

HEIAN PERIOD, 794–1185

Following a decade of court intrigue, the capital was shifted to Heian (modern Kyoto). This transfer represents more than just a change of location. Japanese culture thereafter became more resistant, though not impervious, to mainland Chinese influences; instead the Japanese increasingly developed their own unique cultural style.

Fujiwara Clan. The imperial family increasingly lost real political power, which passed into the hands of the Fujiwara regents and warlords. For several centuries Fujiwara leaders such as Yoshifusa (858–872) and Michinaga (966–1027) wielded real political power in Heian. The emperors were reduced to puppets playing an increasingly onerous ritual role. Many chose to abdicate the throne rather than submit to the endless court ritual under the watchful control of their Fujiwara masters.

Decentralization. The decline of the real power of the emperor was also reflected in the growth of an independent landed aristocracy. The Fujiwara regents increasingly granted their supporters, clients, and temples tax-free status on their lands, which decreased central government revenues. But since Fujiwara power was based on their own military resources and support from clients and vassals, they preferred the additional support they could gain from their clients to the revenues lost by the central government. In the end, real control of land and wealth thus passed to the hands of the provincial aristocracy, providing them with an independent power base from which to develop their own bands of warriors which would ultimately threaten Fujiwara domination and plunge Japan into civil war.

Culture in the Heian Period. The Heian period represents one of the high points in Japanese culture, providing the classical standards which influenced Japanese art and literature for the next several centuries. Court culture centered on the aristocrats of the capital, a small tightly knit group sharing a unique worldview, and consciously setting themselves apart from the Japanese population as a whole. The era is characterized by extreme elegance and refinement in dress, speech, writing, and art. The entire mentality of the age is wonderfully depicted in two works by Japanese aristocratic women, the *Tale of Genji*, by Murasaki Shikibu (978–1016) and the *Pillow Book* (diary), of Sei Shonagon (late tenth century). A person's refinement was demonstrated by dress, etiquette, calligraphy, art, poetry, and esthetic and emotional sensibilities.

The Fall of the Fujiwara Clan. Land and wealth came increasingly under the control of the provincial aristocracy, who began to raise private armies owing ultimate loyalty not to the central government, but to their regional patrons. The military also became increasingly professionalized, with skills in horsemanship, archery, and swordsmanship being especially valued. Many Buddhist temples raised armies of warrior-monks both for their own defense and to influence court politics. By the late tenth century these provincial warbands became an increasing threat to the central government. A series of rebellions and wars ensued; emperors began to play rival military factions against each other, thereby regaining some level of independence in the late eleventh century. This factionalization of Japan into numerous rival military camps—Fujiwara, imperial, temple armies, and provincial warlords—culminated in civil war in 1156, bringing the end of the Heian period.

KAMAKURA, 1192–1333

Military Dominance. The Kamakura age was characterized by the rise of the Japanese military elites to positions of dominance in society. The fundamental restraint on the militarization of Japan was the sanctity of the imperial house; the emperor could not be killed, nor could the imperial title be transferred to another family. Nonetheless, military ideas and values became fundamental in Japan from this period until after World War II.

Creation of the Shogunate. The period had its beginning in a civil war from 1156 to 1185 between the Taira and Minamoto clans. The war culminated in the rise to power of the Minamoto leader Yoritomo (1147–1199), who instituted the shogunate, by which real power in the government was held by a *shogun* (supreme military commander) under the nominal leadership of the emperors. This institution survived in Japan until 1868. Thus by the thirteenth century Japan had become largely militarized on a pattern broadly similar to feudal Europe; real power rested in the hands of aristocratic warriors with relative autonomy in the provinces. These warlords were tied together by oaths of loyalty, vassalage, marriage, and economic and political interest.

Bushido and the Samurai. The system of values of the samurai of this period gave rise to bushido, the way (lifestyle) of the warrior (*bushi*). The principal ideals of the warrior included bravery, pride, honor, absolute loyalty, and a complete disdain of death. "Death before dishonor" was not simply an idle slogan for the samurai; those who failed their masters, were defeated in battle, or dishonored in any way would frequently commit ritual suicide rather than face a life without honor. These martial values are well represented in the most important work of literature of the period, *The Tale of the Heike*, an adventure story describing the intrigues and wars between the Taira and Minamoto factions in the late twelfth century.

Martial Arts. Bushido included skill in the martial arts of swordsmanship, archery, and horsemanship so frequently associated with the samurai of medieval Japan. Many of the military practices, technologies, and techniques of Japan had their origins in China, and were adapted into the Japanese military and social system. The modern association of the martial arts with Japan is largely due to the fact that the isolation of Japan between the seventeenth and nineteenth centuries allowed the survival of archaic forms of warfare, whereas similar martial skills in other parts of Asia, the Near East, and Europe declined in the face of new military technologies.

Social Structure. The social structure of medieval Japan is characterized by several features. The endurance of the imperial dynasty throughout Japanese history (although frequently merely as figureheads) is unparalleled in world history, providing a continuity to the social and political system. Beneath the at least nominal power of the emperor, Japan was divided by strong social stratification and a system of powerful military clans and factions. Aristocratic warriors, with their personal armies of samurai, wielded power in the provinces over the peasant and middle classes. Bonds of loyalty and mutual interest tied warriors to their warlords; similar ties bound the various military clans into networks of alliances which continually struggled for control of Japan through domination of the imperial family and court.

Buddhism. Buddhism continued to flourish and spread throughout the Kamakura period. Its importance is represented by the proliferation of sects and the development of new Japanese schools of Buddhist thought. In times of violence and warfare, many people seek consolation through faith. In Japan this was represented by the rise of True Pure Land Buddhism under the leadership of Shinran (1173–1262), who sought salvation through faith alone in the Amida, the Buddha of the Western Paradise. Others followed the teachings of Nichiren (1222–1282), an ex-monk who believed he was a Boddhisattva, and who preached salvation through faith in and repetition of the Lotus Sutra hymn. Both of these movements became widespread in medieval Japan, and still have numerous followers today.

Zen Buddhism. Among the aristocrats, however, a militant form of Zen Buddhism became the most important religion. Originally known as Chan Buddhism in China, Zen became important in Japan due to the pilgrimages and teachings of the two greatest Japanese Zen masters, Eisai (1141–1215) and Dogen (1200–1253). The most famous form of Buddhism in the West, Zen was quickly adapted to Japanese culture and the Buddhist monastic life. It is noted for its strict monastic discipline, the importance of meditation as a means of Buddhist enlightenment, and the belief that enlightenment comes as a sudden illumination, rather than as gradual understanding. Zen ideas and themes had a tremendous influence on the arts and poetry of medieval Japan.

The Mongol Invasions. Legitimization for the militarization of Japanese society came from the Japanese victories over the Mongol invasions in 1274 and 1281. The first invasion force was destroyed by a storm.

The second, however, with nearly 140,000 men, landed and engaged in seven weeks of campaigning in Japan before their fleet was also destroyed by the gods through a great storm known as the *kamikaze* ("divine wind"), from which the World War II Japanese suicide pilots drew their name. This vindication of the military was not without its cost; the strains of devoting so much of their economic resources to preparing a defense against the Mongols eventually undermined the support for the Kamakura leaders.

MUROMACHI (ASHIKAGA) SHOGUNATE, 1338–1573

After a brief attempt by the emperor Go-Daigo (1333–1336) to reassert the independent power of the emperor, Japan entered a period of factional struggle for the shogunate, culminating in the rise to power of the Muromachi faction of the Ashikaga clan. The foundation of their power was established during the shogunate of Yoshimitsu (1392–1428). This line of shoguns continued the basic military and governmental policies of the Kamakura period, with regional warlords developing into military governors of provinces with semi-independent powers.

International Trade. International trade in a wide range of products with China and Korea flourished during the Muromachi age, leading to the rise of an important merchant and manufacturing class in Japanese society. Organized into guilds, and associated with important temples and military clans for protection, merchants, bankers, and pawnbrokers became increasingly prominent. Cities like Hakata and Sakai (modern Osaka) became important commercial centers. Trade with China brought with it increasing Chinese cultural influence.

Culture. Aristocratic Japanese culture flourished during the Muromachi age. Under the influence of Zen Buddhist theology and Chinese culture, traditional Japanese cultural forms such as the No drama, the ritual tea ceremony, flower arranging, and ink painting reached their height. Japanese architecture was coupled with the development of Zen influences in gardening and ideas of harmony with nature. The splendid Silver Pavilion palace of the Muromachi shoguns is an excellent representative of the mixture of all of these elements in Japanese culture.

The Age of War, 1467–1543. A succession dispute resulted in the Onin War (1467–1477), leading to a century of decentralization and military conflict. Each regional military clan, under the leadership of a *daimyo* (lord), achieved basic independence; ties to the central government were reduced to links of mutual self-interest, which could be broken as the situation dictated. As in medieval Europe, each regional warlord built his own castle, mobilized an independent army of samurai, and hired additional troops from roving bands of mercenaries when necessary. The old martial virtue of loyalty to one's lord became a thing of the past as ambitious soldiers of fortune struggled for power and wealth. As the struggles continued, warlords began to arm their peasants to increase the size of their armies; armed peasant revolts thus became a further source for instability since they now possessed the weapons and skills necessary for rebellion.

THE RISE OF THE TOKUGAWA SHOGUNATE, 1543–1638

Rise of Hideyoshi. This century of military decentralization and war concluded with the rise of the warlords Toyotomi Hideyoshi (1582–1598) and Tokugawa Ieyasu (1598–1616). Although born a peasant, Hideyoshi rose through the ranks to become an outstanding general and warlord. Building on the military foundations laid by his predecessor, Nobunaga, and utilizing firearms first introduced by the Portuguese in 1543, Hideyoshi managed to reunite Japan by 1590. In the process he reorganized the land and tax system of Japan, and disarmed the peasants (the "sword hunt" of 1588), creating strict caste barriers between commoners and samurai. Turning Japan's military strength outward, he unsuccessfully invaded Korea between 1592 and 1598 with an army totaling nearly 300,000 men. A power struggle followed Hideyoshi's death in 1598. One of his generals, Tokugawa Ieyasu, seized the shogunate following his victory at the battle of Sekigahara in 1600, founding the Tokugawa shogunate, which lasted until 1867.

The Europeans, 1543–1638. The Portuguese came to Japan beginning in 1543 with two major goals in mind: trade and spreading Christianity. At both they ultimately failed. The Japanese were initially repelled by the manners and customs of the Europeans; eventually, through culturally sensitive missionary efforts of Jesuits like St. Francis Xavier (1506–1552), Christianity and European trade made some headway, culminating with the conversion of several Japanese lords. Efforts at Christianization collapsed following the unsuccessful Shimabara rebellion of 1637, which was led by Christian Japanese. Christianity was thereafter outlawed, and soon essentially disappeared in Japan. By 1638 a strong anti-foreign reaction had taken hold in Japan, leading to the closing of all ports except Nagasaki to foreigners. Thereafter Japan entered a two-century period of isolation from which it would emerge only under the threat of Western imperialism in the late nineteenth century.

KOREA AND TIBET

Korea

Korean political history is dominated by several major themes. First, its proximity to China meant that Korea benefited from continuous cultural and technological influences from the Chinese—especially Buddhism and Confucianism. It also brought several periods of Chinese political domination.

Second, its proximity to Japan made Korea an important conduit for the movement of both goods and ideas between Japan and the mainland. Finally, Korean political history is characterized by fluctuating periods of unity under strong monarchies, and fragmentation into smaller regional political units.

THE THREE KINGDOMS, 57 B.C.–A.D. 668

Korea was inhabited by relatively backward tribal peoples, when, in 108 B.C., the region was annexed by the Han rulers of China, initiating a period of Chinese cultural influence. Buddhism, a modified Chinese writing system, and Confucianist ideas about government were all introduced, becoming fundamental cornerstones of Korean society. During the period of the decline of the Han dynasty, Chinese political influence waned as the Koreans established three independent kingdoms—Koguryo, Paekche, and Silla—and entered a period of political competition.

SILLA, 668–935

Most of Korea was unified into a single state in the late seventh century by the kingdom of Silla. Based in part on Chinese patterns, the kings of Silla created a strong absolute monarchy, a salaried aristocracy and bureaucracy, a hierarchical provincial government, and a Confucian-style educational system. Korea's indigenous aristocratic parliament, the Hwabaek, was temporarily dominated by the monarchy, but reemerged in the ninth century, and managed to restrict the absolutist powers of the kings. Thereafter Korea became fragmented into several principalities until the early tenth century.

KORYO, 935–1392

The unity of Korea was restored by the kings of the Koryo principality through a combination of military expansionism, diplomatic marriages, and alliances. Government was initially in the hands of a Confucianist civil bureaucracy, but in 1170 a general, Choe Chung-hon, led a military coup and overthrew civilian rule. In a system broadly similar to the Japanese shogunate, the Koryo monarchs remained as figureheads, with real power residing in the hands of warlords.

Mongol Conquest. This warlord system of government was disrupted in 1231 with the invasion of the Mongols; after thirty years of fierce resistance, Korea finally submitted to Mongol overlordship, providing a large number of ships and troops for the two Yuan-Mongol invasion attempts on Japan.

YI, 1392–1910

Following the collapse of Mongol rule in China, General Yi Song-gye overthrew the moribund Koryo dynasty in 1392, establishing the Yi (or Choson) dynasty, which was to remain in power until the Japanese invasion of 1910.

Golden Age. The fifteenth century in Korea is often seen as a golden age, reaching its height under Sejong the Great (1419–1450). Scholarship flourished with the establishment of a royal academy at Chiphyonjon. A Korean phonetic alphabet was developed in 1443, which, combined with moveable-type printing (invented in 1234), led to a renaissance in letters. Buddhist religious organizations, which many considered corrupt, were temporarily suppressed, while Confucian scholarship flourished.

Japanese Invasion. Another remarkable achievement of the Yi dynasty was the defeat of an attempted Japanese invasion by Hideyoshi in 1592. Under the direction of Admiral Yi Sun-shin, the Korean navy produced the world's first iron-clad ships, winning one of the great naval victories in history against the Japanese. Facing relentless guerrilla action on land, the Japanese withdrew in 1598, leaving Korea independent, but with serious economic and cultural damage from the war. This victory, however, was followed by the invasion of the Manchus in the early seventeenth century. By 1637 Korea had become a vassal of the Manchu (Qing) dynasty of China.

Tibet

BACKGROUND

Tibet occupies a unique position among the world's civilizations. Known as the Rooftop of the World, Tibet is a land of massive mountain ranges, glaciers, and lakes, surrounding a network of high alpine valleys and passes where humans can survive. The unique geography of Tibet contributed to its history: The mountainous terrain afforded protection from outside invaders, but also isolated Tibet from trade and communications, and contributed to political fragmentation.

THE TIBETAN EMPIRE, c. 600–889

Until the sixth century, Tibet was inhabited by nomadic pastoral tribes known as the Qiang. In the late sixth century the various clans began to consolidate into a tribal confederation. The unification of Tibet culminated in the reign of Srong-brtsan (608–650), who united all of the tribes and clans, creating the Tibetan or Tufan empire. For the next two centuries the Tibetans were a major military power in Asia. Their armies fought against Turks in Central Eurasia, Arab Muslims in Iran, Chinese, and Indians. The pinnacle of their power was achieved in 763 when they sacked the Tang capital of Changan, imposing tribute on the Chinese. A succession crisis in the early ninth century began the breakup of the empire; by 889 Tibet had again fragmented into various feuding clans.

THE LATER TIBETAN PERIOD, 889–1642

Tibetan Scholarship. During the following centuries, Tibet ceased to be a major political power, becoming instead a center of Buddhist monasticism and scholarship. Buddhist monks from India and China traveled to

Tibet to study, lecture, debate doctrine, and translate. Tibet became renowned as a land of pious and eccentric monks with great spiritual and magical powers.

Tibetans and Mongols. The Tibetans again briefly played a role in international affairs when they allied themselves with the rising Mongol military power in the thirteenth century. The great Khublai Khan selected Tibetans to serve as Buddhist court priests and ministers, the most famous being Phags-pa (1235–1280), who invented an alphabet for writing Mongolian.

Rise of Lamaism. With the collapse of the Mongols, Tibet enjoyed two centuries of independence, but was plagued by internal factionalism and disunity. Unity was finally restored in the seventeenth century by the Yellow Hat (*Dge-lugs-pa*) sect of Buddhist monks, whose abbots were the founders of the line of dalai lamas, and who were influential in the conversion of much of Mongolia to Tibetan Buddhism. By the late seventeenth century Tibet had passed under Manchu Chinese authority.

TIBETAN BUDDHISM (LAMAISM)

Origins. From the seventh through the tenth centuries, Tibetans came increasingly under the influence of Indian Tantric Buddhism. In the following centuries the Tibetans swiftly absorbed and translated a vast amount of Indian Buddhist literature; many texts which are today lost in the original Sanskrit are preserved only in Tibetan translations. Shamanistic elements from the indigenous animistic Tibetan religion called Bon were mixed with Buddhism, which became the fundamental cultural force in late medieval Tibet, influencing all aspects of government, life, and culture.

Characteristics. There are several unique characteristics of Tibetan Buddhism. From the late sixteenth century the spiritual leader of the Tibetan Buddhists was the dalai lama, who combined both absolute secular and spiritual powers. He was thought to be the repeated reincarnation of the spirit of all previous dalai lamas, and ultimately the incarnation of a Bodhisattva. Tibetan Buddhism also boasts a vast pantheon of divine beings. As many as 25 percent of Tibet's population was participating in Tibetan Buddhist monasticism before the Communist Chinese conquest in the twentieth century.

TIBETAN CULTURE

Tibetan cultural expression is fundamentally monastic and linked to Buddhism. Medieval Tibetans were noted both for their remarkable libraries of traditional Buddhist texts, and for the creation of important religious writings which were unique to Tibet. The most famous is the *Tibetan Book of the Dead*, which describes the Tibetan view of the spiritual journey of the soul in the period between death and reincarnation. Medieval Tibet is also noted for its fine Buddhist scroll painting, icons, mandalas (mystical dia-grams), and dramatic ritual dance. Architecture was dominated by fortress-like monasteries built on mountain crags and slopes.

The medieval period in East Asia was one of the most splendid in world history. China remained the center of political, economic, and cultural power in the East throughout this period. Nonetheless, various important regional civilizations—Japan, Korea, and Tibet—came into being initially under Chinese cultural influence, but developed into unique independent civilizations which would ultimately give rise to modern nation states. Mongol domination of nearly all of East Asia during the thirteenth and early fourteenth centuries came to an end as a new outside power appeared on the horizon. The coming of the European explorers and merchants in the early sixteenth century ushered in the end of medieval Asia, as the Europeans began East Asia's integration into the modern age of global interaction and interdependence.

Selected Readings

Blunden, Caroline, and Mark Elvin. *Cultural Atlas of China* (1983)

Ch'en, Kenneth. *Buddhism in China* (1964)

Collcutt, Martin. *Cultural Atlas of Japan* (1988)

Gernet, J. *A History of Chinese Civilization* (1982)

Hane, Mikiso. *Premodern Japan: A Historical Survey* (1991)

Henthorn, William. *A History of Korea* (1971)

Hucker, Charles O. *China's Imperial Past* (1975)

Lee, Ki-baik. *A New History of Korea*, trans. E. Wagner (1984)

Rossabi, Morris. *Khubilai Khan: His Life and Times* (1988)

Sansom, George. *A History of Japan to 1334* (1958)

_____. *A History of Japan, 1334–1615* (1961)

Sickman, Laurence, and Alexander Soper. *The Art and Architecture of China* (1971)

Snellgrove, David, and Hugh Richardson. *A Cultural History of Tibet* (1986)

Twitchett, Denis. *The Cambridge History of China, vol. 3: Sui and T'ang China, 589–906, pt. 1* (1979)

15

Central Eurasia

1040–1170	Selchuqid Turks dominate Near East
1071	Battle of Manzikert; Byzantines defeated by Turks
1206–1227	Chingis Khan, supreme khaghan in the steppe
1219–1300	Age of the great Mongol conquests
1259	Death of Mongke Khan; Mongol empire fragments
1283–1293	Mongol invasion of Southeast Asia and Java
1335	End of Ilkhanid Mongol rule in Iran
1368	End of Yuan Mongol rule in China
1363–1405	Age of Tamerlane's conquests
1502	Fall of the Mongol Golden Horde
1500–1650	Nomads decline; Russians and Chinese conquer steppe

Many ethnic groups have lived in Central Eurasia. Indo-Europeans dominated the region until about the time of Christ, followed by Huns, Turks, and Mongols. Central Eurasians developed a unique socioeconomic system—Central Eurasian nomadism—to deal with the special environmental conditions on their steppe homeland. Their way of life was thus very different from, and in many ways antithetical to, the socioeconomic system of sedentarists (farmers and city dwellers). These and other factors contributed to a constant state of tension between the nomads of Central Eurasia and the surrounding sedentary civilizations. At various times in history the nomads played a significant role in the collapse of sedentary empires and social systems.

Central Eurasia played a fundamental role in premodern world history in several ways. It was a major avenue for the transmission of peoples and goods between China in the east, and the Near East and Europe in the west. Ideas also flowed along Central Eurasian trade routes: Buddhism was transmitted from India to China, while Islam spread eastward along the great Silk Road. Technologies, such as paper, gunpowder, and printing, were transmitted from China to the West via Central Eurasian intermediaries. Thus, Central Eurasia played a paradoxical role, both as an avenue of peaceful interaction and exchange, and as a breeding ground for armies of nomadic horse archers which posed a constant threat to the kingdoms and peoples of China, India, the Near East, and Europe.

PASTORAL NOMADISM

Background

The fundamental characteristic of the premodern history of Central Eurasia is the interplay between the nomadic lifestyle of the steppe and the sedentary lifestyle of the farmers and city dwellers. Nomadism was the dominant social organization of Central Asia until the seventeenth century. On the other hand, the dominant form of social organization in the regions surrounding Central Eurasia—Europe, the Near East, India, and China—was sedentary, a combination of farmers and city dwellers.

GEOGRAPHY

Definition. Central Eurasia (also known as inner or central Asia) is defined geographically as the region extending from Romania and Poland in the west to the Pacific Ocean in the east, and from the Arctic Ocean in the north to borders of Iran, India, and China in the south. It thus covers roughly the same area as the former Soviet Union. Indeed the formation of the Russian empire in the sixteenth century was to a large extent the conquest of Central Eurasian nomads by Russians with firearms.

Tundra and Forest. Climatically, Central Eurasia is characterized by concentric climatic bands radiating southward from the Arctic circle. The northernmost band consists of frozen plains of tundra; the second is a broad band of vast forests, stretching as much as 700 miles wide from north to south. These regions were inhabited by hunting and fishing peoples, or by reindeer-herding tribes. Some people in this area were sedentarized only in the late nineteenth and early twentieth centuries and did not play a major economic, cultural, or political role in the premodern Old World.

Steppe. The most important geographic and climatic strip in Central Eurasia for world history is the steppe (flat grass-covered plains), which is only a few hundred miles wide from north to south, but over 4,000 miles from east to west. Three characteristics give the Central Eurasian steppe its decisive impact on world history. First, the region has limited rainfall, and therefore was of limited agricultural value for premodern technologies. Except in special oases or fertile river valleys in the steppes, premodern farming was not very successful. Second, the steppe grassland provides a perfect environment for herding. Thus most peoples of Central Eurasia were pastoralists, raising various combinations of sheep, horses, goats, cattle, and camels.

Finally, this band of steppe land runs nearly continuously from Hungary in the west to the Pacific Ocean in the east. The steppe thus serves as a natural line of communication linking China to the east, the Near East to the southwest, India to the southeast, and Europe to the west. Its role in history was twofold. It served as a line of trade linking east Asia with Europe, the

Near East, and India. It also served as a center for the development of nomadic tribal confederations, which could use their control over the Central Eurasia steppe as a means of gathering and moving armies to invade and pillage the sedentary civilizations surrounding the steppe.

Desert. The southern band of Central Eurasia is a vast desert, encompassing much of the modern regions of Turkestan, Sianking (northeastern China), Mongolia, and Tibet. Geographically and climatically it is an extension of the vast deserts of the Sahara and Near East. Unlike the Sahara, however, within the broad desert zone of Central Eurasia there are numerous micro-environments which permit both agriculture and pastoralism. Thus throughout this desert there are mountain valleys, river valleys, and oases where human communities could prosper. As with all deserts in the world, there exists in the Central Eurasian desert a mixture of pastoralism and intense agriculture in certain favorable zones.

| *Social and Economic System* | CENTRAL EURASIAN PASTORAL NOMADISM |

The role of Central Eurasia in world history cannot be understood without first analyzing the socioeconomic system of Central Eurasian pastoral nomadism. Most of Central Eurasia lacks adequate rainfall for agriculture. The peoples in this region are therefore largely pastoralists, their herds living on the grasslands of the steppe. Although there were certainly regional and chronological variations, nearly all Central Eurasian pastoralists followed a closely related social and economic pattern.

Nomadism. Nomads were dependent for their food supply—the fundamental human need—on their herds, which lived by grazing in pastures. Thus, as the Chinese astutely noted, Central Eurasian nomads were followers of grass and water. This nomadic lifestyle was necessary, both because of the problems of overgrazing if they remained too long at any site, and because of seasonal changes in rainfall and temperature. Nomadic lifestyle precluded the growth of cities, except near rivers and oases where intensive agriculture was possible. It also made state formation and taxation difficult. If a tribe of nomads became oppressed or unhappy, they could theoretically simply migrate with their herds to another region. Many of the characteristic features of sedentary civilization—cities, writing, monumental architecture, bureaucratic empires—are notably rare in Central Eurasia.

Society. Central Eurasian nomads were organized into patriarchal clans and tribes, with traditional and inheritable rights to certain tracts of grazing land. As families grew, male children received inheritances of part of the family herd. If herds grew too large, or drought reduced the available pasturage, clans would necessarily divide in search of better pasture. Thus arose a constant competition among different clans in nomadic society for pasture land. Women had relatively high status among nomadic groups, performing many important economic functions, and occasionally engaging in warfare alongside the men. Extended groupings of nomadic clans and tribes could combine into tribal confederations known as the *urdos*, which has come into English as the word horde. The leader of an urdos was know as the *khan* or *khaghan* (king).

Tribal Migrations. The nomadic lifestyle of the Central Eurasians had a dramatic impact on history. Their mobility meant that entire peoples and tribes could migrate almost at will. When this occurred within the confines of the Central Eurasian steppe it often went unnoticed by outside historians. However, if a tribe was capable of migrating out of the Eurasian steppe and into the sedentary zone, a chain reaction of dislocation and warfare often ensued, sometimes with tremendous historical implications. Several such occurrences will be described below.

The Horse. Another important characteristic of Central Eurasian peoples was their close ecological relationship with the horse. The horse was originally domesticated by Central Eurasians as a source for food, but they eventually took to using it for pulling carts and riding. These forms of transportation were quickly put to military uses: the war chariot from about 1800 B.C., and the cavalry from about 900 B.C. From then until the early twentieth century, the horse and cavalry played a decisive role in military power in the Old World.

ETHNIC GROUPS

Although there have been many different ethnic and linguistic groups in Central Eurasia, they can be broadly categorized into two main language groups: Indo-Europeans (or Indo-Aryans), and Turko-Mongolians (or Ural-Altaic).

Indo-Europeans, 2000 B.C. to A.D. 800. The Indo-European language family is one of the largest on earth, including English, most of the other languages of Europe, Iranian, and the majority of the languages of India. Since all of these languages bear fundamental linguistic similarities, historical linguists have assumed that at some point in the past, the ancestors of all speakers of Indo-European languages derived from a single tribe of proto-Indo-Europeans. Historic, linguistic and archaeological evidence increasingly points to Central Eurasia as the ancient homeland of this hypothetical tribe, perhaps in the areas north of the Caspian and Black seas.

Turko-Mongolians, 300 B.C. to A.D. 1600. There are numerous modern and extinct dialects and languages within the Turko-Mongolian language family. Modern Turko-Mongolian languages include Hungarian and Finnish in Europe, and Turkish, Uzbek, Azarbaijani, Kazakh, and Mongolian in Asia. Although Turko-Mongolian peoples first appear in Chinese records of the late first millennium B.C., they undoubtedly existed much earlier in eastern and northern Central Eurasia. The period from about 300 B.C. to A.D. 500 is one in which the Turko-Mongolians gradually expanded throughout Central Eurasia, absorbing, destroying, or driving out the Indo-Europeans. Although the Turko-Mongolians' rise to dominance in Central Eurasia represents a significant shift in language, religion, and culture, there was no related transformation of the social and economic order. Pastoral nomadism remained the foundation of Central Eurasian civilization. Furthermore, the patterns of interaction between agrarian and nomadic peoples also remained fundamentally the same.

Government and Warfare

GOVERNMENT

Nomadic "Democracy." Government on the steppes was a strange mixture of democracy and autocracy. Since nomads were not permanently tied to any given tract of land, if they became sufficiently displeased with a situation, they could "vote with their feet," and simply leave. Thus, leaders in the nomadic world necessarily had to acquire the consent of the governed. Government was an extension of tribal patriarchy, with power frequently held by the eldest male of a clan or tribe. However, a strong elective element existed in the steppes, whereby a leader had to earn the right to wield power by convincing his tribal members that he deserved their respect and loyalty.

The Khaghan. The khaghan, or king, held power by a combination of charisma, wisdom and justice, military victories, and wealth. A victorious leader who brought wealth to the tribe through plunder was assured of the loyalty of his followers. Thus, when a great steppe warlord appeared, he could sweep all opposition before him as increasing numbers of former enemies decided to become followers of the new victor. Such a confederation could just as easily disintegrate if the nomads came to believe that the son of a great khaghan did not deserve their respect or loyalty. There was also a religious element in nomadic government, centered on the belief that the success and victories of a khaghan were a manifestation of divine favor.

NOMADIC MILITARY SYSTEM

Cavalry. The horse provided both faster strategic movement (getting armies from their bases to the battlefield) and faster tactical movement (movement of troops on the battlefield). As such, an army with chariots or cavalry had significant advantages over an army composed largely of infantry. The vast grass-covered plains of the Central Eurasian steppe is both the natural habitat of the horse and a perfect region for breeding almost limitless numbers of horses. Thus, throughout history, not only were all Central Eurasian warriors mounted, but frequently they had several horses each, allowing them to switch mounts when their horses became tired in the midst of battle. Although the population of the steppe was much smaller than the surrounding agrarian societies, all adult males were required to provide military service for the tribe; if necessary they could leave all herding and other economic functions in the hands of the women. Thus large bodies of men could be mobilized, especially if the entire steppe had become united by a great khaghan.

Mounted Archery. The primary weapon of Central Eurasian nomads was the recurved composite bow. Made of layers of wood, horn, and sinew, then curved in the opposite direction of the intended draw, the strength of the composite bow was equal or greater than that of much larger bows, while its small size allowed it to be easily manipulated and shot from horseback. The combination of the horse and the composite bow gave the nomads a tremendous military advantage of superior mobility and firepower over the sedentarists for whom horses were often expensive and in limited supply.

Tactics. Nomadic military tactics were often based on their hunting methods. Constant harassment of an enemy on the march was combined with an extensive network of scouts. In battle they would send out flying columns to surround enemy troops in a double envelopment. Independent bands of nomads would ride circles around their enemies, barraging them with a hail of arrows. Only when the enemy was sufficiently weakened and disorganized from the archery assault would the nomads advance for close melee. Feigned retreat was a standard tactic, where the nomads would pretend to flee from an enemy to separate a body of men who could be isolated, surrounded, and destroyed. If an enemy appeared to gain the upper hand, the nomads would simply flee, only to return from another direction on another day.

Trade or War? The Central Eurasians had a product, the horse, which was in high demand in sedentary zones, and for which they could receive high prices. Central Asian tribes also controlled the Silk Road trade route across Asia. Vast trading profits could be made for all concerned if the Silk Road could be kept open and safe. The sedentarists, on the other hand, possessed cloth, metals, grain, and luxury items which the nomads desired. These factors naturally led to numerous cases of extensive trade between the nomads and the sedentary states. Nonetheless, the nomads quickly realized that they could frequently raid and plunder the sedentarists' cities and caravans, thereby gaining enormous wealth and power. This dilemma of trade vs. war led to fluctuating patterns of cooperation or conflict between nomads and sedentarists.

The Conflict of Steppe and Sown. Thus, from a broad historical perspective, the history of Central Eurasia has been described as the "conflict between steppe and sown," referring to the tensions between the nomads of the steppe and the agriculturalists living on land sown with seeds. When the sedentary kingdoms were powerful, and trade was profitable, the nomads would frequently become willing trading partners. On the other hand, if the sedentary states were weak, a charismatic khaghan arose in the steppes, or natural or political disasters forced the nomads to the verge of starvation, the nomads would often attack, and occasionally overwhelm sedentary civilizations. Thus the history of Central Eurasia is in part the story of repeated waves of nomads attacking—with varying degrees of success—the sedentary states of China, India, the Near East, and Europe.

AGE OF THE INDO-EUROPEANS, 2000 B.C.–A.D. 800

The origin of the Indo-Europeans, their initial homeland, and the nature of their tribal migrations are currently the subject of a major debate among historians. It is quite possible that such issues can never be resolved with certainty. It seems likely that the Indo-Europeans originated in the Central Eurasian steppe on the northern shores of the Black and Caspian seas. It is generally agreed that by 2000 B.C. Indo-European tribes were found throughout parts of Europe and in western Eurasia.

Indo-European Migrations

What is more certain is that by at least 1800 B.C., some warlike Indo-European tribes began a monumental migration, spreading out from their original homelands into parts of Europe, the Near East, India, and most of the Central Eurasian steppe lands to the western borders of China. By the end of the period of the Indo-European migrations (c. 1000 B.C.), Indo-European tribes had come to dominate most of these areas.

CHARIOT WARFARE

Development of Chariots. These migrations and conquests were made possible by the development of two new military technologies: the composite bow and the war chariot. The composite bow (described above) gave greater penetrating power to arrows. It was apparently invented in the Near East, but was used by Indo-Europeans in conjunction with their war chariots. In the Near East, donkeys had been used to pull cumbersome heavy four-wheeled war chariots in the third millennium B.C. However, the Indo-Europeans developed a lightweight, two-wheeled, war chariot. This lighter vehicle, when pulled by horses instead of donkeys, was far faster and more maneuverable. Combined with an archer armed with a composite bow, the chariot served as a mobile archery platform, a vehicle to transport elite troops to key places, and a shock weapon for charges against infantry. These advantages soon made it the supreme weapon throughout the civilized and nomadic worlds for nearly 1,000 years.

Spread of Chariot Technology. Chariot technology spread through a combination of conquest and diffusion. Conquering Indo-European chariot warriors naturally brought chariot technology to the lands in which they eventually settled, as seems to have been the case in India. Furthermore, non-Indo-Europeans quickly copied chariot technology when faced with the threat of military conquest. For example, the Hyksos warlords of Syria and Palestine, who were for the most part Semites, adopted chariot warfare in the eighteenth century B.C., allowing them to conquer the delta of Egypt. Thereafter, the Egyptian princes of Thebes also began building their own chariots in the mid-sixteenth century, allowing them eventually to expel the conquering Hyksos and create the empire of the New Kingdom (1560–1085 B.C.). Likewise, the Chinese adopted chariot technology from the Central Eurasian warriors in the thirteenth century B.C. Chariots remained a dominant factor in Chinese warfare until the third century B.C. Eventually chariot technology even reached subsaharan Africa.

THE INVENTION OF CAVALRY

Decline of the Chariot. The age of the great Indo-European chariot warriors lasted for over a thousand years. By the early first millennium B.C., however, the development of horseback riding techniques had advanced to the stage that cavalry began to replace charioteers as the principal military arm of the Central Eurasian nomads.

The Importance of Cavalry. The development of the military uses of the horse had as fundamental an impact on world history as the invention of gunpowder weapons would some two thousand years later. In the steppe the mounted archer became the basic warrior, giving the nomads strategic and tactical military superiority. The development of horse herding and cavalry created the classic Central Eurasian socioeconomic order and military system which would continue for the next two thousand years. Military systems in sedentary states were also transformed, increasingly relying on mounted warriors as the mainstay of their military power. This in turn led to the formation of mounted military aristocracies throughout most of the Old World, best exemplified by the medieval European knight.

The Earliest Horse Nomads

The first great horseback-riding nomadic peoples known to history are the Cimmerians, Scythians (Shakas), and Sarmatians. This group of Indo-European speaking nomads dominated the western steppe (from Romania to Iran) from perhaps 900 B.C. to A.D. 200. Some details of their history are known.

Scythians (Shakas). The Scythian period began about 750 B.C. when the related Cimmerian tribe raided widely throughout Anatolia. They were followed about 670 B.C. by the Scythians proper, who defeated the Medes in 641, initiating a twenty-eight-year period of widespread raids throughout the Near East to the borders of Egypt. The Scythians participated as allies of the Medes and Babylonians in the final destruction of the Assyrian empire in 612. The Persians eventually suppressed the Scythians in the Near East,

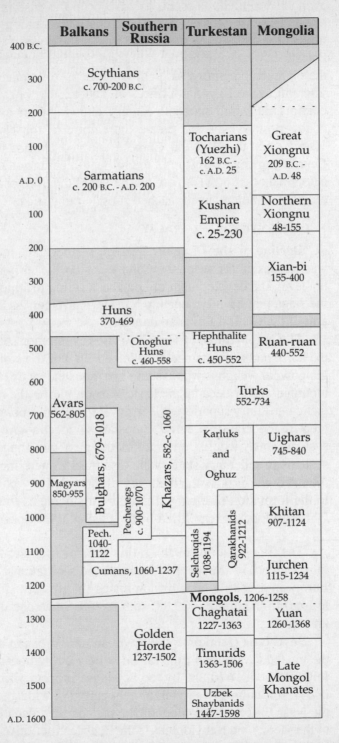

Balkans	Southern Russia	Turkestan	Mongolia

Scythians c. 700-200 B.C.

Sarmatians c. 200 B.C. - A.D. 200

Tocharians (Yuezhi) 162 B.C. - c. A.D. 25

Great Xiongnu 209 B.C. - A.D. 48

Kushan Empire c. 25-230

Northern Xiongnu 48-155

Xian-bi 155-400

Huns 370-469

Onoghur Huns c. 460-558

Hephthalite Huns c. 450-552

Ruan-ruan 440-552

Avars 562-805

Bulghars, 679-1018

Khazars, 582-c. 1060

Turks 552-734

Karluks and Oghuz

Uighars 745-840

Magyars 850-955

Pechenegs c. 900-1070

Khitan 907-1124

Pech. 1040-1122

Selchuqids 1038-1194

Qarakhanids 922-1212

Cumans, 1060-1237

Jurchen 1115-1234

Mongols, 1206-1258

Chaghatai 1227-1363

Yuan 1260-1368

Golden Horde 1237-1502

Timurids 1363-1506

Late Mongol Khanates

Uzbek Shaybanids 1447-1598

Fig. 15.1   Central Eurasian Peoples from 400 B.C. to A.D. 1600

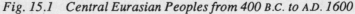

but were unable to destroy their bases on the steppe itself; a major attempt by Darius the Great to destroy the Scythians in the Danube valley in 513 B.C. was notably unsuccessful.

Decline. Scythian and related Sarmatian nomadic tribes continued to threaten the eastern frontier of the Iranian empire for the next several centuries; many eventually became mercenaries and governors for the Persians. Scythian nomads managed to defeat the attempts of Alexander the Great to subdue them in the late fourth century B.C. About 170 B.C. they began raiding India, founding a major kingdom in the region of modern Pakistan in 94 B.C. The Scythians and Sarmatians were slowly overwhelmed and absorbed by Turko-Mongolian tribes from eastern Eurasia beginning in the second century B.C. Nonetheless, many Indo-European nomadic peoples—such as the Soghdians—remained on steppes for centuries to come.

AGE OF THE HUNS, 300 B.C.–A.D. 552

Origins

The homelands of the Turko-Mongolian-speaking Central Eurasian tribes was the region of modern Mongolia and Manchuria. Until about 300 B.C. their history is somewhat obscure. It appears that they adopted chariots from the Indo-Europeans in the fourteenth century B.C. Scattered references in early Chinese sources describing warfare with Central Eurasian "barbarians" are insufficient to provide a detailed history. What can be said, however, is that a fairly continual state of tension existed between the sedentary Chinese in the Yellow River valley and their nomadic neighbors to the north and west. Sometime around the fifth or fourth century B.C., military horsemanship was introduced to eastern Turko-Mongolian tribesmen from the the Indo-European nomads to their west. As in the west, the rise of cavalry and mounted archery transformed the social and military foundations of steppe society, the military system of the sedentary Chinese, and the balance of power between the two.

Early Xiongnu (Eastern Huns), 209 B.C. – A.D. 155

THE RISE OF THE XIONGNU

At roughly the same time as the unification of China by the Qin (221–206 B.C.) and Han (206 B.C.–A.D. 221) dynasties, the earliest Turko-Mongolian tribes emerge into the full light of history. Even at this early time they appear to have developed the classical social and military system of mounted archery which would dominate the steppes for the next two thousand years. In Chinese records the earliest unified steppe state was established by the Xiongnu (who are often associated with the Huns).

Forming a loose tribal confederation, the Xiongnu nomads were united under their first great Shan-yu (emperor) Mao-tun (209–174 B.C.).

The Tokharians (Yuezhi). The rise of the Xiongnu can in part be seen as a decisive division in Central Eurasian history, marking the beginning of the linguistic transformation of the steppe from Indo-European to Turko-Mongolian. Before the rise of the Xiongnu, the Indo-European-speaking Tokharian (Yuezhi) horde lived on the boundaries of China, controlling much of the steppe. A war for domination of the steppe between the Turko-Mongolian Xiongnu and the Tokharians culminated in 176 B.C., with the defeat and expulsion of the latter. The Tokharians moved westward, settling in the area of modern Turkestan and Afghanistan. Their political history culminated with the founding of the cosmopolitan Kushan Empire (c. 100 B.C.–A.D. 224), which represented a remarkable synthesis of nomadic Central Asians with Iranian, Greek, and Indian cultures (see chapter 7).

XIONGNU RELATIONS WITH CHINA

The early phase of Xiongnu history is characterized by a strong symbiosis with the Han dynasty. The relationship was essentially one of mutual threats and extortions. The Xiongnu would threaten to raid China unless they were provided with "gifts" of gold, silk, and grain. The Xiongnu political system was heavily dependent on such Chinese "gifts." The Xiongnu khaghan maintained his power through personal charisma, the strength of his military, and judicious gifts to his vassals. Thus the Chinese tribute was redistributed by the khaghan throughout the steppe in a system whereby all subordinate tribes eventually benefited.

Chinese Steppe Policy. Chinese policy with the Xiongnu centered on four interrelated principles. First, by "using barbarians to fight barbarians," the Chinese meant hiring Xiongnu mercenaries, supporting dissenters within the Xiongnu confederation, and allying with non-Xiongnu Central Eurasian tribes. Second, the Great Wall was built in part as a defensive structure to prevent Central Eurasian raids into China, but it was also a barrier to economic and cultural exchange between the ordered hierarchical universe of Confucian China and what was perceived as the anarchical chaos of the barbarian steppe. Third, judicious use was made of gifts, bribes, and hostages, including marriage of imperial princesses to Xiongnu khaghans. Fourth was military intervention. These overlapping policies remained the pillars of the Chinese Central Eurasian policy for nearly 2,000 years. It is remarkable to note the nearly exact parallels between Chinese policy toward the nomads and that of the Iranians and Romans.

THE MILITARY OPTION

When the extortions of the Xiongnu became too extravagant, the Chinese would bribe other Central Eurasian tribes to attack the Xiongnu in the rear, ferment revolt by supporting rivals to the Xiongnu throne, or mount massive military incursions beyond the Great Wall.

Logistical Problems. The fundamental problem with the Chinese attempts to extend their military power beyond the Great Wall was twofold. The logistical problems were overwhelming: there were no fortified cities to use as bases of supplies, no fields to plunder for food. The Chinese army had to carry all its supplies with it, meaning that in practice they were forced to limit the length of their campaigns to a few months.

Strategic Problems. Furthermore, it was usually quite difficult to force a military decision on the Xiongnu. Realizing the Chinese logistical problem, the Xiongnu would simply move away from an advancing Chinese army, frequently refusing to engage the main Chinese army in direct combat. Eventually, when the Chinese supplies were exhausted, their army was forced to retreat to China. The Xiongnu would then simply return to their temporarily abandoned pastures. Thus, from the Chinese perspective, it was much less expensive and dangerous to bribe the Xiongnu into peace than to mount military offensives. This factor remained a constant in the relationship between all sedentary states and the Eurasian nomads. The fundamental inability of the sedentary states to effectively extend their military strength into the steppes to destroy the power base of the nomads gave decisive strategic advantage to the nomads until the development of effective firearms in the late fifteen century.

Chinese Conquests in Central Eurasia. The most important periods of Chinese military intervention into the steppes came under the emperor Wu (141–87 B.C.). Chafing under the thinly disguised extortion that China was forced to pay to the Xiongnu, the "Martial Emperor" Wu decided to change the international order by crushing the Xiongnu and annexing the steppe once and for all. In an extended series of bloody campaigns from 130 to 90 B.C., Chinese generals were temporarily successful. Ultimately, however, the problems of logistics and the generals' inability to destroy the mobile power base of the Xiongnu prevented a permanent military solution. In two campaigns in 99 and 90 B.C., the Chinese army was nearly destroyed, and the general Li Guang-li was captured. The emperor thereafter abandoned the policy of conquest.

Ban Chao's Campaigns (A.D. 73–102). A second major period of Chinese intervention beyond the Great Wall focused on a rather different and more obtainable military goal: securing the Silk Road trade route. Between A.D. 73 and 102 the Chinese sent a brilliant general, Ban Chao, to maintain a protectorate over the Tarim basin in order to control trade on the Silk Road. Uneasy Chinese control was maintained in the region for those three decades. In 97 a Chinese expedition even reached the eastern shore of the Black Sea. Following Ban Chao's death, however, an extensive anti-

Chinese rebellion occurred, and all Chinese troops were withdrawn from Central Eurasia in 107.

LATER XIONGNU AND CHINESE NOMADIC STATES, 155–557

As long as the Han dynasty retained its economic vitality, internal unity, and military strength, the balance of power between the Xiongnu and the Chinese remained basically intact. However, the decline and collapse of the Han dynasty in the late second century disrupted that order, leading to a period of political flux both on the steppe and in China itself. Another major factor was the military incursions of a new Turko-Mongolian group, the Xianbi. Barbarian warlords such as the general Cao Cao initially served as mercenaries for the Chinese, rising in rank until they became kingmakers. Some ultimately attempted to seize the throne, while preserving the facade of Chinese imperial order for another century.

Small Kingdoms. In the long run, however, even this pretense vanished. Eurasian nomads, under the leadership of Liu Zong, sacked the greatest Chinese cities of the day, Louyang (311) and Changan (312). These events had repercussions in China similar to the sack of Rome by the Vandals in 410. Thereafter Eurasian warlords who had adopted a thin veneer of Chinese culture ruled a bewildering array of barbarian successor states in northern China from 311 to 557. At the same time, a new Central Eurasian people, the Ruan-ruan, displaced the Xiongnu and Xianbi as the dominant power on the steppe. From c. 450 to 552 the Ruan-ruan formed a new imperial order on the steppes. The age of the Xiongnu in China had passed.

The Western Steppe, c. 300–552

Xiongnu and Huns. There is disagreement among scholars as to the exact relationship between the Xiongnu north of China and other peoples known as the Huns in other parts of Central Eurasia. At various times in Xiongnu history, rival khaghans of the royal family or rebel Xiongnu clans fled westward to escape submission. It is quite possible that the Hephthalites of Turkestan and the Huns in Europe—or at least their ruling elites—were descendants of these refugee Xiongnu lords and clans.

However, even if the Hephthalite Huns and European Huns were somehow ethnically or culturally related to the Xiongnu, these different Hun peoples were politically separate and may have had little contact with each other. Nonetheless, it seems likely that the massive tribal movements occurring throughout Central Eurasia from China to France in the fourth and fifth centuries A.D. must be linked by internal historical forces in Central Eurasia, even if obscure to modern historians.

HEPHTHALITE HUNS

Conquest of Iran and India, c. 440–552. As with most Central Eurasian peoples, the origin of the Hephthalite Huns is somewhat obscure.

It seems that in the early fifth century they moved southwest from the Tarim basin into Turkestan, overwhelming and absorbing local nomadic peoples. In the course of the next century the Hephthalites posed a major military threat both to the the Sasanids of Iran and the Guptas of India. Under their great but brutal warlords Toramana (c. 470–500) and Mihirakula (c. 500–520), northwestern India was systematically plundered and devastated. The imperial Gupta dynasty of India collapsed under subsequent political and military stress, ending the classical age in India (see chapter 7).

Collapse of the Hephthalites. Hephthalite power came to an end through the use of a classic military strategy against the nomads. In 557 the Sasanid king Khosrow I entered into an alliance with the rising Turkish khaghan Ishtemi, effectively surrounding the Hephthalites. Simultaneously attacked by Turkish nomads from the northeast, and by the Sasanids from the southwest, the Hephthalite state was crushed. By 561 their power had completely collapsed, and their former domain was divided between the Iranians and the Turks. However, some 30,000 Hephthalite warriors are said to have fled westward rather than submit to new Turkish and Iranian overlords. These nomads, together with other nomadic refugees fleeing Turkish domination, reappeared in a new political incarnation as the Avars in Europe in 562 (see below).

ATTILA AND THE WESTERN HUNS IN EUROPE, 374–469

The Coming of the Huns, 374–434. As noted above, the coming of the Huns to Europe was directly related to political developments within Central Eurasia. In 374 the Huns crossed the Volga river, occupying the homeland of the nomadic Alans, who moved westward and defeated the Germanic Gothic tribes in 375. The Visigoths in turn fled from Alan conquerors into Roman territory, where they crushed the Roman army and killed the emperor Valens at the battle of Adrianople in 378. The collapse of the Roman army left the frontier open for the massive Germanic invasions and the eventual fall of Rome.

Attila the Hun, 434–453. In the meantime, the Huns pushed farther westward, conquering all the tribes in their path, and reaching the border of the Roman empire at the Danube river in 405. In the next decades they sporadically raided the Roman empire, but were finally galvanized when Attila, "the scourge of God," became the khaghan (434 and 453). Between 441–448 he plundered the Balkans at will; thereafter a vast tribute paid by the Byzantine emperor convinced Attila to leave the East in peace and turn his attentions westward. His invasion of Roman Gaul (France) was cut short by a serious defeat at the battle of Chalons in 451. Although checked, he was not crushed; in 452 he plundered northern Italy. Rome itself was spared only by negotiations with Pope Leo I, the promise of a vast tribute, and the hand of the daughter of the Roman emperor in marriage. His death in 453 spared Europe further attacks. Thereafter, Attila's former vassal tribes revolted while his successors engaged in a civil war for the throne; Attila's empire disintegrated. Attila's son Dinzigikh attempted to hold the state together, but was defeated and killed by the Byzantines in 469.

Decline of the Huns. The Huns then divided into two factions, remaining simply as minor tribes among other Germanic, Slavic, and Turkic peoples in eastern Europe. They briefly threatened Constantinople in 559, but were driven off. In the late sixth century they were conquered and absorbed by the Avars, another Central Eurasian tribe. The direct effects of the Huns on European history were negligible. Their armies raided for only slightly more than a decade, and their empire collapsed after the death of Attila. Indirectly, however, they played an enormous role. Their incursions initiated the massive migration of hundreds of thousands of Germanic tribesmen into the Roman empire, destroying the West and laying the foundations for feudal Europe.

THE AGE OF THE MEDIEVAL TURKISH KHANATES, 552–1206

Turkish Civilization

In many ways the basic socioeconomic, cultural, and political patterns of steppe history show great continuity between the Hunnic and Turkish periods. There were, however, four significant developments. First, the rise of various Turkish tribes and states to domination in Central Eurasia created significant ethnic and linguistic changes in the region. Turks became the dominant ethnic group of Central Eurasia and have remained so to the present. Second, the political and military organization of many Central Eurasian peoples became increasingly sophisticated. Indigenous forms of writing and literacy appeared on the steppe, trade increased, bureaucracies and other forms of government became more permanent. Third, the Islamic religion was introduced to the steppes about 750. As time progressed, Islam became the dominant religion of the steppes, thereby increasing the influence and cultural and economic ties between Central Eurasia and the Near East. Finally, the boundary between the economic and cultural spheres of the steppe and sown remained relatively constant in Europe and China; in the Near East, however, the boundaries began to blur following the coming of the Selchuqid Turks.

THE ORIGIN OF THE TURKS

Turkish legends speak of the birth of their ancestors from a she-wolf and of their early life in caves to which many Turks would make annual pilgrimages. Linguistically, Turkic languages have existed in Central Eurasia for thousands of years—indeed the Xiongnu and Huns may have spoken what we call Turkic languages. Historically, however, the earliest mention of Turks comes in the early fifth century, when they appear as a tribe skilled in iron working, serving Ruan-ruan overlords. In 552 the Turks revolted under the leadership of their tribal chief Bumin (546–553), and won a decisive battle against the Ruan-ruan khaghan. Thereafter the Turks swiftly rose to dominance of the steppe. In 560 they allied with the Sasanid Iranians and crushed the Hephthalite Huns in Turkestan, annexing half their former domain. By 564 they were raiding and exchanging embassies with northern China; by 567 they were operating in the southern Russian steppe and exchanging embassies with the Byzantine empire.

Turks in the East

THE RISE OF TURKISH STATES

For the next six hundred years, Turkish khaghans and princes would dominate the Central Eurasian steppe. Like the earlier Xiongnu and Huns, but unlike the later Mongols, the Turks were never able to establish a long-lasting united empire encompassing the entire steppe. Rather, they were divided into a diverse array of states, sharing a common language, social order, and economic system, but frequently differing radically in terms of culture, religion, and political alliance.

TURKISH EMPIRES, 552–840

The First Turkish Empire, 552–734. The "imperial" period of the Turks lasted from 552 to 583, during which they established control over the steppes, with Turkish armies successfully campaigning from Manchuria to southern Russia. From 583 to 630 a succession dispute divided the Turkish state into feuding eastern and western khanates, thereby weakening both their control over the steppes and their relative military strength against China and Iran. Under the resurgent military power of the Tang dynasty, Chinese armies penetrated the steppe, defeated the Turks, captured the eastern khaghan Hie-li, campaigned on the shores of the Caspian sea, and established control over the Silk Road. By 659 the Chinese, for the first time in history, had direct political control over large parts of Mongolia, Tarim, and Turkestan; the Tang empire now bordered the new Umayyad Islamic empire in Iran. Chinese domination of the steppe was short-lived, however, lasting only from 630 to 684. Thereafter, the khaghan Elterish revolted, liberated the Turks from Chinese rule, and quickly reestablished the Turkish empire to nearly its former size. This revitalized Turkish state only endured from 684 until 734, after which the Turkish clan of the Uighurs revolted and established the Uighur dynasty.

The Turks and China. During the two centuries of Turkish domination of Central Eurasia, Turks played basically the same role in relation to China as had the previous Xiongnu dynasty, with fluctuating periods of alliances, peaceful coexistence, military suppression, and outright war. In the initial decades of the seventh century, the Turks used the political chaos in China to extort tribute, raid Chinese cities, and fight for and against rival Chinese armies. Turks increasingly served as mercenaries and advisors in the early Tang period (618–907).

Uighurs (745–840). The Uighurs were a Turkic tribe which rose to power in the mid-eighth century. Unlike previous and later Central Eurasian tribes, Uighur khaghans followed a strong pro-Chinese policy throughout their reign. In 755 An Lu-shan, a Central Eurasian mercenary serving as one of the most important generals in the Tang Chinese army, revolted against the Tang, captured the capital at Changan, and nearly overthrew the dynasty. He was stopped only by the intervention of the Uighurs, who crushed the rebellion and saved the Tang dynasty (although sacking the cities of Changan and Louyang in the process). For the next century the Uighurs remained the dominant power in the eastern steppe.

In many ways the Uighurs were unique in the history of the steppe. Unlike other nomadic khaghans who ruled from mobile camps, the Uighurs built and ruled from an actual city, Karabalghasun. They promoted agriculture and maintained a formal bureaucracy which kept written government records—their script formed the basis of the later Mongol writing system. Although linguistically Turkish, and politically allied with the Chinese, the Uighurs maintained their strongest cultural ties with Soghdian Iranians of the Tarim basin, eventually adopting Manichaeism (a denomination of Zoroastrianism) as the state religion, although also patronizing Nestorian Christianity (see below). They were eventually overthrown by the Kirghiz nomads, but remained an important tribe until the present, serving notably as government officials during the Mongol period.

Turks in the West

TURKISH PEOPLES IN EUROPE

Turkish nomadic tribes also played an important role in the southern Russian steppes. Ethnically Turkish nomads threatened Europe from the fall of the Huns to the rise of the Mongols. The Avars (562–802) dominated the Danube plains, threatening the city of Constantinople and raiding into western Europe. They were replaced by the Magyars (c. 850–955), who spread terror throughout Germany and Italy for half a century. The Magyars were finally defeated by the Germans, converted to Christianity, and created the kingdom of Hungary. Bulgar Turkish nomads created important kingdoms in southern Russia and in the Danube basin (679–1018); the modern nation of Bulgaria derives its name from this Central Eurasian tribe. Khazar Turks (582–1060) converted to Judaism and created a powerful merchant state to the northeast of the Black Sea. The final Turkish tribes in the region were the Pechenegs (c. 900–1122) and Cumans (c. 1060–1237) who dominated the steppe and threatened the Byzantine empire until the coming of the Mongols in 1237. Thereafter, the Mongol Golden Horde remained a serious threat to Russian and eastern European states until the sixteenth century.

THE TURKS AND ISLAM

By far the most significant role of the Turks in world history comes through their relationship to Islamic civilization. By 560 Turks had replaced the Hephthalite Huns as the frontier nomadic state on the northeastern border of the Sasanid empire. For the next century relations between the Sasanids and Turks remained strained, with frequent disputes over trade and Turkish raids. Arab Muslims first came into contact with the Turks as they conquered the crumbling Sasanid empire in the mid-seventh century. As inheritors of the Sasanid empire, the Umayyad caliphs (emperors) initiated an aggressive Turkish policy, which included attempts to control Central Eurasian trade routes, proselytizing in Central Eurasia, and military intervention.

The Battle of Talas, 751. Arab military pressure in Turkestan occurred on and off in the early eighth century. At the same time, the collapse of the Turkish empire in 734 destroyed the unity of the Turks, leaving them open to outside domination. Tang Chinese generals invaded Turkestan, bringing the Chinese and Umayyad Muslim empires into contact. In 750 the Turks rebelled against their Chinese masters, calling upon an Umayyad army for support. In July 751 the Chinese army was crushed by a combined Turkish and Arab force on the banks of the Talas river. Chinese domination in Central Eurasia quickly collapsed. This Muslim victory opened Central Eurasia to penetration from Arab armies, merchants, scholars, and missionaries. From this point on, Central Eurasia came increasingly within the sphere of Islamic civilization. Chinese armies would not operate in Central Eurasia for nearly another thousand years.

Rise of Turkish Muslim Warlords. The military skill of the Turks was highly regarded by the Arabs. Paralleling the use of German mercenaries by the Romans, Turkish mercenaries and slave-soldiers were enlisted in Arab armies and soon rose to positions of prominence. The results in the Muslim world were also similar to the Roman experience: Turks—like Mahmud of Ghazni (998–1030)—eventually usurped authority within the Muslim world, and ultimately established independent dynasties.

The Turkish Invasion of the Near East. Shortly thereafter, a Turkish nomadic dynasty, the Selchuqids (1038–1194), who had been recently converted to Islam, invaded and overwhelmed Iran and Mesopotamia. Their invasion and conquests were to initiate a Turkish period in Near Eastern history. Turkish sultans and warriors came to dominate nearly all regions of the Near East. The Selchuqid Turks defeated the Byzantine army at the battle of Manzikert in 1071, which was followed by the collapse of the Byzantine empire in Anatolia (modern Turkey), beginning the slow ethnic transformation of the region from Greek to Turk. Turkish warlords also led the Islamic conquest of India. Thus by 1400 Islamic Turkish military aristocracies—descendants of Central Eurasian Turkish nomads—were in control of nearly the entire Near East, the former Byzantine empire, and much of northern India.

SEDENTARY TURKISH DYNASTIES

The Turks were the most enduring of any Central Eurasian people. Most nomadic ethnic groups and tribal confederations ultimately disappeared; the Mongols today live in a small, relatively unimportant state dominated by their Russian and Chinese neighbors. Turks, however, remained an important people in the Near East and Central Eurasia until the present. Five major empires were either founded by Turks or dominated by Turkish military aristocracies (see chapters 9 and 11 for details).

Sultanate of Delhi (1206–1526). Building on the Indian wars and conquests of Mahmud of Ghazni and Muhammad of Ghur, Turkish warlords and warriors overwhelmed northern India, establishing a culture that was religiously Islamic, culturally Persian, but dominated by a Turkish military aristocracy.

Mamluks (1250–1517). Mamluks were mostly Turkish military slaves and mercenaries who formed the bulk of the Egyptian army in the early thirteenth century. After instigating a palace coup, the Mamluks established their own dynasty, initiating two and a half centuries of control by Turkish warlords of Egypt.

Ottomans (1290–1922). The Ottoman empire was founded in the early fourteenth century by Osman, a Muslim Turkish nomad who led tribal war bands against the Byzantines. Ultimately, the Ottoman empire became the most powerful state in the Near East, laying the foundations for the modern state of Turkey.

Safavids (1502–1736). The Safavid dynasty in Iran was founded by Ismail Shah (1502–1524), a Turkish warlord who claimed to be sent by God to restore justice in the Islamic world. However, this dynasty quickly became Persianized, loosing its Turkish identity.

Moghuls (1526–1761). The Moghul (Mongol) dynasty of India was likewise founded by a Chaghatai Turkish war band under the leadership of Babur (1483–1539). Under Moghul leadership, nearly all of India was conquered by the Muslims, completing the process which had begun under Mahmud of Ghazni, another Turkish warlord, five centuries earlier.

Thus, ethnic, linguistic, and cultural elements of Central Eurasian Turks became an important part of Near Eastern and Indian Islamic culture, with Turks dominating the military and political institutions of those two regions for centuries following their initial intervention into the Near East in 1040.

However, intervening between the initial eruption of the Turks into the Near East in 1040, and their final rise to prominence in the Near East and India in the fifteenth century, the world underwent a century of domination by another Central Eurasian nomadic confederation, the Mongols.

THE MONGOL WORLD EMPIRE, 1206–1368

The most famous and successful Central Eurasian state was that of the Mongols, who created the largest empire of pre-modern history. The rise and fall of the Mongol empire follows the quintessential pattern of Central Eurasian states. A great warlord appeared on the steppes, uniting the nomads. The nomads subsequently expanded their domain, migrating and conquering surrounding sedentary territory. Under the warlord's immediate successors, the empire continued expansionism, while culturally and economically merging with their sedentary conquered peoples. Ultimately, the empire disintegrated through civil war over succession, and rebellion. The entire Mongol period lasted only a century and a half.

The Origin of the Mongols

As an ethnic and linguistic group, Mongolian peoples had probably existed in northeastern Central Eurasia since prehistoric times. There were undoubtedly ethnic Mongols in many of the Central Eurasian tribal confederations of the Xiongnu and Turks. Socially, culturally, and religiously, there is little to distinguish them from other Central Eurasian nomads. The emergence of the Mongols as an independent important tribe occurred only in the twelfth century, when they appeared as vassals of the Khitan and Jurchen nomadic tribal confederations. Their rise to power in Central Eurasia was the result of the military and political genius of Chingis Khan.

CHINGIS (GENGHIS) KHAN, 1206–1227

Rise of Chingis Khan, 1167–1206. Born in 1167 to a minor Mongol chieftain, Temuchin was orphaned as a young boy, spending his early years in poverty and obscurity. Slowly, on the merits of his military prowess and personal charisma, he gathered about him a growing band of Mongol warriors, engaging in constant tribal warfare with surrounding clans. As word of his military victories spread across the steppe, more and more nomads gathered under his war banner. By 1206 he had united the entire central steppe into a tribal confederation under his supreme authority and assumed the imperial title by which he has become know to history— Chingis Khan, "World Emperor."

Conquests, 1206–1227. He then turned his attention to his sedentary neighbors. His two great campaigns were against the Chin dynasty in

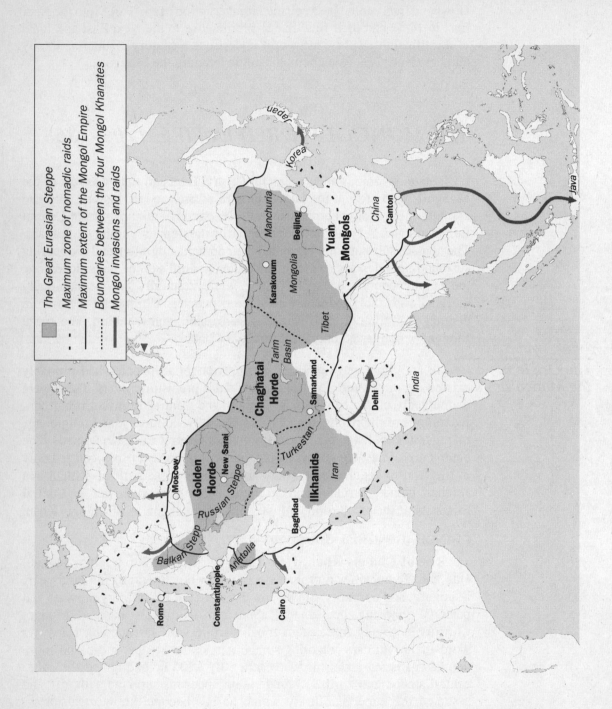

Fig. 15.2   The Mongol World Empire, 1206–1368

northern China (1211–1234) and the Khwarazm-shahs of Iran (1218–1224). The results of these campaigns were horrifying. Millions died in what was probably the worst carnage of premodern times—only with the aid of modern technologies have Hitler, Stalin, and Mao managed to surpass the Mongol record in the creation of human misery. Some scholars maintain that Iran and China took centuries to recover from the devastation. But this was only the beginning of the Mongol conquests.

The Mongol World Empire and the Four Successor States

Following traditional steppe practice for succession, on the death of Chingis Khan the Mongol empire was divided into four sections, each ruled by one of Chingis's sons, but under the supreme leadership of his son Ogedei (1229–1241), who was proclaimed Great Khan of the empire. The Mongol advance continued on three fronts, under the direct leadership of these regional governors. As time progressed, however, each governor became increasingly independent. Ultimately, in 1259, a dispute arose concerning succession to the Grand Khanate and the empire broke into four independent states which began feuding among themselves.

CHINA AND THE YUAN, 1260–1368

The Mongol campaigns against China continued for nearly seventy years, culminating in 1279 with the final conquests of the south under the leadership of Khublai Khan, grandson of Chingis. One of the greatest Mongol khans, Khublai's reign witnessed the culminating success of the Mongol conquests with the fall of China. It also saw the beginning of the collapse of the Mongol empire with its breakup into four states, and the increasing adoption of Chinese culture in Khublai's court. Recognizing that they could not militarily expel the Mongols, the Chinese bureaucrats and intellectuals attempted, with moderate success, to transform the Mongols into cultural Chinese.

Mongol Conquests. Mongol expansionism in east Asia continued throughout the late thirteenth century. Korea was conquered between 1218 and 1259. In what were probably the largest naval campaigns in premodern times, Japan was twice invaded unsuccessfully, in 1274 and 1281. The second expedition involved nearly 200,000 men and over 4,000 vessels, roughly the size of the Allied invasion of western Europe in World War II. Various regions in Southeast Asia were also invaded between 1281 and 1300, including a naval expedition against Java in 1292–1293.

Decline. Chinese attempts to sinicize the Mongols were only partially successful; the Chinese never came to accept their brutal and arrogant overlords. Non-Chinese, such as the Venetian trader Marco Polo, were preferred as government officials at the expense of the traditional Confucian Chinese bureaucrats. In the fourteenth century the Yuan Mongol dynasty progressively weakened, slowly losing control over China. A combination of exploitation, corruption, succession crisis, flooding of the Yellow River, and the Black Death culminated in the 1340s in the outbreak of rebellions led by the secret millennialist Buddhist White Lotus society. By 1368 the Mongol Yuan dynasty had been overthrown and replaced by the native Chinese Ming dynasty.

IRAN AND THE ILKHANIDS, 1253–1335

The fall of the Khwarazm-shahs in 1224 had placed the northeastern half of Iran in Mongol hands. In the ensuing decades, the Mongols were occupied elsewhere, but by 1251 their attention was again turned to the Near East. Under the leadership of Chingis Khan's grandson Hulegu (1253–1265), a large Mongol army invaded western Iran, culminating in 1258 in the capture and sack of Baghdad, the capital of the Muslim caliphate. The Mongols thereafter moved westward to attack the last remaining center of Islam in the Near East, Egypt. But in a forty-year war (1260–1303) the Mongols were finally halted by the Turkish Mamluks of Egypt, who had adopted and professionalized Central Eurasian horse archery, and were thus able to meet the Mongols on an equal basis.

Conversion to Islam. As in China, the Mongol Ilkhanid dynasty in Iran entered into an uneasy relationship with the conquered Muslim peoples. At first, it seemed as if the Khans might adopt an anti-Muslim policy by raising pagans, Nestorian Christians, and Buddhists to positions of authority, and allying with the Crusaders and Byzantines against the Mamluks of Egypt. Ultimately, however, the Ilkhanid Mongols adopted the religion of their conquered subjects, officially becoming Muslims in 1295. Mongol government in Iran was noted for the same short-sighted brutality and extortion found in China, and with the same predictable results: the local peoples felt no loyalty, and often great antipathy, to their Mongol conquerors. Few Iranians or Arabs mourned when the Ilkhanid Mongol dynasty disintegrated in civil war and rebellion after 1335.

THE CHAGHATAI HORDE, 1227–1369

The Chaghatai horde is the least well known of the four successor states to the Mongol world empire. During the civil war that followed the death of Mongke Khan in 1259, the Chaghatai horde became completely independent. Thereafter, its political history revolves around conflicts with other Mongol states, and a series of unsuccessful invasions of northwestern India between 1299 and 1308, which were ultimately defeated by the Sultans of Delhi (1299–1308). The collapse of the Chaghatai khanate as a significant military power came in 1369 when they were defeated by Tamerlane and forced to become his vassals (see below). Thereafter various rulers claiming descent from Chaghatai remained as chieftains of small principalities, but with little political and military power.

EUROPE AND THE GOLDEN HORDE, 1237–1502

Mongol Conquests in Europe. The most long-lasting of the Mongol successor states, the Golden Horde, was based on the steppes of southern Russia, the old grazing ground of the Huns some eight hundred years earlier. Initial Mongol campaigns from 1236 to 1242 had temporarily penetrated deep into Europe. In 1241 the Mongols defeated a German army at the battle of Lignitz and a Hungarian army at the Sajo River. However, the death of Ogedei Khan in that same year had forced the withdrawal of Mongol troops from central Europe. Their conquest of southern Russia, however, was permanent. All of European Russia became either occupied or tributary to the Mongols for several centuries. This "Tatar yoke" of Mongol domination had a lasting psychological and political effect on the Russians, contributing to the autocratic and militaristic nature of their society.

Mongols and Russians. The history of the relationship between Russians and Mongols is generally one of conflict and oppression; feuds, raids, and battle were common. While the northern Russians had some levels of autonomy in return for the payment of tribute, they were under continual pressure from the khans. Although the conquered Russians were Christians, the Mongols of the Golden Horde eventually adopted Islam as their official religion in the early fourteenth century, adding an additional element of conflict between Mongols and Russians. By the middle of the fifteenth century the power of the Horde was waning due to defeats by Tamerlane and internal strife. This created the opportunity for the military expansion of Moscow at the expense of both the Golden Horde and their Christian Russian neighbors. Thus by 1502 the last of the Mongol khanates, the Golden Horde, had disappeared, being absorbed by rival nomad groups and the advancing Russians.

TAMERLANE, 1363–1405

Although the world empire of the Mongols collapsed with the fall of the Ilkhanids in 1335 and the Yuan in 1368, the legend of the Mongols continued for centuries on the steppe. Chingis Khan played the role of an Alexander or Caesar in the minds of subsequent nomadic peoples. Many later rulers claimed descent from Chingis Khan and consciously attempted to imitate the conquests of that great ruler. The most successful of these was Tamerlane.

Conquests. Timur-i Leng (Timur "the lame," known as Tamerlane or Tamburlane in the West) was one of the greatest conquerors in world history. Beginning his life as a soldier in the Chaghatai khanate, he rose through the ranks by his military skill. In 1363 he rebelled against his overlords, replacing the Chaghatai khan at his capital at Samarkand. Never losing a major battle, in the following decades Tamerlane conquered Persia (1381–1387), the Golden Horde (1388–1391), Mesopotamia (1393–1394), Russia

(1395), India (1398–1399), Syria (1400), and Anatolia (1402). He died in 1405 at the age of sixty-nine while preparing for an invasion of China.

Impact. Tamerlane is noted for both his military genius and his great brutality. His troops are said to have built pyramids and towers from the severed skulls of those who resisted his conquests. On the other hand, he also utilized the loot of his conquests to make Samarkand the center of culture in the Asian Islamic world, and one of the fabled cities of the medieval Orient. Although they were never able to hold his extended conquests, Tamerlane's descendants ruled his central empire in Iran and Turkestan for the next century (1405–1506).

CENTRAL EURASIA IN WORLD HISTORY

Central Eurasia Culture

LITERATURE

The literature of the steppe was basically oral, centering around poetry, folk tales, and epics which were told and retold for centuries in different versions around the campfires of the nomads. The themes of nomadic literature were martial, telling tales of great wars and heroic deeds. No indigenous written records exist from the steppe before the eighth century; most of the steppe epics and poetry were recorded after the fourteenth century. The most famous literature of the steppes include the *Epic of Manas* and the *Tales of Dede Korkut*.

HISTORY

The earliest historical records written by Central Eurasians are Turkic inscriptions from the eighth century. Until the thirteenth century we are forced to rely largely on the descriptions by the sedentary enemies of the steppe nomads for an understanding of the history of Central Eurasia. This necessarily creates distortions in our understanding.

Central Eurasian Historians. The beginning of a real historical tradition in Central Eurasia comes with the Mongol conquests. The Mongols instinctively recognized that their empire represented something unique both in the history of the steppe and the history of the world. The *Secret History of the Mongols*, chronicling the rise of Chingis Khan and the beginning of the Mongol conquests, is the most famous and important historical work to be written by the nomads. The *Golden Chronicle* is another Mongolian work detailing the later history of the Mongols following the breakup of the Mongol empire.

Sedentary Historians. Sedentary historians also recognized the significance of the nomads in world affairs. Many observers wrote important histories of the steppe, often based on firsthand information derived from visits to Central Eurasia. The most important works are by the Roman Priscus, the Persians Juvaini and Rashid al-Din, the medieval Europeans John of Plano Carpini and William of Rubruck, and the Han Chinese historian Sima Qian.

ARCHITECTURE AND ART

Architecture. Although there were a few great cities built on the steppe, such as Karabalghasun of the Uighurs and Karakorum of the Mongols, for the most part Central Eurasians maintained their traditional nomadic existence. Cities and monumental architecture were therefore rare in Central Eurasia. Only on the fringes of the steppe, in cities such as Samarkand where nomadic and sedentary cultures merged, do we find great architecture, which is usually associated with the artistic styles of one of the sedentary civilizations.

Art. The most important surviving examples of nomadic art come from metal working. The Scythians were renowned for their fine gold craftsmanship, as witnessed by archaeological finds from Scythian burials. Thereafter, metal carving and ornamentation remained an important art form throughout nomadic history. Artistic wood carving and fabric design were also highly developed, but few such examples have survived. Delightful fresco paintings survive in some of the caravan and oasis cities of the steppe, manifesting artistic mixtures of Chinese and Persian styles.

RELIGION

Shamanism. Although there were many different forms of nomadic religions in Central Eurasia, historians of religion have classified them as shamanism (a *shaman* is a priest or magician who has power over the forces of nature). The fundamental concept of shamanism is animism, that all elements of nature—plants, animals, and stones—are imbued with a spiritual essence or power. Shamans are humans who can contact and, in some cases, control this immense reservoir of spiritual power which fills the universe. Shamans also had the important power to contact and appease the spirits of dead ancestors. With such powers they served the role of priests, prophets, doctors, and magicians in nomadic society. They were especially noted for their ability to transfer their spirit into the body of animals: a bird to ascend into heaven, or a wolf to gain strength and power. Indeed, our legend of the werewolf may ultimately derive from ecstatic shamanistic trances in which the shaman believed his spirit had been transferred to the body of a wolf.

Tengri. In addition to the widespread and numerous variations on these basic shamanistic ideas, the nomads also worshiped a supreme god, called Tengri (Heaven or Sky) by the Mongols. All the other numerous spirits and gods were ultimately subservient to the overwhelming power of Tengri the Sky-god. The Mongols believed that they had been appointed by Tengri to conquer "all under Heaven," or the entire world. In addition to this substratum of shamanism, several outside religions also had a major impact in Central Eurasia.

Buddhism. Buddhism was introduced into Central Eurasia from Afghanistan and India in the third century B.C., and from there spread rapidly throughout Central Eurasia. Between roughly 200 B.C. and A.D. 900 Buddhism was the most important outside religion in Central Eurasia. Most of the major cities and more "progressive" tribes were partially Buddhist in culture. The remains of Buddhist paintings and sculptures dot the caravan centers of Central Eurasia. It was Central Eurasian Buddhist monks, merchants, and missionaries who first introduced Buddhism into China. When nomadic warlords dominated northern China following the fall of the Han they invariably were strong patrons of Buddhism. From the late Mongol period, Tibetan Buddhism became increasingly influential, and it is the dominant religion among the Mongols today.

Islam. Beginning in the eighth century, Islam steadily replaced Buddhism as the major imported religion of Central Eurasia; today the peoples of the central and western steppe are largely Muslim. The coming of Islam into Central Eurasia brought with it strong cultural and economic ties to the Near East. Islamic script, art forms, and patterns of government became dominant in Turkestan and southern Russia from the late Mongol period until the late nineteenth century.

Other Religions. Although Buddhism and Islam were the major world religions in the steppe, Judaism, Manichaeism, and Nestorian Christianity all played important roles in the region. The impact of Judaism among the Khazars has already been discussed (chapter 8). Small minority Jewish communities also existed in various Central Eurasian cities.

Manichaeism is a branch of Iranian Zoroastrianism which developed in the third century A.D. (see chapter 7). Persecutions in Iran drove the Manichaeans to seek refuge in the Central Eurasian caravan towns where they soon became an important scholarly minority. Many Manichaean texts have been discovered in the Soghdian script (a Central Eurasian dialect of Persian). The Uighurs, who were the dominant nomadic power on the steppe from 745 to 840, made Manichaeism their state religion in 763. Manichaean minorities continued in Central Eurasia until the sixteenth century. Their apocalyptic ideas influenced the Chinese White Lotus society's participation in the rebellion which overthrew the Mongols and established the Ming dynasty in China.

Nestorian Christianity originated in the early fifth century as an interpretation of doctrinal controversies over the nature of Christ. Persecuted by the Orthodox Church, Nestorians sought and found refuge in the Sasanid empire. They continued as an important protected minority in Mesopotamia and Iran following the Islamic conquest in the seventh century. The Nestorians were avid missionaries. They had carried their religion into Central Eurasia by the time of the Hephthalites (sixth century). From there it spread among the Turks as a minority religion; Nestorian missionaries even reached China in 635. Nestorianism's greatest success came in the Mongol period, when several entire Mongol and Turkish clans converted. There was even optimistic talk of the possibility of converting the Ilkhanid Mongol rulers of Iran to Nestorian Christianity, but they ultimately joined the majority Islamic religion. In the long run, Nestorianism too declined, being largely replaced by Islam.

Impact on World History

The peoples of Central Eurasia contributed to three major developments in global history: trade, transmission of ideas, and warfare.

TRADE AND THE SILK ROAD

The creation of a unified and ordered steppe empire under the Xiongnu contributed to conditions in which transcontinental international trade could flourish. The Xiongnu quickly recognized the wealth that could be obtained by controlling overland trade to the West in silk and other goods. Thus by about 100 B.C., an organized and basically permanent trade network had been established, connecting China with Iran and eastern Mediterranean states. This trading system became known as the Silk Road. Barring brief times of closure during periods of political anarchy in Central Eurasia, the Silk Road remained the most significant international land trade route in the world until the discovery of the sea route from Europe to India and China in 1498.

TRANSMISSION OF IDEAS

In addition to carrying economic goods, the Silk Road became an important conduit for the transfer of ideas and technologies between East and West.

Religions. Buddhism flourished in Central Eurasia during this period. Mixed with Eurasian shamanism, it remained the international religion of Central Eurasia until the coming of Islam in the eighth century. With the opening of the Silk Road, Central Eurasian missionaries began introducing Buddhism into China. During the period of Central Eurasian dynasties in north China, Buddhism received imperial patronage and established permanent roots. The transfer of Buddhism from India to China via Central Eurasia was to have profound effects on the spiritual life and culture of all east Asia. Beginning in the eighth century, Islam likewise spread eastward into Asia from Iran over the Silk Road.

Technologies. Many important technologies were also transmitted from east Asia to the Near East and Europe via the Silk Road. The most important were paper, gunpowder weapons, and printing (see chapter 14).

WARFARE

The two most important inventions of Central Eurasia were the war chariot and cavalry. Both of these military innovations revolutionized warfare throughout the Old World, establishing basic military patterns until the rise of gunpowder weapons.

Indo-European Migrations. The Indo-European migrations of the second millennium B.C. drastically transformed the political, ethnic, linguistic, and cultural boundaries of the Old World. Sedentarized Indo-Europeans ultimately gave rise to the great civilizations of Iran, Greece, Rome, and India.

The Huns and the Fall of the Classical Empires. Between approximately 200 and 550, three of the four great empires of the Old World collapsed. Only the Sasanid Iranians survived, largely because their military system was based on professional armored mounted horse archers, allowing them to compete effectively in battle against the nomads. Eurasian nomads were intimately involved in this process of imperial collapse. Thus the role of the Huns in Iran and India was quite similar to that in China and Europe. Their arrival initiated mass migration of tribal peoples fleeing their domination and disrupting the sedentary states. Their presence contributed to a state of endemic warfare on the steppe frontiers. Their raids brought devastation and economic decline, contributing to a weakening of the sedentary states, and the eventual collapse of Rome, Han China, and Gupta India. Thus the Huns proved to be a major contributing factor in the collapse of the Classical empires and the rise of new political systems in the Middle Ages.

Turkish and Mongol Conquests. Turkic and Mongol peoples applied continual pressure on the sedentary states surrounding the steppe belt. Turkic invasions of the Near East transformed the military balance of power in the Islamic world, and ultimately significantly contributed to the fall of the Byzantine empire and the Islamic conquest of India. The age of the Mongols was one of unprecedented conquests and destruction, which entailed significant political and military transformations of nearly every kingdom in the entire Old World.

The Decline of Central Eurasia, 1500–1650

In 1500 there were still powerful Central Eurasian tribal confederations posing serious threats to sedentary peoples. By 1650, for the first time in history, the Central Eurasians had been largely conquered by the sedentarists. More remarkably, the nomadic homeland of the Eurasian steppes had been overrun and was increasingly put to the plow. Thereafter Central

Eurasians ceased to play a significant military or political role in world history. This remarkable shift of power was due primarily to two nearly simultaneous developments: the invention of gunpowder weapons and shifts in world trade routes.

Gunpowder. The traditional weapon of the steppe nomads had always been the bow. They possessed the metallurgical technology necessary to provide sufficient bows, arrows, and other premodern weapons for their needs. The production of gunpowder weapons, however, required a level of technology that the Central Eurasians did not possess. Furthermore, their nomadic lifestyle made it very difficult for them to develop their own firearms industries. For the first time in history, therefore, they became fundamentally dependent on sedentary powers for their weapons. Continual improvements in the technology of firearms steadily tipped the balance of military power away from the mounted nomadic archers to the musket-armed infantry of the sedentary states. Ultimately, the nomadic hordes were shattered by the volley fire of muskets and artillery of the Chinese and Russians.

Trade Routes. The second crucial factor in the decline of Central Eurasia in the sixteenth century was the major shift in world trade routes and economy brought about by the discovery of sea routes from Europe to India and east Asia. Before the European voyages of exploration, much of the China-to-Europe trade passed over the Silk Road, enriching the nomadic middlemen. As an increasing percentage of world trade shifted to European maritime merchants, the economic value of the Silk Road declined, creating a depression in Central Eurasia, thereby further decreasing the economic and military power of the nomads.

The Expansion of Russia and China. The creation of the Russian empire during this period was possible due to this shifting military and economic balance of power from the nomads to the sedentarists. Until 1480 Moscow had been the capital of only a small duchy which was under the sovereignty of the Mongol Golden Horde. By 1590, with the benefit of firearms, the Russians crushed and conquered the disintegrating Golden Horde, absorbing the entire western Eurasian steppe into their empire. By 1650 the Russians had conquered most of northern Asia and were establishing colonies on the Pacific Ocean. Somewhat later, the Qing Chinese emperors were also expanding into Central Eurasia. By the mid-eighteenth century the Chinese had incorporated the nomadic territories of Tibet, the Tarim basin, parts of Turkestan, and even the Mongol homeland into their empire.

Some Central Eurasian khanates continued after the decline of their power in the sixteenth century, such as the Kalmuck empire. Nonetheless, Central Eurasians would never again challenge sedentarists for control of the world, as their ancestors had only a few hundred years earlier.

Central Eurasian history can be broadly divided into three major periods: the age of the Indo-Europeans (2000 B.C.–A.D. 800), the age of the Huns (300 B.C.–A.D. 552), and the age of the Turks and Mongols (552–1600).

In each of these periods the invasions and conquests by Central Eurasian nomads of sedentary lands played a fundamental role in shifting the balance of power as well as the rise and fall of great empires. The chariot and cavalry were two great military innovations which were perfected by Central Eurasian nomads, transforming military strategy and tactics throughout the Old World.

The Indo-European migrations and conquests had important effects on world history. Indo-European languages, cultures, and peoples spread throughout much of the Old World. These early chariot nomads eventually became sedentarized and civilized, laying the foundations for some of the most important cultures of the Old World. Indian, Iranian, Greek, Roman, Germanic, and Slavic civilizations were all created by the descendants of Indo-European tribesmen. Furthermore, since the sixteenth century, Indo-European languages have come to predominate throughout the New World and have become the most important international languages today.

The fall of the Han, Tang, and Song Chinese dynasties were all influenced by military intervention by steppe nomads. Likewise, the collapse of Rome was indirectly affected by the coming of the Huns. The Byzantine empire collapsed in the twelfth century under the impact of Turkish nomads. The great medieval Hindu kingdoms were conquered by Turkish Muslim warriors. Thus a great deal of the political and military transformation of the premodern Old World was caused directly or indirectly by military attacks of the Central Eurasian nomads.

Central Eurasians also played an important role in cultural exchange in the Old World. The Silk Road was the major economic highway of premodern times, over which Buddhism spread from India to China, and by which technologies such as paper, gunpowder, and printing reached the Near East, India, and Europe.

Selected Readings

Barfield, Thomas J. *The Perilous Frontier: Nomadic Empires and China, 221 B.C. to A.D. 1757* (1989)

Grousset, Rene. *The Empire of the Steppes: A History of Central Asia* (1970)

Halperin, Charles J. *Russia and the Golden Horde* (1987)

Heissig, Walther. *The Religions of Mongolia* (London, 1980)

Jagchid, Sechin, and Paul Hyer. *Mongolia's Culture and Society* (1979)

Kwanten, Luc. *Imperial Nomads: A History of Central Asia, 500–1500* (1979)

Maenchen-Helfen, Otto J. *The World of the Huns* (1973)

Mallory, J. P. *In Search of the Indo-Europeans: Language, Archaeology and Myth* (1989)

Morgan, David. *The Mongols* (1986)

Phillips, E. D. *The Royal Hordes: Nomad Peoples of the Steppes* (1965)
Rice, Tamara Talbot. *Ancient Arts of Central Asia* (1965)
Saunders, J. J. *The History of the Mongol Conquests* (1971)
Sinor, Denis, ed. *The Cambridge History of Inner Asia* (1990)
Spuler, Bertold. *History of the Mongols* (1968)

16

Renaissance and Reformation

1276–1337	Giotto begins transformation of painting in Italy
1304–1374	Petrarch, father of the Italian Renaissance
1347–1348	The Black Death (bubonic plague) in Europe
1353	Publication of Boccaccio's *Decameron*
1397	Manual Chrysoloras introduces the study of Greek to Italy
1434–1494	Medici dominance in Florence
1450–1535	Sforza dynasty rules Milan
1452–1519	Leonardo da Vinci: the "Last Supper" and "Mona Lisa"
1456	Guttenberg first uses moveable-type printing
1475–1564	Michelangelo: "La Pietà," "David," and the Sistine Chapel
1494	French invasion of Italy
1509	Erasmus's *In Praise of Folly* published
1517	Luther's ninety-five theses
1521	Diet of Worms
1524–1525	Peasants' Revolt in Germany
1527	Rome is sacked by Emperor Charles V
1533	Marriage of Henry VIII and Anne Boleyn
1540	Society of Jesus (Jesuits) founded

1541 Theocracy established in Geneva under Calvin

1545–1563 Council of Trent, the Catholic Reformation

1553–1558 Restoration of Catholicism in England under Mary

1555 Peace of Augsburg

1588 Spanish Armada

1618 Beginning of the Thirty Years' War

1648 Peace of Westphalia ends the Thirty Years' War

The fifteenth and sixteenth centuries in Europe were periods of incredible transformation in all aspects of society. The source of this cultural Renaissance, or rebirth, was northern Italy, where humanist scholars and artists created a golden age of literature and the arts. Classical Latin and Greek texts were rediscovered and widely used as models for writers and thinkers in the humanities and philosophy. Art and architecture reached what many feel is the greatest age in world history. The new invention of printing spread literacy and knowledge throughout Europe, while geographical and astronomical discoveries brought new views of mankind's place in the universe.

The Christian religion did not escape this transformation, both by the humanist scholars of the Renaissance, and by the Protestant Reformers. By the end of the fifteenth century, the "new monarchies" of England, France, and Spain had developed national governments with strong, centralized authority that had effectively challenged the political power of both the nobility and the church. At the same time, the so-called "Holy Roman Empire" was a diverse collection of hundreds of fiefs, ecclesiastical city-states, free cities, counties, and duchies that encompassed most of central Europe and northern Italy. Charles V (emperor from 1519 to 1556) felt it his obligation to preserve the power of the Church in his domain, but his dream of a strong, unified empire was little more than a grand illusion. Trade was expanding in Europe, wealth was growing, and the population was increasing. But there were also signs of tension, none of which had more possibility for disrupting society than the smoldering discontent with the Church. The Protestant Reformation became the most shattering and far-reaching upheaval in centuries. It brought an end to a thousand years of Christian unity in the West, gave rise to new political and economic theories, and laid the foundation for ideological conflict and religious-political wars that continue to affect parts of the world even now. The Reformation brought about so much religious and political upheaval, in fact, that it is not inappropriate to call it the Protestant Revolution.

THE EUROPEAN RENAISSANCE

The Crisis in Late Medieval Europe

Social and Political Crisis. Medieval Europe was plunged into a period of severe crisis in the fourteenth century. The Black Death, or bubonic plague (1347–1348) killed as much as one third of the population. Many regions of Europe also faced a serious economic depression. Politically, France and England were embroiled in a century of continuous feuding known as the Hundred Years War (1337–1453). Other regions of Europe also faced numerous long-term wars. The Ottoman Turks were overwhelming the Balkans as Constantinople fell (1453) and European crusading armies were seriously defeated. The authority of the Holy Roman Empire declined, dividing Germany into numerous small feuding principalities.

Religious Crisis. Religiously, the fourteenth century was an age of heresy and schism. The authority of the papacy was undermined both by the scandalous behavior of some of the clerics and popes, and by a schism in which several popes were simultaneously elected. One of the great monastic orders of Europe, the Templars, was falsely accused of heresy, satanism, and various forms of perversion, and disbanded (1312). Although these accusations were false, they nonetheless contributed to the undermining of trust in the religious establishment. The religious crisis culminated when the popes became virtual prisoners of the French monarchy at Avignon (1305–1378), a period known as the "Babylonian Captivity." Thereafter, during the Great Schism (1378–1417), two rival lines of competing popes were elected, further undermining the authority of the papacy and Church. It seemed as if the Church might be rent asunder, dividing into various denominations along political and ethnic lines. Indeed, this is exactly what eventually did happen during the Protestant Reformation of the sixteenth century.

Signs of Renewal. Rather than destroying European civilization, these crises challenged Europeans to develop new social, economic, cultural, religious, and political forms of organization to meet and overcome their problems. Even as most of Europe was still in a situation of social and political chaos, Italy was entering what was to be its most glorious age.

The Italian Renaissance

SOCIAL ORIGINS

Political Independence. For much of Italy, the thirteenth and fourteenth centuries were times of trouble, as Italian city-states and the popes struggled for independence against the Holy Roman emperors of Germany. By the middle of the fourteenth century, however, the German emperors had essentially relinquished their claims to dominion in Italy, leaving the region politically fragmented into numerous competing city-states lacking a strong central government. By the 1380s four city-states had come to dominate northern Italy: Milan, Venice, Florence, Papal Rome. In addition to these major powers, there were a host of smaller, but often significant city-states as well. After a century of decay, the prestige and independence of the papacy was finally restored at the Council of Constance (1414–1417). For the next century under the "Renaissance Popes" Rome became one of the leading city-states in Italy, and a significant participant in the Renaissance.

Social and Economic Foundations of the Renaissance. Unlike many other regions of medieval Europe, Italy had never lost its urban and mercantile foundations. With the withdrawal of German ambitions from Italy, the city-states flourished as never before. Italy's central geographical location made it the natural avenue for trade from the eastern Mediterranean. The great maritime cities such as Venice grew wealthy from their control of the luxury trade to the Orient. An example of the international scope of this trade was Marco Polo's famous trading journey throughout the Orient (1271–1295). Other cities, such as Florence, grew prosperous through manufacturing and banking.

Italian governments were dominated not by a landed military aristocracy, but by alliances of great mercantile families, who directed government policies to maximize their manufacturing and trading profits. Although frequently dominated by dictators such as the Sforzas of Milan (1450–1535) or the Medici of Florence (1434–1494), these rulers recognized the importance of a strong economic policy and became some of Italy's greatest patrons of arts and letters. Thus in the fifteenth century, Italy underwent a period of tremendous economic growth and prosperity. This wealth laid the foundation for the cultural golden age of the Italian Renaissance.

HUMANISM

Learning for the Wealthy Laity. The new literary and philosophical ideas which were characteristic of the Renaissance are called humanism. Education and scholarship in medieval Europe had been dominated by the clergy, whose concerns centered on theology. The rise of the merchant class in the fourteenth century in Italy created a new set of circumstances which led to the transformation of education and scholarship in Italy. Merchants sought educations for their children both as a requirement for the complexities of government, law, and accounting and to provide entertainment and cultural sophistication. Thus a new curriculum developed designed to meet the educational needs of the new upper class. Whereas the clerical and monastic education had centered on the *studia theologica* (theological studies), the new education centered on the *studia humanistica*, the humanistic studies or the humanities.

Humanistic Curriculum. Humanistic studies were based on the seven liberal arts as designated by the ancient Roman philosopher Cicero. These included grammar, rhetoric, poetry, moral philosophy, history, music, and mathematics. The goal of these studies was to create an educated gentleman, who could fulfill his responsibilities in government, law, and trade, but who could also lead a cultured and sophisticated life at the great courts and palaces of Italy. The humanist was thus a person who had been educated in the humanities, as opposed to a theologian, who had been educated in traditional religious studies. It should be noted that there was nothing necessarily antireligious in a humanistic education. Indeed, many of the great Renaissance humanists are often called Christian humanists, due to their efforts to integrate traditional religious studies with the new humanistic curriculum.

The Revival of Classical Studies. The basic texts for the new humanistic studies came from ancient Roman models. Classical scholarship flourished as humanists searched for, edited, printed, and analyzed the great works of the Greek and Roman world. A wide range of Classical Latin sources were "discovered" in monasteries, where they had been preserved for centuries by the monastic scholarly tradition. The written and spoken Latin of the fifteenth century was "purified" as efforts were made to make current usage conform to the patterns of Classical Roman Latin; the language of Cicero was seen as the supreme manifestation of Latin prose.

The Rediscovery of Greece. While most of the Latin texts used in the Renaissance had been known for centuries, humanists made them a fundamental part of the curriculum and the subject of intense study. In 1397, however, a refugee Byzantine scholar, Manuel Chrysoloras, began teaching in Italy, bringing with him a large library of Classical Greek texts, many of which had been completely forgotten in the West. The intellectual results of the introduction of these new texts was revolutionary. Greek language became widely studied, numerous Greek texts, such as Plato, were translated into Latin, and lost Greek ideas began to have an impact on Renaissance ways of thinking. The search for the fonts of wisdom, art, and literature in ancient Greece and Rome also gave Italian humanists a new sense of history — of the wide differences between their world and the world of the Romans they sought unsuccessfully to emulate.

Humanists and the Bible. This spirit of returning to the Greek and Latin sources of literature, philosophy, and art, infected religious scholarship as well. Scholars began searching both for improved texts of the Bible and early Church Fathers, and to attempt to determine their original meaning after centuries of medieval scholastic commentary. The impact of the revival of Greek studies on religious thought is clearly seen in the great Christian humanist Erasmus, who published the first printed edition of the Greek New Testament in 1516. Other Christian scholars began to study Hebrew with Jewish rabbis in order to reach back to the original language of the Old Testament. These new interpretations of ancient biblical and Christian sources would have a tremendous impact on the development of the Reformation (see below). Thus the Reformation was due in part to the application of new humanistic methods of textual criticism and interpretation to the Bible.

THE HUMANISTIC WORLDVIEW

Views of Mankind. The Renaissance humanistic worldview was essentially that of the educated Italian upper classes. Humans were seen as fundamentally free to choose their own destiny; they could control their lives through exercising will and reason. Christian moral concepts were mixed with those of Classical moral philosophy. For many the "good life" was seen as a search for wealth and physical and aesthetic pleasures. The greatest manifestations of human achievement came in the arts and literature. "Virtue" (in its original sense of manliness), as manifest in discipline, courage, individualism, and genius, was the most important characteristic a man could have. While the Renaissance forms of individualism created many masterpieces of art and literature, it also bred an arrogant egocentrism as manifested in the *Autobiography* of Benvenuto Cellini. The negative side of the philosophy of the Renaissance can be seen in the self-centered hedonism and self-serving political and economic policies which plagued Italian cities.

Political Thought. During the Renaissance, Italy was divided into numerous small city-states, each of which was split by internal factions. While recognizing that this situation created a fundamental political weakness which threatened the independence of Italy as a whole, no one could agree on a solution to the problem. The most important political thinker to grapple with these problems was Niccolo Machiavelli (1469–1527). A typical man of the Renaissance, Machiavelli viewed the Roman republic as the perfect model for political organization. Believing that conventional Christian morality was irrelevant to political behavior, Machiavelli became the quintessential advocate of the philosophy that "the ends justify the means." Indeed, his name has become an adjective to describe the unscrupulous pursuit of power politics. The goal of Machiavellian politics was to achieve power, and all necessary means were justifiable in its pursuit. The ultimate purpose of political power, however, was not the aggrandizement of a single individual, but the restoration of unity to Italy.

Occult Studies. Although the humanists' thought and behavior was in many ways secular, their worldview included elements of both traditional Christianity and the occult. Occult philosophy flourished during the Renaissance, as humanist scholars attempted to merge Christianity, new scientific discoveries, and pagan magic and philosophy into a single unified worldview. Astrology, alchemy, magic, and cabalism (Jewish magical mysticism) were all widely studied in the Renaissance. These subjects were not considered satanic, but rather were the "hidden wisdom" (the original meaning of occult) of ancient days which could unlock the secrets of the universe.

Indeed these subjects were not seen by their practitioners as antithetical either to reason, or to Christianity, but were the ultimate fulfillment of both.

RENAISSANCE ARTS

The economic and political rivalry among the Italian city-states stimulated the arts in a manner which would have been impossible in a single united kingdom: instead of one king and royal court patronizing the arts in Italy, there were dozens. Renaissance cultural competition through patronage of the great artists, architects, poets, and scholars of the age was in many ways similar to sports competition in the modern United States. Just as the civic or college pride of many Americans is intricately bound to their urban sports teams, Italian citizens took pride in the cultural adornment of their cities through the presence and patronage of the great artistic and scholarly geniuses of their age. The results of this cultural competition can be seen in the magnificent works of art and architecture which adorn every city in Italy.

Literature. Literature of the Italian Renaissance was written in many genres, including poetry, short stories, drama, epistles, essays, and histories. Most of these forms were derived from classical models and were frequently written in Latin, although Italian became an increasingly important literary language. The greatest Renaissance poet was Petrarch (1304–1374), who is sometimes called the "Father of the Renaissance," and was noted for his splendid sonnets and odes. Ariosto's (1474–1533) massive poem *Orlando Furioso* is a remarkable blend of fantasy, love story, and chivalrous adventure. The master of the Renaissance short stories was Boccaccio (1313–1375), whose *Decameron* contains a hundred tales told by people during the Black Death. Drama was widely written and produced for Renaissance courts, including works of light comedy by the political theoretician Machiavelli.

The Essay. The essay was the most important literary form of the Renaissance, represented by moderate-sized rational and erudite discussions of important topics. The subjects of Renaissance essays were limitless, ranging from science to magic, or from love to war. A remarkable example of the Renaissance essay was *The Courtier*, by Castiglione (1478–1529), which describes the ideal education, behavior, and lifestyle of the Renaissance courtier. Pico della Mirandola (1463–1494) wrote the famous *Essay on the Dignity of Man*, describing the Renaissance ideal of the unlimited potential of the human mind and will.

Art. Although other genres were represented, the most important forms of Renaissance art were painting and sculpture. Religious themes and imagery were predominant in both art forms, although secular subjects such as portraits became increasingly popular. In painting, Renaissance artists developed a wide range of new styles and techniques, including individualism, naturalism, and the use of perspective. Among the greatest

Renaissance painters were Leonardo da Vinci (1452–1519), Michelangelo (1475–1564), Raphael (1483–1520), and Titian (1477–1576). Michelangelo is also considered the greatest Renaissance sculptor. His "Pietà," depicting Mary holding the dead Jesus in her arms, is widely considered the finest sculpture in the world.

Architecture. Numerous beautiful examples of Renaissance architectural styles grace the great cities of northern Italy. As in the medieval period, cathedrals were the major architectural form in the Renaissance, followed in importance by the palaces of the great political and merchant families. Brunelleschi's (1379–1446) cathedral in Florence formed the prototype for Italian Renaissance cathedral architecture. The masterpiece of Renaissance architecture, however, is the splendid St. Peter's cathedral in Rome, designed by Bramante (1444–1514) and Michelangelo. The largest cathedral in the world, the magnificence of St. Peter's perfectly evokes the arrogant piety of the Renaissance popes.

The Northern Renaissance

CHANGING CONDITIONS IN EUROPE

The spread of the Renaissance to northern Europe was based on changing conditions and circumstances in the sixteenth century. The centers of wealth and economic power began to shift from Italy to the north as the discovery of the Americas and new maritime routes to the Orient undermined Italy's monopoly on the eastern trade. The rise of absolutist monarchies in Spain and France brought a shifting of the balance of military power which allowed those countries to intervene in Italy, undermining the independence and prosperity of the Italian city-state system. Between 1498 and 1516 Italy became the battleground between the great powers of France, Spain, and Germany. In 1527 Rome itself was sacked. The Reformation (see below) also caused the centers of intellectual vitality to shift northward. As Germans, French, Dutch, and English grappled with the great intellectual and religious questions of the day, intellectual inquiry in Italy and Spain was restrained by the Inquisition and official literary censorship. Although Italy had lost its cultural supremacy in Europe by the late sixteenth century, it nonetheless was the fundamental inspiration for the northern Renaissance.

CHARACTERISTICS OF THE NORTHERN RENAISSANCE

Printing. Invented in China in the eighth century A.D., the idea and technology of printing eventually made their way to Europe by the fifteenth century. The first major book printed in Europe with moveable type was the Latin Bible published by Johann Guttenburg at Mainz in 1456. In the next half century printing spread rapidly throughout Europe; there were printing presses in every major European town by the beginning of the sixteenth century.

The social and intellectual effects of printing, both on Europe and on world history as a whole, cannot be overemphasized. Books became less expensive and more numerous, allowing for both the preservation of texts from the past and the dissemination of new books and ideas. With the proliferation of inexpensive books, many more people could become literate and participate in intellectual life; the age of domination of ideas by a small group of literate priests had passed. Printing gave scholars access to a far wider range of ideas and texts than had been possible in the age of manuscripts. This, in turn, created an intellectual environment in which new ideas could be widely published and discussed, laying the foundation for the social and intellectual changes of the Reformation, Enlightenment, and the scientific revolution. The invention of printing thus created a new mechanism for the exchange of ideas; the intellectual revolution brought about by printing laid the foundation for the modern age.

Christian Humanism. Forms of Italian Renaissance humanistic ideas, scholarship, and art spread quickly throughout the rest of Europe, creating similar patterns of intellectual and cultural change. The major difference between the humanism of Italy and that of the north was the increased emphasis of the role Christianity should play in humanist education and scholarship. Christian humanists believed that a proper humanistic education combined Classical and Christian subjects and would lead to increased spirituality and piety in society. The following are among the foremost Christian humanists of the northern Renaissance: Johann Reuchlin (1455–1522) was a leader in the study of the Old Testament in Hebrew. Desiderius Erasmus (1466–1536) published the first printed Greek New Testament (1516) and applied new philological methods to the study of the Bible. Thomas More (1478–1535) published his *Utopia*—a critique of English society in the form of an allegorical journey to an ideal society—in 1516 as well.

Art. Painting, architecture, and sculpture in the rest of Europe lagged behind Italian models. There were nonetheless many notable achievements. The Dutch Van Eyck brothers, working in the early fifteenth century, adopted Italian techniques and naturalism in their oil paintings. Albrecht Durer (1471–1528) of Germany is noted for his strange renditions of mythological and allegorical themes. Although born in Crete, El Greco (1541–1614) became the leading painter in late Renaissance Spain, serving as a transitional figure to later painting styles.

Literature. Literature also flourished in the north, surpassing, in many ways, its Italian models. In France, Montaigne (1533–1592) perfected the art of the humanistic essay, while Rabelais (1495–1553) wrote biting satires of French society. Cervantes (1547–1616) wrote his masterpiece *Don Quixote*, a satire on Spanish society in the form of the adventures of a crazed would-be knight. The greatest literary figure of the northern Renaissance, however, was Shakespeare (1564–1616), whose dramatic works include perhaps the finest plays ever written.

THE PROTESTANT REVOLUTION

Pressures for Reform

Martin Luther is usually thought of as the founder of the Reformation, but by the time he posted his famous ninety-five theses on the door of the church at Wittenberg Castle there was already a climate in Europe charged with religious discontent and highly conducive to change.

THE DECLINE OF PAPAL PRESTIGE

Dissatisfaction was aimed at all levels of the Church hierarchy, beginning with the papacy, whose spiritual and political prestige had been waning for over two centuries. Most disturbing were the negative images bred by papal involvement in secular affairs. Rigid control over income-producing church lands; a military establishment; conduct of diplomacy on the same basis as any secular prince; fund raising, often through the buying and selling of ecclesiastical office; elaborate courts; fortunes dispensed on patronage of the arts: all these and more helped undermine the papacy's spiritual image. In addition, kings, princes, and people of wealth chafed at the political and economic power the pope could wield over them with the mere threat of excommunication.

OTHER REASONS FOR DISCONTENT

Indulgences. Abuses were seen at all levels. One of the most disturbing was the sale of indulgences, which involved relief from the earthly penalties of sin in return for financial contributions to the Church. The opportunity for exploitation was obvious.

Clerical Immortality. Critics were also dismayed at the fact that local parish priests were often in abject poverty, many were nearly illiterate, and the state of priestly morality was distressingly low. Clerical vows of celibacy were broken often; drunkenness, gambling, and other unacceptable behavior were not uncommon.

Personal Piety. At a different level, many people seeking a more spiritually satisfying personal piety were vexed by the pomp and ceremony of church service, as well as the emphasis upon sacraments and the role of the priest. It all seemed to make salvation less a matter of personal faith and more a matter of form, and it was not uncommon for dissatisfied individuals to seek fulfillment in other ways. Some looked for it in the Bible, and some found solace in lay religious fraternities dedicated to simple, pious living.

Printing and New Ideas. Technology and the arts also contributed significantly to the spread of discontent. The printing press had found its way into some 250 European cities by 1500, and books, including the Bible, were becoming common. In addition, a profusion of satire, criticism of the clergy, and outrage at some Church practices appeared with increasing frequency in printed matter as well as in the works of artists.

CHRISTIAN HUMANISM

The most important intellectual movement to help set the stage for religious reform was Christian humanism, whose disciples anxiously probed the literature of early Christianity in their efforts to offer people a better guide to true Christian morality and spirituality.

Erasmus, 1466–1536. The greatest of the humanists was the Dutchman Desiderius Erasmus, who told lay people that they should seek to live by "the philosophy of Christ": an inner piety that was not related to Church routine and ceremonies. His most well-known book, *In Praise of Folly*, was a satire on both the church and the wisdom of the world. But more than that, it was also an appeal to his readers to go back to the simple Christian life. Erasmus was also scandalized at the thought that anyone should be kept from reading the scriptures. He tried to encourage the study of the Bible and published a new edition of the Greek New Testament (1516). He was the most important intellectual forerunner of the Reformation but, ironically, as it progressed he was rejected by both sides: the church because he wanted to reform it, and the leaders of the Reformation because he refused to break with the Church. He wanted reform to come from within.

The German Setting for the Reformation

There was no more likely place for reformation to occur than in the German states. Politically, the power of the emperor had long been in decline. But despite their desire for political independence, most of the German princes found it impossible to resist the Church, with its rich, financially independent hierarchy and its hold on the minds of the people. City governments, too, resented the privileges and immunities enjoyed by clerics, such as the fact that priests, monks, and nuns were exempt from civic responsibilities and paid no taxes, even though religious orders held large amounts of urban property. People at all levels were resentful toward the Church for many reasons, yet too divided to do anything about it.

Martin Luther and the Rise of Protestantism

Martin Luther thus came on the scene at exactly the right time: intellectuals, rulers, churchmen, and lay people alike were ready for reform. Like the humanists, he wanted it to come from within, but the circumstances of time and place moved reform in other directions.

THE INDULGENCE CONTROVERSY

The spark that finally ignited the smoldering conflict was the indulgence controversy.

Origins. Indulgences were initially granted during the late eleventh century, at the time of the First Crusade, as a reward for those willing to fight to regain the Holy Land for the Church. Eventually, the Church proclaimed that it could dispense a "treasury of merit" to free believers from the earthly penalties of sin.

Abuse. By the early sixteenth century, however, the belief had developed that indulgences granted total pardon for all the penalties of sin—both in this life and after—and the sale of indulgences had become a common way of raising revenue for the Church. In 1517, Pope Leo X (1513–1521) revived an earlier indulgence proclaimed to raise funds for rebuilding St. Peter's cathedral in Rome. The archbishop of Magdeburg, who badly needed funds to repay the debt he had incurred in order to hold more than one high ecclesiastical office, then hired the Dominican friar John Tetzel to sell indulgences throughout his territory. Tetzel's sensational advertising campaign appealed especially to the ignorant, who were told that through their donations they could not only buy relief from the consequences of their own sins, but could do the same for their deceased families and friends. "As soon as coin in coffer rings, the soul from purgatory springs," was reported to be one of his more melodramatic slogans.

Martin Luther, 1483–1546. Such tactics brought phenomenal success to the campaign in Magdeburg, but they also stirred Martin Luther to action. An Augustinian monk in Wittenberg, Luther was already aching inside as a result of his long and troubled quest for personal piety and his conclusion that faith, not works, was the only means of salvation.

Martin Luther began his clerical career in 1505 after being badly frightened in a thunderstorm and making a vow to become a monk if he survived the ordeal. In 1507 he was ordained a priest. Later he obtained a doctorate in theology, and in 1512 he became a professor of Scripture at the University of Wittenberg. As a young friar he became deeply introspective, worrying constantly about salvation and living with a highly troubled personal conscience. He found little help in the sacraments and forms of the Church. Only after he gained an insight that moved him in a new theological direction did he begin to find personal peace of mind.

Ninety-Five Theses. After intensive study of the writings of Paul, Luther finally concluded that the external forms of the Church—elaborate ceremonies, formal liturgy, even penance—had nothing to do with salvation. Faith alone was the only way to receive God's grace, and this was a free gift that could not be earned. The indulgence campaign flew in the face of everything Luther believed. On October 31, 1517, he posted on the door of the church at Wittenberg castle a list of ninety-five theses, or propositions, on indulgences. He raised searching questions also about papal wealth and other related topics.

Impact. Luther's intent was to inaugurate a public theological discussion, but the impact was much greater than he anticipated. Printed copies of his theses circulated widely, evoking discussions of even broader theological issues. The most crucial of these was that of the pope's authority: Did he or did he not have the right to authorize indulgences at all? Luther said he did not, for indulgences were not sanctioned by Scripture and therefore had no effect on salvation. His opponents argued that questioning the authority of the pope undermined the Church itself. At first Leo X characterized the affair as merely a "squabble among monks," but eventually he issued a letter condemning some of Luther's propositions, ordering his books burned, and giving him two months to recant. Luther defiantly burned the letter in public and the result was excommunication.

Charles V. It seemed impossible at that point for Emperor Charles V, who felt it his duty to protect the Church, to remain aloof from the controversy, and when he held his first imperial diet (an assembly of the empire's cities and princes) at Worms in April 1521, he summoned Luther to appear. When ordered to recant, Luther again refused, saying that he was bound by the Scriptures and would be convinced by no other authority. The already excommunicated monk soon found himself also condemned and outlawed by the emperor. He went into hiding at the Wartburg castle, under the protection of Frederick the Wise, elector of Saxony. He had little to fear, however, for even the princes who would remain Catholic were antagonistic enough toward imperial power that they would not deliver to the emperor someone who promised to continue to erode it.

LUTHER'S IDEOLOGY AND ITS APPEAL

Salvation by Faith. Luther's most fundamental doctrine was that people were justified in the eyes of God by faith alone—not by good works or the sacraments of the Church. Because of the depravity innate to humans, they were totally incapable of winning salvation through their own efforts. This hardly meant that a Christian could continue to sin, for faith in Christ compelled one to do good works, but in the end it was only faith that would be accepted by God and result in personal salvation.

The Authority of Scripture. A second issue was religious authority, and in Luther's theology this authority rested solely with the Bible. All other forms of authority or channels of communication, including the pronouncements of the pope or of Church councils, must be rejected. God's chosen faithful, Luther declared, constituted a "priesthood of all believers," thus eliminating any need for priests or popes. Luther also denied the efficacy of all the sacraments but the two he saw authorized in Scripture: baptism and the Eucharist (the Lord's supper). In addition, the liturgy was simplified and services were conducted in the vernacular rather than in Latin.

Luther's Bible. The capstone to Luther's life work was his monumental translation of the Bible into German, completed in 1534. It provided families with the opportunity to read the Scriptures for themselves, and actually stimulated literacy among both men and women.

Reception of Luther's Ideas. The attraction of Lutheran teachings was obvious. Princes who had chafed at the rule of Rome welcomed a theology that subordinated the Church to the state. Laymen saw in it the possibility for eliminating clerical abuse. The masses admired Luther's defiance of Church authority, as well as his advocacy of a simpler, more personal religion, based on the spirit of early Christianity and the centrality of the Scriptures.

CONSEQUENCES IN GERMANY

Peasant Revolt. Luther did not anticipate most of the consequences of what he was doing, and he was stunned by some of those he lived to see. His teachings intensified social unrest among the peasants, for example, and in 1525 many angrily condemned their lay and ecclesiastical lords who were imposing new economic burdens. Luther sympathized with them, but he did not believe in using armed force; when they threatened outright rebellion he warned against it. Angry revolts nevertheless broke out in several states, with the peasants using slogans taken directly from Luther's writings. They were soon crushed by the nobility, but only after an estimated 75,000 people lost their lives.

Protestant Origins. As Luther urged the princes to confiscate ecclesiastical wealth and promote other Church reforms, he also strengthened nationalistic feelings in the princes' domains—feelings that fed on opposition to the emperor and to his support of the Church. Rulers throughout Germany took up the cause of Lutheranism by secularizing Church property (a means of bringing the Church and its wealth directly under their control as opposed to that of the pope), and instituting simple, uncomplicated worship services. Luther believed that true worship was an inner matter, and that the elaborate forms of the mass did nothing for personal salvation. The rulers also required that services be conducted in German rather than Latin. In 1529, however, at the Diet of Speyer, the emperor withdrew his policy of toleration. The Lutheran princes responded with their own declaration, "protesting" the emperor's decree. With this the term *Protestant* was born. Realizing that the emperor was not unwilling to resort to military force against them, in 1531 they formed a defensive alliance, known as the Schmalkaldic League, that effectively deterred him for over a decade. When war did break out even the Catholic princes refused to support the emperor. The result was the Peace of Augsburg, in 1555, which formally recognized the right of each prince to decide whether his state should be Roman Catholic or Lutheran.

Protestantism was irreversibly established in Germany, and perhaps half the population of the empire was Lutheran. But the ink was hardly dry on the ninety-five theses before unorthodox teachings began to appear in many other places as well, and in many forms.

Ulrich Zwingli and the Swiss Reformation

Switzerland was a patchwork of small, disunited states and cantons, one of which was Zurich. There, in 1518, came Ulrich Zwingli (1484–1531), a reformer who, like Luther, emphasized the primacy of scriptural authority and rejected the role of churchly forms. But he went further than Luther by rejecting all the sacraments, putting more emphasis on the role of the individual, and teaching that people are inherently good.

By 1529 Zurich and five other cantons had become Zwinglian. Two years later war broke out between them and the Catholic cantons. Zwingli's forces were defeated, and the reformer himself, serving as a chaplain, was killed in battle. Switzerland remained split, however, between Catholics and the reformers.

John Calvin and the Reformation

John Calvin (1509–1564) was second only to Martin Luther in his importance to the Reformation. French by birth, Calvin devoted himself early to the study of theology. When, in 1534, he became identified with Lutheranism, he was forced to leave France. He found his way to Geneva where a friend, William Farel (1489–1565), was attempting to establish a reformed church. Farel persuaded Calvin that it was his obligation to God to stay and help.

CALVIN IN GENEVA

Calvin's Theocracy. In 1537, the year after he was elected a preacher, Calvin's plan for church reform was accepted by the citizens of Geneva, but the following year he and Farel were exiled for making too many intrusions into political affairs. Three years later, however, the citizens invited Calvin to return; he soon instituted a powerful theocracy in Geneva patterned after his idea of the ideal Christian community. It was governed by two councils, the municipal council and a church consistory. The consistory, which had the authority to excommunicate, assumed the task of supervising the morals as well as the religious activities of the inhabitants of Geneva. Eventually the majority were converted; those who remained Catholic were excommunicated and forced to leave.

Religious Laws. The rules in Calvin's Geneva were strict, and the regimen was stern. People were regulated in the way they dressed, were required to attend religious services, and were forbidden to participate in such activities as card-playing, dancing, and even trivial singing. Fines and punishments for the smallest offenses were severe enough, but the most serious offense, open heresy, was punishable by death.

CALVIN'S IDEOLOGY

Calvin's most important work was his *Institutes of the Christian Religion.* Like Luther, he emphasized the omnipotence of God and the total depravity of man. People could do nothing about their own salvation, but

God had already predestined certain individuals, the "elect," to be saved. All the rest were predestined to be damned.

Predestination and Morality. Hopeless as it may seem at first glance, this doctrine actually enhanced faith and piety among believers. While individuals could not know that they were among the elect, they were told to stop worrying about it and act as if they were. If, then, they lived according to God's will, including performing good works and attending services regularly, they could find communion with God, feel his grace in their hearts, and have reason to believe that they were among the elect. They felt an obligation to live just lives, and even though good works saved no one, they were signs of one's election.

Capitalism. Calvinism also helped give rise to modern capitalistic thought, for it justified wealth based on private property and individual effort, on the assumption that economic success was another sign of being among the elect. Thrift, industry, and hard work were among the highest values of the Calvinistic community.

THE SPREAD OF CALVINISM

Calvin founded an academy in Geneva and its students helped spread his ideology far and wide. By the time he died in 1564 there were more than a million Calvinists in France, called Huguenots. In Scotland, meanwhile, John Knox (1505–1572) founded the Presbyterian Church on Calvinist principles, and persuaded the parliament to make it the state religion. In the Netherlands most of the population of the northern provinces joined the Calvinistic Dutch Reformed Church.

The English Reformation

In England, meanwhile, nascent Protestantism flourished among the Lollards, despite the king's attempt to suppress them. The English humanist William Tyndale (1494–1556), in Antwerp, began printing an English translation of the New Testament and sending copies to England with merchants. The Lollards eagerly distributed them, along with some of Luther's ideas. In general, however, the Protestant movement made little headway until the king himself decided it was time to throw off his remaining ties with Rome.

NATIONALIZING THE ENGLISH CHURCH

Henry VIII, 1509–1547. The spark that ignited the English reformation, however, had little to do with church reform and everything to do with the politics of the monarchy. King Henry VIII was married to Catharine of Aragon, who had given him six children but no surviving male heir. He had fallen in love, meanwhile, with Ann Boleyn and wanted to divorce Catharine. He sent a petition to Pope Clement VII asking for an annulment, but Clement delayed, hoping that Henry's own fickleness would make the problem go away. One complicating problem for the pope was the fact that

Charles V, who held considerable political influence over him at the time, was Catharine's nephew. Charles was not about to let the pope hurt Catharine in any way. Henry was not to be denied, however; his personally appointed archbishop, Thomas Cranmer, granted the annulment and, in 1533, performed the marriage between the king and Anne Boleyn.

Formation of the Church of England. Henry soon decided to take the English church away from the jurisdiction of Rome. In 1534 Parliament's Act of Supremacy declared him to be the head of the Church of England. Certain prominent dissenters who refused to recognize this act—including the humanist Thomas More who resigned his lord chancellorship in protest—were beheaded for their opposition. Despite the apparent decisiveness of the break, however, under Henry the doctrines and practices of the church saw only minor change, though he dissolved the monasteries and confiscated their lands.

EDWARDIAN REFORM

Edward VI (1547–1553) was the son of Jane Seymour, whom Henry had married after having Anne Boleyn beheaded because she did not produce a male child. During his reign several significant reforms were promoted. Clergymen were allowed to marry, the liturgy was simplified, and Archbishop Thomas Cranmer produced the *Book of Common Prayer*, to be used in all services in the Church of England. He also revised some doctrines and ceremonies to bring them more in line with reformed churches on the continent, but when young Edward died the reforms stopped.

THE CATHOLIC RESTORATION

The new monarch was Mary Tudor (1553–1558), Henry's daughter by his first wife. Determined to restore Catholicism, she earned herself the nickname "Bloody Mary" by having almost three hundred Protestants burned at the stake. Her brief reign temporarily wiped out all Protestant reforms, but in another way it built support for Protestantism as it created hatred for Catholicism in the hearts of many English citizens.

ELIZABETH I AND THE ANGLICAN SETTLEMENT

When Mary died the throne went to Elizabeth I (1558–1603), the daughter of Anne Boleyn. Ruling as a Protestant, Elizabeth nevertheless resisted pressures from some to conduct a ruthless anti-Catholic witch hunt. But everyone had to attend the Church of England; the *Book of Common Prayer* again became the basis for a uniform liturgy. The Thirty-Nine Articles, approved in 1563, outlined the fundamental tenets of the Anglican Church (i.e., the Church of England), but they were vague enough to satisfy a wide variety of people. This settlement was not universally accepted, however. In Ireland the Catholics bitterly resisted any effort to impose

Anglicanism upon them. In addition, people known as Puritans because they wanted to purify the church by eliminating more of its forms and modifying more of its doctrines, began to challenge the Anglican establishment.

Radical Protestantism: the Anabaptists

There were some similarities among all the reformers discussed so far, particularly their insistence that the church and state were linked, and their retention of some doctrines and practices, such as infant baptism. There were more radical reformers, however, who believed that in order to make the church more like early Christianity individuals must not be baptized until they were adults—old enough to be converted. Their enemies called them Anabaptists, "re-baptizers," for even though they had been baptized as infants they insisted on having this ordinance performed again.

Anabaptists rejected all forms of church authority but joined together in voluntary associations of adult believers. Some formed utopian communities where they abolished private property and shared everything in common. They also believed in the complete separation of church and state and in the ideal of religious liberty. These things, however, alarmed other Protestants as well as Catholics, all of whom insisted that church and state went hand-in-hand and that there was no room for religious dissent. As a result, Anabaptists were brutally persecuted from all sides. Tens of thousands were executed in northwestern and central Europe, while others fled to such places as Bohemia and Poland. They survived as Brethren, Hutterites, and Mennonites, and later some filtered back into Germany and, eventually, to North America.

THE CATHOLIC REFORMATION

The Roman Catholic Church was far from oblivious to the need for reform. Efforts to eliminate corruption and bring about change were taking place long before the Protestant Reformation erupted. The results were limited but, beginning with Pope Paul III (1534–1549), more effective and far-reaching reforms took place. Some were designed to eliminate abuses, others to clarify church doctrines and practices, and still others were intended to root out heresy and, if possible, reclaim the Protestants. The latter effort is sometimes called the Counter-Reformation.

Inadequate Early Efforts at Reform

Though there were some commendable efforts at reform early in the fifteenth century, they depended largely on the whims of individual popes. Julius II (1503–1513) made a few moderate changes but his successor, Leo X, seemed too concerned with the secular splendor of the papacy to pay much attention to reform. Hadrian VI (1522–1523) practically eliminated the luxurious papal court, cut back on the bureaucracy, halted the buying and selling of offices, and curtailed the lavish patronizing of the arts, but Clement VII (1523–1534) had no predilection to continue the effort. Clement VII also became absorbed in political conflict between France and the Holy Roman Empire that resulted, in May 1527, in the emperor's troops thoroughly sacking the city of Rome.

Paul III and the New Reformism

It remained for Paul III (1534–1549) to lay the foundation for permanent internal reform. Determined to reassert papal authority throughout the church and to carry out whatever reforms were needed, in 1537 he appointed a committee to advise him. Its report was a frank, realistic assessment of abuses, and Paul immediately put into effect many of its proposals aimed at the hierarchy. He also decided to call a general church council for the purpose of reexamining church theology and, it was hoped, resolving some of the uncertainties that still plagued it. There was heavy resistance in Rome to such a move, however, and he was unable to convene the council for another ten years (1545). It took nearly twenty years to conclude its deliberations (see below).

THE INQUISITION

Origins. Paul was also determined to root out heresy. Based on medieval models, in 1542 he founded the Sacred Congregation of the Holy Office, with jurisdiction over the Roman Inquisition. Composed of a committee of six cardinals, the Inquisition could impose both religious and secular penalties, and could even order executions.

Abuses. Under Paul III its activities were kept under control but in later years its excesses became notorious. It accepted hearsay as evidence of heresy and other wrong-doing, felt no obligation to inform the accused of charges against them, applied torture, and often destroyed heretics themselves along with their heresies. The mere threat of being called before the Inquisition was a fearsome experience, and the atmosphere of suspicion, spying, and accusation it created seemed to some like a reign of terror. The Inquisition was most effective in the Papal States.

PAUL'S REFORMING LEGACY

Paul's achievements as a reformer set the stage for even more sweeping reforms to come. Realizing, however, that the permanency of reform depended upon his successors, he appointed to the College of Cardinals (which elected popes) men well known for their piety and learning and who were also dedicated to reform. The result was a succession of popes who, by the early seventeenth century, had restored to the papacy and the Church an image of spirituality and morality.

The Emergence of New Religious Orders

Internal reform was strengthened also by the rise of several new religious orders, such as the Capucines, founded in 1528. This group became well known as missionaries and preachers, and their poverty, austerity, and simple preaching even convinced some Protestants to return to the Catholic fold. The Ursuline order of nuns, founded in 1535 and approved in 1544, focused on training young girls for their future roles as wives and mothers. The impact of none of these orders, however, could compare with that of the Society of Jesus, founded by the best-known figure of the Catholic Reformation, Ignatius Loyola (1491–1556).

THE SOCIETY OF JESUS (JESUITS)

Ignatius Loyola, 1491–1556. A Spanish soldier, Loyola received a serious wound in battle and, while recuperating, spent considerable time studying the life of Jesus and other religious works. He went through a period of deep personal soul-searching, and by the time he emerged from the hospital he had decided to devote the rest of his life to becoming a true soldier of Christ. Dressed in the plainest of clothing (some youngsters dubbed him "Father Sack"), he adopted a life of service and total austerity, wandering from place to place, and even traveling barefoot to Jerusalem and back. Eventually he decided to continue his studies in Paris, after which he recruited a small group of followers intent on accompanying him on a return to the Holy Land. They ended up in Rome, however, offering their unconditional services to the pope. Loyola's most important publication, *Spiritual Exercises*, laid out a rigid spiritual regimen for a four-week period of retreat and study. Through it those who joined found the spiritual strength to devote themselves to a new life of strict religious piety.

Creation of Jesuits. The Society of Jesus was approved by the pope in 1540, and it quickly attracted many recruits who proudly went by the name of Jesuits. They took vows of poverty, chastity and obedience, with special emphasis on obedience to the pope. They led lives of service, indifferent to personal discomfort and safety. They also founded schools that provided the best education available for children of both the rich and the poor.

The Jesuits and the Counter-Reformation. As conscious tools of reform, the Jesuits were not above using any means necessary, including spying and persecution of heretics, to bring it about. They preferred to convert heretics rather than kill them, however. They spread rapidly throughout Europe and their Society became one of the most important instruments of the Catholic Reformation, eventually taking their message throughout much of the world as missionaries to the Americas, Africa, and Asia.

PAUL IV

For the most part, the fourteen popes who reigned between 1549 and 1621 were faithful in continuing the reforms begun by Paul III. Paul IV (1555–1559) was particularly zealous, and his nephew, Cardinal Carlo Cafra, pursued the Inquisition with a ruthlessness unprecedented in Rome. Paul also attacked abuses at all levels, imposing heavy penalties on anyone who resisted or evaded his reforms. He tightened discipline among the cardinals themselves, drastically reduced the bureaucracy, and severely punished simony (the buying and selling of church offices), despite the loss of Church revenue. In addition, the Holy Office published an *Index of Forbidden Books* (1559), which banned Catholics from reading the listed books and pamphlets on the grounds that they contained heretical ideas. Books were burned by the thousands, and people were punished for possessing indexed works. His excesses, sadly for him, shocked even his own cardinals and made him highly unpopular in Rome. Nevertheless, building on the foundation laid by Paul III, his reforms permanently changed the image of the papacy and enhanced the unity of the church.

THE DECREES OF THE COUNCIL OF TRENT

Paul III's general council finally assembled in Trent in 1545 and met intermittently until 1563. It had a stormy history, characterized by rivalry and intense disagreement among various national factions. Most of the council's time was spent on doctrinal issues, and in the end most people were amazed that it could agree on so many questions.

Doctrinal Unity. One symbol of this newfound unity was the astounding fact that by the time the final session of the Council of Trent concluded in 1563, the delegates had fully agreed on all the questions of doctrine and reform that had been submitted to them. Moreover, the predominance of the pope over councils had been reasserted, and it was he who had the responsibility for confirming and executing the council's mandates.

The council's most important decrees were those affirming the truth of all the doctrines Protestant reformers had rejected. It also reaffirmed the importance of the priest as well as the elaborate ritual connected with worship services, insisted on sweeping clerical reforms, forbade the sale of indulgences, and required every diocese to establish a seminary where the clergy could be trained.

Results of the Catholic Reformation. The first two popes to hold office after the council concluded, and particularly Pius V (1566–1572), completed most of the internal reforms and expanded the work of the Inquisition. Another pope, Sixtus V (1585–1590), completely reorganized the curia by fixing the number of cardinals at seventy and instituting fifteen permanent congregations to handle specific administrative and doctrinal matters.

Reform was a gradual, sometimes difficult, process, and it never succeeded in making reconciliation with Protestantism, but it added a new vitality to the Church. It appealed to many who were appalled at the austerity and self-denial they saw in Protestantism, as well as the doctrine of predestination; they were delighted to participate in a newly invigorated Catholicism.

LEGACY OF VIOLENCE: WARS OF RELIGION

Background: Complexities of European Politics

Among Charles V's imperial problems was a series of wars with the Valois kings of France over certain Habsburg lands in Italy. These wars helped advance the cause of Protestantism when Charles, in an attempt to gain support of Lutheran princes in Germany, signed the Peace of Augsburg in 1555. All his efforts had failed: the Protestant states were officially recognized, leaving his title of emperor with little effective power.

In 1556 Charles abdicated, dividing his territories between his brother Ferdinand and his son Philip. Ferdinand received Austria and the empire, while Philip inherited Spain, the Low Countries (present-day Holland and Belgium), Milan, Sicily, and Spain's American possessions. As Philip II of Spain (1556–1598), the new king continued the war with France and won in 1559. In England, meanwhile, Queen Elizabeth felt constantly threatened by the presence of Mary, Queen of Scots, a Catholic and rival heir to the throne who was a favorite of many of Elizabeth's opponents. These political intricacies, with religion as one of their most volatile elements, provided part of the complex and often confusing background for the tragic wars of religion that plagued Europe in the Reformation era.

Religious Conflict in France

By 1559 perhaps ten percent of the population of France were Huguenots, but the weak French monarchy could do little to check their growth. Even French nobles became Protestants, which led to inevitable clashes with Catholic lords. Peasants, too, fought and killed each other. Protestants frequently attacked Catholic cathedrals, destroying statuary, stained-glass windows, and other sacred items that, to them, were symbols of idol worship. On August 24, 1572, 3,000 Huguenots were killed in the infamous St. Bartholomew's Day massacre. Within three days thousands more (variously estimated as from 12,000 to 20,000) were killed in well-orchestrated strikes throughout the country.

The Catholic-Protestant struggle soon became intertwined with a three-sided rivalry for the throne that ended, in 1589, with the assassination of Henry of Guise and King Henry III. A Protestant, Henry of Navarre, ascended the throne and reigned as Henry IV (1589–1610). Henry believed that a strong monarchy was the only way to keep France from collapsing. Knowing that only by being part of the religious majority could he promote the cause of the monarchy as well as that of religious toleration, Henry compromised his religious principles and joined the Catholic Church, proclaiming "Paris is well worth a Mass." On May 13, 1598, he proclaimed the famous Edict of Nantes, guaranteeing freedom of conscience to the Huguenots. Nonetheless, many Huguenots fled France, seeking religious liberty in Holland, England, or North America.

Philip II and the Revolt of the Netherlands

ORIGINS OF THE REVOLT

In the Netherlands, meanwhile, the Calvinist population was growing, especially in the north, and gaining the support of wealthy merchants who wanted independence from Spain. The Dutch Protestants openly encouraged resistance to Catholic authority and Philip finally ordered the regent, his half-sister Margaret, to eliminate them. Her answer was the Inquisition. This, along with heavier taxes and other grievances, resulted in a rash of anti-government and anti-Catholic violence in 1566. The response was brutal, as Philip's troops ruthlessly exterminated religious and political dissidents. Civil war ensued.

APPEAL TO ELIZABETH

In 1576 the rebel provinces came together under William of Orange (1572–1584). The ten southern provinces gradually fell to Philip's troops and remained Catholic. The other seven declared their independence in 1584 as the United Provinces of the Netherlands and became Protestant. They also begged Queen Elizabeth to come to their aid. Elizabeth, however, had no desire to offend Philip, either by executing Mary, Queen of Scots, or by supporting the Dutch Protestants. But finally, convinced that if the Protestants lost Philip would invade England anyway, and increasingly fearful of Mary's plots, she did both.

SPANISH ARMADA

Philip's response was to mount a vast armada of 130 ships to escort barges carrying an army of perhaps 30,000 invasion troops across the English Channel. The fleet sailed on May 30, 1588, but it was soundly defeated by 150 British ships. The war dragged on until 1609 when Philip III (1598–1621) finally consented to a truce. Technically, at least, this recognized the independence of the United Provinces of the Netherlands as another Protestant state.

The Thirty Years' War

The most disastrous of all the religious wars of this period was the Thirty Years' War (1618–1648), which grew from religious and political struggles within the German empire and surrounding states. As Protestant-Catholic tension continued to increase, two armed camps arose, the Protestant Union and the Catholic League. The shooting began in 1618 after a struggle relating to the throne of Bohemia. In the course of the war, characterized by a myriad of complex religious and political alliances, all the major powers of western Europe found themselves involved. In October 1648 the Peace of Westphalia finally ended the conflict.

PEACE OF WESTPHALIA

The Peace of Westphalia marked what amounted to the end of any remaining power for the Holy Roman Empire, though it continued to exist in name, and with a politically impotent emperor, for another 150 years. Instead, there were over three hundred independent German states, as well as hundreds of tiny semi-independent principalities. The ruler of each state had the right to determine the religion of that domain. The treaty reaffirmed the Peace of Augsburg, though broadening it to include Calvinism as well as Catholicism and Lutheranism.

Devastation of Germany. The tragedy of the Thirty Years' War was in the devastation it wreaked on the people of Germany and Bohemia. Over a third of them died as disease, pestilence, and starvation followed the marauding armies. Economic devastation was also long-lasting, as the already dwindling trade and commerce of some areas was thoroughly destroyed. The war brought nothing but decline for most of the German population.

Between the fifteenth and seventeenth centuries, Europe had been completely transformed in its religious, cultural, economic, and intellectual life. The old patterns of medieval Christendom had not been destroyed, but were nonetheless thoroughly transformed. The invention of printing and the rise of humanist ideals and methods in scholarship and literature had spread literacy and intellectual life beyond the hands of the clerics. Dominant trends of thought in western Europe were becoming increasingly humanistic, secularized, and individualistic. New Renaissance styles in art and architecture also flourished, producing many world masterpieces.

By 1648 the national states of France, England, and Spain had been strengthened politically, and a few new national states, including the Netherlands, were on the rise. The political power of Rome had been broken, and the pattern for the development of modern political states had been set. The religious world had been shattered by the rise of Protestantism, and there was recognition of the right of each state to determine its own church. Most important, the church no longer controlled the state; rather, the secular authority controlled the church—both with respect to ecclesiastical appointees and church finances.

Some may have asked at the time whether it was all worth the price. The human race's capacity for inhumanity was nowhere better illustrated than in the persecution, thought control, torture, intrigue, executions, murder, and war all carried out in the name of religion. The contending faiths, however, were eventually forced to recognize that there can be no such thing as a universal church with total political and religious hegemony; such religious tyranny only binds the human mind and makes religion a matter of force or bias rather than faith or reason. It was an important start toward the modern concept of free religious worship.

In the long run, the new religions as well as the revitalized Catholic Church all made important spiritual and social contributions to the peoples of the world. The Bible could be enjoyed by all who could read, which led to their own greater spiritual development. Emphasis on Bible reading helped promote greater literacy, opening the doors of the mind to books and new ideas far outside the realms of traditional religion. For all its excesses, the Reformation helped create vital new opportunities of all sorts, along with important new ideas, for the people of the western world.

Selected Readings

Bainton, Roland H. *Here I Stand: A Life of Martin Luther* (1950)

Bouwsma, William J. *John Calvin: A Sixteenth-Century Portrait* (1988)

Chadwick, Owen. *The Reformation* (1972)

Cheetham, Nicolas. *Keeper of the Keys: A History of the Popes from St. Peter to John Paul II* (1982)

Delumeau, Jean. *Catholicism Between Luther and Voltaire* (1977)

Dickens, A. G. *The English Reformation* (1989)

Dunn, Richard Slator. *The Age of Religious Wars, 1559–1715* (1979)

Glimore, M. *The World of Humanism, 1453–1517* (1952)

Haile, H. G. *Luther: An Experiment in Biography* (1980)

Hale, J. R. *Renaissance Europe: The Individual and Society, 1480–1520* (1971)

Harbison, E. Harris. *The Age of Reformation* (1955)

Hay, Denys. *The Age of the Renaissance* (1986)

Jensen, De Lamar. *Reformation Europe: Age of Reform and Revolution* (1981)

———. *Renaissance Europe: Age of Recovery and Reconciliation* (1981)

Kettelson, James M. *Luther the Reformer* (1986)

Kristeller, P. O., *Renaissance Thought: The Classic, Scholastic, and Humanist Strains* (1961)

Martines, L. *Power and Imagination: City-States in Renaissance Italy* (1980)

McManners, John, ed. *The Oxford Illustrated History of Christianity* (1990)

Parker, Geoffrey, ed. *The Thirty Years' War* (1984)

Spitz, Lewis W. *The Protestant Reformation, 1517–1559* (1985)

Index